THE KENNAN DIARIES

Also by Frank Costigliola

Roosevelt's Lost Alliances:
How Personal Politics Helped Start the Cold War

Awkward Dominion:
American Political, Economic, and Cultural Relations with Europe, 1919–1933

France and the United States:
The Cold Alliance since World War II

Russia 1933-1937 | Roughly — Dec. 20, 1933.

The train bearing the ~~members of the~~ ~~so called~~ first American Ambassador to the Soviet Union and his suite - later dubbed "the original Bullitt expeditionary forces" - crossed the Polish-Soviet border in the early twilight of a late December afternoon, ~~and after~~ The ~~silent~~ deserted forests of the border zone ~~[illegible]~~ crowded the single track on ~~both sides~~ either hand, silent, snow-covered and forbidding. At the very barbed wire stood a lone, wooden sentry tower, in a clearing, ~~on the Polish side~~, and on top of it was the dim figure of a Polish soldier, with gun and fixed bayonet, and his great coat turned up against the intense cold. A short distance beyond the border, the ~~Soviet Frontier guards came on board~~

THE KENNAN DIARIES

George F. Kennan

EDITED BY

Frank Costigliola

W. W. NORTON & COMPANY

NEW YORK · LONDON

Frontispiece: Kennan penned this entry around December 20, 1933, ten days after first crossing into the Soviet Union. He later revised it for an unpublished memoir. *Princeton University Library.*

Printed in the United States of America
First Edition

For information about special discounts for bulk purchases, please contact W. W. Norton Special Sales at specialsales@wwnorton.com or 800-233-4830

Manufacturing by RR Donnelley Harrisonburg
Book design by JAMdesign
Production manager: Julia Druskin

Library of Congress Cataloging-in-Publication Data

Kennan, George F. (George Frost), 1904–2005
The Kennan diaries / George F. Kennan ; edited by Frank Costigliola. — First edition.
pages cm
Includes bibliographical references and index.
ISBN 978-0-393-07327-0 (hardcover)
1. Kennan, George F. (George Frost), 1904–2005—Diaries. 2. Ambassadors—United States—Diaries. 3. Diplomats—United States—Diaries. 4. Historians—United States—Diaries. 5. United States—Foreign relations—1945–1989. 6. United States—Foreign relations—Soviet Union. 7. Soviet Union—Foreign relations—United States. 8. World politics—1945–1989. 9. Cold War. I. Costigliola, Frank, 1946– editor. II. Title.
E748.K374A3 2014
327.730092—dc23

2013045016

W. W. Norton & Company, Inc.
500 Fifth Avenue, New York, N.Y. 10110
www.wwnorton.com

W. W. Norton & Company Ltd.
Castle House, 75/76 Wells Street, London W1T 3QT

1 2 3 4 5 6 7 8 9 0

To my former adviser, Walter LaFeber,
and to the memory of my father, Umberto Costigliola,
and my neighbor Carrol Stedman. Like the life of
George F. Kennan, each has been a model of
integrity, persistence, and achievement.

Contents

Timeline

1904: Born February 16

1921–25: Studied as an undergraduate at Princeton University

1926: Appointed to be a Foreign Service officer

1927: Became vice-consul in Geneva, then was transferred to consulate in Hamburg

1928: Posted to Berlin, then to Tallinn, Estonia, and Riga, Latvia

1929–31: Assigned to study Russian language, history, and culture in Berlin

1931: Married Annelise Sørensen

1931–33: Posted to Riga

1933–37: Sent to Moscow

1937–38: Assigned to Department of State, Washington, DC

1938–39: Posted to Prague

1939–41: Sent to Berlin

December 1941–May 1942: Interned at Bad Nauheim, Germany

1942–43: Sent to Lisbon

1944: Worked in London

July 1944–March 1946: Became assistant to Ambassador W. Averell Harriman in Moscow

1946: Wrote the "long telegram" and then was invited to become a professor at the National War College in Washington, DC

1947: Became director of the Policy Planning Staff in the State Department; published "The Sources of Soviet Conduct" in *Foreign Affairs* under the pseudonym of X

1948–49: As Policy Planning Staff director, influenced the Marshall Plan and other policies but also became disenchanted with the rigid Cold War orientation of U.S. policy

1950: Went on leave from the State Department to undertake research at the Institute for Advanced Study at Princeton; advised the Truman administration on its response to the North Korean invasion of South Korea

1951: Gave Charles R. Walgreen Foundation Lectures at the University of Chicago, which are published as *American Diplomacy*; helped to initiate talks with the Soviets that eventually settled the Korean War

1952: Served as ambassador to Soviet Union, May–September; thereafter returned to the Institute for Advanced Study

1957: Broadcasted the Reith Lectures on the BBC advocating disengagement from the Cold War

1959–60: Continued his work as a scholar at the Institute and spoke publically on the issue of Germany and the Cold War

1961–63: Served as ambassador to Yugoslavia; thereafter returned to the Institute and for the next four decades struggled to balance public engagement with scholarly work

1966: Gave televised testimony before the Senate Foreign Relations Committee criticizing the Vietnam War

1968: Gave an early endorsement of the antiwar Democratic candidate for president, Senator Eugene McCarthy; criticized tactics of youthful war protestors

1970s: Researched and wrote two volumes on the history of the pre–World War I Franco-Russian alliance; developed increasing concern about the nuclear arms race

1981: Awarded the Albert Einstein Peace Prize and in his acceptance speech recommended a 50 percent cut in the nuclear arsenals of the superpowers

1982: Joined the "Gang of Four" in calling for Washington to adopt a no-first-use policy on nuclear weapons

1983–91: Worried about imminent nuclear war almost to the end of the Cold War

1990s: Received many honors and awards; spoke out against the eastward expansion of NATO

1990s–2004: Documented his physical and mental decline—even as he published a best-selling book on his personal and political philosophy and another on the genealogy of the Kennan family

2005: Died March 17

List of Major Figures

Dean Acheson. Secretary of state from 1949 to 1953 who increasingly disagreed with Kennan's proposals on Germany and on nuclear weapons

Svetlana Alliluyeva. Stalin's daughter who defected to the United States in 1967 and became a friend of the Kennans' for a while

Joseph Alsop and Stewart Alsop. Influential Washington columnists

Georgy Arkadyevich Arbatov. Founding director of the USA and Canada Institute in Moscow and a welcoming friend during Kennan's research trips to Moscow in the 1970s and 1980s

Isaiah Berlin. British diplomat and Oxford University political theorist who was a friend of Kennan's for many years

Ernest Bevin. Foreign secretary in the postwar British Labour government

Charles E. "Chip" Bohlen. Diplomatic colleague and friend of Kennan's since their days in the Moscow embassy in the 1930s

Charlotte Böhm. Kennan's lover in Berlin during the late 1920s

Constance Kennan Brandt. Kennan's older sister who took him in after his 1924 trip to Europe

Willy Brandt. Kennan's friend who became mayor of West Berlin and then chancellor of the Federal Republic of Germany

David K. E. Bruce. Influential State Department official

Mary A. Bundy. Daughter of Dean Acheson, artist, and Princeton friend of the Kennans'

McGeorge Bundy. National security advisor under Presidents John F. Kennedy and Lyndon B. Johnson, president of the Ford Foundation, and collaborator with Kennan in the "Gang of Four" article in *Foreign*

Affairs urging Washington to adopt a policy of no-first-use of atomic weapons

William P. Bundy. Adviser to Presidents John F. Kennedy and Lyndon B. Johnson, editor of *Foreign Affairs*, and Princeton friend of the Kennans'; husband of Mary A. Bundy and brother of McGeorge Bundy

James F. "Jimmy" Byrnes. Secretary of state from 1945 to 1947

Harry Carlson. Kennan's superior in the Tallinn, Estonia, consulate

Anton Chekhov. Russian dramatist and short-story writer whom Kennan greatly admired

John Paton Davies Jr. State Department expert on China and a friend of Kennan's who was falsely accused of disloyalty by McCarthyite investigations

Anatoly Dobrynin. Soviet ambassador to the United States and an acquaintance of Kennan's

Marion Dönhoff. Editor of *Die Zeit* and a close friend of Kennan's

John Foster Dulles. Republican foreign policy expert and secretary of state, from 1953 to 1959

Elbridge "Durby" Durbrow. Kennan's colleague in the Moscow embassy

Cyrus Follmer. Kennan's friend from the diplomatic corps and the best man at his wedding

Dorothy Fosdick. The sole female member of the Policy Planning Staff and a confidant when Kennan was distressed

Oliver Franks. British ambassador to the United States

J. William Fulbright. Democratic senator from Arkansas and head of the Senate Foreign Relations Committee

John Lewis Gaddis. Yale University historian and Kennan's authorized biographer

Mikhail Gorbachev. An admirer of Kennan and the last general secretary of the Communist Party of the Soviet Union

Bernard Gufler. Kennan's longtime friend and colleague

Eleanor Hard. The daughter of prominent Washington journalists to whom Kennan was engaged before she broke it off

W. Averell Harriman. U.S. ambassador to the Soviet Union when Kennan served as his number two from 1944 to 1946

Loy W. Henderson. Kennan's superior and a friend in the Moscow embassy in the 1930s

Hans von Herwarth. Diplomat in the German embassy in Moscow in the 1930s who befriended Kennan and other Americans

Dorothy Hessman. Kennan's longtime secretary

Jeanette Kennan Hotchkiss. Kennan's older sister and confidant

Charles James. Kennan's cousin

Philip C. Jessup. State Department legal adviser

Annelise Sørensen Kennan. Kennan's wife

Christopher Kennan. George and Annelise's son

Florence James Kennan. Kennan's mother, who died two months after his birth

George Kennan. Cousin of George F. Kennan's grandfather who traveled throughout Russia in the late nineteenth and early twentieth centuries and then wrote about his experiences

Joan Elisabeth Kennan. George and Annelise's second daughter

Kossuth Kent Kennan. Kennan's father

Louise Wheeler Kennan. Kennan's not beloved stepmother

Wendy Kennan. George and Annelise's third daughter

Henry A. Kissinger. A friend of Kennan's who rose from being a Harvard University professor to the national security advisor to secretary of state

Vladimir ("Volodya") Kozhenikov. Impoverished Russian émigré in Berlin whose family Kennan befriended

Walter Lippmann. Widely read columnist and early critic of Kennan's doctrine of containment who later became a friend of Kennan's

John Lukacs. A historian and a close friend of Kennan's

Douglas MacArthur. U.S. military commander in the Korean War

George C. Marshall. Secretary of state from 1947 to 1949 who appointed Kennan to be the first director of the Policy Planning Staff

H. Freeman "Doc" Matthews. Director of the Office of European Affairs in the State Department and a friend of Kennan's

Eugene McCarthy. Friend of Kennan's and senator from Minnesota who challenged President Lyndon B. Johnson in the 1968 primary election for the Democratic nominee for the presidency

Robert McNutt McElroy. Edwards Professor of American History at Princeton University when Kennan was a student there

Constantine Nicholas "Nick" Michaelas Messolonghitis. A Princeton friend who accompanied Kennan on his 1924 trip to Europe

Vyacheslav Molotov. Soviet premier and later foreign minister under Stalin

Herbert Spencer Murch. Professor of English at Princeton who denied Kennan entry into his composition class

Robert Murphy. Influential State Department political adviser in World War II

Paul M. Nitze. Succeeded Kennan as director of the Policy Planning Staff and developed ideas very different from Kennan's regarding nuclear weapons

Carmel Offie. Former aide to William C. Bullitt and State Department officer during and after World War II

J. Robert Oppenheimer. Head atomic physicist on the Manhattan Project and subsequently director of the Institute for Advanced Study at Princeton

Alfons Paquet. German travel writer in the 1920s after whom Kennan patterned some of his own writing

Valentin Patzak. German SS officer in charge of Bad Nauheim, where Kennan and other Americans were interned in 1942

Frieda Por. Hungarian doctor working in Vienna who treated Kennan in 1935 and later, after moving to the United States, became the Kennans' family doctor

Bill and Laura Riley. Friends of the Kennans' who hosted the elderly couple in Florida and in Maine

Frank K. Roberts. Kennan's friend and counterpart in the British embassy in Moscow

Dean Rusk. State Department official under Acheson; later president of the Rockefeller Foundation, then secretary of state under Presidents John F. Kennedy and Lyndon B. Johnson

Arthur M. Schlesinger Jr. Historian, adviser to President John F. Kennedy, and a friend of Kennan's

Strobe Talbott. State Department adviser to President Bill Clinton on Russian affairs and a friend of Kennan's

Charles "Charlie" W. Thayer. Kennan's colleague and friend in the Moscow embassy in the 1930s

Llewellyn E. "Tommy" Thompson Jr. U.S. ambassador to the Soviet Union from 1957 to 1962 and 1966 to 1969

Andrey Vyshinsky. Soviet foreign minister and former prosecutor in the late-1930s purge trials

Grace Kennan Warnecke. George and Annelise's eldest daughter

James E. Webb. Undersecretary of state under Dean Acheson

Cousin Grace Wells. Cousin of Kennan's mother who cared for him and his siblings after their mother died

Frank Wisner. Ambassador and diplomatic troubleshooter in the Clinton administration

Where Kennan Lived and Wrote

935 Cambridge Avenue, Milwaukee, Boyhood

"A dark, strange household. . . . All the windows of the living room almost right up against another house, and the blank side toward an open lawn. So it was a rather dark house."[1]

"We didn't socialize among ourselves. . . . After dinner we always used to go to our own rooms . . . to write letters or read or something."[2]

Berlin, 1930

"Ensconced in a quiet and comfortable suburban apartment, riding horse-back every morning."[3]

Near Riga, Latvia, 1931

"We like our house very much. It probably sounds quite feudal to you. This, after all, is a comparatively primitive country, and servants aren't a luxury. . . . I pay the cook $10 a month and a combination of chauffeur-gardener-butler $16. Household expenses, including some entertainment, shouldn't run to more than $80 a month, in a place where a lamb roast costs 8 cents a pound. . . . I, glowing with fresh domesticity, will go out to saw the wood for tomorrow and see if the chickens have laid any eggs."[4]

Moscow, 1934

"I installed myself for the winter in the Hotel National. . . . Annelise soon joined me and . . . cooked my meals for me, on a whiskey-case behind a screen; and our bedroom served as dining room, living room and Embassy Chancery as well. Within its walls life was lived, food was cooked, toilets were made, friends were entertained, while the telephone buzzed erratically, and official visitors, all of them curious and many of them exacting . . . trooped in and out. . . . Russia, always partial to intimacy and confusion, had promptly claimed its own."[5]

Sanatorium Gutenbrunn, Near Vienna, 1935

"I have already been left alone with my own thoughts for over 180 hours—180 separate hours. Just think of it. Who else could contrive in these harassed days to set aside one hour every day without fail to no further purpose than the contemplation of three walls, a ceiling, two cupboards, a wash bowl, a mirror, a coat rack, and the fading, shifting universe of his own memory?"[6]

"I have been trying, with very indifferent success, to write a novel, and . . . have ground out 8 pages of amateurish fiction. . . . I have now gained 18 lbs since I got here, but my stomach still has to be handled with care."[7]

Jeschke's Grand Hotel, Bad Nauheim, Germany, 1941–42

After Germany declared war on the United States on December 11, 1941, Kennan assumed leadership of the 130 American diplomats and journalists detained in Bad Nauheim, a spa for heart and rheumatism patients about eighteen and a half miles north of Frankfurt. "Kennan became the narrow neck of the hourglass through which filtered the requirements" of both his grousing compatriots and their German masters.[8] He helped organize a makeshift school, "Badheim University," and wrote, largely from memory, a series of lectures on Russia's history and "national character." Ironically, Franklin D. Roosevelt as a boy had spent several summers in Bad Nauheim and had attended school there while his father tried to recover from heart disease.

The Farm, East Berlin, Pennsylvania, 1942–2001

"He wrote on the highest floor in a quest for peace and quiet. A trap door closed it off from the rest of the house. My father had a simple, homemade table and his old Underwood typewriter—the kind that is rather tall with rows of letters in a 'stadium seating' arrangement. Here he would click and clack away for hours in the morning. A bookshelf nearby was filled with old Soviet journals, such as *Pravda*, a filing cabinet, and assorted furniture that was not needed anywhere else. On the wall hung some of his many honorary degrees, awards (National Book Award, etc.) and presidential appointments signed by Harry Truman."[9]

Institute for Advanced Study at Princeton University, 1950–2001

Kennan regarded the scholarly ambience of the Institute—which featured brilliant colleagues, ample staff, and no teaching responsibilities—as "unsurpassed anywhere in the world."[10] For most of his half century there he wrote in Fuld Hall 208. Approximately twenty by twenty-four feet with a fourteen-foot ceiling, the office was packed with books. Four large windows looked out onto the Institute woods, the six-hundred-acre preserve of huge trees where Kennan loved to walk, think, and at times cut firewood.

146 Hodge Road, Princeton, New Jersey, 1951–2005

Built in 1904, the year Kennan was born, the house contained six bedrooms plus a fourth-floor tower that he chose as his study for academic writing. While the height of the tower offered a panoramic view from all five windows, it also obliged him to lug up firewood for the wood stove, its sole source of heat. The stairs became a hindrance in later decades when his knees gave out. He also wrote in a smaller room that contained the only television in the house. The diary he penned downstairs at a desk in the rear living room. The location of the home, a mile from the Institute for Advanced Study, enabled Kennan to bike or walk to the office or into Princeton. He and Annelise lived in the house till their last days.

Sørenhus, on the Dvergsnestangen peninsula near Kristiansand, Norway, 1935–2001

"Sørenhus looks out to the open sea. . . . My father worked in a small bedroom with faded floral wall paper, dominated by a white double decker bed. . . . Under the window, was a metal typing table where his old Royal typewriter stood. Through the closed door we could hear the clacking of the typewriter keys and knew better than to disturb."[11]

"He worked either in the small bedroom . . . or in the shed, probably to get away from distractions in the house. He would wear jeans, an old T-shirt, and a bandana handkerchief on his head pirate-style as protection from insects as he typed away on his old typewriter . . . set up on boards over two sawhorses."[12]

The *Nagawicka* and the *Northwind*, 1960s–80s

Named after a lake outside of Milwaukee where Kennan as a child had spent summers, "the *Nagawicka* was made of wood, with a double-ended, lap-strake hull. She was thirty-two feet long, with a high bow and a simple sail plan. . . . Dad loved the whole boating experience. What he lacked in years and years of boating knowledge he made up for in extensive reading about sailing and boat handling. . . . He was highly organized about our trips, with endless lists and assignments of chores, most of he did himself. When aboard he wrote at the chart table. . . .

"In the early 1970s, Dad acquired a larger, more serious vessel, the *Northwind*. . . . She was a great sailboat and took us all over the Skaggerak, the Kattegat, up into the Baltic, and elsewhere."[13]

Introduction

Though his diary totaled eight thousand pages of elegant, insightful prose penned over eighty-eight years, George F. Kennan was not satisfied with the effort. He faulted himself for gaps in the journal and for failing to refine every single entry into a golden nugget for future readers. With his diary, as with his extraordinarily productive, 101-year life, only the aspirations exceeded the achievements. As a friend observed, "It isn't easy being George Kennan."[1]

The Kennan diary focuses both inward and outward. It reveals the personal life and the political, philosophical, and spiritual concerns of America's most noted diplomat and foreign policy strategist. The journal records how a cosmopolitan, ruthlessly honest, sometimes blinkered, usually insightful "organic conservative" evaluated the changes ripping through the twentieth century.[2] Though Kennan focused on political issues, his was an aesthetic perspective. His "'way-of-knowing' is somewhat like that of a poet," a Washington operator perceived.[3] A long-time aide marveled at his extraordinary ability "to observe and to feel beauty, and just simply to drink it all in like a sponge."[4] The diary sparkles with sumptuous description of such perceptions and feelings. It includes not only astute political analysis but also limericks about birds depicted in Audubon prints, whimsical verse on getting old, and wistful poetry about an aborted romance. The diary for the year 1946, most of which he spent at the National War College in Washington, consists of notes on the books and lectures that shaped Kennan's strategic thought. When the talks grew boring, he sketched faces, farm animals, and the shapely legs of the stenographer.

Though delighting in much about his surroundings, especially the natural world, Kennan could also be critical—most relentlessly about his own shortcomings and those of U.S. society and government. In his various roles as diplomat, policy planner, historian, public intellectual, and peace advocate, Kennan hoped to nudge Americans toward a moderation of their excessive individualism, self-indulgence, commercialism, and exploitation of the environment. He believed the United States should pursue an astute, cautious, realistic, and honorable foreign policy guided by professional diplomats such as himself. Insofar as America pursued any global mission, the nation should focus on becoming a model by perfecting its own institutions. While regarding himself as a teacher and a prophet, Kennan voiced skepticism about the United States instructing, let alone forcing, other nations to adopt its values.

Though his stance on certain policies shifted over time, he himself remained remarkably consistent. From the eleven-year-old boy darting around Milwaukee to catch glimpses of visiting President Woodrow Wilson to the near centenarian watching aghast as President George W. Bush attacked Iraq, Kennan remained the active, reflective, and sometimes-querulous diarist. With a sensibility reaching (or so he claimed) back to the nineteenth and even the eighteenth century, he looked from afar—and askance—at the shortsightedness, vanity, and dubious progress of his own era.

Kennan's perspective on Russia was also distinctive. He authored the containment doctrine that, in its various iterations, became the touchstone for generations of U.S. policy makers and analysts waging the Cold War. Nevertheless, his own feelings about the people of Russia and their rulers were ambivalent. In October 1944, only sixteen months before dictating the "long telegram" that would lay out the rationale for walling off the Soviet Union, he described his experience in walking through the streets of Moscow. He felt "as though I had lived here in childhood, and I react intensely to everything I see and hear." It gave him "an indescribable sort of satisfaction to feel myself back again in the midst of these people with their tremendous pulsating warmth and vitality." He would even "rather be sent to Siberia among them (which certainly would happen to me . . . if I were a Soviet citizen) than to live in Park Avenue among our own stuffy folk."[5] Paul Nitze, who would become a foe on policy while remaining a friend, observed that Kennan "loved the Russian people." Indeed, his empathy with them "became almost passionate."[6] In the diary Kennan confided that "my Russian self . . . [is] much more genuine than the American one."[7] While loving the Russian people, Kennan despised their government, not least because it kept foreign diplomats such as himself isolated from the populace. This mix of feelings fed into the thinking that would prompt Kennan, repeatedly during the Cold War, to call for renewing negotiations and contact with Soviet leaders.

The vantage point of the diarist was remarkable also in another way. It was not just in Moscow that Kennan's senses reached beyond the ordinary. "I read all sorts of mystery and beauty and other things into landscapes and places, and also into music," he explained. "Every city that I went to had not only a different atmosphere but a different sort of music and intonation to it. . . . I was immensely sensitive and responsive to differences in the atmosphere of places."[8]

The atmospheres and places so vividly described include Geneva during the heyday of the League of Nations; Lithuania, Latvia, and Estonia, still bearing the imprint of imperial Russia; a Vienna sanatorium under the sway of Sigmund Freud; rural Wisconsin as seen from Kennan on a bicycle; Berlin in both the Weimar and the Nazi periods; Prague as it fell under the German boot; Moscow in the exciting times before Stalin's purges, as well as during the frightful bloodletting; Bad Nauheim, where Kennan, after the bombing of Pearl Harbor, had to juggle the self-centered demands of both the Germans and his fellow internees; bombed-out Rotterdam and Naples; wartime Cairo and Baghdad; Moscow during the height of the Grand Alliance; Washington in the early Cold War period; both halves of war-wrecked Germany; Moscow again, during the depths of the Cold War; South America in 1950; Oxford in 1957–58; Belgrade in the 1960s; apartheid South Africa; the seas around Norway; Russia in the late Soviet period; the Institute for Advanced Study over the course of a half-century—and many airports and airplanes.

The last Kennan hated. Rancor at the discomforts and impersonal nature of air travel fueled some of his most trenchant diary entries. Automobiles he also found nefarious because they isolated travelers from each other and promoted suburban sprawl.[9] Such vehemence notwithstanding, Kennan could escape neither cars nor planes. The family's weekend getaway, the farm in East Berlin, Pennsylvania, that the Kennans had purchased in 1942, required driving from Washington or from Princeton. And of course air travel was necessary as he pursued a very busy career as a government official and then as a historian and public intellectual.

In the 1930s–40s, Kennan became the top Russian expert in the U.S. government and the author of the containment doctrine. After studying Russian language and culture in Berlin and in the Baltic nations in 1928–33, he journeyed to Moscow with Ambassador William C. Bullitt in December 1933 to set up the first post-1917 U.S. embassy. That tour lasted until 1937, after which he served in Washington, Prague, Berlin, Lisbon, and London. He returned to Moscow in 1944 as number two to Ambassador W. Averell Harriman. In 1946, he was summoned back from Moscow to lecture to up-and-coming military and political officials at the National War College. In 1947, Secretary of State George C. Marshall elevated the forty-three-year-old diplomat to director of the State Department's newly created Policy Planning Staff. Kennan relished the chance to formulate measures, such as the Marshall Plan, that could rebuild the key industrial areas of Western Europe and Japan and thereby thwart Soviet expansion. (Having the ear of the secretary of state, he no longer confided in the diary. The journal for 1947, the year of his peak influence, amounts to a single page of verse.) His career seemed unlimited. Informed by Assistant Secretary of State Dean Acheson, himself a rising star, that Kennan was slated to head the Policy Planning Staff, a colleague acknowledged that "a man like Kennan would be excellent for that job." Acheson snapped back, "A man like Kennan? There's nobody like Kennan."[10]

Within the Truman administration, Kennan first gained praise with the circulation of his "long telegram," a 5,540-word cable, the lengthiest in State Department history, sent from Moscow on February 22, 1946. The American public learned about him when he was revealed as the author of the "Mr. X" article, published anonymously in *Foreign Affairs* in July 1947. The two statements argued that while cooperation with the Kremlin was impossible and war was unnecessary, a policy of "containing" Soviet expansion was feasible. Plus, Kennan suggested, containing the Soviet Union would lead to an eventual mellowing or even collapse of the regime. Kennan's writing in the long telegram and in the Mr. X article was so skillfully crafted that his emotionally charged, exaggerated depictions of the Soviet Union as an existential threat were accepted as being what he claimed they were: hard-headed descriptions of unavoidable reality.

He wrote this hellfire sermon for several reasons. He was concerned with spreading Soviet political influence. From Moscow he underestimated the extent to which U.S. official and public opinion had already given up on cooperation with the Kremlin. He resented the Soviet government for isolating him and other foreigners from the Russian people. Mid-level friends in the State Department were prodding him to speak out. Finally, as a confidant later explained, "he really wanted recognition [from top officials], which he wasn't getting."[11] Determined to be heard, he banged the alarm bells. With the wartime alliance broken, Kennan's notion of "containing" Soviet expansion appealed as a welcome alternative to World War III. The long telegram and the Mr. X article spurred administration officials along the route they were already taking.

Kennan also helped escalate the Cold War by encouraging the newly established Central Intelligence Agency to undertake covert "political warfare," a move he later regretted. "Probably the worst mistake I ever made in government was to accept the responsibility for giving this sort of guidance to CIA."[12]

For the rest of his life Kennan would protest that he had meant containment to remain primarily political. Such intentions notwithstanding, the grimness of the threat so graphically portrayed in the long telegram and in the Mr. X article mandated, most officials concluded, a military buildup against the Soviets. Kennan was also frustrated by the fact that, aside from the reconstruction of Western Europe through the Marshall Plan, most of his strategy for resisting the Soviets was ignored. In the long telegram he insisted that "every courageous and incisive measure to solve [the] internal problems of our own society . . . is a diplomatic victory over Moscow." He wanted the United States to tackle its domestic problems with "improve[d] self-confidence, discipline, morale and community spirit."[13] Having urged such reforms since the mid-1930s, he would continue to articulate this formula in his diary and in public for the rest of his long life.

Even though he had helped launch the Cold War, Kennan soon grew appalled at what he saw as the excessive militarization of U.S. policy. As early as 1948, he was privately calling for a renewal of diplomacy with the Kremlin. (He regarded himself as the official best qualified to conduct such negotiations.) When the Truman administration responded to the explosion of the first Russian atomic bomb in 1949 by debating whether to build a "super" weapon, the vastly more powerful hydrogen bomb, Kennan argued strongly against such an escalation of the arms race. He lost the debate, though he did bond with atomic scientist J. Robert Oppenheimer, who from his perch as director of the Institute for Advanced Study at Princeton, also opposed developing the "super."

Kennan more and more found himself at odds with the hawkish direction of U.S. policy. Moreover, Acheson, who became secretary of state in January 1949, did not share former secretary Marshall's appreciation for the thoughtful analyses of long-term threats and opportunities generated by Kennan and his policy planners. Nor did Acheson and others agree with Kennan's argument that establishing an independent, rearmed West Germany would dangerously harden the East-West divide. Kennan urged instead trying to negotiate with the Kremlin for a reunified, neutral Germany, a deal the Soviets possibly might have accepted. Increasingly marginalized, Kennan vented his frustration in the diary. The journal, which had nearly gone dry during the halcyon years of 1946–48, again filled with rich, though often dour, commentary. In 1950, Kennan briefly moved to the center of decision making as he helped the Truman administration cope with the North Korean invasion of the South. The following year Acheson called on him to initiate talks with a Soviet representative to the United Nations. This parley would later (without Kennan) lead to an armistice in the Korean War. In 1952, his tenure as ambassador to Moscow, which should have been the capstone to his diplomatic career, proved instead an embarrassing fiasco. He became emotionally overwrought in a desperate effort to ease the Cold War. In a bizarre turn of events, the man who loved Russia was declared *persona non grata* and expelled by the Russian government.

In essence fired by incoming Secretary of State John Foster Dulles in 1953, Kennan overcame his humiliation by launching a second career as a historian at the Institute for Advanced Study. "Oppenheimer kindly invited me back after the disaster in Moscow," he later recalled.[14] The director offered the appointment only after surmounting opposition from some faculty at the Institute, primarily mathematicians, who objected to the ex-diplomat's lack of scholarly credentials. Kennan, typically, overcompensated for his initially shaky status. In ensuing decades, he would publish twenty books and win nearly every possible book prize. Even after he retired as the most eminent star at the Institute, he still, he confided to a friend, felt himself under a regimen of publish or perish.

Kennan was looked up to by millions in America and in Europe for his articulate, principled critique of the Cold War. He riveted radio listeners in Britain with his 1957 Reith Lectures and television audiences in America with his 1966 testimony against the Vietnam War. Yet his calls for diplomacy rather than cold or hot war were not welcomed by many, particularly those convinced that dealing with the Soviets was unrealistic, dangerous, and less advantageous than pursuing the Cold War. Dean Acheson reacted with fury to Kennan's urging in the Reith Lectures for negotiations leading to the reunification of Germany and a pullback of both U.S. and Soviet troops from the tinderbox of central Europe. Acheson pursued the attack in the press and in a face-to-face confrontation. There was "blood flowing out from under the door," Acheson boasted to his son-in-law.[15] In 1981, upon receiving the Albert Einstein Peace Prize, Kennan gave a widely publicized speech calling for a 50 percent reduction in the U.S. and Soviet nuclear arsenals, a position that President

Ronald Reagan later would adopt. Kennan remained an inspiration to the U.S. and European antinuclear movements in the 1980s.

When the Soviet Union collapsed on December 25, 1991, Kennan's daughter, Grace Warnecke, called to congratulate him on his foresight. He was not happy, however. "This is all happening too fast," he worried. "It will bring more trouble in its wake."[16]

At age eighty-nine, Kennan published a best-selling book, *Around the Cragged Hill*, a layman's philosophical treatise in which he argued vigorously for the reform of American society.[17] If he could not change the United States in his lifetime, he told himself, he might still have a chance afterward. He hoped that even many years after his death, readers would pick up his books or read his diary and realize, finally, that George F. Kennan did have some answers for America's domestic and foreign policy problems.

In the post–Cold War era, the former diplomat publicly criticized what he saw as unwise interventions abroad and a triumphalist attitude toward Russia. He pointed out the dangers in the ostensibly humanitarian intervention in Somalia in 1992–93. He argued in the press (and privately to friends in the Bill Clinton administration) that expanding NATO to include Poland, Hungary, and Czechoslovakia amounted to a shortsighted provocation of a temporarily weakened Russia. In the fall of 2002 as the George W. Bush administration was gearing up for war against Iraq, Kennan spoke with reporters for the last time. He was in Washington with his friend, ex-senator Eugene McCarthy. Castigating the administration's dangerous policy of preemptive war and its intention to oust Saddam Hussein, he warned that "the history of American diplomacy" demonstrated that "war has a momentum of its own, and it carries you away from all thoughtful intentions."[18]

Not content with his respect among the public, Kennan never gave up on trying to influence policy makers. Even decades after leaving the State Department, he was still, "in the deepest sense . . . a Foreign Service officer," a friend observed.[19] Impelling him were his unceasing drive, missionary impulse, and loyalty to the United States as he thought it should be. He remained, as a former colleague noted, "very ambitious and very intelligently ambitious."[20]

Such aspiration involved his love life as well as his life's work. Indeed Kennan linked the two in his conviction that sexual freedom fostered intellectual and aesthetic vitality. Reading Freud in 1930s Vienna had reinforced his notion of an inescapable conflict between the disciplining order of civilization and the creative impulses of Eros. That dilemma remained agonizingly personal for Kennan, who was torn between a powerful sense of responsibility to his marriage and other obligations, and an equally persistent dread of succumbing to old age and boredom. Already at age nineteen, he feared that while the world now appeared "colorful and romantic . . . in two years time it will be all drab and meaningless."[21] At thirty-one, he expressed a dual concern: "I am afraid that I won't alter the world, after all, before my imagination dies, or have another real love affair . . . before my hair turns grey."[22] Though ever discreet about the details, Kennan filled many a diary page with his struggles over the dilemmas of sex and marriage.

As his pairing of aspirations to "alter the world" and "have another real love affair" illustrates, Kennan habitually linked personal with political concerns. He waxed passionate about Russia, his desire to reform American society, his scholarship, and nearly everything else he cared about. Close associates remarked on these strong emotions. A particularly perceptive friend was Isaiah Berlin, the British political philosopher, who met Kennan in Moscow in 1945. They were drawn together by a shared love for Russian culture and distaste for the Kremlin. Berlin observed Kennan up close in Moscow; at Oxford, where the American was visiting for a year; and in Princeton, where the Briton spent time at the Institute for Advanced Study.

Berlin concluded that Kennan's personality "explains him. . . . All that he has written—his attitudes, his influences, springs from his inner personality, more so than in the case of more . . . conventional people."[23] Aspects of personality that help explain the diary include Kennan's sense of himself as a historical actor with a mission; his ambition, drive, talents, high standards, and charisma; his melancholy and loneliness; his feelings about his mother, stepmother, and wife; and his defiance of old age as he reached, with mixed feelings, the century mark.

Kennan knew he was incredibly smart and talented. As a newly minted Foreign Service officer, he dreamed of becoming "both respected and powerful. . . . [I] might someday make the very pillars of the State Department tremble as I walked through the ringing corridors."[24] An elitist educated in early-twentieth-century America and Germany, Kennan, not surprisingly, embraced aspects of eugenics, a supposed science that was widely accepted in both countries. "For generations," he wrote his sister in 1935, the Kennans have been "breed[ing] an excellent stock. I am sure we are all leading up to someone quite wonderful." While aspiring for what he termed "greatness," he remained unsure whether he could reach it. He knew for certain, however, that he exceeded others in ability. "I have more qualifications for reporting on conditions in northern and eastern Europe than any man I know," he claimed—and he was probably right.[25]

A secretary from the State Department years observed that Kennan "liked to have disciples—people who would sit at his feet."[26] Dorothy Fosdick, a colleague on the Policy Planning Staff, agreed that "he had a strong messianic streak. I always felt he thought he should have been Secretary of State himself." He felt "superior to everyone around him."[27] In the late 1950s, when he was making waves by calling for negotiations with Moscow, Kennan regarded "himself as a world statesman," Berlin recalled. "He said he thought he and [Indian Prime Minister Jawaharlal] Nehru were perhaps unique figures . . . having a political doctrine to offer to the world."[28] Though highly cognizant of his abilities, Kennan also remained self-critical, even humble, about his inability to bring about the changes he believed essential to better the United States and the world.

Moreover, Kennan had reason to feel superior. Presidential adviser and foreign policy expert William P. Bundy agreed that his Princeton friend was often "twenty or thirty years ahead of anybody else's thinking."[29] According to the leading historian of the Policy Planning Staff, the work leading to the Marshall Plan, the rebuilding of Japan, the decision to limit aid to Nationalist China, and the reaching out to Tito's Yugoslavia after its break with Moscow qualified Kennan as "'America's Global Planner.'"[30] His post–State Department books garnered two National Book Awards, two Pulitzers, and a Bancroft Prize. The Einstein Peace Prize was only one of many such awards. He could speak both German and Russian like a native. "No American spoke Russian the way George did," recalled Robert C. Tucker, who also had served in the Moscow embassy. "He speaks an intellectual kind of Russian that really cultured people speak," added Tucker's wife, herself a Russian native.[31] While ambassador to Yugoslavia under President John F. Kennedy, Kennan learned Serbo-Croatian (a Slavic language quite different from Russian) well enough to give a public lecture. Norwegian he mastered, and French nearly so.

Though Kennan complained in the diary of fatigue, he appeared to others as indefatigable. "He was incapable of just stopping and taking a few hours off," recounted a friend and neighbor. After the long drive to the Farm, Kennan would immediately start "the tractor to mow the lawn. Then he'd rush inside and go upstairs to type . . . most of the night." Following an arduous sailing trip in Norway, the exhausted crew lay down, only to "hear a wheelbarrow going back and forth. Here was George . . . with really immense stones . . . building a set of steps."[32] Kennan, who over the years delivered hundreds of talks and "labored over" each one, "would never give a lecture a second time around," a longtime secretary testified.[33] Summing up her boss's approach to life, she marveled, "He never takes the easy way out, even with his bicycle."[34] It was on a heavy, old-fashioned bike lacking gears that he pedaled around Princeton.

Despite all his achievement and energy, Kennan remained fragile. Fosdick recounted that "he could go into a bad slump when he thought he was not being listened to." In such a "crisis," he would "take me to lunch at the old Allies Inn, near the Corcoran Gallery, and pour out his heart to me." At a nearby table they "always used to see J. Edgar Hoover and his friend Clyde Tolson"[35]—this was Hoover's favorite restaurant.[36] Kennan no doubt had turned to other women for solace. This "was a natural role for a woman," he explained to her. "Women throughout history had been confidential advisors to monarchs. Their historic role was to listen sympathetically, to provide comfort, to give private counsel."

Despite his royal expectations, Kennan did not lord it over his staff, take his frustrations out on them, or, according to the evidence, press them for sexual favors. Secretaries typically stayed with him for decades and would later emphasize his unfailing courtesy and kindness. Fosdick did not see her role as confidant/comforter as "demeaning"; to the contrary, she prized it as "a very high compliment."[37]

Although Kennan could strike others as aloof (he appeared as if he were in "a religious novitiate," an official remarked), he could unwind at a party or wind up to deliver a spirited talk.[38] In Moscow Kennan taught himself to play the guitar. He delighted in singing Russian folk songs and other tunes. He and other Americans organized the "Kremlin Krows" to play at dance parties; after the touchy Soviets objected, the band reemerged as the "Purged Pigeons."

He performed in other ways. Perhaps because Kennan, as the diary reveals, was suffering emotional turmoil when he gave his 1951 University of Chicago lectures and his Reith and Oxford talks—and perhaps, also, because he was frantically writing some of the talks until the moment of delivery—his lectures brimmed with feeling. Berlin remembered the "hellfire preaching" at Oxford. His sermon: "The Russians are ruthless; they are powerful; they know what they're doing; they'll certainly conquer. And we've gone a-whoring after pleasure, drugs, God knows what."[39] Each lecture packed in more people than the last. The word went around the university: "Here was a remarkable individual."[40] At Harvard he filled the biggest lecture hall. Listening to Kennan at Chicago was "like an experience on the road to Damascus," recalled a professor. "There was this marvelous melodic flow. It almost has a transforming quality on you when Kennan speaks."[41]

His kind of charisma carried over the airwaves. Kennan's televised testimony before the Senate Foreign Relations Committee in February 1966 proved a media sensation. Millions of Americans watched an elegantly dressed, slightly old-fashioned, and impressively articulate expert—indeed, the author of the containment doctrine—explaining why the war in Vietnam was undermining rather than enhancing U.S. power and prestige. Kennan offered visible proof that opposition to this war was not restricted to long-haired, radical college students. In the following days, the mailman arrived "hauling sacks like Santa Claus," remembered a secretary.[42] Most of the letters contained praise, and many emphasized how engrossing his testimony had been. One woman who had been ironing when he began became so absorbed that she burned the clothes.[43] Twenty-three years later, Kennan again testified before the Senate Foreign Relations Committee, this time to affirm that Soviet leader Mikhail Gorbachev could be trusted. The *Washington Post* celebrated the "Grandeur on Capitol Hill." Kennan, at eighty-five, spoke "with such lucidity, learning, and large-mindedness that the senators did not want to let him go." When he finished after two and a half hours, everyone spontaneously applauded. Queried when that had last occurred, the clerk replied that it was in 1966—when Kennan had testified about Vietnam.[44]

Despite such moments of glory, Kennan, as the diary attests, often suffered melancholy and loneliness. His son, Christopher, recalled that his father had "a deep emotional life that was very regimented and repressed. There was a lot that he didn't say."[45] An associate at the Institute perceived "great vanity" coupled with "permanent uneasiness."[46] Mary A. Bundy, a friend of the Kennans' and a daughter of Dean Acheson's, discerned a "haunting sadness, deep in him. . . . I don't know where it comes from," she reflected, "but it's an awfully big part of him." Nevertheless, "he could be very outgoing. He loves a party."[47] Another friend, the historian Arthur S. Link, described what he had observed at "dozens" of Princeton dinner parties: "Everybody's seated around couches and chairs. . . . [Kennan would] get up, put his hands behind his back, walk back and forth, and give you a monologue. It's marvelous."[48] Afterward, however, the monologist would kick himself for having gone on and on, for having relaxed his emotional control. Assessing the degree to which the unhappiness expressed in the diary reflected his typical mood is difficult. Kennan acknowledged, "I tended to write diaries when I was depressed, and not when I was not."[49] And yet he also believed that his pride and his getting along with others required masking his sadness. Early on he decided that "happiness is simply the practice of skillfully kidding oneself along. . . . Happiness consists in over-looking the truth."[50]

Both nature and nurture seem to have shaped his moods. An older sister, an actress who escaped to New York City, later reflected, "I don't think the Kennan family were very happy people."[51] Their father, Kossuth Kent Kennan, fifty-three years old when George was born, was shy, morose, and careful not to display too much affection lest he undermine his son's manliness. Although smart and ambitious—Kent (as he was known) had researched the income tax in Germany and helped introduce it to the state of Wisconsin—he saw his compensation as a lawyer plummet in old age. His in-laws, the relatively wealthy James family, never thought him good enough for their beloved daughter, Florence. She and Kent had three girls, then George. Only two months after his birth, she died from complications of appendicitis. Baby George was not only weaned abruptly, but also lost out on "the actual holding, the body contact with his mother," a sister later recalled.[52] He suffered another loss when a beloved relative of the deceased mother, who had come to live with the family and take care of the young children, Cousin Grace Wells (after whom George would name his first daughter), had to move out when Kent remarried. The stepmother, Louise Wheeler, was nicknamed "the kangaroo from Kalamazoo" by the Kennan children, who never took to her. "She wasn't a motherly person," explained one of the sisters. Worse, she "was really cruel," Kennan expostulated many decades later.[53] With palpable distaste, he described her as "a highly nervous woman, thin and uncertain of herself," and overly focused on women's clubs.[54] His stepmother embodied traits, characteristically feminine in his mind, that would rile him for the rest of his life.

In explaining his life and his feelings of loneliness and melancholy, Kennan started with the premature death of his birth mother. He began his memoir by stressing that the loss "scarred [him] for life."[55] In the first interview with his authorized biographer, John Lewis Gaddis, he volunteered, "I was affected neurotically by the absence of a mother."[56] His earliest memory, he told his daughter Joan, "was asking my sisters why we didn't call Cousin Grace mother." Decades later, he could still regret that his father had not married Grace; "she would have been a wonderful mother." Though the eleven-year-old writing in the diary seemed happy enough, the boy going through puberty would feel the loss more sharply, or so he would remember. The Princeton student told himself that the absence of a mother explained why "you are twisted."[57] The lost mother—forever beautiful, loving, and beyond reach—flitted through the thoughts of her son and the pages of his diary. Some of the most poignant entries describe her appearing to him in a dream, or his "talking" to her when visiting the family grave. Near the end of his life, Kennan dreamt of "searching for his mother in a crowd of Russian peasants."[58]

If the absence of a mother spurred Kennan's lifelong yearning for things tantalizingly wonderful but beyond his grasp, the presence of a practical wife, Annelise Sørensen Kennan, both grounded and frustrated him. The diary is, for the most part, studiously vague about problems with Annelise or with the children (Grace, born in 1932; Joan, in 1936; Christopher, in 1949; and Wendy, in 1952). Kennan's courtesy, dislike of hurting others' feelings, and reluctance to expose family problems to the gaze of future readers reinforced his innate discretion. Nevertheless, what he saw as the inescapable dilemma of creativity-through-sexual-freedom versus dullness-from-responsible-monogamy runs like a red thread through much of the journal. Sometimes he discussed the problem obliquely or in the third person, other times in Russian, still other times with details about the agonizing guilt but little specific about the sin.

The months leading up to Kennan's marriage on September 11, 1931, marked a sudden reversal of what he saw as a hedonistic course. In January of that year, he referred to "my Russian girl, Renata, who is the nicest of all my girls, and naive enough to love me."[59] In April, he remarked that his "Puritan origin" was "in revolt against the non-Puritan influences" of Europe. His life could be told as "the story of the man who tried to sell his soul and couldn't."[60] On July 9, he declared, "I ought to be getting married to someone or other, this summer because I am thoroughly sick of my bachelor existence."[61] Back on March 22, he had met Annelise, a twenty-year-old Norwegian who, like him, was studying in Berlin. On August 8, just thirty days after declaring his need to marry "someone or other," Kennan was on his way to Kristiansand, Norway, to get to know Annelise's parents before the planned September wedding.[62] "I never told my parents how little I knew him," she later admitted.[63] What stuck in Annelise's mind from her earliest days of knowing George was his emphasizing to her that "he was terribly worried about the United States. I was very young," she added, "and it was hardly the thing you would sit and talk to a young girl about."[64] This initial gap—between George's serious concerns and Annelise's somewhat dismissive, light-hearted approach—would endure throughout their long marriage.

Annelise was by all accounts charming, attractive, intelligent, and devoted to her husband. She and George complemented each other, and stayed together for seventy-three years. She was totally at ease in almost any social situation, a key asset for the wife of a diplomat. Not very interested in intellectual or political issues, she did not try to become the person she was not. With the help of household staff, she managed the home and the children, and took care of practicalities. She helped make it possible for Kennan to accomplish all that he did by being her cooperative and discreet self. He depended on her for many things. When Annelise was away, George, who was color-blind, could appear at the office with outlandishly mismatched ties and socks.

Although the precise inner working of any marriage must remain a mystery to outsiders, some of the bounds of this relationship seem clear. In response to Gaddis's question about the role of Annelise in his life, Kennan started off by saying, "'Well, you must realize that she's not a particularly intellectual woman.'"[65] A friend of the couple's felt Annelise "could have seemed a little boring at times to him."[66] Three years into their marriage, Kennan, in part influenced by the social experimenting still going on in Moscow, offered a stark analysis: "Few husbands are going to be interested in a wife's . . . visits to the hairdresser . . . tea parties . . . [and] participation in club[s]"—the very activities that took up much of Annelise's day. Most men, he continued, "will have far more real community of interest and mutual respect" with their "stenographer-secretary, who shares the trials and triumphs of his day, than with the wife." As a result of this "iron logic . . . secretaries [frequently] cause marital complications." Kennan advocated a radical solution: changing "the character of marriage. . . . The principle of permanent and possessive intimacy must give way to something resembling—aside from sexual relationships—the attitude of college roommates to each other."[67]

Kennan in 1934 was pointing up what he saw as the linked challenges of marriage: sustaining monogamy and common interests. Nearly a half century later, he mused, "'Thou shalt not covet thy neighbor's wife.' My God, I've coveted ten thousand of them in the course of my life, and will continue to do so into the eighties." He added, "All that has to be fought with. But the main thing is to try to play your role in a decent way."[68] The diary shows how Kennan indeed fought with his impulses while striving for decency.

Those efforts were complicated, however, by an underlying difference between him and Annelise. She did not share or sympathize with many of the anxieties, concerns, and ambitions—especially the idiosyncratic ones—that preoccupied him. Instead, friends observed, she "holds him down to earth. . . . She has ways of pricking [his] bubbles."[69] Gaddis, who spent considerable time with both George and Annelise, observed "her really deflate him in an almost merciless way. It's funny, but at the same time it's pretty ruthless."[70] Kennan, who had told Fosdick that women's "natural" role was to console and comfort men, must have felt—as indeed he confided in the diary—abandoned and alone. He once confessed to his daughter, "It's so painful being with your mother because I can't talk with her."[71] Always thin-skinned, he turned elsewhere for succor, solace, and, probably, sex.

He had, as his journal indicates, a series of affairs, flirtations, and fantasies. He reminded himself that he had to perfect the art of hiding from his wife nothing but the big things. A quest for understanding and companionship, even if only from his reflected self and from sympathetic posthumous readers, spurred his writing in the diary.

Elegant writing came easily to Kennan. William P. Bundy, the editor of *Foreign Affairs* and a friend, remarked, "I've never seen anybody whose mind and his pen were so synchronized as his." Bundy remembered waiting for a late train on a "freezing, freezing day" in the barely heated Princeton Junction station. "George sat there with yellow paper, pen flowing across the paper . . . just flowing."[72] Even into his nineties, he wrote with beautiful penmanship, filling narrow-lined paper with perfectly formed letters. When it came to typing, secretaries were embarrassed to discover that he was faster than they were. They also marveled at his ability to dictate long, complex sentences that needed no revision. He could resume the dictation of a sentence interrupted by a phone call. His writing was influenced by his reading the work of two accomplished stylists: Edward Gibbon, the historian of ancient Rome, and another George Kennan, who was a cousin of his grandfather's and a self-taught expert on czarist Russia. Brilliance with language held dangers, however. As Mary A. Bundy, probably reflecting the views of her father, put it, the "seductiveness" of Kennan's prose "excites people all the more in the ideas."[73]

His finely crafted sentences poured forth: verbally and in diaries, letters, telegrams, memoranda, notes, book drafts, articles, lectures, and interviews. All this, plus the photographs, clippings, and other material he had collected, total 330 boxes (136.2 linear feet) in the George F. Kennan papers that are available at the Seeley G. Mudd Manuscript Library at Princeton University. The diaries alone fill twelve boxes. In his later years, Kennan mused about eventually publishing his collected works. He amassed such a detailed record because he saw himself as a historical figure, obligated to document his life as completely as possible.[74]

Kennan also kept the diary as a means to polish his prose and try out material for the fiction that he never quite managed to write. Many of the entries are travelogues, inspired by a German writer from the 1920s, Alfons Paquet, who "made a deep impression on me . . . with the way in which he incorporated the environment, the atmosphere, and the history, with the . . . way things were that day."[75] Kennan wrote about places because "I never liked to write about people, for fear of offending them."[76] He was a playwright who never wrote plays, perhaps because his gift for depicting scenes was not matched by a skill, or inclination, for dialogue.

He characterized the diary as "more personal" than his letters, which tended "to be more political and intellectual."[77] Nevertheless, the journal contains astute appraisals of major political figures. The diary also offers a critique, not much of it positive, of U.S. foreign policy. The diary entries for 1944–45 and 1948–50 stand out for their detailed discussion of foreign policy issues. Running throughout the journal are long expositions of Kennan's political philosophy and his recommendations for improving U.S. society. Also important are his efforts to understand Christian spirituality and to freshen its relevance as a philosophical guide.

As Kennan felt his physical, intellectual, and psychological strength fading in his nineties, he continued, characteristically, to push himself while complaining about it. He still attended dinners, gave short talks and interviews, and penned magazines articles and op-ed essays. At age ninety-six, he published a book, laboriously researched in a multitude of small archives, on the history of the Kennan family. He kept the diary as a way of keeping himself together. Though the journal still touched on national and international issues, it also served as means for self-management and for recording signs of decline—a deterioration that, he groused, family, friends, and doctors refused to take seriously.

To the very end of his 101 years, Kennan's aspiration exceeded his extraordinary achievement. Even as his body was failing, he tried desperately to hold on to his intellect. Shortly before he died, his friend Bill Riley paid a visit. Kennan lay in bed. Riley recalled, "George indicated he wanted me to come closer, and I put my ear near his mouth. Up to then he had not really said much, and what he said was difficult to understand. He said, 'Bill, I had planned everything except this.' What I took him to mean was that he was completely prepared to die, but not to lose his ability to think clearly."[78]

Through his life and his diary, George F. Kennan raised compelling issues that still ring clearly today. He engaged his passion and intellect to question the sacrosanct assumptions in U.S. foreign policy. Is the United States capable of sustaining a sensible foreign policy that is not beholden to narrow domestic interest groups? Can America really serve as a model for countries with quite different cultures? When is military intervention overseas worth the blood and treasure? Is Washington wise to give Israel nearly unlimited support? Should Russia be treated as a has-been great power that cannot prevent the expansion of NATO right up to its borders? Is it necessary to have a domestic transportation system that accentuates dependence on imported energy? Would not the United States and the world be better off if Washington pursued a more isolationist, or at least a more cautious, strategy? Kennan believed that in order to deal with such questions the United States needed to organize a Council of State—a group of unimpeachably respected citizens—who might offer sound, untarnished advice to a president and Congress blinkered by petty concerns.

Kennan also posed difficult issues about love, God, and death. And he did so in ways intensely personal, ways that invite each of us to weigh the questions that agitated him for most of his 101 years. How can we, as human beings aiming for both decency and happiness, reconcile the conflicting impulses of sexual freedom and family responsibility? How should religion (for him a humanistic Christianity) shape our daily lives and ultimate perspective on life?

Even though Kennan in the diary remained guarded about what he said, left unsaid, and said obliquely, reading it brings us closer to him. The entries reveal the vulnerabilities of a great man, weaknesses that we might identify within ourselves. And in knowing him, we better know ourselves, in terms expressed by a gifted writer and an unflinching judge of character. He says things about himself that we might not have yet said to ourselves. And in his documented decay, in his self-aware slide toward the final ending, we vicariously experience the cruel process of dying, as one's small gifts are taken away, little by little. Through Kennan's stubborn effort, we also get a glimpse of how we can reconcile this harsh truth of life, how we can fade into history with dignity, always striving for our best selves, never getting there, but succeeding simply in the trying.

Editor's Note and Acknowledgments

Kennan wrote. In addition to twenty books and thousands upon thousands of letters, lectures, diplomatic cables, and policy memoranda, he penned or typed nearly five linear feet of diary. Readers of this volume should know the criteria I used in selecting from these approximately eight thousand pages. Although Kennan regarded his diary as more personal than political, he did discuss specific foreign policy issues, particularly in the entries for 1944–45 and 1949–50. Moreover, the entire run of the diary contains commentary, often acerbic, about the overall direction of U.S. foreign policy. I have included nearly all of this political discussion, omitting only repetitious details and remarks of interest solely to narrow specialists. In general, I have selected for Kennan's most vivid prose while including representative examples of his various experiences, moods, concerns, and ideas. If there is any topic in the original diary that is slighted here, it is the daily log of sailing in Scandinavian waters aboard Captain Kennan's beloved *Nagawicka* and *Northwind*.

Within entries, excluded passages are marked with ellipsis points. Published entries that begin after, or end before, unselected material are not marked with ellipsis points. I have simplified Kennan's sometimes-idiosyncratic punctuation and silently corrected his rare misspellings. Passages that he wrote in German or in Russian are so indicated with a footnote.

Among the many joys of working with this diary has been the pleasure of getting acquainted with the daughters and the son of George and Annelise Kennan. Grace Warnecke shared her reminiscences as well as her fascinating memoir, *Daughter of the Cold War*. Joan Kennan was extremely generous in allowing me to use her collection of Kennan family photographs. Like Grace and Joan, Christopher Kennan welcomed me into his home to discuss his father's life. Wendy Kennan was also helpful in sharing her many memories. Bill Riley, Mary Acheson Bundy, and Terrie Bramley offered important insights based on their years of association with Kennan. Marcus Padulchick provided details about Kennan's final months. I first came to appreciate the importance of Kennan many years ago when listening to one of Walter LaFeber's elegant lectures.

I would not have been able to undertake this editing project had I not received a vote of confidence from the Kennan Diaries Project Advisory Committee (John Lewis Gaddis, Richard Immerman, Daniel J. Linke, Paul Miles, and Bradley Simpson) set up by the Seeley G. Mudd Manuscript Library at Princeton University. Richard Immerman offered sound advice throughout the subsequent editing process. John Gaddis was generous in replying to queries and in reading through a draft of the introduction. Archivist Dan Linke was unfailingly helpful in mobilizing the resources of the Mudd Library to facilitate this project. I also benefited from the assistance of Mudd staffers Amanda Pike, Adriane Hanson, and Christie Lutz. At the Institute for Advanced Study at Princeton, administrator Marian Zelazny and librarians Marcia Tucker, Christine Di Bella, and Erica Mosner were helpful. I appreciate the generosity of Mark Lawrence and James McAllister as well as that of Hannah Gurman and Anders Stephanson in sharing their ideas regarding the Kennan project. Michael Cullen was also helpful. A great help during the editing process was the expert typing of Dara Hall and the careful translating of Ksenia Tatarchenko and Marcia C. Schenck. The publication of the diary has been aided by the crisp professionalism of Andrew Wylie, the good advice of Drake McFeely, the capable copyediting of Mary Babcock, and the hands-on dedication and shrewd judgment of Jeff Shreve.

My initial interest in George F. Kennan was quickened during a year at the Institute for Advanced Study in 2009–10. Nicola Di Cosmo's suggestion that I offer an "After Hours Conversation" on Kennan spurred me to examine the newly opened Kennan papers. That informal seminar led to conversations with Kennan's former associates at the Institute, including Glenn Bowersock, Morton White, Irving Lavin, Marian Lavin, and Freeman Dyson. Dyson was also generous in sharing his correspondence with Kennan. IAS Director Peter Goddard, taking an active interest in my work, invited me to return to the Institute during part of the spring and summer of 2011, when I commenced work on the diary project. Avishai Margalit opened some key doors for me.

I have benefited from solid family backing while working on this project. My brother, Charles Costigliola, was there 24/7 with cheerful, savvy technical support. My daughter, Jennifer Nancy Costigliola, and son-in-law, Josh Tarsky, were inspiring in terms of their own hard work, while my granddaughter, Aviva Tarsky, offered delightful reasons to take time off. My mother, Nancy Costigliola, has approached George F. Kennan in longevity while remaining just as vigorous. My deepest debt is to my wife, Diann Bertucci, who has been loving enough to allow me to believe that she is indeed interested in yet another story or aspect about Kennan. She is a wonderful partner in terms of sharing ideas and fun.

I cannot conclude these acknowledgments without also thanking George F. Kennan for caring so passionately about making the United States a more cautious, thoughtful, stable, and hence less commercialized nation. He was a conservative in the traditional sense of one who wants to work toward—or back to—a good society, and then protect it. Despite some prejudices with respect to race, ethnicity, and gender, he stands out as an intellectual who thought otherwise—indeed, as an intellectual whose thought was often wise. I am grateful for this opportunity to transmit his ideas to a wider audience. Often in despair that his concerns about peace, foreign intervention, and the environment were falling on deaf ears, Kennan wrote this diary in part because he hoped that it, along with his books, would be read and taken seriously long after his death.

Frank Costigliola
Storrs, Connecticut
September 2013

THE KENNAN DIARIES

Chapter One

Milwaukee and Princeton, 1916–24

1

Diary
of
George Kennan, 11 years old,
Beginning
Jan. 1, 1916.
If found return to
935 Cambridge Ave.,
Milwaukee,
Wisconsin.
Born, Feb 16, 1904. U. S. A.

In this simple, little book,
A record of the day I cast;
So I afterwards may look
Back upon my happy past.
George Kennan.
11 years old.

Diary
of
George Kennan, 11 years old,
beginning
Jan. 1, 1916

If found return to:
935 Cambridge Ave.
Milwaukee,
Wisconsin
U.S.A.

Born Feb. 16, 1904

In this simple, little book,
A record of the day, I cast;
So, I afterwards may look
Back upon my happy past.

George Kennan.
11 years old.

1916

George Frost Kennan grew up in Milwaukee, Wisconsin, in a bookish, upper-middle-class family composed of his father, Kossuth Kent Kennan, a lawyer who had helped introduce the income tax to the state of Wisconsin; his stepmother, Louise Wheeler Kennan; his older sisters, Jeanette, Frances, and Constance; and his younger half-brother, Kent. George's mother, Florence James Kennan, had died when he was only two months old. The young boy displayed an interest in larger affairs, especially in the military training that many Americans regarded as precautionary because of the war raging across Europe since August 1914.

Though Florence had succumbed to peritonitis from a burst appendix, her son grew up believing she had died giving birth to him. That guilt would help foster George's lifelong melancholy. Nevertheless, such sadness does not seem evident here. Eleven-year-old George portrays himself in this fragment of a diary as a physically active, curious boy, smart but not a grind, and generally happy.

Milwaukee, January 21

We had an awful geography test today. We're having our January thaw now; and to-day you had to rush and push in slush and mush. I came home right after school on account of the slopiniss [*sic*]. I think I can have the wood-work in my room painted white.

January 29

I walked down-town this morning and worked in the office all day. Papa gave me a quarter for it which I spent at Weber's for a half-a-pound box of (it was supposed to be) cream candy, but which tasted like automobile grease.

January 31

We didn't have any school this afternoon because of the President's[1] visit. I went to hear him speak at the Auditorium first only it was packed full.

1. President Woodrow Wilson visited Milwaukee.

Then, in going to Uncle Alfred's office to see him, I watched his auto go past only never knew it. At last I saw him standing in the observation platform of his train with Mrs. Wilson behind him. My room is being painted over.

February 20

This morning I walked to Sunday-School, stayed to church and walked home. In the afternoon, Kenty, Papa and I walked down [to the] Town Club and watched them play billiards. I went to the patriotic service at the church tonight and was very much pleased with Dr. Jenkins' sermon on "Preparedness."[2]

February 21

This afternoon I walked home from school and played outdoors with Kenty. After supper Papa read to me the book of Esther and part of Job, out of the Bible.[3]

February 25

This afternoon after school I played marbles with Art Morsell and Leonard Barry. After supper I went down to the Auditorium to see if the Naval Militia was drilling only I was disappointed.

March 3

I went down to Dr. Taylor's office to be vaccinated for Typhoid. It isn't supposed to hurt, only on me he struck a blood vessel and it burned like fire. There are 244 cases of typhoid and 5 deaths from it in the city.

March 4

Censored by G.K.[4]

March 23

This morning when I woke up there was about 20 inches of snow on the ground and everywhere else including Kenty's cart and my bike. I worked for an hour before breakfast shoveling snow and going for rolls.

2. Though the service may have been strictly religious, a campaign for military and moral "Preparedness" was sweeping the country as Americans observed a Europe engulfed in total war.

3. George's father, who used his middle name, "Kent," read the Bible almost daily.

4. Even at this early age, Kennan was sensitive to what his diary might reveal. He erased an entry and marked the spot by writing this phrase in large letters.

After breakfast Jeanette[5] and I spent nearly an hour walking to school on the car-tracks as the cars weren't running then and the tracks were the only places where walking was possible. This afternoon I went over to Sam's. I forgot to say there was thunder with the snowstorm.

April 1

To-day was April Fools day. This morning I went to a meeting of the Junior National Security League where I heard two very interesting talks, one by General King and the other by an ensign in the Navy. Then I monkeyed around and shot off the Hotchkiss Revolving Cannon.

April 8

This morning I went down to Mr. Santer's soccer field where the National Security League held its meetings. We were drilled for an hour and a half by a naval officer.

April 22

This morning I did some errands for Mother and got down to drill just before it was dismissed.

April 23

Today was Easter and Charlie's[6] birthday. After Sunday-School I went to his house and saw his presents. He got ELEVEN DOLLARS from his father.

May 1

This afternoon I walked home.[7] Then I went down to Grandpa's with Kenty and Mother to see the kittens. Aunt Mary's cat has five or six baby kittens about four days old. Our report cards came out today. I'm tenth on the honor roll, again, my average being 87⅛%.

May 15

This afternoon I went to practice and rode home on the car. I got to bat lefty after this because I can do it pretty well and it confuses some pitchers.

5. Jeanette "Netty" was the older sister with whom George felt closest. He would bare his soul in letters written to her in the 1920s–40s.

6. Charles James was the son of Kennan's mother's brother, Alfred James. The wealthy, socially prominent Jameses regarded Kent Kennan, with his less advantaged background and austere personality, as not good enough for their beloved daughter Florence.

7. Other times George rode the streetcar to and from school.

1924

This fragment of a journal, written during the last weeks of Kennan's junior year at Princeton, is apparently all that has survived of a more extensive diary from his college years. Despite Kennan's later memory that his Princeton years were unhappy ones, he seems to have led an active social life. While serious about his studies, he enjoyed only mixed success. Perhaps the most startling revelation here is that Kennan, who later won awards for his prose style, was refused admission into a composition course.

Princeton, April 28

This morning, to McElroy's[8] precept, where someone asked him what he thought of Wilson.[9] He said he thought Wilson would eventually be recognized as one of the greatest figures in history because he interpreted the Great War to the country so that the country could enter it and make sacrifices with a clear conscience.

April 30

This was a rainy day, most of which I spent studying that marvel of literary condensation, Gooch's "History of Modern Europe."[10] It is really a great aid in the allopathic treatment I am taking this spring to cure my imaginative tendency, because it takes real assiduous mental concentration to dope out a sentence of it.

8. Robert McNutt McElroy was the Edwards Professor of American History at Princeton University.

9. Former president Woodrow Wilson died on February 3, 1924. Wilson, who had promised Americans that their participation in World War I would help "make the world safe for democracy," saw his dream shattered at the 1919 Versailles peace conference and in the rejection by the U.S. Senate of the Versailles treaty and membership in the League of Nations.

10. George Peabody Gooch, *History of Modern Europe, 1878–1919* (1923).

May 1

A walk out through the Pyne estate[11] with Eric & participation in the Clio discussion group upon the subject of the Japanese exclusion bill[12] were the chief events. Although the discussion group, naturally enough, reached no clear conclusion upon the subject I may as well record what I decided before I forget it. The existing conditions, under the "Gentleman's Agreement," were unsatisfactory. That did not, however, warrant the sudden passage of an exclusion act without any prior warning or negotiations with the Japanese government. Neither did the protest of the Japanese ambassador warrant such indignation on the part of the Senate; the protest was not an attempt to dictate America's immigration policy; it was merely a reminder that the act of the House of Representatives, if allowed by the Senate to become law, amounted to an expressed opinion of the U.S. that the Japanese government was not a gentleman, for reasons which Japan was given no opportunity to explain.

May 2

Today I did practically nothing but study. After nearly fifteen years of "education," I am just now beginning to learn how to assimilate knowledge; perhaps next year I can start on the assimilation.

May 6

Having only one class, today, & that an 8 o'clock, I spent a good part of the day trying to read history out at the Pyne estate, but found it so much more diverting to watch the ducks & fish that I returned early to get some studying done. Took some time for a swim as soon as I got back. This evening I studied until 8:30 & then went over to see Army,[13] who argued race problems with me and showed he knew considerably more about it than I did. He half-converted me to his "extermination of the lower races" idea. I cannot see why it is wrong in principle, although, like most sound theories, it seems impossible when one thinks of the

11. The Moses Taylor Pyne estate, called Drumthwacket, lay on Stockton Street not far from the Princeton campus.
12. The 1924 Immigration Act angered Japan not only by prohibiting its nationals from emigrating to the United States but also by violating the Gentleman's Agreement by which the Japanese government had agreed to itself bar such immigration. Many saw the act as needlessly insulting to Japan.
13. Army was a friend.

practical difficulties. However, I'm a theorist as long as I'm in college, and as long as possible afterwards. On with free trade & birth-control!

May 9 and 10

Worked on my Waterway theme[14] most all of Friday. Late in the afternoon went over and played a banjo in Campbell [Hall]. All of Friday night down on Prospect Street at the house-parties, chiefly at Cloister's, as Ed Green's guest—pretty good party, no drinking. Legs got so tired I wasn't good for any walking all today. To bed at six this morning, up at 7:30; studied & loafed all day, to dance again tonight. Marvelously peppy party—even I enjoyed myself—profitable, too: 2310 Delancy St., Phil.[15] Think it's about time I got to sleep.

May 12

Whittlesey[16] gave the third & last of his lectures on American industrial growth. They are the lectures which one follows with close interest but which one couldn't repeat a word of, afterward. He enlarged upon our natural dislike of change, & I was tempted to tell him my pet theory of that, but didn't. McElroy's precept was interesting, with much discussion upon imperialism & "the right of men everywhere" etc. Wrote to both Connie's[17] this afternoon, to thank her for a box of fudge she sent me & to advise him to study this summer instead of accompanying me to Europe, which advice he will undoubtedly ignore, since he has little faith in my prescience when it conflicts with the beautiful future his myopic vision presents to him. Connie is just the wrong mixture of the visionary & the practical: a trip to Europe with him will certainly mean an eternal alliteration of toil, trial, trouble, & tribulation; but still human nature is so unreasoning that I look forward to it.

May 17

Came home about 10:00 o'clock. A fellow dressing for a dance in the room just below mine locked himself out, sans everything, as he came upstairs

14. Kennan was writing a term paper that pointed up the advantages of what decades later would become the Saint Lawrence Seaway. With the help of the Seaway, ships could steam between the Great Lakes and the Atlantic Ocean.
15. The young woman whom Kennan met and who lived at that address subsequently wrote to him.
16. Charles R. Whittlesey was a professor of economics at Princeton.
17. Constance Kennan Brandt was an elder sister of George's. Constantine Nicholas Michaelas Messolonghitis, whom Kennan referred to as "Connie" or "Nick," was a Greek American student, also from the Midwest, who would accompany Kennan on his ramble through Western Europe in the summer of 1924.

to shave. So I raked out an old pair of military-school white ducks; he held onto one end and I the other, and I climbed down the outside into his window, thus earning, apparently, his eternal gratitude.

It was the most perfect night I can remember: the moon practically full, & so bright that none of the stars around it were visible; a light, warm breeze, smelling fully as sweet & by no means as sickening as a prom-trotters perfume. I smoked a pipe & sauntered out across the golf links below the grad college. The bushes which fringe the course, along the road, were in full bloom, and looked silver in the moonlight, and all was complete.

> "Oh lady, by yonder blessed moon I swear,"
> "That tips with silver all these fruit tree tops."[18]

Above the pool, the tee has been made into a sort of parapet, and back and forth across that there was pacing a dim white-clad figure, muttering & talking. Whether or not he saw me coming I don't know but as I drew near, he marched away with long strides, still talking unintelligibly to the moon, as a dog does. All of which goes to prove that there is more than one damn fool in Princeton.

May 18

Spent most all day reading alternately American History & Conrad's "Almayer's Folly."[19] Went out [to] the Grad College to hear the organ recital, this afternoon. Somehow I didn't enjoy it as much as I have enjoyed them in the past. Down to Key & Seal[20] with Harry for dinner this evening.

May 19

Wasted an incredible amount of time today. About one o'clock I strolled out to the Pyne Estate, and finished "Almayer's Folly," sitting in a tree. Met Mr. Murch[21] this evening, who informed me that my previous English record was exceedingly poor and that, in effect, I might as well effect the international abolition of armaments as to get into his composition course. My vanity was sorely wounded.

18. *Romeo and Juliet*, act 2, scene 2. Kennan penned "by yon blessed moon."
19. Joseph Conrad's first novel, *Almayer's Folly* (1895), depicts the quest for gold by a Dutch trader in the Netherlands East Indies.
20. Key & Seal is the social eating club that Kennan would quit in his senior year.
21. Herbert Spencer Murch was a professor of English at Princeton.

May 20

Had a conference with McElroy at noon, and he "set me up" for the rest of the day by telling me I "showed an unusual grasp of these things," and that I ought to get a first group in his course. Went in and had a long chat with David White this evening; it is the last stage in my social deterioration. Refusing to associate (or being unable to) with the conventional was the first phase; associating with the unconventional is the second.

The news that the Senate had passed the Bonus Bill inspired me to write a comment on it & send it to the *Princetonian*. The wisdom of old age, however, dictates that I commit it to these pages, instead.[22]

It is with a sense of profound awe that one must regard the Senate of the United States, for the men who compose it stand alone on the pinnacles of achievement to which they have attained.

Some of their predecessors have, to be sure, done great things; in the period since the Civil War there have been examples of accomplishment which it is difficult to rival, say nothing of excel. The "Republican majority" of 1866 who foiled the nefarious designs of President Johnson, the great body of men who took so active an interest in the building of the Union Pacific Railroad, and, in our own time, that group of staunch patriots who kept our country out of the deadly tentacles of the World Court—all these have set records which will long endure in the hearts of Americans.

But now these records have fallen and greater deeds have been done. All honor & glory to the 67th Congress of the U.S.! In the field of legislative bungling it has proved itself supreme; it has achieved the last word in pettiness, the ultimate in stupidity!

May 23

Studied almost all day for tomorrow's history test. This afternoon I took time off for a swim & this evening I went for a walk. The parts of Gooch, Morocco, the Balkans, & the Anglo-Russian treaty of 1907 I know pretty well—the rest I am wholly ignorant of, but I don't think it's important.

May 27

McElroy gave a good lecture this morning. He was talking about Roosevelt, but got side-tracked on Wilson & quoted a remark to the effect that Wilson went up in a fast elevator but came down running it himself, which quite struck me, for there is more in it than meets the eye.

22. What follows is, of course, sarcastic.

Cousin Grace[23] & Miss Reese & some other "Miss" drove down today & Charlie[24] & I had lunch with them at the "Peacock Inn." After that we drove around for a while.

This morning, by the way, my conscience so bothered me that I ascended to the heights of Witherspoon [Hall] & notified Ed Greene that I was writing to his girl. I feel better.

May 29

Studied internal European history (since 1850) this afternoon, with Bob McKinley. Also indulged in the dumb and doubtful luxury of buying another dance record, which was wholly unnecessary. Bob, by the way, maintains England favored Germany in 1900, which, if it be indeed true, will make all my potent argument to explain why she favored France (on Walter's[25] last test) look extremely sick.[26] Bye-by—first group.

June 6

The end of this book[27] makes a convenient breaking-off-place for the year. On Saturday I went up to New York & got the required note. There then followed ten days of loafing, visiting and other forms of sin. When we start for Europe I shall resume diarizing.

23. Cousin Grace Wells won the hearts of the Kennan children when she came to live with and take care of them after the death of their mother. One of the reasons why the children resented their stepmother, Louise Wheeler, was that she replaced the beloved caretaker. Kennan would name his eldest daughter after this cousin of his mother. Grace was the caretaker of Miss Reese.

24. Charles James, Kennan's cousin, was a fellow student at Princeton.

25. It remains unclear who Kennan meant by "Walter." The history professor was McElroy.

26. Decades later, Kennan would write two volumes on the diplomacy of this pre–World War I period.

27. Kennan penned this diary in a college exam booklet.

1924

During the summer after his junior year in college, Kennan, accompanied by Constantine Nicholas "Nick" Michaelas Messolonghitis, "a big Greek boy with a broad grin" and a fellow Midwesterner at Princeton, traveled around Europe. Bankrolled with only the six hundred dollars Kennan had gotten from his father, the travelers hoped to find work in Europe.

June 21

This morning we got packed up by ten or eleven o'clock & by noon we were en route to Ridgewood. Our one ride, from Princeton to Rutherford, N.J., was with a gent who flunked out of Princeton in 1911. Was an interesting bird; told how he got money one time in Los Angeles by swiping a bunch of subscription receipt blanks from a newspaper office, soliciting forty dollars' worth of subscriptions with them, and then shipping out of town. Also told us how he was in a political gang in a small town, and how they used to thumb-mark the ballots so that they could tell whether the individuals voted the way they were paid.

A college friend came over in a Packard & took Nick & I [*sic*] up to the Ridgewood Country Club, which is so located that it has a wonderful view over to the ridge along the Hudson. He says there are no Jews in Ridgewood; we have probably discovered already a place far more remarkable than any we'll find in Europe.

June 25

We proceeded once more up-town to the 57th St. Y.M.C.A., where we asked in vain for a room. It being then 3:30 or 4:00 a.m. we made up minds to save expense & dragged ourselves into Central Park where Nick lay down on a bench and I on the ground, & spent the time in real hobo slumber until about 6:30.

By 8:00 a.m. we were again down at the Battery, where we waited in the park for the steamship offices to open. We were about the seediest looking persons in Battery Park, which is saying something: soiled; wrinkled clothes, two day beards, unkempt, hot as usual, & tired to death. Our morale was utterly shot.

At 9:00 a.m. we made inquiries concerning the *Berengaria*, which was to leave at 5:00 p.m. the same day. They told us we could get third-class passage at $97.50 a piece. That, plus visas & tips would use up well over half our funds but, as I said, our morale was shot.

"Nick" sez I, "on board that boat there must be a bath & a bed." With that thought our reason fled, & we bought tickets forthwith on the S.S. *Berengaria*.

June 26

My God! We are with a bunch of deportees! Of all the scurvy, seedy, filthy, low-down, diseased, wrecked, ignorant, miserable human beings that God ever made a bad job on, these wretches hold down first place. There is a one-eyed man; there is some dark-skinned devil in a turban who grins unceasingly; there is a negro-woman; there is a bearded, consumptive old devil who looks like Santa Claus out of a job in Constantinople; there is an infernal Hunyak who sits on a bench on deck, with hair like a mop & a mouth like a cavern & bla-a-a-a-s, idiotically, under the impression, I guess, that he is rendering a native folk song; there is a worthy matron with two children, a sullen air, & a jaw like the movie political boss, lacking only the unlit cigar; there is an enormous Englishman with a similar wife, both completely expressionless; there is a huge Teutonic-looking man who seems to be afflicted with a combination of epileptics & St. Vitus Dance; there are at least a hundred spaggettis [*sic*] who all look alike, with long brown mustaches & several layers of dirt; there are as many hefty matrons with weird boudoir caps & dull faces; there are fifty dirty & squalling kids who fall down the gangway & swear at each other in pidgeon-English [*sic*]; there are three English nurses with the proverbial large feet, astounding taciturnity, & severe expressions; there are innumerable cockney stewards whose only philosophy is the prospective tip, and who all have that weazened, angular appearances which cockneys should have; and finally there are two respectable, civilized, American female school teachers, who don't associate with the rest of the vulgars, & to whom Nick & I hope to address ourselves if we can summon the courage.

The actual accommodations are not bad. We have a room to ourselves (thanks be to God), & it's all right except that the port-hole is so near the water it can't be opened, so that it is eternal night inside. . . . There is a smoking room which wouldn't be so bad if there were nice people in it. It includes a bar which we have refrained from patronizing, owing to financial considerations. The food is passable but none too good; I am probably prejudiced against it by watching the people who eat it. Taken all in all, it would be quite a comfortable trip, were it not for the fellow-passengers.

Fortunately they are not communicative, as a rule. Those who have attempted to be I have squelched by true Princeton snobbery. If I have gotten nothing else out of college I have at least learned to discourage sociability when I so desire. There is a manner of glowering angrily at the culprit by way of preparation, then sticking the main blow by a choice bit of frigid & conclusive civility, & finally capping the operation by a return to the pose of wearied indifference, a manner learned to a nicety by all Princeton men, & to perfection by those from Yale & Harvard. It is of great use in a third class cabin.

Southampton, England, July 2

Somehow we evaded the customs officials & found our way out to the street where we got quite a shock! The taxis, all following the left hand side of the street, are the most antiquated, fantastic, ancient hacks I ever imagined. All the private autos are so small that they make the Fords, of which there are many, look like Stanley Steamers. Many of the trucks, by the way, are steamers and resemble a combination of ocean yacht, locomotive, & plain common truck. The street cars are curious double-decked affairs, merely 5th Ave. buses on tracks, and are always called tramways. The streets are quite narrow, most of the houses old, & none of the buildings at all high. The dress of some of the male inhabitants would create a good riot in the U.S.A. Imagine the town Beau Brummell,[28] solemnly dismounting from a ridiculously high bicycle, wearing a derby, a wing-tipped collar with a colored 4-in-hand tie, striped shirt, & pants, short by design, further elevated towards the knee by a pair of bicycle clamps. Every third emporium, on the main streets, bears some long rigmarole painted on its white plaster about wines & spirituous liquors, which means that it is a saloon. They are often very ancient

28. Beau Brummell was an arbiter of male fashion in early–nineteenth-century Britain.

& sometimes brand new; the whole place, in fact, is a curious mixture of the XVIIIth century & the XXth. By the side of The Harbour Inn or some such thing, established by appointment of William, King of Great Britain, France, & Ireland, by the Grace of Allah, etc., in 1695, and seemingly being part of this edifice, one often sees a familiar-looking building labeled "F. W. Woolworth—3d. & 6d. Store."

Neither of us having had anything to eat for a long time, we set out, after finding a hotel, for a meal, & found a place where we got a good steak dinner, although at no slight expense. The early part of the evening we spent walking around the town & later we got bread & cheese & beer at a restaurant, before going to bed. The hotels here are more in the way of boarding houses, & always charge so much for "bed & breakfast." The beds are astoundingly comfortable.

July 3

Arriving by train at Exeter about 5 p.m., we sauntered up the main drag, & stopped in a second-hand book store where I picked up a couple of Shakespeare's plays. After that we sought out hotels and finally located one for 4 & 6.[29] A hotel, in England, merely means a house where they give transients bed & breakfast for twice as much as it's worth; it is generally sort of a sideline to something else for the proprietor. The one we stayed at in Southampton was an appendage to a salon; this is an appendage to a bakery shop.

Friday, July 4

We started this morning, about 9:30, for the "Lorna Doone" country. By dint of some 6 or 8 miles of walking & as many in two automobile rides, we reached Tiverton by about 2:00 p.m. There we lunched & looked around. We wanted to see the old "Blundell's School," where John Ridd went,[30] but we didn't want to take the time, figuring that the longer we fool around before we get settled the more money we lose, because traveling is so expensive.

Asking [for] the road out of Tiverton, we struck [up a conversation with] a garrulous old lawyer who had himself gone to Blundell's School,

29. Four shillings and six pence.

30. John Ridd is the young protagonist in Richard Doddridge Blackmoor's *Lorna Doone* (1869). The romantic novel, set in the Exmoor region of England, became a favorite among Ivy League college students.

& who dragged us into his dwelling like a Jewish clothes-monger, to tell us about himself & his curios. He was about seventy, but tough & spry, with his lip discolored by the innumerable cigarettes he smokes. He had several interesting antiques, of which he was immensely proud. Among them was a picture of the old school-house where John Ridd went, framed in the wood of a panel which the old boy had swiped himself from the school-room.

After a half-hour or so we broke away & set out for Dulverton, hoping to reach there by evening, for it was then about the middle of the afternoon. The first three or four miles we walked, and then we were invited to ride by a farmer's wife in a sort of dog-cart. It was only a two-wheeled affair & contained already herself, a baby, the baby-carriage, a pram (as they call it), & several bundles, but we managed somehow to add ourselves & our luggage to the party. She was a sociable soul and we passed a pleasant half-hour discussing, for the most part, the trials & problems of the farmer. She asked us if we didn't think a tariff would help the farmers, & I don't think we succeeded in explaining to her that because an article is produced in one's native country it is not necessarily cheaper than it would otherwise be. After we left her we got an auto ride which took us right to Dulverton. The road between Tiverton & Dulverton was along a very pretty valley, with neat fields & hedges, & quaint thatched farm cottages. The country gets more rugged & less populated as we go north.

In Dulverton I went to the post-office while Nick filled his stomach in someplace or other. I wrote a note to Father, requesting the other $100.

July 6

This morning we breakfasted & immediately walked out of town to make inquiries. In good plain American: there wasn't much soap; they were all the same. The women are always at the door; God knows where the men are. "Do you know of anyone around here who takes in lodgers?" "No-o-o! I daon't think I dao." "Would you take some yourself?" "No-o-o," horrified, "Us never does that. Perhaps the villagers dao; ye might a-a-ask they." And so the interview is over. By noon we gave up and returned to town, where we finally found a restaurant open. In English towns like Exeter very few things but the churches are open on Sunday. We had a long wait at the R.R. station, during which I read my "Lorna Doone" & Nick slept. At four o'clock we got our train and at 8:15 or thereabouts we were deposited in the city of London.

Neither of us knew a soul in London nor anything whatsoever about the city. But Nick recollected that the Association of American University Clubs, or some such thing, was on Russell Square, so he took great delight in asking the way of a Bobbie, (which he loves to do), & we got on a bus, bound in that direction. When we were somewhere in the vicinity of the Square we asked another Bobbie if he knew where the place was. He didn't know about the association, but directed us to the American Y.M.C.A., nearby & they offered to put us up here for 5 & 6, which seemed good enough. We were delighted anyhow to talk to an American & to get the luxury of a real bath.

We talked for a while to the man in charge here, an American. He told us he doubts very much if we can get any kind of a room for less than 5 shillings a night, because there are some 250,000 visitors in London just at this time. So it seems that we'll have to scout around, & get a job somehow, despite the unemployment, for we have very little money left above our passage home. We went over to a little restaurant this fellow recommended, & there we got a quite sizeable dinner for only 2 shillings a piece, which is considerably cheaper than it would be in the provinces.

July 7

In sizing up London I find myself unconsciously comparing everything about it to New York, or rather contrasting, for it is rather the points of difference than those of similarity which I notice. Outstanding, of course, are the lack of high buildings, & the multitude of double-decker buses, which take the place of trams in the "down-town" districts running on not only two or three streets, as in New York, but on practically every street of any importance, & of those there are many. Their subway, or "underground system" seems to me an improvement over ours. Serving a complicated & confusing city, it is itself necessarily complicated & confusing, & seems to be composed of several independent lines which wind around indiscriminately and with no apparent semblance of order. But service, what little I have seen, is frequent & the cars are very much more clean, comfortable & generally attractive than ours. Both buses & subways cost a tuppence, ordinarily, but if one doesn't know the ropes he must often pay more by riding past a station. The traffic being on the left hand is very confusing—I should think sometimes disastrous—to American pedestrians; it is surprising how the habit of looking to the left when one starts to cross a street does cling to one.

July 11

We composed prayers, this evening, for recitation at the close of each day until we shall be safely on the way to America.

I say:

> Dear God, who got us in this town
> Without a solitary crown,
> For Christ's sake, get us back again,
> And make it snappy, God—Amen.

Nick says: (being more concerned with food)

> Oh Lord, it gives us both a pain
> To eat this rotten London hash;
> Please ease up on the goddam rain,
> And send us down a little cash

July 12

We ate dinner up at a Lyon's Place by St. Giles Circus, & exchanged pleasantries with another pretty waitress who let us off easy on the bill. We now have three, two at the Express Dairy, who know enough to bring great big glasses of water when they see us coming, and who will generally overlook an item or two for us on the bill.

July 16

I decided that we should move on to the Continent & to hell with finances. We could go to France—beat our way down to Marseilles & make the consul there send us home. Why in the world should two Americans, young & able-bodied, stay a month in England & never see the continent, merely for a few paltry financial considerations?

July 17

We reached Paris at 6:15 in the morning. . . . I have never seen any city even remotely resembling it. It has all the magnificent distances of Washington, the boulevards of Philadelphia, the metropolitan freedom & gaiety of New York (but more so), the time-honored mellowness of London. The streets and boulevards are so wide & open that the street traffic is never jammed or even crowded, as far as I can see: the taxis spin gaily along the boulevards, choosing their own road, and disregarding restrictions as to speed just as they do in Chicago.

July 20

This was a quiet day. I spent the time until two or three o'clock writing letters, etc., in the room. I then went out to a little park . . . & finished "Lorna Doone." At five or six o'clock we both went over to the Hotel des Invalides to see Napoleon's tomb, but it was closed. So we went by subway to the Place de la Bastille, where we had dinner, Nick in a frenzy of happiness because I urged him to have a double order of steak & potatoes, which he did. He is nevertheless quite incensed because I tell him his thoughts, wishes, regrets, dreams, hopes, interests, etc., are bound up completely in his own body. Maybe they are not *completely* so bound, but I have never seen anyone yet who was so downright miserable when his bodily senses were annoyed and so supremely happy when they were satisfied. We walked back by way of the Cathedral of Notre Dame. I am curious to know where the movie of *The Hunchback* was made: if in California, how did they reproduce the Cathedral so well? If in Paris, how did they make all the surroundings fit the 15th century when they are so obviously the 20th?

I have been doing considerable thinking about an essay I want to write next fall on "Princeton Democracy." I want to defend Princeton from the extreme accusers who shout "snobbery," etc., & yet attack that element there which is not democratic, namely, those whose vision extends no farther than graduation & who accordingly make social prestige during undergraduate years the sole aim of life. It suggests a number of things to think about. What causes the super-sensitiveness which underlies Princeton's stratified society? Is this stratification a good thing? On what is it based? On what should it be based? I want also to write on the difference of Princeton now from the "golden nineties." Has the "glory that was Princeton" died away, or has it only been undergoing a change of form? In either case, to what has it been due?

July 21

I had a most terrific hang-over all today, & about all I did of any moment was to improve my personal appearance a bit, for tomorrow. . . . Feeling most depressed & sentimental, after a bottle of wine, I wrote a short note to Harriet.[31]

Still on the track of my epoch-making criticisms of Princeton life, in regard to the latter one, I want to remember to bring in this summer's pet generality, namely, that the only virtue is strength, & the only fault weakness. Much can be said with that for a foundation.

31. Harriet was probably a young woman Kennan knew back in the United States.

July 22

Versailles is fully as luxurious & enormous as it is reported to be. It seems unbelievable that people could have built such a place in the old days. I had a good chance to review my history, looking at the hundreds of historical paintings on the walls of the palace, but as far as fidelity to fact is concerned those paintings make one smile. For they always represent great occasions, such as Napoleon giving the standards to his regiments, or Henry IV making his triumphal entry in Paris, & every one knows that all big ceremonies like that, from weddings to coronations, invariably are disappointing, sometimes even grotesque. The participants & the attending multitudes are all in too much of an excitement to realize fully the seriousness of the matter and it takes on a sort of comic opera aspect.

In that regard, I always think of the unveiling of the battle-monument in Princeton, and of poor [President Warren G.] Harding sitting in a glaring sun on the white concrete steps, mopping his brow with a handkerchief, & caring more for a glass of good, cold beer, than all the heroes of history.

From Versailles we took a little trolley line out to St. Cyr to see where Napoleon went to school. But when we arrived we found it was only open to visitors on Wednesdays & Sundays, & a gent told us Nappy never went there anyhow, so that was somewhat of a fiasco.

Back to Paris about 6:30 & went over to the Boulevard St. Michel for dinner, stopping for a glance at the Sorbonne, afterwards. Then, it being a fine balmy evening, we sauntered down to & across the river, then up to La Place de la Concorde, & Madeleine. There we hailed a horse-taxi, & after having a drink of cognac we drove up the Champs Elysees to the Arc de Triomphe, a damn fool luxury for two individuals who are just six days from starvation. Walked home from the Place de l'Etoile, in full agreement that, if there is no place like home, neither is there any place like Paris.

July 24

To dinner about eight-o'clock at a restaurant over by the Gare St. Lazare, where I had a small bottle of "vin rouge," as usual, & afterwards a "vertreuse jaune," as unusual. Then we walked east a ways, & I had another glass of wine somewhere. Walked some more & went into another place where we had whiskey & soda. Here I was holding forth in a loud tone about how I would "do" Chicago when I became rich.

July 25

Up early this morning (ten o'clock) & down to the American Express, all with a bad headache. I found two bits of mail, one telling me there is no soap in trying to get back my money from Southampton, the other saying that a certain sum of money had been cabled to me in England. So I wired for it to be sent here. If it is less than $25 we will probably go to Marseilles; if it is between $75–$125, we will probably go to Italy; if it is more than $125, we will probably go home, while we have the chance.

On the way home, I figured it all out how I can make my millions by starting an airplane express company in the United States; I'll be the Harriman[32] of commercial aeronautics.

On the way home I stopped for a swim at one of those places along the Seine. The water was very filthy and the spring-board was terrible; also the air was pretty chilly, but I enjoyed the swim and it cost me only about fifteen cents.

This evening I went down to tell the chambermaid to wake us at eight and found the whole family seated around in the office. The old man lit into me at the rate of sixty words a second, about our sleeping all day. His main point seemed to be that we drank too much beer & not enough wine. He even wanted me to get up tomorrow morning at 5:30 to go along with him & see some market which is the biggest in the world, said he'd come up & wake me himself, pour water on me, etc., if necessary. I would have done it, just to show him I could, if it hadn't been that we have a hard enough day tomorrow anyhow. I got the worst of the argument, all right, but he had me at a disadvantage because all my arguments were limited to things I knew how to say in French.

July 26

At the American Express promptly on the stroke of nine, this morning, but the mail hadn't been sorted. Went out for a bite to eat & returned at ten to find a cable of a hundred dollars from Fran[33] with the message: don't be afraid to cable Father for money; he is willing to send all you need, or words to that effect. Poor Franny; she evidently got scared by the letter I wrote her from London & told the whole tale to Father, who, of course, gritted his teeth, boiled with rage, & assured her he would send me all I needed. She couldn't have meant better; she couldn't have

32. E. H. Harriman was a railroad baron. Two decades later, Kennan would be working in the Moscow embassy assisting the tycoon's son, Ambassador W. Averell Harriman.
33. Frances was an older sister of George's.

done worse. She paved about a good solid mile of the way to hell, with her own good intentions, & the result is that I'm afraid it will be some time before I visit 309 Cambridge Avenue again.[34] But

> "to mourn a mischief that is past and gone
> Is the next way to draw new mischief on."[35]

So that's that. There's nothing to do about it at present; when I get to America I'll have to pay back Fran, & I think I'll carry on all communication with home from a long distance.

We decided to use Fran's money as if it were Father's $100, go to Italy on it, & pay the $100 Father sends, back to Fran when we reach New York.

[George and Nick traveled by train from Paris to Turin.]

Turin, July 27

We found a room for 14 lires, after some casting about, & got installed in it about noon. For lunch we went down to a little restaurant next door. There was a number of young Italians there, about our age, and they were nice clean-cut looking fellows, considerably more neat in appearance than we were. I was remarking on it to Nick when the one sitting next to me started to talk to us in English. It seems his Mother runs a restaurant in New York, & he had been there some five years himself. So we had an interpreter during our meal, & learned a lot which we wanted to find out about Italy. We had a great time exchanging versions of the song "Yes! We have no Bananas." It seems that they play that very much over here, now (they stopped playing it a year ago in America), and he was anxious to learn the English words to it. So we wrote them out for him & he, in return, wrote out the Italian for us.

We came up to the room right after lunch & slept until eight o'clock. I had some very terrible & weird dreams not of the usual kind & woke up very much depressed. I dreamed of the family & pondered about it all & for a moment I managed to grasp the whole thing and see it just as it is, but now I can't remember it. It is very peculiar, one of those things which are always just around the corner. All I know was that it was very sad. There are two kinds of dreams. One, of which I must have hundreds every night, is the usual kind: hundreds of impressions and

34. This was the address for his father's home in Milwaukee.
35. Shakespeare's *Othello*, act 1, scene 3.

brain pictures of the last day or so, flashing around in the brain at will, with no semblance of order. Our imagination & memory, released from the control of the mind, run rampant by themselves, and react on the mind while it sleeps. The other kind of dream I can't explain. There is more order in it & sometimes hints of originality: that is we see and hear clearly interesting things which we know we have never heard or seen in real life, & we seem to do some clear & logical thinking about them. It seems to me that the only possible explanation for these lies in the action of some kind of mental telepathy.

Genoa, July 29

Today began again the sad parade of the waterfront. If there be anything in this world more discouraging than trying to get a job on a boat I have yet to find it. We struck the consul in the usual ceremony: that is, we lied to him about how much money we had & he lied to us in return about our chance of working away from this dump. He tried, of course, to get us to cable for money, told us how utterly impossible it would be for us to get jobs, how many experienced seamen were already waiting for them, how one American was repining at present in the Genoa jail, etc. He won't help us out until we're flat broke or until he's convinced that we can't be scared into wiring for money. Even then Nick thinks he isn't obliged to get us a job. Of course, when we go broke we'll go to jail. The consul will then kindly offer to advance the money for a wire; and we, I, at any rate, refuse to wire for money. Then, the question is, must he send us home or can he let us stay in jail as long as possible?

July 30

This morning, while heading for the office of the Dollar Line, I stopped in to inquire, in a curious rather than hopeful manner, what was the price on the Holland-American Line, railroad fare included. I could scarcely believe my ears when the woman there told me it was about 1400 lire from Modane. Now Modane being but 50 lire away from here, the total, plus meals, is scarcely more than 1500 lire, which is a vastly different tune from that about 1900 lire which we have been hearing at the other places. I made her look it up two or three times, but, strange as it seems, I could locate no monkey-wrench in the machinery, so I dashed home, woke up Nick, dragged him over there, & after some more inquiries we made first arrangements for passage on the *Volendam*, leaving Boulogne-sur-Mer August 6. It may be that all the cabins will be booked & it may also be that the $100 we are expecting from

Father fails to arrive this week (or any other week, for that matter), in either of which cases we will again be up a tree, but, God being with us, there is now a prayer of our getting home. The money can possibly reach us tomorrow morning, it can possibly never reach us until we send for it. So there we are.

This afternoon we saw a little of Genoa, walked out the road that runs up the bluff. Looking seaward, it reminded me strongly of Milwaukee, the blue Mediterranean, surging peacefully around in the rocks at the bottom of the bluff, looked quite like Lake Michigan does from the east side of the city at home. But simply to turn around was enough to realize that this is 4,000 miles from Lake Michigan. The palm trees, the square houses of the town, the dirty, cobbled streets, and the hazy, barren, rolling mountains, down among which the town is set, have no resemblance to Milwaukee. . . .

We hunted around some, today, for a cheaper room, & found a couple which were fine except that the attendant "sanitary conveniences" were neither sanitary nor convenient.

Walking around the waterfront this afternoon set me to dreaming about the boat I want to have when I live in Milwaukee, if such a misfortune really does befall me. It will be about twenty-five or thirty feet in length, long enough to hold a comfortable cabin with one or two bunks, but small enough to be handled by one man, if such limitations are compatible. What I will do with it, how I will have it fixed inside, & where I will go in it, furnishes infinite food for contemplation.

July 31

No mail. No telegram. Stalled for time. Nick slept until one o'clock. I went out on a little exploration party in the morning & discovered the Genoa stock-exchange, which would make the one in New York sound like a Quaker meeting wrapt in silent prayer. Italians are by nature inclined to generous articulation & gesticulation, particularly in crowds, so a stock market brings out the natural tendencies to the full. Also got a free ride on a Genoan street-car, which pleased me mightily.

August 1

We started out about 11:30, after ascertaining that there was no mail, & went to scale one of the hills, in order to see the fortifications on top, on Nick's part, and to get the view, on mine. . . .

At the gate there were some Italian sentries, who told us we could not go into the castle, for such it seemed to be, but one of them very kindly went & got a canteen full of cold water for us. In return we gave them some American cigarettes & we had quite a social time for about a half an hour, while we rested. They were a coarse, rude, sloppy bunch. But we had a good time talking to them, although it was laborious conversation. They explained that their pay was 40 centissimos (2 cents) a day, that the old castle was now a big government wireless station, that there were some fifty of them stationed there, plus some sailors (because here, as in our country, the navy runs the wireless service), that they didn't like Italy nor Mussolini, and that they were all coming to America as soon as they might have the chance.

August 2

This afternoon we invested in two paper-backed volumes, one of Shakespeare & one of Conrad, for 8 lire a piece. Then we came up & read & slept. I read Pericles & afterwards tried to perfect a poem I have been thinking about. I haven't finished it, but I have part of it rudely outlined. It's great for passing time.

Men say that Truth is Beauty, Beauty Truth!
Fools! who will trust a word without a try!
Fools! who believe the gaudy dreams of youth!
Beauty is but a rank, eternal lie!
A flower which, only sought, will fade and die,
A jest of our own poor hopes. Outside our brains
It has no real being. A curse I cry
Upon the God who, knowing that it pains,
Will sing of freedom but ne'er release his bondmen's chains.

And yet—I know not if He be so bad
That he deserves a curse. Almost at will
A thousand other pleasures may be had,
More solid and less fierce, but pleasures still,
Which are no kin to beauty; they instill
A sense of gratitude in Man. Then, too,
Does it not prove the mind is but a sill
Upon the soul's abyss, that we once knew
Great things,—and may, in time, know them anew?

(Pretty far-fetched)

August 4

I am making a strong effort to be more equable in temper & disposition, by restraining myself when I find myself too congenially inclined, as well as otherwise.[36] I think the trouble with human beings is not so much that they are unable ever to see the light of reason on things, but that they are able to hear it only in flashes, & for the rest, being weak, they are unable to face it & turn their heads the other way. That, of course, borders on philosophy, in which, of course, there is no pure reason, but I am assuming in this that the beings in question have already laid down some unreasonable assumption as an axiom, & build on that. Then, if they were strong, they would at least follow out the logical conclusion even from the illogical premises, as in geometry, but as it is, their brains are so weak they shrink from even such a show of reason, & yielding to emotions, pile one inconsistency upon another.

August 5

Having no mail this morning, we talked with the steamship agents and with the man at the American Express, & I sent home a cable for money which set me back more than half of our worldly funds. They say we will probably get a return in about four days.

This afternoon we went to the beach on the other side of the point & went swimming. The water & the whole place were exceedingly filthy. They are much more careless about the bathing dress than we are at home. Most of the men wear only trunks, & the babies wear nothing at all.

We struck the proprietor or "Padrone" for a room somewhat nearer the ground, the one we have being five floors above the level of the entrance. At first he said 4 lire more & then he came down to 2, where he stayed. So we told him we guessed we'd have to look around for another room & left him. After a while he hailed us & said we could move into a lower room tomorrow. All of which goes to show that you've got to bicker with Europeans or you get stung.

I've been getting intestinal trouble from this Italian food, & tonight I was really sick—had to spend 4 of our few lire on some castor oil. I guess if I stay in tomorrow & then watch what I eat, I'll be all right.

36. Kennan would throughout his life berate himself for not living up to this resolution.

August 6

I passed the time writing doggerel about an Italian, after the fashion of something I've read somewhere. An example of it:

When at the tender age of four
He went away to college,
To gather up some business lore
And other useful knowledge.
His course of study was begun
With "Elements of Begging."
Then came "Fruit-selling 201,"
And "Practical Bootlegging."
He also read a lengthy book
On "Breeding Cats," but finding
That too dull, he changed and took
"Advanced Handorgan-Grinding."

There was no mail today and we have decided that there must be some hitch somewhere along the line, neither of us having had a letter yet.

August 8

Despairing over our financial condition & worrying over my physical condition, which seems to be with me for good, & which is, I suppose, dysentery, or something like that, caused by bad water. Nick kindly informs me people die from it.

At about 11:00 I got up & wavered down to the American Express, hoping to ask Bliss, the solemn, systematic, blond Englishman there, if there was an English-speaking doctor in Genoa. When I arrived I was most agreeably surprised to find that the money had arrived, & might be had by calling at the other office of the American Express, where the shipping & banking business is done. So I tore over there, arriving just in time to get the money, $130, before the office closed down at noon. Then I had a little snack, not having had a square meal for about 48 hours, & after lunch we went curiosity-hunting while we waited for the steamship offices to open at 2:00. We went to the art shop where they sell all the marble things. I found an alabaster miniature of the Lion of St. Marks, in Venice, which I want to send to Con for her wedding present, but not being able to afford it at the time, I made arrangements to send the money from America when I can get it.

Our train for Paris left at 6:20. We made a few last arrangements, very hastily, & at 5:45 we went to depart from the hotel, whereupon there followed great strife & altercation between Nick & the Padrone. The latter wanted to charge us for another day because we hadn't told him soon enough that we were moving out. I wish I could repeat the conversation; it all worked up to a grand climax something like this.

Padrone. I can't help it. You must pay ze bill.

Nick. We won't pay for—

Padrone. I get ze police!—I—

Nick. Police! Say, big boy—we'll have the American consul over here so—

Padrone. (shaking with rage)—Oh—I—(motions with his fists).

Nick. What'll you do? I come around the counter and—

Padrone. (swelling up to a bursting-point)

Sacre Dieu!!!

Nick. (in same tone).

Sacre Bleu!

Padrone. (collapsing, & muttering thru his teeth). All right. You pay ze bill up to zis morning.

Changed trains at Torino, & got into a carriage with two old French soldiers, retired veterans, another Frenchman who was suffering miserably from a swollen jaw, & a big, bull-necked, bronzed, Teddy Roosevelt type, Englishman, with a strain of Indian blood in him, "a taint, as you call it," he remarked rather bitterly. He had a bottle of Scotch whiskey, & we a bottle of mineral water, so we cooperated & mixed flat drinks for a while. At midnight I left Nick & the Englishman arguing over whether or not one could buy a college degree in America, and went into a half-empty compartment, where I stretched out & slept until we reached Modane, about 2:00 or 3:00 a.m.

August 8

I was trying to puzzle out one of the time-tables hung on the wall of the station, when I was assisted by the most interesting specimen I have met this summer. I thought at first he was colored, but when I saw that his white shirt & collar were covered with the same dark grime as his face I realized that it was only the natural result of the Italian railroads. He was diminutive (in fact he later referred to himself as a "little shrimp") & a pair of spectacles completed the effect of innocent & almost pathetic harmlessness. His appearance was really disreputable, "quite filthy-dirty," as he expressed it, for his sooty face was set off above by an ancient headgear rivaling Nick's in its utter dilapidation, & below by a linen duster, once white, but now correspondingly tinted by the Italian State Railways. It was evident at his first word that he was decidedly British, & it was the British solemnity flowing from so unimposing a source that made the striking effect.

He was a cyclist, an ardent one. By profession he was some sort of a chemist, but during his two weeks' vacation each year he pursued cycling with unique British seriousness & earnestness. While he was on the road he apparently gave no consideration at all to physical limitations. He thought nothing of cycling thru mountainous country & he considered 150 miles a good day's ride. . . .

Once, he remarked, he had been caught by the Moroccan Moors, who are notoriously fierce & lawless. Under urging, he told us about this, in his quiet tone of injured innocent, as though we did him an injustice by considering it at all remarkable.

"One day," he said, "I stopped in a little village about four in the afternoon. I asked there about the road to the place where I meant to spend the night, about 40 miles away. They told me about two roads, one the main road which was the direct way, and the other a camel track, they called it, which was more round-about. I thought I'd try this & I set out, but it turned out to be very hilly & I didn't get along as fast as I expected so that when it got dark I was still pushing up hill in the dark & I hadn't yet reached the town.

Pretty soon I came to a place where there was a camp fire just off the road, but I thought I'd go right on. Then three of these big fellows came out and stopped me. I couldn't speak their language so I made signs that I wanted to go on, & I started to leave but (this in a most aggrieved tone) they held my bicycle & I couldn't get it away from them.

One of them pointed up the road toward the town where I was going & then raised his gun to his shoulder as if he were going to fire it. Yes, they had guns & they had sort of knives or swords under their sashes. They motioned me to follow them, & there was nothing else to do so I went with them to their tent. It was one of these things, you know, where you have to climb in on your hands & knees. They gave me some black bread & a sort of coffee & then we all lay down & went to sleep.

In the morning they gave me some breakfast & let me go." So it seemed that rather than trying to harm him, these fellows were protecting him for the night against real marauders.

When day broke he bade us a solemn farewell, & jumping on his bike just as he was, without even removing his coat, he pedaled away out of sight in the morning fog.

August 9

I rose early & spent the morning doing errands. Just after lunch I went to see an American doctor by the name of Robinson, who told me I had a form of dysentery & gave a couple of prescriptions which I had filled at a nearby drug-store.[37]

August 13

Up, shaved, packed, fed, & at the office of the Holland-American Line at 9 o'clock this morning. We were examined again & vaccinated. Then they gave us our tickets. . . .

An undergraduate from Brown, class of 1925, joined us. We have in him the typical Eastern collegian, if there be any such thing. I often think that human beings defy classification, but there are certain qualities which undergraduates in the smaller New England colleges all seem at least to emulate and, to a more or less degree, to bear. Smoothness is the most comprehensive term for all of them. It is really quite literally descriptive. All of Mr. Samuel Balou's[38] relations with other human beings run along with a sort of smooth, sinuous ease. There are no congestions, jarrings, interruptions, unless caused by the other person. Mr. Balou knows exactly how he should behave in every situation & even if the other parties make mistakes, his equanimity is not greatly upset; he merely feels the same mixture of surprise, contempt, & indignation which an actor feels when a comrade fumbles his lines, & he generally rises to the occasion by playing still better himself, as a good actor would. He is of middle-size, with clean, dark features. He would be a good dancer although not exactly graceful: modern dancing does not altogether demand grace. What I mean is that he would be perfectly at home on a dance floor, & any girl would feel perfectly at home dancing with him, not greatly thrilled, nor bored, but satisfied in the knowledge that he was a solid & respected unit in her stag-line.

37. Recurring intestinal trouble would plague Kennan for the rest of his life.
38. Balou was the Brown undergraduate.

The method by which he achieves such phenomenal "smoothness" is simple. It is nature, not him, he was born to personify or to embody all the things which the Eastern college man tries to be. Emotions, for example, are the discordant notes in social communication. Revolting against the manifold hypocrisies of inter-human relations, particularly in "polite society," they chime in at the wrong moments & spoil the music. Perfect urbanity is of necessity unemotional. The collegian recognizes this & tries to squelch his emotions. Balou goes him one better, & becomes the ideal by not receiving any at all.

I don't mean to malign poor Balou or the implication that he is a cold, cruel automaton. But his virtues are patterned & made to order. He is perfectly human & likeable. After a month or so of almost incomprehensible foreigners, he is a great relief, in his complete naturalness & simplicity.

August 13

The journey may as well be treated as a unit rather than as a series of days, for though all the days were enjoyable, they were also very much like one another, in most ways. So here is for the trip.

The item of first importance in an ocean journey is probably the boat. This I have already mentioned a little. I liked it more & more throughout the trip, & almost wish I could remain with it as part of the crew. . . .

Of fellow passengers, I had perhaps thirty, in the third class. Nick, of course, was present, although he spent most of his time below, what with seasickness & reading. . . . There was a group of eleven Germans, among whom my particular friend was a good-hearted old boy with grey hair, who was coming to live with his son in Milwaukee. I conversed with them a good deal & got in some good linguistic practice in that way. There was one poor Dutch woman, lean & haggard, who had seven children with her, the oldest of whom was not over 12. She was alone with them, & I felt very sorry for her, for she was seasick & so were most of the children.

There was an American family from Los Angeles, consisting of a mother with two daughters. The mother was typically & depressingly bourgeoisie, having been originally a children's nurse in England. She reveled in the Jap immigration law, wished either Hiram Johnson[39] or Henry Ford were president, scoffed at the League of Nations, etc. The

39. Hiram Johnson, presidential hopeful and California's Republican senator from 1917 to 1945, helped pass legislation blocking emigration from Japan.

eldest daughter was only thirteen, but a little old for her age, pretty, & at the crest of youthful illusions; she liked to devour romantic literature. The other daughter was about the cutest & therefore probably the spoiledest baby I have ever seen. Her name was Jeannette & she was a terror & a stunner.

I seldom take a violent dislike to people but I did to one man on board. He is a typical dago—wears a cap, a bushy, black, moustache, a brown flannel shirt with the collar buttoned but without a tie, sleeves unrolled but not fastened, blue serge pants without a belt, & brown army shoes which he is too lazy to lace up, thus revealing white socks & long, grey woolen underdrawers. He is talkative in a weak, ignorant, furtive, sneering way. Well, God help him. There are a few indiscriminate, unnecessary, & uninteresting low-caste Dutch people, & two filthy & slovenly shaven-headed Polish youths of about 16 or 17. This constituted the passenger list of the S.S. *Veendam* on her 14th voyage.

I saw nothing of the cabin passengers except at a distance, & what I did see of them did not interest me much. Even the sight of pretty girls up on the promenade deck doesn't demand another glance from me, having long come to the conclusion that if only the brave deserve the fair, only the smooth receive them. And indeed, Sam Balou has been up there quite regularly, even to their dances, because if one has the clothes & ability it is not hard to fool the stewards. After a few days he got to know the captain & got his permission to stay there regularly.

My time was taken up mostly with patient & intense observation of the weather, which interested me much, & with reading. I read some of Shakespeare, "Captain Blood" by Sabatini,[40] & some magazines. I find a sort of fascination in watching the behavior of a large body of water under various conditions.

August 23

The quarantine inspector came aboard this morning about 8:00 o'clock & examined us for lice, etc. After a time we moved on into the harbor & we docked at Hoboken at 10:15, by New York time. It required about a half hour to get by the customs officials & make farewells, so about quarter of eleven we stepped forth again on the soil of the New World. We had $2.25 a piece, the proceeds of one pound we had saved & cashed

40. Rafael Sabatini's *Captain Blood* (1922) is an adventure novel set in the late-seventeenth-century Caribbean.

on the boat. Nick decided to stay a night with his friend Joe in New York & go thence to Princeton, where he would see about his job with Mrs. Dickinson. I figured my best bet would be to strike out for Schenectady & get some money from Connie, and after I could return to Princeton & make plans. We went together over to the McAlpin, where Joe works (that cost me a dime) but Joe wasn't on duty yet, so we separated & I started for Schenectady. A subway took me to 242nd St., & a street car from there thru Yonkers to Hastings. There I had a lunch, which with all the transportation brought my fortune down to $1.60. From there I hit the road & bummed rides to Albany where I arrived about 9:00 p.m. The rides were of the usual various nature: a well-educated old gentleman, a truck, a non-descript youth, a kind-hearted electrical contractor, two drunks, an amateur mechanic who wasted a half-hour of my good time while he tried to fix the valve on an old Jeffries, & a hard-boiled horse jockey who took me the last forty miles into Albany at a surprising pace, in an old open Ford. It seemed that on this occasion he was racing with time, for he had a date with a chorus girl in Albany & he was already a couple of hours late.

From Albany I took an electric car & slept thru to Schenectady, where I transferred to a street car. It was not very easy to find Connie's bungalow, but I finally managed it, & rang the doorbell until Crowell[41] got up. They pretended to be real glad to see me, fixed up a meal for me & I got to bed about 12:30 p.m.

August 25

Went downtown this morning with Connie. I went around with her for a while, & then she went home while I further civilized myself by a haircut, a shave, & a pair of garters which she had insisted upon my buying. The afternoon I spent loafing, writing letters, etc. After dinner I went to Albany by trolley, whence I took boat for N.Y. on the Hudson River Night Line. The boat was a terrible old tub by the name of *Fort Orange*, a huge thing, large enough indeed, & all.

Here ended, by exhaustion, the account of the European trip of George F. Kennan.

41. Crowell was Connie's husband.

journey to Reval. Beyond us, on the barren heights of a coastal island, a stolid white tower looms up against the metallic, unreal sky. They tell me that the sense of unreality is produced by the slanting angle of the light-rays, in this nordic latitude. Be that as it may, the sight of this tower and its forlorn island proves to me again that Helsingfors is only a unique phenomenon, that the country itself is not modern America, but the Northland itself, - bound irrevocably to its sadness and its incurable unreality.

Reval. 10. Oktober, 1928.

Ich interessiere mich besonders für die Begeisterung, die in jeder Grossstadt in Europa bei der Kriegserklärung geherrscht haben soll. Ich kann es mir so echt vorstellen. Es war nicht nur Hass gegen die anderen; es war nicht nur die Ueberzeugung, dass man eine heilige Sache vertritt. Der Krieg wurde als plötzliches Allheil angesehen; jede kleine Spannung des Einzelnen, jeder unter dem Joch der langen bürgerlichen Aera gebändigte Wunsch durfte sich im Kriege ins unpersönliche erlösen. In einer gelangweilten Welt, der es lange an Kreuzzügen gefehlt hatte, bot sich der Krieg als Aenderung, Abenteuer, Hoffnung, an. Ich wäre auch unter solchen Umständen wie toll durch die Strassen gelaufen. Die laue Sommernacht wäre mir auch als Schauplatz geheimnissvoller, grossartiger Ereignisse vorgekommen, and ich hätte, wie die anderen, beim Anblick eines jeden Sternes, in jedem fernen Geräusch der Nacht, eine Verkündung der neuen, besseren Zeit gespürt, die nun schliesslich über Europa heranbrechen sollte.

Narva, 4. November, 1928.

Es ist alles Wirrwar. Nichts hängt zusammen. Es gibt keine Lösung. Die Kleinigkeiten häufen sich sinnlos vor dem müden Auge zusammen, und wollen ihr Geheimnis nicht enthüllen.

Ich habe nie meine eigene Bodenlosigkeit deutlicher gespürt als heute. Ich sehe keine zwei Bilder von demselben Standpunkt, kann also nie vergleichen, und muss hilflos den unendlichen Zug unverständlicher Eindrücke über mich ergehen lassen. Wie ein echter Deutscher, ringe ich tagtäglich um eine Weltanschauung, aber eben weil ich kein Deutscher bin, finde ich keine.

# # #

The first thing on the day's program was a walk through the Crenholm mills. These mills are located at the falls of the Narva River, which runs from Lake Peipus to the sea. They were founded over senty-five years ago by A russian Baron Kroop, but the capital later passed into British hands. Before the war, they

Chapter Two

Berlin and Riga, 1927–33

1927

After graduating from Princeton eighty-third in a class of 219, Kennan spent the summer of 1925 working as a deckhand on a coastal steamer. He then studied in Washington for the Foreign Service exam, becoming an officer in September 1926. To his sister Kennan confided, "I have a lot of respect for Coolidge and most of his cabinet, but they are all tiresomely sanctimonious." He added that while the State Department was "a vast improvement on the old days when William J. Bryan convulsed the diplomatic corps with his grape-juice dinners, it does make itself a bit ridiculous at times."[1] *At age twenty-three, Kennan took up his first foreign post, as vice-consul in Geneva, Switzerland. In August 1927, the State Department transferred him to the consulate in Hamburg, Germany.*

Geneva, May 16

As we steamed down the lake, Mont Blanc faded out, and, as though for compensation, a brilliant full moon emerged deliberately and dramatically from a bank of clouds and threw down its corrugated path of light upon the water. It was no wan, frail, feminine moon—this—but a great, strident, sexless disc of light, that mounted the sky with the assurance of a star actor making his appearance on the stage.

As I write, this same moon still commands the heavens and the earth. It lights up the vague cliffs of the Saleve mountains, across the lake; it transforms the lawns into deep, soft carpets of same [*sic*] strange material; it floods boldly in the window before me; it excites the placid Genevoises so that the whole town is out strolling on the quais; and finally, it so overawes my poor nightingale that he has gone out of business

1. Kennan to Jeanette Kennan Hotchkiss, December 3, 1925, box 23, George F. Kennan papers (hereafter "Kennan papers"), Seeley G. Mudd Manuscript Library, Princeton University. A teetotaler before Prohibition, Secretary of State Bryan had forbade the serving of alcohol at official dinners.

entirely for the night, and has left the field to crickets and grasshoppers and distant tram cars.

May 24

I ponder again on the homo americanus, or however you write it. . . .

Now Mr. A. is the genuine, keen, American business man, transplanted to European soil. He is apparently quite without individual character. He has no distinguishing physical characteristics at all. He is clean shaven, expressionless, wears shell-rimmed glasses. He is neither fat nor thin. He has an American car, and tells us with pride how he drove from Havre to Geneva in so many days.

He has a good analytical mind, and does considerable thinking about the future, from a purely technical point of view. He has carved out a remarkable career, first with the General Electric Company, where his ability was so well recognized that they, with all the genius of American business, sent him over to Geneva, severed official connections with him, and let him become one of the tsars of the European lamp cartel, knowing full well that he would always be their own unofficial representative. Here he lives, quietly, placidly, unobtrusively and would generally be classified as a Babbitt.[2]

Yet he has none of the silly exaggerations of the Lewis-Tarkington[3] types. He doesn't scoff at art and beauty; he doesn't care enough about them to scoff. He has no disappointments, to disillusions, no longings, nothing but pure objective interest in the manufacture and sale of electric lamps. He tells us: "I'm not one of those who say they wouldn't be in business if it weren't helping humanity, but I do believe that this industry *is* improving and helping humanity," and he went on to explain how better lighting improved the efficiency of labor.

He may be right. Yet tonight, after dinner, I walked up and down the terrace, smoked a pipe, and wondered about it.

May 26

This clear, transparent city—strange study in white and blue—has a sort of dual individuality. There is the old Geneva: a group of about a hundred thousand sober French-Swiss people, who are homely and

2. George F. Babbitt, the paragon of conformist pro-business values, is the chief protagonist in Sinclair Lewis's *Babbitt* (1922).

3. Like Lewis, Booth Tarkington explored in his novels the illusions and narrow vision of middle-class America.

industrious and contented with a sphere of interests as limited as those of small-towners the world over. The real Genevese thinks about how business is going, and about municipal politics, and about whether Jacques will be able to go to school next year, and about whether it wouldn't be a good plan for the family to go picnicking on the Saleve at Pent-cote [*sic*], and about how the new railway station will look when it is completed. "The League of Nations," he ruminates, "was a fine thing for business, and it brought a lot of tourists to the town, and besides it is probably a good thing if it will keep these other nations from going to war." But it is by no means a central fact in his life. Diplomats, statesmen, tourists: the Genevese accepts them all as part of existence, and as equals; he minds his own business and when his business brings him into contact with these others, he treats them neither with awe nor with contempt. And when business is over, he is content to go his way and to let them go theirs.

Like all the Swiss, the Genevese people are essentially what might be called innocent bystanders. They are eternally watching something. The boats, for example, must leave twenty or thirty times a day from the dock by the Pont du Mont Blanc. Yet every time that a boat leaves, there is sure to be a crowd of placid Genevese citizens staring as though they were watching the departure of the *Leviathan*. The traffic cop at the main corner, making magnificent gestures which nobody ever obeys, is always the cynosure of at least thirty or forty pairs of wondering, Swiss eyes. A tire being repaired on the streets will draw a sizeable crowd of silent watchers. A building being torn down on one of the main streets has so fascinated the public that for two weeks special guards have been posted to keep the curious at a safe distance from the flying bricks. They are a nation of rare philosophers, these Swiss, who like to watch things, not necessarily because they want to learn and imitate, but simply because they feel that things are interesting to watch. In spite of all they tell of the hardships they suffered during the war, I have a suspicion that as they stood up here on their mountain tops and watched the rest of Europe fight, they had the same solemn air of attentiveness on their faces as they have when they watch a building being torn down, and I think they must have enjoyed it just as much.

July 4

In the afternoon, I was unbearably sour and sleepy, and still suffering from a damned lunch I ate yesterday in Lausanne, but I had to get dressed up and go down to the Hotel Beau Rivage for the 4th of July reception.

In there came all the Americans, the women eager and fresh in their best flouncy summer clothes, all eyes to see who was there and all that sort of thing, the men frankly disgusted and bored, except two or three college students, on European tours, who flopped in, looking very sleek, and were impressed at the number of celebrities. Tuck,[4] with professional cordiality, did the receiving, and, there not being much for me to do, I escaped to the lobby and read a magazine during the first part of the affair. Then tea was finished, and everyone crowded into the ball-room and Admiral Hilary Jones[5] read a speech, which made it the women's turn to look bored and the men's to look eager, because it was all about the Arms Conference, and it slapped Great Britain deftly on both cheeks. And immediately afterward, I found myself explaining to a British acquaintance that it was all "Conference fodder" and I suddenly thought with horror of the effect that would have on Tuck, if he ever should discover that his vice-consul was going around, explaining away the delegate's speeches.

July 14

Everybody here is simply furious about the Sacco Vanzetti case,[6] and they send us all sorts of petitions,—even painted up the side-walk outside the Consulate, one time. The evening papers, tonight, announced that S. and V. are to be executed on August 10, and as I was leaving the Consulate, the little wisp of an old woman who is the wife of the concierge waylaid me in the hall, simply quivering with indignation, and announced in an accusing tone: "Monsieur: Sacco et Vanzetti vont être executes!"—and then she stood waiting belligerently, expecting me, I suppose, to announce that I would cable the President immediately to let them off. Unfortunately, I could do no more than mutter something about a "mauvaise affaire" and slink shamefacedly out of the building, but I couldn't help feeling that there was something glorious in the fact that that poor little dried-up woman, who putters around all day in the dirty basement of a Geneva office building, should quiver with indignation and want to

4. S. Pinkney Tuck was U.S. consul in Geneva.

5. Admiral Hilary P. Jones was naval adviser at the Geneva Disarmament Conference.

6. Nicola Sacco and Bartolomeo Vanzetti were Italian American anarchists accused of executing a guard during a robbery in Massachusetts. Despite doubts about their guilt, they were executed—retribution, many charged, for their radical beliefs and foreign birth.

assault a vice-consul because she considered that somewhere, thousands of miles away, human beings were going to be cruel and unjust to two of their fellows.

Hamburg, September 10

This was a particularly bad day to attend a foreign colony wedding. No one should ever go to a wedding particularly to such a one when he feels as though he were tuned up to vibrate to all the struggle and tragedy and discord of the world as well as to all its harmony. But that was the way I went to the ball-room of the Hotel Atlantic, there to see poor H——, mild, unimpressive H——, with his still less impressive bride, the two of them kneeling there, before the pastor of the British Church, kneeling with all their faults and their weaknesses and their petty pretensions, kneeling and trembling and dedicating their lives to each other, and behind them a small company of uneasy acquaintances, assembled to lend dignity to the occasion. It was pitiful, pitiful, pitiful: this faint, struggling gesture toward the vision and the dream.

The horrible wedding breakfast followed the ceremony: conversation dragging like the ticking of a clock, the jarring uncertainty, when somebody proposed a toast to the bride, the half-hearted attempts at festivity, the completely out-of-place feeling, as though that gay table, with its heaped red roses and its dainty place cards and its tall wine glasses were not for us miserable exiles, just gathered from our dusty desks and ledgers, but rather for some truly happy, triumphant marriage party, celebrating the symbol of all the strength and the glory of two people's lives.

Sometimes I am afraid that we are all expatriates, we humans, no matter where we reside. I am afraid that we are expatriates from another more kindly, more genuine world, the memories of which fade from us with our childhood.

But these are bad, dark days, and horror hovers on the horizon of things like distant thunder.

October 10

I went to a premiere tonight. . . . It is really alarming, how I fall for any presentation of the lonely, innocent girl whom all the world deceives and mistreats for three acts, and tonight, when the widowed mother, in the court scene, took the accused Cinderella in her arms and cried: "Now, now, that's all right: I am a mother, too!"—I wanted to lay my head on the expansive shoulder of the fat lady ahead of me and heave vast blubbers. Only the sense of my consular dignity, and the realization that the leading lady, after all, has probably committed her own share of injustices on others, in the course of her career, restrained me.

October 30
It is a strange thing about cities: there are some which are simply collection of buildings, like Geneva or Philadelphia, inanimate, impersonal things, and there are others, like Hamburg, which reach out for you, when you live in them, and spread the tentacles of their beauty and their evil quietly around you. They establish a personal relationship, which you can never shake. And just so, here in Hamburg, the city talks to me personally, talks with a melancholy, autumnal beauty through its splendid, quiet boulevards and its inland lake, talks with a thrilling, breathless strength through the restless machinery of its harbor, and yet talks with the voice of unutterable horror, through the lurid, repulsive alleys of St. Pauli,[7] and their inhabitants who come to the seaman's division in the Consulate and inflict their lives on mine.

November 1
It is a peculiar little world of its own, this European political world, a world which lives in an atmosphere of speeches and declarations and editorials, which the bulk of the people know nothing about. A Belgian cabinet minister unveils a war memorial in some small town and says the Germans are a bad bunch of people, who are just waiting for another opportunity to hop on Belgium. Nine out of ten Belgians, as well as the same proportion of Germans know nothing about the speech and don't want to know anything about it. But the next day every nationalist paper in Germany is up in arms and writing stormy editorials about the death of the "Locarno Spirit"[8] in Belgium and prating interminably about the "franc-tireurs," and wailing about a "straining" of diplomatic relations, and a new "tension" in the political atmosphere. It never seems to occur to them that what they call the "political atmosphere" is, after all, only the atmosphere around a certain thin strata of professional politicians and suspicious journalists, and that underneath it, the great fundamental forces of the nations and the classes grow and change, quite unaffected by all this prattling of bitter little men.

7. St. Pauli was famous for its red-light district.
8. In 1925 at Locarno, Switzerland, Germany signed a treaty with France and Belgium reaffirming cessions of territory to them after World War I.

November 7

Yesterday was a rainy Sunday. I walked down to the post office, in the morning, and ran into a huge communist demonstration, thousands and thousands of people standing in the drizzling rain before the Dammtor Station, with their red flags and arm-bands, listening to soap-box orators, singing the Internationale, marching around behind sickly fife and drum organizations, buying propaganda literature, and Sacco-Vanzetti postcards.

I stood around and watched, listened to snatches from the speeches, looked at the people themselves. And the strange thing was: that, for all my contempt for the falseness and hatefulness and demagoguery of Communism, I had a strange desire to cry, when I first saw those ranks of people marching along the street: ill-dressed, slouching brutalized people.

It was the first time in my life that I have ever caught a hint of the real truth upon which the little group of spiteful parasites in Moscow feeds, of the truth that these stupid, ignorant, unpleasant people were after all human beings, that they were, after centuries of mute despair, for the first time attempting to express and to assert themselves, that under the manifold hokus-pokus of the red flags and the revolutionary ritual they had found something that they considered to be essentially their own, something that they believed in, and were proud of, that tomorrow, just as yesterday, these same people would again be mutely absorbed in the work of the world, with barges, railways, drays, factories, street-cars, and what not, while other people—the industrialists and journalists and politicians gathered the fruits of their labors and held the center of the stage,—but that today was *their* day, and they were marching under *their* banner, sullied and cheapened as that banner might be, that they were marching sullenly and defiantly, but with hope and with a tremendous earnestness.

Here, it seemed to me, was certainly error and hatefulness and pathos; but here, also, was seriousness and idealism. And after all, in the present state of the world, I am inclined to regard any sort of idealism, be it ever so beclouded with bitterness and hate and bad leadership, as a refreshing phenomenon.

November 12

This afternoon there was a charity tea dance in the new *Cap Arcona*, the latest and largest liner for the Germany–South America service. She lay out in mid-stream, along the dolphins, and we went out to her on a tender. . . .

I felt an irrepressible yearning to exchange, as though by some magic transformation, my cutaway for sailor's dungarees and the brilliant comfort of that gay ballroom for the sooty forepeak of the tramp steamer, to ride into the darkness and the night rain.

November 30

Last night I went to the "Dom." . . . A city of blinking lights, tents, booths, and tawdry shacks of all descriptions, long, dirty streets of trampled mud, gambling booths, food booths with sugar canes and sausages, shooting galleries where the guns shoot crooked, Ferris wheels, alligator shows, crazy houses, scenic railways, peep shows, Wild West, the whip.

The thick crowds move slowly along the street. A little bald man stands on a platform before a tent, haranguing the crowd. Behind him, attired in brilliant but somewhat threadbare evening wraps, stand a half dozen miserable creatures who once were women, shivering with the cold, pale even under the smears of paint. . . . A hoarse voice shrieks: "Oh ye faint-hearted! Of what are ye afraid?" and one looks around, expecting to see an evangelist, but it is only a gambling booth. Slushed stenographers swing, shrieking, around the whip. . . .

Men yell, wheels revolve, lights blink, whistles blow, people laugh, people eat, human life flows along in all its variety and all its monotony, in all its pretension and all its pathos, and behind it all, as Franz Werfel[9] writes, the gods themselves dance on, in high indifference!

December 20

Reading *Die Buddenbrooks* (Thomas Mann),[10] this *Forsyte Saga*[11] of old Lübeck, I cannot help but regret that I did not live fifty or a hundred years sooner. Life is too full in these times to be comprehensible. We know too many cities to be able to grow into any of them, and our arrivals and departures are no longer matters for emotional debauches, for they are too common. Similarly, we have too many friends to have any real friendships, too many books to know any of them well, and the quality of our impressions gives way to the quantity, so that life begins to seem like a movie, with hundreds of kaleidoscopic scenes flashing on

9. Franz Werfel was an Austrian Bohemian novelist and playwright.
10. Mann's *Buddenbrooks* (1901) chronicles the decline over four generations of a German family beset by the disruptions of modernity.
11. John Galsworthy's novels detailed the lives of three generations of an upper-middle-class British family.

and off our field of perception, gone before we have time to consider them.

I should like to have lived in the days when a visit was a matter of months, when political and social problems were regarded from simple standpoints called "liberal" and "conservative," when foreign countries were still foreign, when a vast part of the world always bore the glamour of the great unknown, when there were still wars worth fighting and gods worth worshiping.

1928

In January, Kennan left Hamburg for leave in the United States. Discontented with the Foreign Service, he thought about resigning. Moreover, he was engaged to Eleanor Hard, the daughter of the Washington journalists William and Anne Hard. She then broke off the engagement, and Kennan felt crushed.[12] *He was also deflated by the "real tragedies" suffered by his lover, Charlotte Böhm, and other Germans whose lives were wrecked by war, hyperinflation, and depression. He despised the "boundless optimism" felt by many Americans about their "perpetual prosperity. . . . That's why I am probably always going to be a considerable radical."*[13]

His career, however, was lofted by his acceptance into a new State Department program for three years of language study. He chose Russian, as had another George Kennan (1845–1924), the cousin of his grandfather, who was a role model. The two men shared a birthdate, and there were many other parallels in their lives. The State Department sent the younger Kennan first to Berlin, then to Tallinn ("Reval" in German), the capital of Estonia and a window on the Soviet Union. He was already teaching himself Russian.

New York, March 1

At 33rd Street and Broadway, there are five layers of transportation, five layers of gleaming rails and thundering wheels!

Deep under the city, the electric suburban trains glide away from the echoing crypts of the Pennsylvania Station, to plunge through the

12. Decades later, Kennan would note that Anthony Lake, the State Department official who became President Bill Clinton's national security advisor, was the son of his former fiancée.

13. Kennan to Jeanette Kennan Hotchkiss, October 20, 1928, box 23, Kennan papers.

bowels of the earth until they again rise to the light on the flats of Long Island. Above them, in the 33rd Street Station of the B.M.T. subway, the long express trains plunge in and out between the crowded platforms, with a grinding of brakes and a sparkling of the third rail contacts. Above them stands the cavernous terminal of the Hudson Tubes, with its tawdry white pillars and arches, its never-ending flood of humanity, its jingling of fare-boxes rising over the roar of the trains. On the street above, the surface cars rattle along between the pillars of the "L," while over them the elevated trains glide in and out of their station, in a plane and a world of their own.

North of Grand Central a new skyscraper is sprouting up. There is nothing unusual in this in itself. But the elevated streets which skirt the station and converge to form Park Avenue, are not going to be led around this new building. Instead, two huge archways run through the new structure, from north to south, and at some date in the near future, the streams of traffic flowing through these archways will recall vaguely the innumerable tourist prospecti of California, where an automobile is invariably portrayed, passing through a hole, in the base of a great tree.

Following my whim, I wander abroad in the early hours of the morning, and drink in the infinite variety which, even at that hour, springs from the inexhaustible city.

Washington, March 17

I pace the city like a man who is lost: across the viaduct, into the muddy paths of Rock Creek Park where the snow has not yet melted, through the lines of white-pillared houses between Sixteenth Street and the Park. I know this city as I know my own name, and yet there is something which I cannot find. Somewhere, in one or another of these quiet streets, there must be genuine beauty and life, to solve the riddle. Somewhere there must be the hidden key of significance, to unlock the meaning of this preposterous, mocking Sunday afternoon!

Or is there no key? Does all the life and purpose of this country flow so relentlessly into its workshops and its offices that on the days when these are closed there is nothing left but a vast, senseless desolation of stone and steel and aimless motion? A world of lost faces, drifting helplessly in the vacuum of their own restlessness?

The cars roll silently on, and give no answer. An all-engulfing boredom, a depression too great to describe, weighs on the city. Only at the corner of U and Sixteenth Streets, the fresh face of a young girl, smiling behind the window of a limousine, is like a breath of wind from the mountains, redolent of life and of spring.

March 26

On this night, I make my last reluctant obeisance to the obscure gods of Washington, to the cool, derisive deities who have taken without compensation the two best years of my life. They are the gods of my own personal Washington, not of the tourist center nor of the political capitol, but rather of the wistful, nervous Washington, the Washington of ceaseless promise and ceaseless denial, throbbing on through the years, behind the glittering hauteur with which it is clothed.

In the knowledge that I am finally leaving this Washington, leaving it in a sense far deeper than the purely physical one, memories of it become suddenly doubly keen: memories of the hurdy-gurdy man in Church Street, on hot summer evenings, of grey and white buses streaming along Sixteenth Street, in the shadows of the shuttered Russian Embassy, of well-dressed people; dancing placidly in great ball rooms, of charity balls in the Willard Hotel, of nightclubs, where the softness of the atmosphere and the subdued lilt of the music contrasted so cruelly with the cheapness and vulgarity of the guests, of paths along the Tidal Basin, on spring afternoon, of shady streets in Georgetown, where the old brick houses sung to themselves the songs of a still, deep past, of winding bridle-paths in Rock Creek Park, of children playing around the fountain at Dupont Circle, of the cold shaft of the Monument and the pillars of the Lincoln Memorial in the moonlight, of lights shimmering across the Potomac on frosty winter nights, of cool, dark corridors in the State Department. These and a thousand other memories return now to taunt me for the homage I have done them. They sear like fire, for in every one of them lies the glow of failure!

Berlin, April 18

In the formal drawing room of the American Embassy, a crowd of unvivacious gentlemen, in black coats and striped trousers, chatter perfunctorily. Only Stresemann,[14] swaying his portly figure back and forth as he talks, is animated and dynamic. One wonders at the secrets of Europe

14. Gustav Stresemann, foreign minister of Germany from 1923 to 1929, sought to reconcile his nation and the victors of World War I.

which must lie within that broad, shaven head and feels it almost a sacrilege that a man with such responsibility should joke and laugh.

May 6

My window overlooks the square before the Schöneberg Rathaus. It is a great place for political demonstrations. . . . Tonight the roll of a drum calls attention to a demonstration coming across the square. It is no colorful, enthusiastic procession, this time. It is a small group of the well-disciplined Social Democrats, with one or two banners, and a couple of squeaky instruments. They pass my window, four abreast, women and men, shabbily-dressed and unimposing. They are not the virile, overall-ed proletarians of the Communist posters. I doubt, despite their professed socialism, whether they are members of the proletariat at all. They are more apt to be members of the great ragged overlap of the classes, the lower bourgeoisie, each with his few marks in the Sparkasse [savings bank], and his petty social ambitions.

It is an unimpressive parade, and pathetic by virtue of its very unpretentiousness. Yet there is significance in this quietness and unpretentiousness, something stronger than in all the blaring and roaring of the communists and the *Stalhhelm*.[15] These poor voiceless people from the garrets of Berlin: they have carried, all unwitting, the idealism of the German character through the horrors of war and revolution and economic collapse, and on their narrow shoulders rests the fate of future generations.

August 5

Week-end visit to Carlson in Hapsal.[16]

I leave Reval [Tallinn] in an execrable humor. I feel physically tired and repulsive; I hate the world, and the world hates me. I resent Reval, and all the people in it; it angers me that I should have to visit Carlson when I do not want to. . . . It was kind and good of Carlson to ask me. He meant well by it. Yet what right have these people to force on me their drab world and their timorous, middle-class standards? What right have they, to demand, as they will, that I adapt myself to their conventions, that I play up to their weaknesses and their prejudices?

15. The "Steel Helmets" was a right-wing, paramilitary organization composed of World War I veterans and sympathizers.

16. Consul Harry Carlson was Kennan's superior in Tallinn. Hapsal was the location of Carlson's vacation house.

We sit a long time at dinner, the Carlsons and the Britisher chatting, while I sulk. I hear the band outside playing the Dance Macabre, which we used to play at Princeton, in the University Orchestra. Once we went on a trip, and played the Dance Macabre at a girl's school, a boarding school at Saratoga Springs, N.Y. It was midwinter, and I remember still how the great bare elm trees arched over the snow-covered streets against a starry, winter sky. The hope and mystery of those days has never been realized, but I can feel them still. And what can these people know of that hope and that mystery, sitting here and chatting their foreign-colony gossip? Their whole lives have degenerated into foreign colony gossip and they would like to pull mine down to the same level.

The Britisher asks me if I play bridge. I say yes, but that I do not intend to play it in Reval. I say that I expect to do some studying and in general to be pretty busy.

The Britisher laughs. "That's what they all say", he replies, "but before long they are playing around and having as good a time as the rest of them."

That makes my blood boil. Damn him, do I look like the "rest of them?" Does he think that I, too, have so little strength of character, so few resources within myself, that I will be forced to seek refuge from boredom, as they have done, in the dull pettiness of foreign-colony social life?

In the morning I feel stuffy and bilious. Sunshine floods the cool garden, mocking my bitterness. At breakfast, I sense the hostility. I am not surprised. I deserve it. Before the others are through eating, Mrs. Carlson suggests that I amuse myself as I see fit. I take the hint and excuse myself. As I walk away, I can feel the remarks which I cannot hear. They are all against me. I am not their kind.

I hire a rowboat and set out on the bay. A fresh, strong wind blows in from the west. The water dances and seethes and bubbles in the sunshine. Sailing parties pass me, tacking up to the mouth of the bay. Their white catboats lean tautly on the wind, cut swiftly through the whitecaps with a swishing noise. I head toward the west, into the teeth of the breeze. I enjoy the difficulty of rowing against it. It is something physical, on which I can vent my ill-humor, something I can fight frankly against. By the time I reach the mouth of the bay, my hands are blistered, and it is time to turn back.

In the afternoon, the Britisher suggests that we go out in a paddleboat, across the bay, in one of those thin, frail craft which one sees in such abundance on the lakes around Potsdam. We start out, diagonally into the wind. A wave immediately comes over the bow, splashing both of us, drenching our clothes. It soon becomes obvious that we will soon be wet to the skin, if we keep on. Yet we are both stubborn. He is not going to complain, and neither am I. So on we go, into the wind, cold spray dashing in at us, in a continual, chilling stream. My arms and wrists are sore from the morning's rowing. They ache at every stroke.

We reach the other side of the bay, pull the boat up on a little island, take off our dripping clothes, put them in the dry compartments at either end of the boat, and start back, in swimming suits. It seems an interminable trip. My left arm is so cramped that I can scarcely paddle. We are both chilled to the bone, and very miserable.

Now I am on the train, coming back. The Britisher, thank God, is staying over another day. The somber Estonian landscape flows past the train window, and the black tops of the distant pine trees form a jagged, dark horizon, against the glowing sunset. Across the clear red sky are stretched thin, horizontal ribbons of cloud, some of bright gold, others of a dark, greenish blue. Slowly, steadily, the glowing sky behind them fades, and with it, my unhappy week-end nears its close.

September 4

The Americanization of Europe, the flooding of the continent with the cultural as well as the economic goods of the New World: all this is something which Europe owes to its own imperfection. Americanism, like Bolshevism, is a disease which gains footing only in a weakened body. I have lost my sympathy for the Europeans who protest against the influx of American automobiles and American phonograph records. If the Old World has no longer sufficient vitality, economic and cultural, to oppose these new barbarian invasions, it will have to drown in the flood, as civilizations have drowned before it. The wheels of history cannot be halted out of a love for tradition and a respect for past accomplishments.

Two or three nights ago, I dreamed that I again encountered C, whom I had not seen since we left college.

I asked him about his work—(it was back in the States).

He replied: "Oh, it's all pretty routine stuff, and one wonders sometimes but when one sees all the good it does."

I had to turn away. I was overcome with an unbearable depression. It seemed to me that America was full of puzzled young men living tragedies, seeking pitifully in the results of their occupations some excuse for the throwing away of their own lives.

September 6

I feel, sometimes, the temptation to escape from the ordinary futile trend of our times by visiting strange places, doing strange things, seeing strange people. There is always the allure about the place where no American has ever been, and one feels, when one gets there, that one has shaken off the shackles of his own environment, and has elevated himself above his fellow-citizens who stayed at home.

It is a dangerous mistake. The period of discovery is nearing its close. Scourged by boredom, nitwits pursue the rare and exotic to the ends of the earth. There is little that remains unseen, undescribed. Milliburton's[17] travel lecturers, wealthy professors, they all swarm through the few dim regions that have thus far resisted the twentieth century. Anybody can travel, who has health and persistence. Talking movies, radio, radio movies: these will soon destroy the few small fragments of the unusual which have still been preserved from the profane view.

Where, then, lies the escape from the squirrel-cage? Where is the opportunity to raise one's self, by sacrifice and hardship, if need be, out of the whirlpool of the commonplace?

It lies in *depth*, rather than *breadth*. Our civilization is like a body of water which, lacking profundity, spreads out over its own banks and floods the countryside with a thin sheet of stagnant water. Like a glutton reaching for new and rarer morsels, leaving undigested those which he already has, it fastens with fleeting, uncomprehending curiosity on one thing after another, strips each of its coverings, gapes idiotically at it, and finally discards it again in a library or museum. Always something new, for God's sake, something new.

Yes, the solution lies only in depth. There is nothing new under the sun, in the ordinary sense except ourselves. It is not farther away from all that we are familiar with, that we are going to make discoveries, but rather deeper down in our own selves, about which we know everything, and understand nothing. . . .

17. Most likely Kennan was referring to the prominent travel writer Richard Halliburton.

[In his quest for vestiges of pre-1917 Russian culture, Kennan traveled to the fifteenth-century monastery of Pskovo-Pechorsky and to Narva in northern Estonia. Though studying Russian he was also perfecting his German.]

Narva, Estonia, November 4[18]

Everything is confused. Nothing is connected. There is no solution. The petty details are piling up before my tired eyes but they remain meaningless, they do not reveal their secrets. I never sensed my own groundlessness more keenly than today. I do not see two pictures from the same point of view, thus I can never compare. I have to endure helplessly the never-ending train of impressions. I struggle daily to attain a world view, like a real German, but precisely because I am not German, I do not succeed.

18. This entry is in German.

1929

In early 1929, the State Department appointed Kennan to the legation in Riga, Latvia. While there, he traveled throughout the Baltic area. Inspired by the travel writings of the German journalist Alfons Paquet, whom he admired, Kennan worked hard at describing what he observed. The fledgling diplomat was assigned to study Russian language and history at the Friedrich Wilhelm University of Berlin. Kennan did not comment on the stock market crash in October.

March 5[19]

Berlin is thawing out, rather dirty and colorless. A mute depression lays a heavy atmosphere on the endless rows of houses. Politics are bankrupt. The economic crisis rules. In Paris the reparations issue is being negotiated without hope or idealism.[20]

Books by Remarque and Renn,[21] which are visible in every bookstore, paint the extreme horror of the *last* war, but no one has any idea how the *next* one can be avoided. Life goes on by dint of habit, without enthusiasm, and only a pair of foolish tourists laugh meaninglessly on the Kurfurstendamm.

En route to Dorpat, Estonia, March 29

Our second class carriage, like all the rolling-stock of the old broad-gauge Russian lines, is roomy and sturdy. The wide, flat benches, with their leather cushions and varnished wooden backs, are much preferable to the stuffy and odorous upholstery of the Western European cars. The other travelers are composed of a couple of Jews, some natty Latvian

19. This entry is in German.
20. The Young Committee of international businessmen arrived at a plan to reduce Germany's reparation obligations stemming from the Versailles treaty of 1919.
21. Erich Maria Remarque wrote *All Quiet on the Western Front* (1929). Ludwig Renn wrote *War* (1928).

officers, with their Sam Browne belts, several members of the Riga bourgeoisie, going to the country for the holidays, and a remarkably intelligent-looking family, speaking Latvian but sporting Canadian Pacific suitcase labels of the world. Some of the people smoke, some chatter in German, Russian, or Latvian, some read the morning papers, some curl up on the sunny benches and sleep, some stare out the window.

There is much activity at the little way-side steps. In front of the grey, wooden stations, inherited from the Russians, the dirt platforms are lined with country people, in ill-fitting, holiday clothes, waiting for a train in the other direction to take them to the city. Seedy-looking railway officials, in khaki overcoats, push officiously through the crowds. Peasant women carry milk cans between the baggage cars and their dingy carts. Railway station loafers lean against the railings, surveying the train and the crowd. They are always present in considerable numbers, wearing muddy Russian boots, dirty mackinaws, and the big Finnish fur-caps, with a leather covering, and ear-laps tied across the top.

Dorpat, March 30

Estonian students, sitting in a café, impervious to the sparkling weather out of doors, impervious to the far roar of the world. It would not be so bad, if the café had an atmosphere of its own, if it could encourage the growth of an Estonian Boheme, throughout these winter months. But it has nothing of the sort. It is only a shabby reproduction of that indescribably vacuous institution: the typical northern-European café, where heavy red draperies shut out the healthy light of day; where coffee and cake is served on little tables with sticky imitation-marble tops and paper-napkins, where bored traveling salesmen read the daily papers and look at the women; where women sit patiently, by themselves, hoping to appear mysterious and romantic through their anonymity, hoping someday to encounter the shadowy Prince Charming, as he is encountered in fiction magazines; where a second-rate orchestra scrapes out tunes to which nobody listens—in short, where there is not even the lure of intoxication and vice and despair, but only sickening pretension, dullness, boredom, and stale air.

Kovno, Lithuania, April 9

One must go far to find the law or necessity which lies behind the creation of these bright new walls, which are to be government buildings and banks. No capital in the world has been created by more freakish turns of fortune than this. Threads of Fate, leading to all parts of Europe and America, are responsible for the fact that this scrawny Jewish village, lying by its frozen river in the morning sun, may call itself the capital of the muddy, impoverished countryside which stretches out around it.

It has accepted its strange Fate without thanks, without emotion, as a hungry animal accepts an unexpected meal. When the tide of fortune turns, when the officials and diplomats go away, leaving the government buildings as empty as the shops of the little Jewish merchants, there will be snarling and recrimination, but there will be no real sadness, for there has been no real hope.

Riga, Latvia, May 26

Summer has come to the Baltic, and with it the long white nights. A summer sun bathes the city in golden, vibrating warmth. The Kaisergarten is a mass of bright foliage, and the dandelions float on a sea of high, thick grass. Crowds stroll along the gravel paths, sun themselves on the benches, listen to the soldier's concert at the bandstand. There is a confusion of human voices, talking in Russian or German, a hum of invisible insects, a rush of warm breeze through the fresh foliage, a rumbling and honking of distant meter-cars, a crying of children, and a laughing of young people.

It is all too rich, too full, this summer day. It is more than one can stand. One would like to cry out to the gods to take it away again. We, on whom these gods have spat the venom of their snow and rain for so many months, how shall we receive this sudden surfeit of warmth and tenderness? We are not prepared for it. We would like to clutch it and hold it, but it is too immense, too illusive, to be grasped. We have no loves, no triumphs worthy of this day, we can only walk blinking and bewildered through the hot paths of the park, in the disturbing knowledge of a glory we cannot share, a glory in which the indomitable pettiness of our own lives prevents us from participating.

Evening comes, and driven by an irresistible restlessness, I find myself again in the paths of the park. It is dark under the tall trees, and only the still lagoon holds something of the glow of the sky. The human beings, still strolling on the paths, have lost their identity, their hideousness, and have become shadows, endowed with mystery and beauty.

[**Following a personal visit to Sweden and Denmark in the summer**]

After two and a half years in the war-stricken parts of Europe, the most startling and significant thing about Scandinavia is that here is a part of the world which never really experienced the war. Everywhere else, there are only two great divisions of history: before the war and after the war; but here, incredible thought, the years between 1914 and 1920 brought no famine, no revolution, no inflation, and no break in the perpetual, imperceptible merging of the generations.

[During a personal visit to Hamburg in the fall][22]
How can one explain the appeal of Hamburg? Why should this city, more than any other, take the visitor in and fascinate him? Why is it that while other cities become empty and boring, Hamburg always sings its multi-sonic, buzzing song in which all hope and all fear of humankind finds its expression? I know no answer. I simply avow myself to this city as to a goddess and am exuberant that the city exists.

22. This entry is in German.

1930

Kennan spent most of 1930 in Berlin studying at Friedrich Wilhelm University as well as with private tutors. The State Department paid for his educational and living expenses. The department instructed him to acquire an education similar to that of a well-off Russian before the Russian Revolution. Kennan also delved into the nature and the outlook of communism as he sought to formulate his own judgment of the claims and promise of Soviet ideology. Although bored with much of his life, he found Russia "one place which never seems to lose attraction."[23]

January 18

In reviving this long-neglected diary, for reasons scarcely known to myself, I am first of all going to preserve . . . an unmailed letter,[24] written in Riga:

"As a matter of fact, I am rather disgusted with both branches of the service, and with the Department. As for the diplomatic service, one can say that it offers opportunities for interesting and profitable work. That despite the fact that the increasing ascendancy of business over politics has brought about a corresponding decrease of importance in diplomacy, as an active agency in world affairs. Yet I should not care to remain much longer in our diplomatic service, in Europe.

When I see the way in which it functions over here, I have to go back and question its real raison d'etre. What do we establish these missions over here for, after all? Merely to comply with international custom, to maintain cordial relations with the European governments, and routine communications which pass back and forth? Or to maintain a wide-awake information service capable of reporting, interpreting, and predicting political trends with which our Government will have to reckon

23. Kennan to Hotchkiss, November 16, 1930, box 23, Kennan papers.
24. Kennan did not reveal to whom the letter was addressed.

in its foreign policy? I think it is true of most of our European missions that the emphasis is laid far more on maintaining a back-slapping cordiality with members of the government and the diplomatic corps than on the real work of the mission. The elements of social prestige and 'contacts' are given an importance far exceeding their real value. For a country actively participating in the fray of European politics, it is valuable to have diplomats whose intimacies are such that they can get the low-down at any given moment on just what is taking place in the town. I listened in, one evening, on one of the Swedes here, who was pumping a gent from the Latvian Foreign Office on what had been going on at the Foreign Office during the day, and I appreciated the necessity of it, for the Swede.

But we don't have to do that sort of thing; the minor scandals all come out in the newspaper wash, anyway, with time, and it is quite possible for our diplomats to be respected without being parlor-entertainers. Yet we go ahead in our own fashion. We play our bridge, dance with other people's wives, give our dinners, exert ourselves, as though our lives depended on it, to make ourselves agreeable to that vacuous and transitory society which is called diplomatic and governmental. We succeed, God knows. Our revered representatives in many a European capital are more native than the natives; the local press sings paeans to them; they get every invitation that comes along; official faces beam at every wreath they lay, and at every gift they present. But what for? I have yet to see the results. I have yet to see any genuine affection for the U.S. spring from the carefully cultivated popularity of its representatives. As a matter of fact, it seems to me that we rarely even attempt to cash in our standing for anything of real value to the government, and that even when we do attempt it, the Europeans are not as responsive as one might expect. They are pleased indeed at our attentions; they are very glad to come to dinner and all that; but they know that it is not necessary to give anything valuable in exchange, because the dinners will continue whether they do or not. Thus they reply to our curiosity, if at all, by whispering in a tone of greatest confidence the same line of patter which they have released to the press in the morning, and go home laughing contentedly up their sleeves."

January 26

"Hello. Miss L——? This is the American you talked to the other night at the Russian opera. Look, I find myself unexpectedly free, this evening, for the first time in months. I'd sort of like to go out and paint the town red, and I wondered if you'd come along.

Very red?

Well, pretty red. Besides I haven't been out with an American girl for pretty nearly two years.

All right, I'd be glad to.

Fine, I'll call for you. . . ."

Home. I drink another whiskey-soda, and wax expansive over the virtues of my fellow countrymen, at the same time wondering what it is that forces me to act like a gentleman, when I am with an American woman.

March 3

A train of huge barges, headed by their colossal river tug, is moored along the shore, below me, and a crowd of loafers, including myself, watches a sick woman being carried off one of the barges on to a prim little municipal, horse-drawn ambulance. I am filled with my usual curiosity; I would like to hire on one of these barges as a deck-hand, accompany it upstream, learn what sort of people work on it, what they hope from life, and what they get out of it. The fact of this barge's having come up the Elbe with the others, at this time, will, to be sure, receive the due official attention of the American Government. It will make a slight alteration in the figure cited by the American Vice Consul who will write "Upstream freight traffic on the Elbe River in the month of March amounted to XX tons, valued at YY million marks, in comparison to AA tons, valued at BB million marks, for the same period in 1929." Somebody in the Department of State will then read this, to see whether there are typographical errors; and somebody in the Department of Commerce will read it, to see whether the figures check with those sent in by its own foreign service (in the hope of catching the Consular service off its guard), and it will then be relegated to its grave in the archives. But no one will have told the story of the sick woman who had to be carried off and placed in the horse ambulance, and who shall say that this story is of any less significance than the freight statistics?

Aboard a train from Riga to Vilna, April 15

My poor, beloved Duna, flowing out of Soviet Russia, flowing across the dull Latvian countryside, on this sunny spring afternoon, do you not wonder about the secret of your existence? Do you not rebel a little, inwardly, at the silence and the forsakenness of the country through which you have come, and do you not ask yourself what great things lie at the end of your journey? You will flow on down to the city of Riga (so much I can tell you) and you will flow under the iron railway bridge, and the traffic-laden pontoon bridge; you will slap gently on the sides of docks and ships and stone embankments and pilings; you will carry tugs and ferry-boats on your glittering back; you will then slide silently down the few remaining miles of sandy channel to a strange and lonesome sea. But what will become of you when you have reached the sea? I cannot tell you. Your life will be over; your personality will be merged in a far greater personality. But will it have been worth the long, mysterious trip, all the way from the highlands of the province of Pskov? Will the promise of the sunny skies and the fresh spring breezes have been realized? Will you know the answer to the universal question of this wistful, waiting, Russian countryside? You must wait and see. But I feel sorry for you, just the same, and I wish for your sake, that you might flow through great cities and great harbors, into teeming seas, so that the tremendous bustle and to-do of civilized humanity would at least give you the impression of purpose and adventure in the part you play.

August

Question: Communism does not pretend to be any less materialistic a doctrine than capitalism. It is only state capitalism carried to its ultimate conclusion. It does not pretend to make men better, but only to make great masses of them more comfortable and freer.

Answer: Communism destroys the individualism arising out of individual property, together with the hypocritical ideals created to sanction this property. This alone constitutes a moral improvement and, in freeing humanity from its religious and moral prejudices, opens the way for true development.

Question: But does it? Would the human being, adapted completely to the communist mold, living in a barracks, working in a factory, surrounded (let us assume) by physical comfort, believing neither in the superhuman nor in the human individual, filled with a truly oriental conviction of the worthlessness of his own soul and all his human relations, taught that the history of man for the untold eras had been motivated solely by the desire for material aggrandizement,—would this man be any more decent, humane, unselfish and courageous than his capitalistic forefathers?

Answer: How about the unselfishness and courage of some of the communist leaders?

Question: The elevation and self-sacrifice of the present communist generation is in some cases pure desperation, in others the religious fervor to be found in every class battle. What will become of this when the battle has been won, when the backbone of militant communism, the private industrial establishment has been eliminated?

Answer: How can one claim that the industrial unemployed is the backbone of militant communism? The backbone of all communism is the industrial worker, employed or unemployed, the proletariat. And the proletariat after the realization of communism, will not only continue to exist, but will itself compose human society.

Question: But is there, in the ideological sense, any proletariat other than the unemployed? The minute a man gets a job and an income, what becomes of his proletarian zeal, unless it is constantly formed by a fanatical dictatorship? Where does his psychology then differ from that of the petit bourgeois? What interests has he, other than his own personal gain? Other than the increase of his salary and the improvement of his living conditions? What does he think about other than the feathering of his own individual little nest?

Answer: There is of course no difference there. The material selfishness of the factory worker is no different from that of the hardware retailer. But the factory worker does not exploit human labor; the hardware merchant presumably does. And the factory worker does not try to conceal this desire for material gain under a cloak of illusory ideals and false institutions, but acknowledges it as a given factor, affirms it as something natural and consequently right, attempts to build on it instead of ignoring it and denying it.

Question: You grant, then, that even in the communist millennium self-interest—enlightened, perhaps, and deprived of the possibility of exploiting others through the control of capital, but self-interest nevertheless—will continue to be the guiding motive of individual conduct?

Answer: Yes, but we feel that the two reservations mentioned will in themselves bring about a definite improvement over the self-interest of the capitalist regime.

[Kennan returned to the United States on a personal visit.]

New York City, August 9
We ride up-town in a taxi. I had forgotten how dirty the streets in this town were, and that slum children splattered around in bathing suits under public outdoor shower-baths. . . . Little Italian boys cling to the spare tires of the taxicabs. They ride all over town, this way, going in gangs. They are the citizens of the future. Their nerves are strong. Neither the shadows of the tremendous buildings nor the masses of their fellow creatures oppress or impress them. When they are adults, possibly they will be better equipped than we, to cope with their environment.

[En route to Europe,] October 14[25]
Superb weather, yet again. The deck chair was prepared for me and I spent the entire day reading Dostoevsky. I was lying awake many hours yesterday evening and thought about whether a radical, anti-democratic party, a fascist party in essence, could have any success in America. Whether the party would have to start as a lawful or unlawful party and whether the necessary material existed. Somehow, I just can't conjure up an image of the American who is prepared to put the public good before their personal lives, including love and society. However, there is a real possibility in the naïve seriousness of the young generation.

October 21[26]
I finished reading Feiler's *The Experiment of Bolshevism* today.[27] That has led me to think about the future of the bourgeois rather than the communist world.

If one sees the main factors of decline of bourgeois culture in overpopulation, overproduction, and intellectual collectivization, one is allowed to draw some conclusion as to how to rescue this culture. Any person that wishes to bring about such a rescue would have to advocate for state capitalism. This would, if nothing else, at least eradicate the competition of the biggest trusts. This person would further have to support the regulation of births. Thirdly, this person should demand the total freedom of the written and the spoken word, as well as safety measures in the interest of the small publisher. Moreover, it needs to be considered what to do with the "Book of the Month Clubs," the radio, and the cinema. It is possible that nothing could be done against them. It is obvious that the state cannot directly intervene pedagogically in a democratic system.

25. This entry is in German.
26. This entry is in German.
27. Arthur Feiler, *The Experiment of Bolshevism* (1930).

However, it does not seem too much to hope for an intellectual differentiation of production, and I wouldn't demand more. It merely means that one shouldn't let the *Saturday Evening Post* culture become exclusive, so that we have to accept the mediocre because there is no alternative, as we see presently in the newspaper business.

[Undated, probably November–December]
Has it never occurred to anyone to accept socialism in the economic sense without any of its political connotations? The capitalist countries have a choice. They can let their capitalistic economic structure work itself into such a chaos that it collapses of its own accord, drag the cultural achievements of centuries down with it, and succumb to a new Middle Age of bolshevism, as our abandoned tropical plantation succumbs to the vegetation of the jungle. Or they can separate politics from economics, and their intelligent classes can put business life on a socialist basis from above, without turning political power over to the proletariat. If the intelligent classes in these countries haven't enough force and stamina to do this, then Western European civilization is already dead and gone and there is no hope. . . .

Can anyone seriously maintain that the desirability and necessity of a revolution for the realization of socialism were precisely the same in Tsarist Russia as they now are in England or Sweden or China or the U.S.A.? The entire international aspect of the communist dogma, presupposing as it does only one psychological element, the dubious one of class-consciousness, and ignoring all differences of political and social development and character between the different nations, is an obvious absurdity.

1931

In January, Kennan, who would soon turn twenty-seven, wrote his sister that "if I were a private citizen, I should become a Boheme and attempt to think. Being a Foreign Service Officer, I can only choose between marriage and stupidity, on the one hand, and nervous exhaustion, baldness, and futility, on the other. I choose the first; and I shall act accordingly as soon as I can."[28] *Only months later, he met and fell in love with a twenty-year-old Norwegian woman, Annelise Sørensen. They wed on September 11, 1931, and would remain married for seventy-three years.*

Swiss winter resort, March 8

A row of sleigh-taxis, and the coachmen, looking rather exotic and un-Swiss, with their sun-blackened faces chattered all day in an almost unintelligible German. A lively and alarmingly unorganized traffic churned through the main street from morning to night; hatless, strolling pedestrians, with canes and dark glasses, grim, determined skiers, whose precipitous approach was announced only by the dry rustling of the skis on the packed snow, hotel flunkeys, transporting trunks and suitcases on little hand-sleds, sturdy yellow post-buses, with chains on their tires and trailers behind for the skis of the passengers, tractors hauling little dump carts of snow, and the little sleighs of the natives, drawn by pairs of excited, straining police dogs. There was a jingling of sleighbells, a music honking of the bus horns, and strains of rasping, throaty music from the loud-speakers of the distant ice-rinks. . . .

Fellow guests, scraped from the bourgeois of four countries. Germans of all sorts, including a young sheik, with wavy grey hair, fashionably sunburnt face, and a weak, unpleasant mouth. Young British women, without their husbands, rather hard-boiled, and trying ineffectually to be gay. An American college boy, with a tremendous physique and no

28. Kennan to Hotchkiss, January 3, 1931, box 23, Kennan papers.

forehead, who maintained frankly: "I'd rather have a good body and be dumb than vice versa." A French family, and one Dutch couple, who stood out clearly among the rest through their breeding and poise.

In the evenings one danced in the casino. There was one listless table of roulette, where people sometimes risked as much as ten francs. On the dance-floor the usual European "Kurort" [spa]-crowd, even to the professional dancer with the padded shoulders and shiny-glued hair, with an eye to the young British women. And the evenings were long, as only such evenings can be when one feels one's youth sliding gently but firmly away without the compensations of either vice or virtue. "Have you been here very long? Have you done any shee-ing? Do you like to play bridge?"

In the music which droned across the dance floor, the notes of a Negro cornetist danced and played and ran circles around the conscientious rhythms of his less-imaginative European colleagues.

"I'm dancing with tears in my a-a-a-e-e-es. . . ."

(Well, well, just think of that. You are dancing with tears in your eyes, are you? Dear me, that's quite serious, you know.)

"No, I haven't done any shee-ing. I came here for the skating, you see."

(And what might be wrong with you, my good fellow, that you in your young years should be dancing with tears in your eyes? Do you think that is manly and proper?)

"For the girl in my arms isn't yo-o-o-o-o-ou."

"Yes, I can imagine it must be wonderful, if you know how."

(But after all, now, don't tell me that you, an upstanding American young man, as we must presume, would cry,—*cry*, mind you, like a damn baby, because you had to dance with some other girl than the one you wanted to dance with.)

"No, I haven't played any bridge since they started contract; I've never had time."

(Don't you think, really, that there is something unnatural, something positively abnormal about a young man dancing around with tears in his eyes for such a reason? Don't you see that in this condition you scarcely present that bulwark of strength and self-assurance which a woman has a right to look for in a man? Don't you see that you really don't want a woman at all, as a woman? That you only want a mother to hold your head on her shoulder and dry your dancing-tears and flatter your delicate little egotism and tend to your little physical necessities for you. This, my hypothetical young man, is very very bad, and you had best take immediate steps to correct it. You had better stop dancing with this poor unappreciated girl if you can't amuse her any better than by spoiling her make-up with your messy tears, and you had better go out into the open air and realize that mother is far away and that no one is ever going to understand you and that it is not very important whether anyone ever does; you might even try to understand someone else for a change.)

Berlin, May 30

Was rather surprised to find myself developing to V,[29] with something approaching fervor, certain ideas which I had not formerly known were in my own mind. I rejected the communists, I said, because of their innate cowardice and their intellectual insolence.

They had abandoned the ship of Western European civilization like a swarm of rats, when they considered it to be sinking, instead of staying on and trying to keep it afloat. Abandoning the ship, they had grasped at a theory for economic adjustment, possibly right though somewhat antiquated, and had hoped by means of this theory to cross at a bound the gulf across which the rest of mankind had been struggling through centuries of slow and painful progress. They had credited their own intelligence with powers far greater than those of all previous generations, had laughed at all the things which have stirred and troubled men for centuries, had called all their forefathers and most of their contemporaries hopeless fools. I was not a religious man, I said, but this impertinence struck me as a form of sacrilege, cultural and intellectual sacrilege, if you will, as a tremendous blasphemy against all the previous struggling and suffering and sacrificing of the human animal. I felt that it must some day be punished as all ignorant presumption and egotism must be punished.

I tried to make it clear that this applied to communism only in its international aspect. As a purely Russian phenomenon it might have a different meaning; for Russia it might be a constructive necessary development in a certain sense. For us in the West, though, it could only be regarded as an *Untergangserscheinung*, a sign of retrogression.

Granted this, I failed to see, however, why it should change matters

29. Kennan befriended the impoverished Russian émigré Vladimir (Volodya) Kozhenikov, Vladimir's mother, and his sister, Shura.

for us. Was it for us to stand aside and stop fighting because things were going against us? Did a football player leave the field when the score turned against his team? Did a real soldier stand anxiously watching the tide of battle, in order to decide whether or not to fight? We were born and bred with certain principles of decency in individual conduct and with certain hopes in the efficacy of these principles for the improvement of the human race. Such principles had little to do with economics; they belonged to us not because we were capitalists but because we were humanists. No mere changes in the economic system could take them away from us. It was up to us to preserve and defend them, but not to abandon them because they were in danger.

Enter Kennan, the moralist.

[**Undated**]

Note—one of the leading traits of the Russian mind: the inability to compromise. Before the war the allegation: *ma komupouuce* [willingness to compromise] was enough to spell the end of a political career. To the communists (Russian) compromise is equally repugnant. They acknowledge "temporary retreats" but never compromises. Contrast to the Anglo-Saxon political theory, which regards compromise as the essence of political development.

[**Undated**]

It seems to me that Dostoevsky could have such a reputation as a psychologist only in countries which are extremely naïve in this respect.

There is not one reasonably normal, decent soul among all his characters. Not one is really tangible, to no one of them does the reader have a sense of personal relationship. There are saintly heroes and despicable villains, and characters in which these two contrasts carry on a lurid, feverish fight. There are also weak contemptible characters. But there are no kindly, philosophic, respectable souls who know the value of work and regularity and health and good humor and self-discipline.

Dostoevsky was not a cultured man. He understood only the life of the Moscow and St. Petersburg boheme: an abnormal, distorted, feverish life, in which dirt and darkness and sloppiness were the prevailing elements. He had a hatred and complete lack of understanding for foreign countries. Yet what was it he longed to get back to? Certainly not the Russian countryside, which he never noticed and cared nothing about. Certainly not the mass of the Russian population, with which he had very little connection. It was the mental, moral and physical disorder of the Russian city boheme, which he loved and longed for. Here there was no discipline, no deportment, no regularity, no cleanliness, no honesty, no moderation, no restraint. Here Dostoevsky felt at home.

[**Undated**]

Question: Has not communist education, with its emphasis on dialectics and neglect of independent scientific thought, with its wealth of preconceived conclusions and poverty of constructive mental discipline, has not this ruined a generation? Will the generation now growing up in Soviet Russia ever be good for anything? Will it not do Russia more harm than good, in the last analysis? Will one not eventually have to undo most of what the communists have done and return to the point where Chekhov,[30] the last of the humanists, left off,—to the ideal of hard, conscientious and unpretentious endeavor? The communists have carried out one part of the Chekhov ideal. They have sought the improvement of society through pressure on the mass and not the individual. But they have made two tremendous mistakes. In the first place, they lost human respect and sympathy for the individual whose fate is after all the end of all human improvement. In the second place, they have repudiated modesty. They have become cocky and supercilious *hochmütig* [arrogant]. With that they have lost every chance of extending real help to Russia.

May 14

Wherein lies the difference between communism and state capitalism, in the minds of the communists themselves? There are of course a number of points at which the two conceptions differ. True communism, for example, would reward endeavor according to the needs of the subject, not according to his productivity. In true communism money would no longer exist; even the state itself would become superfluous.

Now in Soviet Russia as it is today, none of these characteristics of communism are at hand. Wages are not equalized. Money continues to exist and all attempts to depreciate its importance are stamped as heresy. The state is very much in evidence and, according to Molotov,[31] is to remain so far many years to come.

Wherein, then, does Soviet Russia, as it is run today, differ from the

30. Anton Chekhov was a playwright whose life and works Kennan greatly admired.
31. Vyacheslav Molotov was Soviet premier and later foreign minister under Stalin.

communist conception of state capitalism? The Soviet leaders themselves would answer this question as follows: under state capitalism, in its most advanced form, national economy is centrally controlled and administered in the interests not of the population as a whole, or even the majority of it, but only of a particular group, the oligarchy of high financiers. Thus the populace suffers. In Soviet Russia national economy is controlled and administered in the interests of the proletarian class.

Now it might be claimed that in Soviet Russia, too, the state has utilized its economic power in the interests of a particular group. It might well be maintained that in the ruling group of the communist party, the love of social and political power per se replaces the desire for wealth which motivates, or is said to motivate, bourgeois financiers. But for the sake of argument, we will acquit the communist leaders of all self-seeking, and assume that they are not running the economic life of Russia in their own selfish interests.

But is this economic life being run in the interest of the proletariat? By no means, no more than it is in capitalist states. The very material conditions under which the Russian people are now living bear evidence to that fact.

The economic life of Russia is being run in the interests of a doctrine, the doctrine of the inevitable violent communist revolution in all countries, the doctrine of the limitless predominance of the class struggle in every phase of human activity. This doctrine has created and necessitated the continual hostility between Soviet Russia and the rest of the world. It has necessitated the maintenance of the Red Army and the entire military-industrial development program expressed in the Five Year Plans. Indirectly it has necessitated the never-ending material sacrifices of the population, the physical, mental and moral ruin of a generation.

June 26

Has Bolshevism any goal? "From each according to his ability; to each according to his needs." That means anything and everything. Where are the limits of man's ability? In his mental attitude toward his work? Where are the limits of his needs? There are none. Man needs infinity.

It will not do to confine ourselves to the mere material. The elimination of the exploitation of man by man, if it should ever occur, would not be so important as the Bolshevists think.

If communism is ever to mean anything to men, it must satisfy spiritual as well as material needs. Bolshevism shows as yet no signs of doing this. It has not even a program for it. Questions of sex, children, the family, artistic expression—these have been only temporarily regulated to meet the demands of the intermediate epoch. This regulation has in some ways been a very happy one. It has relieved the younger generation to a large extent of the curses of egotism, romanticism, day-dreaming, and neurasthenia. But at the same time, it must have decreased their natural resistance to these diseases. And what about the future?

There are two possibilities.

a) The materialistic phase of the development, the phase on which all energies are now being concentrated, succeeds. What then? Industrialization and economic expression—frigidaires, autos, radios—have their limits. The greater the success, the more surely one may expect a relaxation, [in Russian] a disposition to demobilize, a resting on one's laurels, a looking about for rewards, the return of the soldier from the front. The young communist will again be forced to turn his attention inward, and to ask himself what there is to live for.

b) The materialistic phase fails. The policy of rapid and forced industrialization turns out to be an economic mistake. The tempo of construction cannot be maintained. Collectivized agriculture cannot reabsorb the masses of transient labor, nor do these masses, uprooted and inspired with undefined hopes, wish to be reabsorbed. They pile into the big cities. Discontent; increasing expenses of government. Foreign credit breaks down. Depreciation gains the upper hand over production. Catastrophe. Breakdown of the system.

In either of these two cases, what will we see? We shall see the disappearance of those conditions which maintain the self-confidence and the mental health of the younger Russian generation, which kept it from egotism, romanticism, day-dreaming, and neurasthenia. We shall see the disappearance of the war spirit, of the immediate, concrete objective, of the ready-made philosophy. And then where will our young Russian be? Totally untrained to think for himself, unaccustomed to face his own soul, guided neither by tradition, example, or the steadying influences of personal responsibility to persons near him, he will be as vulnerable as a babe in the woods. The demons of uncertainty and introspection will make short work of him. From the most morally unified country in the world, Russia will become, overnight, the worst moral chaos. The political and social results are horrible to think of. And those will be the fruits of Bolshevism.

A year and a half ago, I once had lunch with a Russian communist official in Berlin. I told him the greatest danger for Bolshevism lay in its success. He said he understood what I meant.

June 16–18

Berlin to London & back again.

In the afternoon we fly down the valley of the Rhine, at an altitude of some 2,000 feet.

I can no longer feel any particular excitement at the sight of the Western European countryside from the air, at the rapid crossing of borders, at the thought: this, below me, is such and such a country. I suppose it is because I have come to know the meaning of the word "province", and that this is an international conception, which does not change with the flags and people. I see not only the quaintness of historical tradition, from my lofty perch; I see also modern life in all its manifestations. I see the stupid newspapers, the tawdry moving-picture houses with their Hollywood films, the stuffy restaurants and saloons, the narrow streets with their gossips-mirrors, the reflections of material and intellectual poverty in the little shop windows, the jails and poor-houses and insane asylums and maternity hospitals, the barber-shops with their illustrated magazines, the undertakers' establishments, the churches, the country railway stations. They are all practically the same, in one country as in the next. The only result of their careful investigation by an intelligent man would be another "Main Street."[32] Over them all, like an all-enveloping poisonous gas, lies a sinister pall of boredom, the suffocating boredom of petty, timid life, waiting for the senseless slaughter of the next war to shatter its lethargy. . . .

In a way, one feels a little sorry for the British. When they once get to like you, they give themselves away. I don't think they will ever be quite a match, individually, for a clever American. But I can conceive of no greater catastrophe than for us to take advantage of that fact. As a rule they are extraordinarily decent people, and endowed with an instinct far healthier and wiser than our own. It is up to us to understand them, to learn from them, to humor them and to put them in their place on occasions, to stand our own in their relations to us and support them in their relations to others. To ruin them would be to cut off our own roots. For outside of a certain fundamentally Anglo-Saxon tradition with some new world modifications, what is there in America capable of forming a lasting ideological basis for a great nation?

32. Sinclair Lewis's novel *Main Street* (1920) criticized the pettiness and hypocrisy of small-town America.

1932

The year 1932 would prove a difficult one for Kennan. Having completed his Russian language study in Berlin, Kennan was transferred not to the Soviet Union, which Washington still refused to recognize, but rather to Riga, Latvia, the listening post on the pariah nation. Although happy with his wife, Annelise, he chafed under the restrictions of family life. Those bonds were tightened by the birth of Grace Kennan on June 5. A few weeks earlier, Kennan had received the news that the inheritance from his mother had been lost in stock market speculation by his brother-in-law. In addition, the State Department was cutting salaries.

The diary indicates that Kennan found difficulty in confiding all his problems to Annelise. Though feeling stifled by his job of writing official reports from outside Russia, he dared not resign. To his sister he confided, "What I should most like to write is fiction, and my life is a very unfavorable one for that."[33] *The worsening Depression darkened his view of the future for both himself and the world. Yet late in the year a light glimmered. "Election day today," Annelise wrote George from Norway on November 8. "I expect Roosevelt will win. . . . I wonder what they will do about Soviet Russia."*[34]

Riga, May 7

Perhaps it might not be a bad idea to cover the last year—it is nearly that much—in retrospect, as a penalty for my laziness.

I returned from London on the *George Washington*, as I recall. There were several hundred Rotarians on board. I find this entry in a notebook:

Several hundred Rotarians on a boat. I seek their company, somewhat

33. Kennan to Hotchkiss, October 18, 1932, box 23, Kennan papers.
34. John Lewis Gaddis, *George F. Kennan: An American Life* (New York: Penguin Press, 2011), 69.

shyly, not because it affords me any pleasure or profit, but because I want to find something in their way of thought to which I can attach myself. After all, if I am not an American, then I am nothing at all.

It strikes me that while they are all nice people, there is not a real lady or gentleman among them. These are the people whose interests I am supposed to defend. I am not sorry to do it; they are good naïve people, most of them—kind and generous. They work hard at home and deserve their place in the sun. But they are children, and it is a bore to have to protect children from their environment when you cannot discipline them and teach them to protect themselves.

Also from the notebook:

Golf is a game for people who like walking but are afraid of being left to their own thoughts.

Bridge is a game for people who don't even like to walk.

It is strange: now that I begin to write this, I realize that this year, examined closely, has been a preposterous, incredible, heart-rending year. Yet it has surely been not more so than any one of the years since I came to Europe. Evidently life itself, whenever examined closely, is heart-rending, incredible and preposterous.

Of the remaining Berlin days, in June and July 1931, I remember little, and would like to remember less. Besides, they were too varied in their monotony, and too monotonous in their variety, to be recalled here in retrospect. In a way, it is a pity to have lost them, with their intensity and poignancy. Even tragedy has its charm. But they are gone now, in any case. Anything I might attempt in the way of recalling them would be very inadequate.

I left Berlin early in August 1931.

A bad road to Stettin. Harvesting going on in the fields.

It is a Saturday, August 8. Banners are stretched across the village streets. . . . One can hear voices all over the far Pomeranian countryside: "No one has any money. The French have taken it all."

In Stettin, I drive direct to the dock. Two drunken stevedores are having a fight by the corner of the warehouse. The thud of fists and the scuffling of shoes on the cobblestones echo across the quiet water of the slip.

While waiting for the ship to sail, Volodya and Shura, who have come along to bid me goodbye, disappear. After a while, they come back, laden with armfuls of flowers. With their last few marks, they have bought out an entire flower shop. They take it very seriously, this departure.

Instinct, rather than any logical process of thought, tells them that while we may meet again soon, this day and this departure mark the termination of my residence in Berlin and that this is the real goodbye. As the ship is moving away from the quai, a taxicab comes driving up with much honking, and a stout lady descends, clutching a dozen parcels and waving an umbrella at the boat. We maneuver back to the dock, and while the stout lady is bundled over the rail we have a chance to shake hands again, and Volodya hands me their new address on a crumpled slip of paper. Now we are off again. The engine pounds determinedly as we move down the slip. I stand in the stern and wave my handkerchief like the German-est German until the tiny waving spots of white on the dock have finally faded from view. (Oh my children, my children. What was there for me to say to you? What is there now for me to write about you? Has not the injustice, the insanity of the world been sung a million times, and always imperfectly? Is there any use for me to add my voice?)

It is after six o'clock as we steam down the river. This trip has lost its romance, since I made it three years ago, on my way to the Baltic for the first time. Which only means that I have other eyes. Or perhaps I am just tired.

June 13

Boredom, boredom, boredom! Boredom that aches, that crushes, that makes the mind writhe this way and that in its search for some sort of relief. Boredom that kills the appetite and saps the energy. The world moves on senselessly and impotently.

June 14

Women are like the leaden centerboards on sailboats. They keep the boat upright and steady in its course, but they are not the motive power that makes it go. In fact, if you want to take a chance and go fast before the wind, you have to eliminate them at times. And one of them is all you can use; any more pull you down.

[**Undated**]

Saturday afternoon pot-pourri.

What a comedown we are, in comparison with our ancestors. Why should pioneers and adventurers beget timid, petty officials?

Why are we so much more intimate with those who are absent than with those who are present? To someone living in the same house, we would never think of saying the intimate things about ourselves which we readily put into letters to absentees. Hypocrites, all of us, we write in such a way as to demand the sympathy of our correspondents. If they were here with us, we would not dare to demand a thing. They would see through us too readily. They would see how little sympathy we actually deserve.

July 13

Nothing good can come out of modern civilization, in the broad sense. We have only a group of more or less inferior races, incapable of coping adequately with the environment which technical progress has created. . . . This situation is essentially a biological one. No amount of education and discipline can effectively improve conditions as long as we allow the unfit to breed copiously and to preserve their young. Yet there is no political faction in the world which has any thought of approaching the problem from the biological angle. Consequently there is really nothing positive to be expected from any political movement now in existence. There is nothing which any of them can do except to give the present generation of inferior beings a training and discipline which will in no way alter their offspring. . . . These political factions may profoundly influence environment; they will not alter heredity!

August 4

This is a mental crisis I am in the midst of. Thinking back, I can recall many such crises. Yet here, as is the case of the present economic crisis, there is the intimation that this is not *a* crisis but *the* crisis. Just as there have always in the past been new markets to absorb the flood of economic expansion, tumbling over itself in its uncontrollable rush, so there have been new illusions and new hopes to absorb energy and attention, to give the false sense of motion and direction. That is all changing now. The world is at the end of its economic rope. I am at the end of my mental one.

I am beginning to comprehend that I am condemned to a rare intellectual isolation. Be it a compliment or a reproach, the fact remains: my mental processes will never be understood by anyone else.

December 17

The crisis is predominantly one of overproduction and will become more or less chronic in time. The only solution to this, under capitalist conditions, lies in the return of great masses of people to the land, not as industrial farmers growing cash crops, but in a capacity—bitter as it may sound—like that of the semi-independent European peasant. . . .

Capitalism entails democracy, and democracy is too powerless to put people back on the land or do anything else of any importance. And economic dictatorship, socialism, has unfortunately stranded on the shoals of political radicalism. I believe in dictatorship, but not the dictatorship of the proletariat. The proletariat, like a well-brought up child, should be seen and not heard. It should be properly clothed and fed and sheltered, but not crowned with a moral halo, and above all not allowed to have anything to do with government.

1933

Feeling boxed in by the personal and professional limitations of his life, Kennan spent most of 1933 brooding in Riga. The previous year the State Department had turned down his request to visit the Soviet Union. He despaired that despite his fascination with Russia, he would never get there. Upon learning that his father knew the newly installed secretary of state, Cordell Hull, Kennan urged the sending of a note lauding him as "a specialist in Russian matters."[35]

The breakthrough moment, however, came only in December when Kennan, on leave in Washington, talked with the newly appointed ambassador, William C. Bullitt. Impressed with the young man's knowledge of Russian, Bullitt tapped him to help set up the new embassy. A few days later they departed for Moscow.

[The next entry is apparently Kennan's third-person rumination on himself.]

Riga, January

The sad fact that government is a conspiracy is largely the result of democracy. Democracy for people to accomplish by means of deceit what formerly was accomplished by means of force.

The great statesman, the public figure, has the advantage of being able to forget himself and his private fortunes for a time and to subordinate his petty personal interests to the glory of the game he is playing.

The little man, the honest independent farmer for example, can call his home his castle and live the dignity of his personal life.

The petty official can do neither. He sacrifices his private life without even the reward of public accomplishment.

35. Kennan to Kossuth Kent Kennan, April 7, 1933, Joan Elisabeth Kennan papers (in private possession).

The technique of marriage is nothing more or less than the art of dissimulation.

Only hopeless or surfeited eyes see clearly.

Woman is flattered and pleased when treated like a rational being, but cannot refrain from taking advantage of it.

The Kennans never knew anything about love. They knew only friendship. Their expression of devotion consisted in standing by someone when he was in trouble, not in showing useless attention to a perfectly healthy and prosperous human being, who might have been expected to get along well enough by himself. Friendship, after all, was a much more useful relationship under frontier conditions than love. The Kennans rarely took responsibility for other people (this applies of course only to the men of the family), in the spiritual sense. They left that to God. If another person was unhappy without any obvious tangible reason, they concluded it could only be the result of his liver or his sins and recommended castor oil and church attendance.

It seemed to him that he would have made a talented academician, with the proper training. As a matter of fact, he felt that he could have done well in almost any field except the one which interested him, fiction.

But what difference did it make, after all, if he had talent. Was not all life a story of undeveloped talents? How many talented men had there been among those millions who died during the war? No, no. God alone knew why talents were born into the world, but it was quite evidently not for the enrichment of humanity. Nature was generous.

He was thoroughly pessimistic in his outlook on his contemporaries. He believed that the race was definitely declining. The decline of the race did not, in his opinion, mean that there would be no decent, intelligent, courageous people. It meant that such people would become fewer and fewer, that they would be comparatively powerless and mistreated and would live in the consciousness of being doomed to failure, ineffectiveness, and early elimination. In general, their position would be like that of the Russian emigres in Western European cities.

For years he had rejected all serious study of the Russian emigration, as of a movement without a future, as the condemned relic of a society whose limitations were only too well known, and he had devoted all his attention to the Bolsheviks, in the conviction that to them belonged the future of society. This conviction did not desert him. But upon the realization that he himself, in any case, was not a Bolshevik, his attention gradually changed and had oriented itself on the emigres, for in them he saw the reflection of his own personal future. He scrutinized them with a dread eagerness in order to learn whether they had developed any philosophy which might lighten their burden, or whether their plight was one of unmitigated suffering and tragedy.

At first he was unhappy in his marriage. It forced upon him what was in reality a thoroughly bourgeois mode of life. This horrified him. It was apparent to him that bourgeois life was an acceptance of death. It was one long, careful preparation for a fine funeral with an ornate coffin and the town's best undertaker. No wonder revolutionists had felt no compunctions in exterminating the bourgeoisie. It was the essence of the philosophy of the good burghers that they were ready for their extermination.

But the demands of marriage were inexorable, and after two years of perplexity, he began to face the facts and finally ended up by capitulating entirely. What else could he do? He had taken on a responsibility which was in direct conflict with his own work, his own hopes, his own life. It was no one's fault. It just *was* that way. The only thing to do was to recognize that you had been caught and to make the best of it: not to beat frantically against the bars of the cage. One might well dream of the past. One might well watch life outside, through the bars. But one could not participate in this life. Personal pride and spirit were inconsistent with responsibility for other people, and the time had come to capitulate.

So he became a model married man. He was faithful to his wife in the ordinary sense as well as in the intellectual. He knew that faithfulness, taken by itself, was a ridiculous and unhealthy ideal. But if one were to take at all seriously his own personal life, then there was no choice but to observe order and clarity in sexual matters as in everything else. Promiscuousness was not sinful, it was merely sloppy. It was a lack of neatness. It was always accompanied by confusion and disorder and uncertainty. And if monogamy was unhealthy, then a certain amount of physical discomfort was the price one paid for one's personal dignity, for the sense of neatness and definiteness in one's personal life.

I saw him again, a year after the capitulation. He complained a little. To abandon hope: that in itself was not so hard. That could happen to anyone. But to feel how you gradually got stupid, how you gradually lost the ability to see yourself with any sense of proportion, to lose the sense of the tragedy of the whole thing: that was hard. That made it seem as though life had lost its last significance.

If his wife had been less dependent on him he would probably have committed suicide at this stage. He had abandoned so many lives with so little hesitation and with so little concern over what was coming next, he said, it could surely not be hard to abandon this one.

He had long since lost everything resembling patriotism. "Why?" he used to ask, "should I love my country? It deceived me repeatedly and taught me nothing. My birthplace was completely indifferent to me. Why should I not be indifferent to it?

"America, after all, is too broad and confusing a conception to warrant any genuine loyalty. What have I in common with the average southerner, or the New York Jew, or any one of a hundred types? America is hardly a national conception anymore. It is a sort of international entity. The overflow from the entire world has seeped into a great territory and has drowned out the heritage of my fathers. There it lies now, this human overflow, sprawling out over the continent in all its ignorance and all its sordidness, a society conceived in selfishness and dedicated to the proposition that one man's suffering is no other man's business, incapable of regulating its own public life, waiting stupidly for the advent of catastrophe."

When I saw him last, he was still despondent. But if you were to have asked him the causes of his despair, he would not have been able to tell you. That which he feared had come to pass. He himself had forgotten, and perhaps his mind and spirit were no longer capable of reviewing the delicate processes through which the abandonment of hope had been brought about.

But this lapse of memory was not important. For hope and despair, like so many other manifestations of human nature, were primarily matters of habit, rather than the results of any immediate stimuli.

"*Deutschland erwache!* [Germany awake!]" screamed the slogan on the newspaper.

It was, he said, a matter of indifference to him whether Germany woke up or not. It was equally distasteful to him awake or asleep. Like many an individual, it was pitiable and slightly repulsive in its sleep, loud-mouthed, and obstreperous in its waking hours. God knew which condition was preferable.

In any case, he did not consider the Nazi revolution a real awakening. He was sure that it was only a nightmare.

February 26

In the evening to a Buster Keaton talkie, where we saw the tragic effect which the talkies have had on good pantomime. Instead of one of those marvelous farces where the very silence of the participants is half the charm: an absurd gangster film with a sickening moral tinge and sentimentality of incredible crudeness, the horror relieved now and then by flashes of the old pantomime genius.

June 22

I am bored with myself and with everyone around. Horrible spectacle. Intelligent, splendidly educated people, frittering away their time and decaying, in this life, for lack of anything else to do. All these preparations gone to waste. They serve something, of course, the British particularly. But nothing like what their education would warrant. Well, well, next thought. I used to think that my perpetual exhaustion came from demanding too much, from a horror of wasting time. Apparently no such thing. Here I have demanded nothing, have wasted time without compunction for a year. A few more years of this sort of thing and I'll be a timid, dried-up old clerk. Yet there is no relaxation, no adjustment. I have only supplanted the strain of intellectual endeavor with the strain of being head of a family. What are the odds?

July 2

Given that, for the sake of my family, I am lost, then at least family life should be dignified, calm, and beautiful. But for this one needs income. How am I to get it?[36]

I can't write. No imagination. I can only describe what I have seen, and that is impossible, under the circumstances. But is it? Granted complete detachment?

July 21

Advice to a son.

Whenever you are moved by a woman's charm to trespass upon her honor, recall that if you do so she will never forgive you for it, and that whenever you encounter her in the future you will be met with resentment and reproach. No matter how little honor a woman may have, the price she sets on it is infinite, and it stands to reason that she always considers herself to have been underpaid for her sacrifice. Women never completely forgive those to whom they have yielded.

Never make plans for personal contacts. It leads to day-dreaming. Know what you want and act accordingly. Know neither shame nor self-

36. This paragraph is in Russian.

satisfaction. Both are beside the point. Everything is concentration. Only concentration can overcome the petty pitfalls which lie before sensitive natures.

[Undated]
Returning to America after six and a half years of residence in Europe, he found the American accent as affected as the British. Was it really necessary for all these people, even nice-looking young girls, to appear so hard-boiled, so formidable, so emotionless? Any more than it was necessary for the British to place in their voices the intimation that their own personal lives were mysteriously superior and complete and that speech, for them, could only serve to ward off unnecessary intrusion from inferior elements or to express bland amusement at the ridiculousness of the rest of the world? What dangers threatened these good Americans, that they should arm themselves with so much bitterness and gruffness and harsh forebodings? Was it the omnipresent lightning of disrespectful ridicule, so prevalent in their whole social life? The exaggerated American sense for the unheroic in human nature?

Despite unusual intelligence and potential ability, you have only the position of a glorified clerk, and hardly earn enough to support your family. You are so little representative for even the position you hold that people refuse to believe you hold it. For two years, you have marked time completely, gaining little knowledge, no health, and losing, if anything, in mental vigor. Your health is poor; you are almost a nervous wreck; your ability to work, and consequently the security of your family, are in constant jeopardy.

Yes, there are certain extenuating circumstances, but they do not alter the fact that there is one predominating cause for the whole situation. You know what that is.

[While the precise nature of that "one predominating cause" for his unhappiness remains unclear, evidence suggests that it might relate to Kennan's difficulty in reconciling his obligations as a husband with his impulses for sexual freedom. He believed that his creativity and vitality depended on such freedom.]

(But I would be almost crippled by this change. I would have to live in a sort of vacuum. I would be speechless and dull.)

Amputations are always crippling. There never was a better chance.

August 17

The first years after marriage I let myself be carried along by matrimony, the third year by the excitement of going to Russia. Neither one was worth it. The only result was that I lost my self-respect.

Every time I try to think, I fall into melancholia and inactivity. All manifestations of activity are vanity and wastes of energy which later revenge themselves.

I gave up intellectual activity because I thought it was tearing me to pieces. I would now gladly be torn to pieces if I could only recover self-respect.

August 20

I am no longer fascinated by the mystery. The struggles of the spring have taken the heart out of me. To be a diplomat is bitter enough, to be a married one is still bitterer. Russia is, to me, a forbidden world, and the iron of this realization has struck so deep that I am becoming indifferent to it, as we become indifferent to all things which we really know we cannot have.

October 31

If you think you are going crazy, never fear. Lunacy is not self-consciousness, and if you think you are crazy: you aren't.

If you think you are achieving greatness, never hope greatness is not self-conscious; and if you think you are great, you aren't.

We aren't civilized. We're still only a generation from spittoons and shirt sleeves and the Chicago's World's Fair. We're still a bunch of farmers, of obscure genteel origin.

December 20—a reminiscence

The train bearing the first American Ambassador to the Soviet Union and his suite, later dubbed "the original Bullitt expeditionary force," crossed the Polish-Soviet border in the early twilight of a late December afternoon. The deserted forests of the border zone crowded the single track on either hand, silent, snow-covered and forbidding. At the very barbed wire stood a lone, wooden sentry tower, in a clearing, and on top of it was the dim figure of a Polish soldier, with gun and fixed bayonet, and his great-coat turned up against the intense cold. A short distance beyond the border, the train slowed down at a little cottage, beside the tracks, and the Soviet border guards, with their long, snug overcoats and the blue caps of the O.G.P.U.[37] uniformed forces, came on board. A few minutes later there were lights and voices outside the windows and the train pulled up in the station at Negoreloe. People crowded around. A dapper little individual, who turned out to be the Foreign Office's agent in Minsk and who had been sent down to the border for the occasion, pushed his way through to the Ambassador's compartment and delivered a ceremonious little speech of welcome.

A banquet had been laid out in the station restaurant. We sat down in company with the Soviet and American journalists (some of the latter with their wives) who had come to meet us. The dumpy shaved-headed waiters from the dining car bustled about and gave voice to their distress at our failure to eat, an experience which for most of us was to be repeated many times in the course of our contact with Russian standards of festivity.

The big Russian sleeping-cars, bearing the impressive placards: "Stolpce—Vladivostok," were waiting on the tracks. The snow gleamed from their roofs; wood smoke emerged from the chimney's light showed only dimly behind the frosted double windows, but single lamps over the doorways glowed invitingly. These roomy vehicles were not cramped cubicles of steel and glass, like the Western European cars on which we had come this far. They were wooden ships on wheels, designed to be inhabited by the same persons for periods considerably longer than the average Atlantic crossing. Despite their advanced age (the so-called "international" cars of this type all appeared to date from before the Revolution), they were comparatively cozy and comfortable.

It was already eight-o'clock by Russian time when we left Negoreloe. Throughout the evening, the Ambassador sat in the dining car and fenced with the journalists in his inimitable manner.

I shared a compartment with the Moscow representative of TASS, the official news agency. He stretched himself out in his underwear and slept the sleep of the innocent. I cannot begrudge him that space in retrospect, for he has subsequently almost surely gone the way of most Soviet citizens who had professional contacts with foreigners in those days, and has either lost his head entirely or is laying it on a less comfortable pillow.

As for myself, I sat up nearly the whole night, looking out at the sleepy, winter-bound station of White Russia and the western *oblast*. To me this first contact with the Soviet Union has an exceptional meaning.

37. O.G.P.U. was the secret police.

I had spent five years in intensive preparation for it. I had a greater command of the Russian language than I had ever encountered in any foreigner born and bred outside Russia, save two or three of my colleagues who had also undergone special training in preparation for their service there. I had a knowledge of Russian history and literature equivalent to that of the average educated Russian of the old school and considerably better than that of the average product of Soviet education. Finally, I had spent the last two years compiling and analyzing Soviet economic statistics as a principal occupation and collecting materials for a biography of Anton Chekhov as a hobby. The result was a consuming curiosity about all things Russian, and an intense excitement at the first actual contact with the Soviet world.

Chapter Three

Moscow and Vienna, 1934–37

1934

The diary for 1934 only hints at the turbulence in Kennan's life during his first year in the Soviet Union. "Moscow had me somewhat on the run," he soon after admitted; "I was too fascinated by Russia." He chafed under "the compulsion to political inactivity, self-restraint, and objectivity" mandated by his position as a U.S. official and by his marriage. These limits were rendering him "sterile." He found it "incredible" that in a world as interesting as the U.S.S.R. "we should have to reconcile ourselves to anything as boring and as out-of-date as life in the Moscow diplomatic corps."[1] *The mix of frustration and excitement would lead to Kennan's physical and mental breakdown in December 1934, a year after he had first arrived with Bullitt.*

Moscow, April 5

Woke up with a headache from a party at the French Embassy. Went for a walk before breakfast to clear my head. Tried to keep in the thin March [*sic*] sunshine as much as I could. Stared at the little church in the midst of the subway construction on Lubyanka and decided it was probably Moscow baroque.

. . . Had pains in my groin today so badly that I decided to stop drinking until summer. In accordance with this decision, stayed home from a party tonight and studied up on Soviet art.

April 8

I have always thought of literature as a type of history: the portrayal of a given class at a given time, with all its problems, its suffering and

1. Kennan to Charles W. Thayer, May 22, 1935, box 3, Charles W. Thayer papers, Harry S. Truman Presidential Library, Independence, MO.

its hopes, etc. For that reason, the diplomatic corps has always defied literary approach. From that point of view, it is too insignificant, too accidental, to warrant description.

Perhaps that is all wrong. Perhaps they should be described simply as human beings, not as diplomats (so-called) of the twentieth century. If Chekhov could describe Russian small town folk with an appeal so universal that even the American reader gasps and says: "How perfectly true," why cannot the Moscow diplomatic folk be written up the same way?

[Undated]

Russia is a filthy, sordid country, full of vermin, mud, stench, and disease. The rulers try hard to make it look brighter, in Moscow, at least. They put palms and orchestras in the station restaurants, for example. But these pitiful efforts don't scratch the surface. In the waiting room the peasants who haven't got money to go into the restaurant, camp on the floor, for days and nights; the grown-ups sit on the bundles of belongings and stare hopelessly, patiently into space, while the ragged children sleep like little animals on the floor.

[The metaphor in the next entry suggests frustration that duties were forcing Kennan to conceal his true, Russian identity from "his own" family. The phraseology also suggested that while he held the position of parent, Russians figured as "the children."]

August 31

I am among the Russians like one who has to wear a mask among his own children.[2]

September 3

Here human flesh lives in one seething, intimate mass—far more so, even than in New York. It streams slowly, endlessly, in thick, full currents, along the boulevards, between the dark trees, under the gleam of the street lights; it is carried, as herded, tired animals are carried, in box-cars, in the long trains of street cars. And it is human life in the raw, human life brought down to its fundamentals—good and evil, drunk and sober, loving and quarreling, laughing and weeping—all that

2. This sentence is in Russian.

human life is and does anywhere, but all much more simple and direct, and therefore stronger.

There is something unmistakably healthy in it all: not the health we strive for by the elimination of microbes and danger and physical hardship, but the health bred of the experience and survival of all these ills. Revolution, like nature, is lavish and careless. Its victims are no more to it than the thousands of seeds which are cast to the wind, in order that one tree may grow. But in its blind masterfulness, it has at least given new scope for the survival of the fittest, the nervously and physically fittest, who are by no means the most intelligent, or the freest from dirt and disease. The principle of natural selection, deprived of its beneficial operation by vaccinations and nursing homes and birth control, has been allowed to come into its own in its full ruthlessness. This is the answer to the question: how do the Russians stand it? Many of them didn't stand it. And these whom you see on the street: they are the elite, not the elite of wealth or of power or of the spiritual virtues, but nature's own elite, the elite of the living, as opposed to the hoi polloi of the dead!

It is this tremendous health, this earthy vitality, which attracts the over-civilized, neurotic foreigner. The fact that he himself could not stand it for six months, that it would crush him as it crushes all forms of weakness, does not dissuade him. There is something in its very cruelty which appeals to his sick fantasy. It is a form of flagellism [flagellation], perhaps, like all deliberate self-abnegation.

September 18

Read *Lady Chatterley's Lover*.[3] Not a very good book. Frankness is unimportant, one way or the other. It is more scientific rather than pornographic. The main thing is that it is not a very good book anyway. It gets nowhere and proves nothing. The only reaction is: "What of it?" Surely no one believes that the characters in the book, or anywhere else, are going to find real happiness in life in general through having discovered that there is such a thing as contentment in bed. The end, instead of being the triumph and enlightenment that it was intended to be, is actually tragic. Imagine this ill-suited pair, setting out in life with no common interests, no common society, nothing in common, as a matter of fact, except a certain sexual compatibility of doubtful duration.

It is no wonder that the expression of the sexual instinct mounts up

3. D. H. Lawrence, *Lady Chatterley's Lover* (1928).

to a tremendous problem for many people, as it did for the characters of this book. Sex is not a thing to be examined and analyzed in a non-scientific way by the subject himself. It is not a field for introspection. It is not something which can be made an end in itself. The normal sex life is led by persons to whom sexual expression is, as it should be, only incidental, and who spend as little time contemplating its pleasures as they do worrying about its results. Sex ceases to be a complicated and terrible problem when there are other things vastly more important.

September 26

Bad day. Rainy day. Permeated by the suspicion that I am worn out and depleted by—oh, what the hell's the use?

Things seem to have no significance. I know that they should be recorded, but I am too tired to distinguish the essential from the trivial.

Tea at the Embassy, with British liberals including Sydney Webb. They think very abstractly and find it easy to be enthusiastic about communism because their attitude is a complete pose. In their hearts, they never dream of being Bolshevistic or anything else except plain British.

1935

After Kennan's physical and nervous collapse in December 1934, the State Department granted him months of paid leave to recuperate in the Sanatorium Gutenbrunn in Vienna. Annelise and Grace were with him for part of the time. The diary for early 1935 offers the deepest, most candid self-appraisal that Kennan would venture in the nearly ninety years that he kept a journal. His perspective on his psyche was influenced by his medical doctor, Frieda Por, who espoused the teachings of Sigmund Freud, and by Kennan's own reading of the Viennese psychiatrist. Though Kennan remained a skeptic about psychoanalysis, he also came to see as central to the human condition Freud's notion of an inescapable conflict between the creativity inspired by sexual desire and the restraint insisted upon by civilization.

Even after his release from the sanatorium in late April, Kennan continued to live in Vienna—and to agonize about his life. The thirty-year-old felt himself "still in that stage of inner rebellion against middle age and futility. . . . I am afraid that I won't alter the world, after all, before my imagination dies, or have another real love affair, on one of these summer nights, before my hair turns gray."[4]

The State Department assigned him to light duties at the Consulate General in Vienna and then to the legation, where he became friends with the influential minister George Messersmith. In November, George, Annelise, and Grace returned to Moscow.

Vienna, January 31

Is it not possible that the neurosis, instead of being the cause of nervous and physical ill health, is the only prevention? That only those people

4. Kennan to Jeanette Kennan Hotchkiss, June 28, 1935, box 24, Kennan papers.

are truly healthy in the physical and nervous sense who are able to take refuge successfully in unreality? Our dreams, Freud tells us, are designed to protect our sleep from the influence of the unfulfilled wishes, the unfinished battles, the frustrations, repressions, and failures which have dotted our past lives. Is this not equally true of our day dreams, our pet illusions? Are they not all that save us from a realization of the futility and absurdity of existence, and consequently from complete acquiescence in physical dissolution and death?

Conversely, cannot ill-health, nervous and physical dissolution, be the sign of the only true health of the spirit: the ability to be distracted by dreams and illusions from the contemplation of the fascinating, ruinous, destructive thing called "truth"?

February 4

[Dream] . . . A crowded restaurant. Old Petersburg, as if I lived there. And was that not the Tsar, who had just been murdered and who lay in state, where the orchestra should have been, on a bier, and were those not his plainclothes men, who sat at the table around about?

I went out, and as I did so I passed a table where all the marines were seated. When I got out the door, it was night. A great watchdog, a Doberman, came running up out of the darkness.

I was frightened and started back for the door. The dog sensed it, and reared up on his hind legs as though to jump for my neck. I raised my arm and shoved the forearm, heavily wrapped, into his jaws. We stood that way, the dog not daring to bite, I not daring to move. The dog moved around so as to show me a sign on his back, indicating that he was an imperial watchdog, with full official status. I bowed in acknowledgment. "Kennan," I introduced myself stiffly, "Secretary of the American Embassy."

[The following is a letter to Cyrus Follmer.][5]

February 6

Most of the time I stand the monotony all right but now and then, and this is one of the times, I am seized with a stinging restlessness and a longing not so much for action as for the associations of other days and above all the rare friends in whose eyes and words the world and life

5. Cyrus Follmer was Kennan's colleague from Berlin and best man at his wedding.

were once so nicely mirrored. There were no friends like this in Moscow or even in Riga. Marriage, insofar as it limits complete individuality, is hard on friendship. So I must think back to the days of Berlin and the many times when we turned the material of our tormented, breathless, consular existence over and over and scrutinized it in the glow of the old oven and the warmth of the evening teapot, in the "Slums," until it seemed to take on life and significance itself, and I felt that all we would have to do would be to put it down on paper and we would have immortal literature.

Those times have never returned. Never since has life glowed so richly and so deeply. It probably never will. And I cannot avoid the somewhat bitter reflection that all the experiences of those full days, experiences which we regarded as struggles away from impending catastrophe toward some glorious future, were possibly the fullest that we will ever know, and that what we took as preparation for life was actually the nearest we were ever destined to come to life itself.

In any case, Cyrus, the glow remains in memory. Let's not let it die out completely. Set the clock of your emotions back three or four years, as mine has set itself, and let me have a real letter to take off the chill of a Western Europe which I don't seem to recognize.

February 10

Dear Netty:

For nearly two weeks now I have been lying in bed in this sanatorium, gazing at the walls and ceiling of my room, without other distraction than the daily visits of the doctor (a Hungarian Jewess) and the consumption of my scanty meals. This existence bids fair to continue for some time longer. . . .

I had supposed that my mind, once freed like this from outer stimuli, would fall back on its own resources and begin to construct magnificent plans for the future or new worlds of the imagination. In a subconscious fear of putting it finally to the test, I exhausted every possibility of distraction. I read a dozen books, and innumerable newspapers and magazines. I studied Italian grammar, although there is no reason in the world why I should learn Italian. I got a radio set and twiddled with it by the hour, although I no longer enjoy listening to music and am not interested in weather reports or in broadcasts of the international skating championships. I whiled away time trying to think out a plot for a novel, wherein a self-sacrificing young man nobly assists his lady love in arranging an abortion for which he is not responsible, in order that her weak and pampered husband may have the peace of mind to be successfully famous, and this I have done although I know full well that I am incapable of inventing a literary character and that I shall never be able to relate anything with any semblance of veracity, except the truth.

But all these efforts have been of no avail. I ended up just where I had started: staring at the ceiling and waiting for inspiration. And as the hours came and went, and inspiration failed to put in its appearance, there was nothing else to do but capitulate and admit to myself that, when you get down to rock bottom, the only things which I am really interested in doing are sailing on the Norwegian coast and taking walking trips in the Austrian Alps, and that my only real incentive to work is the concern lest poverty take the bloom off my little daughter's cheeks and lest my wife be subjected to the kicks and blows which humanity loves to administer to anyone who is down. These are the "resources within myself," those priceless assets which we are constantly accusing others of not possessing. These are the dreams and ambitions, the hopes and fears, the intellectual and spiritual results of a Princeton education and eight years of the cultivating influences of Europe.

But if there is no present and damned little future, there is at least a past. It is this past which I am moved to consider. But I must restrict myself to my experience abroad, as a foreign service officer. It is, after all, only since I came abroad that my eyes have been even half way open. All memories prior to this time are only fantastic visions, reflected and distorted in the mind of a child who trailed too many "clouds of glory" onto this matter-of-fact world, and trailed them too long.

What could there possibly be to tell about these eight years of life in Europe? I am no longer naïve enough to think I have "discovered" Europe. Poor Europe! It is, to be sure, a closed book to most of the hundreds of thousands of American tourists who visit it annually. But its mysteries and enchantments are those of the past, not of the present. "Main Street" runs with scarcely a break from Land's End to Bucharest, and from Palmero to the north coast of Norway. For those who want to know its content, there are such books as *Little Man, What Now?*, *The Adventures of the Brave Soldier Schweik*, *Alexanderplatz*, etc.[6] I except Russia, where there are still mysteries of cruelty, suffering, horror, hope & self-

6. Hans Fallada, *Little Man, What Now?* (1932); Jaroslav Hašek, *The Good Soldier Schweik* (1923); Alfred Döblin, *Alexanderplatz* (1929).

sacrifice which few Americans could ever hope to penetrate and which would be beyond the comprehension of the average American mind. But here, too, I have nothing to relate, for my own impressions rest more on literature than on experience.

My personal life provides a still less fertile field for literature. Adventures! I have had none. Experiences? Of what interest are the unhappy little adjustments of a scared young American, who cracks up now and then with a loud thud against the realities of life? The bag of false ideas about life and himself, the top-heavy equipment with which he faced the Old World, to him so new, all this may have been unusual in its quantity, but it was nothing unusual in its character. And experience at home would probably have forced him to get rid of most of it, piece by piece, just as Europe did. That, too, is a story which has been told too often.

Yet no two people think alike, and each of us probably sees a few things, in the course of his life, to which the eyes of others are closed. As I look back on these years, there are many vivid impressions; their sheer variety makes it a pity to forget them. Perhaps if one were to collect all those on paper, to reproduce them with sufficient honesty and simplicity and fidelity, they might unite themselves into sort of a picture, and among them the elements of this picture one might discern, (oh wonder of wonders), the semblance of an individual point of view. Drawn by this hope, scourged by boredom, I move reluctantly, uncertainly, and unhappily, to a consideration of the past.

[In what follows, Kennan recounts his departure from the United States eight years earlier, when he took up his first foreign post as vice-consul in Geneva.]

On a fine sunny day in late April 1927, the good ship *President Harding*, trembling to the roar of her own whistle, moved slowly, slowly out from the dock into the Hudson River, pointed her nose downstream, and began to slide quietly towards the misty, smoky reaches of Lower New York Bay and the Narrows. On board were four young foreign service officers, bound for their first posts: one for Bremen, one for Stuttgart, two for Geneva.

What a lark! What an adventure! How gaily the white handkerchiefs of friends and relatives bobbed up and down in the distance, on the dock! How deep, how full-throated the roar of the harbor and the city! How bold and free the crying, wheeling gulls!

The shores of New York were disappearing in the background. Great distance was growing up between these young men and the soil that had nursed them.

But what of it? Was it not spring? Was not their destination only Western Europe? Did not everyone go to Europe in the spring? The only difference was that they had diplomatic passports and the government was paying for the tickets.

They did not realize that this was the beginning of a separation in time far more important than the separation in space. It did not occur to them that they were exiling themselves voluntarily from all that they understood and from all that understood them. They could not know that this was a form of death that was taking place this fine gay, morning: the termination of a life where mileposts, clear and familiar, had marked the path from the weakness of infancy to the strength of maturity, and its replacement by another life, where other mileposts, fantastic and ominous, would mark a path from strength back to weakness.

The dining car on the boat train from Cherbourg to Paris swayed and rattled through the night. We sat long over the novelty of legal wines and liqueurs.

I stared through the sooty window pane into the blackness of the night. In the lights of village stations, whisking past the window, I already sought an imagined enchantment. The anticipation filled me with a sense of freedom and elation. Wicked, alluring, liberating Europe! Gone was the everlasting moral tension of our own prim country. Gone the fears and repressives and false hypocrisies. We are back now in the land of Rabelais and the Vie Parisienne. Here, where the good, round cast-iron urinals decorated the center of every self-respecting boulevard, we would have no more shame-faced, dirty murmuring about the "washing of hands." Here, where a mistress was a joke and not a scandal, we would have no more necking in the back seats of automobiles.

I did not recall, as I stared into the window pane, an incident of childhood days in Germany, how I had watched, with a fierce childish jealousy, the spectacle of a little German boy happily performing his devoirs, with the tender cooperation of his mother, in a public park, and how I had envied him that intimacy which made his mother a partner, rather than an enemy, in those forbidden things. Had I recalled this incident, I might have understood more about myself and my tendency to seek an erotic tinge in the Brittany landscape which lay in darkness outside the dining-car window. I also did not know, at that time, that Europeans, absorbed in a sterner struggle for existence, subjected by tradition to a more exacting social discipline, had less room in their lives than Americans for any inordinate eroticism. Had I known this, I might have understood more about the world which I was entering, and done better in adapting myself to it.

But none of these things was in my mind. And when the train reached Paris in the early hours of the morning, and I walked, too restless to go to bed, through the tawdry, unreal dawn of the Montmartre, I was already moving into that most dangerous of all the haunts of the human spirit: the world that does not exist. . . .

The summer of 1927 was hot and sunny in Geneva. The year ripened, as not every year does, to a deep, full maturity. The place surged with sunshine, and with an unprecedented influx of foreign visitors. The Naval Disarmament Conference was in session for weeks.[7] Its hundreds of delegates and hangers-on played and danced in fidelity to the diplomatic traditions of the Congress of Vienna. The university held a summer school for foreign students, and American girls strained idealistic eyes through shell-rim glasses to discern the glories of the League of Nations. Day by day, the greatest tourist season in Europe's history poured its tired, bewildered stream in and out of the city's gates. The permanent officials of the League of Nations played golf conscientiously and tactfully and disapproved severely of the Germans. Day after day the international crowd promenaded along the quais; the big white tourist boats docked and cast off in a steady procession; the bridge across the Rhone carried its heavy stream of automobiles with foreign licenses. On Sunday mornings the great fountain in the harbor cast its sparkling waters high up into the sunlight. The war was over. The crisis had not begun. The city—always passionless, always dignified—took on something of the fragile, unreal elegance of 1913.

Outside of my official duties, which were only too directly concerned with the tourists, I was happy enough to take very little part in all this transitory confusion. . . . But withal this, I was neither happy nor peaceful, and wasted in impatience and introspection what might have been a uniquely enjoyable summer. There were occasional little trysts which remained memorable. . . .

I spent a day in Lausanne. It seemed to me that I sensed in old hotels with their great gardens and in the parks along the lakefront the languorous boredom of pre-war Europe. I thought of a brief entry I had

7. During this conference, U.S., British, and Japanese negotiators attempted without success to extend to smaller vessels the 1922 agreement limiting the tonnage of large battleships.

seen in a forty-year old record book at the Consulate at that time, during the height of the Victorian era. A wealthy American couple had been touring Europe with their young daughter. They had stopped for some time at the Hotel Beau Rivage. One evening, the young lady had rented a row boat and had rowed alone far out into the beautiful lake. Here she had quietly jumped overboard and had shut herself off forever, by a mass of cold black water, from the life of vast hotel dining-rooms, of corsets and bustles and towering hats, of trains and carriages and stupid parents. I could picture the scene so well to myself: the quiet of the evening on the lake, the dark purple masses of the mountains to the east, the ripple of the water against the prow of the boat. The white excursion steamers will have puffed by, now and then, with the orchestras playing on the docks. Perhaps one of the stone barges, with its red sail, lay becalmed at a little distance. And then the empty row boat will have drifted on through the night, invisible on the black water, while the lights that rimmed the lake went out, one by one. It will have drifted and lapped against the little ripples of the fitful night breeze, until the sky grew red behind the mountains and the lake became grey and luminous in the dawn.

In general it seemed to me that this prim and decorous Swiss town, with its abundance of strict girls schools and with its historic role as a shelter for homesick political refugees, must have been hallowed or cursed by all the unruly dreams, the sorrows and frustrations and longings which had taken place within its walls. Poor Lausanne! Like all international watering places, it is a shrine where pilgrims from all the world, wealthy, pampered pilgrims, come to do homage to a beautiful scene, and to learn, if they stay long enough, how little escape there is from one's self, even amid the most beautiful scenery, and how few places there are, between the womb and the grave, which can lay claim to the title of "home." . . .

Geneva had been an unreal pageant of irresponsible power and wealth. Its connection to the earthy fundamentals of human life had been, for a casual outsider like myself, disturbingly hard to discern. The sight of the ships and merchandise and dock-workers of Hamburg harbor encouraged me. Here there were no facades. Here life was lived! . . . I came to love Hamburg, as I have loved no other city. It was probably coincidence. I was at an impressionable age, and romantically imaginative Hamburg was at the peak of its[8]

8. The letter/memoir ends here.

February 12

You feel the need of unburdening your soul to the Frau Doktor. You are anxious to tell her that you are depressed; that your meal in the dining-room, the first one, was too much for you; that the sight of these people, who still felt themselves so much a part of life that they could stare and gossip about one another, that the sight of these people had brought you to the realization that you must gradually abandon your cloistered seclusion and go back into the life which you left so cheerfully; that your thoughts, so pleasantly occupied until now with the past, had been rudely directed to the future; that you had no confidence in this future, no desire for it, no idea how you were going to cope with it. You had not, after all, coped with life successfully in the past. That was clear enough from the very fact that you, a perfectly sound and successful young man, in the prime of life, should be lying in this sanatorium together with a lot of old syphilitics and anemic women.

Why did you want to tell all this to the Frau Doktor? Whence this urge to confession? Did you really think that she could help you? You knew she couldn't. You knew no woman could, unless she were beyond the last trace of femininity and treated you with the unsparing frankness and the contempt which you deserve. What, then, is the idea? Where do you get that stuff?

—Well, after all, she is in charge of my treatment. She is a doctor. Should she not know the state of mind of her patient?

—Oho, you goddamn hypocrite! None of that stuff! No sir! None of your limp excuses! You are in a sanatorium, not a psychopathic clinic. It's your stomach that is being treated, not your head. If you think your head needs treating, then face the facts and go to a psychiatrist, but don't come sneaking around to lady stomach doctors with your little intimate confidences.

Learn to take it, Kennan. Don't run away. It's your problem. It won't help you to enlighten the Frau Doktor about its complexities. It won't even make her share your unhappiness, which may be what you really want. She doesn't care whether you face life successfully when you get out of here. No one does, and for that reason you can't spite anyone but yourself by being unsuccessful. Cut it out!

February 14

Further conversation, this time with the he-doctor. "You see, doctor, I have no foundation for a normal, healthy spiritual life. And the only way I can overcome this deficiency is by subjecting myself to constant external discipline. The steady pressure of active responsibility helps a great deal in this respect. And I dare not relax. If I relax, there will be no renewed health, but only complete collapse. I am like a man on a bicycle: as long as I keep going, I can balance; if I stop, I fall."

"Very well, my young friend, but if I tell you that your physical equipment will stand the strain no longer? And that if you go farther, you will only encounter repeated physical collapses, each one worse than the one before?"

"Then it does indeed look bad for me. But perhaps there is an escape. In the first place, I said I could not relax at all. That was an exaggeration. I have two forms of relaxation. One is sleep, the other is sport. I can increase the indulgence in both of these, without danger. And in addition to that, I can treat my body so carefully that there will be no excuse, almost no physical possibility, of a breakdown. I can lead a life as Spartan as that of Marcus Aurelius."

"And your wife? Who is going to share her interests? Who is going to give her companionship in youth, gaiety, and human society?"

February 15

Once upon a time there was a little boy. On Saturdays there was no regular school, but he was supposed to go to dancing school in the afternoon. He had to put on a Buster Brown collar and patent-leather pumps, and go to dancing school at the "Atheneum." He hated this. It was an insult and an outrage to deprive him of his holiday in this horrible manner.

There was no way he could get out of it. The family was firm. But there was one thing he could do. He could get revenge. He could make the family take the consequences of their own action. He could make his misery so conspicuous that they could not ignore it. He would go, all right, but he would never give them the satisfaction of thinking he liked it. He would get up Saturday morning with sealed lips and the air of a martyr. He would refuse to speak the entire day. He would refuse to go out and play. In the afternoon he would sabotage the procedure of dressing to the best of his ability. And when the heroic efforts of the family had finally gotten him into his Buster Brown collar and his patent leather pumps, he would suffer himself to be led off to dancing school like an animal to the slaughter. They had beat him, but not broken him.

(How could this have been avoided? What could the family have done about it, more than they did? Their great mistake was probably in trying to make him like it, in their desire that he should like it. That gave him a chance to get his revenge. They could get him there but they couldn't make him like it. They should have grinned a hard-boiled grin, the family should have, and have said: "We don't give a damn whether you like it or not, you silly little brat. It's school, like any other school, and your own feelings make no difference about it.")

Six or seven years later, the boy was a cadet in military school. In the dark late afternoons of autumn, his company used to be sent out for a quick two mile march on the country roads. The Wisconsin countryside had become cold and bleak. The barrack to which they would return would be still bleaker. As he pounded along in ranks, through the chilly dusk, the boy, who was very lonely, would dream great day dreams of glorious love, in which he, in his little cadet's uniform, was a figure as romantic as a prince.

Then the long-awaited Christmas holidays came. They meant good food, comfortable clothes, soft life—and girls. In tremendous excitement he rode home. But the first couple of days brought nothing. The city had forgotten him. The city ignored him. He began to sulk and to mope around the house. His elder sisters would come with suggestions. Wouldn't he like to go to this or that little party or take such and such a girl to the movies. And he would recoil in horror from these pitiful little suggestions. That should be his Christmas holiday? After all the dreams of the lonely afternoons? Never! What he wanted was understanding, understanding and sympathy for the blows and insults and hardships and loneliness of the academy, and retribution, retribution in the form of some vague, indistinct but glorious realization of his day dreams. They were responsible for him. Let them feel his bitterness. Let them realize what a difficult child they had raised. He had his pride. They could bend it but they could not break it. And let them pay for their folly in bending it.

So he would refuse to go out. He would stay home and sulk, and read the dirty poems in his father's edition of Robert Burns, which stood in the living room book shelf.

Instinctively, perhaps, he was trying to warn the grown-ups that they were raising an unruly, neurotic child, and he was appealing for help.

In later years, in the years of maturity, he gradually acquired responsibility for others. This responsibility he could carry well enough. But let the slightest attention be paid by anyone, either himself or others, to his own happiness and welfare, and the old rebellious defiances returned with a savagery which astonished even himself. He was not happy. No one should ever believe that he was happy or that he could be made happy. A martyr he was, and a martyr he should remain, to the end of his days, and let there be no mistake about it.

Illness was his only refuge, and he would not be cured. . . .

You have the bitterest of all lessons to learn—but also the most necessary: humiliation!

That is the only solution. You must have no interest in your life or your work or yourself, but you must pretend to have. It is the only way you can beat down your own ego and at the same time save your family.

No one must ever know it. The moment you ever consider seriously anyone else's knowing it: in that moment, the ego gets its chance again and you are off into the same wilderness.

You no longer have any personality. You yourself are dead. It is only your body that lives on and behaves itself this, that, and the other way.

That is all the purest nonsense.[9] It's all completely unrealistic. This is all just excuses. One has to affirm a life lived in health. One must have the power and courage to achieve that. It makes no sense to say that you don't have this capability. That's a matter of will. You have it if you want it.

You won't change anyway. You will talk and brood and write, but everything will stay the same old way. It will lead to no result. You will only gradually grow older and cooler. Finally you will become impotent. Nothing further.

The greatest difficulty is that this pride is so tightly bound up with the zest for life. When I concede that it really doesn't make a difference, that it's totally the same to me what people think about me, then the zest for living disappears. Then everything is meaningless to me. I don't want to read any books or newspapers—I don't want to speak with anyone. What's the sense?

There is only one other possibility: that is to arrange things in such a way that I could be a martyr by getting well. If someone could convince me that recovery was a difficult and strenuous process, which for my own good, I ought never to attempt, if people shook their heads with disapproval and concern at every meal I ate, every hour I rested, and every pound I put on, then I might get well in short order.

9. This paragraph and the following two are in German.

February 18

[Dream] Home on leave, I walked into his office, in the Division of F[oreign] S[ervice] Administration in the State Department. I wanted to ask him where they expected to send me next. To my utter dismay and astonishment, he replies that they were going to drop me from the service entirely. A Moscow colleague, H-n,[10] had turned in to the Department a little chit I had once written him in the office, and this little message contained so much foolishness and lack of judgment that the Department could no longer retain me in its employ. Furthermore, my accounts, for that month when I had administered the office, had been an awful mess.

I thought of my family—it seemed to me I even heard Grace's voice. I thought of the poverty into which I should immediately be plunged when my job was gone. I pleaded with H.,[11] told him I was willing to go to any post they wanted. They could even use me for typewriting, if they wanted, but please not to fire me. He said he might think this over. I realized then that what he had said had been partly only sadism, and that he had probably not made up his mind entirely to fire me, but had at least wanted to give me a good scare. However, I knew that H-n had gotten after me behind my back and that H. had it in for me.

[Undated]

Possibly we could describe the situation as follows. Men are unfortunately impelled by certain natural instincts, one of which is the instinct to reproduce his kind. This instinct cannot be satisfied under the conditions of our civilization without troubles and complications. Our high social organization objects to the vagaries of nature in this respect, and tries to tame and regulate instinct with its taboos and penalties. The man who lets himself get caught between the cogs of nature and those of society gets rubbed to pieces. One can defy the laws of society, make himself an outcast and satisfy nature; or one can take the banns in a spiritual sense, undertake an early acceptance of death, a renunciation of one's own life, and let it go at that. In the latter case nature is eager for revenge and even society is not entirely satisfied. But it is better than being rubbed to pieces.

10. "H-n" refers perhaps to Loy W. Henderson, Kennan's superior.
11. It is unclear whom "H." refers to.

April 9

It seemed to me that I had wrested at least one *Erkenntnis* [insight] from the mysterious strongholds which guard the laws of human life. This is the sense of a universal sadness that covers human life wherever industrialization has forced its entrance. It is a sadness not confined to factories. It lays its hand in every manifestation of life with which it comes into contact. When combined with poverty and dirt and disease, it can turn to horror and despair. When combined with the pomp of power and the magnificence of nature, it takes on a hue of tragedy which makes the most splendid theme of modern literature. It gleams in the illumination of cities at night. It weighs on the Sunday crowds around the great cities, wherever they are. It lays bare the nastiness and pettiness and ugliness of provincial towns, against the background of a violated countryside. It is the pathos of these centuries. It arises not from our "relationships of production" as the Marxists would maintain. It arises from the damage which the machine has done to the human body and the human soul. It is akin to the sadness of police dogs who live in apartment houses and lean out the window to sniff the air and see the sunshine.

There is no escape from it, for the time being, at least. But life is less puzzling and less terrifying when one sees its activity, its inevitability, and its beauty.

As they were leaving Vienna, Annelise and Grace leaned out the car window. It was a new, shiny blue car. Annelise tried hard and unsuccessfully not to cry. Grace ran her lips dreamily along the metal rim of the window. I stared hard, for a while, into the blue glaze of the side of the car.

Annelise could not reach down far enough to kiss me, so she gave me her hand, and I kissed it. Then Grace took off her woolen glove and held her hand out, too, for the same purpose. That saved the moment—if not the day.

April 10

In the afternoon I sat in the Kurpark on a bench, read Austrian history off and on, watched the nurse maids come and go and reflected sadly on the invidious effect which years of consort with a real lady have had on my qualifications as a bachelor.

April 20

Pondering, as I have so often pondered before, over the idea of staging a little revolution in one's unfortunate personality, the sad realization came to me that you can't change human beings radically, all of the sudden. The best you can do is to influence them, like plants, over a long period of time, by gradual changes in their environment. It is only a question of what changes.

May 10

Reading Russian history, this morning, about the passing of the corporative idea of the state, in the 16th century, it occurred to me to question whether the proletarian conception of the state, so powerful and fascinating throughout the world right after the war, had not already outworn its freshness and passed into history in accordance with that inevitable mysterious law of change which makes Wagnerian music, the apotheosis of all that was vital to our fathers, no longer vital to us but only an interesting monument of the past. Will human nature ever again be violently repelled or attracted by this idea of the dictatorship of the proletariat and the eventual achievement of the classless society? Has not the Russian experiment proven, if it has proven anything, that the proletariat, once given power, does not necessarily exercise it with any particular altruism or intelligence by virtue of its own economic chastity, but readily hands it over to the most ruthless and determined political element, which in turn, as a consequence of its ruling position, only inherits the fears and interests of former regimes and exploits the people, under appeals to their patriotism, for the maintenance of its own foreign and domestic position?

The Russians will continue to brag about economic superiority for some time, because their low standard of living & the undeveloped state of their country will free them from the particular problems which are bothering more advanced states. This bragging may even continue to impress the short-sighted. But it is only an argument for state capitalism, not for communism, and will appeal to liberal bourgeois, rather than to proletarian circles. Will the pathos of the burly, over-alled worker, with his sleeves rolled up, brandishing a red flag and striding over the bodies of top-hatted capitalists, ever grasp the hearts of people as it did just after the war? I doubt it.

June 4

I am an officer in the foreign service of the U. S. Government. I am stationed in Vienna. Here I fulfill a small part of the current bureaucratic administrative work of the government. Soon I shall go to another post, and then to another and another. I shall get paunchy and bald and set in my ways. Maybe, in the course of time, I shall get up to a high position and even exercise a moderate influence on some field of foreign policy, before I retire. Meanwhile I shall be visited on occasions with a normal share of the misfortunes of a father and a husband and an individual, and as compensation there will be days and nights, now and then, saturated with intimations of a bounty and a glory we have never known. Finally, I shall die, and there will be an obituary in some Foreign Service Journal, and my children will throw away my old letters.

June 25

Again a vista opens up. (How many more? How often?) This time it must not fade like the former ones. It must not!

We build on the fierce dignity of responsibility, self-sacrifice, resignation, determination, all that sort of thing. It is the renunciation of personal life. I know it.

(Why not renounce it? You are beaten. Acknowledge it. You have been knocked down, shamed, and humiliated beyond description. You have no personal dignity any more. All that remains is your dignity as a husband, a father and an official.)

Say good-by to this world. You have failed. Get that, god damn it,—you have failed.

July 16

Felt horrible this morning and groaned around the office. It was hot and sultry. It was the day of Frau Schuschnigg's funeral.[12] The sky was overcast and a storm seemed imminent. The funeral was in the afternoon. The Minister came back from it, in tails, a top hat, at five o'clock. He told how the Chancellor had been on the verge of breaking down and how, while the crowd was returning from the cemetery in the weird, sultry sunless heat of mid-afternoon, a naked woman had dashed out into the crowd from a nearby house and the police had had to overpower her and take her away, and one of the diplomats had seen a dagger in her hand.

November 11 [*sic*]

Arrived in Moscow, from Poland, on Thursday noon, November 14. Went to the Ambassador's for lunch, then drove to the Mokhovaya and went to bed in our new apartment, to cure my cold.

12. Kurt Schuschnigg was chancellor of Austria.

Felt a little strange at first. Things seemed too quiet and well-organized. I felt better as soon as I discovered that the chain on our toilet was busted and had been repaired by some ingenious soul with one of the wire paper clips from the office. When I discovered that the bathtub faucets leaked and that the water later appeared, generously mixed with bad plaster, between the cracks of the linoleum floor, everything was all right. A couple of broken door knobs were just a needless luxury.

On Friday, the decree appeared, abolishing the Torgsin and Intourist valuta business, and providing for a stabilization of the ruble.[13] I wanted to jump out of bed when I saw it. Annelise, unimpressed, shoved my head over a bowl of chamomile tea, covered it up with towels, and refused to listen to my cries of anguish. Later in the day, we spent hours discussing the matter. We sang the song about "Bring me a lei from Hawaii because leis are too expensive here." It was decided that Durby and Charlie[14] would have to take on engagements at the Metropol [hotel] in the capacity of ruble boys, to take the place of the departing "valuta girls." We ate the "last supper," and visions were conjured up of six old men in rags, at some future Red Square parade, watching the top-hatted proletarians saunter past: the remainder of the Moscow diplomatic corps.

13. The ending of these special arrangements for foreigners made it much more expensive for Kennan and other diplomats to purchase Russian rubles.
14. Elbridge "Durby" Durbrow and Charles W. Thayer were embassy colleagues.

1936

In November 1935, the Kennans returned to a changed Moscow. Stalin's bloody purges were now under way. In addition to other innocent victims, Soviet artists, intellectuals, and officials who had socialized with foreigners were being imprisoned, exiled to Siberia, or executed. Kennan, who had worn himself out in the exciting, relatively open social and cultural environment of Moscow in 1933–34, grew frustrated, angry, and despondent at the crackdown on contact between Russians and foreigners. By December, he had decided, "I am ripe for a transfer. The isolation of foreigners has never been greater." He added that "the atmosphere of suspicion and fear" weighed particularly "on those foreigners who have a real interest in Russia."[15]

On a happier note, George and Annelise welcomed the birth of their second daughter, Joan, in April. The previous month, Kennan took an adventurous journey through the Caucasus region.

The Caucasus, March

Kutais and Tiflis were too much alike to be described separately. They are essentially oriental cities, cities of the Near East. Hot sunshine, dust, overcrowding, intense street life, poverty, disease, and deceit seemed to be their main characteristics.

The Georgians are a lazy, dirty, tricky, fiercely proud, and recklessly brave people. They never seem to work unless they have to. The Transcaucasus is the spiritual home of the drug store cowboy. The streets are packed with loafers at all hours of the day.

Transcaucasian filth is the filth of the Orient. Compared to it, Russian filth seems earthy and wholesome.

The Georgians claim to have acquired their trickiness from their dealings with the Armenians. However this may be (and to the outsider

15. Kennan to Hotchkiss, December 6, 1936, box 24, Kennan papers.

it seems an idle question), Tiflis and the entire Transcaucasus seem to be rampant with corruption, speculation, and crookedness. It is commonly believed that every cashier in Tiflis makes an average of two or three hundred rubles a month on the side, by crooked means. Many of the state funds flow into channels other than those for which they were allotted. Arrears in the payment of wages are a chronic evil which not even the best efforts of the state have been able to alleviate. The teachers seem to be the hardest hit in this respect.

The pride of the Georgian is well known. He looks down on all the neighboring races, with the possible exception of the Turk, for whom he has a certain respect as a fighter. The Armenian he hates virulently, and the Russian he holds in contempt.

Being an intense individualist, he has a typically romantic conception of honor and dignity. He will stand being cursed better than he will stand being laughed at. He considers that it is better not to live at all than to live with besmirched dignity. He is willing to fight at the suspicion of a sneer or a slight.

As a result of this same individualism, he shows great daring and spirit in an individual, hand-to-hand encounter, but makes comparatively poor material for a military organization. The Caucasian military units (I understand there are two divisions of locally recruited troops stationed in the Transcaucasus) look sloppy in comparison with Russian units.

Although the Georgian nationalists do not like Stalin, they have every reason to be thankful to him. They are still the only remaining independent people of any importance in the Soviet Union. This is borne out by thousands of little indications: by the faces and behavior of the people, even by the number of loafers and beggars in the Tiflis streets.

The Georgians have never regarded themselves as having been conquered by the Russians, or as being a subject race. The Russians, in their view, simply bribed their princes and gained access to their towns. Russian soldiers, they told me, had never subjugated the country districts. At the present time, the Russians were only a tool in the hands of one faction of ambitious Georgians. To hell with them.

Since the Kirov murder, Moscow's grasp on the Transcaucasus has begun to tighten up.[16] It is doubtful whether Stalin, in the face of the

16. The murder on December 1, 1934, of Sergei Kirov, Stalin's comrade and potential rival, led the dictator to launch the bloody purges of 1935–38 that wiped out much of the leadership of the Communist Party and of the Red Army. Gone, too, were many of the Russians who had befriended Kennan and other foreigners.

consolidation of his power and his economic successes in Russia, will be willing to tolerate much longer the laziness, the backwardness, the corruption, and the defiant, romantic nationalism of his compatriots.

Georgia will be a hard nut to crack. But Stalin's nutcracker has cracked hard nuts before, and at the present moment it is stronger than ever. Outside observers who have had an opportunity to study Georgia at close range for a long time feel that this contraction of the Moscow nutcracker, when it occurs, will be the best thing that ever happened to the Georgians. . . .

The country was rich with the remnants of every sort of old culture: Roman, Greek, early Christian, even pre-historic. It was evident that man had scratched out a scanty existence on these barren, almost biblical hills for many a century.

We passed a dam and a hydroelectric station, built some years ago by a German firm. Over it stood a statue of Lenin. The outstretched arm pointed downward, and local wit had it that he was indicating to the faithful where they should look for his soul.

One wondered whether some day that electric station and the statue of Lenin would not join the rich assortment of historical ruins and mementos which littered the surface and the bowels of those hills—whether, a thousand years hence, the era of Russian domination might not be recorded by historians as merely a brief and minor link in the long chain of the history of the Caucasus. It was difficult to believe that the crude stamp of Soviet Muscovy would leave a mark deeper than the mighty cultural influences of Greece and Rome.

The train left Tiflis in the afternoon. . . . When the train finally approached the southern suburbs of the city, Moscow—crowded, turbulent, semi-barbaric Moscow—loomed out to the hardened eye as a welcome haven of culture, civilization and progress. . . .

Stalin never comes back to his home town of Gori. His mother, a simple and portly old woman, lives very modestly in two rooms in Tiflis. The other communist leaders sometimes come to see her when they are there. Voroshilov[17] dropped in, on the occasion of his recent visit to Tiflis. She expressed the opinion that he was "a nice boy."

Communist historians have recently unearthed some of Stalin's school report cards. He got good marks in everything but deportment.

Stalin has three children. The eldest, Sasha, is described as a good-for-

17. Kliment Voroshilov was defense commissar and a member of Stalin's inner circle.

nothing roughneck. He likes to drink and fight. He lives in Moscow (he is already a young man) and apparently has a job of some sort. He comes to Tiflis on his vacations, and raises hell. The second son, Basil, is still in school. The third child is reputed to be a small daughter.[18]

There seems to be as much difference of opinion among common Soviet citizens as among the diplomats concerning the circumstances of Stalin's last marriage. I overheard a long conversation on this subject between a Jew from Dnepropetrovsk and a Georgian from Stalin's home town of Gori. The Jew thought the new bride was Kaganovich's sister; the Georgian thought it was Mikoyan's.[19] Neither knew the cause of the death of the former Madame Stalin. Both thought there was something phony about it.

[Undated] Bookkeeper on a Collective Farm

I picked this man up at night one time, driving into Moscow from the country. He never saw my face, nor did I see his. He sat in the back seat while I drove. He called me "Comrade Mechanic" throughout and did not dream that I was a foreigner.

He was greatly delighted at the prospect of having a ride in a machine.

"You're a lucky devil," he said. "Just think of being able to go joyriding all day long and get paid for it."

I asked him what his job was.

He was a bookkeeper for a collective farm near Moscow. He had an apartment and a family in Moscow, and commuted out to the farm on suburban trains every day. He got 200 rubles a month, in addition to 60 kilograms of potatoes, 30 kilograms of milk, and some vegetables in season.

How were conditions on the collective farm?

Horrible.

What was the trouble? Wasn't the harvest enough to go around?

Enough to go around? There wasn't a penny left for distribution. Here it was March and he hadn't even made up his accounts for the year 1935. He didn't dare. The trouble was not with the harvest. The trouble

18. Stalin's three legitimate children were Yakov Dzhugashvili, Vasily Dzhugashvili, and Svetlana Alliluyeva. In 1967, the last would defect to the United States. Though Kennan helped Svetlana get settled and publish her memoir, theirs would prove a rocky friendship.

19. Lazar Kaganovich and Anastas Mikoyan were longtime members of Stalin's inner circle. It seems unlikely that Stalin married either sister after his second wife, Nadya Alliluyeva, committed suicide in 1932. See Simon Sebag Montefiore, *Stalin: The Court of the Red Tsar* (New York: Alfred A. Knopf, 2004).

was corruption. The leaders on the farm stole everything. There was nothing left for the peasants. The leaders made a practice of writing out "kommandirovki" for themselves for trips to Moscow. The peasants made paper boxes during the winter, and the leaders would obtain such "kommandirovki" on the pretext of going to town on business, in connection with the box-making. They would draw 18–20 rubles each time from the treasury, to pay the expenses of the trip: train fare, meals, et cetera. They would stay right there in the village, drink the money up, and claim their day's pay, in addition. The whole cash turnover for 1935 had been only some fifty thousand rubles, and these kommandirovki alone had cost over five thousand.

"Doesn't the Party take an interest in such a state of affairs?"

"The Party?" My friend snorted. "Why the manager of the farm was a party member, and he was the worst one of the bunch. He's out now. He's gone to a consumers' cooperative society. He'll steal even more there. We've got a woman in his place, now, but she can't do anything. She hasn't got enough authority."

"But how do they get away with this? Doesn't anyone stop them?"

"I've been trying to stop them myself for months. I got a couple of investigations started, but nothing came of it. Yesterday I was up at the Soviet Control Commission and I hope to have an inspecting committee out there pretty soon."

"They must love you out at that farm."

"Love me? Brother, it's a regular war."

We were coming into town. He was still stricken with awe and admiration at the mechanical perfection of the car.

"It's just as though it were alive. It's just like a living thing. You'd think that it did all these things of its own accord. Who'd ever believe that it was just because you push all those gadgets?"

I let him off on the Arbat, very pleased with his experience but sighing at the adversities of fortune which had made him a bookkeeper on a farm instead of a chauffeur.

1937

Worn out by the travails of life in Moscow, Kennan awaited his transfer. The State Department first decided to send him to Jerusalem, then ordered him to Washington, where he was assigned to the European division to deal with Soviet affairs.

[As the next entry suggests, Kennan still pursued flirtations and fantasies regarding other women.]

Moscow, April 19

At the ballet I was tired, and had nothing to say to the diplomats who smoked their cigarettes in the lobby between the acts. Twice, during those entre-acts, she flitted past me, weaving like a wraith through the crowd, and was gone before I could do more than stare, and I had a feeling that she came because I was there.

May 17

Home alone this evening, fell to reflecting that no passionless democracy like our own, no state which is only the accumulation of millions of individual philistinisms, can have much in the way of a foreign policy.

May 23

Sunday. Arose in clouds of black despair. Went alone out to the dacha. . . . In the afternoon, took Grace and her little friend to the park of culture and rest, and for a ride on a river boat. Kept up a running fire of summonses and admonitions all afternoon and felt like a dried-up old governess. Whiled away the evening by lying on a sofa and doing nothing at all except reminisce.

May 27

Played tennis with H.[20] at the German Embassy in the afternoon. It sprinkled faintly. Sat on veranda and drank beer afterwards with him and the German Ambassador.

May 30

Drove out to dacha with Grace in afternoon, to get forgotten glasses. Was passed by Stalin on way in, riding in the extra, middle seat of an enormous Cadillac limousine, followed by a big Packard. . . . Stalin, when he went by us, stared gloomily out of his window at Grace & myself and we stared back.

June 9

Warm. Full summer. A hard and perturbing day's work in the office. Arrests and demotions. Went to the open air café on the Red Square with Loy, at 6 o'clock.[21]

June 11

The Tukhachevsky Trial.[22] Hot. Tennis & garden party at the Finns in the afternoon.

June 13

Worked until 2 o'clock. Went out to the dacha and played tennis. Came in and went to view the body of Lenin's sister, laid out in state in the Hall of Columns.

June 23

News of my transfer.

Washington, October 17

Out to Mount Vernon in the morning. Magnificent weather. Bracing cool air, cloudless sky, warm autumn sunshine. Shapeless, droopy people,

20. "H." probably refers to Hans von Herwarth, a German diplomat who would remain a friend of Kennan's for many decades.

21. As Stalin was purging much of the Soviet leadership by execution, Franklin D. Roosevelt was, in Kennan's mind, "purging" the State Department's Division of Eastern European Affairs by merging it into the Division of European Affairs. That shift would dilute the influence of Soviet experts, such as Kennan and Loy W. Henderson, his companion at the café.

22. The trial for alleged treason and the execution of Mikhail Tukhachevsky, marshal of the Red Army, figured among the horrors that hardened Kennan's opposition to Stalin's regime.

stuffy from Sunday morning waffles and funny papers, tired from not walking, staggered out of shiny automobiles and dragged themselves around the grounds of the old mansion.

We went for a long walk. It took time and patience to find a place where we could get off the automobile highway. Meanwhile the cars whirred by us monotonously, each depositing its streak of blue fumes over the landscape. But finally we branched off onto the shady quiet side roads. Grasshoppers flicked themselves around before us. An occasional late bird sang from the hard, many-colored foliage. The corn was stacked in the fields. Two or three times, some old car full of negroes rattled by. Once we passed a boy throwing stones at the branches of a hickory tree to make the nuts fall. Dogs from the negro shacks came out and barked disconsolately at the rare phenomenon of a pedestrian. It was very nice and encouraging but in the distance, the roar of the Sunday traffic on the big turnpikes was never lost, and it was never clearer that man is a skin-disease of the earth.

October 24–25

The buses to Alexandria are full of negroes and unhealthy, unbeautiful whites. The drivers wear floppy caps, chew tobacco and spit out the little window by their side. At the front of each bus is an advertisement to the effect that "you can trust us with the most delicate apparel."

Across the river, past the gas stations, past the airport with the barbecue restaurant, past the junk heaps and the automobile graveyards, past the sign boards, the nigger shacks and the real estate development announcements. On the other side, runs the railway embankment. All America is passing before our eyes on this short ride out to Alexandria.[23]

A day of despair, in the middle of such a horribly senseless city, and of wondering whether there were not still, somewhere in America, a place where a gravel lane, wet from the rains, led up a hill, between the yellow trees and past occasional vistas of a valley full of quiet farms and woodlands, to a house where candles and a warm hearth defied the early darkness and dampness of autumn and where human warmth and simplicity and graciousness defied the encroachments of a diseased world and of people drugged and debilitated by automobiles and advertisements and radios and moving pictures.

23. The Kennans rented a house in Alexandria, Virginia.

on the objects. "It is incumbent on the authors of persecution," says Gibbon, "previously to reflect whether they are determined to support it in the last extreme. They excite the flame which they strive to extinguish; and it soon becomes necessary to chastise the contumacy, as well as the crime, of the offender."

Before we undertake any extensive responsibilities for the running of internal affairs in Germany by means of force and coercion, we would do well to reflect, as Gibbon suggests, whether we are determined to go through with it, come what may. It may require an exertion of force quite out of proportion to the positive results obtained. It may require a ruthlessness now foreign to our troops; a ruthlessness which can serve only to brutalize those troops themselves and to give them the worst possible lessons in the practises of government. It will certainly require, to be successful, a far greater degree

CHAPTER FOUR

World War II, 1938–45

1938

Kennan spent the first part of 1938 working at the Department of State in Washington. In June he took a long bicycle trip through his home state of Wisconsin. The State Department assigned him to Prague in August, just weeks before German demands for the Czech Sudetenland threatened imminent war and led to the Munich conference.

Washington, February 9

[Dream] It was in Moscow, in [illegible] apartment. They had all gone to the theater. I was alone there, except for the maid, C——, who sat before a mirror in her best dress, fixing her hair.

Things were breaking up. D[1] was leaving. In another day his things would all be out of the apartment. We would all be separated. The world would again become strange and cold.

My eye fell upon the bare corner of the room. The furniture had been taken away and the bare floor, dirty and discolored, leered at me in the blaring light. This brought home to me the whole tragedy of what was happening. Panicky with horror and revulsion and loneliness, I turned to the maid, threw myself down on my knees beside her. I wanted to embrace her and to cling to her and to stop the passage of time that was going to tear us all apart.

But she was indifferent. She had made money all these years, working for D. She was happy for her new dress and faced the future with confidence and pleasure. She was young, and the only one of us to whom the separation had no particular significance.

February 11

To the office. Gastritis. Argued bitterly and savagely with Guf[2] about isolationism. Realized that I must adjust myself.

1. "D" probably refers to Elbridge "Durby" Durbrow, a friend in the Moscow embassy.
2. Bernard Gufler was Kennan's longtime colleague and friend.

To reception at Latvian Legation in afternoon.

In Europe, it is possible; here it is difficult.[3]

[Undated]

Homecoming

The writer is one of those comparatively few people whose American origins and upbringing are unimpeachable but who, as a result of circumstances which could not possibly cast doubt upon his patriotism, has been condemned to spend most of his mature life abroad.

On the occasion of his last visit to this country he was a little puzzled over the discrepancy between the America of boyhood recollection and the urban façade of American life with which he was now confronted. Travel, whether by railway or by auto, did little to dispel this bewilderment. For the sleek, air-conditioned trains slid quietly and swiftly down their long avenues of steel, affording only fleeting glimpses of industrial sidings, abandoned houses, junked automobiles and a semi-desolated countryside; while the great highways, leading from filling station to filling station through a gauntlet of billboards, warning signs, and hot-dog stands, were only projections of the city street, the identical city street, which lay at either end.

It was with a view to clarifying his own mind and to ascertaining whether the "country," with its connotations of the genuine and the simple, still existed, that the writer availed himself of a recent opportunity to return to his own state and to travel for a couple of days on a bicycle through a section which he could justly consider as his native soil.

In addition to its being the scene of his boyhood, the state had other qualities which commended it as the scene of an expedition of this sort. For one thing, it was a predominantly agricultural state. It was also fairly representative: neither too old nor too new, too far east nor too far west. Finally, it was a relatively prosperous and socially progressive state where, if anywhere, the most encouraging results of modern Americanism might logically be sought.

My jumping-off place was one of those occasional spots in the landscape of the central northern states where a touch of bizarre scenery: a rocky glen, a waterfall, or a precipitous elevation, has broken the beautiful monotony of the countryside and has provided a convenient excuse

3. This line is in Russian.

for waylaying the passing motorist and extracting a few dollars from his pocket before releasing him to pursue his swift, boring flight across the plains. This place, with its aggressive tourism, its advertising, souvenirs, information booths, hotels, and tourist homes, has something of the atmosphere of the religious pilgrimage points in central Europe, and I was glad to shake its dust from my tires in the bright sunshine of a hot June morning and to pedal out of town over the hills toward the east.

The air which trembled in the sunshine over the road ahead was heavy with the fragrances of early summer: of new-mown hay and of the teeming small life of the swamps. The road, although not a very important one, was broad and excellently covered with a dark oil surface.

Indeed, all the roads, both county and state, over which I was destined to ride in the course of the following days were beautifully graded and surfaced. They led through prosperous and thickly populated farming country. They were lined with quiet, spacious farmhouses, which stood back behind tree-covered lawns and gravel driveways. Towns and villages were interspersed at intervals of roughly ten to fifteen miles. Yet it seemed to me that these beautiful highways were the most deserted places I had ever encountered. In the course of a one hundred mile journey I was destined to encounter on the open road no single fellow-cyclist, no single pedestrian, no single horse-drawn vehicle. And as for the occupants of the occasional machines that went whirring by, they obviously had no connection in the social sense with the highway over which they were driving. Slumping back on the cushions of their stream-lined models, traveling at such rates of speed that the world on either hand was only a blurred, flowing ribbon of green, they had no more real association with the highway than their fellow-travelers in the cabins of the transport planes which occasionally droned overhead. They were lost spirits, hovering for a brief period on another plane, where space existed only in time. To those of us who inhabited the highway—to the birds and insects and snakes and turtles and chipmunks and the lone cyclist—these motor cars were only an abstract danger, a natural menace like lightning, earthquake, or flood, which had to be reckoned with and coped with (here the turtles, whose corpses strewed the pavement for miles, seemed to be at the greatest disadvantage) but to which we had no human relationship and which only accentuated rather than disturbed our loneliness. To anyone who complains of lack of seclusion in our modern life, I recommend walking or cycling on the highways. He may go for days without meeting any of his own kind. But

I should not commend this course to anyone inclined to the feeling that the free and unrestrained association of human beings is a prerequisite for a healthy social and political life. He will think back with regret to the vigorous life of the English highway of Chaucer's day and he will ponder with misgivings the extensive isolation of the modern traveler in his movements from place to place.

Be that as it may, the morning sun, to whom a deserted highway is as good as any other, began to bake lustily, and after a couple of hours of pedaling I was relieved enough to find a village by the side of a lake. The inn was a relatively new building, on the site of an older hostelry of pioneer days, and fitted out with "antiques" from the surrounding countryside. I was not sure that it was not an improvement over the black leather settees and the cuspidors of the country hotels I had known as a boy. In any event, I had a swim and, for sixty-five cents, a luncheon consisting of young onions, white radishes, broiled pike garnished with slices of apple, bread and butter, salad with cherries and pineapple, milk, ice-cream, and strawberries. Thus it was with an almost unpleasant consciousness of the generosity of nature in my native habitat that I set off again in the burning sunshine of early afternoon, on the second leg of my journey.

That leg was a particularly dry one. The only community along the way was a village by the ambitious name of Endeavor, which I passed through in the middle of the afternoon. Unfortunately, the manifestations of Endeavor on the part of the city fathers were principally of a moral nature. The place where, according to all accepted standards, the "tavern" should have stood was occupied by a stern "gospel tabernacle" and two men in overalls, of whom I inquired concerning the possibility of getting a glass of beer, grinned widely and replied: "Not here you don't. The place is stone dry." Their hearts were not stone dry, however, for they caught up with me in a Ford, when I had gotten a short distance out of town, and shouted: "About a mile further, on your left." And sure enough, a mile further on the left was the ubiquitous beer sign and back of it the roadhouse with its dark, cool bar room and with four enormous drunks who pawed each other affectionately at the bar and inquired of each other repeatedly in tones of earnest solicitation: "Is you tough?"

Four o'clock brought me to my day's destination. This was a backwater village, abandoned by both highway and railway. The new concrete road had been put through a half mile away. The railway had discontinued service on the branch line which led to the town and had added insult to injury, the inhabitants told me, by tearing down the "depot." So the community slumbered on peacefully, soiled but not engulfed by the flood of standard urban influence which flowed through so much of the surrounding countryside.

For me, its attraction lay chiefly in the fact that it was adjacent to a large piece of property which my paternal grandfather had acquired upon his return from the Civil War and much of which he had himself cleared for the plow and fenced in with a five-rail fence. I had at home the record of my father's boyhood reminiscences, written shortly before his death, and I was curious to see what had become of the land where, seventy-five years ago, communication with the outside world was still maintained by the wood-burning steamboats which plied the narrow streams and the Indians and the ducks gathered by the hundreds every year to gather the wild rice which grew in such profusion in the marshy places.

Upon entering the village, I repaired to the saloon as the proper source of all useful information. I was not disappointed. The company consisted of the barkeep, a German farmer, and an elderly newspaper editor from a neighboring small town. They were listening to a radio account of a baseball game between Washington and the White Sox, and discussing the prospects for the outcome of the Louis-Schmeling fight.[4] The editor, however, was interested in my quest, offered some suggestions of his own and then referred me to the village's oldest inhabitant.

I found the latter's house without difficulty. He was a well-preserved man, in his nineties, with a dignified beard. We sat together, side by side, on a swinging settee on his front porch, while he told me about old times. He remembered the pioneer days, before the Civil War. . . . Upon the old man's advice, I set forth to find one of the farmers who now lived on what had once been the family property. . . . He was a fine-looking man, with soft blue eyes and a firm, sensitive mouth. While the wagon rolled slowly round and round the field and the young farm hand stowed the hay that rolled inexorably up the conveyor from the mechanical hay-rake, I walked alongside, in a rain of chaff, and discussed family history with the farmer.

I gladly accepted a laconic statement that I was to pass the night at the farm. The house had both bathroom and dining room, but all

4. The June 1938 boxing match between the African American Joe Louis and the German Max Schmeling was seen as an epic struggle with racial and international significance. Louis won.

of us washed and ate in the big kitchen that stretched clear across the middle of the building. The dinner company included the farmer and his wife, their son, three farm hands (one of whom was a young Indian) and myself. The wife had prepared the meal herself. She had no "help." It consisted of smoked carp, onions, creamed potatoes, sweet buns with this season's strawberry preserves, chocolate cake, strawberries with cream, and lemonade.

After dinner the farm hands withdrew and the rest of us sat in the "parlor" and talked. The son was a short-sighted, good-natured, stupid fellow about twenty. He contributed little to the conversation. Later in the evening the daughter of the house arrived. She had been spending the day with friends in the city. She had been to college and was now preparing to become a physical training instructor. The entry of such a person—smart, well-dressed, confident, blooming with health and energy—into the tired evening atmosphere of the old farm house was a breath of air from another world. It was idle to speculate whether this contrast was for better or for worse. It seemed doubtful that she would ever make a farmer's wife, like her mother. Yet she was doubtless better educated and more wide-awake than her mother had ever been. In reality, the city, at once so menacing and so promising, had claimed her for its own as it had so many other farm children, and her future lay, for better or for worse, in its copious lap and not on the farm. . . .

The next day saw me ride over forty uneventful miles. . . . That evening I walked back to the house where I had my room. No one was at home and I sat for a time alone on the porch in the darkness. The tree-lined street stretched away down the hill, under the arc-lights. The side-walks were deserted, but a steady stream of sleek dark cars flowed between them, moving in and out of the town. Each car had its couple or its foursome inside, bent on pleasure, usually vicarious pleasure, in the form of a movie or a dance or a petting party. Woe to the young man or young woman who could not make arrangements to be included in one of these private, mathematically correct companies of nocturnal motorists. All the life of the evening flowed along the highways in this fashion, segregated into quiet groups of twos and fours. There was no provision for anyone else. There was no place where strangers would come together freely, as in a Bavarian beer hall or a Russian amusement park, for the mere purpose of being together and enjoying new acquaintance. Even the saloons were nearly empty.

It seemed for a moment as though this quiet nocturnal stream of temporary moving prisons, of closed doors and closed groups, was the *reductio ad absurdum* of the exaggerated American desire for privacy. What was in England an evil of the upper class seemed here to have become the vice of the entire populace. It was the sad climax of individualism, the blind alley of a generation which had forgotten how to think or live collectively, of a people whose private lives were so brittle, so insecure that they dared not subject them to the slightest social contact with the casual stranger, of people who felt neither curiosity nor responsibility for the mass of those who shared their community life and their community problems.

I recalled the truly wonderful fashion in which, as had so often been proved, these same people would rise to the occasion and subordinate their personal interests to collective efforts in the event of a natural catastrophe such as a flood, a hurricane, or a war, and I could not help but feel that one ought to welcome almost any social cataclysm, however painful and however costly, which would carry away something of this stuffy individualism and force human beings to seek their happiness and their salvation in their relationship to society as a whole rather than in the interests of themselves and their little group of intimate acquaintances. That such a cataclysm was imminent, within the span of a decade or two, seemed probable enough; and I found myself looking forward to it in much the same way as Anton Chekhov, in the eighteen-nineties, looked forward with both hope and trepidation to that "cruel and mighty storm which is advancing upon us, which is already near and which will soon blow all the laziness, the indifference, the prejudice against work, and the rotten boredom out of our society."

Before me lay another day of beautiful countryside, lonely highways, hot sunshine, and cooling drafts of beer at roadhouse bars. But nothing which I was destined to see subsequently served to weaken the relief at the thought that this sad breakdown of human association in urban America was something that could not last and that whatever else might be sacrificed in the years to come, the spirit of fellowship, having reached its lowest conceivable ebb, could not fail to be the gainer.

September 16

Disgust with myself for the easy vapidness of existence at this point of early middle-age: the realization that I myself am something of a bore and have damned little of any value to say to anyone.

Washington is beautiful only in its parks, trees, and gardens.

[Kennan crossed the Atlantic en route to assignment in Prague just as the Munich crisis was peaking.]

September 27

Phoned the Embassy from the ship this morning and asked them to make plane reservations Paris to Budapest, in the hopes of getting into Czechoslovakia, through Rumania. Later read in the English papers that the American Legation had left Prague. No mention was made of the destination of the peregrinating establishment, and I have visions of pursuing it through the wilds of Ruthenia.

September 28

We discharged our passengers at Plymouth and started out across the Channel. The ship was almost deserted, the water again calm as a lake. The sea gulls pursued their normal activities, the sun shown benevolently. No one would have dreamed that there could have been turmoil and confusion not far away, on such a day.

But when the gangway dropped into place at Le Havre, a panicky and seething Europe burst upon us in a second. The Consul at Havre boarded the ship at once and told me that it would not go on to Hamburg but would discharge its passengers at Le Havre and start back to the U.S. with a capacity load of escaping Americans. There was a frenzied interval while the family threw things into trunks and suitcases, hasty arrangements were made to leave the car in the Consul's custody, a telephone connection with the Embassy was finally established in the purser's office, and by 5:30 p.m. the whole family was pushed aboard the already crowded boat train for Paris.

Normandy was soft and rich, after our jagged unkempt countryside. The train from Le Havre to Paris keeps running along the tops of hills and one finds oneself staring down into narrow valleys where prim French houses, each with its vegetable garden, behind it, line the winding oil road.

People from the Embassy met us in Paris, in the evening, and we drove to the hotel through streets darkened as a precaution against air raids.

Prague, September 29

Up at 5 a.m., kissed my slumbering family good-bye and rode out to Le Bourget. It had turned out that a plane was again going to Prague and the Embassy had made reservations for me.

We took off in a fog and rode for three quarters of an hour over vast snow-fields of mist. Then things cleared.

At Strasbourg, where we made our only stop, some of the roofs had Red Cross signs painted on them. Otherwise there was nothing in the peaceful countryside to indicate tension.

At Prague I found everyone much relieved over the scheduled meeting of Chamberlain, Daladier, Mussolini, and Hitler at Munich. Nevertheless, things were still upset. Wives had left and most of the American staff had banded together and were living in the Legation, in dormitory style. I share a room with the other secretary and the Consul General. The main reason for their staying here is that the town is completely blackened out at night and it is very difficult to find your way around.

Walked down town this afternoon. Was absolutely charmed with the buildings and the city. I think a year in Vienna must have done a great deal for my appreciation of baroque.

Met Hubert Renfro Knickerbocker and some other journalists at one of the big hotels. Their plight amused me. Here, like vultures, to profit by the mortal agony of a little country, they were supposed to be giving the world hot news right from the center of things. In actuality they were grouped around a borrowed radio in one of the hotel rooms, frantically trying to find out from a London broadcast what was taking place in the world.

September 30

Up early and had a little stroll in crisp morning sunshine, before breakfast. Stood on the parapet by the palace and looked out over the city, which lay, covered with mist, in the valley. The morning broadcast from London brought the details of the Munich agreement, and the morning was spent in speculation as to how the Czech people would take it.

Went down town for lunch. There was a good deal of talking among small groups on the streets. Wherever newspapers were posted, numbers of people stood reading them. Crowds were assembled around the loud-speakers. Otherwise things were fairly quiet.

I was back in the Legation in the afternoon, when the Government announced to the people, over the radio, what had happened.

Later in the evening we went for a walk down to Manesuv Bridge. A slight rain was falling. Things were quiet, but there was real sorrow and bitterness in the faces of the passers-by, and it was no night to be heard talking French or English in the streets.

October 2

Walked down town in the morning and stopped in at the little baroque church on the City Hall Square. It is now used by a congregation of the Czechoslovak Church; a dissident Catholic sect whose origins apparently go back to Hus.[5] The church was full. The people sat quietly while a priest harangued them from the high pulpit on the subject of the recent political events. Here was no mellow benevolence. Here was also no exalted fanaticism. Here was bitterness, harshness, Puritanism, intolerance. Here was still some of the spirit of early Protestantism. And it was justified. This world had betrayed the Czechs. Let them turn their faces from it. Let them abandon all hope of the virtue of the human race and seek their solace in a just, unbending, and stern God.

Noon in a down town café. The tobacco smoke floated in the air. Fat Jews sat gloomily over their coffee cups and German papers.

October 9

Ate a sandwich sitting on a wall with a tree-lined, cobble-stoned road stretching out before me, and very pleased to be back in Europe. Beyond Černošice, up into the woods & hills. Ate more sandwiches, to the accompaniment of a glass of beer, at a country tavern. There was a stout old woman who served the beer, wooden benches around the wall, a young man with a pigeon in a little cloth bag, an old man with an enormously long pipe. Rode back from Karlstein on a train packed to overflowing with demobilized soldiers, who joked grimly about politics.

October 13

Higgins, as courier, & young Kennedy[6] showed up in the morning, much to our amusement, both having started for Prague from Paris by train, thinking that the trains ran through. They had been kicked off at Eger & had made their way here in various ways. I undertook to get them out again, and at 2 o'clock, armed with papers from the German Legation, we left Prague in the Minister's Lincoln, for the occupied territory. Sudeten-Germany seemed a little drab and poor—gone the magic

5. Fifteenth-century philosopher and priest Jan Hus inspired Czech resistance against the Catholic Church.

6. John F. Kennedy's father, Ambassador Joseph P. Kennedy in London, had sent him on a "fact-finding" mission through Europe. The young man's impressions would influence his subsequent book, *While England Slept* (1940).

of Bohemia and central Europe, not yet come the general cleanliness and well-kept appearance of Germany proper.

October 17

Called on Mrs. C.[7] in the afternoon. Why must the wives of American men in positions of authority be so terrifically on the defensive? Having so much power, I suppose they feel responsibility. They fear that their men, who are easy marks for them, might be easy marks for other people as well.

7. "Mrs. C." was possibly the wife of the U.S. minister in Prague, Wilbur J. Carr.

1939

With the German occupation of all of Czechoslovakia, the State Department transferred Kennan to Berlin, where he assumed the heavy burdens of administrative officer of the U.S. embassy. The diary for 1939 ends in June, before the signing of the Nazi-Soviet pact in August and the onset of World War II in September.

Berlin, June 7

Left Prague by train in the early morning. . . . We hung around the border for an hour or so and all sorts of officials asked us for our papers. Grace said: "We don't ask the other people for their passports; why do they ask us for ours?" . . . Berlin was reached in early afternoon. At the station, there was an altercation. Solveig[8] had left the briefcase with Joany's pot in the toilet. When she went back to get it, the charwoman had taken it away. We found the charwoman, but she wouldn't give it up. It was her duty, she said, to turn it over to the *Zugführer* [conductor], who would give it to the lost-and-found. If she gave it to me and someone else claimed it, she would get in trouble. I got furious. Ours were the only children in the car. Grown ups didn't travel with pots. We were in a hurry. We had only a half-hour to get across the city. I finally took it away from her and walked off. It worked beautifully. There were no recriminations, and I reflected smugly as I walked off with the pot that if, like the Germans themselves, I had relied on further conferences and negotiations to recover what I felt I had lost, I might have been talking, as Mr. Hitler says, for twenty years longer.

June 8

Saw the children and Solveig off at the station first thing in the morning. The two little faces beamed out of the train window at us, and Grace

8. Solveig was an au pair.

waved delightedly as the train pulled away. I was too harried and tired to appreciate the full significance of this last separation; it was twelve hours later, and the sunset was fading across an impressive North Sea, when it hit me. . . .

[George and Annelise vacationed briefly in London.]

London, June 11

Sunday. Stayed home all morning. Lunched downstairs. Anna Freud[9] came over in the afternoon, a middle-aged woman with tired, deep eyes and a sensitive, intelligent face which, once seen, will not readily be forgotten.

Later we went downtown. We walked around past Buckingham Palace and past a park where the ponds were beautiful and full of ducks and smelled abominably. . . . Thence to a big movie house, where we saw *Goodbye, Mr. Chips*[10] and I was disgusted at the sentimentality and romanticism with which the British upper-class loves to surround itself.

9. Anna Freud, the daughter of Sigmund, was a psychoanalytic theorist in her own right.
10. Based on the 1934 novel by James Hilton, *Goodbye, Mr. Chips* portrays the long career of a beloved Latin teacher.

1940

In February 1940, the State Department ordered Kennan to accompany Undersecretary of State Sumner Welles on his abortive peace mission to European capitals. Ever the discreet diplomat, Kennan did not mention the mission in his diary. Nor did Welles seem to rely on Kennan's advice. Meanwhile, the widening war was engulfing the personal lives of the Kennan family. George had Annelise fetch their two daughters, Grace and Joan, from her family near Kristiansand, Norway. They made it out only days before the Germans invaded on April 9. Annelise brought the children to the United States while George shouldered most of the responsibility of running the American embassy in Berlin.

Berlin, April 15[11]

Annelise left for Norway in the middle of March. On April 4, I had reason to call her long distance and ask her to bring the children back at once. She left the next day, a Friday; went to Oslo that night and took the sleeper Saturday night to Copenhagen.

I left Berlin by plane on Saturday afternoon for Copenhagen, where I wanted to meet them. It was a clear afternoon, with marvelous visibility. The plane, Swedish by nationality, had to leave Berlin in precisely the opposite direction of its destination and waste an hour flying in a great circle to the southeast, in order to comply with the German military requirements. . . .

Next morning, right after breakfast, I met the family at the station. Gracie and Joany were dressed in twin blue coats, with little Happy Hooligan bonnets, and each of them had a new pleated woolen skirt, of which they were very proud. They were on the crest of the wave, and remained that way all day, on the trip to Berlin. . . .

11. Kennan copied into his diary a letter to his sister Jeanette Kennan Hotchkiss.

Monday morning brought the news of the laying of the British mine fields along the Norwegian coast. That evening we sat by the radio and listened to an account from Oslo of the torpedoing of a German troop ship off Kristiansand. The trusting Norwegians had mobilized all the ambulances in that part of the country and rescued as many as possible of the survivors. They were brought into Kristiansand, under the eyes of thousands of curious Norwegians, who noted naively that they were all young men of roughly the same age and all had military haircuts, and who wondered where they had been bound. Few apparently suspected that they had evidently intended to effect a landing there the following morning.

Tuesday morning I tuned in the United States on the radio and heard the first snatches of news of the occupation of Denmark and the Norwegian ports. At noon, Annelise and I heard together, with a feeling of sickness and horror, of the bombing of Kristiansand and the shelling of the town from the sea.

Since then, life has been a round of the most intense activity in the office and of intermittent moments of hovering over the radio and trying to reconstruct something of the truth from the waves and waves of lies and boasts and prevarications which reverberate back and forth across Europe. Annelise still has no idea what has happened to her parents, her brothers, or her home. The Germans have maintained an ominous and embarrassed silence about everything concerning the situation in Kristiansand and there is every reason to fear that the unfortunate community was treated to a baptism of horror worse than anything else that has happened in Scandinavia. That the family should have come out of it unscathed physically would be almost a miracle, that it could have avoided a terrible shock in every other way is beyond possibility. Annelise has taken it wonderfully, with a composure and dignity which is the admiration of everyone, here. But it is naturally a cruel strain on her, and it is something which I am afraid neither of us will ever quite get over, however it turns out.

It is hard to explain our reaction to all this. Coming direct from Russia or from some of the other less happy countries of this continent, I always had an apprehensive sense of unreality and implausibility at the idyllic state of Kristiansand. It did not make sense that so much decency and comfort and health could exist side by side, within a few hundred miles distance, with such overpowering forces of nastiness and perversion and brutality. The instinct was of course sound, and its confirmation brings almost a sense of relief. Things are at least clear: the two cannot exist side by side, and the feeling of insecurity and anxiety, which so few others shared that I had begun to wonder about its validity, has found its explanation and its justification. There is now no more cause for heart-searching or for fear. We have gotten beyond that. The worst has happened, and there are no more questions to be asked. There is nothing left to do but to take the consequences. There can be no more wondering about who is right and who is wrong. All that is unimportant, as even we ourselves are. It is solely a matter of who gets whom, as Lenin put it. And we know only too definitely which side we stand on. Even our own little persons are no longer so important, and the world no longer revolves around our individual prosperity. We can accomplish little individually, and our own individual demise can have only minor bearing on the issue in which we are interested. We simply have to do what we can, together with the others, like very primitive little humans, and we need bother our heads with moralizing and philosophy as little as our primitive ancestors did. We love and we hate, and we let it go at that.

To get back to the tasks of the moment, I still don't know what to do with the family. I have reservations on the *Manhattan*, sailing from Genoa on May 4, for Annelise and the children. But I can't send her off until she has found out what has happened to the family in Kristiansand, and it may be that she will have to postpone her sailing. Meanwhile, anything may happen in Europe, at any moment, and a return to the United States may very well become altogether impossible, if the war extends to southern Europe. Most foreigners think it quite possible, and many even hope, that it will not be many days before this place itself will taste some of the more bitter realities of warfare. If it does, our own arrangements will depend on the circumstances, and on luck.

Materially, thank God, we are not badly off for a change. I have just had another boost in the service, which raises my salary nominally to $6,000 per annum, and gives me an actual income at this post, including rent allowance, compensation for appreciation of currency, etc., of roughly $13,000. How long the good fortune will last is another matter. But for the moment, I am well ahead of almost every one of my age in the service. I have only three more jumps, which can conceivably but not probably be negotiated in some seven or eight years, to put me at the top of the service and in line for a position as minister. There is not much chance that that will materialize, for the higher one goes the more enemies one makes, but it is a satisfaction to realize that so far, at least,

I have missed no boats, and that even if I should remain at my present rank for years, I would be sure of a respectable income and jobs of responsibility and authority.

For Goodness sake, don't apologize for writing us letters about life in Highland Park. They—together with the *New Yorker*—are the only things that keep us sane and give us a feeling that some day life can be lived again for its own sake.

If Annelise comes over, she will almost certainly want to spend the summer with you at Pine Lake. After that, we'll see. I hope myself to be able to come back before the year is out, but all that seems epochs away at this juncture. No one, in Europe, thinks more than a week ahead, any more.

I still have my awful job here, and see few hopes of getting away from it, for a long time. But there again, why think of more than the coming week. That alone can bring more than years would have brought in the good old days.

You probably wondered that you saw no pictures of me with the Welles mission. I was there, but I have an inherited genius for keeping out of photographs. I saw a picture in LIFE today taken in the special car placed at our disposal by the German government. Every one else in the room was in the picture, but all you could see of me was a hump in the table cloth, which denoted my knee.

[On June 14, the day Hitler's troops marched into Paris, Kennan, armed with a German permit, was traveling to The Hague and to Rotterdam to reestablish communication with stranded U.S. diplomats.]

The Hague, June 14

Left Berlin shortly before one o'clock, on the new express train to The Hague. Prisoners, probably Polish, were working on the fields between Berlin and Hanover. The sun beat hard on the flat, treeless fields, and the armed guards kept the prisoners lined up in neat, Germanic rows.

Beyond Hanover we began to encounter long trains of box cars with fresh prisoners from the west. The only openings for light and air were little apertures cut high up, near the ends of the cars, and through these one could see the crowded heads, the pale faces, and the bewildered eyes which stared, full of boredom and homesickness, out over the cold severity of the north German plain.

I looked at these and at the peasant women in the fields and at the well-ordered railway yards, and I fell to reflecting that whereas at one time, when individual conviction and determination played the decisive part in warfare, it was the free peoples who made the better soldiers, now, in the age of the machine, the slave peoples had the advantage; for it was the machine that counted, and the machine, in contrast to the sword, was best served by slaves.

At the border two train loads of SS, complete with motor vehicles, anti-aircraft guns, and field kitchens on flat cars, were waiting on a siding. Here, in contrast to the prisoners' cars, the sliding doors of the box-cars were thrown open, and the soldiers crowded in the doorways, all looking very much alike, staring at our luxurious train, and devouring the newspapers and magazines which we passengers tossed to them.

There was little damage visible in Holland, at least in the district through which we passed. Now and then there was a burnt out farm house or a gutted warehouse along the tracks, but everything had been thoroughly cleaned up with true Dutch neatness, and the bridge across the Ijssel, blown up by the retreating Dutch, had already been repaired sufficiently by the Germans to permit our heavy train to crawl over it.

By the time we reached Deventer, it was dark, and the blinds had to be pulled in the cars to observe the laws of the black out. I sat through the rest of the evening listening to a conversation between a smug Nazi business man and a successful Dutch fifth-columnist. I had to grip the cushion of the first-class compartment to keep from butting in and attempting to blast some of the complacency and hypocrisy out of the conversation. The German, a cold pompous swine, merely reechoed the *Völkischer Beobachter*[12] and was scarcely worth annoying. But the Dutchman, who had a keen, subtle intelligence and a fine command of language, put my reserve to a hard test. Professing great understanding for national-socialist ideals, he told the German of Dutch tradition and of the bourgeois conservatism of the Netherlands and pointed out regretfully how hard it would be to train Dutch youth, who had only a small country to fall back on and no great conquests to look forward to, to be national-socialists. As the train pulled into The Hague, I could not help remarking to him that he would indeed have a hard time creating a Dutch national-socialist movement: for either it would be truly Dutch, in which case it would be only an unsuccessful competition for the German movement, or it would be pan-Germanic, in which case all

12. This was a major Nazi newspaper.

the values of Dutch nationalism would be sacrificed and the adherents, instead of being superior Dutchmen, would only be inferior Germans.

June 15

In the afternoon, I went for a long walk. The house fronts of the town, prim and well-proportioned, breathed Puritanism and a solid, unostentatious prosperity. The sense of formality was so over-powering that I could only envisage generations of guests arriving for tea and being scrutinized with chilly suspicion by the servants for their social qualifications. This was obviously a country where no grownup who did not walk the primrose path could lay claim to warmth or forgiveness or tenderness. But civilization it was, indeed, and I reflected with sadness on the faults of an education which had left me so dependent on these undisciplined, really uncivilized necessities. . . .

I watched the sturdy, impassive, stubborn people trundling their bicycles and pushing their barges. Their fidelity to habit and tradition was so strong that it seemed as though nothing could ever change them. But try as I might, I could see little but ruin and decline ahead for most of them. What could Germany give this country economically to replace her lost position as a center for the colonial empire, as a transit point for overseas trade? These provinces, like Norway and Denmark, lived largely off their overseas connections. They were Europe's windows to the outside world. But would a Europe dominated by Germany, confined to a continental, autarchic economic policy, deprived, at least in its northern sections, of all its colonial empires, a Europe which had killed the great economic vortex of England off its own coast, would such a Europe need much in the way of windows to the outside world? Rotterdam would remain as a transit harbor, yes. But that alone, together with the growing of some flowers and vegetables, would scarcely suffice to maintain the dense population and the high standard of living of these water-bound provinces.

One could only expect that to the spiritual misery attendance upon the destruction of a great culture and a great tradition there would be added the misery of foreign exploitation and economic decline, and that some day large parts of these Dutch cities, sinking back into the swamps from which they had been so proudly and so competently erected, would become merely a curiosity for the edification of future generations of German tourists and would perhaps help to give the latter a sense of appreciation, tardy and helpless appreciation, for the values their forefathers had so light-heartedly destroyed.

June 16

We[13] drove to Rotterdam. We came into town along a normal city street, with shops open, trams running, crowds of busy people on the sidewalks. Suddenly, with as little transition as though some one had performed the operation with a gigantic knife, the houses stopped and there began a wide open field of tumbled bricks and rubbish. Here and there a wall or even the gutted framework of a house remained, but in most places there was only a gray plain of devastation. The main streets leading through this great ruined area were left untouched. Trams and motorcars ran on them as usual, and the unfathomable Dutch wheeled along on their bicycles as though nothing unusual had occurred. At one of the main corners of the city, traffic was still fairly thick, but not a building was left standing anywhere near, and the impression gained was that it was a crossing out somewhere in the country, between fields that had been used as dumping grounds for debris and refuse.

Most striking of all, apart from the ghastly scope of the destruction (the number of houses destroyed must have run into thousands), was the utter absence of transitions. Where bombs had not fallen, everything seemed in perfect order. Where they had fallen, there was simply nothing left at all. I saw a shop doing business and people living in a house on one side of which there was a perfectly normal city scene and on the other side of which, beginning right at the side of the house, there stretched nothing but a desert of bleached, smoking debris, as far as the eye could see.

June 17

Got up early in the morning, to take a six o'clock train back to Berlin. The five-hour trip across occupied Holland, in the dead hours of Sunday morning, was very dull indeed. It was still raining; the towns were empty; one had a feeling of the world's being forsaken by everyone but the cows. I read the German paper, pondered gloomily on the propaganda patter about "senseless resistance," and reflected that if there were anything in this war that had made any sense to me at all, it was resistance that had produced the ruins of Rotterdam.[14]

13. Kennan and his driver.

14. Kennan, who had edited this typed entry with pen, may have inadvertently left out a crucial "the." He probably intended the phrase to read: "it was the resistance that had produced the ruins of Rotterdam."

1941

In 1941, World War II spread across the globe. Nazi Germany invaded the Soviet Union on June 22, Japan attacked Pearl Harbor on December 7, and Germany declared war on the United States on December 11. Despite such momentous events, Kennan wrote little in the diary.

Annelise, who had intended to wait out the war in the United States with the two daughters, instead left the girls with Kennan's sister Jeanette and returned to Berlin in April. She had somehow found out her husband was having an affair. Decades later, when asked why she had left her children and ventured back to a war zone, she curtly replied, "To save the marriage."[15] *In September, when Jeanette could no longer care for the girls, Annelise returned to the United States.*

Berlin, August 31
The day dawned gray and cold.

Duty in the Embassy in the morning.

In the afternoon Kitty & Annelise and I drove out into the country and went walking in a forest. Damp sandy roads and oak trees. We came to a *Forsthaus* in the middle of the forest and sat there, on the little covered veranda, during a shower, and I sketched the barn across the road. Then the sun came out, and the wet trees glistened in the late sunshine while we walked back, and there was a rainbow.

There was an air alarm for one hour in the evening. We sat in the upstairs room, by the open door to the balcony, and waited for shooting, but there was none. Bright moonlight flooded the balcony, from a lovely half moon, and there were mottled clouds.

We argued long in the evening about America, a sort of shadow argu-

15. John Lewis Gaddis, *George F. Kennan: An American Life* (New York: Penguin Press, 2011), 141.

ment, in which the things that were said were only obscure allegories for the many things we really should have said, and could. Any two of us could perhaps have said them. But "three's a crowd."

September 1

American holiday. I had duty again in the morning. In the afternoon we went sailing. Lake Havel was autumnal and deserted, and compared to the emptiness of the brisk, clear afternoon, the memories of sailing in June—with all the heat and the complexes and the heartaches—seemed like memories of happiness.

1942

Shortly after Germany declared war on the United States on December 11, 1941, Kennan, other U.S. embassy staff, and a number of American journalists were interned in Jeschke's Grand Hotel in Bad Nauheim. Washington and Berlin did not negotiate a repatriation until May 1942. In charge of the group, Kennan had the thankless job of dealing with matters petty as well as major. Much of the complaining circled around the meager food ration.

Though not much bothered himself by such austerity, Kennan agonized over a personal crisis. He apparently felt disappointed and deeply humiliated by an affair gone sour. He did, however, enjoy giving lectures on Russian history at "Badheim University," which he had helped organize.

[The following entry suggests the nerve-wracking responsibilities heaped on Kennan in a typical day. He had to juggle the dictates of the Germans, the concerns of his fellow Americans, and the whims of the Swiss, his link to officials in the Nazi capital.]

Bad Nauheim, January 25

1. Graffis asked whether I had yet sent to the Swiss the memo he left with me yesterday (Saturday) afternoon.
2. Endeavored to get Copenhagen baggage upstairs.
3. Speck and Stadtler came to get stationery.
4. Mr. Morris came to tell about trouble with baggage.
5. Smith came to complain that his wife was missing two bags.
6. Hinkle came to say that he did not want representations made about his wife.
7. Miss de Zaba came to ask about visiting O'Neill.
8. Got Miss Lawson, who wanted to send money to O'Neill, and had her arrange with Miss de Zaba.

9. Chalker came to ask whether he could photograph from my balcony.
10. Talked to Best about his remaining in Germany. Promised to bring in declaration.
11. Mr. Morris came to tell of representations made through Swiss concerning discourtesy of hotel personnel.
12. Wrote memo for Patzak about Miss Humes' lost powder case.
13. Wrote memo to Fischer about the letter he wanted to send to Lisbon.
14. Wrote memo to Howard, transmitting letter from Swiss Legation.
15. Drafted letter to Swiss Legation on Gleboff case.
16. Drafted letter to Swiss Legation submitting Lochner's claim.
17. Wrote memo to Bailey and Laukhuff submitting letter from Swiss Legation, for their reaction.
18. Talked to Oechsner about Graffis' case (Gleboff).
19. Talked to Tucker about his newspaper work, and cards for his English class.
20. Looked vainly upstairs and down for Whitcomb in order to talk to him about his claim.
21. Drafted letter to Swiss Legation about Best's case.
22. Talked to Miss Dehmel about her case and drafted letter to Mr. Morris for her signature.
23. Looked high and low for Caillat-Bordier, in connection with baggage.
24. Talked with Charlie Smith about getting a letter to O'Neill.
25. Went to see Patzak and talked with him re difficulties with baggage.
26. Went to see Mr. Morris re talk with Patzak.
27. Saw Patzak again to explain misunderstandings.
28. Supper.
29. Talked with Mr. Morris and Caillat-Bordier.
30. Talked with Zorn about hotel organization and tips.
31. Drafted rules for Secretariat.
32. Saw Whitcomb about his claim.

April 19

1. The conviction that when in a depression he was nearer to reality, to a certain tragic and melancholy reality, than at other times. It was, in

other words, not the depression which was abnormal, but the irrational hopefulness, which prevailed at other times.

2. Was it a falling into extremes to say that he had to acquire the art of continence [crossed out "abstinence"] in order to be incontinent with gracefulness and self-assurance? *"In der Beschränkung zeigt sich erst der Meister.* [It's limitation that proves the master.]" And how to acquire the art of continence? If through diet and regimen, then it is lost the moment one resumes normal life. And one cannot go through life as a general ascetic, merely to exert control over one particular urge. That is only acknowledging one's slavery to it. Or was he wrong?
3. There is only one solution. You have come to this conclusion over and over again. It is to abandon hope, to acknowledge oneself as old and beyond those things. My God, man, you are no youngster any more. What do you expect?
4. Can you do that without loss of self-confidence, of pride, of energy? That is your problem. Do you see the solution?

April 20

Can one continue to drift like this? Must one not now decide upon some direction, some course?

I should like to lay all the given facts out before me, as one arranges a bridge hand, and make my decisions on mathematical considerations.

What do I actually want in life? Which is within the conceivable realm of possibility? For myself, I would wish (1) a happy, balanced personal life; and (2) work which I considered positive. The first of these is out of the question because of the tragedy that has occurred. The second is out of the question largely because I am an American. If a people were only deluded, you might do something with it. But when it is biologically undermined and demoralized, there is no future for it, regardless of the outcome of the war, but to suffer the consequences of its deficiencies. Someone with power might be able to do something about this. But no one has power in America. The system makes no provision for it. And it is probable that anyone who set about to overthrow the system in order to attain power would, if successful, merely open the floodgates to evils worse than anything he thought to combat and end up by making himself the tool of the forces of disintegration.

The only solution then, personally, is gardening, or the sort of glorified gardening called gentleman farming—that is perhaps the only form of playing with toys which is not ridiculous in elderly men. And it gives us a chance to acquit our responsibilities toward at least a small section of that earth which, in the main, we men have so abominably misused and disfigured.

Stronger, though more defensive in quality, than this wish for myself is the wish for my family: that they may be preserved from the cruelty of others and from natural catastrophe and that the children shall have an opportunity to grow up in peace and health. What offers these assurances? There is a real problem.

Neither the Foreign Service nor farming offers any complete assurances along these lines. The ideal thing would be to combine the two. For the same sort of catastrophe is not likely to hit both of them simultaneously.

The Foreign Service is pure drudgery. Its sole merit is that it pays a cash income. Otherwise it has no significance. If it were not for the family, I should probably not remain in it a day longer than I needed to. On the other hand, having the family, I cannot see my way clear to leaving it. I cannot ask wife and children to follow me into a sort of early-Christian renunciation of this world, such as farming would be, to renounce all the advantages of education and all social amenities. I can try to hold such a thing in reserve, against the possibility of even greater misfortunes. But I cannot sink back into this form of proletarianism at once, on the theory that some day I might have to do so anyway.

Why are you behaving as you are? Be honest now. You are doing it because you are ashamed and humiliated.

Let us rather say I am shocked, discouraged, and humiliated. What I have been guilty of was in my eyes a folly, to be sure, but a minor one, and there were plenty of ameliorating circumstances. That it should have been punished in so grotesque and humiliating a manner is what sets me back. Why, in the name of God, must I be pursued by misfortune in this relentless way?

But you still haven't answered my question. Why are you behaving as you are, and not in some other way?

Because I cannot face these people now. I am burning inside with rage and humiliation. To think that I, George Kennan, should be in the position of having to conceal anything. If I go among them and lead a normal life, and the thing later comes out, I have made myself a double-hypocrite. I should have to withdraw from them anyway, then. I should rather do it now and anticipate them.

Furthermore what, to me, is life among them? I have done my duty towards them. I cannot, in the circumstances, do any more; nor can they, God knows, do anything for me.

But you didn't think of that before.

Yes I did, occasionally. But this gave a great and final push to it. There is of course a certain element of stubborn boyish waywardness in it. I have been thwarted, as I was when I was a boy, and my pride has been hurt. As then, I react by breaking things, figuratively. I say if I can't have the real things, I shall not allow myself to be put off and satisfied with little things.

But is that logical? What are the "real things" you can't have?

Women, there's one thing. Liberty is another. Peace of mind's a third. Isn't that enough?

Yes. I suppose it is.

April 22

The important thing with respect to age is, after all, as in all other things, not what you do but how you do it. A man is as old as he feels, and the time has come for me to feel old, to force myself to feel old. But if I am to do this, then I must do it with good grace and dignity. That takes courage, resolution, *Selbstüberwindung* [willpower]. Above all it takes the strength of character that enables one not to look back.

Why is it necessary that you should feel yourself old? Is this not a stupid, dangerous bit of extremism?

For a man to feel himself young in my circumstances means that he must of necessity be very tough of heart, very gay, very well-balanced in his human relationships, and relatively irresponsible. I am none of these things. I cannot therefore be young successfully. Nor can I continue to be young unsuccessfully. The resultant fiascos would soon be too much for me and would affect not only me but likewise the people I love.

May 5

This morning Patzak[16] told me officially that we would leave here for Lisbon by train a week from today, the 12th, at 10:26 p.m. This was the news that we have been waiting for in this hotel for 136 long days. I drew up a notice about it, got it signed by the chief, took it down and pinned it to the bulletin board in the deserted front hallway and returned to my room without feeling any interest in the reactions of my fellow-internees.

16. Valentin Patzak was the German SS captain in charge of Bad Nauheim.

It represented months of labor on the part of many government officials and months of constant unpleasantness, self-restraint and trial for those of us who were in charge of the group here. For all of this many of the people in the group are incapable of feeling understanding, and they will repay us for it with nothing but ingratitude and criticism when they get out. All of which is not of much importance.

But now that the break has come, I think that I must resume the writing of notes of this sort, as a means of collecting myself mentally and spiritually for the plunge back into life. I am utterly worn out by the strain of living uninterruptedly for 5 months under one roof with 135 other people among whom I have no single intimate friend, and of trying to save them from dangers for which they have had no appreciation. My own personal life and strength have been so neglected that I have felt during the last four days something close to an incipient disintegration of personality: a condition of spirit devoid of all warmth, all tone, all humor and all enthusiasm. If this writing will help me to gather and order my spiritual forces again (and writing sometimes does) it will be worth the time. . . .

The afternoon was made unpleasant by the voices of other internees, including some of the higher officers, who object to letting all their hand-baggage go in the baggage-car except one single over-night bag, and to carrying said over-night bag to the train on the day of departure, as the Germans would have them do. As though it mattered. . . . This on a day when the British have been starting into Madagascar, when the further fate of France hangs in the balance, when thousands of people are dying and hungering cheerfully for what they conceive to be important issues. Oh my tender charges: if you only knew what burdens you will have to stumble under some day, if civilization is to be held up at all, you would not mind practicing a little right now with your week-end bags!

I was so disgusted at the last manifestation of false dignity and sissy-ishness that I couldn't bring myself to go down to dinner and have locked myself in my room for the evening.

May 14

We finally left Bad Nauheim night before last. At 8:15 p.m. I had the outer group assembled, in the hall of the hotel, and we walked over to the rail-way station. It was a warm May evening, but overcast. The inhabitants stood along the curbs or in the windows and watched with superficial impassivity the departure of "*die Amerikaner.*" Inwardly, most of them probably felt, despite all German military successes, a mixture of hostility, envy, and an uneasy questioning: "What if they should win the war after all?"

At 9:30, the wheels began to move and our stay in Bad Nauheim, having lasted just about five months, had come to an end. . . .

About noon-time, we were circumventing Paris on the belt line railway through the southeast suburbs. An abandoned tennis club, with weeds growing three feet high all over the courts, expressed succinctly the horrible rapidity with which a great city can suddenly lose the spirit of a metropolis and become a mere collection of buildings and ruins in the midst of the countryside.

The afternoon found us spinning southward through Orleans and Tours, behind an electric locomotive. Our long train of sleepers, drivers, and baggage cars was evidently a sensation in that subdued, occupied area. At lunch, a missive of some sort broke the window across from me in the dining car. The crash was like an explosion, and we all sat motionless and bewildered as the shower of powdery glass fell on the occupants of the table under the window. Somewhere along the way a man rose up in the middle of a field, unrolled an American flag and waved it as we passed. In a station, where we were passed by one of the few French passenger trains we saw, a woman put her head out of a window and made faces at us.

[**Undated**]

From you—embattled comrades in abstention,
Compatriots to this or that degree,
Who've shared with me the hardships of detention
In Jeschke's Grand and guarded hostelry,
From you, my doughty champions of the larder,
Who've fought with such persistency and skill,
Such mighty hearts, such overwhelming ardor,
Your uninspiring battle of the swill,
From you, my friends, from your aggrieved digestions,
From all the pangs of which you love to tell,
Your dwindling flesh and your enraged intestines:
Permit me now to take a fond farewell.
For five long months you've slept and nursed your bellies,
Or strolled along the Usa's quiet shores,

Eaten your rolls and failed to eat your jellies,
While others toiled and tramped and fought the wars.
The world might choke in food-restricting measures;
Chinese might starve, and Poles might waste away;
But God forbid that you—my tender treasures—
Should face the horrors of a meatless day.

[In September, the State Department sent Kennan on a mission to Lisbon, a center of wartime intrigue. As counselor of the U.S. legation in Lisbon, he was to help block the Portuguese from supplying wolfram to Germany while encouraging them to grant America and Britain naval and air bases in the Azores. George, Annelise, and Joan (Grace was in a Washington boarding school) left for Portugal with a firmer stake in America. In July, they had paid $14,000 for a 238-acre farm in East Berlin, Pennsylvania. The farm was close enough to Washington for getting away on weekends. In a pinch, George calculated, they could wring a living from the land.]

Washington, August 28

After conferences in the Department in the morning, I started back to the country at noon, to enter upon the last lap of preparations for another, and final, tour of war duty abroad. How different these preparations are from the many we have made in the past. Before, there was always the sense of adventure, of hope, of anticipation. This time, these luxuries must go by the board.

Six months ago, I was a prisoner in the heart of Germany. Whether we would be exchanged at all seemed, to those of us who were in the know, nip and tuck. I knew that if we were not released, we faced catastrophe, in the sense of deterioration of personality and of physical strength.

I learned then that for men who are really on the spot, there is nothing worse than a vacillation between hope and despair. The only ones who really have great strength are those who have great faith or resignation, and possibly they are the same thing.

I cannot afford, this time, to hope that I shall come out of this unscathed. The dangers (which, again, few people realize but myself) are not small, and I am just provoking fate, which has once been kind, by going into them again.

In this, my position is no different from that of tens of thousands of men who are now going abroad with the armed forces. And yet I sincerely envy these others. Their responsibilities are relatively few. If they survive at all, they return with the laurels of heroism on their brows, simply by virtue of their participation.

In the task they have given me, I cannot succeed. I can hope to do better than other, less experienced men. But what I can do will be known to very few people, and appreciated by fewer still, and the effort will probably end in personal catastrophe for myself and the family.

That is war. And I record these gloomy prognostications not with any sense of heroism, but because I feel that if I hold them constantly before me I shall be able to do my job with greater detachment, greater humor, less nervous wear-and-tear, and, paradoxically, greater enjoyment.

[What follows is a letter to George's sister Jeanette.]

Lisbon, December 1

I have a good sized job which usually keeps me busy until about 7:00 o'clock in the office. A lot of social obligations go with it. The result is that we have very little time to see Portugal, which is an amazingly beautiful country. We are broke, as usual, but the edge is taken off the hardship by the realization that there is always the farm, at home. . . .

I am neither happy nor unhappy. It's not the place I should choose to live for my own pleasure. I'm used to the accepted seasons of northern climates, and I don't think I'll ever feel at home in a place, however beautiful, where it never snows, where the hot summer is the dead dormant season, and where the grass gets green and the crops are put out in the fall. But I'm doing my job as best I can and, hell, it's war.

1944

Although the diaries lack entries for 1943, the year proved pivotal in the outcome of the war and in the development of Kennan as a diplomat. With fierce fighting in the Soviet Union, Italy, and the Pacific, the Allies finally won important victories. In Lisbon, Kennan confronted confused orders from the State and War Departments regarding negotiating base rights in the Azores. He ignored those instructions and appealed directly to the White House, where President Franklin D. Roosevelt heard Kennan out and endorsed the diplomat's plan for approaching António Salazar, the Portuguese dictator.

By March 1944, the State Department had transferred Kennan from Lisbon to London, where he served as political adviser to the ambassador to Great Britain, John G. Winant. Winant was also the U.S. representative on the Anglo-American-Soviet European Advisory Commission (EAC), whose responsibility was to agree on plans for the postwar occupation of Germany. In June—the month of the D-Day landing in Normandy—Kennan was appointed to the number-two position to the ambassador to the Soviet Union, W. Averell Harriman. With the Germans still occupying much of Europe, Kennan reached Moscow by flying via military transport from Italy to Egypt, to Iraq, to Iran, to Russia. He arrived in Moscow on July 1. Annelise and the children would later join him.

March 1944
In instructions to our [EAC] Delegation, there has been no trace of a foreign policy.

We have evidently preferred to see the [German] satellites sink back completely into the arms of the Axis, rather than to depart from unconditional surrender & make political choices.

In the case of Germany, our lack of policy is having the following effects:

1. We are allowing serious misunderstandings to grow up with the Russians, not over any real issues, but simply through failure to take into account their psychology. War guilt clause. Zones.
2. Our proposals for surrender terms indicate an utter absence of concern on our part over the amount of responsibility we are assuming in Germany. They are so phrased as to give the three allies unlimited responsibility for the future of the German nation. They show no desire, and no real place, for acquiring allies and helpers among the German people.

I doubt the soundness of this even from the military government standpoint. But I am not competent there.

Where I *know* it is unsound is in the sphere of international collaboration in treating the German question.

If we are not to achieve any real understanding with the Russians on political purposes, let us not, for God's sake, rush into unnecessary responsibilities of governing a great people jointly with them, at the most difficult possible moment for any government at all. If we cannot defeat Germany without them, and if we cannot agree with them on the future of Germany, then are we right to insist on our terms of unconditional surrender, with the enormous commitments which they contain?

What else could we do?

We could exploit the fears of the Nazi leaders in order to leave them in control in such territorial & other circumstances that they could not survive. We could drop all talk about war criminals, about our unlimited rights in Germany, etc., and concentrate on such measures of disarmament as would solve the problem of Germany from the standpoint of our war with Japan. This means something like the Russian document. But to be on sound ground, it should be accompanied by a very clear tripartite understanding about the military occupation which is to follow, and in arriving at this understanding, we should press for a minimum, rather than a maximum, of direct allied military government and of interference in German internal affairs. We should avoid all measures of disbandment or demobilization. We should plan our own occupational measures in such a way as to constitute a minimum of interference in the internal life of the country.

Why be so "soft" on Germany?

In the first place, this is not being "soft." Measures of military disarmament constitute the harshest ones, in reality, that we can take, short of actual physical extermination.

Secondly, the other measures, measures other than the ones I have mentioned above, require great policing strength, clear-cut political objectives, and unity of purpose. None of these we have. Without these things, policies of coercion and internal interference have a way of becoming more binding and restricting on the authors of them than on the objects. "It is incumbent on the authors of persecution," says Gibbon, "previously to reflect whether they are determined to support it in the last extreme. They excite the flame which they strive to extinguish; and it soon becomes necessary to chastise the contumacy, as well as the crime, of the offender."[17]

Before we undertake any extensive responsibilities for the running of internal affairs in Germany by means of force and coercion, we would do well to reflect as Gibbon suggests, whether we are determined to go through with it, come what may. It may require an exertion of force quite out of proportion to the positive results obtained. It may require a ruthlessness now foreign to our troops, a ruthlessness which can serve only to brutalize those troops themselves and to give them the worst possible lessons in the practices of government. It will certainly require, to be successful, a far greater degree of unity of purpose and method than can conceivably be achieved at this time between the Russians and ourselves.

What we must ask ourselves is this:

Is it more worth our while to fight the Nazis longer in order to force them to put themselves blindly in our hands, or to ask them to do at once, as a condition of the cessation of hostilities, such things as we wish them to do?

What must we *accept* as our objectives in the case of Germany? When I say accept, I mean, in view of our existing commitments.

1. Complete disarmament of Germany.
2. Complete allied occupation, for purposes of assuring (1) and of psychological demonstration.
3. Removal of Nazi leadership and punishment of war criminals,
4. Reparation and restitution.

17. On his seven long transatlantic flights in 1942–44, Kennan read much of Edward Gibbon's *The Decline and Fall of the Roman Empire* (1776–89). It reinforced his belief in the difficulty of any nation succeeding in maintaining long-term control over another.

Points (3) and (4) are mutually contradictory and cancel each other out.

Suppose we take just (1) and (2).[18] For that the Russian document suffices beautifully.

We must keep quite separate in our minds our program for the treatment of Germany, and the type of surrender document we want. The latter should serve the former.

If we wish to make our participation in the Commission effective we must do the following:

1. Replace Mr. Winant by a vigorous experienced man who can give the Commission his full time and attention.
2. Replace Admiral Stark,[19] as his Naval Advisor, with a *single* young active officer, whose mission would be to advise the Representative, when called upon to do so, on strictly naval matters, and who would not correspond direct with the Navy Department on these matters.
3. Have the Military Advisor, cease to be a representative of the J[oint] C[hiefs] of [Staff], and function solely as an independent advisor to the Representative.
4. Cause the Resolution of the JCS dealing with the work of the Commission to be cancelled.
5. Have the War and Navy Departments[20]

Naples, June 16

I drove around at length with Murphy and Offie[21] in the city. It was not yet a pleasant sight. People looked reasonably well-fed, but ragged and dirty. The worst of their hardships, to me, seemed the complete lack of transportation. Once I saw a train of three incredibly dirty and battered tram cars, crawling along a street on the outskirts, and at one point an American Red Cross bus seemed to be moving civilians. Otherwise, there appeared to be no public transportation whatsoever, and the collection of ancient horse-drawn vehicles which had been pressed into service was ludicrous and pitiful.

We dined at a very melodramatic modern villa on another section of the heights overlooking the city. It was the home of the French representative on the Advisory Council for Italy. We kept off all controversial

18. Kennan wrote, "Suppose we just take (a) and (b)."
19. Harold R. Stark.
20. Entry ends.
21. Carmel Offie, William Bullitt's former adviser, worked for State Department political adviser Robert Murphy.

topics, but behind the pleasant company and the beauty of the evening there loomed the vast tangle of contradictions and complications, both with ourselves and with the Italians, which must inevitably attend the internal and international restoration of France. With us Americans, it will be particularly difficult. The French know exactly what they want, and are quite unreasonable about it. We are the soul of reasonableness, and have only the dimmest idea of what we are after.

June 17

If there is anything more hopeful than the skill with which our military men pursue the responsibilities of conquest, it is the alacrity with which they again drop them, once their possession is no longer in dispute. . . .

Sam Reber,[22] down from Rome for the evening, was also at dinner, with tales of SS torture instruments, of bodies without fingernails or toenails, of tons of high explosives hidden in the German Embassy.

I hear various reports here about German prisoners. Some say they are depressed and discouraged. Others say that they are defiant and bitter, that they reproach us for our action: saying that we are destroying the cultural values of Europe and delivering it up to Bolshevism, that we understand nothing of the continent, and have no plan for its future. To this, my answer would be: if you drop the rot about Bolshevism, for it was not we who first invited the Russians into Eastern Europe and then attacked them, and if you regard Europe as a cultural museum, rather than the seat of a living, organic cultural development, then perhaps the reproach is justified. Let us assume, in any case, that it is, and that we represent a catastrophe for Europe. Then the fault is still with the Germans, for having provoked our intervention. We are bound to come over here every time anyone threatens the security of England, and if continental peoples do not wish to bring down upon their heads this dread plague of un-understanding Americans, they must learn to leave the English alone. Let the Germans take a lesson from this, and not repeat their folly.

Among the things which I saw today were the records kept of the progress of our long-range strategic bombing and its effects. These records were maintained with a scholarliness, a conscientiousness, a devotion to detail, an imaginativeness of portrayal, which were a tribute to the talents of the American people. Tonight I lay in bed, while the thunder pounded and echoed through the hills and the rain roared down

22. Samuel Reber was a member of the Allied Control Commission in Italy.

on the roof of the tent, and wondered why it was not possible to put a thousandth part of that energy, that talent, that devotion, into the conquest of the social and cultural objectives which so obviously lie ahead of our people.

June 18

Lunch at Kirk's[23] "golden brothel," a house near the sea which was once the dwelling of a royal mistress. I sat beside the wife of the Soviet representative, throughout lunch and afterward, and talked to her about Russia. She was, of course, an engineer by training, and was struggling hard, like all official Soviet wives abroad, to reconcile her duties with her feminine instincts.

Whoever would understand Russia today should study the Soviet woman: not just the bar girls in the Metropol Hotel but the great mass of women of the educated official class. They are being trained in a manner which, to my knowledge, has never before existed. Emphasis is on the social, rather than the personal, morals and bearing of the Soviet woman. Her dignity rests not alone on her feminine and maternal functions, but on her function in society. She does not live in order to love, nor does she love in order to live. Our women work, too, and are often independent. But it is a different sort of a thing. With us, the personal note is always there: the straining for smartness, the desire to please as a woman, the limbo of a glamorous and successful personal life in the offing. And with us there is the pride which strives, however unsuccessfully, for independence of thought. In Russia, woman's work is not a decoration to private life but a stern duty to the state. And independent thought is, as in Nazi Germany, a form of self-corruption, unnecessary, dangerous, immoral.

This, in both the women and the men, is to me the most terrifying and discouraging difference from our own mentality. And I see no end to it. People brought up in that way have an unlimited faith in the guidance of those who are in authority. I see nothing that could break that down. Inconsistencies and reverses in the party line are as nothing to them. If the line changes over night, there must have been a good reason for it. Setbacks and suffering in national life, being always the result of the infernal workings of some persons other than their leaders, leave them cold or even strengthen their glowing faith. And what they are told to

23. Kennan would later recall that he had learned much from Alexander Kirk, an eccentric, old-school diplomat.

believe they do believe, with fervor and sincerity, even though it may be logically irreconcilable with something else that they believed, with no less fervor and sincerity, a year before.

After leaving Kirk's, we drove through the harbor district, where I saw destruction worse than anything I had ever seen in one concentrated area, with the possible exception of Rotterdam. Most of it, I am sure, was done by ourselves, and I cannot help but wonder whether it was worth the cost. . . .

The talk turned on political matters, and I soon found myself delivering a bitter polemic about the tendency of intolerant regimes to surround themselves with enemies of wicked and diabolic intent, and about the way in which they often succeed, through their miserable intolerance, in making real enemies out of people who never needed to be enemies at all. When I am asked whether Mikolajczyk,[24] for example, or numbers of decent, unhappy Frenchmen, or let's say numbers of Poles and Finns, are agents of Hitler, my answer would be: "Not yet, but they probably will end up in that camp, if the intolerance and hostility and imperiousness with which they are received elsewhere leaves them no decent choice." As long as these forms of intolerance exist in the United Nations camps, we are going to find ourselves being amazed to learn that still more and more groups of people whom we are accustomed to think of as fairly decent, have turned out to be veritable agents of the devil. And if we join with sufficient savagery in the chorus of hatred and vilification, we stand a good chance of making them, in reality, just that.

Cairo, June 21

These two days were too alike to describe separately. Egypt, that triangle of irrigated desert around the delta of a polluted stream, was suffering from a heat wave. The hot breath of the Sahara enveloped the miles and miles of brown plaster walls; the mud flats on the outskirts steamed and stunk under the fiery African sky; in the streets of the foreign quarter the glare lay, white and burning, between the blank concrete walls of the villas. People barricaded themselves in their houses against the heat, and limousines were parked in shady basement garages, that they should not become too hot to sit in.

In the evening of the first day, when the sun had set and the sky had cooled, the heat could be felt rising back, like steam, from the baked

24. Stanisław Mikołajczyk was premier of the Polish government-in-exile in London.

earth. Elderly Britishers, groggy from their siesta, sauntered out for their game of golf. Itinerant Arabs, who had lain stretched out in the shade of a wall on the pavement through the heat of the day, arose, shook some of the dirt out of their robes, and began to beat their torpid donkeys into a resumption of the interminable trek from nowhere to nowhere. The jeeps and command cars, coming down the road from the pyramids, passed a string of dromedaries plodding slowly, patiently up the timeless hill to the timeless desert. In the Hotel Mena, the doors were thrown open to the terraces. The bar began to serve drinks outside. In the music room, surrounded by elaborate Moorish gratings, a pale-faced Polish refugee woman with a dog played Chopin on the piano; and a lone rat, sick and confused with the heat, ducked miserably around on the tiled floor, among the potted palms, searching for the exit to the darkness and freshness of the garden. . . .

At dawn, when I got up to go to the airport, it had become cool, and a clean fresh air lay over the sleeping city. But the sun was rising, great and ominous, on the cloudless sky, and it would not be long, I knew, before the heat and corruption of the day would descend once more upon the fertile, sinister land.

[Kennan copied the following letter into the diary.]

June 21

My own darling Annelise:

A few random impressions will perhaps give you the best picture of these last few days: a bucket seat in an A[ir] T[ransport] C[ommand] plane from Algiers to Naples, next to a severe and intellectual G.I., who repeated all the clichés of *P.M.*,[25] and took me sternly to task for the reactionary lapses of the State Dept.; Offie at the airport; lunch with Kirk & Murphy & Offie, in a house overlooking the great bay; Kirk full of his usual quips: objects violently to being called the American *member* on the Advisory Council ("particularly for a man of my age"); dinner in a very modernistic & spectacular villa still higher over the city, where our host was the Free-French representative; a tent, all to myself, at a military headquarters, where the heavy summer thunder-showers droned on the roof at night; luncheon with many generals and other celebrities; consultations with an American air force general four years younger than

25. *P.M.* was a left-liberal magazine.

myself and as efficient as any officer I ever saw; the implausible spectacle of slouching, impassive young American kids running much of the life of Naples, and running it pretty damned well; Sam Reber down from Rome, with tales of German cruelties and stupidities; walks in the forests on the hills near Naples; the vast and depressing destruction along the Naples water front; cocktails with royalty, the latter rather laboring the royal prerogative of frankness; luncheon again at Kirk's with the wife of a Soviet diplomat for my table companion, and all the old pot-boilers about the wonderfulness of the theatre in Moscow; 13 hour trip in bucket seats in a blacked-out plane (too dark to read) from Italy to Egypt.

Baghdad, June 23–25

The chief impression of Baghdad in the summer, which I carried away from those three days there, was one of claustrophobia. All day we were barricaded in the Legation (where the temperature never fell below 90°) by the much fiercer heat outside. We might look out the windows (as one looks out the windows in zero weather in the north) and see the burning dusty wind tearing at the eucalyptus trees, and the flat, bleached country enveloped in the colorless sunshine of the desert; a sunshine with no nuances, no shades, no shadows—a sunshine which does not even brown the skin, but only strikes and penetrates and dissolves with its unbending hostile power. Into this inferno of heat only "mad dogs and Englishmen," as Noel Coward used to sing, could dream of venturing. At night, it cooled off considerably, and we slept in reasonable comfort on the roof. But by that time the real mad dogs and the jackals had come in from the desert, and it was not safe to walk in the outlying district where the Legation was situated. The only tolerable time of day, when it would have been possible to break out of the prison walls, was the early morning. . . .

What of the possibilities of service in Baghdad? A country in which man's selfishness and stupidity have ruined almost all natural productivity, where vegetation can survive only along the banks of the great rivers which traverse its deserts, where climate has become unfavorable to human health and vigor.

A population unhygienic in its habits, sorely weakened and debilitated by disease, inclined to all manner of religious bigotry and fanaticism, condemned by the tenets of the most widespread faith to keep a full half of the population, namely, the feminine half, confined and excluded from the productive efforts of society by a system of indefinite house arrest, deeply affected, and bound to be affected, by the psychological habits of pastoral life, which have ever been at variance with agricultural and industrial civilization.

This people has now come just enough into contact with Western life so that its upper class has a thirst for many things which can be obtained only in the West. Suspicious and resentful of the British, they would be glad to obtain these things from us. They would be glad to use us as a foil for the British, as an escape from the restraints which the British place upon them.

If we give them these things, we can perhaps enjoy a momentary favor on the part of those interested in receiving them. But to the extent that we give them, we weaken British influence, and we acquire, whether we wish it or not, responsibility for the actions of the Iraqis. If they then begin to do things which are not in our interests, which affect the world situation in ways unfavorable to our security, and if the British are unable to restrain them, we then have ourselves at least in part to blame, and it is up to us to take the appropriate measures.

Are we willing to bear this responsibility? I know, and every realistic American knows, that we are not. Our Government is technically incapable of conceiving and promulgating a long-term consistent policy toward areas remote from its own territory. Our actions in the field of foreign affairs are the convulsive reactions of politicians to an internal political life dominated by vocal minorities.

Those few Americans who remember something of the pioneer life of their own country will find it hard to view the deserts of Iraq without a pang of interest and excitement at the possibilities for reclamation and economic development. If trees once grew here, could they not grow again? If rains once fell, could they not again be attracted from the inexhaustible resources of nature? Could not climate be altered, disease eradicated?

If they are seeking an escape from reality, such Americans may even pursue these dreams and enter upon the long and stony road which could lead to their fruition. But if they are willing to recall the sad state of soil conservation in their own country, the vast amount of social improvement to be accomplished at home, and the inevitable limitations on the efficacy of our type of democracy in the field of foreign affairs—then they will restrain their excitement at the silent, expectant possibilities of the Iraqi desert, and will return, like disappointed but dutiful children, to the sad deficiencies and problems of their native land.

I had occasion, during the period I was in Iraq, to reflect on the Polish-Russian question. . . . For millions of people in our country this question has become the test of the willingness of Russia to pursue a decent, humane, and cooperative policy in Europe. If Russia is prepared to pursue such a policy, then the tremendous latent possibilities of American-Russian relations have before them an open road to fruition. If not, then there remains for the Anglo-Saxon powers only the division of western Europe into spheres of influence and the establishment of a relationship to Russia which can serve the interests of neither party. For many people in our country, the attitude of Russia in the Polish problem will be the touchstone of Russia's relations with the West.

I think that I understand as well as anyone the complications of the Russian position. It is of course not the territorial question which causes the real difficulty, but the question of the Polish Government. Here the Soviet Government is making things unnecessarily hard for itself, and it is clear that those responsible for Soviet policy are either incorrectly informed by persons within their own sphere of authority or have arrived at an incorrect appraisal of the situation.

Reasonable people everywhere will understand that the current policies of the Soviet Government, with all their tremendous importance for the future of Europe, cannot and must not be compromised by disputes over past errors in judgment of individual groups or individuals within the Soviet Government. I am sure that the Polish Government, whatever tactical mistakes it may have made in the past, would understand this as well as anybody else, at the present moment. The demand in Russia for the complete suppression and liquidation of the Polish Government, with all its records and archives and memories, may serve the interests of certain groups within the Soviet Government who know themselves to be responsible for past mistakes. It will not serve the interests of the Soviet Government or of the Soviet people as a whole. For if the present Polish Government is ruined and driven to despair, it will merely become the core of a Polish emigration which for years will continue to make propaganda over the alleged excesses of Russian authorities toward Polish forces and civilians during the period of the Russo-German Non-Aggression Pact. Whereas if any reasonable arrangement can be made with that government (and such an arrangement would not necessarily preclude either extensive territorial arrangements or the reconstitution of the

Polish Government to include people such as Witos[26] and others) there can be no doubt that the Polish leaders would be willing enough to let bygones be bygones; and the Russian Government would always have, in its own tremendous strength, the guarantee of that undertaking. If the present course is continued, it means that the entire international future of Russia is to be jeopardized for the internal political security of a few individuals in Russia who once gave unsound advice or who took unsound decisions.

Tehran, June 28

I went for a walk in the evening. I was surprised to find myself in a city that seemed, after all, very Russian. In the straight cobbled street, the high fences, the Russian signs, the crowds strolling in the evening darkness, and the cosmopolitan babble of tongues, I could even sense the familiar breath of summer evenings years ago, in Reval. It was impressive to think of those two capitals, so far apart and yet so near, bound together by that vast fluid influence which is Russia. . . .

I began today to read a collection of wartime articles of Ilya Ehrenburg,[27] under the title of *War* and I was greatly disappointed in it. It is nothing but the nastiest type of wartime propaganda: devoid of every appreciation of the tragedy of this war, replete with accusations against the Germans on points which a Soviet writer might better have passed over in silence (unless what is evil in a German becomes good in a Russian), full of the most childish distortion and misrepresentation of cited texts, lacking in any attempt to understand seriously the nature of the enemy with whom we are dealing. Can it be that Russia's case in this war is so weak that it can be defended only by this mendacious, abusive drivel? I find it hard to believe. Ehrenburg's style is no more elevated, his distortions no less ugly and shameful, his intellectual position no loftier, than those of Dr. Goebbels. Either something is wrong with Ehrenburg, or something is wrong with Russia's position in this war. No one with a clean conscience need descend to such abusiveness. Nor are the faults of the Nazis so complex and subtle that they should require such vehement exaggeration to make them plausible to the reader.

26. Wincenty Witos was a former Polish premier.
27. Ehrenburg was a prominent Soviet journalist and novelist.

Moscow, July 1

At Stalingrad, everything except the airport building (which they were still working on) appeared to have been destroyed. . . . How deeply one sympathizes with the Russians when one encounters the realities of the lives of the people and not the propagandistic pretensions of their government.

August 1

Had dinner last night at the British Embassy with the Polish Prime Minister, Mikolajczyk, and the members of his entourage. They had now been here two days. The Prime Minister had seen Molotov.[28] He had not yet seen Stalin. He himself was apparently encouraged by his talk with Molotov. The members of his entourage were depressed.

The British Ambassador proposed a toast to the success of their mission, and since Mikolajczyk had been encouraged to come here by our President and by the British Prime Minister, we clearly had to maintain a general attitude of confidence and good cheer.

I found the evening a hard one. I was probably the only non-Pole present who had enough experience of Eastern Europe to be thoroughly aware of factors involved. I knew that an agreement between the Poles and the Russians would be possible. I knew that such an agreement could even contain strong assurances of the independence of Poland. I knew that there could be solemn engagements on the part of the Russians not to interfere in Polish internal affairs. I knew that the Red Army itself, during its period of occupation, would be entirely dignified and decent in its attitude toward the Poles.

But I also knew that entirely regardless of present intentions the force of circumstances would eventually transform such an agreement from a charter into a harness for the Poles, that Russians, in the long run, would be no more inclined at present than they were a hundred years ago to accept the contradiction of the grant to Poland of rights which were not yet given in Russia, that Russian conceptions of tolerance would not go far beyond those things with which Russians were themselves familiar, that the Russian police system would inevitably seep into Polish life unless sharp measures were taken on the Polish side to counteract it, and that such counter-measures would inevitably be deemed provocative and anti-Russian in Moscow. I knew, in short, that there is no border

28. Vyacheslav Molotov was the Soviet foreign minister.

zone of Russian power. The jealous and intolerant eye of the Kremlin can distinguish, in the end, only vassals and enemies, and the neighbors of Russia, if they do not wish to be the one, must reconcile themselves to being the other.

In the face of this knowledge, I could only feel that there was something frivolous about our whole action in this Polish question. I reflected on the light-heartedness with which great powers offer advice to smaller ones in matters affecting the vital interests of the latter. I was sorry to find myself, for the moment, a part of this. And I wished that instead of mumbling words of official optimism we had had the judgment and the good taste to bow our heads in silence before the tragedy of a people who have been our allies, whom we have saved from our enemies, and whom we cannot save from our friends.

August 2

Much news today. Turkey had broken relations with Germany. In Finland, Mannerheim replaced Ryti.[29] Our troops had broken out of Normandy. The Russians had driven through to the sea, near Tukums.[30] . . . In Riga there would be general relief that the Germans were leaving, rejoicing in a few at the approach of the Red Army, panic among a few others, and finally, among the majority, a sense of bitterness and sadness that the dream of national independence, which for one brief period had once become reality, was never again to be realized in their time. And perhaps it is hardly worth mentioning that if, after the vicissitudes of the last five years, any people still remained in Riga who had been brought up to love the gentler things of life, such things as quietness and privacy and personal dignity, those people must have reached the stage of total despair, for there will be no place for them in Eastern Europe within the field of contemplation of people living today.

Of most of this the Red Army troops, bathing in the faintly salty waves of the gulf, washing off the grime of an unprecedented military campaign, will have been ignorant. To all of it they will have been indifferent. The nationalist aspirations of the Letts they will despise, as lacking power and grandeur. The personal fastidiousness of those who have cultivated the art of living will seem to them, if they ever run across it, a useless and foppish idiosyncrasy. Only the future is interesting, not

29. Carl Gustaf Mannerheim, who negotiated an armistice with the Soviets, replaced Risto Ryti, who had cooperated with the German invasion of the Soviet Union.
30. Latvia.

the past. And theirs, in their own smug conviction, is the wave of the future.

August 3

Lunch at the Embassy with the Polish Prime Minister and his suite. He was due to see Stalin later in the day.

One of the Poles asked me point-blank what I thought of their chances. I replied that I thought the Russians, all things considered, wanted an agreement, but that I could not imagine that they would be inclined to go far out of their way to get it. I thought that the Poles could consider themselves well out of it if they could reach any satisfactory arrangement which would make it possible for Poles in exile to return to their native country and work there for its future. But I warned him that I usually leaned to the pessimistic side, and advised him to take that into account.

August 4

In bed all day with a cold. Perused various documents, including our Government's proposals for what we call, with refreshing simplicity, "an international organization."[31] By this is meant the international organization which is henceforth to keep us all at peace, and which we propose to discuss in the forthcoming conversations in Washington. It was a long and detailed document, designed apparently to preserve a status quo. What that status quo is, we don't know. And official Washington says, in effect, like Woodrow Wilson many years ago: "It doesn't matter what the status quo is, if we get the document."

Ours is a unique system of the conduct of foreign affairs. There are other countries which are democracies, but none of these has our strength or our favorable strategic situation. They are all threatened by dangers so formidable and so permanent that they are compelled to be relatively serious and realistic in their foreign policies. Otherwise catastrophe rapidly overtakes them. None of them can afford to make foreign policy the football of internal popularity-seeking.

In our country, the conduct of foreign affairs, and particularly of policy toward Europe, is governed by strange rules. Our people having grown up chiefly from the most varied European elements, the affairs of Europe rarely fail to strike chords in one sector or another of our public opinion. This is particularly true of the foreign language and recently

31.The United Nations.

arrived groups. And it just happens that these groups, which still retain the European passion for organization, exercise a degree of political power in our country far greater, proportionately, than the older American elements themselves. Almost no step can be taken by our Government in European affairs that does not arouse criticism in one or the other of these groups. But no President wants to risk criticism. The result is that public opinion acts as a constant paralyzing factor on the formulation of policy toward Europe.

To this must be added the fact that the average American of longer standing, being himself incapable of understanding the Europeans, finds it comforting to wish a plague upon them all and to take refuge in the sense of self-righteousness which is his American birthright. In his mind there is something sinful about Europe and about those who interest themselves in it. He regards any serious preoccupation with its problems in a born American as a suspicious thing, smacking of immorality and betrayal of the simple American virtues. The president who gets "involved" in European affairs receives his censure. The president who strikes an attitude of moral superiority and aloofness toward Europe receives his praise.

Newer elements, who still have axes to grind in Europe, exploit this popular prejudice, and when anything is done by our Government in Europe which arouses their displeasure, they quickly interpret it to the country at large as a departure from sound American principles.

All in all, our entire system of Government runs counter to the creation and pursuance of a considered consistent European policy.

Such a policy could be created and pursued only by specialists and professionals. We persist in placing foreign affairs in the hands of amateurs.

Such a policy could be created and pursued only with discretion, without any tipping of our hand. We insist that all our cards should be face up on the table so that the American people, and everybody else, can see them. . . .

The American public is by no means indifferent to Europe. It has certain definite demands to make on Europe. It would like Europe to be well-mannered and peaceful and stable. It would like things arranged in such a way that we would not be bothered by Europe, would not have to think about it, in particular that we should not have to go to war in consequences of Europe's quarrels.

It becomes the duty of every president and every secretary of state to cater to these conflicting demands of the American public: the demand that we should remain undefiled by contact with the sordid and detailed realities of Europe, and the demand that our government should take action to prevent Europe [from] becoming a source of trouble. And the unvarying tendency of these presidents and secretaries, when confronted with this dilemma, is to take refuge in general and abstract schemes, which can serve at once to conceal the absence of a real policy, to cater to the American fondness for dealing high moral principles, and to throw onto other governments the responsibility for future outbursts of violence.

Underlying the whole conception of an organization for international security is the simple reasoning that if only the status quo could be rigidly preserved, there could be no further wars in Europe, and the European problem, as far as our country is concerned, would be solved. This reasoning, which mistakes the symptoms for the disease, is not new. It underlay the Holy Alliance, the League of Nations, and numerous other political structures set up by nations which were, for the moment, satisfied with the international set-up and did not wish to see it changed. These structures have always served the purpose for which they were designed just as long as the interests of the Great Powers gave substance and reality to their existence. The moment that this situation changed, the moment it became in the interests of one or the other of the Great Powers to alter the status quo, none of these treaty structures ever stood in the way of such alteration.

International political life is something organic, not something mechanical. Its essence is change, and the only systems for the regulation of international life which can be effective over long periods of time are ones sufficiently subtle, sufficiently pliable, to adjust themselves to the constant change in the interests and power of the various countries involved.

An international organization for preservation of the peace and security cannot take the place of a well-conceived and realistic foreign policy. The more we ignore politics in our absorption with the erection of a legalistic system for the preservation of the status quo, the sooner and the more violently that system will be broken to pieces under the realities of international life.

The provisions of our proposals designed to prevent a great nation from conquering and dominating a small nation reflect a thinking which is naïve and out of date. We ignore completely the time-honored conception of the puppet state, which underlies all political thought in Asia and

Russia, and occasionally appears in Eastern and Central Europe as well. This conception alone mocks any legalistic formulas for the regulation of international life. Try asking the head of the Outer Mongolian Republic whether Mongolia has any grievances against Russia. He will pale at the thought. He is personally in the power of the Russian police system, and his people live under the shadow of the Red Army. Why should we suppose that it will be otherwise among the regimes "agreeable to Moscow" which are being set up along Russia's western border? Can't we see that the greater the degree of Russian domination, the less apt they will be to complain about it? Can't we see that they will be in the position of prisoners whose terror of their immediate jailors is far too great and too immediate to permit them to risk an appeal to a higher and more distant authority? Or to take another metaphor, the position of those victims of American gangsterdom whose fear of the certain vengeance of the gangsters prevented them from seeking the less certain protection of the police?

The conception of law in international life should certainly receive every support and encouragement that our country can give it. But it cannot yet replace power as the vital force for a large part of the world. And the realities of power will soon seep into any legalistic structure which we erect to govern international life. They will permeate it. They will become the content of it, and the structure will remain only the form. International security will depend on them: on the realities of power, not on the structure in which they are clothed. And we are being almost criminally negligent of the interests of our people if we allow our plans for an international organization to be an excuse for failing to occupy ourselves seriously and minutely with the sheer power relationships of the European peoples.

August 6

Mikolajczyk saw Stalin, as scheduled, day before yesterday. Stalin showed interest in his statements about underground activity in Poland (on which it is unlikely that Stalin had previously been accurately informed), manifested a willingness to explain the Russian attitude about frontiers, but referred Mikolajczyk to the Polish Committee[32] for the all-important question of changes in the Polish Government.

Yesterday the Polish Committee leaders, accompanied by a hitherto

32. This was the Lublin Committee of pro-Soviet Poles.

unknown figure called Bierut[33] who is described as President of the Polish National Council, arrived at the Moscow airport and were received with great pomp and with all the honors usually accorded to very distinguished visiting statesmen. All this was given publicity in the Soviet press, but not a word was said to indicate that the arrival had anything to do with Mikolajczyk. The Soviet public, in fact, has never been told that Mikolajczyk is here.

Meanwhile, in Warsaw, Mikolajczyk's supporters have allegedly seized whole portions of the city and are desperately trying to hold them against the Germans, while Russian troops lie across the river in the Praha suburbs. There is apparently no liaison between the two forces, and there is some suspicion that the Russians are deliberately withholding support, finding it by no means inconvenient that the Germans and the members of Mikolajczyk's underground should destroy each other.

The British here have now sent a written communication to the Soviet Government asking that the Red Army arrange for the dropping of supplies and munitions to the beleaguered Poles. The answer which the Russians give will tell us a good deal about the future of international collaboration in Europe, more, perhaps, than the conversation which Mikolajczyk will be having today with the members of the Polish Committee.

September 18

1. There has been no change in Soviet policy since Moscow and Tehran.[34] The Soviet Government since the time of Munich has never relaxed its determination to have a fairly extensive sphere of influence in certain neighboring areas of Europe and Asia, in which its power would be unchallenged. In the mind of the Kremlin, this has been a sine qua non for Soviet postwar policy. In contemplating and discussing collaboration with other great powers, they have always gone on the assumption that this primary and minimum requirement would be at least tacitly recognized. They have also never envisaged that collaboration with other powers would mean the permanent relaxation of any of the controls they have set up to prevent the outside world from learning too much about Russia and the Russian people from learning too much about the outside world.

33. Bolesław Bierut.

34. The Moscow foreign ministers conference convened in October 1943. The Tehran summit conference met in late November–early December 1943.

2. At the time of Moscow and Tehran and immediately thereafter the Soviet Government, feeling it essential not to offend unnecessarily public opinion in the Western countries, took pains not to emphasize these aspects of Soviet policy. With the improvement in the military situation in the spring of this year, their sense of dependence on the Western powers was lessened and they became more open in the promulgation of these policies.
3. There is probably no threat nor allurement which could cause them to part in good faith and permanently from their sphere of influence policy. Their stand on this matter is made more intransigent by certain past developments with respect to Poland and the Baltic States. These developments have apparently left a sensitive nerve somewhere in the highest Soviet political circles which prevents their being entirely reasonable on this subject.
4. We must find a means to adjust ourselves and our plans to this situation. If we approach it realistically, I do not think that the Soviet position need be a cause for despair on our part or that we need fear that it will jeopardize the peace of the world.
5. If we are to adjust ourselves successfully to Russia's position we must do the following:

   (a) We must reconcile ourselves to the fact that the Russians will insist on having, in addition to those areas which they are incorporating into the Soviet Union, a certain sphere of interest along their western border. They themselves have probably not made up their minds exactly how far this sphere will extend, and are waiting partly to see how we will react to their efforts toward expansion. We must determine in conjunction with the British the limit of our common vital interests on the Continent, i.e., the line beyond which we cannot afford to permit the Russians to exercise unchallenged power or to take purely unilateral action. We must make it plain to the Russians in practical ways and in a friendly but firm manner where this line lies. In this way, without the necessity of any direct discussions with the Russians, I think we can reach an effective understanding as to how far we each can go. We must be prepared to use all the means at our disposal to maintain our position in this respect.
   (b) Having reached a basic understanding in this way, we can proceed to accept Russian participation in whatever arrangements can be established for international collaboration in the interest of peace

> and security. These arrangements may not be as far-reaching and binding as we would have liked to have them, but reinforced by a realistic understanding with the Russians they would probably bear up well enough. In doing this, however, we must remember that broad generalities, such as "collaboration" or "democracy," have different meanings for the Russians than for us. We must not expect them to enter into forms of detailed collaboration which run counter to their traditional conceptions of Russian state security.

[Despite his criticism of the Soviet government, Kennan delighted in the Russian people and their culture. Returning to Moscow after a seven-year absence, he found himself "fascinated with it every minute. . . . It gave me an indescribable sort of satisfaction to feel myself back again in the midst of these people—with their tremendous, pulsating warmth and vitality. I sometimes feel that I would rather be sent to Siberia among them (which is certainly what would happen to me without delay if I were a Soviet citizen) than to live on Park Avenue among our own stuffy folk." That yearning for closeness with the Russians made it harder for Kennan to accept that, because of Kremlin-imposed restrictions on contact between Soviet citizens and foreigners, "I must always remain a distrusted outsider."][35]

35. Kennan to Jeanette Kennan Hotchkiss, October 8, 1944, Kennan papers.

1945

The year 1945 was one of transition for Kennan. With the death of President Franklin D. Roosevelt on April 12 and the surrender of Nazi Germany on May 8, U.S. policy shifted toward Kennan's preference for a tougher line against the Kremlin. During what would turn out to be his last year as a relatively unknown diplomat, Kennan journeyed to Siberia. There he enjoyed mixing with ordinary Russians and even some Soviet officials.

Trip to Novosibirsk and Stalinsk[36]

June 1945

Left Moscow on Saturday, June 9, at 3:00 p.m., on the Trans-Siberian express. . . . Within little more than an hour we were stopping at Zagorsk and suffering the first of those invasions of women and children selling food which were to beset us at every station for four days and nights. Barefoot or be-slippered, but always with clean scarfs on their heads, looking exactly the same at one station as at another, they came bearing their offerings: milk, fresh, boiled or curdled; cottage cheese; cream; eggs, raw or hard-boiled; radishes; berries; pancakes; boiled potatoes; onions; garlic; pickled carrots; in Siberia, butter. Some of them traded at wooden stands set back a bit from the tracks, but most of them did business at train side. There, on the black cinder track, hard-trodden and greasy with the oil and the droppings from the trains, under the feet of the milling crowds of passengers, train personnel and station hangers-on, without regard for the clouds of soot and dust, a thriving business was done: milk was cheerfully poured from old jugs into empty vodka flasks or army canteens; greasy cakes were fingered tentatively by hands black with train soot; arguments ran their course; bargains were struck; passengers pushed their way triumphantly back to the cars, clutching

36. Stalinsk was later renamed Novokuznetsk.

their acquisitions; and timid little girls with bare feet, who had not succeeded in selling their offerings, stood by in sad but tearless patience, awaiting with all the stoicism of their race the maternal wrath which would await them when the train had gone and they would return home with their tidbits unsold. . . .

Sometimes, odd items were offered. American corned beef went for 30 rubles a can. A can of Vienna sausage (Derby Foods, Inc., Chicago) was held up for sale at one station for 125 rubles. (A Red Army officer who looked at it, turned away in disgust. "I've been eating that stuff for four years," he muttered. "He won't get 125 rubles for it.")

There was little bickering. Where it occurred, it was generally over quantity, not price. In view of the great variety of receptacles used by buyers and sellers (each had to supply his own) there was considerable vagueness, and sometimes disagreement, over quantities. Strong words were passed; but they were passed, for the most part, with humor and good nature. I witnessed one scene where a soldier, surrounded by a sympathetic crowd of onlookers, accused an old peasant woman of tricking him over a purchase of milk. "You'd better be careful, little mother," he said gaily, "not to run across me in the other world. The archangels are all my friends." To the crowd's delight, the old girl crossed herself anxiously; and the incident ended in general laughter.

The car was captained and tended by two husky and good-natured girls: Zinya and Marusya. They had a tiny kitchen where they made tea from a samovar for the passengers. They fed the samovar from scraps of wood which they picked up along the right-of-way. It was their duty to emerge with little red flags at every stop, guard the entrance to the car and drive off the ragged little boys and other species of humanity who tried to hide on the steps, the couplings or the bumpers. This task they performed with vigor and dignity, but without exasperation. They took turns at their duties, one sleeping while the other worked. . . .

Most of the passengers were pleasant to me, but we didn't talk much. Only one evening, when I produced copies of our Russian magazine,[37] a lively meeting formed in the corridor of the car. The party organizer at once took charge and made a speech about how they were worried about the future, how they had trusted Roosevelt but weren't sure about Truman, and look at this fellow Hearst. We had a lively hour of fraterni-

37. As part of the wartime alliance, the Soviets allowed the U.S. embassy to distribute a glossy, Russian-language magazine about life in the United States.

zation. Then suddenly everybody began to look guiltily over his shoulder and the meeting quietly dispersed. After that Russian inhibitions claimed their own, and hardly anyone spoke to me for two days. . . .

We were now on the sector of densest traffic; and we were only one link in the long chain of trains, tiny trains against the surrounding distances, crawling eastward like worms, haltingly and with innumerable interruptions, across the dusty, swampy steppes of Barabinsk. We stopped more than we moved; and when we stopped, we could see the freight trains piling up behind us, and hear them whistling for the right of way with the deep throaty voice which only trains in Russia and America have, and which brings nostalgia to every American heart.

There was a warm, dusty wind. Everything in the car was gritty with soot and dust. When the train stopped among the swamps, we climbed down the embankment, took off our shirts, splashed off the yellow scum from the surface of the swamp water, and washed our hands in the cool dark liquid from underneath.

At nine o'clock in the evening, 98 hours out from Moscow, we clattered slowly across the long bridge over the Ob, and pulled up the grade into the station at Novosibirsk. Alexander Vladimirovich Tereshchenko, Deputy Chairman of the Novosibirsk City Soviet, was standing on the platform when the train pulled in, uncomfortable in the necktie, jacket, and hat which had been deemed to befit the occasion . . . sweating profusely, and wondering what the hell he was in for. The sight of my unprepossessing figure, wilted by four days of jolting and fasting, took him slightly aback, and I think he wondered whether the hat, at least, could not have been spared. . . .

Alexander Vladimirovich and I sat down to supper. I had no appetite, and could eat and drink little. Vodka, ryabinovka [a berry liquor], river fish, salmon, cold meat, radishes, cucumbers, cheese, hard boiled eggs, bread and butter, soup, beer, steak, fried potatoes, fried eggs, cake and tea, were all successively set before me. Each refusal was taken as an indication that the respective dish was not good enough, and served only to stimulate my host and the waitress to new feats of hospitality. I had to listen to the first of those cries of "Meestyer Kennan. Why don't you eat? You don't like it, what?" which were to pursue me through—and out of—Siberia. . . .

The construction and operation of one of the world's greatest opera theaters in a remote and still straggling community like Novosibirsk seemed to me to be a rather breath-taking venture. It is interesting to recall in this connection that the funds for the enterprise were refused by the central government and were therefore put up entirely by the oblast [district] itself. . . . There could be no more flamboyant a repudiation of the past, no more arrogant expression of confidence in the future than the erection of this almost mystical structure on the remote banks of the Ob.

There are undoubtedly tremendous engineering and artistic talents in the people of Siberia. I have no doubt that much more will be done in the next few years to elevate human life on the steppes and in the forests of Siberia out of the squalor. . . . But that this life can ever be elevated, at one stride, to the grandiose conception of the Novosibirsk Opera House I would doubt. And unless it is, the building must remain what it is today: an incongruous dream, out of relation to its own surroundings. . . .

My host, Mr. Borodulin, proposed that we "do" Novosibirsk in one evening.[38] (He evidently had a position of considerable importance in the party which gave him a local prestige out of proportion to his official title.) We first repaired to the new railroad station, certainly one of the greatest in the Soviet Union, where we forced an unshaven and somewhat bewildered station master to show us the place from top to bottom. As Soviet stations go, it was not a bad one. I was favorably impressed by the rooms for women with small children where they had nurses and doctors, showers and play rooms. The impression would have been better if one woman had not pulled at the station master's coat tails and howled that she and her children had been there for days and days and had never been able to get a ticket to move on.

From there we went to the park to see the Isadora Duncan dancing troupe. The audience seemed pleased enough; but I was personally glad for Isadora Duncan that she had not lived to share the experience. We ended up at the circus where all that remained was the lion taming act, in which the lion took raw meat from the mouth of a female lion tamer. The appearance of the latter was so formidable that we were inclined to give the lion the edge on bravery, of the two. This act, however, accompanied by somewhat dolorous sounds of the band, made us both drowsy and we decided to terminate our coverage of Novosibirsk night life.

38. Of this occasion Kennan would recall, "[F]or one lovely evening I was, to all intents and purposes, a member of the Soviet governing elite." Kennan, *Memoirs, 1925–1950* (Boston: Atlantic–Little, Brown, 1967), 273.

Kuznetsk, June 20

We went to the "Palace of Culture," which is simply a labor union club. The building had been turned into a military hospital during the war and had only recently been reconverted for use by labor union members. It had various rooms for amateur theatricals, musical organizations, chess, et cetera. There was a good library of several thousand volumes. On the top floor there was a technical museum devoted to the metallurgical plant, with models of all the shops, specimens of the raw materials, finished products, et cetera. In one room there was a great book, mounted on a pedestal with considerable formality, in which were registered the names of Stakhanovites at the plant.[39] (Since seventy percent of the young workers at the plant are now understood to be Stakhanovites, I must assume that only the leading ones enjoyed the honor of being registered in this way). Upon leaving the museum we came upon a large hall in which exhibits were being put up on the walls in preparation for the celebration of the anniversary of the German attack on Russia. To my amusement and to the acute discomfort of my hosts, some of the exhibits were beautiful large scale charts showing the plant production figures which had been so carefully concealed from me up to that time. The result was that we marched through that hall at a fast clip and I was not encouraged to linger over the individual exhibits. . . .

Every reasonable observer understands the strain which the war placed on Soviet life and the sacrifices which had to be made. There are few of these wartime difficulties which would not meet with sympathetic and tactful understanding on the part of any fair-minded foreigner if placed frankly and honestly before him. But what is annoying is the unceasing insistence on the part of the Soviet official that what they are showing is an advanced and highly democratic form of union organization obviously superior to anything that exists in Western countries. As long as this arrogant and unintelligent pretense is maintained, the open-eyed foreign observer will naturally tend to view with skepticism and some irritation the scanty and carefully chosen revelations of Soviet trade union activity which are served up to him; and he will find it much harder than otherwise to forgive his hosts for the glaring inadequacies with which their system, judged by Western standards, still abounds.

39. Stakhanovites were Soviet workers who achieved far beyond the required norms of their factory.

On Thursday, June 21, I returned to Novosibirsk. From the housekeepers who had looked after me during my stay in Stalinsk I parted with a mutual show of emotion which would have done justice to a residence of months instead of days. . . .

I had one day to spend in Novosibirsk before I could start for home. . . . I suggested a swim. We rattled down to the banks of the Ob, in the Gorki flivver. I undressed and swam and then we sat on a rock in the stinging Siberian sunshine. Little naked boys poked along the shore in a leaky old row boat as boys will do everywhere. Down stream, the long freight trains crawled slowly eastwards across the bridge on the main line of the Trans-Siberian, the cars and locomotives silhouetted like little black toys against the bright sky. Across the river you could see the other trains lined up and waiting for their chance to cross. Far upstream were the faint outlines of the other bridge: the new one, for the coal trains from Stalinsk.

The beach we sat on was stony and unimproved. Behind us was a bathhouse, but it was rundown and faded and obviously closed. [The guide] assured me that some day there would be great improvements here: wonderful parks and bathhouses and athletic facilities. That the effort would be made, I did not doubt. I only wondered whether again, as in the case of the opera house, Russian imagination and Russian dreams of grandeur, unencumbered as usual by any desire to connect past and future, would not cut loose from all connection with reality and begin some fantastic colossus of a project, build part of it hastily and with bad materials, never finish it, and then leave the beginnings to rot away or be used for other utterly incongruous purposes. Meanwhile the Ob, of course, would continue to flow its tranquil course toward the northern sea. And probably, regardless of what marvels had or had not been constructed on shore, for countless summers naked little boys would continue to find leaky old row boats and to pole their way up and down stream on summer days, shouting and splashing, cutting their feet on the rocks, and making astounding discoveries about the nature of rivers and the contents of river bottoms.

I had decided to return by air. . . . I sat next to a little old working woman, who had the hands of a man, who was a member of the Central Committee of the Union of Building Trades, and who was going to Sverdlovsk for a meeting. She was illiterate but bright and alert. She talked at length during the flight to Omsk, and her observations on the flight and on life in general had all the pungency and charm of the mental world of those who had never known the printed word. When we stopped for an hour or two at Omsk, in the blinding heat of midday, I shared my picnic lunch with her under the shade of the tail fin of the plane, and she made me read aloud to her from [Alexei] Tolstoi's *Peter the First.* Gradually we were joined by other passengers, and before the time finally came for the take off I found myself reading to half the plane's company.

We arrived at Sverdlovsk[40] in a pouring rain. . . . One of my fellow travelers was the party secretary, Mr. Borodulin, with whom I had "done" Novosibirsk one evening. We had encountered each other again in the plane like old friends, and he now stuck by me loyally. He succeeded in wrangling a room with four beds for the two of us and in keeping out several other importunate passengers who were looking for a place to sleep. His method was very simple. Looking them quietly in the eye he would say, "You take those bundles of yours and get out of here." There must have been something in the tone of voice which revealed the nature of the authority behind this demand, because the invaders invariably withdrew silently and without complaint.

The following morning the rain was still streaming down. . . . It appeared that it might be a technical possibility of finding transportation to Sverdlovsk for the day, but there was no assurance that one could get back. The hours of the morning wore on. Borodulin and I got fed up with the uncertainty and he decided to turn on the heat. He found a telephone and for half an hour he jiggled the receiver and shouted. His efforts were Herculean, and successful. About an hour later, the crew appeared from somewhere, looking slightly shamefaced. The truck was rolled up. We drove out to the leaky Douglas, got the motor started and soon were off into a solid bank of cloud, destined for Kazan. There was no assurance that we would get to Moscow. But the director of the airport at Sverdlovsk had concluded that his Sunday would be more peaceful without us.

At Kazan we were bustled off once more to an airport hotel. Moscow, it seemed, was having a victory parade, and the Moscow airport would accept no more planes that day. We would have to stay overnight. Again, Borodulin and I snatched the best room and barricaded ourselves against all comers.

In the late afternoon we were sitting in the "commercial buffet," which was a room with two or three tables, a little buffet stand, and a

40. Kennan and the other passengers were stranded for a while at the airport outside Sverdlovsk.

few stale cakes for sale at staggering prices. A lady passenger of middle age, in a well-cut grey traveling suit, who had quietly and without question associated herself with Borodulin and me as the most privileged and influential element among the passengers, casually undertook to raise, by a mere telephone call, a car which would take us around Kazan and show us the sights. This rash boast brought the buffet girl to her feet, from behind her little table. "And just where in hell," she asked with crushing weariness, "do you think you would raise a car in the city of Kazan?" Our traveling companion looked at her challenger with a steely eye. "From the N.K.V.D.," she replied.[41] The buffet girl quickly disappeared again behind her cakes.

The telephone call was made, to the head of the N.K.V.D. in person. But an hour went by and the car failed to materialize. We decided to start out on foot. We walked as far as an amusement park. Evening was upon us, and the crowds were gathering there for what was scheduled as a "popular stepping-out." We borrowed twenty kopek pieces from numerous strangers for a public telephone. It was finally decided that the car should come to the amusement park.

We bought sunflower seeds to eat, and started into the park, but soon decided that it was too crowded for comfort, and that we would rather see the center of town. We set out down a long, broad, tree-lined street, with fine big buildings that reflected clearly the university town. Some of the buildings had been made into military hospitals. The soldier-patients, clad in the frightful flannel garments peculiar to all Russian hospitals, sat out in the front gardens, with their accordions, playing, singing, talking, making remarks through the iron fence at all the girls who passed by. It was pleasant and homelike, if slightly vulgar, to be sauntering on the streets of a Volga River town of a summer evening, spitting the husks of your sunflower seeds philosophically before you as you walked. Eating sunflower seeds gave you the same sense of bovine calm and superiority as chewing gum. For a moment I could almost forget that I was a foreigner in a country governed by people suspicious and resentful of all foreigners. But not for long.

We spied a jeep which the lady thought was the promised car. It passed us before we could stop it. We walked all the way back to the amusement park and found it. It was the one, all right. The head of the N.K.V.D. was there in person, with a chauffeur. He greeted the lady with great

41. N.K.V.D. is the secret police.

respect. But he was embarrassed to shake hands with me, and refused to accompany us in the car, preferring to depart on foot rather than to ride publicly with a foreigner. . . .

The following day I sat for a long time on a suitcase in the stern of our Russian Douglas, looking out at the forests and farm country between Kazan and Moscow and trying to gather together into some sort of pattern the mass of impressions which the past fortnight had left upon me.

It was clear that here, spread out below us on the enormous plain, was indubitably one of the world's greatest peoples: a talented, responsive people, capable of absorbing and enriching all forms of human experience; a people strangely tolerant of cruelty and carelessness yet highly conscious of ethical values; a virile, fertile people with great endurance and vitality, profoundly confident that they are destined to play a progressive and beneficial role in the affairs of the world, and eager to begin to do so.

Between them and the world outside their borders stands a regime of unparalleled ruthlessness and jealousy. This regime knows better than anyone else what riches, what possibilities, what dangers lie in the people of Russia. It has those people completely in its hand. It is determined that no outside influence shall touch them. For this it is important that they should be taught not only not to fear the power of external forces but also not to look to them for favors. The Soviet Government must always be made to appear the sole source of gracious bounty for the faithful, and of righteous wrath for the incredulous or the undutiful. For this reason, the entire system is so devised as to obviate every last possibility of foreign influence on the popular mind and to turn to the advantage of the Soviet Government itself every act of foreign governments or individuals which might affect the people of Russia.

The American man in the street, reading of the struggles and sufferings of those Russians who were so recently his allies, feels the urge to help them, subscribes to the Red Cross or the Russian War Relief, does not demur at the extra labor and taxes involved in Lend Lease to Russia, and accepts with goodwill the arguments of those who advocate great credits for the Soviet Government. How much more must the traveler feel who sees with his own eyes the deprivations of the Russian people and the heroism: the young people working twelve hours a day without comfort or relaxation, the middle-aged people who can recall no security and no peace in their lifetimes and who have ceased to expect any for the future, the widows and war-cripples, the crowded homes, the empty cupboards, the threadbare clothes, the pitiful substitutes for comfort and convenience—and with it all the wistfulness, the hope, the irrepressible faith in the future? Surely here, it would seem, in this gifted, appealing people, purged by hardship of so much that is vulgar and inane in the softer civilizations, organized and prepared as no great people has ever been before for the building of a decent, rational society—here, if anywhere, would be a suitable outlet for the practical genius and the yearning to feel themselves helpful to others, which are signal traits of the American character.

But the fact is: there is no way of helping the Russian people. When a people places itself in the hands of a ruthless authoritarian regime which will stop at nothing, it places itself beyond the power of others to help. Gifts presented to it can be given only to the regime, which promptly uses them as weapons for the strengthening of its own power. If these gifts are passed on to the people at all, it is with the innuendo they were concessions which the regime was clever enough to extract from the crafty outside world while foiling the evil designs which lay behind them, and that those who would share in the benefits of them had better keep on the good side of that omniscient power which was so ably defending popular interests. On the other hand, blows aimed in exasperation at the regime itself are no help to the people by whom it is dominated. Such blows are promptly ducked and passed on to the people, while the regime, breathing sympathetic indignation, strikes one fiery attitude after another as the protector of a noble nation from the vicious envy of a world which refuses to understand. And if then, in the train of policies of arrogance and provocation, real catastrophe finally overtakes the nation, the regime promptly identifies itself beyond all point of distinction with the sufferings of the people and takes refuge behind that astounding and seemingly inexhaustible fund of patriotic heroism and loyalty which human nature seems to reserve for all such occasions. The benevolent foreigner, in other words, cannot help the Russian people; he can only help the Kremlin. And conversely, he cannot harm the Kremlin; he can only harm the Russian people. That is the way the system is geared.

This being the case, what does he do? The answer is anyone's. But I should have thought, with the sights and sounds of Siberia still vivid in my mind, that in those circumstances he would be wisest to try neither to help nor to harm—to make plain to his Soviet acquaintances the minimum conditions on which he can envisage polite neighborly relations with them, the character of his own aspirations and the limits of his own patience—and to leave the Russian people, unencumbered by foreign sentimentality as by foreign antagonism, to work out their own destiny in their own peculiar way.

[Eager to see more of the Soviet Union, Kennan welcomed the opportunity to escort a group of U.S. congressmen to Leningrad and Helsinki, which he describes in the following two entries.]

Leningrad, September

I had been in Leningrad three days of my life, and yet it was like coming home. I had read so much about it, and through the years I had spent in the Baltic states I had come to love the flat horizons of the north, the strange slanting light, the wintry bleakness of nature, and the consequent accentuation of all that is warm and rich in human relationships. . . .

This is to me one of the most poignant communities of the world: a great, sad city, where the spark of human genius has always had to penetrate the darkness, the dampness, and the cold in order to make its light felt, and has acquired, for that very reason, a strange warmth, a strange intensity, a strange beauty. I know that in this city, where I have never lived, there has nevertheless, by some strange quirk of fate—a previous life, perhaps?—been deposited a portion of my own capacity to feel and to love, a portion, in other words, of my own life; and that this is something which no American will ever understand and no Russian ever believe.

Helsinki, September 7

We reached the new Finnish border and stopped at the first Finnish station. Here everything was suddenly neat and cheerful. A new station building had been erected: simple and of wood, but with a certain distinctive modern touch. The platform was in good repair, and clean. There was a freshly painted kiosk where newspapers were on sale. Food was the only essential not in evidence. But the station was almost deserted. The sky was grey. And everything was a little sad.

Our Russian locomotive retired, leaving our sleeping-car, together with two "soft" cars full of Russians bound for the new naval base at Porkkala-Udd, to wait for the Finnish train. We had long to wait. I paced up and down the platform in the wind, a slave to the Anglo-Saxon habit of exercise. The Russians stared vacantly out the windows of their car;

and on their faces was that same stoical emptiness with which Russians stare out of train windows all over their vast, melancholy Russian world.

The sidings were full of freight cars loaded with Finnish goods, being shipped to Russia as reparations. Little cars, wheels and tracks for a narrow gauge logging railroad, bright with shiny metal and new paint, were carefully stored and lashed on the big gondola cars. On others there were piles of clean sawn lumber, neatly cut and carefully stacked. All these contributions bore the mark of orderly, conscientious Finnish workmanship. I wondered at first whether such offerings did not sometimes rouse pangs of shame among the inhabitants of the great shoddy Russian world into which they were moving. But on second thought I was inclined to doubt this very strongly.

Except for myself the station platform was almost deserted. A young, lithe Finn, with a knife in his belt, gave side glances of hatred and contempt at the Russian cars as he went about his work as a switchman. Wood smoke from the little switch engine was torn away by the wind and carried across the clearing, its odor reminiscent of the north woods at home. A Finnish railway man in uniform rode sedately up to the station building, parked his bicycle, and went inside to transact his business. A peasant cart drove up with a family in the back. The family might well be hungry, but the horse was fat and sleek and trotted with a happy briskness which no Russian horse possesses. Over the entire scene there lay the efficiency, the trimness, the quietness, and the boredom of bourgeois civilization, and these qualities smote with triple effect on the senses a traveler long removed from the impressions of bourgeois environment.

Moscow, November 24

Went to dinner with the Norwegian Military Attache. One of the other guests was a Colonel Studyenov. I had a long and frank talk with him after dinner. After a long comparative discussion of Russian and American agricultural methods, in which he showed himself to be keenly interested and well informed, we got on to the subject of Russian-American relations and of foreigners in Moscow. I told him that I understood some of the causes of the Soviet reserve toward foreigners, that I knew that there had been many diplomats and other foreigners in Moscow in the course of the last 25 years who had been tactless and stupid, and I had no doubt that many had tried to exploit the position in which they found themselves for purposes which were not proper. This did not, however, apply to all foreigners and I thought that it was the duty of the Soviet Government to see that arrangements were made whereby at least those of the foreigners who were honest and well meaning were treated as they would be anywhere else in the world. I pointed out how much easier it was for us to deal with people like the British for the reason that any one in our government could usually sit down with his British counterpart and discuss frankly questions of common interest, even to the point of examining the correctness of his own government's policy, without being suspected of treason and without giving false impressions to the other party. I pointed out that with Russians this was impossible.

I also drew his attention to the tremendous balance wheel which British-American relations have in the form of tens of thousands, if not hundreds of thousands, of personal associations between nationals of the two powers. I pointed out that at least 10 or 15 thousand of soldiers in England had married British girls during the war, that those women were now being admitted to the United States, and that every one of those marriages provided two more people who would protest violently against development of any real trouble between the two countries. I cited as an example the fact that here in Russia only about a dozen men in the American services had married Russian women and several of those had not been permitted to leave the Soviet Union in order to join their husbands abroad. I said that to these people he must add in his mind the thousands of Americans who normally lived in London and the thousands of Englishmen who normally lived in the United States, as well as tens and hundreds of thousands of tourists who travel freely in the two countries. The colonel did not deny this but remarked that while there were high-level differences in matters of policy no Soviet citizen could be expected to approach contacts with foreigners with anything else than the greatest caution. I replied that if this were true then any real solution of our problems would be very, very difficult. (I neglected to point out, as perhaps I should have, that things were no different in the peak of our war time association when neither country had anything else in mind but the destruction of Hitlerism.)

The Colonel came back very positively with the statement that this was an incorrect way to approach the question. "In our Soviet language," he said, "the word 'difficult' does not exist. If a thing is impossible, that is that. But if it was not impossible, then one should never complain about difficulties."

I told him in parting that there was a lot to be said for his point of view but that if we were to shut our eyes to the difficulties and try to make progress along these lines in the face of all the existing obstacles then both sides, and not only one, would have to give everything they had to the task. To this he agreed.

I found myself wondering later whether the frank answer would not have been to say that in the circumstances I would then prefer to classify this task as "impossible." For as long as personal life of Russian citizens is dominated, as it is today, by a secret police organization which stands above the law, which is hostile to the outside world in general and which fears to admit the light of day into Russian society, I am bound to say that I do not see how any real stability can ever be introduced into our relations. But this is a good illustration of the reason high diplomats cannot always be frank. The one thing which I must not say as an American representative in Russia is that I despair of the future of our relations.

November 26

Talked with the Ambassador[42] this afternoon. Among other things I told him that I thought we should close the Consulate General in Vladivostok in view of the insulting way in which our people had been treated there (their total isolation from the population, the fantastic degree of observation to which their lives are subjected, the flood light on their house, the eternal face in the window across the street, et cetera) and in view of the fact that I could not see that we got enough out of the office to warrant its maintenance. The Ambassador said that he could not agree to this, that he thought the office was of value to our Government, and should be maintained.

Met later in the day with a group of well informed foreigners who were engaged in a careful and competent analysis of Stalin's status. Little developed that was at all definite, but one point was brought out strongly: namely that the roseate days of Soviet triumphs at Big Power conferences are over, and that there could hardly be any further incentive on the part of those who rule Russia to thrust Stalin forward into the tripartite arena. This would apply whether Russia is actually being ruled by Stalin himself or other persons acting in his name, which is debatable. It would offer one plausible explanation why he should retire somewhat from the scene at this moment. I am one of the few foreigners in Moscow, if not the only one, who feels that it is questionable whether Stalin is still the dictator

42. W. Averell Harriman.

that people think he is. I suspect that power lies in the hands of a group within the Politboro of whom Beria and Molotov[43] are the strongest figures. I think it likely that not only will Stalin be eliminated from the limelight, abandoning his position as Chairman of the Soviet of People's Commissars, but that Molotov will also not wish much longer to have to face the representatives of the foreign world in person on one occasion after another and that he will abandon the Foreign Affairs Commissariat, perhaps after the elections, to someone else, taking over his old position of Chairman of the Soviet of People's Commissars.

December 5

Went over to see the Ambassador in the afternoon. Finally arranged with him that I should be free from administrative responsibilities.

[After the rancorous London conference of foreign ministers that had been held in September, Secretary of State James F. Byrnes switched to a more conciliatory stance and proposed holding a conference in Moscow. He held out the possibility of a deal to head off an atomic arms race. In contrast to Byrnes, Kennan and Harriman had grown skeptical of such efforts to continue wartime cooperation with the Soviets.]

December 7

Was called over in the morning to Spaso House,[44] where I found the Ambassador very much upset. He had just received a cable from Washington to the effect that the Secretary[45] proposed to make a public announcement of the forthcoming [foreign ministers'] meeting that same afternoon, mentioning that the talks would include the subject of atomic energy. This had not yet been mentioned to the Russians, and the Ambassador was rightly concerned that they would resent it.

December 12

Atkinson[46] was in to see me in the morning to talk about the background of the conference, and again I felt how inappropriate it was that these

43. Lavrenty Beria was head of the secret police while Molotov was minister of foreign affairs. Both were longtime henchmen of Stalin.

44. Spaso House had been the residence of the U.S. ambassador to the Soviet Union since Kennan had helped establish the embassy in 1933–34.

45. James F. Byrnes.

46. Brooks Atkinson was a correspondent for the *New York Times*.

things should be discussed by anyone who has as little confidence as I in the efficacy of what we are doing.

December 14

This was a lively day. We were expecting the Secretary and his party. A full blizzard was blowing. Calls to the Soviet weather people in the early morning brought forth the information that weather conditions were impossible and no planes would be coming in. About twelve o'clock we were told that the Secretary's plane had left Berlin at 11:00. This came from a minor official of the Foreign Office. The Red Army and the airport people said they knew nothing about it. At 1:30, just as I was leaving for lunch, Brooks Atkinson came in and said he had just been told by the British Embassy that they had heard that the plane had turned back to Berlin. Thinking this very likely, I went home and had a leisurely lunch, came back to find one of the attaches talking on the phone to a distressed Foreign Office official who claimed that the plane was coming in now and might arrive at any time at the Central Military Airport. I asked where the Ambassador was. They said he had gone to some airport 20 miles south of town because he had heard that the Secretary might arrive there. I grabbed Horace Smith and the little duty car and together we went out to the Central Military Airport. A howling blizzard was blowing and the field was just one white blur with no distinction between sky and snow. You couldn't see across it at all. However, a radio sound truck was driving out into the obscurity as we arrived and there were a number of Russian cars there. We were taken up into the little building at the edge of the field. Two or three journalists came along and joined us. In a few minutes we heard the sound of motors and looked out to see a four-motored plane passing over the roof of the building. We rushed out on the field. The snow flurry had passed and visibility was better. Dekanozov,[47] with one Foreign Office assistant and a lot of NKVD, was out there. Somebody had put up two iron posts with the Soviet and American flags. The plane, which had managed to land somehow or other, appeared out of the soup, taxiing up the field, wheeled up and stopped in front of us. The gangplank was pushed out through the snow and we went through with the official reception. The Secretary, in a light coat and no overshoes, stood in the deep snow while he said his hellos and gave his little speech over the microphone while the wind howled through the little company. I

47. Vladmir Dekanozov was deputy minister of foreign affairs.

then took him to the first available car and drove him, together with Ben Cohen[48] and his military aide, to Spaso. There Kathy[49] gave them drinks and soup and kept them busy until the Ambassador arrived from his journey. Then I went back to the office to clear up papers.

Thoroughly enraged by a telegram from the Department asking us to invite the Soviet Government to a conference to work out mutual tariff reductions next March, I spent the evening writing an eloquent telegram demonstrating why it shouldn't be done.

December 17

Lunch at Spaso, where I sat next to the Secretary and had some chance to tell him about some of our minor difficulties.

Bohlen[50] and Isaiah Berlin[51] came to dinner, and we talked until one or two in the morning. Berlin, who is undoubtedly the best informed and most intelligent foreigner in Moscow, said that the only things he had learned on the occasion of this visit were: (a) the continued existence of the conflict in outlook between age and youth, (b) of the tremendous importance to young people of the feeling of economic security which they have under the Soviet system, and (c) the continued vital importance of Marxist dogma in Soviet thought and action. He agreed with me strongly that American policy must find its expression from now on in action and not in words if it is to do any good.

He was firmly convinced that the Russians view a conflict with the Western world as quite inevitable and that their whole policy is predicated on this prospect. I asked him whether they didn't realize that if the conflict came it would be the result of their own tactics and their own insistence that it was inevitable. He said no, that they would view it as inevitable through the logic of the development of social forces. They would say that possibly some of us foreign diplomats and statesmen might consider ourselves friendly to Russia at the moment but that eventually we would find out that we were hostile to them even though we did not know it at the moment.

48. Benjamin V. Cohen, who had helped draft New Deal legislation and agreements leading to the establishment of the United Nations, was counselor to the State Department.
49. Kathleen Harriman was the ambassador's daughter and hostess.
50. Charles E. "Chip" Bohlen, a colleague of Kennan's in the Moscow embassy in the 1930s, had interpreted for President Roosevelt at the Tehran and Yalta conferences. He had become a top Soviet expert in the State Department.
51. Isaiah Berlin, later a political and social theorist and philosopher, worked during the war in the British Diplomatic Service.

December 19

Was invited by Ambassador to attend the Foreign Ministers Conference this afternoon. Unfortunately the session turned out to consist of two brief meetings of about five or ten minutes each.

Bevin[52] looked highly disgusted with the whole procedure, and it was easy to see by his face that he found himself in a position he did not like. He did not want to come to Moscow in the first place and was well aware that nothing good could come of the meeting. The Russians knew his position and were squeezing the last drop of profit out of it. As for Byrnes, Bevin saw in him only another cocky and unreliable Irishman, similar to ones that he had known in his experience as a docker and labor leader. Byrnes had consistently shown himself negligent of British feelings and quite unconcerned for Anglo-American relations. He had conceived the whole idea of this meeting in his own head and had taken it up with the Russians before saying a word about it to the British or giving them any warning that this was to be done. He had offended the British by giving a copy of the Ethridge report[53] to the Russians but not to the British Embassy, despite the fact the latter had opened its files to Ethridge when he was here and that his visit was largely at British initiative. Finally, Byrnes had come to Moscow with a paper to present to the Russians on atomic energy which had been cleared with neither of the other powers which shared in holding the secret of the manufacture of atomic energy, and this within six weeks after Attlee's[54] visit to Washington and conferences with the President. When Bevin had remonstrated against the presentation to the Russians of any document on this subject which had not been cleared with British and Canadian Governments, Byrnes had given him two days, namely until today Wednesday, to submit this document to London and get the approval of the British Cabinet. Bevin thought he had the assurance of Byrnes that meanwhile nothing would be submitted to the Russians, and indeed no other understanding would have made any sense. Nevertheless, on Tuesday evening, with no word to the British, Byrnes had sent the document in to the Russians. Bevin could view this only as an instance of direct bad faith and was furious.

Molotov, conducting the meeting, sat leaning forward over the table,

52. Ernest Bevin was a leader of the British Labour Party and the foreign secretary.

53. Byrnes had commissioned a liberal journalist, Mark Ethridge, to report on charges of Soviet repression in Bulgaria and Rumania. The report was scathing in its criticism of the Soviets.

54. Clement Attlee was British prime minister and leader of the Labour Party.

a Russian cigarette dangling from his mouth, his eyes flashing with satisfaction and confidence as he glanced from one to the other foreign minister, obviously keenly aware of their differences between each other and their common uncertainty in the face of the keen, ruthless, and incisive Russian diplomacy. He had the look of a passionate poker player who knows that he has a royal flush and is about to call the last of his opponents. He was the only one who was clearly enjoying every minute of the proceedings.

I sat just behind Byrnes and could not see him well. He plays his negotiations by ear, going into them with no clear or fixed plan, with no definite set of objectives or limitations. He relies entirely on his own agility and presence of mind and hopes to take advantage of tactical openings. In the present conference his weakness in dealing with the Russians is that his main purpose is to achieve *an* agreement. The realities behind this agreement, since they concern only such people as Koreans, Rumanians, and Iranians, about whom he knows nothing, do not concern him. He wants *an* agreement for its political effect at home. The Russians know this. They will see that for this superficial success he pays a heavy price in the things that are real.

After the meeting I walked home with Matthews[55] and he stayed for supper. Frank Roberts[56] and his wife joined us. By the end of the evening, Matthews looked so crestfallen at the things that he had heard from Roberts and myself I felt sorry for him and had to try to cheer him up. In the introduction of newcomers to the realities of the Soviet Union there are always two processes: the first, which is to reveal what these realities are and the second, which is to help the newcomer to adjust himself to the shock.

December 21

Talked to the Bulgarian Minister this morning. He began by censuring opposition for not taking part in the election and claiming that they had voluntarily cut themselves off from participation in Bulgarian political life. Being somewhat impatient, I told him that what bothered us was not really questions of parliamentary representation or procedure, but the fact that we were faced there with a regime of police oppression which did not hesitate to proceed in the most ruthless manner against the

55. H. Freeman "Doc" Matthews, director of the Office of European Affairs in the State Department.

56. Frank K. Roberts was a friend of Kennan's and his counterpart in the British embassy.

lives and liberties of individual citizens, and it was our belief that in this atmosphere of terror and intimidation no real democracy could live. He became quite excited at this, and spoke thereafter much more frankly, admitting that the Communists were only a minority but pointing to the desirability of concluding peace and getting Russian troops out of the country.

Lunch with Roberts and Cadogan[57] and two or three other people from the British delegation. Chip was there and I think he and I rather shook Cadogan's composure with our observations on the technique of dealing with the Soviet Government.

December 23

I went to Spaso to a stag luncheon for Molotov and Bevin. Sat next to Tsarapkin,[58] who was relatively human. Bevin caused much amusement among the Americans and considerable bewilderment among the Russians by the dour informality of his asides during the luncheon. When a toast was proposed to the King, he added good humoredly, "and all the other dockers." He told a story afterwards to explain this remark. When Harriman raised his glass to the future success of the conference, Bevin assented and added: "And let's hope we don't all get sacked when we get home." Molotov left the minute luncheon was over. Later in the afternoon they were all hard at work again and worked most of the night. . . .

This evening the Russians put on a special performance of *Zolutchka* (Cinderella) at the Bolshoi. I did not learn about it until late in the afternoon, and, feeling that I ought to be there, took two of the last tickets on the list of those allotted to the Embassy. When we got there, the theater was already packed to the last seat, spot lights were trained on the empty imperial box where the appearance of the foreign ministers was expected, and Molotov and his aides were waiting nervously in the hall outside. As is always the case when the big curtain is down, the hall was stuffy and hot and people were fanning themselves with their programs. The orchestra were all in their places waiting to strike up the national anthems. I found myself in a box with the ambassador's aide and one of his private secretaries. After we had waited for another fifteen minutes, I said laughingly to the private secretary that I supposed the Secretary had forgotten to come. "Oh, no," the secretary replied, "they are only

57. Alexander Cadogan was British permanent undersecretary for foreign affairs.
58. Semyon K. Tsarapkin was a Soviet diplomat.

sitting up in his room at the Embassy telling stories and having drinks and no one dares go in and interrupt them." I immediately tore out of the box and ran down stairs to the administrator's office to telephone. The phone was in use when I got there and I stood in the crowded office for a moment waiting for a chance to use it. Just as the phone became free and I was about to dial the embassy a man in the shiny blue civilian clothes so characteristic of the secret police came into the office, walked up to me, and said with a slight smile on his face: "They have just left." I went back to the box and sure enough in five minutes Mr. Byrnes appeared, having kept several thousand people, including numerous members of the Soviet Government, waiting for something like a half an hour.

The performance was absolutely first-rate, one of the best I have ever seen but it fell very flat on the audience. I understand that Stalin was somewhere in the theater, though not in the imperial box. For this reason the audience, except for the diplomatic corps, was apparently composed almost exclusively of secret police people, who were doubtless afraid that any excessive display on their part of enthusiasm for the performance might look as though they were being diverted from their duties.

Saturday, June 24, 1950

Drove up to the farm with Annelise in the morning. Did business with various people most of the rest of the day. Very hot and oppressive.

Sunday, June 25.

Started back to town in early afternoon and arrived here about 4:30. After glancing at the headlines of the Sunday papers, announcing the attack of the North Korean forces against South Korea, I changed clothes and hurried down to the office.

Found the Secretary in conference with a group of people, including Jessup, Rusk and Matthews; they had spent a good part of the day, as I gathered, arranging for UN action and now, the Security Council having acted with almost unbelievable speed and passed a resolution calling on all its members not to assist the North Korean forces but rather to help the UN in its efforts to prevent this aggression, they were getting down to the consideration of what the US action should be. When my views were asked, which was shortly after my entry into the room, I had to plead unfamiliarity with what had been discussed and done so far. I said that one thing seemed certain to me: that whatever else happened it would be impossible for us not to take prompt steps to assure that Formosa did not fall to the communists since this, coming on top of the Korean attack, would be calamitous to our position in the Far East. We continued our discussion until about 6:15, when the Secretary went to the airport to meet the President. It had been arranged that the Secretary, accompanied by a few of the senior officials of the Department, would have dinner with the President and with a number of the military leaders. This had been arranged before I got there. After the Secretary had left for the airport I was told that he had specifically said that he wanted me present at this occasion, but his secretary said that she was certain that somehow or other my name had not been included on the list which was sent to the White House, and that she also knew that only a certain number of places were available for the dinner and that there would be no room for extra plates. I therefore went home for supper and returned later in the evening to be on hand when the Secretary got back from Blair House. This occurred about 11:00 p.m., as I recall it.

CHAPTER FIVE

Cold War, 1946–50

1946

Kennan kept no regular diary in 1946. He was, however, enormously productive with his writing. His elegantly phrased and emotionally evocative "long telegram" of February 22, 1946, was widely circulated by Truman administration officials looking for a comprehensive explanation of Soviet behavior. In the telegram Kennan argued that the Kremlin, driven by Russian nationalism and insecurities—now overladen with Marxist-Leninist ideology—needed a foreign enemy in order to justify its repressive rule. Negotiations with such an implacable foe would yield little, he insisted. The United States should seek neither compromise nor military confrontation with the Kremlin. Instead, Washington should strengthen U.S. institutions and rebuild Western Europe.

Anxious to influence a wider audience, Kennan considered resigning from the State Department. He was enticed instead to return to Washington, give a series of public lectures around the country, and become deputy commandant for foreign affairs at the newly organized National War College in Washington, DC. There Kennan in 1946–47 lectured to military and political officials on the prospects and problems of what would soon be called the Cold War. To prepare for his lectures, Kennan read about strategy, listened to the War College talks of political and military experts, and honed his own ideas. He even schooled himself in the scientific principles underlying atomic weapons. From this study Kennan arrived at the concept that would become known as "containment."

What follow are Kennan's undated notes from reading and from listening to lectures at the National War College. He used the material in this notebook to prepare his own lectures and to develop the strategic concepts that would inform his thinking for decades thereafter.

Having returned to the United States in May, the Kennan family settled in Washington. They spent most weekends at their farm in East Berlin, Pennsylvania.

Notes on Bernard Brodie (ed.), The Absolute Weapon: Atomic Power and World Order (New York, 1946).

The Russians are confident of their own ability to conduct any sort of activities they wish on their own territory, despite all international undertakings to the contrary, without detection. They are no less confident of their ability to detect and reveal, through their widespread intelligence networks in the other great industrial nations, any attempts on the part of those other nations to violate such international undertakings, and they know that they can rely on the power of public opinion in those countries to require the respective governments to desist from such attempts. The Russian proposals, for exchange of information and for the mutual renunciation of atomic weapons, were drafted in the light of these considerations, and are designed to give the USSR the facilities (particularly the know-how) for the production of atomic weapons, while denying them to the capitalist world. . . .

Our task is to plan and execute our strategic dispositions in such a way as to compel the Soviet Government either to accept combat under unfavorable conditions (which it will never do) or withdraw. In this way we can contain Soviet power until Russians tire of this game. . . .

Does not the significance of atomic weapons mean that, if we are to avoid mutual destruction, we must revert to the strategic political thinking of XVIII Century? Total destruction of enemy's forces can no longer be our objective because

(a) in the best of circumstances (i.e. that the Russians lack atomic weapons or facilities for employing them against us) it implies on our part a war against the Russian people and the eventual occupation of Russian territory; and

(b) in the worst of circumstances, the virtual ruin of our country as well as theirs. Therefore our strategic-political aims vis-a-vis Russia should be limited to:

(a) preventing the power of the Soviet Government from extending to points vital or important to US or British Empire; and

(b) without forfeiting the confidence & friendship of the Russian people, to bring out the discrediting of those forces in Russia who insist that Russia regard itself as at war with the Western world.

Can we afford to forego the disarming or destruction of Soviet armed power, as a strategic objective?

Yes. We must forego it, for either the disarming or the destruction would imply the assumption by us of political authority and responsibility in Russia. It is doubtful whether we could or would wish to put forth the physical effort necessary to achieve such authority, and it is certain that we would not be morally competent to exercise it to good effect. Our effort must therefore be to convince the Russians that it is in their interest to disarm themselves—by acceptance of an international atomic energy authority.

[On reading Clausewitz,[1] Kennan concluded that the twentieth-century trend toward all-out war had become outdated.]

This thinking [about total war] has been overthrown by 2 recent revelations:

1. Atomic weapons, which may make war of annihilation impossible, and

2. Increasing political commitments of victory in great power warfare. War of annihilation or overthrow spells enormous and lasting political responsibility for the victor which is scarcely apt to be desirable.

Even in the case of Germany it is questionable whether a war of destruction was desirable. (Chip[2] says it could not have been otherwise: that the U.S. cannot fight a political war.)

In Russia it is certain that we cannot undertake a war of destruction or annihilation. Against Russia we must wage a political war, a war of attrition for limited objectives. Our people are unused to this, and do not understand it. Thence the value of UN.

We are in peculiar position of having to defend ourselves against mortal attack, but yet not wishing to inflict mortal defeat on our attacker. We cannot be carried too far away by the attractive conception of "the

1. Carl von Clausewitz, *On War* (1832).
2. Charles E. "Chip" Bohlen.

flashing sword of vengeance." We must be like the porcupine who only gradually convinces the carnivorous beast of prey that he is not a fit object of attack.

[In the lecture "Measures Short of War," part of which follows, Kennan outlined many of the strategies and concepts that would undergird U.S. policies in the Cold War.][3]

The major national strategy, to be effective, has to be related not, as before, just to the area of violence, but also to this other area in which the acts of the adversary, though not involving direct violence against us, nevertheless are really acts of war by intent.

How do we determine intent? We cannot determine it with scientific exactitude. That does not mean that we should despair of determining it at all, or at least of making a working hypothesis.

And as a basis for such a working hypothesis, we might say the following:

An act of war is any measure taken as part of a policy which aims at the total destruction or subjugation of the state power of another state or its reduction to a degree incompatible with national honor and integrity.

This definition allows for undeclared wars, as well as for declared ones.

It also allows for the two main kinds of wars:

(1) wars of annihilation
(2) wars for limited objectives.

We have been accustomed to waging war with acts of violence or not waging war at all. Others have made no such distinction, on many occasions. We ourselves certainly came very close to waging war by measures short of violence during the months just before Pearl Harbor. We were forced into that position by considerations of self-defense, because the Germans were in effect waging an undeclared war against us, i.e., they were pursuing a policy which aimed at least at a radical reduction in our state power and one which certainly would have been incompatible with our state security.

In this lecture, now, I must deal with acts short of violence. But I

3. For the lectures Kennan wrote at the National War College, see Giles D. Harlow and George C. Maerz (eds.), *Measures Short of War* (Washington, DC: National Defense University Press, 1991).

object to calling them acts short of war; because they can be every bit as much acts of war, by intent and by consequence, as artillery or air attacks. . . .

Totalitarian mentality represents a mutation of species. It is thus like a virus always present in body politic, dangerous only when powers of resistance are weakened. In old days, it could not take on its modern form, even where successful, due to deeply ingrained feeling for hierarchical concept of society, lack of modern police weapons, and attendant necessity for relying on feudal subordinate in holding together any structure of power.

Requirements—therefore

(a) totalitarian element—which is always present

(b) exhaustion of old spiritual & social order

(c) absence of any new order embodying for individual a plausible sense of community

(d) modern technical instruments of despotism

[Kennan interrupted his notes and thinking about geopolitical strategy to chart his personal strategy, below.]

Notes—Personal

What do you want? Adequate income. Ability to live in country part of year. Ability to travel. Some privacy & quiet. Ability to contribute to intellectual & cultural life of times. Independence of choice.

	Requirements of family	Opportunity for quiet & detachment	Moral, intellectual independence	Opportunity for contribution to thought	Travel	Part time in country	Income
Intelligence	X				X	X	
Academic – Soviet	X	X	X	X		X	X
Academic – Russian	X	X	X			X	
Academic – US	X	X	X	X		X	X
Academic Administrator	X					X	X
Foundation Work	X				X	X	X
Business	X						X
Farming		X	X	X		X	

[What follows are Kennan's notes on a lecture by Bernard Brodie.]

Grand Strategy

Drop the word "grand."

Lecture should be entitled: "The Theory of Strategy: A sermon."

Text: Mahan—defining objects of Naval War College. What is practical training? Someone said: if you want to attract men to colleges, give them something that will help them pass exams. War will be a sterner school. Is a college practical?

Lack of deep and systematic study of strategy. We have retrogressed. Mahan was retired after 40 years of service with the rank of captain. His later promotion, in retirement, was routine.

Is it a science? Is it not an exercise or common sense?

Comparison of strategy & economics?

Even such a truism as that "wealth, to be enjoyed, must first be produced" is not understood by many influential people. Ergo—truisms of strategy also must not be taken for granted. . . .

"Highest type of strategy is that which so orders resources of nation that war may, if possible, be averted, or if inevitable, be won."

Moral: that we *must* have theoretical study on a high level as a part of this institution.

[After listening to many lectures, Kennan jotted down "My own comments." In what follows, he enunciated some of the ideas expressed in his February 1946 "long telegram" and again in an article he wrote that would appear in *Foreign Affairs* in July 1947.]

1. Impossible to distinguish between "security" and "world domination."

2. Only 2 possibilities for relief of Soviet pressure:

a. Internal dissension which would temporarily weaken Soviet potential & lead to situation similar to that of 1919–20.
b. Gradual mellowing of Soviet policy under influence of firm & calm resistance abroad. But this will be slow & never complete.

3. Most important thing we can do is to think out a constructive program for Western Europe which can give new hope and new vision to tired & bewildered peoples of Western Europe. We have regarded that area only as a potential subject for an agreement with Russia.

1947

To the extent that writing in the diary was a way for Kennan to vent his frustrations and disappointments, he apparently had little need of it in 1947. The verse that follows constitutes the entirety of the diary during the year when he reached the pinnacle of his career in government. He became the nation's most renowned Soviet expert. Secretary of State George C. Marshall appointed him the director of the newly created Policy Planning Staff, a post he assumed on May 7. Assisted by a devoted staff, Kennan crafted policy statements on a variety of issues. Though his recommendations were not always followed, they were respected. In July, Foreign Affairs *published, under the pseudonym "X," Kennan's "The Sources of Soviet Conduct," in which he likened Soviet expansion to a wind-up toy car that had to be contained. Kennan's authorship soon became known, and his national reputation was made. Much of the thinking that underlay the Marshall Plan was his. In Paris he played a key role in the negotiations leading to the plan for massive aid to rebuild Western Europe, including West Germany.*

Kennan's silence, at least in the diary, regarding personal problems suggests that here, too, he found satisfaction. It would not last.

Homeward bound at dawn over mid-Atlantic, Paris trip, August 27–September 5

From out this world of stars and mists and motion
The dawn—impatient of the time allowed—
Probes sharply down the canyons of the cloud
To find the fragments of an empty ocean.
Let not this growing hemisphere of light
Seduce the house-bound pilgrim to station:

He may not hope—against the dawn's inflation—
To see *his* darkness passing like the night.
The endless flight on which *his* plane is sent
Will know no final landing field. Content
Be he whose peace of mind from this may stem:
That he, as Fortune's mild and patient claimant,
Has heard the rustling of the Time-God's raiment,
And has contrived to touch the gleaming hem.

1948

Despite his standing as America's premier strategist of the Cold War, Kennan in 1948 began diverging from the Truman administration's policy. In 1947, he had quietly criticized the global claims of the Truman Doctrine. Far better, he had thought, to focus on aid to Greece and Turkey. Though he advocated covert operations and "black propaganda" in carefully controlled situations, Kennan also saw the Cold War as a limited engagement. Confrontation with Moscow should be political rather than military and avoided in areas of marginal importance, such as China. Moreover, Kennan suggested in February, the recovery already under way in Western Europe meant that the time might soon be ripe for serious negotiations with Moscow. In describing the diplomat best suited to conduct such negotiations, Kennan in effect nominated himself. In sum, while most officials in Washington and Moscow in 1948 were escalating the conflict, Kennan, though still very much a Cold Warrior, was beginning to look for ways to ease tensions.

Washington, January 22

Regarding nominations for the Nobel Peace Prize. We decided that no member of this Government should make such a nomination this year. I am afraid that there will always be trouble over the allotment of this award. Peace is not an abstraction, and cannot be treated as such. There is no such thing as just "peace." Everybody wants "Peace." From that standpoint, Stalin might be said to deserve the award more than anyone else, having worked harder and more intelligently than any of the rest of us for the particular type of peace in which he is interested. It must always be asked: "What kind of peace?"—"Whose peace?"

There was another meeting devoted to the question of the Secretary's speeches. I held out for a minimum of speaking engagements. I felt that present arrangements spread the Secretary much too thin, cheapened his word and lessened its public effect, diverted him from more important duties, and constituted an uneconomic drain on his strength. My own opinion is that he should never speak unless there is something highly important, and reasonably new, to be said. We should cultivate a state of affairs where every word he speaks will be not only read but studied eagerly by the entire world. Most of the others were against me in this, but I did succeed in having the number of his engagements for the coming period drastically reduced. The public appearances are not to be more than one a month for the next three months.

January 23

People continue to come to me with alarmed reports of the state of affairs in Congress and the press: the bitterness against the Department, the determination that the European aid program shall be cut down in amount and removed from the Department of State. I have no objection to the establishment of an executive apparatus, outside of the regular Department of State organization, for the administration of this program. But the program is primarily political in intent. If the day by day administration of it is removed, formally or otherwise, from the effective control of the Secretary of State, and if officials are sent abroad to administer the program without being subordinate to the authority of the Chief of the Mission in their country of operations, then a situation will have been created in which it will be futile for anyone to attempt to achieve a coordinated and effective United States policy toward Europe. If the aid program, furthermore, is cut to a point where it is no longer basically the program evolved by the Paris Conference,[4] then it will have lost its real significance and will no longer accomplish the purpose for which it is designed. If either of these contingencies materializes, I see no reason why I myself or any of the others of us who are concerned with United States policy should continue to try to accomplish anything useful within the framework of government service. For the damage done will then be past the capability of any individual to remedy by direct action within the Government, and the most that anyone could hope to accomplish would be to bring about some public understanding of the reasons why this country had failed so miserably to cope with any

4. In response to Marshall's June 1947 invitation, Western European nations gathered in Paris to draw up a list of needs for reconstruction. Kennan and other U.S. officials worked unobtrusively to shape the overall structure of the European requests.

Kossuth Kent Kennan
Joan E. Kennan Collection

Florence James Kennan
Joan E. Kennan Collection

George F. Kennan, seven years old. From the back of the photo: "Not quite so sweet an expression as he usually wears." *Joan E. Kennan Collection*

George, about twelve years old
Joan E. Kennan Collection

George at St. John's Military Academy
Joan E. Kennan Collection

The Kennan family when George was about fourteen. From left, Frances, Kent Senior, George, Kent Junior, Louise, Constance, Jeanette. *Joan E. Kennan Collection*

From the passport George used for his trip to Europe in the summer of 1924
Joan E. Kennan Collection

George with a borrowed car
Joan E. Kennan Collection

George, standing on the left, as a deckhand in 1925
Joan E. Kennan Collection

George as a newly minted diplomat

Joan E. Kennan Collection

"TRIUMPHS AND ACHIEVEMENTS"

George F. Kennan

ST. JOHN'S '21

GRADUATE OF PRINCETON UNIVERSITY 1925

Foreign Service School at Washington after one year of study.

He ranked 6th in a class of 110 and was selected for immediate duty, and was appointed Vice Consul at Hamburg, Germany. Then shifted to the Consul General's Office at Geneva during the World Economic Conference and the Naval Arms Conference. Aug 1927 served as Executive Officer for the Berlin Consulate General. After this assignment he served as Vice Consul at Hamburg, and then to Tallinn, Esthonia. Promoted to the position of Secretary of Embassy in Riga. 1929 he was selected to study for three years in the Orientalisches Seminar in Berlin – a super-university for study of Near-East problems. 1930 he has been promoted to the position of Consul (unassigned) and is said to be the youngest officer of that rank in the service.

St. John's alumni magazine in the early 1930s

Joan E. Kennan Collection

George at the Estonian border with the Soviet Union in the late 1920s

Joan E. Kennan Collection

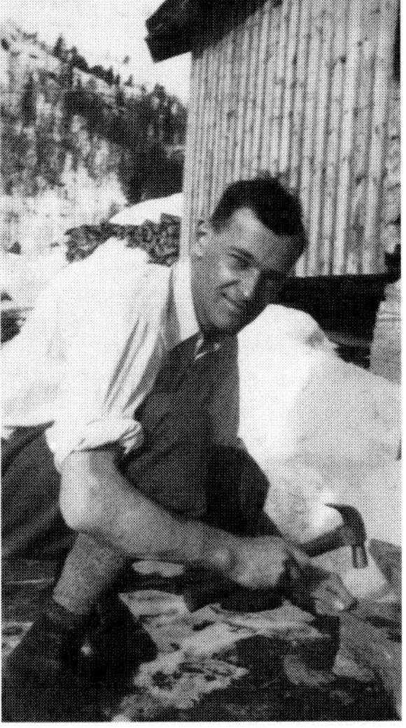

George enjoying the rustic life

Joan E. Kennan Collection

A family gathering in Norway in the early 1930s. George, third from left, focused on his hand of cards rather than the camera; Annelise is second from the right.

Joan E. Kennan Collection

Annelise with daughter Grace in 1932

Joan E. Kennan Collection

Annelise and George enjoying the winter; Grace enduring it

Joan E. Kennan Collection

George with Joan; Annelise with Grace

Joan E. Kennan Collection

Annelise and George in costume for a Moscow ball in 1937
Joan E. Kennan Collection

George in Berlin in 1940 or 1941
Joan E. Kennan Collection

82

were secondary fires. Flash-temperature can be combatted by very light clothing. Fires started among army equipment scattered around on decks. Rare instance of the blistering of paint.

Radioactivities. 2/3 of animals still alive & presumably all-right.

A.F. General: 2 more advantages of Bomb.

1. Difficulty of assembling large formations in bad weather.
2. Greater immunity of individual aircraft – due to limited maneuverability of large formations.

Brody.

Extent of damage which can be inflicted in period before defending state is adequately alerted. – must also be taken into account.

X.

Immunity of only modern building in Hiroshima.

A page from Kennan's notes of lectures at the National War College in 1946. Kennan loved to sketch scenes from his surroundings, including, apparently, the shapely legs of the stenographer in the lecture hall.

Princeton University Library

of the foreign policy problems in the postwar period. And those reasons will strike deeply into the relationships between the Executive and Legislative branches of the Government as well as the attitude of public and press toward the institution of diplomacy itself.

Talked this afternoon with Joe Alsop,[5] who reproached me bitterly for the situation in Congress and insisted that the Secretary had never spelled out in an adequate way to the members of Congress the strategic realities underlying the Marshall Plan proposal. I argued with him at length about the extent of our responsibility for the education of Congress in these matters. I pointed out that personally I had entered a profession which I thought had to do with the representation of United States interest vis-à-vis foreign governments, that this was what I had been trained for and what I was prepared to do to the best of my ability, that I had never understood that part of my profession was to represent the U.S. Government vis-à-vis Congress. My specialty was the defense of U.S. interest against others, not against our own representation. I resented the State Department being put in the position of lobbyists before Congress in favor of the U.S. people and I felt that Congress had a responsibility no less than that of ourselves toward the people. We were not their keepers or their mentors; it was up to them to inform themselves just as it is up to us to inform ourselves. . . . I recognize regretfully, however, that few will agree with this standpoint, and that we might have to see what we can do to make somewhat plainer to members of Congress the overall implications of the question which they are being asked to decide.

January 27

Sat in this morning on a conference concerning presentation to Congress of the bill for aid to China.

The dilemma is this: We all know that this aid cannot materially affect the course of events in China. We are obliged to put the bill before Congress by virtue of our past commitments and of the pressures that exist in favor of aid to China. If, in presenting it, we tell the truth, which is that the Nanking Government is doomed by its own inadequacy and that its power is destined to disintegrate regardless of our aid, we demolish at one blow its remaining prestige in China, hasten enormously the process of disintegration, and lay ourselves open to the charge of having

5. Joseph Alsop and his brother Stewart were influential columnists.

treacherously undermined Chiang's[6] prestige and killed his government by our own action. If, on the other hand, we hold out any hope to Congress that the bill can accomplish anything positive from the standpoint of U.S. foreign policy, we will only be faced a few months hence with incontrovertible evidence that this objective has not been achieved and with renewed reproaches for having urged Congress into another "operation rathole."

January 28

In a state department memorandum on the dispute between Arabs and Jews over partitioning the British mandate of Palestine there was no hint of criticism of the Zionists, who were apparently blameless. The solutions toward which the memorandum pointed were all ones which would have put further strain on our relations with British and Arabs, and on the relations between British and Arabs. Such a policy could proceed only at the expense of our major political and strategic interests in the Middle East. Finally, it seemed clear to me that any further gratuitous effort this Government might make at this time with a view to pushing the execution of the partition plan (and the United Nations resolution does not call on *us* to do anything of this sort) could hardly fail to engage still further our direct responsibility in the matter and to bring us closer to the day when we would be obliged to consent to the use of outside force as a means of enforcing the partition scheme. It is clear that once anything of this sort begins, there is no stopping point short of a state of affairs in which we would really have taken over the major military and police responsibility for the maintenance in Palestine of a state of affairs violently resented by the whole Arab world. I can not conceive that this is in United States interests or that it would be tolerated by the United States people. I therefore see nothing to be gained by starting in that direction.

All in all, I have come to doubt that any arrangement for Palestine worked out by outside powers and enforced either physically or morally by the international community can ever prove satisfactory. Unless the inhabitants of Palestine, both Jews and Arabs, and the international elements which stand behind them, are finally compelled to face each other eye to eye, without outside interference, and to weigh, with a sense of

6. Chiang Kai-shek (Jiang Jieshi) led the corrupt and unpopular Nationalist government in China, which in October 1949 lost the civil war with the Communists.

immediate and direct responsibility, the consequences of agreement or disagreement, I think they will continue to react irresponsibly in the face of the proposed solutions, and there will be no one that can command their loyalty and cooperation. It may be that there will be bloodshed in the wake of a negative American policy. But we Americans must realize that we cannot be the keepers and moral guardians of all the peoples in this world. We must become more modest, and recognize the necessary limits to the responsibility we can assume.

January 30

Talked at lunch with a gentleman just returned from Japan, who told me some disturbing things about the influences behind our policies of extreme democratization and de-concentration of economic life in Japan.

Of all the failures of United States policy in the wake of World War II, history will rate as the most grievous our failure to approach realistically the responsibilities of power over the defeated nations which we ourselves courted by the policy of unconditional surrender.[7]

7. End of diary for 1948.

1949

Kennan concluded that the occupation of Germany by the four victor nations (the United States, the Soviet Union, Great Britain, and France) should end except for the retention of limited military bases. He preferred the reunification of a neutral Germany over setting up West and East Germany as rivals, each allied with one of the superpowers. He hoped that reuniting Germany would pave the way for a Soviet military pullback from most of Eastern Europe. With these ideas meeting skepticism from Dean Acheson, who in January 1949 succeeded Marshall as secretary of state, as well as others in the Truman administration, Kennan went to West Germany to assess prospects.

Viewing the destruction in Hamburg, a city that decades earlier had beckoned him in a mystical way, made Kennan question whether any war was worth the toll it extracted. Such antiwar feelings would intensify in later years.

March 10

Written to a lady—a fellow transit passenger on a Europe-bound plane stranded overnight at Bermuda:

BERMUDA—THE SALUTATION

Frown not, fair pilgrim, on this magic isle
Where unseen fairies toll the bells of night.
Dismiss not lightly, nor with scornful smile
The things that strike the ear and meet the sight
In this implausible, unlikely land:
Fresh lawns, dark cedars, picture postcard sky,
A limpid sea, strange objects on the sand,
White roofs in moonlight; and the aching cry

Of strings of lights along a distant shore
Across a darkened sea. Do not deplore
These things—and others—just because they lie
Amid the vast dread ocean of a dream.
The island's real; and real—I trust—am I.
The distant continents—
Are what they seem.

Her reply:

What seems to you the frown, the smile of scorn,
Dismissal, the deploring of a dream,
Are none of these. The islands are forlorn
Not for their magic or because they seem
Unreal, but just because one cannot stay
More than an instant in such happy air
Before each is impelled upon his way—
Aware of loss but saying "I must not care."
This is the sadness of a bitter time,
And this the final, but unfinished, rhyme.

Berlin, March 12

Late in the evening I took a long walk. The streets were silent and empty and utterly dark. This was the once fashionable suburb of Dahlem. The private villas, those which had escaped the bombing, stood out dimly in the shadows. What pretense, what eager hopes, what plans for personal happiness and prosperity lay behind the building of each of these houses? Whatever were these hopes and plans, they were now dashed. Today the villas stood mute and dark and cold. If Germans lived in them at all, they camped in them like barbarians in the palaces of Italy. There seemed little prospect of doing anything else. It was hard to tell whether this was in itself good or bad, deserved or undeserved. Whatever it was, every one of those dim architectural forms spelled a broken dream, spelled one more bit of frustration for people who had once felt the call of hope and initiative. However you looked at it, it seemed a pity.

Back in the club, I could not sleep. I have lived in this city many years, in its better days, and the immensity of its ruin overwhelmed me. From my window, I watched the events of the night. In little groups, the guests emerged and departed in their cars. Soon the last inebriate colonel had found his way into his jeep. Finally the musicians assembled, with great grumbling and scolding of their own late-comers, and rode off in an incredibly over-loaded jalopy over which they appeared to dispose. And then the tall bare poplars, the same patient poplars which had waited and watched through the final years of the Weimar Republic and the Nazi era and the war and the bombings and the arrival of the Russian army, stood alone again through another night, until the battered cars of the first early subway train came clattering past, through the open cut a few yards away, and the sky lightened to the dawn of a grey, soggy March Sunday over airlift Berlin.[8]

In the afternoon, we drove around town. The sky was the typical winter overcast of Northern Germany. A gusty wind swept around the street-corners, ruffled the puddles of melted snow, and caused the pedestrians to stagger for their balance. The city looked little different than it had three years ago. The ruins, for the most part, still stood in awful and imposing desolation: the piles of rubble flowing down to the sidewalk, twisted iron beams and the remnants of walls standing out above them, portions of rooms hanging giddily in the air like stage settings. Only here and there, it seemed, had rubble been cleared away, on the little narrow-gauge railways set up for that purpose. The massive gutted walls of the Technical High School still frowned gloomily on the vast open space before them. The burned-out steel skeleton of the curtain-tower of the Charlottenburg Opera house was still silhouetted high above the skyline of the surrounding buildings. There was little animation on the streets. Here, a little line of people waited patiently before the entrance to a movie. There, a cluster of young boys huddled in the shelter of a broken wall. Once, in the course of the 20-mile drive, we saw a bus. Two or three times we passed streetcars. They were unpainted and dirty, and had wood in place of window panes.

March 14

Talked this morning, in the office, with two of the American journalists. I asked them why they stayed here in the western sectors of Berlin. After all, this was only an island now, remote from the main current of world affairs.

8. In protest over the progress toward unifying the U.S., British, and French zones of Germany into an independent state, the Soviets in June 1948 had blocked the Western allies from sending trucks and trains through the Soviet zone to supply West Berlin. The United States responded with a massive airlift until the Soviets relented in May 1949.

They were hard put to it to answer the question. They could only fall back on the general consideration that Berlin was a hot spot where some day something would have to happen, and that here one was close to the Russians and had opportunities to observe what they were thinking and doing. But the question rather shocked them. They were dominated by the same state of mind as our Foreign Service people who were startled at the question as to why we still maintained large sections of their office and of military government in Berlin where it only constituted additional strain on the airlift. They could only reply that it was unthinkable that they should leave. The Berliners would think they were deserting them.

Near Frankfurt, March 16

Up early and went for a walk before breakfast, to the amazement and concern of the German personnel. A blanket of dampness and low cloud still hung over the wooded hills. I went down the drive, out of the main gate and into the village. This was a suburban-type village, not a farming community. The square houses stood behind high fences. The yards were used as gardens. Wood piles, garden tools, chickens, and the stalks of last year's cabbage still yielding Brussels sprouts all testified to the primitiveness of life and the vigorous efforts of self-help and subsistence gardening to which people had been driven by the years of hunger and hardship.

It was early in the morning, but people were already on their feet. Housewives were heading for the market with their shopping baskets; white-collar workers, with the usual long rain coat and brief case bulging with the morning sandwiches, clanged shut the little sidewalk gates as they set forth on their bicycles for the day's work. Children were on their way to school with their shiny knapsacks on their backs; and the sight of these knapsacks suddenly brought back a tinge of the sense of strangeness and alarm with which I, myself, as a boy of eight, first went off to school in Kassel in the year 1912, amid a horde of German boys with similar knapsacks, boys who plainly felt so wondrously and securely at home in a world I neither liked nor understood.

After breakfast, back to Frankfurt to attend another meeting. This time it was a meeting of the three military governors. Only three sides of the square of tables were populated this time. The French general, who was the chairman, sat with his cohorts along the middle side; the British and ourselves along the wings.

The meeting was one in which there was a good measure of disagreement. The French general, functioning in his role of chairman, could not have acted or looked otherwise had he been the renegade son of a degenerate French noble family of the ancient regime acting as a military governor for Napoleon somewhere across the broad expanse of Europe. He kept a constant smile on his face, but it was obviously not a smile directed to others. It was a smile of some inward amusement, an almost unbelievably sadistic and arrogant amusement. I had seen nothing like this in anyone since the officers of the European armies before World War I. You could not look at this man without recalling the known facts concerning the fantastic establishment of luxury in which he had surrounded his own person and the disgraceful plundering and carpetbagging which he has not only tolerated but apparently inspired in his own command. You could imagine that it was with this same degenerate smile that he would dismiss German pleas for a more sensible and decent treatment, or inflict some act of arrogance on his own subordinates in the French establishment. Toward General Clay,[9] he was supercilious and indifferent. He made no effort to conceal his intention to appeal their differences to governments or his confidence that the governments would decide in his favor. In the face of this performance, any differences of opinion which we may have had within our American circle about German policy faded completely as far as I was concerned; and my heart went out in gratitude and admiration for the integrity and seriousness and respect for human values and responsibilities which rang out in every word stated on the American side.

Hamburg, March 18

The real destruction we did not come to until we had passed the harbor and the business district and entered the large residential districts east of the Alster River. Here was sweeping devastation, down to the ground, mile after mile. It had all been done in three days and nights in 1943, my host told me. Seventy-five thousand persons had perished in the process. Even now, after the lapse of six years, over three thousand bodies were estimated to be still buried there in the rubble.

In the ruins of Berlin, there had seemed to be a certain tragic majesty. Berlin had been a great cold city, an imperial city, haughty and pretentious. Such cities invited the wrath of gods and men.

9. General Lucius Clay was military governor of the U.S. zone in Germany.

But poor old Hamburg: this comfortable, good-humored, seaport community, dedicated, like so many of our own cities, to the common-sense humdrum of commerce and industry—for Hamburg, it seemed a great pity.

And here, for the first time, I felt an unshakeable conviction that no momentary military advantage, even if such could have been calculated to exist, could have justified this stupendous, careless destruction of civilian life and of material values, built up laboriously by human hands, over the course of centuries, for purposes having nothing to do with war. Least of all could it have been justified by the screaming non-sequitur: "they did it to us." And it suddenly appeared to me that in these ruins there was an unanswerable symbolism which we in the West could not afford to ignore. If the Western world was really going to make valid the pretense of a higher moral departure point—of greater sympathy and understanding for the human being as God made him, as expressed not only in himself, but in the things he has wrought and has cared about—then it had to learn to fight its wars morally as well as militarily, or not fight them at all; for moral principles were a part of its strength. Shorn of this strength, it was no longer itself. Its victories were not real victories; and the best it would accomplish in the long run would be to pull down the temple over its own head. The military would stamp this as naïve, and would say that war is war, and that when you're in it you fight with every means you have, or go down in defeat. But if that is the case, then there rests upon Western civilization, bitter as this may be, the obligation to be militarily stronger than its adversaries by a margin sufficient to enable it to dispense with those means which can stave off defeat only at the cost of undermining victory.

Berlin, March 20

Despite occasional snow flurries, the weather was brighter than last week. It was suddenly the difference between winter and spring. The heavens were no longer all one tone. There were dark clouds, and light clouds; and between them gleamed a new sky—the pale blue sky of spring, on the existence of which one had almost ceased to believe in the endless, dragging northern winter.

Even the children noticed it. On my way to the subway station, I passed three of them, walking an Airedale dog. "Oh look," the little boy was saying, "the dark cloud is the night-fairy and the light cloud is the day-fairy." The Airedale caught the hope and excitement in the boy's tone, and looked eagerly at the others and strained at the leash, to show that he was one of the gang and ready for anything.

(You are right, my little fellow, I thought to myself, there is a day-fairy and a night-fairy, a light cloud and a dark cloud. And which of these clouds will hang over you and overshadow your life in the days of your maturity—which fairy will wield the wand over you—is the great question. The answer will depend partly on you, since none of us is without will and responsibility who is not completely a prisoner. But it will depend more on us Americans. For we have won great wars and assumed to ourselves great powers. And we have thus become the least free of all peoples. We have placed upon ourselves the obligation to have the answers; and anyone can come up and put a nickel in us and ask for an answer, and the rules of the game require us to give one. This, too, you will eventually discover; and, according to the answer we give, you may get mostly the day-fairy or mostly the night-fairy, hovering over yourself and your future. And I'd watch that one, if I were you, come to think of it; because we aren't too sure about all these things, ourselves. And I wouldn't stake too much on the soundness of our answers.[10])

It was plain that if only somehow the inward influences of health and hope could be brought to these children, if it could be shown to them that somewhere, at the end of this afternoon whenever the March sun penetrated the snow-flurries, there were such things as freedom and security and rewards for work accomplished and the chance to walk down the broad vistas of beauty and warmth in the human spirit: if these things could be done, then the ruins, like the charm of a wicked sorcerer, would lose their power over these children, and the day-fairy would once again come into her own.

But whence was all this to come? From the parents? The parents were stoical and hardened and purged of many of their erstwhile illusions. But they were still bewildered, unenlightened people, with a terribly restricted field of vision. From us Americans? We were doing our best. But we had no answer, yet, to the great political insecurity which hung over this area. And our own vision was clouded by our habits, our comforts, our false and corrupting position as conquerors and occupiers.

Near Frankfurt, March 21

Took a last walk through the narrow streets of the little town. Here life was better, unquestionably, than in the great cities of Berlin and Hamburg. The town had been untouched by the bombings. The great Allied

10. This sentence is crossed out.

establishment of the Frankfurt area was all around them, dispensing jobs and marks, and keeping up a high level of economic activity. But not even the best will in the world could concede that this was a good-looking people. The war seemed to have drained it of youth and spirit. And far too high a percentage of those who crossed your path were obviously the same old small-town burghers of the pre-war period: civil servants and pensioners and white-collar workers and petty trades people.

These people had been the backbone of Nazism. Nazism had made them horrible, or had brought out the horror that was in them. Now defeat and frustration had made them grotesque. With their hollowed, grey faces, their thinned, gaunt figures, their long flapping knickerbockers and Jaeger-hats, they reminded me, for some reason, of awkward, aging beetles, who had survived some sort of flood and catastrophe and were still stubbornly crawling around the haunts from which they were supposed to have been removed.

In the evening, I drove down out of the hills to Frankfurt to take the train to Paris. It had been a fine sunny day—the first day of good weather since I came to Germany. Now, although darkness had fallen, the sky was still bright in the west and the stars were out. In the villages, people were out strolling, enjoying the first evening of fine spring weather. There was brisk vehicular traffic all along the road, and most of it German. I thought of the whole bizonal[11] area stretching off behind us in the dusk; and it seemed to me that you could hear the great low murmur of human life beginning to stir again, beginning to recapture the rhythm of work and life and change, after years of shock and prostration. Here were tens of millions of human beings, of all ages and walks of life, reacting, as human beings always have and must, to the myriad of stimuli of heredity and education and climate and economic necessity and emotion. Whatever we did, they would no longer stand still in thought or in outlook. Nothing could keep them from seeking again some outlet for the basic need of the human being to feel that he is doing something important and fruitful and necessary.

Would we be able to feel our way into this sea of human reaction and human will, heretofore so repugnant, so little interesting to us? Would we be able to realize that we are the doctor on whose understanding the recovery and health of this patient depend, without which recovery and health there may be no unity and no success for the Western world? Would we be able to roll up our sleeves, to overcome our own distaste, and to study with cool objectivity the anatomy and pathology of this tre-

11. Bizonia was the combined U.S. and British zones of Germany.

mendous body politic which had wrought so much havoc in our Western world? Would we be able to steer its development into cooperative and constructive lines? Would we be able to give it the sense of participation, the sense of being needed, which it so desperately required? Or would we turn our backs upon it in anger and revulsion, and leave it no choice but to grow again outside of us and against us, in the spirit of those bitter lines by Goethe with which the German Communist Party once used to close its meetings:

> "You must rule and win
> Or serve and lose
> Suffer or triumph,
> Be anvil or be hammer"

In the darkened streets of the suburban villages, in the bustle of the Frankfurt station, in the lights of the little station platforms of the plundered French zone as they slipped past the train windows, there were no answers to these questions; and the misty darkness which hung over the sleeping countryside of the Rhineland was heavy with uncertainty.

Washington, August 23

This morning the question of the U.S.-British talks on Britain's financial difficulties finally came up for discussion in the morning meeting with the Secretary. . . . I pointed out that, at the present moment, with a great question mark hanging over the solidarity of Russian rule in the satellite area and with an extremely tense and unpleasant situation in the Far East,[12] it would be catastrophic if anything happened to disrupt the spirit of confidence and solidarity and the reality of economic stability and progress in the Western world. This, however, was exactly what would happen if something drastic were not done about the British situation. If the British went home empty handed and in despair, I had no doubt that the Labor Government would fall soon thereafter to the accompaniment of a tremendous din of recriminations and bitter words against this country. It seemed to me that there was very little we could do to help the British in the short term, for any help that required legislative action could not be expected in less than a year, on account of the

12. Marshal Tito of Yugoslavia was openly defying the Kremlin. The decades-long civil war in China was nearing an end, with the Communists triumphant under the leadership of Mao Zedong.

Congressional situation, and what we could do for them by administrative action was really very little. No matter what came out of these discussions, therefore, the British would have to return to take some very bitter and difficult measures, on their own hook, in the weeks following the discussions.

But it seemed to me that everything depended on the spirit in which they did that. If they went back feeling that the talks had yielded nothing and that we were going to give them no help at all, even in the long term, the worst results could be expected. If, on the other hand, we could give them the hope that even though we could not provide the short term answers we would be willing to help them face the long term aspects of their problem, I thought the entire picture might be a different one. I pointed out that their dollar drain arose from two factors: (a) their position as banker for the sterling area and (b) the adverse U.K. balance of trade with the dollar area. As to the first, I suggested that perhaps they ought to cease trying to be the bankers for at least a portion of the sterling area, and the respective countries ought to come direct to the U.S. for their dollars. This would mean headaches for us—yes; but it would at least create clarity and public understanding where today there is confusion. As for the British adverse balance, that was a question of adjustment of the British economy to the economies of North America, and I thought that we ought at least to agree to join them in appointing a commission of inquiry to determine what institutional changes, if any, might be made in the relations between the three countries (U.S., U.K., and Canada) which would ease this adjustment and prevent each single component of it from being made a particular issue and bone of contention in the relations between the respective countries. . . .

[Undersecretary of State James E. Webb came to my office and said] Mr. Acheson was a wonderful man, but he was austere and aloof and did not seem to establish a real personal contact with the President and his entourage. If he tried to operate alone he could not carry the opposition of the other people around the President and Louie Johnson[13] and of the Congressional circles who are already beginning to attack him personally in a way they would never have dared to attack General Marshall. He sometimes wondered how it would work out, with the Secretary so reserved and so remote from the White House circle. Besides, the Secretary was a very tired man.

13. Louis A. Johnson was secretary of defense.

August 30

I went out to the Secretary's house in the country, this evening, for a dinner in honor of Chip. We talked particularly about the Yugoslav-Soviet crisis. Chip shares my feeling that while common sense should inhibit the Russians from any resort to direct violence, this is one matter which has really aroused the emotions of the men in the Kremlin in the most extraordinary way, and that anything might happen.

August 31

Spoke very bitterly to [journalist Stewart Alsop] after lunch about the campaign of vilification which his brother Joe had carried on for years against John Davies,[14] and told him that as a result of this smearing, Davies was now going to be transferred to work in some other field, which simply represented a loss of one of the best political minds we had from the field where it could be most useful. When I got back to the office Joe phoned me in white heat about this and talked for three-quarters of an hour straight on the subject.

September 1

Was interrupted for an hour by a visit of the French Ambassador, Bonnet,[15] who seemed to be preoccupied lest the result of the U.S.-U.K.-Canadian discussions be the establishment of some body on which only those three countries were represented. This would "leave France out" and give the impression, he feared, that she was being abandoned by the Anglo-Saxon powers. I tried, evidently without much success, to reassure him about this, yet at the same time to impress upon him our feeling that the French themselves must take the lead in developing union on the Continent, leaving the British outside.

I stand in continued wonder and exasperation at the irrationalism of the French, who are supposed to be the most rational of peoples. They want to be in on everything: even those things which are troublesome and painful and do not require their membership. They want to be in on things where they can contribute nothing and have nothing to gain, rather than have anyone do anything without them. They profess to fears which make absolutely no sense in the light of even the most cur-

14. John Paton Davies Jr., a friend of Kennan's and a Foreign Service expert on China. Republican Senator Joseph McCarthy of Wisconsin was pillorying Davies as treasonous because he had reported accurately on the failings of Chiang Kai-shek's government.
15. Henri Bonnet.

sory glance at reality, and insist that those fears be taken seriously by others. Why in the world they can think that we would have spent ten to fifteen billion dollars in Western Europe and gone through the anguish of negotiating an Atlantic Pact and trying to get that and a military aid program through Congress, if our purpose had been to abandon France, surpasses my imagination.

September 8

Spent the morning with John Davies and Dorothy Fosdick drafting some observations for Mr. Jessup[16] and his group about the suggestions that we should encourage the Chinese to appeal to the United Nations against the violation by the Russians of the clauses of the Sino-Soviet Treaty of 1945 and that we should ask the members of the United Nations to reaffirm at this time the principles of the Nine-Power Treaty (Washington Treaty) of 1921. We opposed both of these suggestions. The first we opposed largely on the grounds that what we did at Yalta with respect to Manchuria could only have meant to the Russians that we were restoring to them the position which Russia had enjoyed there before the Russo-Japanese War, and that a step of this sort on the part of the Chinese would hopelessly confuse and entangle our policies with respect to the Soviet Union with our relationship to the National Government of China. The second we opposed because we felt that it would bind us more than the Russians and would only lead to another revelation of the helplessness of the UN.

September 13

This morning I learned from one of our officers who had been authorized to inform me of the matter that we had received indication that an atomic explosion had taken place in the Soviet Union. The official said that the scientific investigation of the available evidence was continuing, and that we should know the facts in a few days.

. . . Jebb[17] is still skeptical about my own thesis that unification of the Western world should proceed in two parts, with the U.S., U.K. and Canada constituting one part and the Continental countries the other. Jebb feels that in the relationship between the U.K. and the Western European countries there is something tangible at hand: an edifice

16. Davies and Fosdick were members of the Policy Planning Staff. Philip C. Jessup was a State Department legal expert.

17. Gladwyn Jebb was a British diplomat.

which is actually rising and which we should not sacrifice in favor of other edifices which are still only matters of the imagination. He does not feel that there is any chance of the Eastern European countries being freed from communist domination within the foreseeable future; and I gathered that he would not wish this to happen, since in his view it would only complicate the consolidation of Western Europe. His is the pragmatic, tentative British approach, distrustful of logic and of hypothetical considerations, and directed primarily to the short term.

I must still disagree with him. I see no future in relationship of the U.K. to Western European countries which cannot be shared by the U.S. and Canada and which excludes, by implication, the countries of Eastern Europe.

September 19

The whole *raison d'etre* of this [Policy Planning] Staff was its ability to render an independent judgment on problems coming before the Secretary or the Under Secretary through the regular channels of the Department. If the senior officials of the Department do not wish such an independent judgment, or do not have confidence in us to prepare one which would be useful, then I question whether the Staff should exist at all.

This lies in the nature of our work. When Secretary Byrnes called upon the Acheson-Lilienthal[18] group to prepare for him a staff opinion on our policy with respect to the international control of atomic energy, he did not insist that it meet with the unanimous and detailed approval of the Assistant Secretaries before he was interested in reading it. Similarly, when Secretary Marshall first asked this Staff to do work on the problem of European recovery, what he wanted was the Staff's opinion and not a record of the extent to which the Staff could find agreement with the various departmental chiefs on this subject.

This afternoon it became known that the technical study of the evidences of an atomic explosion in the Soviet Union had been completed, and that the conclusion of the scientists was that such an explosion *had* taken place. It was their belief that it was an atomic bomb. Mr. Webb thought that the President might wish to announce tomorrow that such an explosion *had* taken place. The time being thus short, I obtained his

18. David E. Lilienthal, former chairman of the Tennessee Valley Authority, headed the Atomic Energy Commission.

authorization to get together a group at once which would examine the problem of what answers should be given throughout the Executive establishment to the numerous subsidiary questions which would undoubtedly be asked the moment such an announcement were made. My thought was that if we could arrange a uniform set of answers, to be used by all the officials of the Executive Branch of the Government, we could do much to control the reaction to this announcement.

Accordingly, I got together three or four people at my house in the evening, and we threshed out the elements of a set of questions and answers along these lines.

September 21

It is a curious thing how great an influence is exerted on the character of negotiations by the number of people present. They may all be the most trusted of persons, and the relationships between the members of each team may be ones of the greatest intimacy; yet if there are more than half a dozen people around the table there is general hesitation and stiffness and formality.

September 22

This morning, Mr. Paul Palmer of the *Reader's Digest* came to see me. He told me that he had been talking to people around town and had been impressed with the amount of "preventive war psychology." . . . He found a good deal of this sort of thing in the Pentagon. He wanted to know what I thought of it.

I talked to him for fifteen or twenty minutes, and he then said that if I would put in the form of an article substantially what I had told him, they would run it as a feature article in *Reader's Digest* and pay me five thousand dollars besides. I should normally have discouraged him, because no one else among the responsible officers in the Department has any interest in this sort of medium for getting the Government's views before the public. However, in the present circumstances, with the knowledge that the news of the Russian atomic explosion would somehow or other reach the public in the near future, I thought it best not to discourage him entirely and make another try at getting authority to print such an article. It is quite obvious that the news from Russia will add a great impetus to this sort of unrealistic thinking about a preventive war, unless something is done to head off this reaction.

September 24

Judging from this morning's papers, the reaction to the announcement about the Russian bomb was highly satisfactory. A few people naturally jumped to extreme and dangerous conclusions and made statements which can only be harmful to an understanding of the realities of the situation. But for the most part, people took it calmly and the press did a good job of placing the event in the proper perspective.

September 26

This morning, at 12:30, Mr. Webb took me to see the President, ostensibly to report to him on the progress of our negotiations on atomic energy. The President looked slightly tired, but was his usual likeable self. I could understand how such strong loyalties could develop between him and his associates. I was glad, upon reflection, that I had had so little contact with him, for I would not like to be in a position where personal loyalty and affection forced me to close my eyes to the obvious deficiencies in the conduct of foreign policy in this period and to profess enthusiasm for what must remain a confusing and ineffective method of operation. . . .

Americans seem little able to accustom themselves to the thought that their security must rest on the *intentions*, rather than the *capabilities* of other nations and are drifting toward a morbid preoccupation with the fact that the Russians conceivably *could* drop atomic bombs on this country, regardless of the question as to whether it would be profitable or otherwise for them to do so. Europeans, judging from the Foreign Minister's[19] statements, still labor under their own similar preoccupation with the specter of invasion, closing their eyes to the fact that their own domestic Communist Parties represent the grimmer and more real danger and that their own jitteriness about an invasion the Russians have never intended to conduct plays into the hands of those very Communist Parties.

There was great to-do this morning over a new state of hysteria into which the French have succeeded in working themselves. The French Prime Minister had called in Bruce[20] and told him that the events of the past week had indicated that there had been an "historic policy decision of the U.S. Government" to the effect that we would henceforth move only in company with the British and Canadians, leaving France alone on the Continent with the Germans. To back this up, the French pointed to several things which had happened, including statements allegedly

19. Belgian Foreign Minister Paul van Zeeland.
20. U.S. ambassador to France.

made by the Secretary to Schuman,[21] the British devaluation, our talks with the British over the pound and dollar question, etc. This was accompanied by the appearance in this morning's *Post* of an article by Walter Lippmann accusing this Government of exactly the same thing and citing, in support of his accusations, an article by the Alsop brothers in which I had been quoted as favoring a special U.S.-U.K.-Canadian relationship. It was quite obvious that Lippmann's article had been inspired by the French here in Washington, and I could not help but feel that perhaps it also reflected a certain amount of pique over my failure to keep my appointment with him last week.

My only reaction to this sort of thing is one of impatience and disgust. The idea that after the years of work and sacrifice involved in what the Executive Branch of this Government has done with respect to the European Recovery Program [the Marshall Plan], the Atlantic Pact [NATO], and now the Military Assistance Program, we would still be under the onus of trying to persuade the French at frequent intervals that we are not about to abandon them seems to me to have rather dismal implications.

September 28

We discussed the problems relating to the Japanese peace treaty. As in so many other instances, I had the feeling that I was inflicting disappointment and discouragement on others by my inability to go along with ideas which generally commend themselves elsewhere in the Department. I cannot agree that we ought to make ourselves a party to the formal assignment of Formosa to China, when we know that this means only injustice and misgovernment to the natives of the island for decades ahead. I cannot agree that we should insist on a Japanese promise to be democratic and to observe human rights when I know that we have no serious intention of insisting that they live up to such a promise once they have signed it.

Talked this afternoon with Mr. Webb about my own status and told him of my desire to leave government service next June and to be permitted to work on long term studies in the interval. I expressed the wish that I might be relieved of the title and responsibilities as Director of the Planning Staff. This he did not agree to, but he undertook to give as much responsibility as possible to Nitze[22] and to make it possible for me to be relieved of current staff work to some extent.

21. Robert Schuman was the French foreign minister.
22. Paul M. Nitze was Kennan's successor as head of the Policy Planning Staff.

September 30

The morning was marked by new claims staked out for time and energy in the coming period. Nitze and Webb both think that we must work on a reappraisal of U.S. policy in the light of the Russian progress in atomic energy.[23] The [Policy Planning] Staff want a completion of the study on our stance toward European union. In the light of these demands, I had to cancel my plans for visiting the United Nations this fall and to reconcile myself to the fact that efforts on my part to get away from Washington always produce more trouble than success. Reflecting on this development, I realized that I face the work of these remaining months with neither enthusiasm nor with hope for achievement.

October 4

[Talking with Ambassador to India Loy Henderson] left me with a feeling of high uneasiness about any attempts we may make to cultivate a better relationship with Nehru and the Indians at this time. Their views about us are so badly fouled up with arrogance and ignorance, with false assumptions about American "imperialism" and about the comparative aspects of our relationship to Europe and Asia and to the white world and the colored world, that I would almost despair of trying to achieve at this time any relationship to the Indians based on a correct appreciation of the nature of our country and of its aspirations. I have the feeling that with respect to India, as was recently the case with China, things must get a lot worse before they can get better. What I would like to say to Nehru would be something like this:

"We feel that you people have permitted your minds to be filled up with a whole series of grievous unjust misconceptions concerning our country. As long as you entertain those misconceptions we see little possibility of a closer relationship, and even some danger in seeking it. This is primarily your concern, not ours. It is you who will be the sufferers if you stubbornly misinterpret to yourselves the important realities of this world. You think that in the ideas we have been expressing with regard to Southeast Asia we have been pursuing some selfish American aim connected with a power struggle between the U.S. and the U.S.S.R. in which each is seeking some pattern of expanded dominion over other nations. This is a grievous mistake on your part. If the U.S. is trying to make the peoples of Asia conscious of a stake which they have in their

23. The result of this study would be the April 1950 National Security Council Memorandum (NSC) 68, authored by Nitze, which painted the Soviet threat in dark colors and urged a fourfold increase in U.S. defense spending.

own independence from communist ideological and political domination, it is because it is trying to take an enlightened and far-sighted view of world stability, and not because it has some special axe of its own to grind. Viewed from a narrow interpretation of American security and interests, I am not sure that there is any reason for the U.S. to want to oppose Russian expansion into Southeast Asia. And if you insist, you can possibly succeed in preventing us from exerting any useful influence in that part of the world and leaving it, yourselves included, a prey to Russian pressures. You will then find out in the hard way and the painful way who is the friend of the Asiatic peoples and who is not, and you will learn that there is a difference between playing with the ruthless fire of Soviet imperialism and playing with the mellow and modest aspirations of the older and more mature Western world. Now we are not going to woo you or cultivate you. You are the newcomers on the international scene. It is up to you to determine the quality of the relationships you wish to establish. If it embitters you that you cannot receive economic aid from a people whose motives you distrust and malign, we cannot help it; and we are prepared to take that bitterness in our stride. When this present phase of world affairs has passed, you will at least have learned to respect us, whether or not you have learned to understand us."

October 6

Spent the evening browsing in the new biography of Stalin by Isaac Deutscher.[24] While undoubtedly a serious and comprehensive work, carrying the story to a later date than any previous effort has done, I could not find that it added very much to our knowledge of Stalin's life up to his assumption of supreme authority in Russia, and I was not at all sure that Deutscher had done all that could have been done to get to the bottom of some of the more obscure phases of Stalin's early career.

October 7

Spent most of the rest of the morning in a very intensive discussion within the Staff on the question of the Austrian treaty.[25] Since we examined the matter the other evening, two new factors had been added. First, further discussions with the Russians, plus some further reflection on our part, had made it appear that the position the Russians were taking was not

24. *Stalin: A Political Biography* (1949). Kennan attached credence to the claim that Stalin as a young man had collaborated with the czarist secret police.

25. From 1945 to 1955, Austria remained divided into U.S., Soviet, British, and French occupation zones.

seriously at variance with that which had been agreed at Paris. Second, the Austrians had shown us the draft of a letter which Gruber[26] intended to write to the Secretary on this subject. The letter was aggressive, resentful and blunt. It impugned our motives for hesitating to conclude the treaty on the present Russian terms and insisted that we do so. . . .

(1) I now feel that the Austrians are in a very poor position to defend their independence in the face of Russian pressures. (2) In the light of Gruber's views, I feel that the Austrian Government has pretty well signed away the claim that it had, and which I have always sincerely acknowledged, on our sympathy and assistance. (3) This drives home so strongly to me the terrible unforgivableness of getting ourselves into situations of this sort, where we have lost the independence and integrity of our national action, that I would prefer a return to the historic policy of neutrality and isolation to a repetition of the series of mistakes which led us into our present position in the matter of the Austrian treaty.

October 12

[In a discussion with military officials about ABC weapons (atomic, biological, chemical)] they suggested that if our forces were to be expelled from the Continent in a future war, the use of ABC weapons by the Russians might make it impossible for us to return. Similarly, it might be only through the use of ABC weapons that we could prevent our own expulsion. Since they expected that our superiority in the ABC weapons was now at its maximum power, they pointed out that we could conclude from this that the present would be the most advantageous for us to accept an agreement outlawing the use of such weapons.

I cannot overcome the conviction that thinking in these terms reflects a vast over-estimation of Russian capabilities and a misunderstanding of Russian intentions. But I cannot prove this conviction, and the matters in question are too important for anyone to dare act on a hunch.

October 17–21

This week was more full of ideas than of events, and can be treated accordingly.

The first category of ideas were those relating to what we call, for want of a better name, European integration. That embraces a whole bundle of questions, grouped around the following ones: Do we want

26. Karl Gruber was the Austrian foreign minister.

to see closer integration among the European countries (today, perforce, the countries of Western Europe)? If so, do we wish to see it carried to the point of abandonment of sovereignty? And again, if so, when and among what countries? And, regardless of what we may want, is it politic to urge anything like this at the present time? Paul Hoffman[27] is leaving in a few days for Paris, where he must give the opening speech at the meeting of the OEEC.[28] Everyone feels that things are at a turning point, and that the attitude we adopt at this moment will depend not alone on the purpose and function of European Recovery Plan aid in the third and fourth years of the Marshall Plan period, but whether there will be any such aid at all. ECA[29] officials feel that if the European countries will not at least bind themselves to some program of economic union, aimed at the creation of super-national agencies for certain key functions in the control of economic life, there is not much likelihood that they could use further aid effectively; ECA could therefore not recommend it to the Congress very enthusiastically; and there would be little chance of getting the appropriation. ECA would therefore have us bring strong pressure on the Europeans at this time. Since the British are hardly in a position to participate in this sort of arrangement, they would have the Continental countries proceed without the British. All this brings dismay to the European office of the State Department, which feels that this is all too hasty and abrupt, that there is no need for any such intimate economic union and that any suggestion that the continentals proceed without the British will frighten the French and do political damage over all western Europe.

My own position is somewhere in between. I am not sure that the economic arguments for an early step toward real union are very compelling. I have deep feelings, however, about the political necessity of creating in Western Europe an international framework which would bridge national sovereignties to such a degree as to give a different aspect to the German question by providing a home for the German people other than the national home and thus lifting German horizons beyond those national limits with which the Germans have shown themselves so incapable of coping.

27. Paul G. Hoffman oversaw the administration of the Marshall Plan.

28. The Organisation for European Economic Co-operation was a European-based organization that helped coordinate the Marshall Plan while promoting the integration of Western Europe.

29. The Economic Cooperation Administration, an agency of the U.S. government, administered the Marshall Plan.

October 24

An unprofitable day, from the standpoint of office accomplishment, taken up with a long argument in the [Policy Planning] Staff, in the morning, about the U.S.A. itself and the relation of domestic and foreign policy, a lunch with Bill Bullitt, and dinner at the Swiss Legation.

The Staff argument centered around my contention that we are a society which has no control over the direction in which it is moving, socially and technologically, and no assurance that the currents in which we are being involuntarily borne are not ones which carry us away from our national ideals and the foundations of our type of representative government. We argued particularly about the labor movement, and whether it had in it the elements of any real understanding of what constituted progress in human society or whether its concentration on higher wages and more leisure, without regard to the uses to which they might be put, was not merely a demagogic, and basically reactionary, approach. The latter was my idea. I think the others largely disagreed.

Bill Bullitt talked about the problem of European integration. He felt that de Gaulle,[30] with a certain amount of friendly interest and counsel from us, would have been prepared to take real leadership in Europe in the direction of an integration adequate to provide a definite framework for the solution of the German problem. Our failure to take advantage of this opportunity he blamed on FDR and his violent aversion to de Gaulle. He felt that today the governments of the center were essentially paralyzed by the left socialist group; they could not run France with them, and they could not run France without them.

On the Far East, we managed to stay fairly well clear of the painful subject of China. He warned in the strongest terms not to pin any hopes on Nehru and the Hindus. "Build on anyone else you want," he said, "on the Moslems if you will, but not on the Hindus." He said he would rather found a policy on the Senegalese than on the Hindus. He said people who still insisted on letting 30–50 per cent of the food of the country go to sacred animals could never develop India economically. And intellectually, they were brilliant but unsubstantial.

30. Charles de Gaulle led the Free French movement during the war and the French government in 1944–46.

November 7

This was a day of comings and goings. The Secretary and Paul Nitze left in the middle of the afternoon for Paris. Before they left, Vyshinsky[31] down in Washington for the November 7 celebration [of the Russian Revolution] at the Soviet Embassy, paid a courtesy call on the Secretary. I sat in on the conversation, and had the impression that Vyshinsky was really somewhat abashed and lacking in self-confidence in these surroundings and in the Secretary's presence. Not that it means anything now, but I am convinced that he is a bourgeois at heart and secretly would prefer to be Mr. Acheson's first assistant than Soviet Foreign Minister. It is much too late for this, of course. The shadow of his participation in the purges hangs over him, along with other shadows of his past and binds him, with bonds stronger than any prison bars or any emotional loyalties, to the terrible, implacable and contemptuous masters to whom he has sold himself.

November 8

[The U.S. policy of building up West Germany as a more or less permanent state] fills me with forebodings. This means that we do not really want any agreement with the Russians about Germany, now or for an indefinite time to come. But this, in turn, means no agreement with the Russians on anything of any importance. It means that we both carry on for an indefinite period with military commitments extending into the heart of Europe; that there can be no withdrawal for either of us without the other's military influence being sucked, as it were, into the resulting vacuum; that any Soviet military withdrawal from Eastern Europe as a whole becomes increasingly unthinkable; that the wedge across Europe gets driven deeper and deeper; that the settling down of this turbulent world into another period of relative stability becomes more and more unlikely; and that it becomes daily more difficult to see how this deadlock can ever be resolved by peaceful means. Let us make no mistake about this: Germany is the key to the situation. And present Western policy with respect to Germany leaves room for no plausible peaceful settlement with the Russians. In the face of this policy, the German question could be settled in a manner favorable to us only by an internal collapse of Soviet power.

31. Soviet Foreign Minister Andrey Vyshinsky had been state prosecutor during the terrible purge trials of the late 1930s.

And a continuation of the deadlock, which is what we are steering for, must become increasingly difficult for the West, because the U.S. cannot indefinitely satisfy the gap in the food and raw material requirements of the heavily industrialized areas of all Western Europe and the United Kingdom. But the bargaining power of the West will probably decline from now on, in trade matters. Eventually, there must be a considerable expansion of East-West trade. All in all, our policy on the continent takes us along a street to which there are only three outlets: a Russian collapse, a disintegration of our own position, or a terrible war.

November 11

[After dinner with a recently emigrated Russian couple. They] were full of enthusiasm for life here, confident that nothing could be worse than the things they had been through, eager to throw themselves into the new life. I admired this attitude, and was grateful for it. It was a much better one than you would find with many of the displaced persons. But it was clear that they were incapable of knowing, or even imagining, the real nature of the strains they would have to bear in this highly competitive, confusing, and, for a Russian, essentially lonely society. To survive here calls for certain types of strength which are not demanded even by the hardships and dangers of life in the Soviet Union.

November 15

I cannot help feeling the irony of my being called upon for suggestions about how to make a go of things in the western sectors of Berlin at this stage of the game, I having been the one person in the Department who always insisted that the Berlin problem was not soluble in terms of a divided military occupation—that it could be solved only by a retirement of the respective allied military forces in such a way as to throw open an area, including Berlin, which would be contiguous with both zones of occupation, and leaving this area to be governed by the Germans themselves. Such a solution is of course now impossible; and probably it was impossible at the time I advocated it, because it is not likely that we would have had French agreement, even if the Russians had consented to make tolerable arrangements. But we might at least, it seemed to me, have made it clear that this, the only sound solution, was the one we preferred, and that while we would take the alternative one, if others insisted, we did so skeptically and reluctantly, and the responsibility for its success rested with those others, and not with us.

Princeton, November 15

Took the morning train to Princeton, lunched at the Princeton Inn, then walked out to the Institute for Advanced Study, to see Robert Oppenheimer.[32] Talked to him for an hour and a half, both about international control and about the problem of whether to proceed with the development of the super-bomb.[33]

It was Princeton as I remembered it from the moments of my greatest loneliness as a student. I walked out to the back street, far off campus, where I had rented a furnished room during my freshman year, when I was seventeen years old, and looked up at the window in the back of the clapboard rooming-house. A light was on in the room. Perhaps some other student was now there, much like myself, in many ways, and yet, aside from individual differences, surely with some subtle, undefinable differences in outlook. Those are the differences which mark the distance between generations, and they are the great and important mysteries, for they are an integral part of the total mystery of change. . . .

I realized that I was surrounded here by men for whom the people of my generation were partly nuisances and at best regrettable and temporary necessities; that they were skeptical about the difficulties which had stood in our paths and unimpressed with our achievements. In their minds, we were already consigned to the ash-heap of history. Would they soon be rising after us, crowding us, pushing us impatiently toward that ash-heap? Yes—some of us they would be pushing, those of us engaged in the struggle for money or for other forms of power. But those of us to whom it had fallen to try to see behind the realities and to unravel the relationships of our civilization—we would not be pushed. There is plenty of space where we stand, space to the point of loneliness and terror. And any who work themselves into our vicinity, old or young, will soon feel the protecting covering of the generations falling ominously away from them and they will huddle together with us and with the curious ones of all times and ages, seeking warmth and company before the coldness and the endlessness and the silence that confront them.

32. Formerly head scientist of the Manhattan Project to develop the atomic bomb, J. Robert Oppenheimer was director of the Institute for Advanced Study, where Kennan in 1950 would come to live and work.

33. The Truman administration was trying to decide whether, in the wake of the Soviet development of an atomic bomb, to build a much more powerful weapon, the hydrogen bomb. Kennan and Oppenheimer were opposed.

Washington, November 18

Meeting of the Foreign Service Examination Board, with further efforts on the part of some of us to save the principle of professional diplomacy from the envious talons of people ignorant of the meaning of the term. Poor Foreign Service, whose honorary head I now happen to be: you will always be defenseless in a democratic society, and every time your members begin to grow intellectually and imaginatively, into a thoughtful and constructive concept of their own functions, they will attract envy and resentment by their "differences" and will eventually be discouraged and embittered into resigning. And they will leave behind them the mediocre spirits, who will then dominate the Service; and people will continue to say: "How can you ask us to support the Foreign Service? You haven't got any good men in it." In this way, American diplomacy will move along, for better or for worse, with always a few young men advancing just enough in experience and understanding to realize what the profession *might* be with a little support, and then paying the penalty for this dazzling appreciation by being criticized as "de-Americanized" and condemned to ignominy and frustration before they can make this appreciation the basis of any constructive effort.

. . . Went out to dinner at the home of some friends, where one of our former colleagues in Moscow showed us a series of colored movies taken in the Soviet Union. What stood out, to my mind, was how silly all the foreigners looked, compared to the Russians. People generally look silly when they are posing for amateur movies, but it was clear nevertheless from these pictures how idiotic most Western foreigners must ordinarily appear, to the denizens of the Soviet Union, with their endless drinking and partying, their preoccupation with the physical comforts, their desperate pursuit of distraction from boredom, their obvious lack of any serious interests.

November 19

Pondering today the frustrations of the past week, it occurred to me that it is time I recognized that my planning staff, started nearly three years ago, has simply been a failure, like all previous attempts to bring order and foresight into the designing of foreign policy by special institutional arrangements within the Department. Aside from personal shortcomings, the reason for this seems to lie largely in the impossibility of having the planning function performed outside of the line of command. The formulation of policy is the guts of the work of the Department, and none of it can successfully be placed outside the hierarchy which governs operations. No one can regiment this institution in the field of ideas except the Secretary. He can take as much independent advice as he likes from outside the institution; he can take it orally from "special assistants" or "counselors" or other official advisors. But when it comes to any formalized staff effort, anything that has to be put down in writing and is designed to serve as a major guide for action, the operating units—the geographic and functional units—will not take interference from any unit outside the line of command. They insist on an effective voice in policy determination; if one of them cannot make its voice alone valid, it insists on the right to water down any recommendation going to the Secretary to a point where it may be meaningless but it is at least not counter to its views. . . . The only way the thing will work is if a Secretary of State will thresh out a basic theoretical background of his policy and then really set up some sort of an educational unit through whose efforts this system can be patiently and persistently pounded into the heads of the entire apparatus, high and low.

November 20

If the French are unwilling to move . . . toward a normalization of Germany's position in Europe and if none of the Western European countries besides Germany is in a position to take any leadership in the direction of European union, and if no one there has any ideas how this can be done and it is therefore all very premature and impossible—then this is very unfortunate for the Continentals, for it means that they have no real chance of coping with their responsibilities, that in the end the Continent must be dominated by the Germans or the Russians or a combination of both, and that a sound U.S. policy would have to aim at an early readjustment to this sad state of reality. In other words, I would like to call their attention to the fact that while it may be very true that they lack the will and the understanding to do the things we are pressing them to do, there is no satisfactory alternative to their doing these things, and their confession of helplessness is not something we can all cheerfully accept and take in our stride but the evidence of a grim and ominous situation, more tragic for them than it is for us.

November 21

This afternoon the Department announced that it had approached 30 other countries presumed to have consular or diplomatic representatives in Communist China and had requested them to intercede with the Chinese Communist authorities for the release of our Consul in Mukden, Angus Ward.[34] I had not known of this decision before its announcement, and was hard put to answer telephonic and other inquiries about it which came to me late in the day.

To my mind, this is a good example of how we should not behave. The Chinese Communists are under no obligation to us. It is our own fault that we left our Consul there when the place was taken by the Communists. This is a straight bilateral issue between ourselves and them. If we were prepared to behave like a great power, we would treat it as a bilateral issue and not make ourselves ridiculous by asking a lot of weaker powers to assist us in solving it. I am constantly amazed at the manifestations of the stubborn belief on the part of some of my colleagues that we are wicked if we act alone, on our own responsibility, but are moral and praiseworthy if we place ourselves timorously in the company of a lot of others and pretend that we are just one of the crowd.

At dinner tonight I had to listen to sharp criticisms of our policy on Formosa, to assertions that we should be taking the island under our own wing, and to charges that if the military and naval authorities had been consulted the State Department would never have been able to get away with such a pusillanimous policy. It was not easy for me, who recommended months ago that we take this bull by the horns and assume responsibility for the island, to defend our failure to do so. And it was even harder to refrain from pointing out that our failure to do so was largely the result of the unwillingness of the National Defense Establishment to assume the attendant military responsibilities.

November 22

Pondering further the reasons for my own sense of frustration in my present position, I realize that the heart of the difficulty lies in the fact that my concept of the manner in which our diplomatic effort should be conducted is not shared by any of the other senior officials of the Department, and that the Secretary is actually dependent on these officials, for better or for worse, for the execution of any foreign policy at all. Even if he shared my views, he would not be able to find others who did; and lacking such others he would have to operate through people whose philosophy of foreign affairs would necessarily be a different one.

34. Held under house arrest and charged with espionage by the victorious Chinese Communist government, Ward and his staff were finally released in December 1949.

The fact of the matter is that this operation cannot be unified and given real purpose or direction unless a firm theoretical groundwork has been laid to back up whatever policy is pursued and unless the persons most concerned, here and in our delegation in New York and in our occupied areas establishments and in our field offices, have all been thoroughly and severely indoctrinated in this theoretical groundwork, so that they all have the same understanding of what it is that we are trying to do. Since our present governmental system lacks the disciplinary authority for such indoctrination, it can come really only through an intensive educational effort directed toward our public opinion in general and particularly toward the work of our universities. All this impels me to the thought that if I am ever to do any good in this work, having the courage of my convictions, it must be outside the walls of this institution and not inside them.

1950

In 1950, Kennan took a fact-finding trip to Latin America. He found little to like in the people, their culture, or the land. This was also the year that he began to shift from State Department adviser to scholar at the Institute for Advanced Study at Princeton. He nevertheless played a key role in shaping the Truman administration's response following North Korea's invasion of South Korea on June 25.

Along with the entries for 1949, the diary for 1950 is unique in its detailed coverage of Kennan's involvement with top-level foreign policy. Though he remained a key player in 1949–50, growing frustration with the direction of policy and the way it was made led him, it seems, to vent in the diary. In 1946–48, when he had been at the height of his influence, the diary suffered. Before 1946 and after 1950, he wrote about foreign policy, but not as an insider. Kennan's belief that others might someday read his diary also shaped its content. Innate discretion, honed by a career as a diplomat, inclined Kennan against putting down on paper sensitive details about foreign policy, or about his personal life. And yet throughout his life he burned with a desire to have his prescience recognized—preferably by the president and other top officials; but if not, then by the public and by posterity.

Washington, January 8

Began the day by reading the draft of a speech to be given to the Press Club by the Secretary next Thursday on Far Eastern policy.[35] Found it dull and sanctimonious and therefore worked in the afternoon and evening on the beginning of a draft of my own.

35. This was the speech in which Acheson would declare that South Korea remained outside the U.S. defense perimeter in the western Pacific. The secretary would later come under fierce attack by domestic critics for supposedly inviting the June invasion by North Korea.

January 9

Met late in the afternoon in the Secretary's office to consider a plethora of messages from Clubb[36] in Peiping[37] concerning the orders he had received from the Chinese Communists to turn over to them the building in the U.S. compound which now houses the Consulate General, as well as certain other American properties. I pressed strongly for a firm refusal on our part to do this, coupled with a statement that if they seized the property we would withdraw all representation at once from Communist China.[38] I argued this (and was supported by the Far Eastern Office) on the grounds that if they wanted us there they would probably not push it to this extreme; if they did not want us there, there was no use trying to stay anyway. This position was adopted. I fear that it means that the rest of our personnel in Chinese Communist territory (who never should have been left there anyway) will probably become hostages and perhaps even prisoners. But I see no way of avoiding this. Any indication of weakness on our part would merely invite new outrages on the part of the Chinese Communists, and eventually we would come to the same result.

January 11

We were all much interested by the news this morning of strong evidences of Tito tendencies in the Japanese Communist Party.[39] This bears out my view that Tito's heresy will have the effect, in the end, of making Moscow's control over the communist movement roughly coterminous with its military power.

Diary notes of trip to South America, February–March

February 19

The train was moving through the approaches to St. Louis, just east of the Mississippi: a grim waste of crisscrossing railroads, embankments,

36. Oliver Edmund Clubb, a China expert at the State Department, was later falsely accused by Senator Joseph McCarthy of sympathy for the Chinese Communists.
37. Peiping was the name for present-day Beijing favored by the U.S.-supported government of Chiang Kai-shek.
38. The decades-long Chinese civil war ended in October 1949 with victory for the Communists, who established the People's Republic of China. Washington would not recognize that government for three decades.
39. In 1948, the Communist leader of Yugoslavia, Marshal Tito, had declared his independence from Moscow's influence.

viaducts, junk lots, storage lots, piles of refuse, and the most abject specimens of human habitation. . . .

[In St. Louis] On this particular afternoon, the river bank was inhabited by six stray dogs, a bum who sat on a piece of driftwood and held one of the dogs in his lap, two small colored children with a bag of popcorn, and a stranger from Washington who sat on another piece of driftwood and sketched a cluster of four abandoned craft tied up by the shore: to wit, one scow with gasoline drums, one dredge, one dirty motor boat, and one genuine old show boat, still in use but slightly self-conscious. The colored children hovered over my shoulder, chattering pleasantly and dropping popcorn down my neck as they watched the progress of the drawing. The faint sunshine slanted in upon us, across the rooftops. Railroad trains clattered along both sides of the river and across the high bridge upstream. A gull came ashore to dabble in the slime between the cobblestones. And the river moved lazily past: a great slab of dirty-grey water, gleaming here and there in the sunshine, curling and eddying and whispering quietly to itself as it went along.

I walked back through the old business district: a district of narrow, dark streets; of sooty, fortress-like bank buildings; and hotels which once were elegant. (The trouble with American cities is that they have grown and changed too fast. The new is there before the old is gone. What in one era is functional and elegant and fashionable survives into the following era as grotesque decay. These cities have never had time to clean up after themselves. They have never had time to bury their dead. They are strewn with indecent skeletons, in the form of the blighted areas, the abandoned mansions of the gay nineties, the old railroad and water-front vicinities, the "houses by the railroad tracks.")

Mexico City, February 23

On the main avenues: the ostentatious, anxious demonstration of wealth by an ever-changing *nouveau riche,* which boils up like foam to the surface of a society that calls itself revolutionary.

Off the main avenues: the people, the demoralized, urbanized people. The wiry, swarthy little men—violent in temper, lacking in self-respect and self-confidence, over-compensating by a dramatized, romantic abandon and ferocity in personality, yet addicted in large part to every sort of chicanery and petty graft; the women—tiny, pathetic, unhealthy looking; the children—imp-like, with dusty bare feet, with sores and scabies—all of them ridden in large part with inherited and intestinal diseases. These people have lost the virtues of their Indian villages, and have never learned the restraints which alone could give reality to the pretenses of the city.

February 25

The officials of the Mexican government had been friendly, polite and hospitable. We had our problems with them, too, but that was quite another matter. Here, on these streets, you felt neither friendliness nor hostility, only a contemptuous indifference, rooted in experience too profound for any ready analysis. It would have taken the patience and fortitude and persistence of a saint to fathom these murky human souls, with their century-old burden of oppression and frustration, and to find out on what sort of terra firma, if any, one could begin to erect the foundations of confidence and hope and self-reliance and understanding. We, at any rate, were far from this point. And there was, it seemed to me, little evidence that time was working in our favor. The excellent work being done by our experts in improvement of agricultural and industrial practices, in public health, etc., was evidently destined to run head on into the population problem, as soon as their success began to affect the birthrate. Meanwhile, just on the mountains between there and Cuernavaca, already badly deforested and eroded, at least four fires were burning, by my own observation, in the remaining timber, probably deliberately started. And there was no question but that soil was slipping away, and water tables falling, at an alarming rate over important parts of the country. This did not promise basic changes in those conditions which had made Mexico a bitter, tragic country, and which had buried so deeply in the Mexican soul those qualities which enable man to entertain the thought and hope of a way out of his squalor and ignominy.

Cathedral of the Virgin of Guadalupe, February 26

In the scene of the procession, as it moved past us, there was an overwhelming electric starkness that rocked the spectator like a bolt of lightning: the gross, bleary faces of the priests; the desperate intentness of the kneeling, scurrying women; the heads of the choir boys thrown back and their faces uplifted as they sang, their child-eyes glancing upward at the great Roman columns and vaults with their gold ornamentation; the dirty, bursting shoes sticking out from under the priestly and choral robes and shuffling over the worn flagstones. Here was the full-throated utterance of the human mass, with all its age-old vitality, with its spiritual dependence, its will to believe and its readiness to submit to the organization and regimentation of that same will.

I drove back to the airport still saturated with the penetrating eloquence of this scene. I have never taken offense at the thesis of the Roman Church that many men require a spiritual as well as a profane framework of law: a moral order founded on an appreciation of the dilemmas of birth and death and of the requirements of social living, a moral order drawn up by those who are wiser and more experienced than themselves and capable of channelizing into the body of spiritual law the ponderous experiences of the millennia of human progress. For many people it is always better that there should be *some* moral law, even an imperfect one or an entirely arbitrary one, than that there should be none, for the human being who recognizes no moral restrictions and has no sense of humility is worse than the foulest and cruelest beast. . . .

This procession, in Mexico City, 1950, was ominously reminiscent of one held many thousands of miles away, one day in the 19th century, on the dusty outskirts of a Russian village, and recorded so brilliantly by Repin in his famous canvas.[40] The Church will have to plunge deeply into its fund of Christian tradition to find the understanding, the selflessness, the inspiration, and the true charity which alone can save it in such countries as Mexico from the ills which befell the Church of the Eastern Rite in Russia.

I did not find those qualities in the faces of those who walked in this procession, any more than Repin found them in that 19th century crowd moving out of the village to supplicate the Almighty for rainfall to relieve the parched fields.

Guatemala City, February 26

The Ambassador[41] met me there, and we talked about his problems with the local Communists, who are probably stronger in that country than in any other country in Latin America.[42]

Panama City, February 27

I stayed overnight with the Ambassador[43] in the spacious, new Embassy which the Government has built. We talked at dinner about scorpions and snakes and Panamanian Communists.

40. *Religious Procession in Kursk Province* was painted by the nineteenth-century populist-minded artist Ilya Repin.

41. The U.S. ambassador to Guatemala was Richard C. Patterson Jr.

42. In 1954, the CIA would overthrow the democratically elected, left-leaning government of Guatemala.

43. The U.S. ambassador to Panama was Monnett B. Davis.

Caracas, February 28

Here was a tropical country in the subsoil of which reposed great quantities of a liquid essential to the present stage of industrialization in the U.S. Americans were extracting this liquid and hauling it away. The local population had not moved a finger to create this wealth, would have been incapable of developing it, and did not require for its own needs the thousandth part of what was apparently there. However, for the privilege of being able to enter and extract this liquid, our firms were paying hundreds of millions of dollars annually into the coffers of the Venezuelan Government, a sort of ransom to the theory of state sovereignty and the principle of non-intervention which we had consented to adopt. The traffic could bear it. Prices of oil permitted it. The companies could pay this tribute and still make money. . . .

There was plenty of oil under the ground. Perhaps this could go on for a long time. There were signs that the competitive position of high priced Venezuelan oil was falling off, but important iron deposits had been found, and new capital was already pouring in for their development. Still, one could not avoid the conviction that some day, some how, there would inevitably be a terrible awakening: a day when the morphine of oil company or steel company royalties and taxes would no longer enter the system of Venezuelan economy, when the country would be thrown back upon its own resources, and when someone would have the unpleasant task of dealing with a terribly disoriented and intellectually debilitated population. It would behoove us to think about that day, and to anticipate it. . . .

Incidentally, all of nature in Venezuela was a bilious yellow-brown.

Trinidad, March 4

Coming to Trinidad from Central and South America, one senses clearly the difference between English and Spanish colonization, even when it involved super-imposition of a colonial strata onto a colored native population. The colored people of the West Indies, while by no means adjusted to, or satisfied with, British rule, make an impression of relaxation and self-respect and placidity by comparison with the violent characteristics of people in the Spanish colonized areas.

Rio de Janeiro, March 8

The Brazilians have acquired, from the humane and cosmopolitan Portuguese, who were their founding fathers, a gentleness which in my view is the essence of civilization and for which one can only bear them respect and affection. But they are no more free than other Latin American peoples from the addiction to a pathological urbanism, out of all proportion to their resources and strangely devoid of real content, an urbanism that moves them to come to the city to spend their money and to invest in urban real estate that which they cannot spend. In this sense, there is a certain sad futility which hangs over this continent, and he who would understand it must picture to himself these spectacular luxury districts of the great South American cities.

Montevideo, March 10

There is more self respect here, more relaxation. Uruguay is spared the racial problem, has a large mixture of that Italian ingredient which seems so healthy and constructive for South American cultures. People are quiet, and decently dressed, and seem to be going normally about their business, instead of seething with frustrated hatred and indignation about this or that. Yet wool exports to the United States are paralyzed by a communist strike for no other reason than that they *do* go to the United States, and we are conceived to be suffering somehow by their absence. And the long rows of warehouses near the railroad station are patrolled by mounted police lest the strikers get at the stocks of wool and destroy them.

Miami, March 20

I ate breakfast at the airport restaurant and then was driven in, by the State Department representative, to the railroad station. There I had to change my reservation at the ticket window. The attendant was new, and his buddy, who was breaking him in, gave him advice on how to transact this business. Their attitude toward this work in hand was characterized by that relaxed, unemotional but utterly objective and self-respecting attitude which is the mark of our people. The basic reliability and decency and common sense which sprang from the performance of this simple transaction struck me, the traveler—coming in out of the heavens from the tense, charged confusion of another world—with the brilliant force of contrast, and I went out onto the station platform with a sense of deep gratitude and of happy acceptance of this American world, marked as it is by the mediocrity of all that is exalted, and the excellence of all that which is without pretense.

Princeton, June 10

It is with reluctance, and as an act of self-discipline, that I address myself again to maintaining a set of personal notes. So much of life seems a repetition of the known. But with the coming departure from government work, there will be need for a self-imposed discipline of thought: for a greater independent effort to achieve quietness and detachment from environment. Without this, too much can slip by. . . .

After lunch, we went on to Princeton. I was going to stop off there, for a day at my class reunion. Driving around, in the baking heat of mid-afternoon, we finally found the 1925 headquarters at one of the eating clubs on Prospect Street. A burly undergraduate was checking in the arrivals. He checked my name off the list, and coolly asked me for $75.00. I was horrified. I was head over heels in debt. I couldn't have raised $75.00 by any stretch of the imagination. I fled, and repaired in panic to the Institute.[44] Here, fortified by Oppie's genial serenity,[45] I made arrangements to have a telegram sent from my office in Washington, expressing regrets at my inability to attend.

[Unhappy with his diminished influence in the administration, Kennan was intent on leaving government. But, as the following entry shows, he was willing to stay on if he was awarded the most prestigious ambassadorship, to Great Britain. Undersecretary of State James E. Webb, who was close to Secretary Acheson, did not seem eager to pursue the matter. The London post was a plum usually granted to a wealthy political donor, such as the businessman Walter S. Gifford, who succeeded Ambassador Lewis Williams Douglas.]

Washington, June 14

There was a long meeting on psychological warfare. Then talked to Mr. Webb, who said he was still hoping that I would get tired of private life very soon and return to the Department, and that for that reason he was holding the position open. I told him that I really thought it was better for me to be outside of Government at this time and that I was planning to be away at least for the full academic year. I told him that plans for the more distant future would depend somewhat of course on what use

44. The Institute for Advanced Study, which Kennan would make his academic home for the next half-century.
45. "Oppie" is J. Robert Oppenheimer.

they could make of me. Only one thing I would mention, which I had already spoken to him about, namely that if there were really no other alternative to having some completely unqualified person follow Douglas in London, I would be willing to do that rather than see a post of such great delicacy and importance misused in this way. Mr. Webb said he had already spoken to the Secretary about this but that they considered the post was so expensive that I would not be able to afford it. . . .

In the afternoon I received Mr. Heindel[46] of the Social Science Research Council, whose desiderata and purposes in coming to see me remained, after his visit, as fuzzy to my mind as much of the language used by the social science school among the academicians. I had spent an hour on the train on Monday going through the papers he sent me, and from these I gathered that there was a certain feeling of frustration in the social science world over their inability to be of assistance to the Government in its foreign policy tasks. They feel that they are the discoverers of some new technique for the uncovering of knowledge about the world, and that the Government ought to have use for this. They have been promoting concentrated programs of area study in various U.S. universities, which I think is all to the good and much needed as a backstop for study and for governmental understanding of foreign countries. But I told him that I was suspicious of collective effort in this field, in the sense that I felt that while the work of many people could contribute to appreciations which would be valuable, those appreciations would always have to stem from the mind of a single person and could never be greater or wider than that. In other words, there is no collective substitute for plain individual wisdom. The social science techniques may contribute to that type of wisdom, but they cannot replace it or improve upon it. . . .

I asked Clubb whether it had never occurred to him that the present situation bore a strong resemblance to the period between the Boxer uprising and the Russian-Japanese War: a period marked by violent anti-foreign feeling in China, by a forced withdrawal of the Japanese from the mainland picture, and by consequent rapid Russian penetration of Manchuria and Korea. He said that he agreed with the parallel but that if it were to be carried to conclusion, the Japanese would have to be given the wherewithal to play their part again in the Far East, as they had done at the time of the Russian-Japanese War. To this I replied: "Precisely," and the discussion ended on that note.

46. Richard H. Heindel.

June 25

After glancing at the headlines of the Sunday papers, announcing the attack of the North Korean forces against South Korea, I changed clothes and hurried down to the office.

Found the Secretary in conference with a group of people, including Jessup, Rusk and Matthews;[47] they had spent a good part of the day, as I gathered, arranging for UN action and now, the Security Council having acted with almost unbelievable speed and passed a resolution calling on all its members not to assist the North Korean forces, but rather to help the UN in its efforts to prevent this aggression, they were getting down to the consideration of what the U.S. action should be. When my views were asked, which was shortly after my entry into the room, I had to plead unfamiliarity with what had been discussed and done so far. I said that one thing seemed certain to me: that whatever else happened it would be impossible for us not to take prompt steps to assure that Formosa did not fall to the communists since this, coming on top of the Korean attack, would be calamitous to our position in the Far East. We continued our discussion until about 6:15, when the Secretary went to the airport to meet the President. It had been arranged that the Secretary, accompanied by a few of the senior officials of the Department, would have dinner with the President and with a number of the military leaders. This had been arranged before I got there. After the Secretary had left for the airport, I was told that he had specifically said that he wanted me present at this occasion, but his secretary said that she was certain that somehow or other my name had not been included on the list which was sent to the White House, and that she also knew that only a certain number of places were available for the dinner and that there would be no room for extra plates. I therefore went home for supper and returned later in the evening to be on hand when the Secretary got back from Blair House. This occurred about 11:00 p.m., as I recall it.

He said that the President had given orders that the Seventh Fleet was to start north from the Philippines and had authorized the Navy to move other units westward from the Pacific Coast to reinforce it. He had authorized MacArthur's headquarters to give air cover for the evacuation of American citizens from Korea. Finally, he had placed the strictest injunctions on everyone that there was to be no further discussion of this matter pending further decisions.

47. State Department advisers Philip C. Jessup, Dean Rusk, and H. Freeman Matthews.

June 26

This morning, in addition to attending the War College commencement, I sat in on an extensive discussion in the Secretary's office on the attitude we should adopt in the Korean matter. This discussion went on most of the noon hour and carried over into the afternoon. I stated it as my deep conviction that the U.S. had no choice but to accept this challenge and to make it its purpose to see to it that South Korea was restored to the rule of the Republic of Korea. The question of what we should commit to this purpose was simply a question of what was required for the completion of the task. I reiterated my view that something also had to be done about Formosa, pointing out that this matter had great urgency. This whole question was discussed at length and the others present, who were the senior advisers in the Department, all gave their views.

My own concept of the reasons why I felt we should take the position I advocated was expressed in a paper I prepared during the course of the day on a question which had been advanced last night by the President. The President had said that he wanted to be advised at once of any prospects for further Russian action in other areas, and it had been decided earlier in the day that the task of preparing the State Department's position on this point would be assigned to me. I therefore, after discussions with the Policy Planning Staff, prepared during the course of the day the following paper, which constitutes in itself a pretty good picture of the background of my own thinking.

At about 3:30 in the afternoon, the Secretary broke off the discussions we had been having with him and said that he wanted time to be alone and to dictate. We were called in about 6:30 p.m., and he read to us a paper he had produced, which was a first draft of the statement finally issued by the President, and which was not significantly changed by the time it finally appeared, the following day, as the President's statement. I think this fact is of historical significance, since it shows Mr. Acheson's advocacy of the course actually taken by this Government was not something pressed upon him by the military leaders, but rather something arrived at by himself, in solitary deliberation and in the knowledge of all that was at stake.

By the time we had been over the Secretary's draft it was already after 7:00 and he was due at the White House early in the evening. All of us who were in conference with him therefore went with him to the Metropolitan Club, where we had a hasty supper.

Since it was decided that the same group should go to the White House as had gone the night before, I stayed away and went home for a short rest. I arrived back at the State Department at the exact moment that the Secretary and the others returned. The situation was as follows: The President had approved the statement in principle but the text of it was to be finally worked out by the Departments of State and Defense and be ready for release the following day about 12:00 o'clock, by which time the President expected to have received and consulted with Congressional leaders. Meanwhile, it had been understood that the Joint Chiefs of Staff would at once issue orders to our forces in the Far East implementing the decisions set forth in the statement.

We therefore immediately set about the final polishing up of the statement, and were busy with this until after midnight. When it was finished, the text was telephoned to the Defense establishment, in order that we might get their comments the first thing in the morning and submit an agreed version to the President. We then faced the question of communicating to Chiang Kai-shek the decision with regard to Formosa. Obviously it would be improper and undesirable for him to receive this news only from the press and radio, and some communication would have to be made to him at once.

June 27

During the course of Monday's deliberations, I had brought up the problem of what we would do in case our forces operating in Korea were to be opposed by Soviet forces identifiable through their uniforms or insignia. I had stressed the importance, in my view, of our recognizing that this would create a new situation, calling for a new set of decisions; otherwise it would be possible for us to "back into" a war with Russia without meaning to do so, simply through the execution of the orders already given to our forces and designed to meet only a local situation. Accordingly, I had been asked by Mr. Webb and the others to put my views on this subject in writing, in order that the matter might be broached to the Defense establishment. Therefore, I got to work on this first thing in the morning, and produced the following paper. After slight modifications by the Secretary, Jessup and others, this was discussed early in the afternoon with the Secretary of the Army Pace,[48] who undertook to lay the matter before the Defense establishment. It was understood that he would not use my contribution as a State Department paper, but would present it merely as some personal thoughts of mine.

That took up a good part of the morning and the early afternoon.

48. Frank Pace Jr.

The President's announcement was made about twelve o'clock. About half an hour prior to that time Perkins,[49] the head of the European office, phoned me in some perturbation that he had, arriving at that moment, all the envoys of the North Atlantic Pact countries whom he had been instructed to receive for the purpose of communicating to them the text of the President's statement, but that he had been given no briefing whatsoever on what to say to them and did not know what to do about it. The Secretary, Rusk, Matthews, and Jessup had all gone to the White House to be present when the President spoke to the Congressional leaders, and they were therefore not available to give him any help. I therefore agreed to go up and speak to the Ambassadors myself, and did so at once. There was quite a group of them, since most of them had brought at least one assistant. Perkins first read the communique over to them twice, so that they might all take careful note of its contents. He then gave the floor to me.

I had given no prior thought about what to say to them, and had no instructions, so I had to ad lib, and did so along the following lines. First I analyzed Soviet motives, stressing the possible relationship of the Korean move to the problem of the Japanese peace treaty. . . . I also pointed out that the timing might have been determined by the simple fact that they had by this time concluded the training and equipping of the North Korean forces to a degree where they considered them adequate to the task. I then said that in deciding to employ our own forces there we were not acting under any strong convictions about the strategic importance of the territory but rather in the light of our analysis of the damage to world confidence and morale which would have been produced had we not so acted. I analyzed the probable consequences of a failure on our part to act, in their relation to Japan, to Formosa, to the Philippines, to Indochina, and to Europe. I told them that we had no intention to do more than to restore the *status quo ante* and no intention to proceed to the conquest of northern Korea.

I said that if the Soviet Union threw in its own forces against us that would create an entirely new situation, both internationally and from the standpoint of our own internal decisions in this country, and would call for a review of our entire position. I explained the relationship of our action to a resolution which had been passed by the United Nations Security Council, saying that while we considered that we were acting

49. George W. Perkins Jr.

in pursuance to, and in the spirit of, the Security Council resolution, we also recognized that we were in a peculiar situation in this respect in as much as we had a special responsibility arising out of our status in Japan and were the only one of the members of the United Nations, except China and the Soviet Union, who had forces in that immediate vicinity. I said that I could conceive, therefore, that what might constitute our duty in pursuance of the Security Council resolution might be different from what other countries would consider their duty to be. We were well aware, I said, that in what we were doing there was an element of grave risk; we were convinced, however, that the risks of our failure to do this would be greater still.

There were a few questions afterward, and then the meeting broke up. I had the impression that the effect had been favorable and that the ambassadors were by and large sympathetic to our action and to the considerations I had set forth to them.

Later in the afternoon, one of the officials of the Press Section phoned me to say that he had heard that I had given a very successful presentation of our position to the envoys of the Atlantic Pact countries and to ask whether I would not give an off-the-record briefing along similar lines to a group of selected correspondents. I stated that I would be pleased to do it if instructed to do so but that I would not wish to make the suggestion myself. Word came back later in the day that the Secretary had disapproved of the idea and had phoned the President, who also disapproved. So nothing came of it, but I could not help feeling that it was a mistake not to give to the press the most complete presentation of the background of our action.

June 28

At the usual meeting with the Secretary the first thing in the morning, Mr. Webb said that in the evening he had discussed with people in the Pentagon and with the President the questions I had raised with regard to the possibility of our encountering Russian forces and that he had encountered a feeling in both places that MacArthur's[50] orders were quite sufficient and he should carry them out, regardless. I said that never had I ever spoken about anything at that table in the Secretary's office about which I felt more strongly than I did about this, that we were dealing here with a matter of the utmost seriousness and it was of the greatest

50. General Douglas MacArthur.

importance that we know at all times exactly what it is that we were doing and not let ourselves get carried into anything by accident. Rusk then said that a meeting had been arranged later in the morning with some of the people from the office of the Secretary of Defense, and that we were to talk the matter out there.

When we met with the Defense officials, who included two Assistant Secretaries of the Army and two or three officers, I made the initial statement on this subject again, and emphasized that what I was interested in was getting everyone in our Government, including General MacArthur's headquarters and the men on the planes and the ships, to realize that if they encounter Soviet forces this would constitute a new situation requiring new decisions, and that they should therefore, while continuing to defend themselves and to terminate successfully the engagements they were in, make it their main concern to get back and report what had happened and should not needlessly aggravate these conflicts with Soviet forces until this Government had had an opportunity to review the situation. I pointed out that if we did not make this distinction clear, and went on the basis that our existing orders would be followed out, come what may, and required no amplification, then we would be assigning to the Russians or to chance the decision as to whether there would be a new world war. This, I said, was a decision of which we had no right to divest ourselves. Much more was at stake than just Korea or even just the interests of the U.S., and if we were to be led into such a conflict it should be by the most grave and deliberate decision on our part.

The upshot of the meeting was that we drafted a brief statement setting forth the gist of this position, and the defense officials took it back for consideration in the Pentagon.

Immediately after lunch, I went to the White House for a meeting of the National Security Council, attended by the President. Here this same question of the possible widening of the conflict was discussed. Secretary Johnson said that they were not averse to giving MacArthur orders along this line, but that they wanted to wrap them up in a set of orders having a wider scope, rather than issue them to him as an isolated order. They said they would proceed rapidly with this. No objection was voiced.

General Vandenberg[51] set forth the difficulties which the Air Force was facing by virtue of weather and other factors, and showed how their situation would be eased if they were able to operate north of the 38th parallel.

51. General Hoyt S. Vandenberg was the Air Force chief of staff.

After returning to the Department, we met again with the Secretary.[52] In the course of the conversation I said that I thought we might consider an alteration of our position about the 38th parallel, to the following effect: that while we would continue to state it as our purpose not to reoccupy any territory north of the parallel, we would not limit our forces to operation south of the parallel but would say that they would operate anywhere in Korea where their operations might promote the achievement of the mission set forth above. This suggestion was generally welcomed; in fact it was clear that other people had been thinking along the same lines, and I can claim no originality for the thought. But I think it was instrumental in determining the establishment of a favorable State Department position on this point. . . .

In the middle of the day, Wednesday, Averell Harriman and Chip Bohlen arrived from Paris, and Chip threw himself into the work at my side, helping me with problems I faced.

June 29

Upon arrival in the morning, I ordered the establishment of two intelligence analysis teams: one for the intentions and attitudes of the Soviet Government, and the other for the same thing with respect to the Peiping Government.

The code room sent down the telegram copy of Moscow's report on the reply to the Soviet note. It was unprovocative, and appeared to be dictated primarily by a resolve to keep Moscow's responsibility in the affair entirely disengaged in the formal sense. At the same time we got word of a highly bellicose and inflammatory statement issued by Chou En-lai,[53] constituting the nearest thing in communist practice (the communist governments never declare war) to a declaration of war against us and calling on the peoples of the East to rise up against us. While it seemed to me that this statement must have bent the bow of Moscow-Peiping relations pretty far and might turn out to be something of a blunder on the part of the Chinese Communists, it indicated, when taken together with the Moscow reply, a pretty clear pattern of Soviet intentions: namely, to keep out of this business themselves in every way but to embroil us to the maximum with their Korean and Chinese satellites. . . .

All day the news from Korea was most discouraging. The South Korean forces are rapidly melting away and leaving the task to us. The

52. Dean Acheson.
53. Chou En-lai was premier of the People's Republic of China.

picture was brightened only by two things that happened to me during the day. I was stimulated early in the morning by overhearing a radio program in which, immediately following the reading of the news from Korea, a colored woman sang a song with the following refrain:

> Save that Confederate money, boys;
> The South shall rise again.

When we went in the morning to the National Security Council offices, which are in the old State Department building, I observed to Matthews while we were riding up in the elevator that if we hadn't moved out of that old building all these things would never have happened. To my surprise the colored elevator woman turned around and said with great firmness and enthusiasm: "That's right, sir."

June 30

On arrival at the office I was called right into Matthew's office for conference. The Secretary had gone to the White House and wanted our advice on certain matters immediately upon his return. The matters were these: Chiang Kai-shek had offered 30,000 troops for the support of the Korean venture. What should our answer be? It was our view, based on the advice of one of the intelligence analysis teams which I had established, that the Generalissimo's offer of troops was probably motivated by three considerations: namely, (1) his desire to establish himself in the eyes of the American people and the world as a full-fledged, fighting ally and to recoup his own prestige abroad; (2) a desire to place Chinese troops on the Korean peninsula so that, in the event that the Korean conflict enlarges into World War III and the U.S. successfully drives back the North Koreans and Soviet armies, Chinese troops will be in a position to move into Manchuria; and (3) a wish to get off the island Chinese forces of whose loyalty he is not completely confident. . . .

We were told that our military people did not want to have these forces; they would arrive without supplies or ammunition, they would be of doubtful political reliability if they met Chinese Communist forces, etc. . . .

We also discussed the question of what line to take with regard to Chou's flamboyant and bellicose statement, issued yesterday, placing Communist China in effect in a state of hostilities with the U.S. I said that it seemed to me that the Russian game was obviously to play their

Asiatic satellites against us; that this was placing a great strain on Soviet satellite relationships; that these relationships therefore consisted the weak point, against which we should drive. I therefore proposed that we take a position roughly as follows, and assert it with a powerful propaganda campaign:

"We refuse to permit ourselves to be provoked into any conflict with the Chinese people by the screams of this desperate clique in Peiping, which is being revealed more clearly every day as a group of irresponsible puppets sacrificing the blood and treasure of China for purposes which have nothing whatsoever to do with Chinese interests."

The news from Korea was very bad. During the night, General MacArthur had asked permission to throw in ground forces. He had been authorized provisionally to throw in one regiment, and had been told that he would receive further orders as soon as the matter could be discussed with the President.

One more matter was discussed at this early morning conference: namely the question of our attitude in case, as seemed probable, a proposal were to be made in the United Nations for high level four-power conferences. Bohlen made the point that the danger involved in discussions with the Russians had always been previously that such discussions might have the effect of standing in the way of firm action on our part. Now that we had acted there was no further danger in discussion, and we should show ourselves ready at all times to talk matters over. This was approved and our position was determined accordingly. . . .

Chip and I were in agreement on what I had hoped I would have an opportunity to add in my statement to the Secretary: namely, that as the conflict widened it was absolutely essential that we take steps on mobilization here at home which would put us in a position to stand the attrition of such a widening military situation in the Far East.

July 1

The usual morning meeting was begun with a long intelligence briefing, which made it pretty evident that from now on the task was solely ours, the Korean Army having pretty well collapsed, and that in view of weather prospects the Air Force would not be able to develop anything like its maximum capabilities. . . .

I said that in my opinion the Russians had placed us over a barrel: in a position where, if we could not fulfill our mission in southern Korea with existing forces and could not reinforce them without danger of depletion of our present small establishment, we had no alternative but to adopt measures of at least partial mobilization. I said that I could not judge whether the Russians were aware that this was the choice they were confronting us with, and wondered about this, for it did not seem to be in their interests to force us to improve our military posture. But I did wish to emphasize that we had to go through with our purpose in Korea, come what may, and that if this called for more than we could afford now to give to the venture, we had no choice but to mobilize greater strength. I pointed out that if our commanders had been told, toward the close of the recent war in the Pacific, that all Japanese resistance would cease and the only task then was to cope with an army of 90,000 Koreans with 100 tanks and small air support and to occupy Korea to the 38th parallel, they would have considered it a small operation indeed. This, I said, was proof that our ability to cope with this situation was a question of our will and not of our capability.

Following this meeting, the Secretary suggested that he, Averell Harriman, Chip Bohlen and myself go out to Leesburg and talk to General Marshall.[54] A phone call was put through to the General, and it was arranged that we should come for lunch. We departed immediately and got out there soon after one o'clock. The General was in fine form. We sat on the lawn under the trees and had our business talk then and there, over our events of the week and the position in which we found ourselves today. The General listened very attentively and silently, as he always does when a problem is being exposed before him, and then gave us his views vigorously and without hesitation.

Pointing out that all of his statements were based on the very scanty information which the Secretary had just been able to give him and not on any detailed background of fact, he said that there could be no doubt about the proper course for us to pursue. We had begun this thing; now we had to go through with it. His greatest worry had been that for the sake of Korea we might have risked an alienation of public opinion in Western Europe, which was the area of the greatest real strategic importance. What we had told him had relieved his fears on this point, but he was deeply disturbed over what he understood to be the attitudes in the Defense establishment, particularly with their relation to the Department of State. He did not feel that we needed to send more in the way of military support to MacArthur. It was a common failing of commanders

54. General George C. Marshall, the Army chief of staff in World War II, would become secretary of defense in September 1950.

in the field to ask for more than they needed, and MacArthur was far from being an exception to this rule. He should be told to do this job with what he had. He could do it if he applied himself to it. The depletion of the forces on Japan was not dangerous. Any amphibious action against Japan would be a great undertaking, and a very risky one in the face of any sizeable air and naval defense.

He was particularly concerned about the initial tendency of the Air Force to think that they could do this all alone. That, he said, was the same old thing. The Air Force and the Navy were full of ideas about how they could do things, and their functions were indeed tremendously important, but when it came down to the last analysis, you could never get along without the "little fellow in the mud." Also, he felt that our people had made a mistake in the organization of the Korean Army. He had begged them to organize it along the lines of the Philippine scouts, using experienced older American non-commissioned officers and filling up the ranks with Koreans. Instead, they had insisted on trying to build up a new army from scratch, officers corps and all. Nevertheless, he was not discouraged, and he felt that this might turn out to be a good thing in many ways.

On the way back to Washington, we talked matters over and agreed that it was important that the General should have an opportunity to state his views to the President in the very near future. Mr. Harriman undertook to get into touch with the President and to make the suggestion, but we agreed that it would neither be fair to the General nor wise for any of us to try to relay the General's views to the President.

July 3

Chip, who had worked over the weekend, told me that there had been some discussion of a desire on the part of the Air Force to send a large contingent of B-29s to the Korean theater, at the cost of a certain depletion of our reserve strength in these planes. He was worried lest this might reflect in part a preoccupation on the part of the Air Force with their own prestige, and a desire to recoup for their failure up to this time to stop the North Korean Army. If any such motives were present, he was afraid that the Air Force, once it had the planes out there, would want to roam farther and farther afield in their bombing activities and that this might lead to wider complications which we had not bargained for. He was much upset, and I think rightly so, because when I stated this view before a large meeting on Sunday, Averell Harriman had said that this reminded him of the wartime days when he and his advisers had discussed matters of this sort in Moscow, and that then, as now, there had always been timid voices which he had had to override. Chip was much worried about this, because he felt that it was essential to our usefulness that we should feel free to give our honest opinions in instances of this sort without their becoming the occasion of offensive interpretations.

It seemed to him particularly unjust that such a reproach should come from Averell, and above all with a reference to the wartime days; for actually during the recent war the sides were usually just the reverse of that, and it had generally been Chip and I who had been obliged to argue with Averell for a firmer policy vis-a-vis the Soviet Union. He was also afraid that this signified the beginning of another unhealthy relationship between the State Department and the armed services similar to that which had prevailed during the last war—a relationship in which the State Department had no say in the determination of policy and hesitated to state its views on policy matters for fear of being accused of obstructing the war effort.

July 9

Chip told me about the Russian approach to the British for suggestions concerning the mediation of the Korean matter and of his anxieties lest the British mess the thing up. Chip pointed out, quite correctly I think, that Stalin, with his contempt for small peoples, must assume that the ultimate outcome of U.S. intervention will be a reversal of the military fortunes of the North Koreans, and that he is therefore holding open the possibilities of a settlement which would prevent the communist reverse from going too far.

July 12

I said that I thought the most dangerous feature of this view was the assumption that what the Russians might do in the future was somehow without relation to the attitude we would take at this time. . . . I had a long talk with Chip Bohlen in the evening. Discussion hinged on the difficulties we had encountered in arriving at an agreed position within the Government about probable future developments. In general, the nervousness and consciousness of responsibility is so great around Washington that it is impossible to get people to set their signatures to anything as risky, and as little founded in demonstrable fact, as an analysis of Soviet intentions based on the subjective experience and instinct and judgment of persons like Chip and myself.

Plainly the Government has moved into an area where there is a reluctance to recognize the finer distinctions of the psychology of our adversaries, for the reason that movement in this sphere of speculation is all too undependable, too relative, and too subtle to be comfortable or tolerable to people who feel themselves confronted with the grim responsibility of recommending decisions which may mean war or peace. In such times, it is safer and easier to cease the attempt to analyze the probabilities involved in your enemy's mental processes or calculate his weaknesses. It seems safer to give him the benefit of every doubt in matters of strength and to credit him indiscriminately with *all* aggressive designs, even when some of them are mutually contradictory. In these circumstances, I was inclined to wonder, and I think Chip was, too, whether the day had not passed when the Government had use for the qualities of persons like ourselves, for the effort at cool and rational analysis in the unfirm substance of the imponderables, for an estimate of our Soviet adversaries based on their possible weaknesses as well as their possible strengths. In the somewhat childish and abusive atmosphere of a democratic society already disbalanced by McCarthyism, there was use only for the cruder and the starker concepts.

July 14

I have become slowly and reluctantly convinced of the necessity of accepting the analyses of our intelligence agencies which tell us that Germany, the Low Countries, and France, at least, could not really be defended against a Soviet invasion. While I think this represents an over-simplified view, and rests quite possibly on an exaggerated picture of Soviet military strength, I cannot prove my position, and I realize that our government has no choice but to operate on the basis of these analyses.

But if this is the basis on which we are going to operate, then what is the use of pouring these arms into Western Europe? Surely the main deficiency on the Western side, and the decisive one, is the continued military prostration of Western Germany. If we are unprepared to remedy this deficiency, of what avail will be these military shipments to the secondary military powers of Western Europe? I have always approved of some military aid to Western Europe, as a morale builder and a symbol of U.S. support. But to pour great quantities in there is another thing. If there are serious initial Soviet successes, as we are obliged to expect there will be in Germany, then France will probably go by default, and all of this expensive equipment may be lost to the Russians without their having to fire a shot for its capture. Possibly this is too gloomy a view, and I hope it is, but it is the only one warranted to date by the state of French public opinion we have observed: the jitteriness, the readiness to assume a dependence on others, and the tendency to blame everyone but themselves for their situation.

July 17

Nitze dropped in to see me—very tired, harried, and worried. The effort to chart out a tentative set of ideas for our reactions to other possible Soviet moves had bogged down completely in the NSC.[55] The military would not cooperate by sending anyone of real authority to participate in the discussions; we were still stuck on the analysis of the situation and had not even gotten to the question of the possible courses of action; and the State Department itself had as yet done no adequate preparatory work on this latter subject. The initial work along these lines ought, he considered, to be done jointly with the responsible military planners, but there was no forum for it.

All this, I thought, was nothing other than the failure of the President to assign clear lines of individual responsibility and authority, leaving the key portions of the executive apparatus to wallow around in the cluttering impediments of the committee system. . . .

I found on my desk, this morning, an intelligence estimate about the military situation of Formosa, which disturbed me considerably. I feared that we were failing to take sufficiently seriously the threat to the island, were relying too much on the Chinese forces on the island, and were allowing ambiguities to exist with respect to the question of military reconnaissance. I therefore drafted a memo urging the Department to do three things, to wit: (1) make sure that the Defense establishment was fully aware of the seriousness of the danger of a successful communist move against Formosa; (b) make sure that they understood that the Chinese troops on the island would be quite unreliable in the event that any communist forces at all were to succeed in landing there, and that we were therefore entirely on our own in this business; and (c) make sure that there were no misunderstandings between the Defense establishment and ourselves about questions of reconnaissance along the Chinese coast with a view to spotting preparations for an invasion attempt. . . .

As far as I can see, it makes not the slightest difference whether or

55. National Security Council.

not the Chinese Communists come into the UN, and the fact that they might come in would be no reason, in my opinion, why we should feel obliged to have diplomatic relations with them. I hate to see what seems to me a minor issue, on which we should never have allowed ourselves to get hooked, become something which the Russians can use to our disadvantage in the Korean affair.

I was shouted down on this. Mr. Dulles[56] pointed out that if we were to do this it would look as though we were retreating on the Chinese Communist issue in the belief that we were thereby buying some Russian concessions about Korea; that this would not be the case and the Russians would still not agree to anything satisfactory about Korea; and that it would therefore look to our public as though we had been tricked into giving up something for nothing. I recognized the force of this and realize that nothing can be done, but I hope that some day history will record this as an instance of the damage done to the conduct of our foreign policy by the irresponsible and bigoted interference of the Chinese lobby and its friends in Congress.

Had a long talk with John Foster Dulles this afternoon. He was preparing a memorandum urging that we give immediate attention to the rearmament of Germany and Japan. I pointed out to him what I felt to be the significance of police forces as a means of bridging the gap between our need for creating strength in those quarters, on the one hand, and the fears of our allies, on the other.

July 20

Another matter which I raised at the Secretary's meeting this morning was the question of our policy toward Germany at this time. I pointed out that to the extent that we were forced to occupy ourselves militarily in other areas, the amount of energy and resources which we could devote to the problems of occupation in Germany and Japan might at any time be significantly reduced. I said I thought we should not rule out the possibility of a situation in which there would still be no invasion of Germany, and yet we would be forced to reduce our occupational and directive effort. This was already happening in Japan. For this reason, I thought it urgently important to move ahead rapidly with putting the

56. John Foster Dulles was the Republican expert on foreign policy who would become secretary of state under President Dwight D. Eisenhower. Secretary Dulles would humiliate Kennan, who still had some time before retirement. Dulles not only neglected to appoint Kennan to a new position; he also neglected to inform him of that decision.

German and Japanese regimes on a fully independent footing, able to carry on successfully without us.

[On July 15, General MacArthur launched a daring and stunningly successful amphibious landing at Inchon, behind North Korean lines. With the fortunes of war suddenly reversed, MacArthur began driving north of the 38th parallel into North Korea. In this next entry Kennan predicted the disaster that would befall U.S. and South Korean forces in November–December. The Communist Chinese, alarmed at the Americans advancing through North Korea up to their border, intervened with a huge number of troops. The resulting debacle was one of the worst in U.S. military history.]

July 21

We must remember that what we were doing in Korea was, although for good political reason, nevertheless an unsound thing, and that the further we were to advance up the peninsula the more unsound it would become from the military standpoint. If we were actually to advance beyond the neck of the peninsula, we would be getting into an area where mass could be used against us and where we would be distinctly at a disadvantage. This, I thought, increased the importance of a clear concept of our being able to terminate our action at the proper point, and it was desirable that we should make sure that we did not frighten the Russians into action which would interfere with this.

July 24

I had a long session with two officials of the Department on the subject of the propaganda lines which we should follow in the event that we should find ourselves in a state of general hostilities with Russia. I urged that our propaganda effort be rigidly divided into that which was addressed to peoples under enemy control and that addressed to peoples elsewhere. As far as those people behind the Iron Curtain were concerned, it was my proposal that we should treat them from the beginning on the assumption that they were allied with us in our struggle against the political power under which they lived. Proceeding on this assumption, I urged that we make our broadcasts to them as business-like and concise as possible, and addressed strictly to the requirements of their own situation. Since radio listening and attention to other media of our propaganda would always be dangerous for them, I proposed that we exclude all extraneous material, in order that the risk to them from receiving our propaganda might be reduced to a minimum. I argued that we did not need to convince them of the iniquity of the Soviet powers that they knew much more about that than we did. We also did not need to waste breath trying to persuade them of our own virtues as a nation. They would be less concerned about all that than about the question whether we were going to liberate them or whether we were going to fail to liberate them. The main point to be emphasized with respect to the war was the inevitability of defeat and disaster for Soviet power. We would do well, I thought, to show at all times a solicitude for the safety of our listeners. We should therefore tell them at the start that they should not listen unnecessarily, i.e. that they should divide this labor with others if they were confident that they could trust them, and that they should be careful not to provoke their own authorities prematurely, but should take very good care to register in their memories the names and faces of all those acting as agents for Soviet power, so that there would be no confusion when the day finally came.

With respect to the countries outside the Soviet sphere, I pleaded for a differentiated approach. There was no use, I thought, in talking about freedom and human rights to people who had never known either. Again, I urged a soft-pedalling of propaganda about our own virtues, with the one exception of the element of strength. I felt it much more important to convince others that we were strong than to convince others that we were right or idealistic or virtuous.

July 25

This afternoon I received a phone call from Hamilton Fish Armstrong,[57] who spoke along the following lines: In the "X" article, published three years ago, I had set out the policy of containment. It had been followed only in Europe. The significance of the Korean affair was that we were now beginning to follow it in Asia as well. He was calling to ask me to write a second article, this time under my own name, spelling out what this policy meant in terms of Asia. How were we to capture the offensive in that continent? How were we to get around the dilemma of the support of discreditable and reactionary leaders? What were the lessons of our China policy in this respect? How could we exploit the forces of nationalism for the purposes of the free world rather than permitting

57. Armstrong was editor of *Foreign Affairs*.

them to be exploited by the communists? What should be the boundaries of our line of containment? How tightly should they be drawn? What was the range of the effectiveness of sea power and air power as projected into the Asiatic land mass?

I made no effort to give him any answer to these suggestions on the spot but arranged to see him when I go up to New York in a week or two, thinking that I would give him my answer then.

In the evening I dined at the Canadian Embassy. . . . Franks[58] made it evident that their great objection to our China policy lay in our commitment to Chiang Kai-shek, which they viewed as something forcing the Chinese Communists into the arms of the Russians. I pointed out to him that Formosa could not be regarded only as a part of the Chinese problem but must be regarded as part of the whole Far Eastern picture, and that whoever said Formosa must go to the communists to facilitate the emergence of an independent Chinese Communist policy vis-a-vis Moscow was really saying that all of the Far East and the Western Pacific, including possibly Japan, must be abandoned to communism, if necessary, for this same purpose . . . . Franks said that the British people took a longer view of these things: that their calculations were fixed rather on what the situation would be in the year 2000, and that in the stolid advance toward such long term objectives they were prepared to take in their stride whatever trials or reverses might come. He thought that in the long run China was more important than Japan and ought to be given priority in our thinking.

This, I said, terrified me; because China was an entity which would never, in my opinion, be dependable from the standpoint of Western interests; Japan, on the other hand, might conceivably be made so. . . .

Chip and I were partly amazed and partly amused to hear Averell Harriman, when I spoke about the McCarthy business, say "you fellows in the State Department" had to learn the necessity of coming clean with the public about your own mistakes; that "you" could not go on putting out White Papers as "you" did in the case of China, whitewashing the mistakes "you" had made; "you" would have to establish a completely frank relation with the public and not pretend that "you" had always been right, etc. Neither of us accepted the challenge, for we saw no point in arguing the question of responsibility for China policy . . . but both of us at once reflected on the fact that the State Department had had no

58. British Ambassador Oliver Franks.

knowledge whatsoever of the Yalta agreement at the time it was concluded; that the Department remained ignorant of the nature of it for a long time after that; that Averell had been one of the President's advisers at Yalta; and that while the Yalta Conference was going on the Acting Secretary of State, in his innocence, had been wiring the American embassy at Chungking[59] warning them to avoid by all means anything that smacked of efforts on our part to mediate between the Russians and the Chinese.

July 28

In all the discussions of the morning I found myself for the most part in a lonely position of single opposition to the views of my associates. The main point at issue is the recognition of the Chinese Communists in the United Nations. I can see, myself, no fundamental objection, from the standpoint of U.S. interest, to the seating of the Chinese Communists, provided we still wish to cling to the principle that the UN is a universal organization and can eventually be of some use in the adjusting of relationships between East and West by means other than a major war. The seating of the Chinese Communists would, in my opinion, constitute no new reality of any great significance. . . . Our insistence on the retention of the Security Council seat by the Chinese Nationalists was a source of confusion and unclarity in Asia. Our motives were being widely misinterpreted, and it was being alleged that our purposes were governed by ulterior and imperialistic motives. . . .

This view was rejected by Bohlen and Dulles primarily on the ground that it would confuse American public opinion and weaken support for the President's program looking toward the strengthening of our defenses, and this view was eventually upheld by the Secretary. I said that I could very well understand this but that I shuddered over the implications of it, for it implied that we could not adopt an adequate defense position without working our people up into an emotional state, and that this emotional state, rather than a cool and unemotional appraisal of national interest, would then have to be the determinant of our action. The position we were taking seemed to me to imply acceptance of the theory that in the last analysis the U.N. would not be universal but would be an Article 51 alliance against Russia. It seemed further to imply that the basis of our policy in the Far East from here

59. Chungking (Chongqing) was the wartime capital of Nationalist China.

on out would be an emotional anti-communism which would ignore the value to ourselves of a possible balance between the existing forces on the Asiatic continent, would force everyone to declare himself either for us, including Chiang Kai-shek, or against us, that this would break the unity not only of the non-communist countries in Asia but also of the non-communist community in general, and would be beyond our military capacity to support. It rested, I said, on the encouragement in the minds of our people of a false belief that we were a strong power in Asia, whereas we are in reality a weak one. Only the very strong can take high and mighty moral positions and ignore the possibilities of balance among the opposing forces. The weak must accept realities and exploit those realities to their advantage as best they can.

With Bohlen and Dulles, as I say, the objections were laid to public opinion. With Rusk and some of the others, I think there was a real sense of moral indignation about the Chinese Communists. These people, after all, are treading now the paths which we old Russian hands were treading over 20 years ago in our first experiences with the Soviet dictatorship. We were not unaware then, and we are not unaware now, of the fundamental ethical conflict between their ideals and ours. But we view the handling of our end, in this conflict, as a practical matter similar to many other matters with which diplomacy has had to deal through the course of the centuries.

We have learned not to recoil from the struggle for power as something shocking or abnormal. It is the medium in which we work, as the doctor works in the medium of human flesh, and we will not improve our performance by failing to deal with its real nature or by trying to dress it up as something else. In our own consciences, in our own concept, that is, of our obligations to ourselves, we Americans may be profoundly aware that we are "right." In our participation on the international scene, we are only one of the contenders for the privilege of leading a national existence on a portion of the territory of this world, on reasonably favorable terms. Other people are our enemies, and we must deal with them accordingly. But let us recognize the legitimacy of differences of interest and philosophy between groups of men and not pretend that they can be made to disappear behind some common philosophical concept.

July 31

Secretary Acheson said that he wished me to make it my function to keep abreast of all information bearing on Soviet attitudes and views and to be able at any time to give the others an estimate of probable Soviet reactions to any moves we might make. This constitutes a much more direct responsibility than I have heretofore had, in connection with the handling of the Korean matter, and will make it necessary for me to give much more in the way of hour-to-hour attention to developments in the military and diplomatic fields. . . .

Following the Secretary's meeting, a member of the Planning Staff dropped in to tell me that he had learned from one journalist, who had learned it from another journalist, that Mr. Dulles had said to journalist no. 2 that while he used to think highly of George Kennan, he had now concluded that he was a very dangerous man: that he was advocating the admission of the Chinese Communists to the United Nations, and a cessation of U.S. military action at the 38th parallel.

August 1

In the afternoon I watched by television the session of the Security Council which has been awaited with such tense anticipation. The flickering screen gave me a headache and hurt my eyes, and I wondered how children could possibly be permitted to sit for hours every day staring into these squawking boxes.

August 4

Was somewhat annoyed at a suggestion made by Dean Rusk, in my absence, Thursday morning, to the effect that it might be desirable to get three prominent outsiders in to examine the material which had accumulated with respect to Soviet intentions, in order to get a fresh judgment as to whether the Russians were planning war. It seemed to me that the only concept which could underlie such thinking was that the most valuable views on this subject were to be obtained from people who knew the least about it. If this were accepted, I reflected, perhaps after I had been out of the Department long enough to forget a very great portion of what I now know, I might be accepted more cheerfully around here as a pundit on questions under discussion.

August 14

The Republican members of the Senate Foreign Relations Committee today published a joint statement attacking the foreign policy of the Democratic administration with relation to the Far East. . . . Never before has there been such utter confusion in the public mind with respect to U.S. foreign policy. The President doesn't understand it; Congress doesn't understand it, nor does the public, nor does the press. They all wander around in a labyrinth of ignorance and error and conjecture, in which truth is intermingled with fiction at a hundred points, in which unjustified assumptions have attained the validity of premises, and in which there is no recognized and authoritative theory to hold on to. Only the diplomatic historian, it seems to me, working from the leisure and detachment of a later day, will be able to unravel this incredible tangle and reveal the true aspect of the various factors and issues involved. And that is why, as it seems to me, no one in my position can contribute very much more to an understanding of U.S. foreign policy unless he first turns historian, earns public confidence and respect on the study of an earlier day, and then gradually carries the public up to a clear and comprehensible view of the occurrences of these recent years.

August 22

Held a press conference this afternoon in connection with my departure from the Department. . . . In reply to a question about how we can achieve our objectives without a major war:

First, while being adequately prepared for every eventuality we should never make the mistake of regarding war as inevitable and of underestimating the chances for peace.

Second, we have to maintain an adequate defense posture for ourselves, if necessary, over a long period of time.

Third, we should give our friends the impression that we are determined people, reliable allies, but that their interest is as strong as ours in the achievement of a more stable and happier world. We must not give them the impression that we have some sort of selfish or ulterior interest in the maintenance of their independence and the maintenance of a firm international attitude in the face of Bolshevik pressures.

Fourth, we must keep our flag flying high here at home, to demonstrate that we are making a success of our own national life, that we are getting on with our problems and see to it that other people understand what those successes mean.

I think that is about all you can do. The main thing I would add is that we should demonstrate that we have the courage of our convictions and that we have confidence in ourselves here in this country. Beyond that the only thing I would recommend is that we be very careful now that we are entering an area where political and military considerations are closely intermingled, to avoid hasty and emotional judgments, to deal with our problems coolly and carefully, realizing that we are now really for the first time as a nation facing the test of maturity and of world leadership.

In reply to a question about why I believe Russia does not want a major war, I said that I thought I could not expand on what was included in the X article and in the *Reader's Digest* article. I said that I still believed that the actions of the Kremlin, which have caused such great concern to people elsewhere in the world and have led to the troubles we have today, are ones which are based on a deep misestimation on their part of the nature of the world around them and a tragic failure to realize that international progress can never be made on the basis of hostility and hatred and antagonism and can be achieved only by freedom of association among peoples and the principle of "live and let live." . . .

Was invited this evening to join in a discussion between some of the officials of the Department and for Senators about our information program and about the proposals that have been made for some staggering increases in the American informational effort. . . . The main audience to which our broadcasts should now be addressed is the audience which actually does most of the listening, namely the privileged and influential members of the ruling group itself. In approaching these people we need no claims to virtue on our part. There is no point in trying to gain their sympathies. They are hard-boiled creatures, with blood on their hands, and not, for the most part, people we want to make friends with. Our approach to them should be designed primarily to sow doubts and hesitations and suspicions in their minds about the path of crime on which they are embarked. We must somehow or other insert in their minds the wicked demon of doubt about the wisdom of their leaders, the soundness of their cause, the loyalty of their comrades and superiors, and the prospects of victory. This is dirty business, admittedly; this is political warfare, and no warfare is pleasant. If we want to broadcast to Russia effectively, this is the sort of thing we have to go in for.

August 23

Two years ago, when the North Atlantic Treaty was being negotiated, I had written a formal Staff paper opposing the admission into a North Atlantic security pact of any single country beyond the North Atlantic area. This had particular reference to Italy. I had stated in that paper that if Italy were admitted, this would constitute a precedent and would almost certainly lead to a series of demands from states still further afield that they be similarly treated. Failure on our part to satisfy these further demands, I had written at that time, would then be interpreted as lack of interest in the respective countries and as evidence that we had "written them off" to the Russians.

We now had to recognize that having solicited and accepted the Turkish offer of ground forces for the action in Korea, we were to all intents and purposes, in an alliance with Turkey and under an obligation to assist her, in the event she were attacked—an obligation far more solemn and serious than any treaty clause. . . . I could not see what the Turks possibly could stand to gain by being brought into the Atlantic Pact.

Princeton, September 10

My first day at the Institute [for Advanced Study] . . . I installed myself in my new office, with windows looking out over the fields to the woods, and had a sense of peace and happiness such as I have not had for a long, long time.

[December]

On Friday morning, December 1, Bohlen phoned me from Paris. . . . There was no indication that any one with a deep understanding of Russian reactions was involved at this time in the formulation of our policy.[60] He said, "I am calling to implore you to go down to Washington and insist on seeing General Marshall, who I know has a high regard for your views, and the Secretary, to try to impress upon them the real considerations which undoubtedly underlie the Russian and Chinese reactions and on which you and I have been consistently in agreement." . . .

On Saturday afternoon, I received a call from John Davies, saying that the Secretary wanted me to come and that he had been authorized by Paul Nitze to tell me that. I therefore took the next train to Washington. This was the first time that I had been called upon by the Secretary since I left the Department in September. I had been in Washington for one day of consultation with subordinate officials in October, but the subject of discussion at that time was only the general considerations involved in the problem of negotiation with the Russians, and had no relation to the specific problems of our Korean or general Far Eastern policies. . . .

60. As U.S. troops neared the Chinese border, Communist Chinese leader Mao Zedong ordered his forces to intervene. Suddenly overwhelmed, the Americans reeled southward in retreat. The Truman administration was near panic.

I came to the Department of State at 10:00 a.m. Sunday morning, December 3, and reported for duty. . . . I joined Mr. Webb and three or four other people for the usual briefing on the battlefield situation in Korea, which was not too revealing. Afterward, Webb talked to me, first in the presence of two or three others, and then alone. He was obviously in a state of considerable agitation. He said that the military leaders felt that a complete withdrawal from Korea was the only alternative to the loss of what was practically our entire ground establishment. They thought that we had perhaps 36 hours for a decision as to an orderly withdrawal. If that decision were not made the result might be complete disaster and effective loss of the entire force. He said that discussions were in progress concerning the attitude which we should adopt in the United Nations and in the conversations with Attlee, who was expected to arrive the following morning. No course would be decided until we had talked with the British. One of the variants which would be discussed with the British would be a direct approach to the Russians with a view to bringing about a cease-fire in Korea. What they wanted from me, he said, was a view as to the prospects of negotiation with the Russians on this problem at this time. . . .

As he left the office, the Secretary asked whether I would like to come home with him for supper. I said that I had another engagement at 9:00 but that I would be glad to come if he did not mind me leaving by that time. Accordingly, we went to his home. The servants had been excused and the Secretary, Mrs. Acheson, and myself had a light supper which Mrs. Acheson prepared. Before and during supper, the Secretary spoke at some length about his problems. Beginning by pointing to a new portrait of himself which was in the living room, he said that the artist had expressed himself as impressed with Mr. Acheson's imperviousness to the crescendo of attacks which were being made upon him at the time the portrait was being painted and had tried in the painting to emphasize what he felt to be that aspect of his character. The Secretary told this about himself in a humorous vein, and ironically, but there was no question how deeply he felt about this matter. He then went on to speak of the strangeness of his position and the fact that at times he felt that he seemed to be the only person in Washington who fully understood the seriousness of the situation in which we found ourselves.

On arriving at the office Monday morning (December 4), I sat down and wrote out by hand the following note to the Secretary:

"On the official level I have been asked to give advice only on the particular problem of Soviet reaction to various possible approaches. But there is one thing I should like to say in continuation of our discussion of yesterday evening. In international, as in private, life, what counts most is not really what happens to someone, but how he bears what happens to him. For this reason almost everything depends from here on out on the manner in which we Americans bear what is unquestionably a major failure and disaster to our national fortunes. If we accept it with candor and dignity, with a resolve to absorb its lessons and to make it good by redoubled and determined effort, starting all over again, if necessary, along the pattern of Pearl Harbor, we need lose neither our self-confidence nor our allies nor our power for bargaining, eventually, with the Russians. But if we try to conceal from our own people or from our allies the full measure of our misfortune, or permit ourselves to seek relief in any reactions of bluster or petulance or hysteria, we can easily find this crisis resolving itself into an irreparable deterioration of our world position, and of our confidence in ourselves."

The Russians had never seen the United Nations' connection with the Korean affair as anything other than a screen for action carried out by this country in its own national interest. Looking at it this way, they were prepared to accept the fact that we could claim some strategic interest in South Korea, on the basis of our responsibilities in Japan, but they could not see how we could claim a strategic interest greater than that of the Chinese Communists and themselves on the Yalu River frontier.[61] What they were saying in effect was: "You had your chance to settle this business at a reasonable point. You did not do it. What possible motive could you have had for going further, unless it was a thought of making war on Communist China?"

. . . I suggested to the Secretary that he might, if he agreed with them, read aloud the main passages of the note which I had written to him this morning and which I presented to him at that point. This he did, and I had the impression that the thought expressed in them was generally appreciated. I gathered that the Secretary proposed to bring the passages to the attention of the President, and Matthews suggested that I might draft something along these lines, perhaps using the identical language, as an opening passage for the President's speech later this week.

Rusk then introduced the question as to whether we were really obliged to abandon Korea altogether and whether it might not be a good thing for us to attempt to hold some sort of a beachhead, particularly in

61. The Yalu River marked the border between North Korea and China.

the light of what I had said about negotiations with the Russians. I took occasion to reinforce the point he had raised. I was afraid, I said, that perhaps our military leaders were not sufficiently aware of how similar our position had become to that occupied by the British for a long period in the past and of how necessary it was for us, on occasion, to hold stubbornly, on the basis of sheer political instinct, to positions which military logic might declare to be useless. One could never know about these things. I recalled the battles in North Africa during the recent war and the drastic and repeated changes in military fortune which carried the front hundreds of miles back and forth along the North African littoral. Had the British not stubbornly clung to a position just short of Cairo, in the face of discouraging odds, they would never have won their final victory. If we could prove, I said, that we could hold some sort of a line or beachhead in central or southern Korea, which would pin down a large number of enemy forces, I was not sure that the prospect of continuing such a contest in the face of air attacks on their lines of communications would prove attractive to the enemy.

The Secretary indicated that he was impressed with these points. The meeting broke up at that point, but shortly afterward I received a telephone call asking me to go to the Pentagon together with Rusk and Matthews to talk to General Marshall along these lines. . . . The General recalled his experiences in the past in the case of Bataan and Corregidor, and cited this as an example of the virtue of hanging on doggedly for reasons of prestige and morale. . . . Upon our return to the Department of State, we lunched with the Secretary in his office. He said that the President had had no patience with the suggestions that we resolve to abandon Korea and had felt that we should stay and fight as long as possible.

saloons and the drug-stores and the flashiest motor-car sales agencies were open. You met men with no hats, blue overcoats, no ties, hair uncombed, shoe-strings dragging. They ~~as~~ all looked as though the had hang-overs. On a street-corner, three older men stood silent and motionless, staring up a side-street. I looked, too, but could not see what they were staring at.

I went into a drug store, thinking that, ~~I~~ having had no lunch, I ought to get something to eat. The soda-fountain counter was wet and dirty. There was no one serving. There was a man pushing the litter off the floor with a wide push-broom. I waited until his ~~pile~~ little heap of paper cups, celaphane wrappers, and cigarette butts had passed under my feet. Then I gave up the idea of eating and went back to the hotel.

On the way, I thought of the things I had seen, and of the Chicago Tribune I had been reading in my room. It had had an article on communism at Harvard, among other things, which I wanted to clip and send to Grace. I also reflected that my grand-father and my mother had come from this town. I heard some boys on bicycles screaming at each other across the street, and realized that even the language was unfamiliar to me.

So I shuffled along back to the hotel, in the depression born of hunger plus ~~a vast~~ an over-powering sense of lack of confidence in my surroundings; and a small inward voice said, gleefully and melodramatically: "You have despaired of yourself; now despair of your country!"

I knew that the challenge, however, melodramatic, was not unfair, and that this—too—I would have to learn to bear in my wanderings in the nether regions.

Detroit, Monday, April 9, 1951.

Walked miles, this morning, first to find an envelop—large-size, and then to find a post-office. Stewed inwardly over the deterioration of public services in our country; thought I might collect comparisons in Europe and write an article about it; dreamed of how pleasant it would be if you had a government strong enough to make everyone in Chicago clean the side-walk in front of his house and keep his car off the street at night so that others could clean the streets.

Lay down in my room, to rest for the lecture. When I try, as I did then, to bring the spirit to a state of complete repose, shutting out all effort and all seeking, I become aware of the ~~impulses of~~ remnants of

CHAPTER SIX

Princeton and Oxford, 1951–60

1951

The year 1951 was a turbulent one for Kennan. In April, during the very days when he was at the University of Chicago delivering the Walgreen lectures (later published as American Diplomacy, *his most widely read book), he agonized over the fallout from an apparent affair or flirtation. He was appalled at the growth of McCarthyite hysteria and feared that the nation would blunder into World War III. Though he played a key role in initiating talks that would eventually lead to an armistice in Korea, and was invited to become ambassador to the Soviet Union, he felt increasingly uncertain about his purpose in life. A visit to southern California underscored Kennan's view of American society as childish and abusive of the natural environment.*

Princeton, April 2

The following notes are thought of as an aid to a process of spiritual self-discipline and reformation. They are designed to help me combat forgetfulness and fluctuations of attitude, to stand as a reproach to inconsistency, to guard against escape into extremes and unreality. They are to stand as the record and reminder of an inner life which, I can only hope, will stand recording.

I know of only one prayer I can make that would seem to have any reasonable and satisfactory foundation. It would be that by every bit of discomfort and effort and hardship I may lay upon myself in this effort at self-strengthening, something might be lifted from the pain I might otherwise bring to others. If I might be permitted to expiate in this way something of the damage I have done, perhaps then something might properly and rightly be deducted from the fullness and disastrousness of eventual revelation.

If there were not this hope, the situation would indeed be desperate. I should find it hard, even if fortune favored me, to adjust to the consciousness of the jeopardy in which I have placed the happiness of other people. And not being sure that the blow would not still fall, I would continue to feel myself half a murderer, to have horror of myself, and to place limitations, in my own mind, on my ability to be useful to any one else in any personal intimacy.

I am like a person who has placed poison in one of two glasses before a person he loves—and looks back upon his act with horror and incredulity—but still does not know from which glass the person will drink.

I must remember that it is bad for me to look too far ahead. This will be a long process. I must let the victories of one day be enough. And if they come hard to me—and if it seems improbable that I should ever win in the long run—then I must be sure, nevertheless, that I win for today; and I must say to myself: tomorrow it will be easier.

If the evil day should come (this is a question) must I not be strong enough not to let it crush me entirely? Must I not say: "In one tremendous field of life, the one in which failure was personally most horrible and painful, I have failed; in others I have proven to have usefulness; I will stand outside of myself and, loathing one part of me, nevertheless talk quietly and sensibly and with respect about the rest?"

April 3

When walking alone, I noticed that when I was forgetful of my problems and limitations I walked faster; when I bethought myself of them, my pace slackened and I began to walk more like an old man. Someone else—an impartial observer, a doctor, let us say—would be inclined to conclude that forgetfulness was good, awareness bad. Yet he would be wrong. For me it is right and necessary that I should become much older in a short space of time. . . .

In general, it seems to me, the training of the spirit is most difficult on normal, practical work days, when the concrete details of life demand attention of a semi-routine sort—and particularly in offices and other places of work, where people wear their professional personalities like uniforms. Then, if ever, habit and forgetfulness are at their strongest.

I am somewhat bewildered by the reflection that I have a guilt-complex vis-à-vis my family in dozens of small matters that make no real difference. How ironic this is. I must teach myself to have nothing to conceal but that which is really worth concealing.

On Saturday evening I leave for two weeks of lecturing in Chicago. I will look upon this as an exercise. I shall live in a hotel on the South

Shore. I have left myself plenty of time between lectures, and have asked that extraneous social engagements be ruled out. Here there will be all the things that are difficult for me: a strange city, a hotel, solitude, boredom, strange women, the sense of time fleeting, of time being wasted, of a life pulsating around me—a life unknown, untested, full of mystery, and yet not touched by myself. Let us see whether I can preserve deliberateness, thoughtfulness, awareness of all that is involved, patience, forbearance. Let us see whether, if I can stand the first day, the next will not be easier. It will be a real test, an opportunity for a real triumph; no, that is an exaggeration. There are no triumphs, only an opportunity to inch a tiny bit along the road.

April 4

Woke up with a dream so appalling that had I taken it seriously I should have had to say to myself: here is something that must undo all that you are attempting. Then, in thinking about it, it dawned on me that the subconscious mind, like the workings of history, is often years out of date in its causality. Even were I to bow before the suggestions that the dream contained—were I to say to the subconscious: you are right, you are unanswerable, I will cut all the fateful knots and follow you—none of it would work out. Ten years ago, it would have; not today. How dangerous a guide, in later age, is then that which is most powerful or nearly the most powerful (for that remains to be seen) within us.

Except insofar as you may have work to do for which certain minimum services from the body are required, what happens to the body is of little importance when you have passed the age of 45. The best you can do with it is to keep it as tidy as possible, limit as well as you can the evidences of its increasing stagnation and obsolescence, and try to see that the light that still shines from it through the eyes does not partake of its sordidness and its obvious decline. Beyond that the vicissitudes and dangers to which it is exposed should not be permitted to trouble you.

April 5

These last two days have been bad days, tired, unwell, strained. I have dragged myself around—too ill to be at my best, not ill enough, and too busy, to stop. The time wasted? No. I have written one whole lecture, rewritten another, talked to a student, talked to Earle,[1] lunched

1. Edward Mead Earle, a specialist on the role of the military in foreign relations, was on the faculty of the Institute for Advanced Study at Princeton, where Kennan was a visiting scholar.

with Oppenheimer, and done a dozen necessary and unavoidable little things. But how does one hold to an inner life when trivia and the body take over to this extent?

The answer, I suppose, is that one tries all the harder, forces one's self to be composed and to look, even though it may be as through a mist, for the more important realities one ought to bear in mind, and hopes, again, that if one can gain something, or even hold one's own today, tomorrow it will be easier. . . .

This morning I had another unpleasant dream on the subject of concealment. Unquestionably, there is an abnormality here: a dread of being found out. This can probably be repaired only by making my life such that there is genuinely nothing to conceal and that means making it such that it will no longer, in a sense, be *my* life at all, but a certain amount of personal activity dedicated entirely to outside purposes.

April 6

I have never been any good at training children or dogs; that is why I am no good at training myself.

Chicago, April 8

I went into a drug store, thinking that, having had no lunch, I ought to get something to eat. The soda fountain counter was wet and dirty. There was no one serving. There was a man pushing the litter off the floor with a wide push-broom. I waited until his little heap of paper cups, cellophane wrappers, and cigarette butts had passed under my feet. Then I gave up the idea of eating and went back to the hotel.

On the way, I thought of the things I had seen, and of the *Chicago Tribune* I had been reading in my room. It had had an article on communism at Harvard, among other things, which I wanted to clip and send to Grace.[2] I also reflected that my grandfather and my mother had come from this town. I heard some boys on bicycles screaming at each other across the street, and realized that even the language was unfamiliar to me.

So I shuffled along back to the hotel, in the depression born of hunger plus an over-powering sense of lack of confidence in my surroundings; and a small inward voice said, gleefully and melodramatically: "You have despaired of yourself; now despair of your country!"

2. Kennan's daughter was a student at Radcliffe College.

I knew that the challenge, however melodramatic, was not unfair, and that this, too, I would have to learn to bear in my wanderings in the nether regions.

April 9

Lay down in my room, to rest for the lecture. When I try, as I did then, to bring the spirit to a state of complete repose, shutting out all effort and all seeking, I became aware of the remnants of anxieties and desires still surging and thrashing around, like waves in a swimming pool when the last swimmer has left; and I realize in what a turmoil the pool of the soul usually is, and how long it must lie untroubled before the surface becomes calm and one can see to the bottom. . . .

The papers today were full of MacArthur and Truman, and I was full of premonitions of trouble.[3] It seemed to me that we were like a crowd of drunken men on a raft, squabbling and gabbing while we drifted down to the brink of the falls. Soon, I thought, we must all go to war, and how desolate war really is. And, with these thoughts in my head, I was struck to encounter, in Churchill's *Gathering Storm* the following couplet from Sassoon:[4]

> "Shoulder to aching shoulder, side by side
> They trudged away from life's broad wealds of light."

Princeton, April 15

I have not written for several days, taken with forgetfulness about personal problems, which became unreal with distance and preoccupation, but also overwhelmed with public ones, flowing from the experience of being in Chicago through this time of the dismissal of MacArthur, and perforce aware of local reactions to it. These impressions, combined with general impressions of Chicago, have left me with some extraordinary appreciations. For the first time in my life I have become conscious of the existence of powerful forces in the country to which, if they are successful, no democratic adjustment can be made: people, in other words, to

3. General Douglas MacArthur, commander of U.S. and UN forces in Korea, was challenging President Truman's insistence on keeping the conflict in Korea a limited war. On April 11, Truman relieved MacArthur of his post. Though the president was at first loudly criticized by the public, opinion turned when top generals testified that it was indeed dangerous to expand the war.

4. Siegfried Sassoon was a British poet whose work captured the initial romanticism and subsequent disillusionment of the generation fighting in World War I.

whom there is no reasonable approach, to whom the traditions of tolerance and civil liberty are of no real importance, people who have to be regarded as totalitarian enemies. I have to recognize that these people have already become dominant in the part of the country from which I came; that I have lost out here, as have all moderate and reasonable people who try to see both sides; that my homeland has turned against me—is not, in fact, the same place, in the human sense, that it was when I was a boy but rather only the same battered stage on which, for the most part, new sets have been erected and non-actors, who do not understand me and tolerate me only because they are unaware that I would dare to disagree with them, play their parts. I am now in the truest sense of the word an expatriate. As an individual, my game is up in this part of the world. I am glad I did not go to Milwaukee. I hope never to go there again until McCarthyism has burned itself out there and people are thoroughly ashamed of it; but such a time is not likely to come, it seems to me, for people rarely repent of their political follies and hysterics, they merely exchange them for other ones and persuade themselves that they were right all along. . . .

It would be a miracle if, with this combination of personal and public problems, anything remained for me personally in life. Let me recognize that I live at one of those times when it is not given to men to live out quietly the golden days, in harmony with nature and at peace with society. This will be a time for leadership or for martyrdom or for both. I may as well prepare myself for it.

April 17

In private life I have come up against fairly formidable barriers. They seemed to me surmountable only with a big degree of dedication to something outside myself. Now I have to face the fact that public life is equally closed. At one time, I was an actor in the conduct of foreign policy. I became convinced that I was accomplishing nothing in that capacity, that the problems were deeper, that the answer lay in a direct approach to the public and in an effort to explain to the public what it was really about. Today, even that seems futile. Myths and errors are being established in the public mind more rapidly than they can be broken down. The mass media are too much for us. There is nothing that can be done about it. To correct this, you would have to educate the educators. I must say that I have lost all confidence in the freedom of the mass media. The fact of the matter is that in this country McCarthyism has already won, in the sense of making impossible the conduct of an intelligent foreign policy. The result is that there is no place in public life for an honest and moderate man. . . . I should not be speaking out here in Chicago. It will do no good, any of it. I must stop this public speaking, this writing for publication.

But what *can* I do? Well, consistency is a virtue by itself. I can finish what I have set out to do, the actual intellectual work at Princeton, insofar as time is available. We must assume that war will break out within two years. Our people have no control over the situation, and they will become more erratic as their frustrations increase. Except for the little boy,[5] the best thing that could happen would be that I should go with the services and get myself killed.

Farming, otherwise, is the only real outlet and salvation. It is to that that I must steer the course, with a view to taking it up as soon as the pension is earned, or forfeited (for the latter seems more likely). That at least gives a goal, and something to work toward. Meanwhile, the work at Princeton must be finished, for consistency's sake. That will see Joany through school, and provide the best time for a change.

[With the fighting in Korea stalemated, Secretary of State Dean Acheson asked Kennan to try to open a back channel of communication with the Soviet ambassador to the UN, Jacob Malik. In keeping with his training as a diplomat, Kennan made a detailed record of his conversations and actions. He kept copies of the letters and memoranda he sent and received, and included the most important records in his diary.

In the original version of the first memorandum, in the next entry, Kennan had, for security reasons, identified the players only by a letter, such as "O." In February 1968, he added a code to identify individuals by name.]

May–June

On Friday, May 18, having been called to Washington by P [H. Freeman Matthews], I talked with O [Secretary Acheson], who . . . asked me whether I would be willing to undertake the project in question, and I told him that I would. It was agreed that arrangements would have to be made by a U.S. official in New York, and that I should see him when I was up there the following week.

On Monday, May 21, I talked at length with [that official] in New York.

5. The Kennans' third child, Christopher, was born in 1949.

It was agreed that he would seek an opportunity to communicate again with X [Ambassador Malik] and to suggest that it might be both useful and interesting for him to talk with me. He was to give X [Ambassador Malik] an opportunity to think it over and was to offer to arrange the meeting.

On Tuesday, May 22, I phoned O [Secretary Acheson] and told him that I had started the ball rolling. I suggested to him that he and a tiny circle of his associates sit down immediately and arrive at some clarification, to be communicated to me, of the areas which might profitably be explored and those areas which it would be better not to have explored at all. I explained that I would be speaking solely as an individual and without commitment of anyone else, but that it was nevertheless obviously desirable that I know what things it would be wise to talk about and what things had better not be discussed. He said that they were planning to do this. I said that I thought that someone, probably F,[6] ought to be kept in a state of readiness to come to see me in Princeton at any time, to bring me this information. I said that I would want him also to be able to brief me on everything that I should know involving things happening elsewhere, such as the Paris discussions or the Japanese peace treaty discussions, which might have a bearing on the subject at hand. I was sure that X [Ambassador Malik], if he consented to talk to me, would be thoroughly briefed on these matters, and I thought I should be too. . . .

May 26

Dear Mr. Tsarapkin:[7]

You will remember our official acquaintance in Moscow. You also know, I suppose, that I am now on leave of absence and engaged in academic activity here in Princeton.

I am writing to ask you to be good enough to tell Mr. Malik (whom I know very slightly) that I think it would be useful from the standpoint of both our governments if he and I could meet and have a quiet talk some time in the near future. I think that my diplomatic experience and long acquaintance with problems of American-Soviet relations should suffice to assure you that I would not make such a proposal unless I had serious reasons to do so. . . .

6. "F" was not identified in the code Kennan supplied in 1968.

7. Semyon K. Tsarapkin was the Soviets' deputy representative at the UN.

May 31
Mr. Matthews:

[Malik] received me very cordially and pleasantly in a sort of a summer pagoda adjoining his house, and we talked for some two and a half hours. His general attitude toward the visit seemed to be: "I am, as a diplomatic representative of the Soviet Union, always happy to meet with worthy Americans and to talk things over with them." He complained, incidentally, that he was isolated, that people were afraid to see him, etc. I naturally told him that I understood his position very well, having served so long in Moscow, even though I personally deplored the decline of normal and free contact between diplomatic representatives and others.

I told him that what I had come to talk about was the problem of a possible cease fire in Korea. I explained my own status and emphasized that as an official on leave, occupying no responsible post in the Government, I obviously could not treat with him formally on behalf of our Government. I realized, I said, that this problem of a cease fire was a very complicated one involving numbers of other countries, and that its final solution would require many things besides just such conversations. But I was convinced that if we were able to ascertain that there was some identity of view between our two governments as to how we should proceed toward it, the other difficulties could all be surmounted, whereas if no such identity of views existed I feared that any efforts to arrive at agreement elsewhere would be apt to be unsuccessful. I wanted to find out, I said, how he felt about this: whether he thought that it might be worthwhile for us to talk about these matters, bearing in mind my status, or whether he thought it would be better for us not to do so, or whether perhaps he thought there was some other forum where the matter ought to be discussed. While he refused to be drawn out on this question, he did say that unless he had thought there might be some use in our talking he would not have agreed to meet with me. In the discussion which ensued, he turned the subject time and time again to general political questions, advancing the usual Soviet propaganda theses. It is my impression that his reason for doing this was probably that our conversation was being overheard and recorded; at least I assumed that to be the case, and his words seemed fully in accord with this hypothesis. I tried generally to avoid this type of discussion by saying repeatedly that I was sure we would not agree on these wider matters, and the best we could do would be to see whether we could not get on with the practical matter at hand. What is set forth below, therefore, about our actual exchanges on the subject of a cease fire represents not a single continuous conversation but a series of things which came out in the course of this prolonged dialectic exercise.

He wanted to know what I thought about the proposal that all foreign troops be withdrawn from Korea. I said I thought that was desirable as a final solution but did not believe that anything of this sort could be done immediately: the Koreans, I thought, were not in a situation where they would be able to take over the handling of their own affairs at once. I feared that the immediate departure of all foreign troops would only mean the renewal of civil war on the peninsula; nothing could be worse than to have the whole thing start all over again in this way. I thought that once hostilities ceased under some sort of cease fire agreement we would have to face the question of the future of Korea, but I was afraid that agreement on that would not be easy for us to reach and negotiations might take a long time. What, he asked, did I think my Government's position was with regard to the future of Korea? I replied that as I understood it it was the position adopted by the United Nations, in a series of resolutions, namely that Korea should eventually be an independent and democratic state, but I did not think this goal had to be achieved to the satisfaction of everyone concerned on the day following termination of hostilities.

He asked on what basis I thought a cease fire might usefully be discussed—what terms, that is, I thought my Government would approve. With the usual disclaimers about not binding my Government, I said I thought it might be useful if we could examine the problem on the basis of termination of hostilities approximately in the region where they are now taking place, recognizing that there would have to be some sort of control authority which could give the respective sides assurance that the armistice would not be exploited by the other side for the purpose of amassing new strength and launching a new offensive. When he pressed for further details, I said that unless I knew whether his Government was interested in seeing hostilities ended on something like this basis I did not think any useful purpose would be served by my going into greater detail. I said there would be plenty to discuss under this concept if we both felt in principle that it was a concept worth pursuing.

When he brought up, as he did repeatedly, the question of our wider differences with the Chinese Communists, I told him that I thought no useful purpose would be served by trying to couple consideration of the cease fire question with the wider problem. I thought we could make progress only if we took the specific question of a cessation of hostilities in Korea and looked at it alone and without relation to the wider differences concerning general Far Eastern problems. He said that in this case my remarks contained "nothing new," and he was at a loss, therefore, to know what to say in reply to them. He did indicate, however, that if I could make more detailed proposals his Government would be interested to hear them. To this I replied, as indicated above, that I thought no useful purpose would be served by my trying to go into greater detail at the time, in the absence of any indication from him of the views of his Government on the general desirability of such a cease fire. I felt that if I were to try, in these circumstances, to go into greater detail about this, I would be only airing views so personal that I did not think they would be useful to him.

When I pressed him to say whether he thought that it would or would not be useful for us to meet again, he was evasive but not negative, saying that he thought that it was a good thing in general for people to talk things over and that he would always be happy to receive me and to pass the time of day. I had the feeling that his reluctance to say anything more definite on this point stemmed from an unwillingness to indicate that he would ask for further instructions from his Government. I therefore said that I would like to give further thought to what he had said and would come back on another occasion at his convenience, if this were agreeable to him. When I suggested several different days on which I thought I could do it, he selected Tuesday June 5 as the most agreeable to him, provided his duties as Chairman of the Security Council did not interfere. We therefore left it that I would return next Tuesday afternoon at 3:00 p.m. in the absence of any further word from him.

I think I should add that during the course of the conversation he repeatedly turned the talk to the problem of the Chinese Communists and our relations with them, going into the usual propaganda line about how sensitive they were, how we had offended them, etc. I think my own replies to these charges are scarcely of sufficient interest to recount. I did say to him that I thought it would be a great mistake to underestimate the extent to which the conduct of the Chinese Communists had been offensive to the American people. I was sure, I said, that ten years of good behavior toward this country on the part of the Chinese Communist regime would not suffice to wipe out in the minds of many of our people the memories of the provocative and hostile attitude which they had exhibited toward our representatives and toward this country in general in these recent months and years, not to mention their gratuitous and uncalled for entry into the hostilities in Korea. The frequency with which he introduced this subject and the emphasis which he laid upon it seemed to me a strong indication that it was in this area, namely of its relationships with the Chinese Communist Government, that the Soviet Government felt itself inhibited in discussing the subject of a cease fire in Korea.

June 5

Mr. Matthews:

The following is the report which I promised you by phone a few minutes ago. The reception today was the same as the other time, if anything even more cordial and with a greater freedom of exchange.

After some talk about other things, I again introduced the subject of Korea. I said I had thought at length about our last conversation. I could understand, I said, why the Soviet Government might not care to express itself in this way on the questions I had introduced. But there was, as I hoped he would recognize, good reason on our part for making the inquiry. If we were to approach with a view to arriving at a cease fire, the regimes whose forces were opposing us in Korea, a number of questions would certainly arise in which the Soviet Government would surely experience an interest and in which it would be useful for us to know their views. . . . I pointed out, as an example of the problem, the dilemma we would be in if the Chinese Communist forces just disappeared again from the Korean scene. Who could give us any assurance, in this case, that they would not reassemble their forces and intervene again in Korea at some future date.

My host then stated that he was in a position to say the following to me:

The Soviet Government wanted peace and wanted a peaceful solution of the Korean question, and at the earliest possible moment. However, since its forces were not participating in the hostilities in Korea, it did not feel that it could take part in any discussion of the question of a cease fire.

He did not know whether I wanted his personal advice, but if I did, it would be that the United States Government get into touch with the North Koreans and the Chinese Communists in this matter.

I told him that I found his statement a clear one and would take careful note of it. I could understand, as I had said before, why his Government might wish to take this position. I could not tell him, what action my Government would take—whether or not, that is, it would wish to pursue the line he had suggested. But if it did, and if questions arose in the discussions which were of interest to the Soviet Government but on which, in the circumstances, its views could not be directly consulted, then I trusted his Government would take note of the fact that an effort had been made on our side to take account of a possible Soviet interest, and our conversations with others would not be taken as an indication that we were trying to solve the Korean problem for all time with no regard whatsoever to Soviet views and interests.

I said that if, as matters developed, they felt the need of any further discussion of this sort I would be glad to be useful in any way that I could. He replied by reiterating that they did not feel that they could take part in discussions of this subject for the reason that he had indicated. (I gathered that this was simply because his instructions allowed for no other reply).

In order that the Department may have a full record of what was said, and not that it adds anything to the picture of Soviet reactions, I may add that I said to him, in the course of this discussion, that I thought we would find it hard to rely on anything the Chinese Communists or North Koreans might promise. He could, I conceded, counter this by saying: "Do you find it easy to rely on what *we* say?" My answer to that would be that I did not believe in the relevance of the word "trust" to the relations between great powers with conflicting ideologies, but I did believe in the value of what one actually *knew* about other party. The Soviet Government, so far as I could observe, was run by people who took a serious and responsible attitude toward what they conceived to be their own interests. The Chinese Communists, on the contrary, seemed to us to be excited, irresponsible people, on the consistency of whose reactions there could be no reliance.

He replied by charging that we were the people who had excited them, and by complaining about American statements to the effect that no agreement with the Soviet Union was worth anything. I said that in my opinion it depended on the subject of the agreement and the extent to which it corresponded to the interests of both parties. I was sure, I said, that he realized that there could be various attitudes towards agreements, even in the communist world, and reminded him of the reassuring words of Lenin to a disturbed party comrade who had deplored the Brest-Litovsk treaty[8] and had said that at least he hoped it was not being observed on the Soviet side. Lenin, I recalled, had replied: "What the hell do you think we are? We have already broken it forty times."

In general, the conversation, like the first one, was replete with efforts on the part of the other gentleman to bring up the global complaint against American policy.

So much for the conversation. Now a word or two about my own analysis of it.

With regard to the reply, the following seems to be evident:

1. It was plain that he had memorized this statement and attached great importance to it. (I got him to repeat it before I left, so that I am quite sure of its tenor.) There is no question in my mind but that it represented precisely what he had been instructed by Moscow to say. I am also certain that an instruction of this nature on such a subject must have had Politburo approval. It should therefore be taken as a major policy statement of the Soviet Government—more significant, rather than less, by virtue of the fact that it was intended for communication in a non-public channel.

2. The words "at the earliest possible moment" are, in my opinion, highly significant. They would not have been used without most careful consideration. They may even contain a note of warning: namely that if Korean hostilities do *not* cease in the near future, Soviet interests, in the view of the Kremlin, will be adversely affected. In any case, this is a hopeful sign, from the standpoint of arriving at an early cease fire.

3. I take this reply to indicate that Soviet influence has already been brought to bear on the North Koreans and the Chinese Communists to show themselves amenable to proposals for a cease fire. This should not be taken to mean that their attitude in any such discussions will be characterized by good will, sincerity, or cooperativeness. They will make all the trouble they can, and probably advance extreme and absurd demands initially. I would think it likely, however, in the light of the Soviet reply, that cease fire arrangements could finally be obtained from

8. In the Brest-Litovsk treaty of March 1918 with imperial Germany, the hard-pressed Bolshevik government gave up a huge amount of territory so that it could focus on fighting the Whites in the Russian Civil War.

them with firmness and persistence on our part and at a cost in nerves and temper no greater than that which was involved in the final settlement of the Berlin blockade.

4. It is significant that on this second occasion no mention was made of the wider problems of international affairs in the Far East, such as Formosa, the Japanese peace treaty, etc. I think this *may* mean that the Soviet Government would like to see a cease fire even if it did not involve a solution of these wider problems. We would make a mistake, however, in my opinion, to conclude from this that the Soviet Government would be willing, or indeed able, to put over-riding pressure on the Chinese Communist regime to abandon (initially, at any rate) its desire to see these questions coupled with the Korean question. While I would accordingly attach no absolute and final significance to this Soviet omission, I think it nevertheless an encouraging sign and would doubt that the Chinese Communists would be able to maintain their position indefinitely, in the absence of Soviet support.

5. While the Soviet Government has been reluctant to participate directly in discussions looking to a cease fire, we may expect that its desires and interests will find *some* reflection in any positions that may be taken by the North Koreans and the Chinese Communists. The North Koreans would be more likely to appear as the exclusive mouthpieces of the Kremlin; but the necessity to coordinate their statements with those of the Chinese Communists may mean that we cannot take even their statements as the pure distillation of Kremlin views. Nevertheless a high degree of Kremlin influence will be reflected in any discussions that representatives of those two regimes may conduct, and it will be up to us to figure out where one thing begins and the other thing ends.

For whatever it is worth, I would like to add a word about my impression of my host, whom I had not met before. I hold him to be one of the better Soviet types: not just a secret police agent like some of his colleagues. I believe that he is substantially sincere in his enormous bitterness and plaintiveness against the conduct of our Government—his sincerity having, of course, a respectable admixture of that genius for rationalization which distinguishes the Soviet mind. I told him that he was making a great mistake in viewing the statements and activities of our Government as the end-product of some Wall Street conspiracy, and that insofar as these views of his might ever have had any relevance to reality they were at least twenty or thirty years out of date. This made no impression on him nor did I expect it to: I was just keeping up conversation. He is interested in this country but tortured, in his interpretation of it, by his ideology, his genuine disgust with certain manifestations of American life, and the pathological envy and sense of inferiority that overcomes many Soviet personalities when they view our material achievements. The result is a distortion of vision more pathetic than sinister. "You see our country," I said to him when leaving "as in a dream." "No, this is not the dream," he replied, with a certain air of desperation, "this is the deepest reality."

One word more, for whatever it is worth. I hope that we will not hesitate to grasp at once the nettle of action directed toward achieving a cease fire. We may not succeed; but I have a feeling we are moving much closer to the edge of the precipice than most of us are aware and that this is one of the times when the dangers of inaction far exceed those of action.

June 19

More and more I feel myself becoming a receptacle for the confidence of other people. Am I not deceiving them all? Especially when I have so little confidence in them—not in *them* as good and worthy people, but in the strength and understanding they can bring to the solution of their problems? I have not *tried* to deceive them. I have never concealed my own views. In fact, were they to read carefully what I have written or spoken for publication just in the past six months, they could be under no illusions about the chasm between my ideas and theirs. But they never do this. They are not sufficiently interested, ideologically. They will come to all this only later. Now they only look at me and believe that I am an honest man and are thereby relieved. Have I any right, in these circumstances, to accept their confidence?

[Kennan included in his diary a copy of the following letter to Secretary Acheson.]

June 20

Dear Dean:

I am taking this informal means to say to you something which is much on my mind, these days. I will ask you to forgive the penmanship, which is not improved by a dislocated collar bone (the penalty of my old-fashionedness in riding a bicycle, and my new-fashionedness in riding it too fast).

It has long been my conviction that ever since our entry into the Korean hostilities the dominant elements in the Kremlin's attitude toward the Korean situation have been (a) a reluctance to see this situation develop into an outright U.S.-Soviet conflict (meaning a world war), but (b) a mortal apprehension of the appearance of U.S. ground forces either in Manchuria or on the Soviet-Korean border, and of any U.S. air action against Soviet strategic positions or facilities in Manchuria, coupled with a readiness to go to great lengths to deter us from any such actions and to resist them if they occur.

Nothing that has happened since the beginning of July last year seems to me to have thrown any doubt on this hypothesis, on the contrary, Soviet behavior has confirmed it at every turn. Of course, the Soviet leaders would like to see us tossed out of Korea; that would solve all their problems as far as *we* are concerned. But having once made their initial mistake of starting this business on the chance that we would not come in, and having realized the extent of their miscalculation, they are now concerned primarily to liquidate the business on terms not too damaging to their prestige or too disruptive of their relations with the Chinese communists.

On the other hand, they are congenitally suspicious of our motives, and inclined to regard us as unfathomable and unreliable opponents (in the sense that "God knows what they will do"). Our talk about principles and the UN and aggression is to them only a sign of wily hypocrisy and devious motives on our part. And to this must be added the fact that they are pathologically sensitive about their borders and the areas adjacent to them, and for this reason the presence of our forces in that vicinity for nearly a year has been for them a nerve-wracking and excruciating experience, straining to the limit their self-control and patience.

Now when we went north of the parallel the first time, I believe it was with reluctance that the Kremlin encouraged the Chinese communists to intervene—that this was, in fact, a rather desperate measure on their part, taken because the only alternative seemed to be their own involvement, which they did not want.

Now that card has been played, and it hasn't worked. Today, if we continue to advance into North Korea without making vigorous efforts to achieve a cease fire, I fear they will see no alternative but to intervene themselves. And my reason for writing you is simply to give you my impression, which I admit to be instinctive and not supportable by "intelligence," that the silence and scrupulous non-interference in the

Korean fighting on the part of the Soviet Union may conceal the most extreme turmoil of decision in the Kremlin, and that the hour of Soviet action, in the absence of a cessation of hostilities in Korea, may be much closer than we think. This action would not necessarily take the form of immediate intervention in Korea; it could be diversionary in nature, in which case a renewal of trouble in Berlin or some special effort to capitalize on the Iranian situation would seem the most likely possibilities. But my antennae tell me that if the Korean fighting does not stop soon, we should watch out for trouble.

For this reason, I hope the fighting *will* stop soon. For a war with the Soviet Union would probably prove a catastrophe for everyone concerned, including ourselves, when all was said and done. And the Korean operation has brought us much greater blessings than we seem to realize, even if it stops now at, or near, the parallel. Whether they show it or not, the Chinese communists have been taught a terrific lesson. Our action in Korea, so often denounced as futile, may prove to have been the thing that saved Southeast Asia and laid the foundation for the renewal of some sort of stability in the Far East.

[From late June to early September, the Kennans vacationed near Kristiansand, Norway, where they and Annelise's family had a summer house on a peninsula that overlooked a fjord. In late July–early August, Kennan interrupted his vacation to testify before the State Department's loyalty board on behalf of his friend, the China expert John Paton Davies Jr.

Spending much of the summer in Norway would become a decades-long tradition of the Kennan family. Even while vacationing, George kept up a busy schedule of reading, writing, and working outside.]

En route to Norway, June 30

The adult world is a broken-hearted world, since World War II, because there is no leadership in it, and no inspiration.

New York City, August 3

I was annoyed with myself for my habit of staring after women. What could they give me? Nothing but trouble and disillusionment and the dissipation of valuable strength. I must teach myself to remember that I do not really want them: that this habit is a sort of an echo of youth, and a very misleading one at that. In this endeavor, I reflected, I have the best of all possible allies: increasing age.

I went into St. Patrick's cathedral and prayed. And then I walked again down the Avenue, and before me and around me was the parade of women going to work. "How ready I am," I reflected, "for a new seriousness and dedication in life. If I could only see the light, however tiny, at the end of the long road."

August 4

I think I detect an affinity between my own state and that of the old continent of Europe. While the great conflicts raged, people thought that great decisions hung by their issue. But when they were over, it was found they had left nothing in their train but weariness and desolation, and that much that was irreplaceable had really died. Stubbornness, it seems, can be an extremely destructive quality.

When I reach the stage where my distaste of myself is more intense than my laziness and gregariousness and love of comfort, then I shall be getting on, and life may begin to have a content.

Physical desire, in a man my age, is often like the experiment the teachers of psychology used to use as an example: where a finger pressed to the brow for a time is removed, but the sensation, and the illusion of its presence, lingers after.

What is there to be said of a family? There comes a time, with the passage of the years, when one can love only small children. There is no love more certainly transitory than this. It warms the soul only as the faint sunshine of late autumn sometimes warms the body: briefly and without promise. But by that time one is grateful for very little.

It is reasonable that I should look forward with a sense of relief to the prospect of again being an ambassador.[9] It is just about the only profession one can have these days in which nothing, but really nothing, is either expected or required of you.

September 5

As I leave Europe, my only message to myself, in the light of this thoroughly wasted summer, is: Write, you bastard, write. Write desperately, frantically, under pressure from yourself, while God still gives you the

9. In July, Acheson had mentioned the possibility of Kennan's becoming ambassador to the Soviet Union in the following year.

time. Write until your eyes are glazed, until you have writer's cramp, until you fall from your chair for weariness. Only by agitating your pen will you ever press out of your indifferent mind and ailing frame anything of any value to yourself or anyone else. Think neither of rest, nor relaxation, nor health, nor sympathy. These things are not for you. For you the written word, but in quantity—in order that there may be enough grain among the chaff. The discipline of language alone can overcome your innate laziness and lack of interest.

If dislike for one's self were really, as the religious teachers claim, the beginning of virtue in the sight of the Lord, then I should be on the verge of saintliness. . . .

I am ill, of course, with the old malady which is a condition and not a disease. But I am resolved that this time I will not cure it by flying from reality, by running away to the phony protectedness of a hospital bed and a nurse's uniform. If I cannot live in the full contemplation of facts: of the mess I have gotten myself into, of the responsibilities I have incurred, of the long road I must go to arrive at something that would make sense in my life, if I cannot live in this natural hardship, then it is high time I ceased to live entirely. Let the damned sore do its worst, burn through to the surface if it must. Perhaps then we will finally get some clarity and harmony into this warring combination of flesh and spirit. But let it not be cured by delusion.

Pasadena, California, November 4

My thoughts are full of this southern California world I see below me and about me. It is easy to ridicule it, as Aldous Huxley and so many other intellectuals have done—but it is silly, and a form of self-condemnation, to do so. These are ordinary human beings: several million of them. The things that brought them here, and hold them here, are deeply human phenomena, as are the stirrings of anxiety that cause them to be so boastful and defensive about it. Being human phenomena, they are part of ourselves; and when we purport to laugh at them, as though we stood fully outside of them, it is we who are the ridiculous ones.

I feel great anxiety for these people, because I do not think they know what they are in for. In its mortal dependence on two liquids, oil and water, which no individual can easily produce by his own energy, even together with family and friends, the life of this area only shares the fragile quality of all life in the great urban concentrations of the motor age. But here the lifelines of supply seem to me particularly tenuous and vital. That is especially true of water, which they now have to bring from hundreds of miles, and will soon have to bring from thousands of miles, away. But equally disturbing to me is the utter dependence on the costly, uneconomical gadget called the automobile, for practically every process of life from birth and education, through shopping, work and recreation, even courtship, to the final function of burial. . . .

But alongside the feeling of anxiety I have at the sight of these people, there is a questioning as to the effect they are going to have, and the contribution they are going to make, to American society as a whole. Again, this is not conceived in terms of reproach or criticism. There is really a subtle, but profound difference between people here and what Americans used to be, still partly are, in other parts of the country. I am at a loss to define this difference, and am sure that I understand it very imperfectly.

Let me try to get at it by overstating it. Here, it is easy to see that when man is given (as he *can* be given only for relatively brief periods and in exceptional circumstances) freedom both from political restraint and from want, the effect is to render him childlike in many respects: fun-loving, quick to laughter and enthusiasm, unanalytical, unintellectual, outwardly expansive, preoccupied with physical beauty and prowess, given to sudden and unthinking seizures of aggressiveness, driven constantly to protect his status in the group by an eager conformism—yet not unhappy. In this sense, southern California, together with all that tendency of American life which it typifies, is childhood without the promise of maturity, with the promise only of a continual widening and growing impressiveness of the childhood world. And when the day of reckoning and hardship comes, as I think it must, it will be, as everywhere among children, the cruelest and most ruthless natures will seek to protect their interests by enslaving the others; and the others, being only children, will be easily enslaved. In this way, values will suddenly prove to have been lost that were forged slowly and laboriously in the more rugged experience of Western political development elsewhere.

It is not meant as an offense to the great achievements of the Latin cultural world if I say that there will take place here something like a "latinization" of political life. Southern California will become politically, as it already is climatically, a Latin American country. And if any democracy survives it will be, as in Latin America, a romantic-Garibaldian type of democracy, founded on the interaction of an emotional populace and a stirring, heroic type of popular leader. When, as in many Latin countries, this sort of political system must operate within the framework of a great ecclesiastical and civil tradition, it is still compatible with a respectable civilization. But what will be the effect where it starts from the wrong end and represents the disintegration of liberty rather than, as in Rome, the raising of a structure of law and custom from the chaos of primeval despotism? Will it not operate to subvert our basic political tradition? And if so, what will then happen to our whole urbanized, industrialized society, so vulnerable to regimentation and centralized control?

1952

After arriving in Moscow as the new ambassador in May 1952, Kennan took personally the virulently anti-American propaganda posters plastered on the streets. He was indignant at Soviet restrictions that isolated him and other foreigners from officials, intellectuals, and ordinary citizens. He was also dismayed at the Truman administration's lack of interest in serious negotiations with the Soviets on such pressing issues as Korea, Germany, and the atomic arms race.

On September 19 while on a stopover in Berlin, Kennan vented his resentment by telling reporters that his isolation in Moscow paralleled that imposed by the Germans after they had declared war on the United States in 1941. On September 26, the Soviet newspaper Pravda *sharply attacked Kennan. On October 3, the Soviet government declared him* persona non grata. *He would be the only U.S. ambassador thus expelled by the Soviet Union. Kennan felt devastated and alone, rejected by both Washington and Moscow, two capitals seemingly able to agree on nothing except further escalating the tensions between them. He despaired that nuclear war was imminent.*

Princeton, January 1

The President having announced during the past week his intention to nominate me for appointment as Ambassador to the U.S.S.R. upon the resignation of Ambassador Alexander Kirk (thereby making me—as far as the public is concerned—already half-way the Ambassador), and this being plainly a mission of which some sort of chronological record ought to be kept, for historical purposes and for personal convenience, it occurred to me that this day, the first of the new year, might be a good time to undertake it—for the assignment will begin at once to affect my life in various ways and its execution will in turn be affected by impressions I receive and things I do at this time.

The papers today carried the news of a most curious New Year's message that Stalin had sent to the Japanese people. While the complete text was not carried, it was plain that the message had special significance and that it was in terms offensive to this country—comparing the present situation of the Japanese people with the position of Soviet territory under German occupation in the recent war. When one tries to interpret this move, a number of things spring to mind, including the obvious Soviet discontentment with the terms of the peace treaty, the rivalries between the Moscow and Peking[10] factions in the Japanese Communist Party, and the present military vulnerability of the Japanese islands in view of our preoccupation in Korea, all of which must have been prominent in Stalin's mind; but all one can conclude is that the Kremlin attaches exceptional importance to the Japanese situation at the present juncture.

January 7 and 8

Received a visit Tuesday afternoon from Professor Herbert Frankel, a South African who I understand to be at present a professor at Oxford. He wanted to talk about colonial questions, linking his interest to the approach he felt he had noted in the publication of my Chicago lectures.[11] He wanted to know what I felt we could do in general about the great arc of underdeveloped peoples spreading from Africa to southeast Asia, about the development of their attitudes toward the West, etc. Explaining to him that my views were those of no one but myself, I told him that I did not think one could generalize about this problem, there being tremendous differences between various countries and regimes. In most instances I did not feel that the local popular leaders were capable at present of looking at the problem or discussing it in calm and rational terms. It seemed to me that things would have to happen that would cause them to become conscious, on the basis of their own experience, of their need for ties with the West and of the necessity for regarding Western nations with respect, as a prerequisite to the maintenance of such ties.

If these things could be brought home to them no other way, I thought the West had no choice but to leave them strictly alone in their own affairs, merely retaining (and if need be, by force of arms) those facilities and sources of supply which had already been available to western

10. Peking was the English name preferred by the government of the People's Republic of China for present-day Beijing.
11. Kennan, *American Diplomacy* (1951).

nations for long periods of time and had entered into the pattern of our security. In this, I said, the West ought not to be terrified by threats that such and such country would "go communist" if it were not cultivated and wooed by the West; the effect of any wide spread of communism in that area would certainly be to enhance the centrifugal forces within the communist orbit. The raw materials, except in parts of Africa, were not really vital to us at this time nor would they be wholly denied to us. And as far as attitudes were concerned, an hysterical and childish nationalism was little preferable to, or different from, what we would see if they were "to go communist"—so far as our interests were concerned. What we needed were cool nerves, the determination to hold—by force of arms, if need be—such strategic and economic facilities as were vital to us and could be held without excessive cost and effort, and a continued readiness to work loyally and helpfully with any group in that part of the world that was willing to recognize the realities of our own position and the respect we deserved as a decent and serious force in world affairs.

January 18

In writing today to Rev. John Bodo of the First Presbyterian Church of Princeton, New Jersey, to inform him that I wished to meet with the Session and be received as a member of the church, I added the following:

"I am afraid that even as a member of the Church I shall be a very imperfect Christian. But I find myself weighed down, these days, with the realization that responsibilities are now being placed upon me so unusual and so vast in their implications that I have no chance of coping with them to any good effect except in a spirit of dedication to purposes higher than myself and greater than myself. What I have to do can be successfully done only from an inner posture of humility, conviction and self-renunciation. This imposes a duty of preparation and self-discipline, for which I need the help of the Church; and I believe I would be guilty of the sin of pride if I did not accept it.

"I am aware that this is not a fully adequate approach to the duties of a confessing Christian, and that in particular I should be thinking not of myself but of what I might be able to contribute to the Church community. But the burden I am to shoulder is not one of participation in any local community: it is one that I must bear far away and in loneliness—in an atmosphere of the most heartless and contemptuous challenge to everything the Church stands for, where people can even exhibit all the evidences of outward success and power to bolster their thesis that man is most responsive to appeals to his fears and jealousies and resentments and least responsive to those sides of his nature that Christianity values. To reside in this place that we can, without exaggeration or poetic liberty, describe as the most impressive example of hell on earth that our time has known—and to reside there as the leading representative and exponent of the world with which the Christian faith is today most prominently identified—is surely a heavy and unusual task for any Christian; and perhaps this one may be forgiven if he concentrates his attention at this time on the problem of how he can best cleanse himself and brace himself spiritually for the ordeal."

[Kennan included in the diary a note he wrote to Chip Bohlen and Dean Acheson, which follows in the next entry.]

January 23

There is one thing, however, that hangs over me so heavily . . . and that is my concern at the continued evidences of what seem to me to be a sweeping and fateful misunderstanding underlying our approach to the peoples of Asia and the Middle East. I am no specialist on these areas myself, but the evidence seems to me so eloquent and incontrovertible that I fail to see how its major lesson can be mistaken or questioned. Would you mind if I spoke my mind to you on this subject with complete frankness and informality?

Surely one of the reasons for our continued failures throughout these areas has been our inability to understand how profound, how irrational, and how erratic has been the reaction generally of the respective peoples to the ideas and impulses that have come to them from the West in recent decades. This applies particularly to the intellectuals who play so prominent a part in political leadership and in the molding of public opinion. To ascertain the reasons for the intensely anti-American attitudes manifested by these people would be to delve deeply into psychological reactions and the origins of various forms of neuroses. I have thoughts about these matters, but will not take up your time with them here.

Only one thing I would emphasize. The respective reactions are obviously emotional and subconscious, and not likely to be altered by any attempts on our part to meet them by any verbal appeal to rational processes. If our Asiatic friends are to be brought to a more sober and sensible frame of mind it will be through their own experiences. And these we can help to condition through our actions, hardly through our words.

The sort of actions likely to be useful in this connection are severely limited. To date, it seems to me that most of what we have done has had the effect of pouring oil on the fire. Since what is eating at the hearts of so many of our Asian friends is really the question of status, aggravated by a burning sense of inferiority and jealousy of us for our riches and for the relative security of our position, anything that gives them the possibility of demonstrating weakness or vacillation on our part, or a degree of dependence on them, indulges their yearning to feel themselves important and is grist to the mill of their preconceptions. The maw into which our favors and concessions and acts of generosity are entering is bottomless. These people can consume an infinite number of our kindnesses just as they can consume infinite quantities of our material goods, and when all is said and done, there will be no more to show for the one than for the other. On the contrary, favors and kindnesses will be normally hailed as evidences of our weakness, our dependence, and our ignominy, and exploited as proof of the cleverness of those who succeeded in extorting all this beneficence out of the silly Americans. The main psychological effect of our pressing various forms of aid on individual governments will be, it seems to me, to convince the peoples generally in that part of the world that in addition to being white and imperialistic we are stupid, uncertain, weak, and obviously on the skids of history, and that they are more important than anybody ever told them they were. . . .

Let us not deceive ourselves into believing that the fanatical local chauvinisms of the Middle East represent a force that can be made friendly or dependable from our point of view, or one to which we would have any right to engage ourselves in the moral sense.[12] It may, in certain circumstances, be useful to our short-term interests that such movements should continue to exist and to manifest themselves as independent movements, since nationalistic fanaticism and extremism are obviously less dangerous from our standpoint than an association of the respective peoples with the more powerful and disciplined force of Soviet Communism, which might be the alternative; but both these forces, the nationalist and the communist, are dangerous and revolting; they have

12. Beginning in 1951, the democratically elected Iranian government of Mohammad Mosaddegh attempted to nationalize the rich oil fields and refineries owned by the British-owned Anglo-Iranian Oil Company. In 1953, the CIA intervened to overthrow Mosaddegh in favor of the shah.

similar origins and traits; both are by nature hostile to us and incapable of contributing anything positive to the type of world we must seek. The Iranian message demanding withdrawal of the British Consulates was Bolshevik in tone, spirit and content, and reflected the debasement and medievalism of international practice common to both movements. If, then, we encourage nationalism in that area, we should do so in the cold light of calculated self-interest, and should let our people know what we are doing. Above all, we should not deceive ourselves into hoping that out of it can come anything with which we ought to be associated either morally or politically. These chauvinistic movements, permeated as they are by violence and immaturity, will breed bloodshed, horror, hatred, and political oppression worse than anything we see today; and the only relevant question is whether they do it in a way susceptible of exploitation by the Kremlin to the advantage of its purposes and the detriment of ours, or whether their workings have a different effect.

Let us then, first of all, avoid associating ourselves with these forces in any relationships of military alliance. . . . The answer to this will of course be: But what of the strategic importance of the territory of these countries, and what of the facilities and privileges we require in that part of the world for the security of the Atlantic community? I fully grant the validity of this consideration, but I draw a sharp distinction between this problem and that of our political intimacy or popularity with the local regimes. To retain these facilities and positions we can use today only one thing: military strength, backed by the resolution and courage to employ it. There is nothing else that will avail us—least of all, attempts to incur the benevolent predisposition of these dreadful characters who in many instances bear the responsibility for local political leadership and on whose bizarre frames the trappings of statesmanship rest like an old dress suit on a wooden scarecrow.

The Western world has no need to be apologetic about the minimal facilities and privileges it requires in the Middle East. Most of these have already been in existence for long periods of time, and there has grown up around them a right of usage similar to that of my country neighbor whom I permit for years on end to drive over my property to reach his own. The thesis to which we acquiesced in Iran: that such arrangements can be cancelled or reversed abruptly, on the basis of somebody's whim or mood, is preposterous and indefensible. It is a dangerous distortion of the concept of sovereignty. But beyond that the British and ourselves have a responsibility of the most solemn and far-reaching nature which prohibits our being spendthrift and over-generous with things that represent the strategic assets not of ourselves alone but of the entire Western world. The commitments we have undertaken to our allies in continental Europe and elsewhere place us in a new position: that of an agent as well as a principal—and charity, by consequence, is beyond our competence. Such things as Abadan and Suez are important to the local peoples only in terms of their *amour propre*—and an artificially inflamed *amour propre* at that.[13] To us, some of these things are important in a much more serious sense, and for reasons that today are sounder and better and more defensible than they ever were in history. . . .

It would be nice to have the entire Middle East remain permanently amenable to Western influence, but that is simply not in the cards today. If we leave these people to their own devices, two things can happen: either they continue to stew in their own tantrums and furies, exacerbated by the revelation that the United States is not going to continue to fuss over them and tickle their sense of self-importance, and they finally get tired of it or fight among themselves, or they yield in one degree or another to Soviet influence and lose in whole or in part their own power of decision. In the latter event, pro-Soviet regimes are to be expected, but not necessarily, or even probably, any attempt at full Soviet occupation, unless there is a world war. In either event, our basic interests can best be guarded if we have quietly and firmly dug in, betimes, at those places that are really vital to us. Had the British occupied Abadan, I would personally have no great worry about what happened to the rest of the country. . . . Similarly, if we and the British were to consolidate the position at Suez with utmost determination, relying on no one but ourselves, who would there be to challenge it? The Russians? Possibly, but again only in the case of a third world war. The local peoples? Can we really seriously maintain the thesis that at a time when we are spending thirty or forty billion dollars a year for defense, we cannot, despite the Korean campaign and our other urgent commitments, handle a military problem which the Israeli Army was easily able to handle several years ago with very little manpower and with equipment that would surely constitute an infinitesimal part of what we turn out in one year? . . .

What I would plead is that we make up our minds at this time precisely what, in physical terms, it is essential that we and the British hold

13. Abadan is home to a major oil refinery in Iran. The Suez Canal is an artery of global commerce.

onto in the Middle Eastern area (I don't pretend to know what it is, and I speak here of Abadan and Suez only by way of illustration) and that we then take steps in whatever manner is most suitable to see that these objects, if they are in any way jeopardized by local hostility, are militarily secured with the greatest possible dispatch. If we do this quietly, with determination, and without being apologetic about it, there may be a great many flamboyant words and a certain amount of brandishing of weapons against us, but I doubt that there will be much more. . . .

I am afraid we are once more, in this case, up against an ultimate reality of world leadership—the one we see in Korea, and one many of our people don't like: and that is that there are situations in this world where not even worthy and necessary ends can be achieved without the application of force—and not just force applied in great blind occasional surges, to the blare of trumpets, but rather taking the form of wearisome, endless, unpleasant vigilance in extremely unpleasant places.

Pasadena, February 2

A young man in the Foreign Service sent me for my comments an article he had written in the hope that it might be placed in *Foreign Affairs*—a profession of faith in the possibility of human perfectibility and the achievement of world community through the agency of individual freedom. Pounding out an answer to him on the typewriter in a sleeping car, I found myself saying the following, which I then judiciously extracted from the draft and confide, instead, to the present record.

". . . I do not take so optimistic a view of the chances for human progress. In general, man is a weak and bad creature, who has lost most of the virtues of the beast and acquired very few of those of the angel. He is not perfectible by education or enlightenment. When supported by a firm social fabric, he can be made to place acceptable restraints upon his less pleasant instincts, and to give a good imitation of walking like a man, but in the great majority of cases the threshold of savagery is never far away. It requires only a minor disintegration of the social fabric to break the barrier and release the demon that resides inside. I have seen little in the development of our egalitarian democracy that would encourage me to believe that it will be capable, operating on its present principles, to continue for long to provide a social fabric adequate to prevent a deterioration of social behavior. Nor can I fully accept the thesis that man's best future lies in the unrestrained exercise of his individual freedom. The exercise of this freedom in our own country is leading to the ravaging of its natural resources and to a serious deterioration of social environment, through the operation of uncontrolled technological change. Plainly, American man, at any rate, is going to have to submit to greater discipline if he is not to suffer a lowering of his own cultural level, and the question is: from whom shall the discipline flow?

"The totalitarians understand the mass of men probably better than we do, but feel no pity for them and for this reason do not hesitate to take advantage of them. They debase men with equanimity, calculating correctly that the more men are debased, the easier they are to control. In the end they, or their successors, must share in the evil consequences of this debasement, but that will be by the workings of nature and should lead to no light-hearted rejoicing or self-congratulations on the part of the democracies, for the debasement will by then have become a fact of history, not quickly or easily repaired.

"Men will be governed to good effect when those few souls who are capable at once of understanding human nature and of pitying it muster the ruthlessness and decision necessary for the conquest and exercise of political power. Such episodes have already occurred in human history, but usually through the evolution of some hereditary oligarchy not through the workings of democracy. The chance of anything of this sort occurring in our own country is infinitesimally small."

Princeton, April 22–23

The President's intention to appoint me Ambassador to Moscow was made known on December 27, and it led immediately (the thought being taken for the deed) to the usual flurry of letters and phone calls and requests for interviews. . . .

On April 1, I went to Washington and paid a *pro forma* call on the President. He had at that time just announced his intention not to run again, and was in a relaxed and genial frame of mind. He indicated that he shared my views as to the motives and principles of behavior of the Soviet leaders, and had never believed that they wanted another great war. He asked me to write to him from time to time, saying that he liked to have personal reports from our representatives abroad. Beyond this, he gave me no instructions of any kind.

The following day I was sworn in, and lunched privately with Secretary Acheson. He, too, was cordial but very reserved; and he said nothing that could give me any clue to the basic line of policy I was to follow in my new capacity.

The next day, April 3, I went to the Soviet Embassy, accompanied by Dick Davis (who now has the Soviet desk in the Department) and lunched with the Ambassador, Aleksandr Panyushkin, and his Counselor, whose name was something like Karavaev. They were cordial and pleasant and we had a reasonably amiable talk, keeping off the more painful issues of the day, concerning which neither of us had any instructions to say anything authoritative on the part of our Government. Panyushkin of course referred to Stalin's most recent press interview, published only the day before, in which he had again affirmed his belief in the possibility of co-existence between the two countries and had cautiously allowed that there might be circumstances under which a new meeting of heads of states would not be entirely useless. Panyushkin wondered why similar statements were not made on the American side: a suggestion which I am sure he had instructions to put forward. I had the feeling that both the Soviet officials were somewhat worn down by the hostility with which they and their Government were now confronted in the United States. Human nature, and particularly Russian nature, is such that this state of mind is not at all incompatible with a complete understanding of the deadly hostility of the entire communist movement toward us and a general knowledge of the restrictions and insults to which the diplomatic corps in Moscow has been subjected for a period of three decades.

Some days later (April 14) I made a similar call on Mr. Malik in New York. I found him much more bitter and sour, mouthing the same things he had said to me when I had occasion to talk with him nearly a year before. He professed to believe that American business circles wanted war and cited as proof of this the frequent statements in the press that an abrupt back-tracking on the rearmament effort would produce another major depression. He, too, asked why there was no reply to Stalin's statements. I told him that we did not wish to mislead people by making vague general statements. At the end of our talk he spoke of the Soviet Union being threatened. "Are you sure," I asked, "that your Government does not prefer to be threatened?" "Positively," was his answer.

Reflecting, when back in Princeton, on my visit to Washington, as well as on the various evidences of Soviet willingness to enter on some new phase of discussion and negotiation with the Western powers, I became concerned to realize that I had had absolutely no real instructions of any sort either from the Secretary of State or from the President, and not even any proper guidance as to their attitude with respect to the acute problems of the moment, such as Germany, the Korean armistice talks, the disarmament discussions in the United Nations, etc. I therefore telephoned Chip Bohlen and arranged for a meeting with the Secretary and his top advisers on April 18. The meeting took place immediately after lunch, and lasted only an hour—the Secretary having an appointment at the White House in mid-afternoon. I was disappointed to find that it was left entirely to me to set the trend of the discussion. The official attitude, as far as I could see, was: "You have asked to see us; we are obliging and have come together at your request; now what is it you want of us?"

I began by describing the delicacy of my coming position in Moscow, pointing out that the publicity attending my appointment, together with the fact of my previous experience there and the positions I had held in the Department and also the general importance of the American embassy in that place, all meant that anything I said in that city would be listened to with great eagerness and interest; and that even statements made to other diplomats, correspondents or visitors would get back to the Soviet Government in the majority of cases; that these and any other evidences of my opinions would be scrutinized with intense curiosity by the Soviet leaders and might well have the result of affecting their attitudes. For this reason, I said, I felt that I ought to have the clearest possible understanding of just what sort of thing our Government wanted me to say and what sort of impression I should try to convey.

I then brought up the question of Germany. From the discussion which ensued I could only gather that our Government did not want any agreement with the Soviet Government about Germany at this time and wished if possible to avoid any discussion that would carry us along that path. We were staking everything at the moment on the attempt to get the new contractual arrangements with the West German Government and the agreement on the European defense force both signed and "in the bag" before any discussions with the Russians could complicate matters. I said that this position worried me very much: I thought it likely that the Russians would press us mercilessly along the lines of their recent notes and would say in effect, "If you don't like our proposals then tell us and the world what your own ideas are for the unification of Germany." I thought we ought to state clearly the terms on which we could consent to unification but say that we would not hold up progress on the West German arrangements for a day in favor of negotiations on the four-power level. The reply was that unless we could get these two agreements signed within the next few weeks, our whole European policy would be grievously affected, and nothing should be done which could possibly detract attention from this program.

With respect to Korea, I gathered that what our Government wanted was simply a termination of hostilities, with the idea that we would garrison lightly the resulting truce line and rely henceforth on the sanction of major war in case it was violated. I pointed out immediately that this left open the question of "major war against whom?" and asked whether it was not considered desirable to get the Soviet Union back into North Korea as a responsible partner. On this I could get no clear guidance and gathered that policy thinking had not advanced this far. I was only able to conclude, therefore, that our Government is indifferent, at least for purposes of contact with the Soviet Government at this time, to the question of *which* communist authority should bear responsibility in northern Korea in the event that a truce is concluded. I did not even bring up the doubts I have about our attitude toward Chiang and about the wisdom and inflexibility of the peace treaty arrangements we are making with Japan, for I knew there would be no point in attempting to discuss these matters.

I raised the question of our attitude in the disarmament negotiations at Geneva, and it was agreed that I should be furnished supplementary data on our position and the background thinking that lay behind it. I was depressed to hear the Secretary say that it was our idea to get some real measure of disarmament first, in the hope that this would render the political problems less acute and easier of adjustment. If there is any one lesson to be plainly derived from the experiences we have had with disarmament in the past half-century it is that armaments are a function and not a cause of political tensions and that no limitation of armaments on a multilateral scale can be effected as long as the political problems are not tackled and regulated in some realistic way. As far as I was concerned, therefore, I felt that our Government could not be more on the wrong tack.

I ended up by saying that I had come down there not to make suggestions about policy, rather to find out what I should know about it, but that nevertheless I could not conceal my concern at the general pattern that seemed to me to flow from what I had been told. As far as I could see, we were expecting to be able to gain our objectives both in the East and the West without making any concessions whatsoever to the views and interests of our adversaries. Our position seemed to me to be comparable to the policy of unconditional surrender in the recent war. This position, I thought, would be fine if we were really all-powerful, and could hope to get away with it. I very much doubted that this was the case, and I thought we ought to reflect very carefully on these matters and see whether we were sure that it would not be better to attempt to solve at least some of these problems by accommodation with our adversaries rather than by complete defiance of them.

The more I thought about this meeting, after returning to Princeton, the more darkly I viewed the chances for my mission. I was depressed not only by the meeting itself but by observations Chip Bohlen had made to me privately about our atomic weapons policy in which it seemed to me that he had succumbed entirely to the flat and inflexible thinking of the Pentagon, in which the false mathematics of relative effectiveness in the weapons of mass destruction was given a sort of an absolute value and all other possible factors dismissed from the equation as of no demonstrable importance. The philosophic difference between this view and my own was so profound, and the hour of our conversation so late, that I could not even bring myself to argue with him about it, but it shocked me deeply, for he and I have been closer than any other people in Washington, I think, in our views about Russia generally, and I realized that the difference of view implicit in his remarks would go very deep and would really prevent any further intellectual intimacy on the questions of American policy between the two of us.

I returned to Princeton, then, feeling extremely lonely. There was, it seemed to me, no one left in Washington with whom I could discuss matters fully, frankly and hopefully against the background of a common outlook and understanding. There would surely be no one of this sort in Moscow, for the doubts I had cut much too deep to be revealed in any way to junior members of the Mission, for whom they would only be discouraging and demoralizing. It seemed to me that I was being sent on a mission to play a game at which I could not possibly win and that part of my obligation consisted of assiduously concealing from the world the fact that I could not win at all and taking upon myself the onus of whatever overt failures were involved. I imagined that I was not the first person who had labored under such handicaps in the strange profession of diplomacy, but it was with a very heavy heart that I set forth, thus empty handed, uninstructed, and uncertain, to what is surely the most important and delicate of the world's diplomatic tasks at this particular juncture.

[The following entry is from a separate notebook kept by Kennan as he flew from Moscow to Berlin, and then on to London. He recorded his reactions to the explosion in Moscow after his Berlin comment that the Soviets treated foreign diplomats almost as badly as the Germans had done during the war.]

This is the notebook used by G. F. Kennan to record ideas for the questions that might be asked him by reporters at Tempelhof Airport in Berlin, in September 1952. This is the incident that resulted in his expulsion from the U.S.S.R.

Where are you going?

I am on my way to London to attend a meeting of some of our European chiefs of mission with the Under Secretary of State, Mr. Bruce.[14] This is one of the gatherings of chiefs which we hold at fairly frequent intervals. The subjects of discussion will presumably cover the entire range of the important problems of American foreign policy on Europe at the present time.

Are you going to report on (the Communist Party Congress, the Chinese talks, etc.)?

I am prepared to report to my colleagues my impressions on any phases of the Soviet scene that may be of interest to them.

What do you think about (the Party Congress, the Chinese talks, etc.)?

I do not think it would be appropriate for me to comment on internal developments in the Soviet Union.

Is the situation more hopeful than it was when you went in last spring?

The situation is not worse.

Have you seen Stalin?

There has been no occasion for me to ask to be received by Premier Stalin.

What do you think of the last Soviet note on Germany?[15]

It shows that the Soviet leaders do not wish the discussion of precisely those matters which will have to be discussed first if there is to be a really free and united Germany.

14. David K. E. Bruce.

15. In the note the Soviets were trying to head off Western agreements that would strengthen the West German army and integrate it into the U.S.-led alliance.

[Kennan wrote the following paragraph with a different writing instrument and in a shaky hand—perhaps because of air turbulence.]

Don't be a boy, and don't feed the little ego. Be deliberate. Learn not to mind pauses and silences. Expect the lonely and the boring. Get used to it. Never be a raconteur unless you are desperate.

Have consulted with Department through Chip. Desire is that we simply ignore *Pravda* attack and that I return & resume duties normally.

From Shakespeare's *Henry VIII*

> Nay then, farewell!
> I have touched the highest point of all my greatness;
> And, from that full meridian of my glory,
> I haste now to my setting; I shall fall
> Like a bright exhalation in the evening,
> And no man see me more.

I have had no real successes, and I dare not hope for any. I shall be satisfied if, when I complete my contribution to public life in our country, I can say: because of me and of what I have done the things my father cared about died a little harder, and a little later, than would otherwise have been the case.

[The Soviet government waited until October 3 to declare Kennan *persona non grata* for his remarks in Berlin comparing the Soviets with the Nazis. Not knowing that this blow would fall, Kennan attended a State Department conference in London, then traveled to Penzance (probably for a vacation), and then to the U.S. embassy in Bonn.]

London–Penzance, September 20

There remain two academic years until I shall be ready to retire. What to do then?

The following possibilities exist:

(a) Public life—*mitmachen* [participation], so to speak.
This could be more diplomacy, more Princeton and boards of directors.

(b) Private life.
This could be farming, or writing—which could be social-political, historical-biographic, Russian-specialized, or teaching.

There occur to me random thoughts that seem to precede and underlie any decision. Among them:

A man of fifty, which I shall be when I retire, has little to lose in life, and no reason to spare himself. Productive work is all he has to live for, unless it be his children. And children are not really thankful if you sacrifice yourself for them. They would rather you should be something. Being something, in this sense, has nothing to do with fame or popularity. A man who isn't anything must be ashamed before his own son, unless he has great humility. That is perhaps the best and wisest of all—to have great humility. But I fear it is not my dish.

What is to *be* something? Is it not to do something? In the case of a man, at least, as opposed to a woman? I think so. It is difficult, in this day and age, to glorify the individual as such, aside from his function. There is no setting for it, and no real training. One can perhaps avoid the worst ill-graces of increasing age: the flabbiness, the garrulousness, the coquetting with one's years as a means of claiming the respect and applause of others. But few are apt to live in a manner which is its own justification. Productive work is needed to carry the inescapable embarrassments and humiliations of age: the need for rest, the yearning for regularity and routine, the slower tempo of the physical habits.

A woman, as she grows older, should become more sociable, and should seek her compensation in service to others, without asking too much from them.

A man, as he grows older, should withdraw. He should avoid, like the pest, all forms of bonhommie, of exhibitionism, of false, forced, or empty conviviality. He should refrain entirely from telling his anecdotes, rather than run the risk of telling them twice.

And because, as I said at the outset, a man of fifty has little to lose, he should, if possible, be scourged relentlessly, like a failing horse, into silence, into physical leanness, into self-discipline, into solitude, into useful activity.

[The following entry only hints at the intense emotions engulfing Kennan as ambassador. He believed that unless someone such as himself halted the escalation in tensions, nuclear war—and thus the end of civilization—would likely ensue. The Truman administration, however, regarded tensions with Moscow as useful in pressuring Western Europeans to accept the rearmament of West Germany and its integration into the Western alliance. Frustrated with Washington, Kennan hoped that the Kremlin might be more forthcoming. He argued that the Soviet leadership was divided between hardliners and another group, who knew about his background, appreciated what he was trying to do, and who might consider negotiations, particularly over Germany, to ease tensions. Fearing that despite his efforts war might erupt and that he might then be tortured by the Soviets, Kennan asked the CIA to provide him with cyanide capsules.]

Bad Godesberg, West Germany, September 29

The following is a classified record of certain events surrounding my service to date as Ambassador to the Soviet Union. It is meant to be kept in secure Government files until duly declassified, after which time I would wish it to be placed with my personal papers.

Before leaving for Moscow I sought, and was granted, an interview with the Secretary of State and other officials in the Department of State, for the purpose of discussing my mission. . . . [But] there was no real interest in Washington at that time for any possible basis of agreement with the Russians on the matters, particularly Germany and Japan, which seemed to me the most important. It seemed to be the thought in the Department that once we had completed our "building of strength" we would attempt the negotiation of a multilateral treaty of disarmament. Germany, and with it Europe, were apparently to remain divided indefinitely.

All this seemed to me quite unreal, and I resented being forced to go out on this delicate assignment with no objective in mind, and with no realistic suggestions to make as to the terms on which we would agree to a settlement of our differences. Bohlen came up to Princeton for a weekend, about that time, and we argued bitterly about this the most of one night. On my way to Moscow I had to fend off numerous press inquiries by saying that I hoped to be able to do something to reduce tension. There was nothing else I could say.

Once in Moscow, I became exhilarated by the challenging and stimulating atmosphere and by the pleasing degree to which I felt within myself the ability to feel my way into its mysteries and nuances. I soon sensed that to at least one faction within the regime my presence there was a source of alarm, precisely for the reason that it was realized that my views were moderate and conciliatory, that it was hard to make me out as an enemy or an ignoramus, that if things came to a point where

I was able to talk to anyone in authority, it would be a "real" talk rather than a protocolar one or the usual diplomatic sparring. I was encouraged, furthermore, by the appreciative responses from Washington and our diplomatic missions in the field to the interpretative messages I wrote and by the extent to which, as it seemed to me, my views were respected by my diplomatic colleagues in Moscow. These things gave me, after the long frustrations of Washington, the sense of having a certain amount of influence and power; and I hoped that if I could establish any sort of quiet communication to the Soviet leaders and get any idea of their real views, this might give me sufficient authority and self-confidence to challenge our existing lines of policy, with the advent of a new administration, and to bring about the evolution of a more constructive and hopeful approach, at least with respect to Europe and the Soviet Union itself.

However, the circles in Moscow to whom my presence was unwelcome did not lose much time in taking measures of self defense. The anti-American campaign was pushed with great vehemence immediately after my arrival, and I could not help but feel that this was done partly as a warning to Soviet circles, particularly the intelligentsia, to have nothing to do with me. In the beginning of July a man who, at least until recently, had been a Foreign Office official in a responsible position, appeared in my office with proposals of so wildly criminal a nature that I could not tell whether this was an incredibly clumsy effort at provocation or an elaborate form of insult. In either case, it boded ill for the future, insofar as it revealed that I was the object of burning resentment somewhere in the Soviet hierarchy. It was also clear that this "somewhere" included at least a portion of the police apparatus.

There seemed, in the circumstances, to be no possible way to defend myself against intrigue and hostility within the Soviet Union except to keep my skirts clean and to give my enemies no openings for compromising me. But that meant, at best, simply continuing to lead a life of wary isolation. I had no means of breaking through the barriers with which I was surrounded and establishing any contact with the people at the head of the regime. I did indeed put out hints that I would be glad to have some sort of informal contact through a cut-out; but not only was this barren of positive results—the incident of the [July] provocateur actually seemed to have been an answer to it, of a peculiarly malicious and insulting nature.

My only other recourse would have been to request an interview with Stalin himself. This I was most reluctant to do. Had I asked for the usual formal type of interview, he would have put me on the spot by merely inquiring what I wanted of him and what proposals I had to make. I would then have had to admit that I had no desiderata whatsoever, whereupon I would be ushered out with the implication that I had taken up the time of a busy man to no good purpose. By obtaining such an interview I would also have exhausted whatever credit I had for obtaining interviews with him generally, and would have placed myself in a weaker position to insist on being received by Stalin on a subsequent occasion, if and when I ever actually had anything to propose. Similarly, I saw no possibility of arranging for an informal talk with him. I had no channel through which to approach him but the Foreign Office. I knew the Foreign Office to be under the direct control and supervision of the police. Their game would plainly be to turn any request for an interview into a formal one. It would be hard to stop them. They would have Mr. Vyshinsky present at the interview, and would publish the fact that it had taken place. This would not only have made quite impossible any frank, informal exchange of views but would also have raised a host of anxious questions and mountains of speculation in the Western press as to what had been said.

I therefore had no choice but to bide my time and hope for some sort of a change in the situation. Such a change could have come only if the Soviet Government had provided me with some informal channel of contact with its leading people and if our own Government had evolved a positive and realistic set of desiderata which could warrant some sort of initiative from my side. As it was, however, with no constructive suggestions to bring forward from our own side, and with no help from anyone in Moscow in arranging any informal channel of discussion to the Soviet authorities, I was simply left helpless, and could only wait.

It is characteristic, I fear, of weaknesses in my own nature that despite this set of circumstances I still continued to hope that some day I would be able to achieve something in effecting compromises between the communist and non-communist worlds on the bitterest issues and avoiding the calamity of another war. In the course of the summer I did all I could on the American side to moderate the asperities and dangers of misunderstanding. I placed the Embassy under much stricter discipline with respect to the assembling of intelligence, insisting that our people remain within reasonable limits in their efforts to obtain information on the Soviet scene, and not make themselves guilty of overt violations of Soviet laws and ordinances. This was not easy to do, for the restrictions placed upon us by the Soviet authorities were outrageous, and I could not help but place myself in a somewhat invidious situation by asking that our people respect them. In addition to this, I used my influence to modify, and in some instances even to prevent, NATO activities which seemed to me to be of relatively minor military value to us but of a very considerable potential provocativeness vis-a-vis the Russians. Finding myself embarrassed to explain my views on some of these matters by telegram, as a result both of my own ignorance about many of the pertinent facts and of the delicate nature of certain of the questions, I voiced the hope that sometime I might have an opportunity to discuss these matters orally with the proper NATO authorities. These suggestions appear to have had something to do with prompting the Department to arrange a meeting of certain European Chiefs of Mission in London on September 24–26, which I was invited to attend.

Realizing that my objections to some of the behavior of our military and the NATO authorities rested on a divergence of views between myself and most of them concerning the Soviet attitude toward NATO, and indeed toward the major problems of peace and war generally, and that to attempt to explain these matters orally at the London meeting would take up a great deal of time and probably not be wholly effective, I sat down in early September and wrote a dispatch on this subject, a copy of which is appended.[16] I hoped that by this time my influence was great enough in Government so that this dispatch would make a real impact and that I would find our people in London, and the NATO people in Paris, somewhat softened up by it for the recommendations I would have to make to them. Finding myself up against a blank wall on the Soviet side, I thought I would at least see what I could do to modify our own position in such a way as to put us in a better position to negotiate with the Soviet Government when the time came, and meanwhile to present as few openings as possible to the Soviet propagandists who were constantly accusing us of wanting war and of preparing for an attack on the Soviet Union. Bearing in mind the generally respectful and interested reactions I had had to a number of other interpretative telegrams and letters I had sent from Moscow, I was buoyant enough to hope that perhaps the efforts would not be without some effect.

Shortly before my departure from Moscow, an incident occurred

16. Kennan published the memorandum as an appendix in Kennan, *Memoirs, 1950–1963* (Boston: Little, Brown, 1972), 327–51.

which, as I now realize, should have given me greater pause for thought. This was the detection in my Spaso study, by one of our Government technicians, of a listening device of so advanced and amazing a nature that it evidently represented a product of long and careful research and development. Its discovery and removal must have been a bitter blow to the Soviet secret police, who were of course its sponsors and operators. It seemed to me that immediately after its discovery (with which I myself had nothing whatsoever to do) the atmosphere around the house became even chillier and more menacing.

The meeting at London began on September 24 and lasted three days. On the second day we had a briefing by one of the highest American officers in the NATO organization. Together with the observations of several of the other people, this briefing came to me as a great shock.

I realized, first of all, from the military briefing that my dispatch had fallen on stony soil; that there was, and would be, no understanding there for the sort of things I had written about; and that the NATO people, as well as our own military authorities, were completely captivated and lost in the compulsive logic of the military equation. From now on, it was clear, that logic would press them continually to do those things which would make war more likely and to refrain from doing those things which would tend to stave it off. For this, they were not really to blame. The fault lay with the failure of the political authorities to provide a firm line of guidance in which both military and political factors would have had their place. Secondly, I was extremely disturbed by the statements of the others present about our policy with respect to Germany. I had hoped that the long exchange of notes with the Soviet Government, running back over the past half year, had brought us to a more thoughtful and flexible position in these matters and that we might be approaching a time when we would be prepared to contemplate negotiations for a unified Germany based on the possibility of an eventual withdrawal of United States forces. I had been urging since 1948 that we state this as our objective and make clear to others the terms on which we would be prepared to consider such a solution. These terms did not need to be ones which would deliver Germany up to the Soviet Union. This line of thought had always been rejected in the Department. But the exchanges of notes with the Russians had demonstrated what dangers lay in too rigid a rejection of this possibility, and I thought perhaps our position might have softened. What I learned at the meeting showed that this was anything but the case. As far as I could learn, not only were our people not interested in pursuing any scheme for German unification at this time and not only were they basing their entire hopes on the ratification of the German contractuals and the European Defense Community agreement, but they were unwilling to contemplate at any time within the foreseeable future, under any conceivable agreement with the Russians, the withdrawal of United States forces from Germany.

I explained to them in detail what it was that terrified me about this outlook. This simply meant no agreement with the Soviet Union at all. The only conceivable terms on which I could see the Soviet Union agreeing to abandon the Eastern Zone of Germany would be ones that provided for the departure of both Soviet and American forces from Germany and probably from Western and Central Europe generally. For them to evacuate the Eastern Zone and relinquish it to a Germany garrisoned by the Western powers would be to invite the collapse of communist power throughout all of Eastern Europe. I was not objecting to a collapse of communist power in Eastern Europe, but I was maintaining that it was hopeless to expect the Soviet Government to agree to any such thing as this. Our stand therefore meant in effect no agreement with Russia at all and the indefinite continuance of the split of Germany and Europe, with the only hope for overcoming that split lying in the possibility that communist power might collapse anyway. But the split, I was sure, was bound to become increasingly dangerous and onerous both to ourselves and to our allies; and to put ourselves in this awkward and difficult situation, with the only hope for overcoming it lying in the possible collapse of Soviet power in Eastern Europe, would be to embark upon a path the logic of which would eventually bring us squarely to the view of John Foster Dulles: that the accent of our policy should lie on an attempt to subvert and overthrow communist power. Again, I would not have objected to this had I thought we were capable of carrying it through without getting ourselves into a disastrous world war and had we had any alternative regimes to put in the place of the ones we were aiming to overthrow. (Even then, I would hold such a policy to be inconsistent with the maintenance of diplomatic relations between our government and the governments of the Soviet bloc.) But these conditions were not present, and in the circumstances, I could see no end to such a policy but failure or war. In short, the only possibility I saw of avoiding a continuance of the trend toward war lay in an agreement with the Russians about Germany, based necessarily on the eventual agreed withdrawal of both Soviet and Western forces. And while I recognized the fears which the prospect of a revived and fully independent Germany engendered in some of its neighbors in Europe, I felt these possible dangers to be less, for everyone concerned, than the certain catastrophes of another war.

I left the meeting at the end of the second day profoundly depressed and cast down. The others had listened with respect and interest to what I had to say, but they knew—and I, too, recognized—that they had cast their die and were far too deeply involved in the present policy to withdraw from it. They had taken a strong position urging the continental countries to ratify the EDC agreement.[17] Once this was ratified all possibility of any agreement with the Russians, as it seemed to me, would be out the window; for an agreement would then hardly be possible without the participation of all the other EDC members, and it seemed unlikely that they would all be able to agree, even if we did, to any arrangement for Germany acceptable to the Russians. On the other hand, we had now put ourselves in a position where, if the agreement were not to be ratified, we would take a tremendous prestige defeat in Europe, with dangerous and unpredictable consequences for the whole political balance between East and West.

In these circumstances, what, I asked myself, could anyone do in Moscow? Why did they want an Ambassador there? How must I conduct myself on my return? In these circumstances, I could not possibly permit myself to be lured into a conversation with the Soviet leaders. Suppose they were to ask me: "What is it you want of us with respect to Germany? What is your idea of a solution to the German question?" My only answer would have to be: "the collapse of your power," whereupon they would have pointed out that that was precisely what they had always said about us, and hardly provided a fruitful basis for discussion between the two Governments. . . .

For the first time, after years of resistance, it seemed to me that war had to be accepted as inevitable, or very nearly so—that the only alternative to it lay in the collapse of our political position in Europe, which might have consequences almost as disastrous. And to think that I would have to return to Moscow and live through further weeks and months of exposure to foul, malicious, and insulting propaganda and yet realize that there was just enough behind a portion of it to make it impossible

17. The European Defense Community (EDC) agreement was a plan to make the military revival of West Germany less frightening by integrating the new German army with the armies of France and other Western European nations. French opposition killed the proposal in 1954.

for me to challenge it (because we *were* actually following to a dangerous degree the false logic that would lead to war in one way or another)—this reflection seemed to me as bitter a one as a representative of our country could ever have had.

The following morning came the news of the *Pravda* attack on me. What the United States Government started on one day, the Soviet Government finished on the next. As though to leave nothing to chance—as though to make sure that by no possible turn of coincidence could I ever be permitted to achieve anything in this position, *Pravda* seized on the slender pretext of some statements I had made to reporters at the airport in Berlin and denounced me as a slanderer and an enemy of the Soviet Union. This introduced a whole new series of complications. I could at first not conceive of myself going back, for I had been brought up to understand that the function of a diplomatist was to serve as an acceptable agency of liaison between his government and the foreign government, and I could not see what further value I would have in Moscow. It could be argued, of course, that I had had no value even before, and had always been treated as an enemy of the Soviet Union. All that was true. But there was still always the chance that if my own Government were ever to provide me with something to say, it might just be that someday there would be someone in Moscow to say it to. Now that chance was gone. From now on, I could expect nothing in Moscow but the utmost effort on the part of the Soviet hierarchy and everyone subordinate to them to make life unpleasant for me. What function could I conceivably have, and what good could I possibly do, in these circumstances, was hard to imagine.

Thinking of these problems, I realized that there was probably hardly a person in the world who could be expected fully to understand how they appeared to me. Such hopes as I had entertained for a yielding or a relaxation from the Soviet side were based on realizations too subtle and too delicate, too deeply founded in the peculiarities of Soviet reality, for people in the outside world to understand. In my feelings about our own policies, most of my colleagues did not agree with me. Even those who agreed with me about policy (for there were a few, though they were not present at the meeting), did not agree with me about the question of returning to Moscow. I felt that in the circumstances my wife and children and foreign servants ought to leave Moscow at once; yet I knew that my wife would not wish to do this but would insist on remaining, and that from now on the fate of the family would be a constant concern to me.

Among these complexities, I would surely find no full understanding or agreement anywhere.

With this moment, I realized for the first time that in this exposed position, which so easily became the center of world attention, I was actually the victim of a loneliness greater than any I had ever conceived, and that it was up to me to brace myself for the prospect that nowhere would I be likely to find full understanding for what I had done, or full support; that there would never be any tribunal before which I could justify myself; that there would be few friends whom I could expect ever wholly to understand my explanations. By being tossed into this impossible position between the two worlds, I had entered an area into which none could be expected to follow me in his thoughts or his imagination. From now on I had nothing to look to but my own conscience. The realization, while hard, was not intolerable, but I think that with that moment I lost the last shred of any desire ever to be associated with public life for any moment longer than was absolutely essential.

1953

Kennan was deeply hurt when the incoming secretary of state, John Foster Dulles, not only did not appoint him to a new post, but also failed to notify him of that fact until months had passed. Kennan would, however, continue as a consultant, for the CIA and for Project Solarium, President Eisenhower's secret review of national security policy. Anguished over the direction of both his personal life and the country, Kennan pondered the connections between spiritual and political issues.

Washington, March 13

Relations with the New Administration concerning My Future Position

At the time of the election I had had no communication with anyone in the new administration concerning my own personal position. . . . Having known both General Eisenhower and Mr. John Foster Dulles personally, I expected to be approached at some point before the new administration took office and to have an opportunity to give them my views not only concerning the state of U.S.-Soviet relations but also concerning the future of the Moscow Embassy and the disposition that was to be made of myself under the new administration. However, the weeks passed and nothing was said to me. . . .

In view of the position I had just occupied in Moscow, the experience I had previously had in Soviet affairs, and the extent to which my name was publicly associated with the problems of Soviet-American relations, I could not help but view this as a very serious and disturbing situation.

I was worried, furthermore, about my duty to the many people outside the Government who had given me their confidence and encouragement in the past and who, I knew, would wish to have some indication from me as to my feelings about Soviet-American relations after the Moscow experience. I had returned from Moscow deeply preoccupied with these problems, to which I had been exposed probably as intensively and painfully as any other American. The outgoing administration had shown no serious interest in my views on these subjects, but this was natural, since there was nothing more that they could do, and they were all tired and in the throes of departure. But if the new administration were also to be uninterested, and if I were to say nothing to the public, it would mean that my feelings on this subject, whatever they were worth, would remain wholly unexpressed and would be of no use to anyone anywhere. For approximately a year, since I was first told of the intention to appoint me as ambassador to Moscow, I had remained silent and had given no personal statements about Soviet-American relations. In view of the significant silence of the new administration, it was clear that if I waited until they took office, I would not be able to speak at all on this subject, since I could not speak for them and yet could not talk about these matters publicly without consultation with them. It seemed to me, therefore, that any statement I might make on this subject should be made during the incumbency of the old administration, in order that the new one might remain wholly uncommitted by what I said.

I therefore accepted the invitation of the Pennsylvania State Bar Association to address its annual meeting at Scranton on January 16, and addressed my remarks on that occasion to the subject of Soviet-American relations. I did this with specific regard to the fact that the incoming administration had made no attempt to get in touch with me on these questions. Had I been given any reason to suppose that the new administration intended to use my views on this subject, and had I been in any sort of communication with them, I would have been happy to submit the speech to Mr. Dulles as well as to Mr. Acheson for clearance and to adjust it to his requirements. But since he had made no effort to communicate with me about these matters, I saw no reason to do so and feared—quite correctly, as it turned out—that unless I stated my views at that time I would have no further opportunity to do so in the coming period. . . .

The news arrived of Stalin's mortal illness, and then his death. I naturally wondered whether in this crisis I would be called to Washington for consultation. The first news of Stalin's grave condition came on Wednesday morning. It was not until Friday morning, however, that I received word from the government. That was a telephone message from Bohlen to the effect that he would like to talk to me about the situation produced by Stalin's death, and wanted me to come to Washington as soon as possible.

On Saturday, March 7, I arrived in Washington on the night train from Boston, and spent most of the morning talking with Bohlen. He had still heard nothing about my own future. In the afternoon he took me with him to see Allen Dulles, now Director of the Central Intelligence Agency, and we discussed for short time the situation resulting from Stalin's death. I then returned to East Berlin by the afternoon train.[18]

On Monday, March 9, I learned that Mr. C. D. Jackson, special aide to the President for matters connected with the Cold War, was trying to get in touch with me by telephone, and I arranged with his office to call on him in Washington the following day.

I therefore came down to Washington that evening. First thing in the morning I had a call from Dr. Raymond Sontag of the CIA asking me to continue to function as an occasional adviser to the Agency, as I had done during the period that I spent in Princeton.

I should add that sometime before this I had agreed only with some doubt and reluctance to appear before the Jackson Committee (the President's Committee on International Information Activities) which was examining questions of psychological warfare on behalf of the new administration. Now, confronted with these new demands that I give advice to the Government at lower echelons, I thought I had better ask for some official clarification of my status in this respect and also to repeat my request for some information about my future. . . .

At 2:30 on the afternoon of March 10, I called on Mr. C. D. Jackson, who told me of certain problems with which he was concerned and asked my advice. I pointed out to him that my status under the new administration was entirely unclarified; that I had seen no official papers to speak of for a period of five months; that I therefore had knowledge of the present state of affairs largely from the newspapers; that I had had no opportunity to be instructed in the thoughts of policies of the new administration; that I could not speak in any way for the Department of State; and that therefore I felt inhibited in giving him any advice. He said he realized all this but that he would nevertheless like to get, simply, my reaction as an individual to certain of the ideas he had advanced. On this basis, I gave him my reaction.

Before I left he said he was sure there was some misunderstanding about my position in Government. He could not believe that the President had meant to convey to me the impression I had received; he

18. The Kennans' farm was in East Berlin, Pennsylvania.

proposed to speak with Mr. Dulles about it and see whether the matter could not be clarified.

I returned to the farm that afternoon. The following afternoon I received another message from Jackson's office to the effect that he would have something toward the end of the week that he would want to show me. I therefore came down to Washington again on Thursday, March 12, and arranged to call on Mr. Jackson the following morning.

That afternoon I received a call from Mr. William Laurence of the *New York Times*, who said he had heard that I was to be retired and wanted to know whether I could confirm that. I told him that I had received no communication of any sort from the new administration with regard to my status. The following morning, March 13, the *New York Times* carried a front page story by Mr. Laurence to the effect that he had learned from "high administration sources" that I was to be retired in the near future.

April 6

Later on March 13 I received word that the Secretary wanted to see me, and I called on him in late afternoon. We discussed the question of my future. He said that he knew of "no niche" for me at present in State Department or Foreign Service, feared difficulties with regard to my confirmation if I were appointed to a position requiring senatorial approval, and considered that it would not be worthwhile to risk such difficulties merely for the sake of appointing me to a minor and unimportant post. To this I agreed and said that in the circumstances I would be prepared to retire. I did emphasize to him, however, that I would not be able to conceal from my friends or the public the fact that no position had been offered to me. He then told me of his views concerning the situation resulting from Stalin's death and the problems it imposed from the standpoint of American policy, and inquired my own. These I expounded to him. He professed himself much interested, said that he always found it stimulating to talk to me, and hoped that he would have further opportunities to do so. . . .

General Smith[19] dropped in and told the Secretary and me that Mr. Allen Dulles was anxious that I should take a position with the Central Intelligence Agency, as an alternative to retiring, and wanted me to get into touch with him about this. The Secretary indicated that he hoped

19. General Walter Bedell Smith was undersecretary of state and former director of the CIA.

something of this sort could be worked out, and felt that meanwhile nothing should be said publicly about my retirement.

I called on Senator Ferguson[20] as scheduled and found that what he wished to speak with me about was the Bohlen appointment. I told him what I knew about Bohlen's personality and qualifications, and his role with respect to the Yalta agreements, and came away with the impression that the Senator had been impressed with what I said (he later cast his vote for Bohlen's confirmation).[21]

In the course of the conversation, Senator Ferguson asked me how it came about that I was living up on my farm and not at work in Washington. I told him what I could of the situation, whereupon he said: "Why, Hell, you wouldn't have had any trouble getting confirmed."

I also spoke again to General Bedell Smith, who warmly recommended that I take the position with CIA.

I returned to the country that same evening.

The following day, March 17, I went to Princeton for a two-day visit. While there I took occasion to consult with a number of my friends. With one exception, they all felt that I should make the break a clean one and not permit the situation to be obscured by getting loaned to CIA. The more I thought about it, the more this seemed to me to be the correct answer, too.

On Thursday, April 2, Annelise and I drove to Villa Nova to dine with the Bohlens at the home of Mrs. Bohlen's mother, on the last evening prior to their departure from the country. His tales of the circumstances surrounding his confirmation did nothing to enhance my desire to remain in Government.

The following morning, April 7, I was received again by the Secretary, Mr. McCardle[22] being present. The Secretary said that he was afraid that perhaps he was under a misapprehension about my position: that he had received the impression that I had wanted all along to retire, and would be glad if I could tell him really what my position was on this subject. This I did, explaining that Government service was not a personal pleasure for me at this stage in my life, but represented a sacrifice in

20. Senator Homer S. Ferguson, a Republican from Michigan, served on one of the committees investigating alleged problems in the executive branch.

21. After a heated debate during which some senators questioned Bohlen's loyalty to the United States because he had served as interpreter at Yalta, where President Franklin D. Roosevelt had supposedly given Eastern Europe to Joseph Stalin, Bohlen was confirmed as U.S. ambassador to the Soviet Union.

22. Carl W. McCardle was assistant secretary of state for public affairs.

certain respects; that I would nevertheless be glad to make this sacrifice and to serve if he felt that I were needed for any important purpose; that I had had the impression that I was not needed for such a purpose; that I did not want to be simply "taken care of"; and that in preference to this I thought I should leave Government service. I explained that I had full understanding for the fact that it was felt that there was a need for "new faces" in the Department and had no quarrel with this position at all. To my mind, everything hinged on the question as to whether he and the President really wanted me in Government or whether they did not.

He inquired whether I had any reason to prefer to serve abroad. I said that I did not. He said he would much prefer that I remain here at home, and thought that I could be generally useful to Government, if after retiring and entering on some sort of scholarly academic status, I would continue to serve the Government as a consultant, particularly with respect to Soviet matters. He said that he himself had often felt the need to get my views, and regretted that the preoccupations of the initial shakedown period had prevented his calling me in on conferences within the Department. He said he would like to feel that I was available on some regular basis not only to other agencies of the Government, but also to the Department of State itself. He mentioned particularly the Policy Planning Staff. He said that if something could be worked out along this line he would be happy to speak to Dean Rusk of the Rockefeller Foundation and ask him to support it. The Secretary intimated that he would like to have a longer talk with me and asked me to be in Washington again the following day.[23]

June 1

On May 8, I went to see Dean Rusk[24] in New York and told him that I would like to return to the Institute in the fall. I gathered from him that he felt there would be little difficulty in presenting to their Board of Trustees a request for a grant of $20,000 to cover my work at the Institute next year—$15,000 for the work itself and $5,000 as a contribution toward the expenses. I pointed out to him that the $5,000 would not fully cover this in my own case, and told him why. He indicated understanding of this, but thought it would be difficult to ask for a larger grant and hoped that the Institute would be able to help in making up whatever gap

23. The diary does not indicate what they talked about the next day.

24. Dean Rusk, who would become secretary of state in the Kennedy and Johnson administrations, was president of the Rockefeller Foundation.

might remain. It does not seem to me that this should constitute a serious problem, and I indicated to him that I thought it would be entirely satisfactory if the Foundation could make available $20,000.

July 29

Today was the day of my final retirement from Government. In the morning I worked (on a forthcoming lecture) down at the Department, in an empty office I was able to use only because the place has become so enormous that organization breaks down, and no one in high authority really knows what goes on in such matters. After lunch, however, I was through with my lecture and it was time to leave for the day. I was resolved not to come back there to work there any more, though no one would have known the difference. I went down stairs to check out with Dorothy,[25] who is remaining for another two or three weeks and has a regular job elsewhere in the Department. She was not at her desk. I left her a note, saying I was leaving and would not be back—ever. Then I said goodbye to Mary Louise, who used to work in the Secretary's office, and to Mary Ruther, the fifth-floor receptionist, and we all nearly wept. Then I took the elevator down, as on a thousand other occasions, and suddenly there I was, on the steps of the building, in the baking, glaring heat: a retired officer, a private citizen, after 27 years of official life. I was not unhappy.

The Farm, East Berlin, Pennsylvania, August 18

These past three weeks were anti-climax, because I still had my teaching job[26] to finish and all sorts of people in Washington to see, the house to close out, etc. It was not until today that retirement seemed to me really to begin. All morning I was occupied with last minute errands. After lunch I did the last chores around the house, packed the Austin to the brim, and set forth on what I hope will be the last of several hundred motor trips between Washington and the farm. At that time, driving out of Washington, I had, for the first time, the full feeling of being retired. I drove slowly all the way up to Pennsylvania, reminding myself repeatedly that there was no hurry.

Once here, I changed clothes and sat on the porch a while before unpacking the car, letting the peacefulness impinge itself on me. Before me, literally, stretched the two fields: the first in wheat stubble, the second

25. Dorothy Hessman was Kennan's longtime secretary.
26. Kennan ran a seminar at the School of Advanced International Studies in Washington.

in corn, both parched and lifeless from the long drought. Behind me, figuratively, stretched 27 years of foreign service, and behind that an almost forgotten and seemingly irrelevant youth and boyhood. Ahead of me, figuratively, was only a great question mark: somewhere between 1 and 30 years to live, presumably, and for what? I was numb inside and had little zest for the question. One thing seemed clear: if there were to be any meaning and satisfaction in life, I had to teach myself not to live it for my own sake, only for creation. What nonsense for an older person to live for the physical pleasures. Those of the flesh become ridiculous, unimportant, and hardly dignified. Eating and drinking are mere invitations to obesity. Love takes the form of an intense concern for other people.

For me, as it seemed, there were only three things: solitude, depth of thought, and writing. And since all of these things were best achieved by addressing one's self to the third, then the great dictate seemed to be: to sit at a desk and write. The thoughts will come—they always do. Just no laziness about writing.

Princeton, August 20

Drove down to Princeton alone today, from East Berlin, the little car piled high with pieces of baggage & bundles of all sorts—a bicycle on top. It was wonderful weather, in keeping with the dry, cool autumnal August we have been having.

Found the house[27] in dismal shape: empty, battered, barn-like, electricity and telephone shut off, the yard neglected and unkempt. An enormous broken branch hung precariously from a tree, its foliage trailing on the ground. Poison ivy was growing in abundance along the drive. Rats had managed to burrow into the gravel protection I had so careful placed alongside the house. In the garage, a family of cats was living, and their dirt had created an abominable stench. My little hand-cart was gone, likewise the hose. It was evident that, willy-nilly, there was going to be another beginning in life.

August 21

Fell to reflecting on a possible article for *Foreign Affairs* on the subject of morality in foreign policy.

What I would like to show is that the conduct of the foreign relations of a great country is a practical, not a moral, exercise. What is at stake

27. The Kennans had purchased a house on Hodge Road in Princeton within easy biking or walking distance of the Institute for Advanced Study.

is the adjustment of conflicting interests. These interests are in part, but never entirely, identical with the "national" interest of the given people as a whole. "National" interest is a matter of interpretation, and a matter to be interpreted by governments, not peoples. Such interpretation is one of the functions of government. It is only through government that it can be made.

But a government, as it appears in the capacity of spokesman for a people, always has a dual character: that of the interpreter and defender of the general interest of the national community vis-a-vis other such communities, and that of the interpreter and defender of the interest of the dominant political element within a given country vis-a-vis other political elements in that country. Partly, it speaks on behalf of the whole national community; partly, it speaks for a *portion* of it against another portion. The aspiration and pretensions which it voices in the international sphere are thus only in part actual desiderata of external relations; in part they are domestic political desiderata, designed to further the fortunes of a dominant political faction or coalition at the expense of other ones.

Thus the interpretation of a national interest at which a government arrives and which then becomes the basis of its foreign policy is neither disinterested nor objective. Nor can it be said to bear any moral quality. It is the product of two factors, and one of those factors is, in its turn, the momentary product of the internal power struggles within the given country. Yet this internal power struggle never is basically of a moral nature; it is of a political nature. It encompasses, in one way or another, the adjustment between rival claimants to dominant internal power. Where internal political rivalry is savage, unrestrained, and based on physical retribution and intimidation, the absence of moral values in this struggle is self-evident. But even where the restraints of a republican form of government are operable, the contest for internal power is not a moral one. . . .

Wherever internal political power is *sought* and becomes a source of contention, the process of government becomes fouled up like no other process with egotism, personal aggressiveness, insincerity, hypocrisy and falseness. It is free from these encumbrances only where men independent of government and reluctant to participate in it are drafted by popular demand, but these instances are rare, and never wholly unsullied, for though an individual may himself be uncorrupted by power, he will not be able to avoid surrounding himself with others of whom this cannot be said.

October 28

Last night the Assistant Dean of the Chapel and two undergraduate seniors came out to the house to ask me to speak at the opening of a conference on religious matters which they hope to hold in early December. It evolved from the conversation that what they really want to know is: What I believe.

I told them that I would consider the invitation provided what I might say would be solely for the undergraduates. Since then, I have been thinking about a possible statement, and want to jot down some thoughts as a reminder:

Human nature not perfectible.

Civilized life a compromise with nature

Das Unbehagen in der Kultur.[28]

No perfect human relationship.

No perfect solutions in political matters.

The dangers of romantic love:

(Love is at best a friendship and a practical partnership, complicated by an intensely intimate, impermanent, and usually unstable element that we call sex).

Possibility of exaggeration of sense of sin in sexual matters (even biblical injunction against adultery envisaged marriage as a polygamous affair and women as a slave; it was easier to observe when you had 35 of them)—some sort of coefficient required to reduce all this to modern terms—what is important is that one learn to live satisfactorily with one's problems, avoiding dissipation of one's physical and emotional powers, because this reduces rather than enhancing possibilities of real health & satisfaction, bringing the minimum of pain to other people, accepting with humility those demands of one's nature that come into conflict with civilized environment, and bear with dignity and without protest whatever humiliations and restrictions this may impose on one's general effectiveness.

The dilemma of happiness & sorrow.

The pleasure without its opposite.

Pleasure only the overcoming of hardship and pain.

2 ways *not* to enjoy:

1) To refrain entirely

2) to be surfeited

28. "The Uneasiness in Culture" is a literal translation of the title of Sigmund Freud's book, which was published in English as *Civilization and Its Discontents* (1930).

Hence the necessity for a certain stoicism in a life, a stoicism which differs from Puritanism in that its purpose is to enable life to be lived to completion, not to inhibit its completion.

And to what end—life?

Do you think you are the first generation that has asked this? Become frightened, hungry, lost, endangered, filthy—then suddenly again achieve opposite of all these things—you will then not inquire into the purpose of existence. There are a thousand things worth living for: beauty, friendship, the sea. . . . [Kennan's ellipsis]

Satisfactions depend on terms of civilized life, to be sure. This, for you, is no laughing matter. American aberrations. Need for slowing of pace of change. Need for improvement in conditions of life—for rapprochement of man with nature. Nature, not machines, is man's real environment. Error of the chemical farmers.

Mystery of life, and its continuity. The tremendous web of human culture, the excitement of being a part of it.

November 9

In the midst of the strenuous exercise of trying to be a scholar in addition to being a husband and parent, and in defiance of the pressures still flowing from the fact of having once been in public life. Success? Indifferent, perhaps barely sufficient.

More thoughts for students:

One should not exclude the possibility of great and enduring happiness in romantic love, but one would be wise to accept its improbability, & not to regard it as one's due.

Surely the Almighty will not lightly forgive us for the things in which we debase ourselves and are unworthy of ourselves, but I find it hard to believe that He, who placed these dilemmas upon us, is going to be seriously wroth with us if we do not find perfect solutions to them. In other words, I do not believe that human beings are destined to rot in hell because their efforts to combine an animalistic nature with the discipline of civilization are not always successful. What is important is that one not be needlessly selfish & inconsiderate, that one not bring needless suffering to others.

And now, how about the relation of ethical & moral belief to civic obligation?

I know of nothing in the Christian religion that tells you whether you have an obligation to collaborate actively with it. There is, it seems to me, a presumption that one should accept it and not rise against it unless it is really pretty awful and hopeless, for plainly some form of public order is required if the Christian virtues are to be practiced at all, yet no perfection is possible here, and we know that attempts to promote or achieve a utopian perfection usually lead to a great horror, confusion, and bloodshed.

Is there, then, a social obligation beyond the passive obligation of ordinary citizenship? An obligation to take part in government actively? Not, I think, unless one is drafted by one's fellow citizens through due electoral procedure or by process of law. Our society does not rest on any voluntaristic foundation. The Constitution provides that government shall bear certain responsibilities & decrees by what processes government should be formed.

It is not to be known by us, and not really of vital importance, whether our society may be said to be advancing or declining.

En Route by train—Washington to Princeton, December 28

Again—the brooding.[29]

For me this country presents no interest whatsoever. This is an infinitely boring country, which, though it has not the slightest idea about this, is condemned to a sad and pitiful fate.

Oh, it is impossible to write, too much jolting.[30]

29. This sentence is in German.
30. These three sentences are in Russian.

1954

Still smarting from his failed ambassadorship to Russia and his rejection by Dulles, Kennan settled uneasily into the life of a scholar at the Institute for Advanced Study. In April, he testified before the Atomic Energy Commission's personnel security board that J. Robert Oppenheimer, the atomic scientist and Institute for Advanced Study director, was indeed a loyal American, despite his pre–Cold War association with a leftist organization. Kennan faulted U.S. culture for hatching such McCarthyite attacks, which had also wrecked the career of his friend John Paton Davies Jr. After Oppenheimer lost his security clearance, Kennan asked him why he did not leave the United States. "He stood there for a moment, tears streaming down his face." Then he stammered: "Dammit, I happen to love this country."[31] Kennan was not sure he loved the United States. Nevertheless, he briefly flirted with the idea of running for Congress.

Princeton, June 12

The "herpes zoster," commonly called the shingles, is my heaviest physical burden. I get mild attacks of it several times a year, which have a marked general physical and psychic effect. When they are upon me, all is dark and sad.

I have such an attack now. Last night I dreamed, with much vividness, that I had returned to Russia as Counselor of the Ethiopian Embassy, a sort of foreign advisor person, as I permitted myself to infer. The ambassador was an unhappy, silent little man, leaving that day to go abroad. He lived in a large hotel. No room had been reserved for me, and not knowing where even to put my suitcase, I left it in his room, hoping he would not object. I found myself wondering why I had accepted such an assignment—it had seemed at the time a loyal and self-effacing and

31. John Lewis Gaddis, *George F. Kennan: An American Life* (New York: Penguin Press, 2011), 500.

almost heroic thing to do. Now I had my doubts. I wondered whether I should call on ________[32] and my other erstwhile colleagues at the American embassy. Would they understand? Not likely.

Read, last night, an excellent article by Stephen Spender, in the British magazine *Horizon,* on "The Situation of the American Writer." He dwelt on the loneliness of the American writer, either in success or failure, on the absence of a literary community in America, on the stultifying and dangerous effect of success, on the fact that if a literary product is successful it is for "merits which are not its true quality."

These things could not be truer, and one is immensely grateful to a British writer for perceiving them.

What this means, of course, is that what is considered to be success is not success at all; that real success does not lie in public appreciation; that the material rewards must normally come from something else than the literary quality itself, which poses a difficult technical problem for many of us, a problem of time and peace of mind.

[Kennan traveled to Massachusetts to speak at the commencement ceremony at Radcliffe, where his daughter Grace received a degree.]

June 14

We drove on to Boston, taking a forty-mile shortcut on a back road, through a sort of abandoned, grown-over portion of Connecticut. What a dead thing is the old southern New England: grown over by scrub forest, inhabited by Italians and Portuguese, the tone set increasingly by the Catholic Church.

Cambridge. I took a long walk in the late afternoon, down to the river, where the cars poured along both banks in a never-ending stream and it was hard to get across the street, down the riverbank, past the Harvard boat house, looking rather forlorn and out of date among all the traffic, down to the next bridge, then around the university and back again. A sooty, over-shaded, dampish town of somewhat bedraggled wooden houses, with streets choked with automobile traffic. I find it a depressing place: a crowded island of intellectualism and some pretension, amid a sea of Irish-Catholic industrialism.

Out to dinner, where I talked too much.

32. The diary leaves the name blank.

June 16

Radcliffe commencement . . . My remarks, to my own surprise, seemed to be very well received. They were directed in part against the views of which Mr. Joseph Alsop is a leading exponent, with regard to the atomic bomb. I was amused to see him in the crowd, as the procession moved into the auditorium. Large buffet luncheon at the home of the president of the College. Joe was there, proclaiming the speech a "personal attack," but actually very pleased over the personal attention.

June 19

[Received a visit from China expert John Paton Davies Jr.] back from Peru for the next round of the hearings that have been going on now for three solid years. He had been cleared by the State Department's Loyalty Board and by the President's Loyalty Review Board, both headed by Republicans. He had been questioned at length, on two occasions, by the lawyers of the Internal Security Subcommittee of the Committee on the Judiciary of the Senate—men who made no effort to conceal that they were out to prove him guilty, for ulterior reasons, largely ones of personal ambition. They had recommended, over the course of years, to the respective Attorneys General that they institute Grand Jury proceedings against him on grounds of perjury. Neither Attorney General, that is, neither the Democrat nor the Republican, has thus far found sufficient evidence to do this. Mr. Dulles, on taking office, let it be known that he would institute his own new administrative review of the entire case, with a view either to finding against him or rehabilitating him. When the review had been completed, Mr. D. said he would personally examine the evidence and make his decision. He examined the evidence, and plainly found himself lacking the courage to make a decision, for the only possible decision would have been to clear Davies, but that would have displeased the Republican Senators. This dilemma is now to be solved, once more at Davies' expense, by the submission of the case to an entirely new investigation.

The Farm, June 22

Left Washington at 2:15, to drive back to the farm. The heat beat down fiercely onto the helpless city. The streets were almost deserted, though twenty or thirty thousand people were at work, all around in the government offices. At the parking lot there was a negro in attendance. He was stripped to the waist, and streaming with perspiration, and complained of the heat. I drove up to Connecticut Ave., but then cut over to Wisconsin and drove to the farm via Highway 240 and then Highway 27—the way we used to take between Washington and the farm in earlier years. On the way I passed many places which, I realized, meant something to me, or had once meant something to me, from these past trips: the place where the man was building the new dairy barn (now looking shabby and worn and somehow as though people were disillusioned with it); the place where we once asked about the crop the men were harvesting in the field beside the road and found out it was worm-wood (we were traveling in Ronny Allen's new Buick, and he could not go more than 30 miles an hour, and the trip went fast nevertheless, and Ronny is now dead); the place where Grace and I once had a flat tire (there was then a little brick school house there, in a grove of trees, and the school house is now some sort of a store or a pop joint, and people dump tin cans in the little woods next to it); and the place where the roof blew off the house; and the place where the view is so lovely; and the place where they bulldozed everything down and put the cement-mixing plant and later somehow there was something faintly beautiful about it, after all. All of these things had meant something to me, and it was perfectly silly that they had. I meant nothing to them. They didn't know they had meant anything to me. Perhaps they didn't even mean anything to themselves. Well, anyway, they would now mean nothing to me any more. Something had happened to me, now. I realized their emptiness, their indifference. But God—the world was dull, and still, and hostile—lying there in the heat.

[Invited to speak at the University of Frankfurt, Kennan gave a series of lectures in German on Soviet-American relations. With the family along, they vacationed afterward.]

At sea, en route to Europe, July 8

Fell to thinking tonight about myself and my future, with an utter lack of success.

Initially, this is all that comes out of it.

1. So far as my own feelings and interests are concerned, I have nothing to live for, yet fear death.

2. I abhor the thought of any occupation that implies any sort of association with, and adjustment to, other people. This is particularly true in the U.S. Nowhere there can I share any of the group or institutional enthusiasms.

3. So far as I myself am concerned, I may as well live in Europe as in the US. I am an exile wherever I go, by virtue of my experience.

4. I do not see any way in which I can use any of my own past in approaching the problems of the future. That has all got to die on the vine: the languages, the intellectual interests, the acquaintances. It makes no whole. It is a museum of odds and ends and left-overs, and whatever value it had is declining day-by-day in geometric progression.

5. Intellectual life is barred for me, partly by the way of life forced upon me by the family whenever we are anywhere near other people, partly by the fact that intellectual exertion comes, with me, only from outside stimulus and constitutes a nervous and psychic strain, yet I have no means of relaxing from it and preserving the balance of life.

6. If I live in Europe, I create an uncertainty with regard to the pension. Theoretically, I could always be ordered back into the Foreign Service, grisly thought. What would I do if I were living in Europe when that happened? However, the pension is a weak reed anyway. There is no reason to rely on the U.S. Government to keep faith with an employee in this sort of an arrangement. It is rapidly getting into the totalitarian habit of judging all these things from the standpoint of the ideological fads of the moment.

7. Farming would be the best solution, but there would be an endless hassle over whether the skimpy cash proceeds, if there were any, should go to the farm or to the family.

8. Teaching would be very difficult, particularly in the US. It requires too much in the way of intellectual exchange with other people. I should never be able to conceal my own intellectual despair, above all, the despair with US society. But to reveal it would be inconsistent with the mythology of any American educational institution.

9. There is a basic conflict, anyway, between my own approach to the financial problems and the interests of the family. The former would demand a great simplicity of life and the maximum reduction of expenditure; the latter would demand maximum income and maximum expenditure.

10. In Goethe's *Urfaust* the following passage occurs:

> "The spiritual world is not shuttered,
> Your senses are closed off, your heart is dead."

11. My older children do not love me. That is a sure sign that I am inwardly unlovely, or at least, what they see of me is. But what they see

of me is full of an embittered sense of duty. What has that to do with me?

12. Business? I shall be 52 years old before I can turn to anything else. And again—an employee relationship in business, implying any sort of group loyalty, would be intolerable. It would have to be a small, tough, independent business.

13. The only possibility that arouses in me any note of hope or anticipation is a professorship in Scotland or England. I should, after all, be able to lecture in Russian history or literature. This could begin in the fall of 1956. I could become a British subject, and thus liquidate the claim the U.S. Government would otherwise have on me. So long as the pension lasted, I could probably contrive to keep some sort of a country cottage, and perhaps even fix it up so that in the end I could retire there. As an older naturalized citizen H. M.'s Government would be content, I am sure, to leave me alone.

Near Frankfurt, West Germany, July 26

One day I took a walk up into the woods. Noticed the smell of corpses throughout the whole area and finally came on a forest cemetery, that was the source of the odor. I didn't see the cemetery at first, but only the courtyard of the building that stands at its gate. I had also forgotten, at the moment, about the odor, and had my mind on quite other things. Then suddenly I found myself looking into this courtyard, and I noticed a special sort of stillness and emptiness in it, and a dampness, and strange, bluish shadow over it all, and it was beautiful, but at the same time sinister. And then suddenly I saw the cemetery beyond it, and realized that for the first time in my life I had been close to the mystery of death.

Freudenstadt, July 30

Took a little walk around town & returned to the hotel black with despair, in the face of the impressions of the day and of the past weeks.

Of the Americans I will not speak. I had despaired of them long before I came over here. But their presence here infuriates me. Everything about them I view with loathing: their callousness, their softness, their imperviousness to things around them, their spoiledness, their garrulous conviviality. Except for the soldiers, nine-tenths of them have no legitimate business over here; and even the soldiers don't need their special waiting rooms in the railroad stations, their requisitioned hotels, their general services clubs, etc.

It is the Europeans that worry me. Suffering seems only to have eliminated the quiet, the thoughtful, the earnest, and to have left everything that was crude, grasping, cynical, & materialistic. For most Germans, the highest spiritual aim seems to be a motorcycle. The country, except for the very simple people who do the work, seems abandoned to a hedonism terrible because it is devoid of all taste. One sees, today, how much the Jews added to Germany.

Is there, one asks, a corner of the world where one could live quietly and decently, in a natural environment not ruined by man, and in a human environment that doesn't remind you of Hogarth?[33]

God, how I wish at least the summer were past.

[The last two sentences in the following entry suggest that for all his complaining about the U.S. government, Kennan still hankered for involvement with it.]

Princeton, December 29

Well, the summer is past, and an autumn of historical research has gone by, and likewise all the excitements of Christmas. . . . Yesterday evening I went in to New York to the annual dinner of our little Committee for the Promoting of Advanced Slavic Scholarship. What a happy mixture this is: good food and drink plus the most innocent and useful of activities. We debated whether to support the publication of a 17th Century Russian dictionary, based on a manuscript prepared by a German merchant in Pskov; a manuscript on the early influence of the western principalities on Moscow, etc.

It was an abnormally warm day yesterday: 60°—rainy, muggy, trains and N.Y. buildings vastly overheated, because no one can take time to adjust heating to outside temperatures.

I understand, incidentally, that there is now a new gadget at Grand Central: an automatic porter, a little baggage cart, available on the platform, which can be induced, by the insertion of a quarter, to make itself pushable; one puts one's baggage in it and trundles it off to the taxi loading platform; nearby is a place where it is to be deposited; and if one deposits it there, it yields up a dime, again, as reward for this correct treatment. This innovation will be solemnly admired and approved, and to almost no one will it occur that the experience of travel, once a

33. William Hogarth was an artist who satirized the disorder and injustice of eighteenth-century Britain.

humanly-fruitful social experience, has become just one bit lonelier, one bit more impersonal. It is as though people were determined to rule out every sort of personal contact in their lives, other than with their own meager families, until one moves, wordless and in utter loneliness from morning to night, through a cold and gleaming push-button world. . . .

Oppenheimer asked to see me, in another connection, and took occasion to say some very agreeable things from which I gathered that the Board of Trustees of the Institute for Advanced Study would be glad to have me there as a member, & to help me with the attendant financial problem, for some years to come. Nothing could have been more gratifying to me; it solves a great many problems. But it raises the question: shall we keep the farm? It is in many ways too much like Princeton, & too much in the same climatic zone, to provide the sort of contrast & relief it did when we were in Washington. Would we not be better off to take a place somewhere in the north, in the hills or on the coast? Yet, if at any time the Government calls me to Washington, the farm is then ideal. No easy answer.

[During these years, Kennan was researching and writing what would become his prize-winning two-volume history, *Soviet-American Relations, 1917–1920.*]

December 30

Reflected on this strange, lonely life of a scholar. Here I was, it seemed to me, trying to warm myself exclusively, as a bystander, at the fires of human situations that existed nearly forty years ago. It gave only a pale, faint warmth, like the moonlight. But were our situations today any more real? Their contemporaneousness was ephemeral, passing. Intrinsically, they were even inferior, for the people were inferior. If the warmth exhaled by the earlier ones was wan and uncomforting, it was surely because I was a poor historian, incapable of recreating the flesh-and-blood images of the characters I was studying. For I am only an observer, here as there.

How, though, to preserve tone as an observer? I notice at once the effects of the lack of stimulus. I become a dull boy, sluggish, uninterested, uninteresting. Can this not be mastered? Is there no way to retain tone in loneliness?

1955

Kennan's failure to receive a high-level appointment from the Eisenhower administration continued to gnaw at him. He felt not only humiliated but also anxious about how to provide for his family of six, which included six-year-old Christopher and three-year-old Wendy. Determined to prove himself at the Institute for Advanced Study at Princeton, where his appointment was at first only temporary, he completed the first of two volumes on early U.S.-Soviet relations, Russia Leaves the War *(1956).*

When the Institute's director, J. Robert Oppenheimer, proposed Kennan for a permanent position, the faculty split thirteen to five in favor. Opposition centered among the mathematicians, who objected to Kennan's lack of an advanced degree and his involvement in policy. Outside evaluators were also divided. Gordon A. Craig, a historian at Princeton University, wrote that despite Kennan's brilliance, his "thinking is not the thinking of a professional historian." He was apt to "stop being the objective historian and slip into the role of the polemicist, arguing the case of 1950 from the circumstances of 1917."[34] *That present-mindedness was what impressed Theodor E. Mommsen of Cornell. "Not many people in this world" were as "profoundly humane" as Kennan, Mommsen declared. He found particularly praiseworthy the man's "deep sense of moral and civic responsibility."*[35] *Although Kennan was not privy to the specific content of these letters and he did secure appointment to the faculty, he remained sensitive about the controversy. He later confided that a principal reason*

34. Gordon A. Craig to E. L. Woodward, March 18, October 16, 1955, Faculty Series, box 19, Kennan folders, Institute for Advanced Study archives.
35. Theodor E. Mommsen to Ernst Kantorowicz, March 17, 1955, ibid.

for the "appalling accumulation of detail" in Russia Leaves the War *and in a subsequent volume was to forestall criticism for superficiality from colleagues at the Institute.*[36]

During the course of the year, Kennan reflected on a variety of matters, including his mother and father, the nature of American society, and what made California distinctive.

January 1
Toward evening Oppenheimer called me up, and I went over to his house and helped to straighten out a most unfortunate misunderstanding that had arisen over a television program Ed Murrow had undertaken to do about the Institute.[37] It involved a good deal of phoning around and manipulation, and reminded me so much of the immeasurable minor crises of diplomatic life, particularly in Russia, that I suddenly realized how long it was since I had "operated"—how passive and placid and eventless, in other words, is the life of a scholar.

[During the course of the year Kennan took several research trips to Washington.]

Washington, January 3
It is hard to express the revulsion I feel toward this city. A neurosis, no doubt. But nonetheless real . . . If my family had been agreeable to our moving to England and becoming British subjects, I should have left the shores of New York without a regret and without a backward glance. It is not I who have left my country. It is my country that has left me, the country I thought I knew and understood. As for the rest, I could leave it without a pang: the endless streams of cars, the bored, set faces behind the windshield, the chrome, the asphalt, the advertising, the television sets, the filling stations, the hot dog stands, the barren business centers, the suburban brick boxes, the country clubs, the bars and grills, the empty activity, the competitiveness, the lack of spontaneity,

36. Lee Congdon, *George Kennan: A Writing Life* (Wilmington, DE: ISI Books, 2008), 73–74.
37. Edward R. Murrow, the CBS radio broadcaster who had reported from London during World War II, hosted the television show *See It Now.*

the sauciness, the drug stores, the overheated apartment stores, the bus terminals, the crowded campuses, the unyouthful youth and the immature middle-aged—all of this I could see recede behind the smoke of the Jersey flats without turning a hair. I could regret the growing distance from a few friends, but in reality it could be hardly greater than the distance that already separates us by virtue of the compulsions of this thin, tight, lonely American life. Here in Washington, at the center of it, is the facade of a great city, but behind it—bureaucracy, provincialism, superficiality, and a weary helplessness.

January 30

I am beginning to believe that Mr. Dulles was quite right to fire me. People don't want such characters as myself in government, and it runs very well without us. The determining realities are deeper than any of us can see, and there is not much room for the inquiring mind. True, we could save people a lot of effort & time & money. But they don't care very much; they wouldn't know it was being saved; and if they had to choose, they would probably prefer the extra cost and effort and time to having people like myself around.

Even this recognition should not make a person so unhappy. Here, of course, the trouble is with me. Basically, it is I, not the others, who have nothing to say. I sometimes ask myself whether there is anything I am interested in—*anything* I would like to do. The answer is: a few things, but they are all out of the question. None of them produces $30,000 a year, and on less than that, you see, one cannot live. As to what one *does* do to earn $30,000 a year, I am wholly ignorant, but the problem is 7 months away, and I shall not worry about it yet.

Now what would I like to do if the $30,000 were not involved? Become a recluse and an esthete, I suppose. Live on the west coast of Scotland, travel, read, give attention to the beauty man has created. And to what end? Perhaps, looking at it enough, imbibing it, living in it, I might someday create some of my own. What else is there worth doing?

February 2

Worst of all, I see no future, and not even any past. As this period of loneliness and withdrawal takes its course, the significance of my past life changes before my eyes, and I feel less and less desire to resume it. I am like the man in Chekhov's story who lost a bet and was obliged to spend thirty years in a friend's library, and when he finished his thirty years he had no desire to come out and remained there the rest of his days. All that went before now seems to me unreal. I even understand very well the victims of the Soviet purges, and their prison repentances and confessions. For I am coming to feel that Mr. Dulles did well to fire me, that I had not been useful as an officer, particularly in the State Department. If I had been useful anywhere, it was in the field, as a chief of mission, but even then not for my work, only for my ability.

March 9

Spent the day, or most of it, at the Pentagon, going into the Military Intelligence records on Robins.[38] Not much there. Had lunch with a high-ranking general, who asked me questions about Russia, and could not help marveling at how quickly the whole, half-forgotten atmosphere of government frustration again took possession of me: the inability to get ideas across, the feeling that even if you could make this one man understand there would still be a thousand others whose minds would also have to be won before any intelligent and intelligible action could flow, the hopeless realization that what is needed here is not a single briefing or explanation but rather education itself, and education of a sort that, once acquired, would make men no longer quite the Americans we know and thus put them to a degree at odds with their countrymen. The reason we will never have wise and able conduct of our foreign relations is that the qualities essential to this, an understanding of history and of human nature, are simply incompatible with Americanism. To be an American is to distrust these things. To know them is to become de-Americanized.

March 14

I do not think the most influential men in our country are ones with whom you can reason—the exception being the President, who knows what should be done but does not dream of doing it because he has no intention of governing.

[Researching the second volume of *Soviet-American Relations, 1917–1920*, Kennan traveled to St. Louis to work in the papers of David R. Francis, ambassador to Russia under President Woodrow Wilson.]

38. Raymond Robins, the American Red Cross official in Russia, had taken on diplomatic responsibilities during the Russian Revolution. He figured in Kennan's book *Soviet-American Relations, 1917–1920: Russia Leaves the War* (1956).

St. Louis, March 19

Today was the anniversary of my mother's death, 51 years ago, and as I got up & made my preparations to start the day, my head singing with the infection, and doozy all over, I undertook to imagine that my mother was near me and to live through the day as I think she might have wished me to live through it: unhurriedly, with grace and dignity, secure and relaxed in the consciousness of her love and her forgiveness, not pecking at myself for past faults nor worrying about present limitations.

[Continuing his historical research, Kennan traveled by air and bus to the Hoover Institution on the Stanford University campus.]

Flying to San Francisco, March 23

The West is to the East, in the U.S., as the U.S. as a whole is to Europe. To us in the East, the West looks standardized, bumptious, shallow, crude, and uninteresting, just as all America does to a European.

The trouble with the American West is primarily its uniformity, the complete lack of contrast and inner tension. Where there is no tension, there can be no real growth, no development of new form. The American West grows physically, in the sense that it multiplies endlessly its own cells. But this is just multiplication of what already exists, it is not the creation of the new. . . .

I feel that somehow or other I must force myself to phrase the reasons why I feel such despair of this country and such a powerful compulsion to have nothing to do with it, to shut it out of my consciousness, to be in it but not of it. It is, I suppose, because I feel that there is no bottom to it, and that if one even attempts to put a foot on it, he will sink down hopelessly, as in quicksand, and finally be swallowed up and rendered sterile, like everything about him. American life has become one long, mildly agreeable narcosis, from which one is awakened only for brief moments of helpless lucidity, during which one is miserably aware of one's condition and aware, also, that there is absolutely nothing one can do about it. On occasions such as this, when I rub elbows with this great hive of activity, I have to keep saying to myself: none of this is going to prove anything; these are people in a dream.

At this moment, we are crossing the Sierra Nevadas. Before us stretches the whole great Pacific Coast. My only thought, as we approach it is: throughout the length and breadth of it not one single thing of any importance is being said or done, not one thing that gives hope for the discovery of the paths to a better and firmer and more promising human life, not one thing that would have validity beyond the immediate context of time and place in which all of it occurs.

I hear someone saying, "Ah, but these people are happy. Why not better join them? Forget that you have ever been a mature person. Learn to play and to be amused, again, like a child, learn to live by childish things. You'd be amazed at the easy contagiousness of escapism and unreality. You'd be amazed, how easy it is to vegetate between the sunshine and the television set, to live for the day, to forget what is coming, to watch rather than to create, to hold humanity at a distance by encasing conviviality rather than to meet it soul to soul. You are simply jealous. That's all that's the matter with you."

Perhaps, perhaps. But elsewhere in the world there are evidences that man has from time to time risen to great dignity and to immense creative stature. I have lived too long in the neighborhood of these evidences to forget them so easily.

March 29

California is a country, rather than a state. . . . Environment does affect the nature of the civilization. Here climate plays, probably, only a relatively minor role. By largely obliterating seasonal differences it serves, perhaps, to reduce the minor subjective tensions in the individual: the test of patience involved in the enduring of dreary rainy days and endless winter months, the minor inconveniences presented by ice & snow & house heating problems. At the same time, the Californian is deprived of the keen emotional experience of the passage of the seasons and the endless philosophic lesson, the lesson of the cycle of life, that is taught by it. These differences are, however, only relative and minor.

A much more important quality of California life that strikes my attention is the lack of inner social and intellectual tension. The uniformity of outlook and custom, the uniformity of circumstances and interest, contrasts with the situation of areas longer settled, with the jumble of old forms and new ones. The "sameness" lies, it seemed to me, like a heavy hand on the intellectual, and even on the emotional life of the place, for it is only from the reconciliation of differing and conflicting elements that true creativeness can exist. In the uniformity of outlook and custom that marks California life there lies an immanent sterility for which no cure is apparent.

[Along with his sister Jeanette Kennan Hotchkiss, Kennan made a pilgrimage to the graves of his parents.]

Milwaukee, July 17

On our way into town we passed the Forest Home cemetery, and stopped off there to see the Kennan graves. We didn't know where they were, but at one point we all sensed the nearness of them. I got out of the car, and walked, dazed and excited, among the headstones, a little panicky, like a lost child (Father, Father where are you?) and it was as though, if I did not find the grave, we would be forever lost and separated.

Jeanette was the one who first saw the family name-stone, a little off the road. We went in, and there they lay: the tombstones still sturdy, respectable in a Victorian sort of way, and uncompromisingly legible and specific, the mounds still showing where the bodies had been lain:

First—my mother, Florence James Kennan, whom I never knew, struck down by death only a month after the birth of the fourth of her children. (Here, buried and helpless, all the love that could not be expended, all the tenderness that could not be bestowed. Dear Mother, it must have been hard and bitter to leave your little children. We have all held you in a sort of awed adoration: our ever-young dead mother, beautiful, unworldly, full only of love and grace for us, like a saint. In imagination, we have received all you would have given us. Pity, only, that we with our youth could not have borne some of your frailty, could not have breathed back into you some of the strength you gave us. (May our love, somehow or other, reach you.)

Next to her, my father, Kossuth Kent Kennan—(God be praised, that they lie side by side; it was a real marriage, full of difficulty, embarrassment, and pain—family differences, differing social origins, and what-not—but full of real love and a total mutual commitment).

My father: awkward, shy almost to the point of cowardice, often putting his foot in it, unable to explain himself, oversensitive, proud, slightly boyish to the end of his days; always in some ways a yokel, in others a man of noble intellect; capable of being utterly broken up and disinterested by too much beauty, a sentimentalist like the rest of us; a man from whose taut, severe, lawyer-like face the love of some one else could suddenly shine forth with great warmth and intensity; a man of much loneliness and much suffering; gaunt, tough, abstemious, scarcely knowing illness after his youth, he lived life to the very end: to a dark and tortured and lonely old age. Myself a moody, self-centered, neurotic boy, as shy as he, and confiding in no one, I must have given him little solace in his old age, but I loved him as I have loved no other man but my son. We never grated on each other; I appreciated his silence and his forbearance. And I understood, perhaps better than anyone in the family, his loneliness, his unhappiness, his despair, and his faith.

Flying home from a research trip to Europe, October 21

I ponder what relation to seek in future with this American society to which I am returning. That I am seriously and in some respects decisively estranged from it seems quite plain. Not that I am unappreciated. A portion of the public appreciates me. But it does not know the depth of my estrangement, the depth of my repudiation of the things it lives by. And on the people that really hold power—the Texas oil men, the slot-machine owners, the politicians—I have no influence and am not likely to have any.

Does this matter? Should one bother about whether the tide of battle seems favorable or not? Should one not fight anyway, on principle? Certainly. But where and how? If defeat is certain in any event, if all one can hope to do is to slow the tide in minor ways—how, then, does one choose one's place in the battle? Is it not there where the things one stands for and the things one has to offer come out in their purest, clearest, and most unsullied form? Surely, then, not in government, where one has to take on so largely the coloration of one's environment.

December 26

I realized what a vital but almost unnoticeable turning point I have passed in my life. Is it right that one should become, when this side of fifty, suddenly without anguish? That the torture of the constant presence of the other sex is abating is all to the good, but that other forms of anguish disappear is not. Chekhov was lucky, in a way, that he died so young, with an enormous labor accomplished. I still have work to do, and am doing it, but it seems too easy, too little challenge. Men, or at least such men as I, are no good unless they are driven, hounded, haunted, forced to spend every day as though it were the last they were to spend on earth.

Perhaps one must make old age a sort of self-torture—not driving one's self, as some do, to pretend to be younger than one really is, but forcing the muscles of body, intellect & capacity for sympathy to work full time, even at the cost of shortening life, so that one does not drift into the long, barren, desiccated old age of our cellophane civilization. . . .

The Princeton paper proudly announced that within a year or so we are to have dial phones. Great achievement! From one more process of life, the human element will have been removed. There will be one less reminder, in our daily lives, that other human beings are around us. There will be one voice less—an impersonal voice, perhaps, but human and sometimes reassuring. What, one wonders, do people want? How far do they wish to carry the process of automation? Are they yearning for day when all the processes of life will be automatic, and there will be nothing left for human hands to do, and we will all sit, in a hushed, perpetual stillness before our television sets, let the span of life pass by us, hardly noticed, and wonder sometimes, vaguely and briefly and without too much curiosity, how it used to be when people were alive?

Washington, December 29

I went to the Mayflower [Hotel] and delivered my contribution to one of the panels of the annual meeting of the American Historical Association. The subject was given as "History & Diplomacy"—so wide, in fact, as to be meaningless. . . . The function was in the main ballroom. Several hundred people were present, for once the ventilation was good. I spoke about the political philosophy to which diplomatists incline: their skepticism about the enlightenment and disinterestedness of governments, their aversion to the spectacle of internal political competition. The speech was not meant to be wholly serious, although some passages were, and I begged the reporters who were present to point out in their stories that this was all in a lighter vein. (I noted the next day that the *New York Times* wholly failed to do this, and the excerpts it carried made a strange, bitter, desperate impression).

1956

While working on the second volume of his history of Soviet-American relations, 1917–20, and writing a number of lectures and essays, Kennan reflected on his meeting with Democratic candidate Adlai Stevenson, the Suez and Hungarian crises, and the significance of Eisenhower's reelection victory.

Princeton, January 8

Our friends from the under developed areas have us boxed in, ideologically speaking, to a position where we are damned if we do and damned if we don't. We are charged with imperialism, *but*, it seems, on further examination, we cannot help being imperialistic whether we wish to be or not. Thus if we attempt not to push other people around, we can be blamed for not using our influence in the right direction. What, then, I find myself asking, could we do to divest ourselves of this tremendous load of sinfulness which the non-European world (and even partly the European) insists we bear? Blow ourselves all up with the atomic bomb? But then there would be complaints about the radioactive fallout, and we would obviously be to blame for the sudden cessation of benefits to which the rest of the world has become accustomed. Plainly, the U.S., no matter what it does, is not to be without guilt. I see no answer, therefore, but to admit quite frankly that we are villains and proceed to play the part with great gusto, warning everyone that nothing good is to be expected of us, so that when the complaints come in, we can say: "Why, what did you expect of us?" Perhaps in this way we could eventually come to rival in popularity our friends the Russians, who have succeeded in establishing in peoples' minds the thesis that they are monsters, and now reap a rich harvest of astounded gratitude and praise every time they act with anything resembling normal courtesy.

I have now started my Volume II.[39] The study and writing of history

39. *Soviet-American Relations, 1917–1920: The Decision to Intervene* (1958).

is marked by the fact that one's own life, in contemporary terms, is very eventless and dull. One is a lackluster companion to one's contemporaries. The present is merely a necessity: to be an historian one has to live in some age other than the one about which one writes. It is a nuisance, because all ages other than the one about which one writes are relatively uninteresting. One is, in other words, a reluctant and not very welcome guest of another time, unwelcome because no age forgives anyone for not being primarily interested in it during his lifetime. Each generation is egocentric and thinks that history revolves around it and its experiences.

January 9

Ice storm again last night for the second time in a fortnight. Looked out the window first thing in the morning and observed with regret that the unctuous city fathers already had sand strewn along the street. In such encounters between the elements and the automobile my sympathies are always with the elements. I wish the ice would stay good and smooth and slippery for days. Let them slither and struggle, I say to myself, until they comprehend what a frivolity they have committed in selling their habits and their souls to the automobile. Anyone with any real humility and taste for life would have known better.

January 21

Three weeks ago, I became a professor here,[40] with what amounts to security for life. Yet not for years, it seems to me, have I been as deeply and consistently depressed as in these last days. My attachment to the present age has worn down to the smooth, cold bedrock of obligation. I see many years of duty before me, nothing else. Scholarship would be a pleasure if personal life were serene and if the privilege of addressing one's self to one's work did not have to be fought for daily among such a host of outside pressures.

January 27

I admire Stevenson[41] as a sensitive, intelligent and valiant person. I consider him the sort of man to whom the people of this country ought to entrust the administration of public affairs, and probably never will. Dulles, furthermore, has thrust me into a position where if I am to be

40. The Institute for Advanced Study at Princeton.

41. Adlai Stevenson, a former governor of Illinois, was the Democratic candidate for president in 1952 and 1956.

an adherent of either party it can be only the Democratic. But what sort of a Democrat am I? So far as domestic affairs are concerned, I am much closer to the Republicans. I think the protection of the farmer is mostly a lot of nonsense. I wish there were much more of what we have become accustomed to call unemployment. The labor union movement in this country strikes me as short-sighted, reactionary, and partially corrupt. . . .

I read this morning, in the *New York Times* magazine, a reflective piece by Allen Nevins about the Civil War, in which he portrayed that development, despite its squalid, horrible and depressing nature, as largely a good thing in the sense that it did "make the nation." Why this confidence that it is good that this nation was made? Does our subsequent experience bear it out? I can conceive that it might have been much better if the South had gone its own way. I hold no iron-clad brief for unity. I am not sure that we would not be much better off without California and Texas and Florida. By shedding our Latin American fringe, we might have preserved something like a north-European civilization in the remainder of the country. There would, in any case, be more diversity, and there is nothing we need more.

February 29

Watched President Eisenhower inform the nation, on television, that he would run for a second term. Then went for a long walk by myself, trying to digest the combination of realizations:

(a) that the country is going to go for another five years without a government;
(b) that its international situation is going to deteriorate greatly and disastrously;
(c) that people really want it this way; and
(d) that I have no relation to all this personally, and am a foreigner in this country.

In the face of this despair, I wonder what I was doing when I accepted invitations to speak three times this spring, and twice publicly. What in the world can I say to people?

This carries very far, even into ordinary social life, even into the relations with one's friends. . . . There can be, for me, only one refuge: learn, at long last, the art of silence, of the commonplace, of humor, anything but serious discussion.

[Many of the archival sources that Kennan needed for his second volume on Russian-American relations during the Russian Revolution were at the Hoover Institution in Palo Alto.]

Palo Alto, California, May 13

California reminds me of the popular American Protestant concept of Heaven: there is always a reasonable flow of new arrivals; one meets many, not all, of one's friends; people spend a good deal of their time congratulating each other over the fact that they are there; discontent would be unthinkable; and the newcomer is slightly disconcerted to realize that now, the devil having been banished and virtue being triumphant, nothing terribly interesting can ever happen again.

The Farm, August 5

How is one to bring up children in this country? If one succeeds in communicating to them one's own tastes, they recoil from the life around them. If one lets their tastes be determined by the prevailing milieu, they soon recoil from their parents.

If one could believe that the life of this age was a healthy one, likely to develop them well physically and intellectually and spiritually, one could easily muster the self-abnegation to abandon them to the influence of the age and make no effort [to] influence them in any contrary direction. But one cannot believe this. How can one sit by and see them become older without really maturing: socially uncertain, imitative, conformist, nervously over-wrought by too much television, exposed first to the false excitement of teen-age hot-rod adventure, then moving into some premature liaison with the opposite sex, missing normal group association both with members of their own sex and with mixed groups. In this false life innocence is lost before maturity is achieved. To say nothing of the poverty of education, the incoherence of speech, the never-ending mumbling of stereotypes, the pretense of tough, disillusioned taciturnity. To all of this one is asked to consign one's children for the sake of social adaptability, in order that they may feel comfortable in their time.

[Kennan visited his sister Jeanette Kennan Hotchkiss and her husband, Eugene, who lived in Highland Park.]

Highland Park, Illinois, August 23

Grace, on her way east from the Pacific coast, has now joined me for a day or two here in Highland Park. Tonight, when I got home from South

Chicago, she told me there had been a phone call from Adlai Stevenson's home in Libertyville. I called back and he took the phone himself, said he had heard I was here, asked me to come over for family supper. I asked if I could bring Grace along, and he said she would be welcome. So we drove over almost at once. Found him very weary and harassed. . . .

It was the night of the acceptance speeches at the Republican convention. While we ate, Nixon's speech boomed out through the house from the television set in the next room. When the President's speech approached, photographers arrived who wished to take a shot of Stevenson listening to Eisenhower. He was willing, in principle, but when they wanted to move the whole room around his patience ran out and he called the whole thing off. Grace and I, who had hidden in the dining room while this went on (so as not to attract curiosity and add another complication) then moved into the living room and all watched the President give his acceptance speech. Mr. Stevenson took it very calmly, thought it, in fact, a very good speech, but we both agreed that it had absolutely nothing to do with what the Republican party actually did. (The strength of the Republicans in the forthcoming election rests, actually, in the fact that so many people have ceased entirely to expect any substance behind the words of the administration; the phrase and the deed have somehow come apart; if you *say* you are for liberation, that means you are liberating peoples.)

When it was over, we talked foreign policy for a short time, and then Grace and I took our departure. Mr. Stevenson accompanied us out to the parking lot back of the house. There was a bright moon, and the fields were in mist, and looked like a sea. We both felt intensely sorry for him: he seemed so tired and harassed and worn; he had so few people to help him; and his whole equipment for going into this battle was so shabby compared with the vast, slick, well-heeled Eisenhower organization. And not the least of his problems is to carry on his shoulders the whole miserable Democratic party: disunited, undisciplined, unenlightened, itself already having unconsciously imbibed and assimilated about half of the McCarthyism of the past few years.

It is clear that regardless of the outcome of the election this country is still removed by decades, and by phases of vast suffering, from anything like enlightened government.

Princeton, September 20

I am still being whip-sawed between the demands of the second volume of my history of the early period of Soviet-American relations (the first draft of it is about half done) and the constant temptations to participate in contemporary discussions. Last night the President gave a speech about peace, a campaign speech, and I itch to get at it in some sort of a public statement. He says, "we witness today across a vast middle area of our earth a struggle by its peoples for freedom—for freedom from foreign rule or freedom from domestic poverty." He says nothing about freedom from native dictators. He speaks of the Communist world ambition turning to new devices, political methods, an "effort to win with the ballot what they have been unable to win with the bayonet." What nonsense. What does he mean by "bayonets"? He is here confusing police & military power. And what does he mean by "ballots"? What have "ballots" got to do with the Middle East? He says our atomic power has "forged the saving shield of freedom." This is a preposterous misimpression. What people has been delivered from servitude by our atomic power? What people has been rescued from it? How can one sit by and let these abuses of fact pass unchallenged? No one in the Democratic camp seems to have the wit to challenge them.

Do I have the right to participate in the public discussion of contemporary problems when I have set my shoulder to the wheel of scholarship?

Do I have the right to decline to participate when so many people look to me with confidence and are prepared to accept my guidance?

September 28

A dinner guest asked me what I would have had the U.S. do about Suez. I said the older I got the more I approached the status of an isolationist. It occurred to me, afterwards, of course, that I should have explained that there are two kinds of isolationist: those who hold the outside world too unimportant or wholly wicked and therefore not worth bothering about, and those who distrust the ability of the United States Government, so constituted and inspired as it is, to involve itself to any useful effect in most foreign situations. I . . . belong to the latter school.

[The next entry was written after the initial withdrawal of Soviet troops from Budapest and before the reentry of those forces, which would crush the Hungarian rebellion.]

November 1

To my mind there must be something in this picture, especially with regard to Hungary, that the public does not know, which explains Russian behavior. There is nothing I know that would give adequate explanation of the way they have behaved and it seems to me there must be something stirring in Moscow which would have caused this extraordinary behavior. The whole thing is that they could have crushed this revolt in Budapest if they had wished to. The physical possibility was there. The only explanation of their withdrawal is by some domestic inhibitions. . . .

What I suspect is that the Red Army leaders, Marshal Georgy Zhukov and perhaps some of the others, have been very impatient with the idea of having their forces used for suppression of popular disorders and used as gendarmes in Eastern Europe. . . . I think this is bound to raise the question of Western forces in West Germany. It will become an acute question because it is evident if agreement could be reached for withdrawal of forces, it will include Poland and East Germany, and I think the East German regime won't last three days. It seems to be by the looks of things they will try to hold on to East Germany, but surely for bargaining purposes. It seems clear that a general withdrawal of forces from Germany would lead to end of communism in East Germany but would cleanse the Polish situation. I would think that they would want to get out of their commitment in East Germany because it will be uncomfortable for them there after what has happened in Poland and Hungary. . . .

I have also always said their rule might come to an end if it could be done gradually and without loss of prestige.

November 7

The events of these recent days[42] have been so shattering that I am at a loss to know how to react to them, personally. I am obliged to note the following:

1. My own fears and warnings, both with regard to "liberation" and with regard to the appeal to UN majorities and the effort to cultivate popularity with the new nations, are being vindicated beyond my wildest dreams.

2. The Administration has involved us in a situation of extreme danger, and one over which it has practically no control.

3. Despite this, it has just been re-elected with a huge majority.

4. My own views have been available to the public for some years and my own position is known to anyone who is at all interested.

5. It is of course dangerous to attribute a personal significance to

42. Soviet military forces put down the rebellion in Hungary.

events in which one played no appreciable part, but I *did* speak my piece and it *was* contemptuously over-ridden by the public, just at this moment of extreme danger. This means that my contribution, and whatever I stand for, has been rejected by my own country at just about the last moment when it could do any good.

6. It seems to me that in these circumstances, it is no good my attempting to contribute any further. I must regard my role in the public life of this country as played out. My future is purely private life; and my task is to learn how to lead this, God granting, with good grace and with philosophic acceptance. I am, after all, not the first person who has suffered this fate.

If war comes, as it probably will, I had best seek a military commission and serve wherever I am then asked to serve. I shall probably not survive it; one rarely really survives two world wars in responsible public service. Nor will it make any difference what I do, for a government so unable to use serious counsel in time of peace will scarcely be able to make better use of it in time of war. But by holding a commission I shall give my family a better break in a country which has no use for civilians in war-time, and which prefers that people serve uselessly in uniform rather than that they serve usefully in civilian clothes.

November 8

I couldn't believe the Russians wanted a world war at this juncture. Russian behavior was conditioned by

(a) The desire to distract attention from Hungary, by heightening the tension concerning the Middle East.[43]

(b) The belief that the Western alliance is split over the Middle East, and that Russia can safely make trouble for Britain and France, confident that we will remain neutralized by the stand we have already taken.

I thought the Russians would drive matters to a high state of tension, whereupon they would seek a dicker with us, whereby we would purchase peace in that area by selling out French and British interests there. This I thought it likely we would do, since no one in authority in Washington cared anything about those interests, or realized that they were ours as well.

43. After Britain, France, and Israel invaded Egypt in response to President Gamal Abdel Nasser's nationalization of the Suez Canal, the Soviet Union threatened the attacking countries with nuclear war if they did not withdraw. Acting separately, the United States applied financial and political pressure to get its allies to pull back.

Thus, if things went as the Russians planned, there would be no world war, only a political conquest of the Middle East by the Russians who would henceforth dominate the area and use the oil, to the extent they could control it, as an instrument of blackmail against the West. But one had to realize that the situation was partly out of hand, from their standpoint as well as ours. From this circumstance, given the high degree of tension everywhere, war could very well develop.

[On November 6, Eisenhower and Nixon won a sweeping reelection victory.]

November 11

My impulse is to say: This is now Nixon's America, not mine. It has nothing to do with me. It wants no part of me, and I, as things stand, no part of it. Why, then, should I take any further part in the discussion of public problems? Why not *really retire* from the public eye, and become completely the forgotten man?

I have to face the fact, after all, that my adversaries have won. Their ideas, not mine, have commended themselves to the overwhelming majority of my countrymen. Is there any use trying to talk to the tiny minority who are interested in what I have to say? Yet they *do* expect something; and it is no doubt myself who is responsible for the fact that they do. Should one not at least try to tell them why one proposes to remain silent? . . .

[Those who look to me] cannot all emigrate and take on some foreign citizenship, as I should like to do. What advice does one give them? To withdraw into apathy and private pursuits, to do as the others do: lose themselves in any sort of empty sublimation, occupy themselves with anything—baseball, camping, television, crooners, Cadillacs, golf, California—anything, so long as it is not real? What else could one say?

The hardest part of this, for me, is that I am quite confident that in most respects I am right. What does one do with such a burden? It would have been much easier had I been wrong. But I have not been wrong in the main. Almost alone, in 1945, I foresaw both the horror of Russia's rule in the satellites, and the necessity of its eventual disintegration. My diagnosis of the weakness of the totalitarian society in Russia proper has proven substantially correct. The Marshall Plan approach was my idea, and I calculated correctly the components of its political success. Had the government accepted the Planning Staff's program for the handling of the German problem, Germany would probably be united, and eastern Germany clear of communist control. Alone among senior officials in Washington I urged, six years ago, that Formosa be put directly under MacArthur's control, & no nonsense about returning it to China. I warned against the attempt to invade North Korea. I am sure that I am substantially right today when I say we are making a fatal mistake in basing our security on the majority of the UN Assembly, rather than on those allies who have a traditional stake in our future. What to do with these perceptions? Bury them? Hide them? Die with them? They are not wanted.

November 27

The Arabs are smiling at us and we are permitted to bask, briefly, in what seems to be what the American political mentality has always yearned for: the approval and admiration and gratitude of the little nations for our support to them in the face of the greedy depredations of the great imperialist powers. The shades of John Hays' Open Door notes fall again over American diplomacy at this juncture. Then, as now, we had said the right words, and everyone was happy about it, even though it failed to affect the situation. Then, as now, the public was content to believe that our posture had somehow shamed the imperialists and won us the gratitude of the helpless little people, whom we could patronize and whom we could show the paternalism which our own political system inhibits at home. In those days, it was the Chinese of whose gratitude we were confident. Yet see where they are today. Now it is the Arabs. Where will they be tomorrow?

1957

Kennan's work in the previous few years came to fruition as his first scholarly book, Russia Leaves the War, *swept the field by winning several top prizes. In November while holding the prestigious Eastman Professorship at Oxford, he broadcast the Reith Lectures over the BBC. In these talks he urged the superpowers not to install nuclear weapons in central Europe, but rather to disengage from that region, thereby allowing East and West Germany to reunite into a neutral state. The lectures aroused a storm of controversy in Western Europe and America.*

Princeton, May 6

Today, Volume I[44] received the Pulitzer Prize—the fourth it has received. I am mildly pleased, somewhat incredulous that it can be that good, but somehow not the least excited about it. Why this lack of enthusiasm, I cannot explain, even to myself. I have done these volumes in as tidy and thorough and workmanlike manner as I could, but my heart has not been in them. There are things that interest me far more; but they are things I never write about. Perhaps it is fiction I should write.

May 23

Came into New York this afternoon for a dinner of the Society of Friends of American History, at which I was to be the first recipient of an award they had established for the best annual work of American history as *literature.* It was a very warm & pleasant occasion. Allan Nevins[45] presided. Norman Armour[46] presented the award.

This event completed the series of awards this spring, which has included:

44. *Soviet-American Relations, 1917–1920: Russia Leaves the War* (1956).
45. Allan Nevins was a prize-winning Columbia University historian.
46. Norman Armour was a career diplomat and assistant secretary of state while Kennan headed the Policy Planning Staff.

the National Book Award (non-fiction)
the Bancroft Award (U.S. History)
the Pulitzer Prize
the Benjamin Franklin Award (best magazine article on public affairs)
the Francis Parkman Award (tonight's)

I don't know what to make of this flood of honors. I cannot believe that the book was that good. . . . I suspect it must have been a dull year in the non-fiction field. But it pleases me, in that it means that I have established myself in the non-fiction field, and that a love of language and writing, which never found any appreciable recognition in government, has found recognition in a wider field. At the same time, it is a responsibility. It means that I now have the ability to be widely heard on my own merits and not just by virtue of a governmental office. It implies an obligation not to fritter away wind and energy, to try to speak only when there is something worth saying and in a forum which will preserve the worth of the voice. The ability to be heard, to be listened to widely & with respect, must be treated, in other words, as an asset in itself, as something which may have come to me largely by chance, but which represents, deservedly or otherwise, a rare possibility of usefulness, in a world where the din of the mass media has drowned or compromised a great many other voices, and which must therefore be cherished and protected, wholly aside from its chance relation to my own person.

July 28

I worry about my utter lack of enthusiasm for the Reith lectures. Christopher[47] just asked me what I was interested in. I couldn't answer him! What, indeed? Boats, I said, vaguely. And I added that I would be interested in growing things, if life permitted. Plainly, the one thing I am not interested in is what everybody expects me to be following most passionately: international affairs. And why not? It has been taken out of me. The frustrations and disillusionments have accumulated in such numbers that I have only pessimism left, and I am too healthy to be interested in what I am pessimistic about.

To be fully honest, I should give these lectures on: "Why there is no hope in the international situation." But then I should have to start with the sterility of our own American society, with the inadequacy of

47. George and Annelise's son, Christopher, would turn eight in November.

our institutions, with the failure of the permissive system. From that I could then go on to the overpopulation, the nastiness, the recklessness of the outside world. I should have to urge the retrogressive society, the declining population, a large measure of autarchy, and a strict political isolation. For whom? England, Canada & the U.S., I suppose; and then I had just as soon see it four U.S.'s—the East and Middle West, combined, the South, Texas, and California, with the Northwest left to choose—all this on a federal basis with Canada & the U.K.—Washington to disappear (and very good riddance indeed) a federal capital to be created, say, near Windsor or Ottawa. As for alliances: Scandinavia & the Siberian Peninsula to be neutralized, continental Europe on its own. The Atlantic group to pursue, then, a policy of rigorous population reduction and the cultivation of autarchy, involving the weaning of our respective peoples from the motor car.

How would all this sound over the BBC?

And what would be the use of advocating such things, in the face of the fact that we in Canada, England, & the U.S. are, after all democracies, and popular opinion will never wake up to these facts. The truth is that democracy in the Western world could be saved from itself only by 50 years of benevolent dictatorship which would, like a doctor, restore the patient to a reasonable state of vigor and then put him on his own again.

Since none of this is going to happen, what can one say that is honest? Warn people that they are in for it, and advise them to cultivate the virtues of early Christianity, based on the belief that the world is going to come to an end in our lifetime?

August 28

Oxford! Serene courtyards. Magnificent old towers, graceful but strong, seeming to swim against the background of the blowing clouds. Breakneck traffic plunging incongruously through the streets. Great phalanxes of bicycles . . . ridden by young women with strong limbs and healthy complexions, not delicate but not unattractive. At home: a chilly, empty apartment in a huge empty house. Endless loneliness, days without the exchange of a single social word. Long walks in the fresh, damp wind: through the parks, along suburban streets which have the prim, rectangular bluntness and blankness of so much of the modern urban scene in England, along the banks of quiet rivers where lovers lie in the deep grass, as lost, as desperate, as helpless, as the heroine & hero of the *For-*

syte Saga.[48] (Ah, love in England, so frail, so handicapped, so overwhelmingly without a chance, and so terribly poignant by consequence!) Meals in tiny little hotel restaurants, where there are only two waitresses, and the menu never changes, and all is so quiet that people whisper in order not to shatter the churchyard stillness. Old common-rooms, with the paneling, the candles and the port, and the feeling of people clinging, clinging to what is really past, and for how long? The contrasts of the English personality in the casual encounters, running all the way from the most beautiful politeness and helpfulness to occasional ferocious flashes of rudeness or condescension. And everywhere, the little groups of summer tourists, camera, and guide-book in hands, dragging their feet, duty written into every line of the visage.

I have been in that stage of loneliness where I feel contempt for others because of their indulgence in the false balm of companionship, contempt for myself, but less, in this instance, for being unable to repress triggers of envy. How weak is man, that he has this need to warm his ego daily in the polite reactions of others, playing his little past, telling his little jokes, maintaining the fluff that is his personality, deceiving himself into believing that others were deceived by it! He is as weak socially as he is physically. Deprive him of food and sleep for two or three days, and you have a quivering bundle of shattered nerves. Deprive him of the companionship of others, and he falls into melancholy and self-pity: his ego starved by the removal of false nourishment, chilled by the unmitigated presence of his own cold, empty self.

In these days, I have finished the lectures for the B.B.C. And damned poor lectures they are, by and large. This is no longer my forte. I sent them down by mail. The editor has been reading them lately. Tomorrow we must have it out. If they will not do, I am inclined to ask to be permitted to withdraw. What miseries I let myself in for when I accepted this invitation.

[In the following entry, Kennan reflected on the intensely hectic and, despite his self-criticism, productive fall term at Oxford.]

Doddington, England, December 22

Three months have now elapsed since I wrote the last of these words. They seem like three years. Thirteen academic lectures at Oxford, six

48. *The Forsyte Saga* is an early-twentieth-century series of novels by John Galsworthy depicting the trials of an upper-middle-class British family.

Reith lectures, one dinner speech at the military commentator's circle, and one television interview have come and gone—all hastily prepared, none as good as they might and should have been. All were well received, the Oxford lectures drawing generally 150 to 200 people, the Reith lectures achieving an enormous notoriety and outward success. I don't know what to make of it all. It is obvious that I am not capable of putting the whole matter into proper perspective. Three times I came away from the studio in the Reith lectures absolutely neurotic with remorse over having, as it seemed to me, made such a mess of it, muttering to myself, comforting myself with the reflection that I had not asked to give them in the first place, afraid even to look at the morning papers, the next day, for fear of seeing there the confirmation of my shame. I felt like Anton Chekhov after the frightful flop of *The Seagull* in Leningrad. How that squares with the public success of the lectures, I do not know!

My feeling now is that I have thoroughly exhausted the working capital of knowledge about international affairs with which I left government five years ago, and wish never to open my mouth about them again until I have some opportunity to learn all over again.

[The Kennans were on the Continent for Christmas break.]

Luxembourg, December 31

People say the Reith lectures made a great splash, and no doubt they did. But the governments certainly could not have been less impressed, or a lot of the press.

I said in the lectures that the attempts to reach agreements about general disarmament were a waste of time. Yet most of the talk about renewed negotiation is cast in terms of the discussion of disarmament.

I said they couldn't negotiate successfully with Russia as a coalition. The NATO communique implies that the NATO countries expect to negotiate, if at all, as a group.

I said they would have to have exploratory feelers and talks, first. Yet everyone persists in speaking as though we expected the Soviet leaders to put all their cards on the table before we have committed ourselves at all.

I said I thought no outsider could draw up a plan for disengagement in central Europe. The world press persists in speaking of the Kennan plan.

I said they should not try to outbid the Soviet Government for the favor of the Asian-African peoples. The Soviet representative at the Cairo

Conference promises unlimited aid to all of them, a promise Moscow could never meet, and people in Washington immediately respond by talking about a new $1,400,000,000 aid program.

I said we should not put nuclear weapons in Western Europe. The statesmen at Paris respond by instructing Norstad[49] to draw up a plan, designating the places in Western Europe where he wants them.

49. U.S. General Lauris Norstad was NATO commander.

1958

The storm over the 1957 Reith Lectures continued into 1958. Kennan had challenged Cold War orthodoxy by suggesting that a deal with Moscow over Germany was possible and desirable. Former secretary of state Dean Acheson jabbed that Kennan "has never, in my judgment, grasped the realities of power relationships, but takes a rather mystical attitude toward them."[50] *Konrad Adenauer, the chancellor of the Federal Republic of Germany, personally thanked Acheson "for the firmness of the way in which you dealt with the unrealistic thinking of Mr. Kennan."*[51] *Kennan faced, in addition to this criticism, an arduous schedule of public lectures at Oxford. As always, he rose to the public challenge even as he privately complained.*

[The Kennan family went on vacation in Switzerland.]

Crans, Switzerland, January 5
A Western position which suggested that the West might under any circumstances withdraw its forces from Germany would, we are told, even though unacceptable to the Russians today, demoralize NATO. If this is true (I am not sure that it is) then I can only say that there could be no more striking proof of just what I have charged: namely, that NATO has become not a means to the negotiation of a European settlement, not something that could be modified or altered to meet counter-concessions on the other side, but an end in itself, something valued more highly than any concessions for which it could possibly be traded, ergo a barrier to any real political compromise.

50. *New York Times*, January 12, 1958.
51. Konrad Adenauer to Dean Acheson, February 20, 1958, box 30, Dean Acheson papers, Sterling Library, Yale University, New Haven, CT.

I am intrigued, generally, by the reaction to the lecture on Germany. It embraces two elements

(1) The Russians wouldn't accept it.
(2) To propose it would weaken NATO.

These two arguments are actually contradictory. If it is so clear that the Russians wouldn't accept it, why should NATO be endangered? Either there must be a fear that these proposals might be accepted, or it must at least be admitted that the virtue of the existing proposals is that they reveal no real interest in a settlement at all, that they are not real proposals.

January 12
Was confronted this morning, wholly unexpectedly, with Acheson's reply to my Reith Lectures, which appeared on the front page of the Sunday *Neue Zürcher Zeitung.* Wandered around half the day, in the snow, trying to adjust to the blow. It is not only that what I said was dreadfully misinterpreted, but it means that there is now really not the faintest hope for American policy, in either party. There is not a man in public life in the U.S. today who is interested in a political settlement with the Russians. We are determined that the contest shall be a purely military one, & shall be settled only that way; we are determined, in other words, to plunge blindly, recklessly ahead with the weapons race, wherever it leads us. And where can it lead us? . . . I am now in the truest sense a voice crying in the wilderness; and never, I think, have I felt a greater sense of loneliness.

January 21
The die is now cast. There will be no European settlement. The arms race will go uncontrollably ahead. These people will have their war, on which they all seem so intent. What will remain of our world when it is all over, is beyond human reckoning.

Oxford, February 2
I find myself wondering at the loathing I experience for Oxford on returning here. . . . I ask myself why I am unhappier here than in Princeton. Individuals here have been kind and hospitable to me. In Princeton, too, I am essentially a guest. Aside from our own circle of good friends, I have no relation to Princeton, either. I detest ⅘ of the manifestations of

contemporary American life. But in Princeton there is the garden; I can work outside; I can get to the farm occasionally; the children can play, informally, out of doors, and it does not necessarily take pre-arrangement to get them together with other children; the house is warm and spacious and pleasant; there is a greater sense of space and freedom over everything; one breathes more easily. In Princeton, too, there is a great deal that one must fight against, but the fight seems more enjoyable, more colorful, more hopeful. Here, all is habit—as forbidding, as unassailable, as cold, and as unimaginative as the stone of the walls.

I have been forced to realize, in these last days, that I have come to a point where I can no longer reconcile my profession of scholarship with any participation in the discussion of current events. The two are like oil and water; they have nothing to do with each other; attention given to one is given at the cost of the other. It is, of course, as a commentator on current affairs that I am valued. It is here that all the pressure is applied. Nobody cares anything about me as a historian. . . .

I am inclined to agree that now, for the first time, the past is largely irrelevant to the present. With the acquisition of the power to destroy their own environment, men have landed themselves in a situation without precedent. If there were anything I could do to help prevent them from destroying it, this would be the most useful purpose to which I could put the remainder of my life. But the moment I turn from scholarship to journalism or politics as a profession, my voice will lose a great deal of the power it possesses for the public, and it is a question whether I could preserve the complete independence which is the real source of my strength as I see it. Therein lies my dilemma.

February 3

Heard the voice of an American woman this morning . . . and suddenly realized how much this period abroad has caused me to love my own people, who are so hopelessly behind the eight-ball and destined within my children's time to know unprecedented horrors and miseries and probably to pass entirely from the scene of world history, but who nevertheless have certain qualities of modesty and candor and helpfulness for the death of which the world will some day be poorer.

The older I become the more I value the female of our species in relation to the male. I know of scarcely a country where she is not stronger and greater than her male counterpart. The man, with his chaotic and destructive sexual urge, so terribly at odds with the ordering and theorizing quality of his mind, vacillates in the various cultures between brutality and a neurotic, hyper-refined helplessness. The woman in both cases has to be the strength: protecting the continuity of life from the reckless male despot, breathing vitality and discipline into the intellectual-aesthete, and preserving for him the endangered bond with reality.

[After a flight to Lisbon, the family vacationed near the Portuguese capital.]

Lisbon, April 11

Went into town in the afternoon and paid my courtesy call on Dr. Salazar.[52] Found him looking well, thoughtful, & sensitive. But it is always difficult to discuss with great public figures the finer nuances of a situation. One hesitates to hold them and bore them with what seem to be minor points. I tried to make plain to him that there were sides to the Soviet character that were positive and where one could appeal to something like honor and self-respect, but I don't think I got very far. "No one trusts them," he said, gloomily. He was obviously not for disengagement, as I had suggested it. He feared turning a united Germany loose in Europe, without firm political (and in Europe that means "military") commitment. He did not fear the atomic weapon: thought it so terrible that no one would use it. He did not seem to realize the implications of the missiles: the very brief warning-time, the premium on surprise. He also did not seem worried about the pollution of the atmosphere through tests of atomic explosives. He did agree that the placing of atomic weapons in the hands of a number of governments, beyond the three that now possess them, would raise new difficulties in the path of any agreements on atomic disarmament.

London, May 15

Seeing *The Cherry Orchard* stirred all the rusty, untuned strings of the past and of my own youth: Riga, and the Russian landscape, and the staggering, unexpected familiarity and convincingness of the Chekhovian world—it stirred up, in other words, my Russian self, which is entirely a Chekhovian self and much more genuine than the American one—and having all this prodded to the surface in me, I sat there blubbering like a

52. António Salazar was the longtime Portuguese dictator with whom Kennan had negotiated to allow U.S. bases in the Azores in World War II. Kennan admired Salazar as a statesman.

child and trying desperately to keep the rest of the company from noticing it.

Kristiansand, Norway, June 21

Do we in the West deserve to survive? I am not the first who has asked this question. Has the time really come for the Russians to teach us, as Custine suggested, "how we can be, and should be, ruled?"[53] I cannot believe it. The truth is that the Russians, once subjected to the wind of material plenty, will be as helpless as the rest of us, even more so, under its debilitating and insidious breath. They have certain potential advantages, in their socialism, just as they have certain actual disadvantages. We could well use a sufficient internal economic discipline to enable us to avoid senseless waste, the wastage involved in such things as advertising and built-in obsolescence, but by and large, America & old Europe, however great their need of new stimulus and invigoration, are not to be saved by Russia. If they are to be saved, it will be only by impulses from within themselves. Russian triumph can have, to Western civilization, only the same significance that the barbarian invasions had to ancient Rome: there might be buried somewhere in it the seeds of another civilization, destined to mature centuries hence, but not necessarily a higher one.

[En route to Warsaw, Kennan stopped off at the U.S. embassy in Copenhagen. Mingling with the embassy staffers, he suddenly grew homesick.]

Copenhagen, June 27

Oh my countrymen, my countrymen, my hope and my despair! What virtues you conceal beneath your slouching self-deprecation: virtues inconceivable to the pompous Continental. How strong you are in all that of which you are yourselves not conscious; and how childish and superficial you are in your own concept of the sources of your excellence. Being one of the most unintrospective of peoples (until very recently, at least) and one of the most insensitive to the impression created on others, you unfailingly hide your real distinction and court the ridicule and envy of the world. You may be punished, in the life to come, for your obstinate immaturity, for your failure to put away childish things

53. Marquis de Custine was a nineteenth-century French writer on Russia. Kennan edited *The Marquis de Custine and His Russia in 1839* (1971).

when the years of childhood have passed, for your unwillingness to bow your heads before the tragedy of the human predicament; but God will reward you, I do not doubt, for your humanity, for your quiet helpfulness, for your lack of pretense, for your naive pragmatism, for your very ineptness in all forms of representation, for your inability to put your best foot forward, and above all for the measureless envy and ridicule and detraction which have been poured upon your heads in recent years by the vain, the spiteful, and the envious of other lands. . . .

Take heed, you scoffers, you patronizers, you envious and malicious detractors, you conceited and superior Europeans, you Nassers and Khrushchevs: if you continue with your efforts to tear us down, you will rouse us yet to maturity, to introspection, to disillusionment, and to cunning in our own defense; and when you do, you will discover in us reserves of strength such as you never dreamed of; and then you, even more than we, will come to regret the passing of the days of our innocence.

[Invited to give a lecture in Warsaw, Kennan paid his first visit to a communist country since leaving Moscow in 1952. Afterward, he sent CIA Director Allen W. Dulles a memorandum describing the Poles' gradual self-liberation from Moscow's grasp. Dulles sent the report to President Eisenhower, who read it carefully.]

Warsaw, June 30–July 3

It is extremely hard to describe the people of Warsaw. They look somewhat smoother, better-dressed, more Western than the Russians. They do all the normal things. We know that they enjoy a freedom of speech unknown in Russia. There is little terror anymore for the common man. And certainly they are not, by nature, a servile race.

And yet, there is a certain wariness and quietness about them that strikes the visitor from the West. They are like people recovering from a shock, or an injury. They walk a little carefully, and they do not wear their hearts on their sleeves. . . .

Only one of the Poles I met was a communist, and this was a woman. She was one of those rare phenomena: a genuine, sincere communist, which meant that she was a person of idealism and courage who understood neither communism nor the non-communist world. My heart went out to her, trying, as she was, to build something cheerful and hopeful on this dismal foundation of error and grim despotism. No one, it seemed to me, would ever be able to restore the genuine *joie de vivre* under this grinding, humorless system. She was, in any case, an exception, a sheep among wolves when it came to the other communists, one destined, unquestionably for disillusionment and tragedy. Still, she was, as a person, vastly more human and approachable than the equivalent Soviet girl guide, with her stern denial of her own femininity, her lack of personal style, her harsh, parrot-like orthodoxy.

The Poles I met were first and foremost nationalists, stubborn, wistful nationalists. A curious thing, this Polish nationalism. It is, of course, an intense love of country, but it is also a desperate consciousness *of not-being-a-part* of anything else but Poland. The Poles are Poles because they are not, and cannot be, anything else. The present-day ones, in Warsaw at least, tell you that they have given up being romanticists, that they are now trying to practice realism, the art of accommodation, the art of not being heroes. Poor people! They do not see (or do they?) that in this very effort to accommodate to Russia they are indulging themselves in just another romantic, implausible gamble.

The imbalance in the present situation of Poland is occasioned, and conditioned, by the appalling memory of Hitler. It could scarcely be otherwise, yet I cannot help but feel that this is a very confusing factor. In the very long run, the Poles would be better off in a close association with the Germans than with the Russians. But try to tell them that today. . . .

One sensed very quickly that Russia was just something one didn't talk about. One passed, in tacit silence, by the Russian-built skyscraper in the center of town, neither praising nor blaming. When the talk turned on German atrocities, one did not mention the massacre in Katyn forest.[54] When the subject was the Warsaw uprising of 1944, one refrained from recalling that the Soviet radio had urged armed action but that the Soviet army made no effort to help the beleaguered Poles, and that when the Americans inquired whether they could use the American shuttle-base in Russia as a landing place for planes dropping supplies to the Warsaw insurgents, the Soviet answer was "no." When one is shown the evidences of the preposterous and criminal destruction of Warsaw by the Germans, no one cares to mention that the Soviet army sat quietly by the entire time, in the suburb of Praga, across the river, and allowed this destruction to proceed without interference. Soviet power, in other

54. While occupying eastern Poland in 1940, the Soviets executed some 22,000 Polish army officers and buried them in the Katyn Forest. When the Germans in 1943 discovered the graves, the Soviets insisted that it was the Germans who had perpetrated this atrocity.

words, is something of which everyone is aware, but of which no one cares to speak, and in this studied silence there is a condemnation more devastating than any words.

Crossing the Atlantic, August 1

What does one do with this contemporary America? . . . Does one try to contribute, to help? Does one admit the futility of any such effort, bow to the overwhelming force of error now prevalent, and retire, to cultivate his garden, to preserve the serenity and clarity of his own vision, and to write books that a handful of people may read and that will probably burn up, anyway, in the imminent atomic holocaust? . . . When governments, in their obstinacy & passion, come into the possibility, & even the probability, of destroying the natural environment of life, can the scholar or the philosopher stand aside? Must he then not enter in to this wretched, brutal, cynical game, and play it for whatever it is worth, sacrificing his own possibilities for contributing to the life of the spirit, in order that this life may have a chance of surviving at all?

Here I am within 45 hours of arrival in the U.S., and I have no answers to these problems at all, but spend my time playing ping-pong with the captain and rushing from one side of the ship to the other to see whether any ships are visible. I may, as friends assure me, be an unusual sort of person, but assuredly, with this lack of will & of concentration, I am not a great one.

September 8, Miscellaneous Reading Notes

Daniel J. Boorstin, *The Americans, The Colonial Experience*

Boorstin seems to derive satisfaction from these differences and to feel that the positive innovations in the colonial experience well outweighed what was lost or neglected from the European heritage. To my mind, this is, rather, a depressing picture that emerges from his pages: a society without poetry, without art, without esthetic feeling, the home of superficiality, of smatterings of knowledge, of crude individual observation in the place of science, of newspapers instead of books, of sloppy, destructive farming, and of a stubborn selfish indifference to the problems of external defense, which it was left to the British to solve (all defense, that is, on other than a local basis).

Is it any wonder that a society so heedless, so selfish, so contemptuous of its own cultural heritage, should find it difficult today to act as a mature nation?

The colonial experience was, in fact, in many ways an unfortunate one: a deterioration rather than an improvement in the state of those who underwent it, a weakening of the social and cultural disciplines that had made the colonists what they originally were, a provincialization of what had before been cosmopolitan, an escape from, rather than a projection of, the greatness of Europe.

[Reinhold Niebuhr, who considered himself a "Christian realist," believed that original sin ensured that almost any human endeavor, if unrestricted, could lead to evil. While deploring the totalitarian tendencies of the communist nations, he also warned the democracies not to succumb to hubris. Kennan found Niebuhr's thought congenial. It remains unclear which particular manuscript Kennan was reading. In 1960, Niebuhr published new editions of both *Moral Man and Immoral Society: A Study in Ethics and Politics* (1932) and *The Children of Light and the Children of Darkness: A Vindication of Democracy and a Critique of Its Traditional Defense* (1944).]

Thoughts on reading Reinhold Niebuhr's manuscript

The question is the relation of the Christian ethic to the process of government.

Let me take as a standard of comparison to the governmental process the realm of the bodily functions and instincts. These things exist, and are inescapable. It is part of the human condition, as given to us by God, that we should be, so long as we live, a part of the whole great physio-chemical process of organic life: that we should endure the humiliation of having bodies in which the cycle of corruption and renewal is daily re-enacted; that we should harbor overpowering instincts for the preservation of our own flesh from danger and injury and for its perpetuation through the process of procreation; that there should stand at the center of our psychic constitution a libido the demands of which, as Freud has demonstrated, we ignore at our peril.

This condition is, from the Christian standpoint, neither good nor bad. It is not good, because it is one which we share with the lowest of the beasts, perhaps even with the plants: it represents merely a part of the general development of organic life on this planet, a development which would seem to be tending to no good end; in fact, in the case of human beings, to some form of self-destruction. The responses which this condition evokes from us are ones not only devoid of dignity but often in conflict with any spiritual distinction, ones which can only be compromised, never reconciled, with the demands of Christian love.

On the other hand, this condition is not bad, because it was given to us by God: it was plainly His purpose that we should be required to endure it and that the endurance of it should in fact be a precondition for the very effort to practice Christian virtues. Plainly, the demands presented to us by this condition, while a part of the human predicament, are not the particular part through which Christian purposes are to be realized: Christian purposes can be realized, in fact, only in the process of a conflict with these bodily demands, only at their expense, only by resisting and overcoming them to a degree. I say "to a degree," for to resist and overcome them entirely is to deny the human state entirely: suicide, in short. . . .

Is the process of government essentially different, in its relation to Christian purposes from these bodily functions and instincts? It, too, is concerned only with the demands of man's body and his self-love. This is true whether it be order or justice which the state is trying to assure. The state exists as an agency by which man requires himself to subordinate, indeed, certain of these selfish demands in the short term, but only to the end of their better realization over the long term. Theft is inhibited, because people can better enrich themselves if it is ruled out. The state, in other words, does some of the things the Christian individual is required, in principle, to do: it combats the selfish, the anarchic, the aggressive tendencies in *some* men, and at *some* times. But it does this for no Christian purpose. It is not for the glorification of God that the state disciplines and restrains individual men. To the extent that the state reflects the love of some men for exerting power over others, it is founded on precisely that self-love which belongs to the category of bodily instincts. To the extent, on the other hand, that it reflects a human preference for order, we must ask: what is the source of this preference? Is it Christian love? Scarcely. The need for order is probably an historically-conditioned necessity: the product of man's surprising ingenuity in the development of weapons and means of communication, an ingenuity which destroyed the presuppositions of primitive life and made the primitive state intolerable. If so, the state reflects merely a more sophisticated and contemporary expression of the human need for physical security; again, an instinctive need, not, as Christ Himself demonstrated, a Christian one.

We must recognize, too, that the basic means which the state employs for the accomplishment of its purpose are not ones by which Christian purposes can be served. The state is, as Lenin correctly recognized, essentially an agency of coercion. It merely transmits the element of violence, in the individual's own interest, from the individual to the community.

We can concede that both the purpose of the state and the means it employs to promote this purpose are necessary and unavoidable. But this is true merely in the sense that the functioning of the state represents another form of the concession we are required to make daily to the animalistic side of the human condition. This being the case, the process of government, like the bodily process, is neither good nor bad in the Christian sense. It is part of the human condition: a necessity certainly sad and seemingly regrettable, but who are we to raise this last question? It is our duty to accept government and to give it its due, to the extent of not attempting to destroy it altogether but of attempting to find some tolerable compromise with it that will still permit a reasonable effort to realize Christian ideals within the framework of individual life and behavior. What we should *not* do is to attempt to find in the governmental process, unsuited as it is both by purpose and by method, a channel through which Christian purposes can hopefully be pursued. . . .

The human predicament with which Christianity deals is, in short, a lonely one, which can be confronted only on an individual basis. This loneliness can be mitigated by the Christian love that is possible between individuals, never between the community and the individual. Only genuine human intimacy—the affection of the family tie or individual friendship or, in some instances (more seldom than we suppose), the illumination brought to him by the pastor or the priest, can moderate the loneliness of man in the face of his Christian duty. And even human intimacy is a weak reed, subject as it is to the same fragility and brevity of human tenure which is the individual's own problem. . . .

There is an element of soundness in the pacifist view. I tried to draw attention to it in the Reith Lectures, with rather disastrous results, for what I said was not understood at all. It is that in the last analysis, one country cannot impose its will permanently on another except by military occupation or the threat of occupation, and then, on the latter instance, only if it can find a local regime to do its bidding. But Russia cannot actually occupy, in permanence, much more than she is now occupying; and another country which had the fortitude to resist the threat of occupation, and the internal discipline to deny power to its own communists, does not, as the Finns have proved, need atomic weapons, or any sizeable military establishment at all *for external purposes,* to defend the integrity of its national life. Our own country, or Britain, could probably purchase, by a policy of withdrawal and unilateral disarmament, a tolerable privacy of its own internal-political processes, comparable to what the Swiss now enjoy, *but* it would have to abandon its allies. It would probably lose all effective control over its sources of raw material, and it would be, as the Swiss indeed are, largely without influence on the course of world affairs—it would live, in other words, by the kindness of circumstances and by the good grace of others. It would be a precarious existence, without dignity or glory; one would require a high degree of internal discipline, and one would have to be prepared to stand long periods of siege.

Washington, December 28

All morning and the lunch hour at the American Historical Association meeting in the Mayflower. The long main corridor was packed from end to end with historians, and the air was beyond belief bad. (When will my people, who pride themselves in other respects on hygiene, ever get a taste for ventilation?) . . . [In Washington] I feel like a ghost, like one who has been permitted to come back and move, lonely and unnoticed, among the living.

The Farm, December 31

Shoveled the pile of rubbish out of the cellar in the morning, while the others skated. Took it out to gullies this afternoon & brought back a load of wood, which I sawed up for the fireplace. With this, together with the trivia, the day passed. Its evening brought the end of the year 1958. Personally, I look back on it with a total absence of enthusiasm. The only accomplishments by which it was marked were: the completion in a reasonably creditable manner of the lectures in England and Poland, the successful removal of the family to the U.S., and the rather expensive rescue of the farm from a state of desolation and neglect and its restoration to a sturdy utility.

Can I make anything more out of the next year? It promises to be a disastrous one internationally, and God knows, of course, what privacy that will leave us. To the extent I am left alone, I can at least write a decent history of Soviet foreign policy and perhaps make a start on Vol. III of the basic study, plus marrying one more daughter. Not much, not very exciting. Perhaps I should force myself to write, in my spare time, the book about domestic life & public policy generally, snatches of which mill around in my head.

What may this year be expected to bring? Mikoyan[55] will come here in January. Nothing will be achieved. The U.S. Government will be unable to offer anything, partly because it has no positive negotiating position, itself, partly because it could in any case not commit its allies. The Soviet Government will not be able to offer anything, because it is determined to save Grotewohl & Ulbricht[56] and because it has nailed its flag to the mast of an unconditional capitulation of the Western interest in Berlin. The result is the situation will be, if anything, worsened by Mikoyan's visit. The crisis will then ripen until by April–May it will assume an extremely acute and menacing form. If by that time the situation in either Iran or Quemoy,[57] or both, has not blown up again, some sort of a tortured and miraculous compromise in the Berlin situation will probably be worked out, with the help of the UN, at the last moment. This will involve delays, so that the crisis will, in the best of circumstances, endure into the summer. If, on the other hand, the Berlin situation is complicated by other crises, in the Middle or Far East, then war may well come.

To the above should be added that the crisis will, at some stage, probably produce a top-level, or senior-level, meeting. It may in fact be by this means, rather than by the UN that the final effort is made to resolve the Berlin situation.

55. Anastas Mikoyan was the Soviet deputy premier.
56. Otto Grotewohl and Walter Ulbricht were East German leaders.
57. The disputed island of Quemoy, occupied by the Nationalist Chinese government on Taiwan, was under bombardment by the Communist Chinese on the mainland.

1959

Kennan continued to agonize over how to reconcile the demands of his public engagement and his scholarly commitments. He also grew frustrated as the Berlin Crisis, which he believed disengagement could have averted, threatened to blow up into a nuclear war.

Princeton, January 14

Dreamed last night, for the first time in my life, that I encountered, twice in fact, my own mother. I recognized her instantly. There was in the face something so infinitely close and familiar—it could, I knew at once, be no other. She was younger than I had thought of her as being and of course more human. The eyes struck me with the intensity of the life that shone through them, and in the mouth, sensitive, sometimes slightly pouting, drawn between laughter and weeping, I was startled to become aware of a real human being, with all her own conflicts and trials and inadequacies, not the angel I had always pictured.

She was dressed rather luridly as befits death in the old-fashioned concept of her time, in a long dark blue or purple robe. She was silent, which was also fitting. She showed no recognition of me; she was plainly preoccupied with something else, but she accepted with politeness and with an enigmatic smile my own instantaneous gesture of recognition and joy and tenderness. She was, for the moment, the main thing in my existence; I was not the main thing in hers.

Now that I am awake and writing, at a table in the Firestone Library, I have no doubt that I saw her as she really was.

How to explain this, after 55 years? I do not know. Again, as on the occasion, two or three years ago, when I sat in a car on Cambridge Avenue, and stared at the old house, I was overwhelmed with the sense of the unreality of the present, with the feeling that this part of life is a long afternoon which will soon be forgotten, that the more important thing is coming. . . .

I wonder whether this is not a sign that death, which has remained so far from me in so remarkable a way through so much of my life, is now coming closer.

[Kennan went to the White House in connection with his advising on the forthcoming U.S. science exhibit in Moscow.]

Washington, January 23

We were taken into the Oval Room and arranged in a single circular line to fit the outlines of the room. When we were all assembled, the President came in after us and stood at the door, and the line filed out past him to the dining room, each of us shaking hands as we went by. He didn't look as old as I had expected; his face had that sort of waxy smooth youthfulness which, it seems to me, one often finds in old generals. He started a bit on seeing me, looked again, and said, "Why, hello, Kennan. It's some time since I've seen you." I am sure he had no idea, before, who was on the list.

February 4

At 4:30, I went to call (at his request) on Senator John F. Kennedy, who came down for this purpose from the floor of the Senate, where he had been battling over the labor bill. He began by talking about this, practically admitting that the Administration bill was a better bill, but saying that his had more chance of passage, and it was better to have something than nothing. (What a typical instance of the politicians' dilemma.) He seemed very harried and pressed, and while most courteous toward me, I felt that internal politics gave him little time to reflect on the state of the world.

February 7

Talked with Fulbright[58] at some length and was at a loss to know what to reply when he asked me what he and like-minded senators could do with regard to foreign affairs. He said that there was very little interest in membership on the Foreign Relations Committee. His colleagues felt that there was no "political mileage" in foreign affairs, only dangers and pitfalls. They much preferred places like the Appropriations Committee, where, as one of them had expressed it, they could have their hand in the

58. Senator J. William Fulbright, Democrat of Arkansas, was chair of the Senate Foreign Relations Committee.

till. He confirmed entirely my own impression of Lyndon Johnson as a skillful tactical parliamentarian without wider interests or ideas. He said the last thing Johnson[59] wanted was any debate of any sort on the floor of the Senate. He wanted everything arranged in advance, with action on the floor being confined to voting.

February 20

[Driving out of Amsterdam, New York,] we passed four more young toughies, striding along the street, hatless, gloveless, leather jackets gleaming in the lamplight, legs spidery in the tight, bowed blue jeans, faces hard and sullen and arrogant. Oh my country, my country, what is it that you do to your youth? How do you continue to make this life on the fringe of criminality—this life with its desolate nightly streets, its seamy luncheon counters and pool halls, its brawls and brutalities, its never-ending profanity and obscenity of speech, its cultivated cynicism, its wretched sexual encounters in the back-seats of cars, its proudly-worn gonorrheas, its hangovers, its cruelties, its bad faith, its absence of prospects—how do you contrive to make this more attractive than all that love and beauty have to offer? And what becomes of us, of our children, when these young monsters, as some day they must, lead all the rest?

Good Friday, March 27

As we approached Harrisburg, on the Turnpike, it suddenly turned weirdly dark, & everyone had to drive with their lights on. (I heard later that this occurred at precisely the hour of the day when Christ is supposed to have been crucified. Many people were deeply impressed.)

The Farm, Easter Sunday, March 29

Lay this afternoon in our bedroom, resting, watching the light fade outside the windows, and pondered the easy, not at all intolerable, but none the less genuine dead-end at which my life has arrived. History has palled on me. The farm, for the first time after 17 years, is losing its meaning. I haven't the faintest idea what now to do with myself.

It occurred to me, in this connection, that never have I lived any place where the present did not seem to represent a deterioration as

59. Lyndon B. Johnson, Democratic senator from Texas, was the majority leader in the Senate.

compared with the past. All the European cities I lived in, except perhaps Lisbon, were wraiths of their former selves: Riga, Berlin, Prague, Vienna, Moscow—not one of them which was not reported to have been a far healthier, more attractive, more liveable place before the first world war. How should one, then, believe in progress? The same is true in this country: wherever one finds any place where life can be made in any way attractive, the problem always is, how soon before it will be ruined? What better proof that we are experiencing the rapid decline of a civilization? Even as a historian, I feel that we are fighting a losing race against forgetfulness, indifference, and the deliberate cultivation of untruth.

I see no life for my children. If the boy were to ask me: where, in this world to which you have introduced me, do I seek genuineness of experience, a life rich in meaning, the development of myself to the utmost, what could I say? Only at the ends of the earth: in the Arctic, perhaps, where almost no other men live; where nature, not man, is your companion and your challenge.

For my own country, I have not a shred of hope, not one. Its institutions are only too obviously inadequate to the position and responsibilities at which it has arrived. And it will not change these institutions, at least not with anything like the requisite speed. The possibility of amendment of the Constitution has come to be used only as a medium for moral gestures, no longer as a real means of improving a political system.

April 13

[At a Council on Foreign Relations dinner] for German Defense Minister, Herr Franz Josef Strauss. He turned out to be a likeable young man, with a wholly genuine charm and jollity, yet obviously able. He has a great fat face, but a strong and not overly obese body. In his speech, he was obliged to give the party line of his government, but he answered questions with candor and considerable skill. He was, I think, quite sincere in the belief he expressed that to separate the German army today from the NATO framework would be unthinkable, that it would have no value on its own.

The dinner was chaired by Mr. Conant,[60] & the room was full of my ideological opponents. Not only Mr. Conant but some of the others were

60. James B. Conant was former president of Harvard University and former U.S. ambassador to Germany.

obviously surprised and nonplused to find me there—as if the Devil had been found occupying a pew in church. When the question time came, I held my peace until the very end. Then, in a hushed and apprehensive silence, I put my questions, not too well, I fear.

I noted that Herr Strauss had said that there was no use trying to negotiate a Germany settlement with the Russians because their aims ran to the control of all of Europe and the world. I pointed out that on this basis there would be no advantage in trying to negotiate with them about anything at all. I further pointed out that if a flatly negative answer were given to the Russians, the Berlin situation would nevertheless continue to be an unsatisfactory and dangerous one from the Western standpoint.

[Kennan went to Chicago to give a speech to a businessmen's conference and another to the Chicago Council on Foreign Relations. He did not further identify "X."]

Chicago, April 17

In the afternoon, I took X to tea. Forlornly, we wandered around the labyrinthian lobby of the Palmer House, looking for a place where we could get a cup of tea. We finally found one, but it was not very *gemütlich* [congenial], and I longed for a good Viennese café. X was her old self: impulsive, warm, and very foolish. She told me her troubles, which was all right, but when I left her on State St., her final word, flung over the heads of the startled passers-by, was: "Sorry to have been so miserable." Thereby she illustrated, by the negative example, the sound rule of human behavior: namely, if you have tendencies which you know yourself are wrong, which you cannot control yet cannot leave, don't apologize for them—brave them out; they are, after all, a part of you.

Washington, April 22

I have to struggle to avoid a certain bitterness to which I am constantly prompted (as I am sure are Acheson and others) by Mr. Dulles' latter day acceptance in Western opinion as a statesman of titanic dimensions. I cannot help but compare with my own powerlessness and relative obscurity the eulogies now heaped on this dying man,[61] with whose physical sufferings we all have greatest sympathy but who, I

61. Secretary of State John Foster Dulles was dying of cancer.

cannot forget, secured his position with the Congress at the price of demoralization of the foreign service and by sacrificing some of its most deserving members, as well as by mouthing inflammatory slogans ("liberation," "massive retaliation," etc.) to which he had no intention of adhering in practice, and who in his years of office has taken no political leadership of any sort, has relied entirely on a negative and defensive military policy as an answer to the Soviet political challenge, and has permitted the division of Europe to congeal, has in fact connived at its congealing, to a point where the eastern half of the continent must now be considered as added in permanence to the Russian empire. What is to be done, one tends to ask oneself, with a public which mistakes this for statesmanship?

June 17

So far as Berlin is concerned, things have worked out very much as predicted in these notes, on December 31 [1958].

I have found myself thinking that we ought to trade complete recognition of Eastern Germany for the best face-saving device we could get with respect to Berlin. . . . Berlin, mind you, has of course, by the implications of present Western policy, no future. When we moved to save it in 1945, we were kidding its inhabitants. In a divided Europe, Berlin is an anomaly. Yet we cannot let it go altogether. What, then, is to be saved?

The answer is, of course: face. Whatever happens, must not happen too flagrantly or abruptly. What you want is for the place to die decently on the vine, for young people to leave it in increasing numbers, for economic life to be gradually curtailed, for plants to move away, for cultural life to fade, for the whole place to dwindle and shrink, in the human sense, until a final absorption of it into the Soviet zone would seem unimportant and scarcely noticeable, even to the remaining inhabitants.

These things are, of course, not my idea of the desirable—precisely the opposite. I am merely trying to adjust my own thinking to the implications of Western policy. In the views I put forward a year and a half ago in England, I am now prepared to admit defeat. If there was ever a time for what I was talking about, that time has now passed. There is to be no disengagement. Germany is to become increasingly an atomic power. The line of division in Europe is to be made steadily sharper, more meaningful, more ineradicable. Starting from such a premise, what can the policy maker do, or the man who tries to put himself in the policy maker's place? Only one thing, it would seem: and that is to try to make this division as comfortable, as relaxed, and as little dangerous, as possible.

June 19

Future archeologists and historians, stumbling on the remnants of these roads, could wonder what great wasteful ruler it was who flung them across the forests, what imperious ruthless potentate had whipped these energies out of his subjects. They would be amazed to learn that this time it was not a man but a machine in whose service all this was done, and that men gave to it, in the belief that they were serving their own convenience, an obedience they would not have dreamed of paying to one of their own number. Law No. 1 of the American empire will be found to have been this: wherever it is thought in any way desirable that the internal combustion engine should go, there it shall find access, at whatever cost.

July 21

Again, as on other occasions, I reflected that I would rather take my children to the ends of the earth, to Alaska or a Norwegian valley, to any place where life was real, for their sakes even to the Soviet Union, than to see them grow up in this cradle of luxury that corrupted and demoralized them before they even reached maturity.

[Leaving Annelise in Princeton, Kennan spent much of September in Europe. Near Basel, he participated in a seminar, held by the noted French intellectual Raymond Aron, on political philosophy. In Hamburg he met with Marion Dönhoff, his friend and the editor of *Die Zeit*. Kennan admired her aristocratic lineage, resistance against the Nazis, and courageous escape on horseback as the Red Army advanced through eastern Germany. In London he gave a talk over the BBC and then in Oxford participated in a conference on the issues facing NATO. The voyage to Europe afforded Kennan time to record the events of previous months, including his visit to Averell Harriman and a meeting with Erich Fromm, Norman Thomas, and David Riesman.]

At sea, September 5

Imaginary conversation with a Russian Communist:

He: But we are going to win.

I: Probably you are. Your people have double the vitality of ours (a situation, incidentally, that has nothing to do with Communism). Besides, you want more than we do to win. You care more about the whole contest. You are like the football team that attaches more importance to the game. Barring accident (for you do also have certain weaknesses which could fly up and hit you in the face), you ought, by all the rules of probability, to win.

He: Why, then, do you oppose us?

I: Because it is my role to do so. It is, let us concede, your destiny to conquer the society I belong to and to destroy all that I, in the personal sense, hold dear. But it is my destiny to influence you, as the more decadent and highly civilized society always influences the more robust and primitive one by which it is conquered. Even if there were no absolute values in loyalty (and there are), there would be no salvation for me in not opposing you. The acceptance of your values would mean, already, the sacrifice of my own, and the sacrifice of them in a manner more painful and ignominious than rapid death. You, the primitive, are the people who are easily swayed by the spectacle of superior force. The indifference to it is the one weapon of the truly decadent.

If a stranger were writing of my life at this time, he might say something like this:

He had certain assets which, in combination, were rare and susceptible, one might have thought, of employment in some good purpose: a clear, if neither well executed nor brilliant mind, a certain feel for all the variations of the human personality, experience in the ways of governments, the ability to command the understanding and sympathy of others through the spoken and written word, and a knowledge of the basic political problems of the time, in both historical and contemporary cross-section, surpassed by only few of his generation. He had, presumably, another five years of intellectual and ten, perhaps, of physical vigor in which to employ these gifts to some useful purpose. And yet it seemed an impossible task to ascertain what this purpose could be. He would passionately have liked to find it.

September 6

I had what might be called a political-intellectual visit from Erich Fromm, Norman Thomas, and David Riesman.[62] They came, at Riesman's initia-

62. Fromm, a German-born social psychologist and humanistic philosopher, was the author of *The Art of Loving* (1956) and many other books. Norman Thomas was a pacifist and longtime presidential candidate for the Socialist Party of America. Riesman coauthored *The Lonely Crowd* (1950), a sociological study of modern conformity.

tive, to discuss ideology. Fromm had prepared a draft program for a new socialist party, and this we used as a basis of discussion.

What a strange quartet we were: Fromm, the old-fashioned and profoundly humane German-Jewish Marxist; Thomas, once the American upper-class maverick of the World War I era, neither theorist nor poet but driven by a sort of a gallant and stubborn irreverence & sympathy for the underdog, the scarred veteran of a thousand brushes with the protagonists of what Galbraith[63] calls the conventional wisdom; Riesman, the brilliant, subtle, and hugely imaginative student of the modern age, far superior to the other two in the sophistication of his understanding for the American scene, trammeled neither (as was Fromm) by the waning power of Marx's magic spell, nor (as was Thomas) by the memories of the struggle over the distribution of wealth which so captured the energies and emotions of American liberals of an earlier day; myself, the newcomer to all the problems, a man whose sturdy Booth-Tarkingtonish Wisconsin background, super-imposed on the obstinate independence of a Scotch-Irish family, had given him little sympathy, from the start, with the inherent self-pity of the socialist cause, who had been further alienated by his first impressions of Russian Marxism in Eastern Europe, who had, therefore, never known a Marxist period in his life, and who had been more deeply influenced by XVIII century thought: Burke, Gibbon,[64] Tocqueville & the Federalist papers, and by Russian XIX century literature, than by any of the thinking of the present century.

There we sat, in the hot third-floor of the farm house, regulating our deliberations with parliamentary formality, under Riesman's chairmanship; below us, the hot fields, the dusty lane, the great fertile countryside of toil and pragmatism, where for fifty miles around there would scarcely have been a touch of understanding or sympathy for our labors.

The result, as is so often the case with such meetings, was outwardly sterile, but only outwardly. Neither Riesman nor I could accept the term "socialism" at all. It was too far, we felt, from the significant issues of the present age, too encrusted with confusing associations from the past. To Thomas, Fromm's ideas were far too theoretical and impractical in

63. John Kenneth Galbraith, the Canadian American economist and aide to Democratic presidents, wrote *The Affluent Society* (1958) and other studies.

64. Edmund Burke, the eighteenth-century British writer and member of Parliament, was the intellectual forebear of conservatism. On long transatlantic flights during World War II, Kennan read through the six volumes of Edward Gibbon's *The Decline and Fall of the Roman Empire.* This eighteenth-century classic influenced not only Kennan's writing style but also his skepticism about the long-term viability of spread-out empires.

the immediate political sense, to be worth more than an amused, head-shaking wonder.

Actually, susceptible as I was to the warm, cozy charm of Fromm's kindly Central European love of humanity, I could not have disagreed more than I did with many of the basic points in his paper. All my Scottish-Protestant antecedents rose in protest against this egalitarianism. This really wild belief in the general goodness of man, this obliviousness to the existence of original sin, this ignoring of conscience and the will, this grievous Marxist oversimplification of the sources of aggressiveness and bad behavior in the individual as in the mass.

Had we been able to come to some real meeting of the minds, I could have contemplated, for the first time in my life, something in the nature of a real political affiliation. As it was, the effect of the meeting was to thrust me firmly back into the organizational isolation where, evidently, I belong. Nevertheless, it was stimulating and greatly enjoyable. We all, I am sure, gave each other something, but it was hard for me, at least, to define what it was.

September 8

I got a telegram from Averell Harriman[65] asking me to come out to Long Island to give him and Charlie Thayer[66] a hand with the book they were preparing about their recent trip to Russia. . . .

Averell was a bit more stooped than I recalled him, otherwise unchanged, apparently, by his recent experience as governor of New York. Politics was now his single-minded calling, as had been, at various times in the past, polo, the Union Pacific Railroad, and diplomacy. He emerged from the house and advanced to meet me as I left the car, attired in shorts and a flapping shirt, beneath which a tanned, thin, elderly chest and belly gleamed as impersonally as that of a Gandhi. He flashed upon me, by way of greeting, his handsome and utterly contrived smile (the mirthless grimace he has recently practiced, with such ferocious determination, for political purposes), led me into his office, and plunked me abruptly down before the 14 chapters of the manuscript. The place was full of papers, the air vibrating with tense, relentless interrogations about every detail of everything that was going on. In another room, a harried stenographer, bland, tight-lipped, and philosophic, with

65. Ambassador W. Averell Harriman was Kennan's boss in Moscow in 1944–46.
66. Charles W. Thayer and Kennan were friends and colleagues from the Moscow embassy in the 1930s.

an "I just work here; I ain't sayin' nothing; you don't know the half of it" air about her. It was all just like Moscow again.

In another part of the house, Mrs. Harriman,[67] who had obviously also had it, stalked around by herself, accepted such intruders as myself with the detached civility which was all we had any reason to expect, and led such of a life as she could in the neighborhood of this tense, driven, literary confusion.

The manuscript, I thought, was pretty ghastly, if approached from any literary or scholarly standpoint, but of course it shouldn't have been approached that way. It did include the recount of a number of really interesting things Khrushchev had said during the course of the long hours he and Averell had spent together. (At one point, incidentally, Khrushchev had said to Harriman something like this: "We don't always reject in toto everything that is said in the West. You take what George Kennan says: a lot of his ideas are of definite interest to us.") But the intellectual basis was superficial. Such style as Thayer had been able to infiltrate into the initial draft had been largely wrecked by the agonized collective editing in which Harriman loves to indulge. The whole seemed to me to reflect, in inordinate measure, a determination on the part of the author to appear as the rigorous, hard-boiled opponent of communism, who was not having any of their tricks, who was not permitting himself to be lulled by any of this wishful thinking about their having internal problems of their own, and who would hold us all sternly to our task of expanding military preparation. There was in the entire book not a word about Moscow's position as the center of a complex modern empire. Nowhere was there a hint that any of the issues that divided us from them could conceivably be compromised.

I did what I could by way of comment, without trying to write their piece for them. It was hard, at times, to remember that I was no longer the obsequious counselor of embassy, & he no longer the imperious ambassador. But I did my best. I boldly advised him not to let the book end on quite so negative a note—a fault which, characteristically, he immediately wanted to correct, then and there, by doctoring a couple of sentences. Manfully, I resisted the pressure to become involved in collective drafting. After 24 hours, having done the best I could, I left again. I never heard from him again—no note of thanks or appreciation. But then, I never wrote a thank-you note to Mrs. Harriman, either—was a bit uncertain as to what category I was in, from her standpoint.

67. Marie Norton Harriman was Averell Harriman's second wife.

September 10

What is it that causes me, on the occasion of such a trip, to make such a fetish of my loneliness, to take so grim a satisfaction in a total abstention from contact with anyone else, is even to myself a mystery. That it is a neurosis, I know. Yet even while I say that, I feel the force of the compulsion. . . . No one else cares. It is for myself that I do this. It is because I want no tenth part of what I no doubt want most desperately. I am determined that if I cannot have all, or the greater part, of what I want, no one is going to deprive me of the glorious martyrdom of having none of it at all. Freud would perhaps deny that there are inherited neuroses. Yet I have an idea that my father was much the same way.

In any event, let this diary know that I have been very heroic: I have resisted all the cheap temptations of loneliness; I have lived for a week in studied solitude among the crowd of people; I have had a drink with no one at the bar; aware of my age and dignity, I have let the ladies all pass me; I have resisted the temptation to hear myself talk. Am I not impressive and deserving of deepest sympathy? The truth is: not a bit.

Hamburg, October 6

I sat on a cafe terrace across from the main railroad station, watching the people move along the sidewalk and the stream of traffic coming and going before the station, and pondering the nature of this new Europe—this materialistic, impersonal, semi-Americanized (but in some ways more modern than the U.S.) Europe—with which I have so little to do. Never had I realized more keenly the extent to which the Europe of my youth, and the Europe about which I had cared, had left me and receded into the past, just like the America of the same description. A man's life, I reflected, is too long a span today for the pace of change. If he lives more than a half-century, his familiar world, the world of his youth, fails him like a horse dying under its rider, and he finds himself dealing with a new one which is not really his. A curious contradiction, this: that as medicine prolongs man's span of life, the headlong pace of technological change tends to deprive him, at an earlier age than was ever before the case, of the only world he understands and the only one to which he can be fully oriented. It is only the world of one's youth, the nature of which is absorbed with that tremendous sensitivity and thirst for impression which only childhood and early youth provide, it is only this world that answers to the description. The Western world, at least, must today be populated in very great party by people like myself who have outlived their own intellectual and emotional environment, and who are old in relation to the time if not in the physical and emotional sense. We are the guests of this age, permitted to haunt its strange and somewhat terrifying halls—in a way part of its life, like the guests in a summer hotel, yet in a similar way detached from it.

Near Basel

Swiss Rheinfelden was itself a constant joy to me: the tidy, well-kept old houses, always neatly painted and with flower pots everywhere; the pleasant maze of narrow streets; the intactness of the old town, with residence and all other functions continuing vigorously and in full harmony; and the school, the church, the little modern shops, the offices, and even the mechanical workshops all functioning amicably side by side, and everything yet aesthetically so pleasing. The meadows above the town were a particular delight to me, with their tree-lined paths and the wooded hilltops in the background; and it was a joy to see how the suburban houses with their gardens, merged so naturally and imperceptibly with the countryside. This harmonious fusion of town and country is what we Americans so rarely achieve.

One afternoon, just before departure, I took my passport along and crossed the bridge to the German side. I was overwhelmed by the contrast. Here, more clearly than anywhere I had ever been, one saw the difference between a country which had involved itself in two world wars and one which had not. On the Swiss side one had in every way this wonderful feeling of intactness, both in space and in time. . . .

On the German side, all was different. Whether or not there had been physical destruction by bombing, I do not know, but the place had the air of a town that had been torn to pieces and was being reconstructed: no harmony, no center, little beauty. And the people were as different as night from day. There was, compared with the prim Swiss, a ravaged, desperate, and brutal quality to their faces. One saw at once that here was a place which had been through moments of something like a breakdown in civilization. There was still a tinge of wolfishness in the way people viewed each other. . . . On the other hand, there was, as compared with Switzerland, a certain wide-flung, careless energy on the German side. The Swiss, too, were energetic, but with them this force was contained, well-bred, bourgeois to the core. In Germany, these middle-class values had disappeared, so that one had, along with the sense of coarseness and the brutal competition, a sense of greater scope and power and ruthlessness of action.

Curiously enough, the women on the German side had also been in some way affected by this disintegration and looseness of values. They had the sheer, coarse, sexual attractiveness of primitive women, which again contrasted strongly with their prim and repressed sisters across the Rhine. Surely, one thought, this cannot be just the force of environment: this must reflect the fact that in Switzerland, over the course of generations, the discreet influence of parents, interested less in the girl's physical attractiveness than in her qualities as a person and a member of society, has been important in shaping marriages; whereas in Germany the children of this age are the products of the catch-as-catch-can sexual mores that have prevailed in that country for the past forty years.

London

England has become the most provincial country on this side of the ocean. Now that her own empire is so largely gone, one sees that in those decades and centuries of her status as a world power, the rest of the world learned much more from England than England learned from the rest of the world. The English are today on the side of the stream of world happenings. Although some of their newspapers are among the best in the world in their reporting of international events, the people seem alarmingly content with their own provincial world of jobs, money-making, football games, darts, motorbikes, and television. The Dutch and Norwegians and Swiss are today in many respects citizens of the world; the English are not. . . .

[In this next entry Kennan writes about Isaac Deutscher's *The Prophet Unarmed: Trotsky, 1921–1929* (1959) and books of similar ideological bent.]

Princeton, November 1

All these books affect me the same way. Here was an image of life as a vast moral conflict, no less romantic than the world of the European fairy tale. Here were the virtuous, deserving, ill-treated masses, who didn't have a chance, incapable of doing or thinking evil, thirsting always for the right things—the people over whose condition it was right to be flamingly indignant, and for whose rescue it was right to sacrifice all. Among them were the workers, who were even purer than the rest, positively shining, in fact, with virtue, paragons—always—of nobility, courage, generosity, and all the right instincts. Here, beside them, were the peasant masses, whose color changed kaleidoscopically: seen against the background of the upper-class (the landlords and the exploiting bourgeoisie), they, too, were virtuous and belonged to "the masses" and one ought to be indignantly solicitous for them; against the background of the proletariat, however, they seemed to have elements of corruption, associated with the ownership of property, so that only those of them who were unsuccessful and wholly indigent deserved your full sympathy (and even then, not as much, of course, as though they worked in factories), whereas those who prospered were somewhat suspect. (There was . . . no connection, ever, between success in private enterprise and any recognized virtue. Frugality, efficiency, industriousness, love of productive work for its own sake; these were evil if you worked for yourself or for a private employer, good only if you worked for the "movement." Conversely, failure and poverty were never the products of personal inadequacy. Laziness and improvidence had nothing to do with them; these were solely the products of exploitation. Failure and poverty proved that you were unwilling to better your lot by making yourself the accomplice of the money-lender or the landlord. Hence, the more you failed and the poorer you were, the more you were virtuous.) Near the peasantry one could discern the massed ranks of the petty bourgeois: quite evil and worthless people, really, but close to "the masses" by all sorts of personal ties. . . . Beyond them loomed the dark cohorts of the real enemy: the upper bourgeoisie, the capitalists, the landlords, the feudal aristocracy, with all their lackeys and accomplices—lost souls, all of them, corrupt, compromised, sold to the Devil, incapable of doing or thinking good, their vision blinded by greed and corruption—people to be dealt with implacably, their faith to be ridiculed, their sufferings to be no cause of pity.

Of course, life was a bit complicated: if such people were to be found in a colonial or under-developed country, itself the victim of imperialistic exploitation, and if they resented the presence and the economic predominance of foreigners and yearned for national emancipation, then they were, for the moment, despite the taint of original sin that rested on them, in part redeemed; for economically weak countries partook of the virtue of economically weak individuals. Here, too, poverty was never in any degree the reflection of one's own deficiencies. Here, to be against the imperialists was a positive trait even in a member of the upper bourgeoisie, and it could make him temporarily your ally. . . .

Such was the romantic image, such the juxtaposition of forces in the great moral struggle in which, exclusively, life was supposed to have its meaning. If you accepted this, as a starting point, then everything fell into place, then this whole tangled tale had its logic. The tortured ideological controversies lost their air of arid scholasticism and began to make sense; the whole sharp savage vocabulary of Russian communism, replete with betrayals, exploitations, hostages, lackeys, and beasts of prey, found its justification.

But of course if this image was faulty, if this was not the way the world really was, if workers were not all heroes and their interests were not all pure, if the content of man's moral dilemmas was not determined exclusively by class interests, then this was all a semi-madness, and a man like Trotsky, whose life was one long outpouring of the most ferocious summons to class warfare and violence, became not a saint, not a prophet, not a high-minded benefactor of humanity, but something very close to a criminal.

December 13

President Robert F. Goheen of Princeton University took me aside at a dinner where we chanced to meet and said that a group of gentlemen from this section of the state had asked him to join them in urging upon the Governor that I be considered as a Democratic candidate for the U.S. Senate in the forthcoming election.[68] He had thought it best to speak to me before speaking to the Governor. I told him I didn't think there was a thousandth chance that anything should come out of it, but that he was welcome, if he wished, to speak to the Governor about it and to find out whether there was any seriousness behind it.

The following day (yesterday) I spoke to Oppenheimer about it. He was very discouraging. At a minimum, I gathered, I would have to go on leave without pay from the 1st of July, thus sacrificing at least a year's salary. But even then, he thought it would be taken by some of my colleagues on the faculty, and possibly by some of the trustees, as a violation of the assurance I gave when I was taken on the faculty here, that I was accepting scholarship as a permanent vocation. . . .

That, so far as the candidacy is concerned, is that. But so far as my own attitude and plans are concerned, it is another matter. If I am to acknowledge myself to be trapped in this manner, then I think my usefulness as a commentator on political affairs, and in fact my usefulness to this country, has really come to an end. And if this is the case, then I shall really have to regard myself as finally retired, and learn to devote myself exclusively to aesthetics.

68. Robert B. Meyner was the Democratic governor of New Jersey.

1960

By 1960, the Eisenhower administration, which had refused to appoint Kennan to a top post, was drawing to a close. Though Kennan tried telling himself that he was too much of a maverick for even a Democratic administration, he could not suppress all hope of again serving in government. Still only fifty-six years old, he believed that his diplomatic instincts remained sharp. In 1958, Senator John F. Kennedy, ignoring Acheson's scathing criticism of the Reith Lectures, had complimented Kennan for highlighting "the right questions."[69] In 1960, Kennan interrupted the family's traditional summer vacation in Norway to visit Berlin and Belgrade, two hot spots of the Cold War. Upon returning, he sent Kennedy, now the Democratic nominee, an eight-page letter on how to revitalize U.S. foreign policy. Though Kennedy replied to the letter, he did not contact Kennan about an appointment until two months after his narrow presidential win in November. By then Kennan had just about given up hope.

The Farm, New Year's Day

As far as I am concerned, my public career, both governmental and literary, is now finished. I hope that life will be, after a while, a bit less hurried. But the next months will not be easy. Twelve lectures at Harvard, five other speaking engagements already accepted, total of seventeen to be prepared in six months—nearly three per month—one in every ten days.

February 29

Notes (unused) for remarks to students and faculty at Woodrow Wilson School

"As you all know, I have spoken publicly from time to time, over the course of the past 13 years, on questions involving the Soviet Union and

69. Gaddis, *George F. Kennan*, 531.

American foreign policy. . . . When I spoke out, in 1947, for example, against the pro-Soviet policies of the wartime years, there was loud applause, and all was well. When I said we ought to remain strong in the face of Soviet power, there was general agreement. We were all on the side of the angels. But there, substantially, the honeymoon stopped. When I ventured the opinion that the hydrogen bomb perhaps was not the best thing to build strength around, there was only bewilderment. When I voiced skepticism that the Russians were aiming to attack us, and urged that we think of our armed strength not so much as a deterrent to a Russian attack, and not as the central feature of our policy, but rather as an unobtrusive background for a policy aimed at peaceful accommodation, there was great and enduring incredulity. When I suggested that some of the things the Russians did were reactions to things we were doing, people thought I was mad. And when, finally, I suggested that we ought to be interested in negotiating a great power disengagement in Europe and the Far East, there was general indignation.

"At no time in the last ten years has U.S. foreign policy resembled what I thought it ought to be, and at no time has it been based on an interpretation of the nature of Soviet power similar to my own. We are now embarked on paths which seem to me to be false ones, conducive to no good end, and we are so far advanced along these paths that I am obliged to recognize the views I held in former years as having now largely lost their relevance. It is indeed today too late to talk any more about getting the Russians out of Eastern Europe; they are there to stay, and I know of no more shabby hypocrisy on the part of Western statesmen than the pious pretense that they wish it were otherwise. We have now just concluded a new security treaty with Japan which will effectively deprive us of all initiative in that area for many years to come, and will commit us in effect to waiting passively for the situation in Formosa to blow up in our faces. The atomic weapons race, to the promotion of which our policy seems to have been directed with singular intensity over the past 15 years, is now roaring along with such momentum that there is not the faintest chance of stopping it; and those who may once have feared that impediments of some sort might be placed in the way of the spread of atomic weapons into the hands of X numbers of other governments can now set their minds at rest. There will be no such impediments: all who wish may have it. The effort of the Poles to provoke discussion of the possibility of barring atomic weapons from the armaments of central Europe has been successfully repelled.[70] The last of our reluctant NATO allies are finally being persuaded to accept the missile sites on their territory and to shape their own forces around tactical atomic weapons. The Russians are evidently giving such missiles to the East Germans, and it must be assumed that they will have no choice but to give them to the Chinese. In the light of these facts it would be quixotic to talk now of trying to halt or avoid the race in atomic weapons.

"Finally, I have said all these years that if we acted as though war were inevitable, we would help to make it that. If we treated the Soviet leaders as if they had no thought but to make war on us, we would eventually have them that way. If we acted as though the military danger were the main thing, we would end up by making it that. Today, for all I know, these prophecies have finally begun to come true. I can no longer say to you that they are not interested in attacking us, or won't be, soon."

Stavanger, Norway, June 15

[Regarding the U-2 crisis] for the life of me, I can come up with nothing but blank pessimism.[71] The worst of it is that one must despair, above all, of American public opinion. The lesson of this incident to me is that any policy on the part of the U.S. government that brings us into sharp controversy & altercation with an unpopular opponent will be supported by U.S. public opinion precisely because it has done just that. So overpowering is the American sense of innocence that when words fly, it is never doubted that we are right & "they" are wrong. . . . No one has ever seriously questioned (no one, that is, but a couple of obscure historians) the steps that brought us into the war with Spain. There was great recrimination after World War II over our policy towards Russia, because that involved good relations with another country, but there has never been any serious examination of the steps that led us into the war with Japan, because once war was a fact, Japan became identified with the characteristic American image of "the enemy," & it was clear that the enemy, being of course totally wrong in his relationship to the war, could have been nothing other than totally wrong in his part in the chain of events that led to it. He having been totally wrong, we, his adversaries, must have been totally right. So what was there to reexamine?

70. In 1957, Polish Prime Minister Adam Rapacki proposed a nuclear-free zone in central Europe, a scheme in keeping with Kennan's idea of disengagement by the superpowers.

71. On May 1, 1960, the Soviets shot down over their airspace an American U-2 spy plane. After Washington denied that this was a spy plane, the Soviets produced the pilot, who had confessed. The incident torpedoed an East-West summit conference scheduled for only weeks later.

The U-2 incident is the product of a chain of action and reaction, as between the Russians and ourselves—a process formed, of course, by many factors, including the more difficult & problematical sides of the Soviet personality, but also including and indeed very prominently, the insistence of the Western governments in viewing the problem of their relationship to the Soviet Government, as primarily a military one, and acting accordingly. At no time was it necessary to send those planes over Soviet territory, in order to make sure that the Soviet Government was not planning a surprise attack. I could have told our people this—did, in fact. So could anyone else who knew anything about Russia. But the American official mind finds it easier to live with its own familiar images than to wrestle with an unfamiliar problem which requires the recognition of subtleties, imponderables, & contradictions. It was easier, therefore, to identify the Soviet personality with the familiar one of Hitler, whose intentions were so boundlessly ambitious and aggressive that he could be expected to intend only the worst, than to try to understand what a fellow like Kennan had to say about Russia.

Berlin, June 16–22

. . . My first day in Berlin was the 17th of June, the seventh anniversary of the day when the workers of the eastern sector revolted, and the East German government came within an inch of destruction. Towards evening, I attended a mass commemorative event on the square before the Schöneberg Rathaus. In 1928, 32 years ago, I had lived on this square. It was then a market place. My windows had looked down on the canvas roofs of the stands. The place was then the end station of one of the double-decker bus lines that combed the city, and all night you could hear the chugging of the idling motors of the buses waiting to start uptown again. Now, the apartment house where I then lived was gone, destroyed in the bombings, gone with all the life that then had filled it. Even the eager, nervous, bewildered boy of 24, who once sat at that window on the fourth floor, was really largely dead. Little remained of him but some silly habits and memories in a graying man of 56. . . .

Later that evening, I sat with Brandt[72] and his Norwegian wife . . . and others, in a restaurant, and whiled away the hours of the night. I had feared they would embarrass me with questions about international affairs, but they appeared to accept me largely as one of themselves, no

72. Willy Brandt, the mayor of West Berlin and a future chancellor of West Germany, had spent the war years in Norway. He would become a friend of Kennan's.

pressure was put on me to contribute, and I had the feeling conversation would have been much the same had I not been there at all.

We talked, among other things, of the Berlin problem. They all had the impression that Khrushchev did not wish to go ahead with the peace treaty, because it was a card he wished only to sell, or to frighten with.[73] Once he played it, he would no longer have it. "Berlin," he is said to have said to Ulbricht,[74] on this last occasion, "is for me only a whip with which to beat the Western powers."

On Monday evening, I went to the theater over in the eastern sector, with Marion Dönhoff.

Fear—guarded, concealed, nameless fear—presided over the whole performance, and we, the hushed, defensive, haunted audience, were as much a part of the strange spectacle as were the actors. Marion and I sat, in stony silence, in the second row, behind two silent figures in some sort of communist officer's uniform. Even when the curtain was down, there was not a sound among the audience. A whisper would have been heard all over the hall. It was clear: I was back in Russia: not the Russia of today, but Stalin's Russia. The dreadful, furtive spirit which Khrushchev had exorcized among his own people, had found refuge here, in this distant Russian protectorate; and it now presided, like a posthumous curse of the dead Stalin on the "faithless" Germans, among the ruins of the eastern sector.

The first of the two parts of the play, 1¾ hours of the wretchedly primitive ideology of the early Stalin period, was all I could take.

Belgrade, July 6–8

I visited President Tito, at his request, and spent an hour with him. . . . He said quite bluntly that we Americans would, in effect, have to pull our socks up if we were to retain our power and prestige. He was interested in Cuba. He did not argue when I said that I thought we had shown all the patience one could possibly show, but merely said with a smile, as though laughing at his own prejudices, that where the issue was between a large and powerful country and a small and economically dependent one, Yugoslav sympathies would always tend to be with the latter. He wanted to know who I thought was influencing the

73. If the Soviet Union signed with East Germany a peace treaty formally ending World War II, the latter, it was feared, could block Western access to West Berlin, which lay deep inside East German territory.

74. Walter Ulbricht was the leader of East Germany.

Cubans, the Russians or the Chinese. I couldn't tell him. I thought it suited them both.

The talk moved on to Germany. He observed that nobody wanted the unification of Germany any more. Khrushchev, he thought, was interested in Berlin only as a lever for getting wider concessions out of the West; aside from this, Khrushchev had no interest in the place. He talked about Khrushchev's proposal for a free city of Berlin and said he thought this ought to include all of Berlin and not just the Western sections. I heartily agreed. . . .

People at home were under no great illusions about the possibility for agreement with the Chinese in any substantive issues. With the Russians it was one thing: we had our differences but there was no real underlying hatred; in many ways we respected and admired each other, and there was a bond of mutual appreciation among our peoples. With the Chinese we had the feeling that we were up against real emotional prejudice of the most violent sort, and that while we might have made our mistakes in policy toward China at one time or another that these mistakes did not justify or explain the violence of the Chinese Communist hatred directed toward us. Things would have to change therefore on the Chinese Communist side as well as on ours before any progress could be made, and it would be a long process. . . .

I asked him whether he was satisfied with the state of American-Yugoslav relations and he said everything was proceeding very smoothly here. The only specific criticism he had to make of American policy was that we often defeated ourselves in our foreign aid programs by first making generous undertakings and then destroying the psychological effect of them by petty restrictions and demands.

Kristiansand, July 19

Thoughts for a book on tragedy of U.S. postwar foreign policy

U.S. errors do not mean that others are not also at fault. Least of all, Russians. Measure of guilt men have taken on their souls for this misanthropic, poisonous police outlook, with its narrow fanaticism, suspicion, falsehood, malice, and hatred—is another thing. I have my share of U.S. conscience. Let some Russian examine responsibility of those who have made it their business to try to arrange human affairs by inducing one half of mankind to hate, trick, and destroy the other.

World War II mistakes. How war which up to December 1941 was not worth our entry suddenly became great universal moral contest, where absolute values were at stake & where respective causes of our associates were as holy as our own. Mistakes vis-a-vis Russia & European war.

Mistakes vis-a-vis Japan & China. Needlessness of U.S. embroilment with Japan. Its price. Once embroiled, only sound solution would have been compromise peace, once Japan was willing to admit defeat on Pacific–Maritime level, leaving her to settle her Asiatic mainland connections in her own way.

En route to the United States, August 10

I think back, now, on the rumination of the summer, and on the months that lie ahead. . . . There are, of course, sharp questions which others would put to me, and which I have been obligated to put to myself. Why should a man who receives annually 500 to a thousand more invitations to speak & write than he can possibly accept feel unwanted? Why should a man who has had unprecedented student response to his lectures feel no sense of achievement as a teacher?

The answers to these questions are:

To the first—because these invitations envisage me only as an entertainer, and concern efforts which constitute only a further fragmentation of time; nobody ever has me do anything really worthwhile;

To the second—because I myself do not really believe in the lecture platform as a means of teaching; because the things I lecture about are not really important to these students; because, again, I am valued mostly as a species of entertainer; and because I think our entire civilization is rigged against the things education ought to achieve, it is a losing battle. Finally, because in the things that do count, the only positions from which one could really be a teacher are the senior political positions, & these are barred to me.

The deepest source of my sense of frustration is that I know my own insights and ideas in the political field to have been largely right—more right than anyone else I know, over these past years. Yet they were listened to only with a detached, amused interest because I stated them engagingly. They have not been used, nor taken seriously—either by the government or (in the U.S.) by public opinion. This will not be different, or not essentially different, under the Democrats. I am, so far as my ability to contribute to public life is concerned, a finished man, partly because I am poor, partly because I have aroused jealousy, partly because I have said the right things too soon, partly because the appeal to the public, in our country, has to go through the mass media, and these media are incapable of appreciating or transmitting that which I have to offer.

I have, of course, a certain real public, which is interested and appreciative, and understands. In principle, it would be desirable to continue to speak for these people. But this is made complicated by the difficulty of getting at them in any other way than through the mass media (which is always confusing), and by the conflict which exists between an interest in contemporary affairs, and on the other hand, my work as a scholar. . . .

[If I were back in office] in Washington, I should only find myself once more a lonely minority of one amid a mass of people who see the world quite differently. There I could only function, as from 1947 to 1950, as a critical voice: a voice which amuses and occasionally stimulates people, to which they listen with a certain benevolent condescension, but which they shake off like a fly whenever any real work is to be done in the shaping of policy.

January 10, 1961

Annelise and I left New Haven at 9:00 a.m., and drove directly to LaGuardia, where we arrived about 11:30 a.m. After some poking around, I found Mr. Kennedy's plane, went on board, and read newspapers until he arrived.

After the take-off, he came into the main compartment, sat down next to me, ordered lunch, and talked with me all the way to Washington.

He began by telling me of the many approaches made to him from the Soviet side, particularly through Menshikov, in recent weeks. He said that to put an end to the many indirect approaches, he had asked Bruce to talk to Menshikov and find out specifically what he had in mind; and he showed me the memo Bruce had written about this talk, to which there was attached an unsigned and unletterheaded document in which Menshikov had set forth what purported to be his own personal thoughts. (This document, which bore -- to my eye -- all the earmarks of having been drafted in Khrushchev's office but cleared with a wider circle of people, was considerably stiffer and more offensive than Menshikov's own remarks.) Both documents stressed the urgency of negotiation and invited exchanges looking towards a summit meeting. Mr. Kennedy asked me what I thought of them, and what he ought to do about them.

I explained that I thought there were two camps in the Kremlin -- not neatly and clearly delimited but nevertheless importantly different -- one of which did not care about relations with this country, because it considered that we could be successfully disposed of despite ourselves and without need for any negotiations, the other of which was reluctant to burn all the bridges. I thought Mr. Menskikov's statements (which specifically mentioned his being in touch with Khrushchev, Mikoyan, and Kozlov) indicated that he was speaking personally for this latter group. On the other hand, the written document had probably had to be cleared with a wider circle, and was therefore tougher in content. I said that I saw no reason why he should take any official cognizance of the written document or give it any specific reply. As for Menshikov and his urgings: I said that in his position I would make no reply to Menshikov or to Khrushchev before taking office; these people had no right whatsoever to rush him in this way, and he was under no obligation of any sort to conduct any communication with foreign governments prior to his assumption of office. As for the subsequent period, I was inclined to think that it might be well to send a private and confidential message to Khrushchev saying in effect that if people on that side were serious in their desire to discuss with us any of the major outstanding differences between the two governments, including disarmament, there would be a positive and constructive response on our side, but when it came to suggestions for summit meetings, the burden of proof -- first of all -- would be on anyone who wanted such a meeting, to demonstrate why these questions could not better be treated at lower and more normal levels, and in any case it was difficult to see how an American President could conceivably meet with people who were putting their signatures to the sort of anti-American propaganda which had recently been emanating from Moscow and Peking. I reiterated that I thought such a message ought to be drafted so as to bear publication in case the Russians spilled it or it

Chapter Seven

Belgrade and Princeton, 1961–70

1961

On January 23, 1961, three days after his inauguration, President John F. Kennedy offered Kennan the position of ambassador to Poland or to Yugoslavia. Kennan chose Belgrade.

Princeton, January 2

The election came and went. Contrary to my usual practice, I permitted my name to be used on Mr. Kennedy's behalf. I had written him on August 17, setting forth my own views as to what most needed to be done in the field of foreign affairs. I had a reply from him on October 30, one week before the election, thanking me for these suggestions and expressing the hope that, win or lose, there might "be an opportunity of seeing you after the election is over."

Nevertheless, it is now nearly two months since the election, and I have heard literally nothing from anyone in Washington in or around the new administration. There is a repetition of the silence of the months November to March, 1952–1953. Meanwhile, most of the senior appointments in the foreign affairs field have been made, and to a large extent to people whom I thought of as friends. . . . Concerning myself, the press has not printed a single word. Things have advanced to a point where, even if I were now to be offered a position, it would be clear that I enjoyed no particular confidence among the members of the new administration.

During these Christmas holidays, I have had to face up to the implication of this situation. I can see it in no other way than as a double failure. I have failed as a public servant. That I was not wanted in government by Foster Dulles was no proof of this. That I am not wanted by my friends makes it unmistakably clear. I have also failed as a publicist. For eight years I have put my views forward currently, in articles and lectures and speeches. Today, at the end of this time, not only do the views command no confidence, but there has not been a single voice raised publicly to regret the absence of my person or my voice from the counsels of the new administration. The fact that this new administration has not called on me may be at least partly explained by the influence of Acheson. Even this cannot explain the indifference of the press. For this, I can say have only myself to blame.

[President-elect Kennedy asked Kennan to fly with him from LaGuardia Airport in New York to Washington.]

January 10

After some poking around, I found Mr. Kennedy's plane, went on board, and read newspapers until he arrived.

After the take-off, he came into the main compartment, sat down next to me, ordered lunch, and talked with me all the way to Washington.

He began by telling me of the many approaches made to him from the Soviet side, particularly through Soviet ambassador Mikhail Menshikov, in recent weeks. He said that to put an end to the many indirect approaches, he had asked Bruce[1] to talk to Menshikov and find out specifically what he had in mind. He showed me the memo Bruce had written about this talk, to which there was attached an unsigned and un-letterheaded document in which Menshikov had set forth what purported to be his own personal thoughts. (This document, which bore, to my eye, all the earmarks of having been drafted in Khrushchev's office but cleared with a wider circle of people, was considerably stiffer and more offensive than Menshikov's own remarks.) Both documents stressed the urgency of negotiation and invited exchanges looking towards a summit meeting. Mr. Kennedy asked me what I thought of them, and what he ought to do about them.

I explained that I thought there were two camps in the Kremlin, not neatly and clearly delimited but nevertheless importantly different, one of which did not care about relations with this country, because it considered that we could be successfully disposed of despite ourselves and without need for any negotiations, the other of which was reluctant to burn all the bridges. I thought Mr. Menshikov's statements (which specifically mentioned his being in touch with Khrushchev, Mikoyan, and Kozlov)[2] indicated that he was speaking personally for this latter group. On the other hand, the written document had probably had to be cleared with a wider circle, and was therefore tougher in content. I said that I saw no

1. Kennedy appointed David K. E. Bruce ambassador to Great Britain.
2. Anastas Mikoyan and Frol Kozlov were deputies of Premier Khrushchev.

reason why he should take any official cognizance of the written document or give it any specific reply. As for Menshikov and his urgings: I said that in his position I would make no reply to Menshikov or to Khrushchev before taking office. These people had no right whatsoever to rush him in this way, and he was under no obligation of any sort to conduct any communication with foreign governments prior to his assumption of office. As for the subsequent period, I was inclined to think that it might be well to send a private and confidential message to Khrushchev saying in effect that if people on that side were serious in their desire to discuss with us any of the major outstanding differences between the two governments, including disarmament, there would be a positive and constructive response on our side, but when it came to suggestions for summit meetings, the burden of proof, first of all, would be on anyone who wanted such a meeting to demonstrate why these questions could not better be treated at lower and more normal levels, and in any case it was difficult to see how an American president could conceivably meet with people who were putting their signatures to the sort of anti-American propaganda which had recently been emanating from Moscow and Peking. I reiterated that I thought such a message ought to be drafted so as to bear publication in case the Russians spilled it or it leaked in any other way. . . .

He asked why I thought Khrushchev was so eager for a summit meeting. I said that I felt that his position had been weakened, and explained why. I thought there was a real sense of urgency in Moscow about achieving agreements on disarmament, and that this stemmed largely from concern over the Nth country problem, and particularly China. Khrushchev, I thought, still hoped that by the insertion of his own personality and the use of his powers of persuasion he could achieve such an agreement with the United States and recoup in this way his failing political fortunes.

Senator Kennedy said that he was giving thought to the problem of staff with relation to foreign policy. He wondered whether he should not have around him in the White House a small staff of people who worked just for him and did not represent other departments. He said that he did not want to be put in a position where he had only one or two people to whom he could turn for certain types of advice. He said that Rusk[3] had already come to him about our possible intervention in Laos. He felt that

3. Kennedy had appointed Dean Rusk secretary of state.

this was too narrow a basis of advice for decisions of such gravity. He did not want to be in the position of Mr. Truman, who had in effect only one foreign policy adviser, namely Mr. Acheson, and was entirely dependent on what advice the latter gave.

I said that it was, and had been for long, my emphatic view that the president should have staff of his own and should not be dependent merely on advice that came up through the various departments and agencies. . . . I described in detail General Marshall's view of the position and function of the Policy Planning Staff, and explained why I felt that the Staff had been useful to General Marshall.[4] For these reasons, I said, I thought it important that he should have a few people whose only task was to assist him in the exercise of his broader responsibilities and who had, in such advice as they gave to him, no other institutional loyalties or motives. . . .

We talked about the foreign service and the state department. I told him that I thought both were grotesquely over-staffed, and that for this reason no patience should be shown in future with people who did not really buckle down and work effectively. I felt that we were on the spot, generally, in the world, that the situation had deteriorated seriously since last spring, that it was a global challenge, and that there was not a single area in the world that did not deserve careful study and the most painstaking review of our policies and possibilities. Everything ought to be re-examined afresh, and this ought to be done energetically and imaginatively. I thought there was too much good fellowship and mutual back-scratching all through the department and foreign service; we needed greater discipline and firmness of administrative vigor all the way through. In this connection, I reverted to the discussion we had had of the privacy of communication and said I felt there must be a greater severity with regard to leaks and contacts with the press. . . .

At some point in the conversation, incidentally, he said that he had made it a rule not to consider any diplomatic appointments prior to his assumption of office. In pursuance to this ruling, he had resisted some very heavy pressures from the political side. He had done this for the sake of the career service and that he hoped the men in the service realized this and would repay him in loyalty and application, accordingly.

4. George C. Marshall was secretary of state from 1947 to 1949 when Kennan headed the Policy Planning Staff.

He asked me at one point about Thompson[5] and the advisability of his remaining in Moscow. I said I thought it would be an excellent thing if he could keep Thompson there, at least for the immediate future, but I thought he should be called home at a very early date and consulted by the President about the problems of our relations with the Soviet Union. This, I said, would not only give the President an opportunity to get his excellent advice, but would also strengthen his hand in any further dealings he might have with the Soviet government.

[George and Annelise Kennan arrived in Belgrade on May 8.]

Belgrade

I felt a certain nervousness, I must confess, over the similarity of these dates to those of my journey to Moscow, nine years earlier: I believe we even sailed on the same day of April, and I must have reached Moscow within a day or two of the date of the later arrival in Belgrade. I hoped history was not preparing to repeat itself.

The initial period in Belgrade was very pleasant. It is always stimulating and absorbing to take over a new post. I presented credentials May 16 at Brioni, where I was well-received by Tito. I was slightly disappointed, to be sure, over the conversation we had, for it was very much the same as we had had the previous summer, and it seemed to me to suggest that the fact of there being a new administration in Washington had made no impression at all on President Tito. This turned out later to be true, and I was compelled, in the end, to recognize that I had been under a mis-impression, before coming to Belgrade, in believing that Tito had been importantly affected by some of the distortions of the Eisenhower policy and that if only these latter could be corrected, his attitude toward us could be improved.

However, at that early moment, this was not yet fully demonstrated, and the attitude of Yugoslav officialdom towards me personally was so cordial and respectful that I continued to hope, if only moderately, that with the course of time I could make some sort of impression on the thinking of the regime.

Something of the depth of the problem was soon made clear to me as

5. Llewellyn E. "Tommy" Thompson Jr. served as ambassador to the Soviet Union under Presidents Eisenhower, Kennedy, and Johnson.

I began to read the Yugoslav official press. At every point, it seemed to be against us. Suspicion of our motives, and opposition to our undertakings, shown through practically every article on world affairs. The line was not, as so many people at home suspected, pro-Soviet, except insofar as Russia was never criticized, whereas we frequently were. What was represented here seemed to be an extreme anti-Westernism and anti-imperialism, *in competition with* that of the Kremlin, not in subordination to it. Insofar as it had any point of orientation, this seemed to be on the most violently anti-European and anti-American factions in Africa. I might be cordially received, personally, in Belgrade, but when it came to the Yugoslav press, we Americans were sinister, wicked, scheming people—imperialists and neo-colonialists.

1962

Ambassador Kennan grew frustrated in his effort to improve relations between Yugoslavia and the United States. The Kennedy administration did little to prevent the U.S. Congress from withholding most-favored-nation trade tariff status on goods imported from Yugoslavia. Meanwhile, President Tito continued siding with Moscow or other neutral nations on issues of concern to Washington. Tito's actions further antagonized Congress. Kennan found himself shuttling between Belgrade and Washington in an effort to minimize offensive legislation while keeping the Yugoslavs in line. Written in Kennan's calendar desk book, the diary for 1962 does not contain the long discursive passages of previous or subsequent years.

Washington, January 11

Spent afternoon briefing the Senate Foreign Relations Committee on Yugoslav matters.

To dinner at Mac Bundy's home where there were, among the other guests, the Phil Grahams, Bob Kennedy & wife, the Schlesingers, and M. Monnet, the father of European integration, with whom I got into a vigorous argument, just before leaving.[6]

January 15

Fearfully hectic & not wholly satisfactory day . . .

Called, at his request, on Allen Dulles.[7] From there to the White House, for discussion & decision on problems of my area. (President asked me to prepare brief for use in presentations to Congress).

6. McGeorge Bundy was Kennedy's national security advisor. Phil Graham was the publisher and co-owner, with his wife, Katharine Meyer Graham, of the *Washington Post*. Attorney General Robert F. Kennedy's wife was Ethel Kennedy. Arthur M. Schlesinger Jr., the historian and assistant to President Kennedy, was married to Marian Cannon Schlesinger. The French economic and political strategist Jean Monnet did perhaps more than anyone to bring about the integration of Western Europe.
7. Allen W. Dulles was former director of the CIA.

Secretary Rusk spoke to me after White House meeting, asking me to see David Rockefeller[8] in New York, re private banking policies vis-a-vis Yugoslavia.

May 28

Went to the White House & spent nearly an hour with the President. Came out & gave press conference to a handful of correspondents.

> [In June, key legislators in Congress proposed denying all communist nations—including Yugoslavia, which claimed it remained nonaligned in the Cold War—most-favored-nation trade status. Other proposals would cut off nearly all foreign aid to Yugoslavia. With President Kennedy's support, Kennan flew to Washington to lobby against this legislation.]

July 2

At 5:00 p.m., to the President, who called in Lawrence O'Brien,[9] made it clear that while it was not thought wise that I should see the House Foreign Relations Committee as a whole, he did think I should see individual legislators, and lobby for all I was worth. He told O'Brien to go ahead & work out a list of people I should see, asked me to give him some suggestions for his press conference, & told me also to go on TV.

Out to dinner, at a pub on Wisconsin Avenue, with Chip and Avis[10]—very enjoyable.

July 3

Down early to Department, for an 8:30 meeting with G. Ball,[11] which did not add or detract much from my problem. Thence to the White House, where I was brought into the President's office; Senator Hubert Humphrey and Speaker John N. McCormick were already present. At the President's suggestion, I spoke my piece to them (badly, I fear, because I was not sure what was wanted of me). . . . In pouring rain, I then traveled all the way to Gettysburg, where I called on General Eisenhower. He saw things just as I did, picked up the phone, & called Congressman Walter Judd. I then went on, still lunchless, to the farm, released the driver, ate a

8. David Rockefeller headed Chase Manhattan Bank.

9. Lawrence F. O'Brien was a political adviser to President Kennedy.

10. Chip Bohlen, a colleague from the 1930s Moscow embassy, and his wife, Avis, were longtime friends of the Kennans.

11. George W. Ball was undersecretary of state.

snack, & spent the rest of the day (except for supper at Juanita's) happily trying to bring to light, from the jungle of the vegetable garden, what was left of Joany's bravely-planted vegetables.

July 5

Down to Capitol Hill, for a frustrating day of tramping from one legislator's office to another.

> [Despite Kennan's efforts and Kennedy's wishes, Congress passed the legislation punishing Yugoslavia and the other communist nations. Kennedy would soon find out about a problem far more serious: the Soviets were installing nuclear-armed missiles in Cuba. Although the president respected Kennan, he did not consult him during what developed into the most dangerous crisis of the Cold War.]

October 14

Fearful agonies of decision, in morning, whether to resign or not. Allowed myself finally to [be] persuaded (not just by Annelise's remonstrations alone, but by these as last straw of many) not to do so, but went off for long walk, totally discouraged—feeling defeated as I have not felt since 1953.

December 11

[Dream] Wildest fantasies. There was some sort of convention-like gathering, at which were present both various parents & various young ladies. A. was dead. I was evidently in the category of eligible bachelors; for twice, when it was suggested to me that I marry one of the young ladies, I amiably agreed—a different one each time. To add to this, Eleanor H.[12] popped up, looking very youthful and beautiful, and we also forthwith decided—I with a certain sense of relief that this time it was someone I knew—that we would marry. The whole horror of my situation did not dawn on me until all 3 commitments had been undertaken. There was no doubt in my mind that of the three it was E. I should marry. There were various adventures; but as I woke up, I was still trying to get the parents of one of the other girls aside to effect the painful explanation of why I could not live up to my commitment.

12. Eleanor Hard was the young Washington woman who decades earlier had broken off her engagement to Kennan.

1963

"I sit helplessly in Belgrade," Kennan complained in reference to Congress's withholding of most-favored-nation trade status to Yugoslavia. He hated being "the exponent of a course of action . . . which I can neither influence nor defend."[13] *A few months later, he offered his resignation, effective July 28. Although Kennan admired and respected President Kennedy, he did not mention the latter's assassination in the diary.*

Washington, January 16

At 4:30, went over to the White House, where I first saw Bundy & then, at 5:00, the President. He told me that an effort would be made through Senate action on the aid bill to get the most-favored-nation restriction removed, though it would take some months. He had in mind making some statement at any early date, in reply to press question, and he asked me to give him my idea of what he might say.

[After attending a NATO meeting in Paris, Kennan spent a few days traveling with his son.]

Valkenburg, The Netherlands, June 24

I feel that I have been dead for months. I do not even recognize my former self. This evening, strolling around town with Christopher, I suddenly saw, staring me in the face from a bookshop window, my own name on a Dutch translation of *Russia & The West*. (More than Gettysburg or Niagara Falls would have.) I had the feeling of "Hello, stranger," & I wondered whether the fellow who wrote that book would ever return.

What bothers me is a total separation of personal life and intellectual

13. Kennan to Walter Lippmann, December 2, 1962, box 81, Walter Lippmann papers, Sterling Library, Yale University, New Haven, CT.

life, so that when I tend to personal affairs, even to the children, the intellect stagnates. . . .

Have the feeling, even now, that I ought to be writing about this trip. But writing: what? About this Western Europe? I used to think there was something mysterious & wonderful about it. Today, I know there is not. I looked at this place tonight and I realized that here there could not even be a literature, because there is no nature except in parks & without nature, as a foil at least, there is no real human experience.

Why was it different in the railway age? Was it really only that I was younger?

[Although in the next entry Kennan did not mention what he had discussed with Kennedy, he evidently remained on the president's list of people worth talking with.]

August 22

At 4:30: to White House to see President who received me about 5 p.m. and kept me for an hour.

[President Tito of Yugoslavia was visiting Washington. Even though Kennan was no longer the ambassador in Belgrade, his expertise on Yugoslav matters and his rapport with Tito ensured him a role in the visit, as indicated in the next entry.]

October 16

At the White House we wait, for a time, in the Cabinet Room, staring out the windows over the lovely autumn flowers of the garden. Then the President comes in, asks some very pertinent questions, requests me to get to work on the official communiqué and the statement of greeting he has to make, and we are finished. . . .

At the "helicopter pad" of the Pentagon. There we stand for a few minutes in a sunshine as hot as the Sahara until a Marine helicopter arrives, very smart and shiny, and settles noisily down on the pad, banging and flailing its great blades and almost blowing us off the green. Swiftly, we are hoisted up into the haze and whisked across the Anacostia River. . . .

At the entrance to Colonial Williamsburg, we descend and are reinstalled, this time in open carriages—big ones, faithful reproductions of the colonial ones, with young Negroes in 18th century costumes as footmen behind us. I am pleased; I see it as a fitting answer to the Lipizzaner horses[14] at Brioni. Slowly now, we weave back and forth, through the streets of this stage-set city, with its picket fences and its housewives in their colonial bustles—this monument to America's nostalgia for a past the last remnants of which it is busy destroying but which it likes to regard as its age of innocence and about which it loves to sentimentalize. It is getting dark now. In general, there are few people in the streets. Such as there are reveal no emotion other than a mild and respectful curiosity. But a small crowd has gathered around the house assigned to Tito and Madame Broz for their personal use. When we pull up there, there is, to my pleased astonishment, a little ripple of polite applause. (Would, oh would, that all other Americans were as well-behaved!)

14. The Lipizzaner horses, a breed dating back to the sixteenth-century Habsburg empire, were noted for their prowess in classical dressage.

1964

In one of the sparsest years of the diary, Kennan reflected, yet again, on why he felt so out of place in California. He also enunciated a view of domesticity that could, with charity, be termed cranky.

[En route to Japan, where he had been invited to speak as a guest of the International House of Japan, George and Annelise stopped to visit with Grace, who lived in California.]

San Francisco Airport, May 21

I find myself immediately struggling once again with the sense of strangeness & aversion that always overcomes me when I encounter the West Coast, strangeness because it seems genuinely a foreign country (all the rest of America does, too, for that matter, but not in the same degree), and aversion because, I suppose, one resents strangeness in a scene which purports to be one's own and is outwardly so much like one's own.

And I realize, as I think of this, that the struggle is not really with California, about which I can do nothing, but with myself, who cannot take it. I go through the same sort of struggle the Englishman goes through when he first visits any part of this country: a resolve to be tolerant and receptive and perceptive of the reasons for things. But it does no good. I start, dutifully, by thinking of the many valued friends I have who come from San Francisco, and from this I move rapidly to the conclusion (entirely consistent with what I think I know about biology and genetics) that there is really nothing wrong with Californians but the environment—take them out of it and they would soon be just like anyone else, that they are in other words, the victims of a pervasive mass psychosis, engendered by the place itself. Could it be, I ask myself, that the settlement of this western Piedmont by Protestant Anglo-Americans was an historical misunderstanding, something that should never have been done, that this was a region which should properly have been populated by Iberian settlers, who would have exploited and wrecked it in *their* way, which somehow seems much more appropriate to it and to them than does the equivalent exploiting and wrecking of it by our people? But then I realize how unkind this thought would seem to them; I think: Oh dear! Here I go, again, being critical.

Sacramento, May 24

The front doors are all tightly locked; I looked in vain for an open window. There is, in all these hundreds of miles of front lawns, not a bench, not a place to sit. The backyards, obviously, are better, more used, more accessible from the houses, but how one longs for the sociability of the European courtyard, even the modest one, with its flagstones, and a fountain, well, and some chickens pecking about, and a spot or two of real, untidy agriculture, and a balcony or two that people really use.

The American front lawn has become an absurdity. What little justification it really had was never really adequate, and it died with the introduction of the automobile. What this country needs is a revival of the gate, the wall, and the used courtyard.

> [After their sojourn in Japan, the Kennans hoped to take the Trans-Siberian railway across the Soviet Union and then connect with other rail lines to Norway. Though Kennan requested travel assistance from the Soviet embassy in Washington, he received a curt reply from the notoriously unhelpful Soviet tourist agency. Miffed, he decided to fly from Tokyo to Oslo via Bangkok, New Delhi, Tehran, Beirut, and Geneva.]

En route, Bangkok to Beirut, July 1

Stopped in the wee hours of the morning at New Delhi, where the heat still rose fiercely out of the burning concrete of the apron, where sleepy, surly Indian officials hurried us around with terse commands in their curious, rapid-fire English, and where the routine showcase of peasant handicraft in the dead transit hall seemed particularly pathetic, surrounded as one knew it to be, by the misery of this vast, teeming, squalid country.

On again, into the night. As we approached Teheran, the dawn, slowly overtaking us, gleamed in a lovely streak under the bright stars from the northeast horizon. At Teheran, for the first time since leaving Japan, we had a cool, sweet-smelling air from the mountains.

Oslo, July 5

For the imaginary letter: "Think, every time you see one of these alluring, even exotic female forms: what lies behind those magic and enticing gates is domesticity unlimited: children, diapers, illnesses, relatives, tiresome questions of money, the sex-destroying question: 'Have you remembered the key?'; and, finally, old age, ugliness, and dependence."

1965

Increasingly troubled by the escalating U.S. war in Vietnam, Kennan in May wrote Annelise, "I am absolutely appalled at what is going on. It looks to me as if [President Lyndon B. Johnson] had lost his head completely."[15] *By the end of the year, Kennan had gone public with his opposition to the war. A trip in February to his father's alma mater, Ripon College, sparked an emotional reconnection. In the summer he visited Russia with his son, Christopher.*

Princeton, January 9

This record book was purchased, hopefully, yesterday, with the thought that it might be helpful to me in reforming my habits of thought and feeling, in deepening my sense of the present and its implications, in learning to bear in mind steadily and constantly, not just in rare moments of remorse or depression or insight, the tragic dimensions of life; in seeing my strivings and problems, if you will, in wider perspective. It is not the first time I have tried this. It will, if it succeeds, be the first time I have tried it with success.

May I begin by reminding myself, on this dark and rainy January afternoon, of certain of the unsolved problems I now face.

It is reasonably clear that in this Princeton life I am now leading the combined pressures of family and household, on the one hand, and what might be called "public life," on the other, are such that I shall never be able, so long as I lead this life, to give more than a small and inadequate fraction of my time to creative activity. This life assures me of a good income, keeps the family nicely, permits us to provide a center for children and grandchildren, and makes possible very nice vacations. Also, it makes it possible for me to fulfill in many ways the functions of a prominent retired diplomat and senior scholar: giving speeches, serving

15. John Lewis Gaddis, *George F. Kennan: An American Life* (New York: Penguin Press, 2011), 591.

on boards, reading manuscripts, receiving visitors. But it gives me little satisfaction. It is not the healthiest of lives. And since, in my case, a sedentary, intellectual life raises—well, let me say it in Russian[16]—provokes well-known needs which could be satisfied only at the price of well-known risks to the happiness and tranquility of the family; therefore such a way of living is not without its serious hazards.

Should I not, in these circumstances, have the willpower either (a) to break away both from family demands and from "public life" at least for large periods of each year and address myself exclusively to creative activity, or (b) to reconcile myself to a certain sort of sterility, and to retire, really, to a country existence which would have, at least, the virtue of being healthier and for me happier? (For you, yes. For Annelise?)

Am I not just marking time, out of a lack of the power of decision?

Enough for once.

January 14

Received this morning the proofs of some portrait photos I had had taken for publicity purposes, and was so appalled at the hideousness of my own visage, in this confrontation that I went off for the morning to the library and worked alone there, that others might be spared the ordeal of looking at me. I was determined that whatever it might be that I had to do to my habits and my life to stop looking like that, I would try to do it.

January 15

Others speak of the satisfaction of teaching. I do not experience them. The process of teaching is useful to me, personally, forcing me to read, to think, to order thought. But beyond that? The students are a mixed bag: 4 or 5 thoughtful, really interested ones. But one fights, even in the best of them, the habits and spirit of the time: its restlessness, its egocentricity, its lack of true intellectual discipline, its lack of detachment. This is a losing battle. Clutch as one may at these young intelligences, the environment—dizzy, spectacular, meretricious, and out of control—will claim them and consume them in the end.

January 20

Today, Mr. Johnson was sworn in as president. I spent the day laboriously endeavoring not to read, hear, or think about the event. Is this

16. The remainder of the sentence is in Russian.

just sour grapes, the fact that I am rejected by Washington? In part, perhaps. But what this man represents—this oily, folksy, tricky political play-acting, this hearty optimism, this self-congratulatory jingoism, all combined with the whiney, plaintive, provincial drawl and the childish antics of the grown male in modern Texas—this may be the America of the majority of the American people, but it's not my America. And while it is probably true that I would like, deep down, to be called upon to serve again, I know I should dread, on closer contact, having actually to do so.

January 25

I am wracked by my own emptiness of spirit. I seem incapable of any serious work, or feeling, or thought. Yet I am unwilling to try to gloss this emptiness over by mere distraction. I long for something to happen to me that would absorb me & force me to come alive again. I should rather suffer than to be like this. Oh Heavenly Father: Is this a crisis of the soul or is it age? How terrible if it should be the latter!

[Having accepted an invitation to give a lecture at Ripon College, Kennan traveled to Wisconsin and kindled a mystical tie with his father.]

Milwaukee, February

The area around the station: the sooty little park, the Public Service building from which the "inter-urbans" once departed, the various pubs with the Blatz signs, looked just as it always did. A raw, dirty wind sneaked out of the railway yards and the dim alleys, bringing clouds of stinging dirt, and over it all lay the familiar flavor of cheap, sinister sin—of back rooms in saloons, of sailors in bus stations, of the stage doors of burlesque theaters, and of dirty picture cards—the same flavor that hung over it, so repulsively and yet so unsettlingly, when I was a youth arriving and departing from this square on my trips to and from the military academy. . . .

At Ripon College I was assigned to a guest apartment. It is, I learned the one in which my father lived, in his senior year. Even today, looking at its scuffed floors, its blank, graceless windows, and the battered tongue-and-groove of its interior partitions it was not too difficult to imagine what it must have been like when my father inhabited it. . . .

In the evening, in the bare-boned gymnasium, with its shiny floors, its over-hanging basketball boards, and its faint smell of sweaty tennis-shoes, I delivered my formal lecture, to an audience of several hundred. I came away, as usual, disliking what I had said, feeling that I had hacked my way through the delivery of it like a droning snow plough, unable to gauge the effect and wishing I had never undertaken the effort. Afterwards, rather mercifully, there were drinks at a professor's house.

Back in the guest flat, I darkened the rooms and sat by the window, watching the storm and the night scene: the drifted campus, white and deserted now under the street lights, the black bare tree trunks, swaying slightly as they reached up past the window and disappeared into the gloom above, and everywhere the clouds of blowing snow: the blessed snow that everyone professes, these days, so to dislike: sweeping, drifting, cleansing, covered everything, mercifully and impartially, with its shroud of momentary purity. Staring thus out into the night, I was suddenly struck with a surge of feeling for my long-dead, honored father: this shy and lonely man; this misplaced esthete, struggling to bestow the imprint of true spiritual distinction and elegance on the shabby, stuffy, claustrophobic existence of the house on Cambridge Avenue; a man whom almost no one understood and whom I myself came to understand properly only after he was gone; a man whom I must have hurt a thousand times in my boyhood by inattention, by callousness, by that exaggerated shyness and fear of demonstrativeness which is a form of cowardice and a congenital weakness of the family. I thought of his one time presence in this place, of our respective lonelinesses, of our diffident, fumbling, helpless affection for each other, disrupted—always and everywhere—by the chatter and irrelevance of daily life, of the chasms of time and death that now separated us. I wondered suddenly whether we were not, at that moment, very close. He must surely have stood, on just such a night, at one of these windows, in his shabby farm-boy clothes, and looked out at the storm, must have been conscious, as I was now, of the land falling away from the hill into the darkness on every side and of the great snow-bound countryside beyond; and his wonder of what lay further afield in the night could scarcely have been greater, for all his youth, than the questioning I now felt, for all my wanderings and experience. Were these chasms of time and death real ones? Was there not a unity and a fellowship in the sensing, the living of this moment? Was this not the tapping of his hands (à la *Wuthering Heights*) that I heard in the dry crackling of the snow against the window?

And so the silly dialogue formed itself and rattled away in my mind through the unslept hours, like the notes of some idiotic song that goes, unwanted, through your head.

"Father, father. Have I done right to come all this way to make myself close to you through the scenes of your youth? Or was this an act of maudlin sentimentality? There is so much I could have given you, and didn't. Does this help?"

"Soft, soft, my son. You should know better than to provoke these mysteries. The moment is indeed the same as you suspect. This is the same snowfall. The ninety intervening summers are as nothing. Beyond that, it is not given to you to know. Do what your deeper nature tells you to do. Give it, if you can, a break, in the face of all the dust and rubbish of life. And meanwhile, take comfort in the beauty of the storm and the night; see the strength and indifference of the snow for all it falls upon, sense its lesson. And if you feel a nearness, then know that it is true. Your own sense of time and space is of no consequence. For the sort of nearness you long for there is no theater, anywhere or at any time, other than in the soul."

Later in the day, there was a final reception and dinner in a restaurant called the Republican House. It was only a few paces from the little structure that is ticketed as the birthplace of the Republican Party. From this proximity and from its name, presumably, it draws trade, I suppose, combining (like the Princeton barbers with their pictures of past football teams) the professions of an institutional allegiance with a desire to make money. How characteristic, I maliciously thought. Signed photographs of celebrated Republican figures decorated the walls. The collection had included one from the late Joe McCarthy, but the students had a habit of stealing it; and the proprietors, commercial instincts prevailing as usual over the political ones, had finally decided to leave the place vacant. Even without McCarthy, I had a sense that I was breaking bread there under the scrutiny of baleful, unbenevolent eyes, not directly hostile, but imperious, contemptuous, and intolerant of all my weak-kneed philosophizing and theorizing. The faces in the photographs evidently thought so too, for the food disagreed with me. I spent another, and final, sleepless night: no father this time, only the Republican Party glaring huffily and unkindly, in the bright moonlight, through the window.

Washington, February 4

To lunch, in the Senate restaurant, with Senator Frank Church of Idaho for whom my admiration, so seldom excited, remains at peak intensity. Also there: Mr. Marten, of the *Washington Post*, & a German correspondent: Mr. Meyer.

Both Church & I were annoyed at Walter Lippmann for having taken words out of our mouths with his article on neo-isolationism.

[In response to a Viet Cong attack on the U.S. air base at Pleiku in South Vietnam, President Johnson ordered a bombing attack on North Vietnam. The Johnson administration had been waiting for such an opportunity to implement Operation Rolling Thunder, a sustained bombing campaign against North Vietnam.]

February 7

News of the retaliatory raid in Vietnam. The provocation, admittedly, was great, but this bombing of points in Vietnam is a sort of petulant escapism, & will, I fear, lead to no good results.

April 24

It occurred to me today: What matters now is no longer what I am (that, after all, could matter only to me) but what I appear to others to be. From now on, I must live for appearances, since the realities have failed me. But to the extent I am successful in creating these appearances, I must not be misled by them. To others, they can mean something; to me, nothing. Nor should I seek occasions for appearing. I must be like an actor who appears on stage as rarely as possible, but then: well.

Think: with every appearance before people how to satisfy the highest and most exaggerated opinion anyone in the group might entertain of you. This means, however, not just empty pretending; it means content as well, but not for its own sake.

Geneva, May 4

[After a successful public lecture] I lay on my bed in blackest depression until dinner time, dined alone, & then went, again, for a long, lonely walk in the rain, through the darkened, dripping parks, in utmost agony & helplessness of spirit. Tried to teach myself to look at everything as though I were dead, but privileged to peek once more through the curtain: disembodied, unhumanized, aware that nothing I saw could possibly mean anything to me.

May 21

Rather ghastly day—not as much so as yesterday, but still bad, with no firm ground under the feet.

Morning taken first with preparations for departure. Then, at 11:30, phone call from Eric Goldman in White House, transmitting the President's invitation to me to deliver luncheon address at White House Festival of the Arts, June 14. Great flap of readjusting travel plans.

June 10

Sitting in the hot, stuffy transit lounge of the London airport . . .

I look back, now, on these weeks of misery, futility and frustration that have passed since I left the U.S. in April. I don't know what I want to do in future, but I know it is not what I have been doing these past weeks.

I am conscious that all this agony marks a great change in my life. Is it in my age? Is it in the circumstances of my life? Hardly the last, for they have changed so little. Presumably, then, the change is in me, and if not connected with age in the absolute sense, it is at least connected with the stage of life at which I have arrived.

What answer do I come up with? Roughly this:

Yield to everything but the trivia—those resist. What does this mean? It means this: Life, in the sense of accomplishment & the pursuit of happiness, is over. Life, from now on, consists principally of waiting to die. My piece is spoken. My usefulness to my time is exhausted. The circle of existing responsibilities, unavoidable responsibilities, is now as large as I can stand. These scattered responsibilities: the family, the Institute for Advanced Study, the National Institute,[17] the various properties; these, plus a measure of study and writing decent enough to make my status at the Institute for Advanced Study something more than a sinecure, both exhaust my available strength and preclude the accomplishment of anything really substantial. This is the unpitying reality. . . .

I must not attempt to teach or to meet with students. The reason for this is that they want from me what I much dislike to give them, dislike to give them, at any rate, in the form they demand it: namely in snap answers on my part to casual, irresponsible questions about current events, on theirs. I *could* teach within a discipline, but I should like, in the first place, a long time for the necessary preparation and it would be difficult for me in any case to find the environment in which I would be permitted to teach in this way. My mere appearance on a campus stirs up a host of other expectations. My reputation follows me around like a shadow or like a mask that I am obliged to wear, so intriguing a mask

17. Kennan had been elected president of the National Institute of Arts and Letters.

Kennan in his State Department office

Princeton University Library

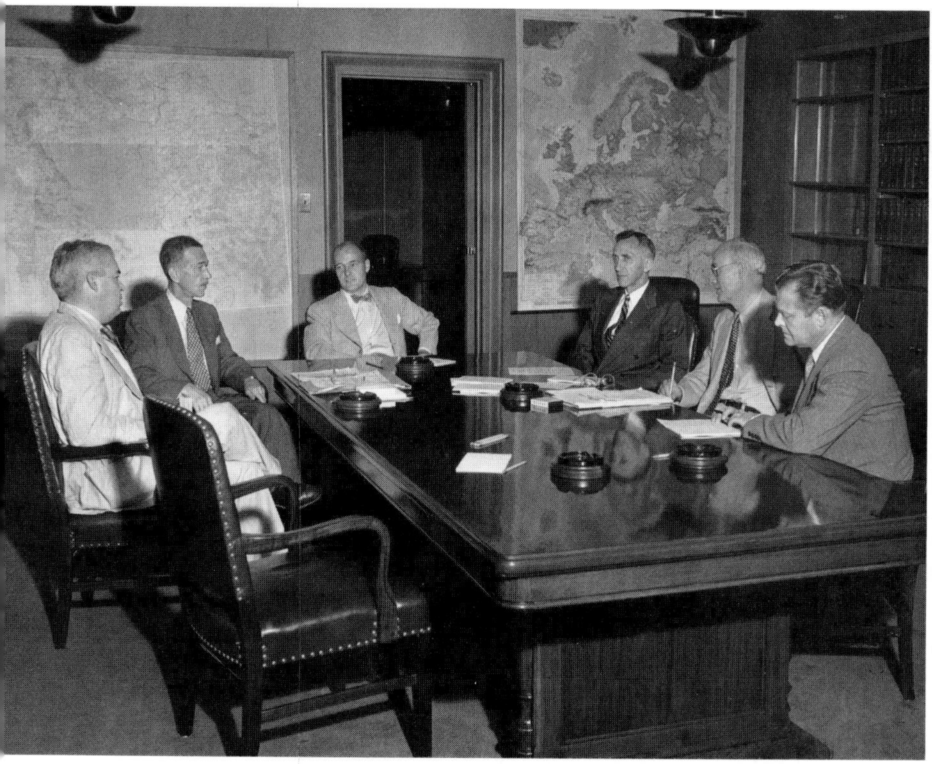

Kennan with his Policy Planning Staff. From left, Bernard Gufler, George Butler, Kennan, Carlton Savage, Harry Villard, and Ware Adams.

Princeton University Library

Kennan family, ca. 1950

Joan E. Kennan Collection

Kennan enjoyed working outdoors, especiall[y]
at the farm in East Berlin, Pennsylvania,
which he and Annelise had bought in 1942.

Joan E. Kennan Collection (left), Princeton University Library (above)

Kennan en route to Moscow in May 1952

Joan E. Kennan Collection

During the stressful months in 1952 when he was ambassador to Moscow, Kennan wondered how to make contact with the Kremlin, visible from his window and yet beyond his reach.

Princeton University Library

Kennan writing at home in the early 1950s
Photographer unknown. From the Shelby White and Leon Levy Archives Center, Institute for Advanced Study, Princeton, NJ, USA.

Aside from what he confided to his diary, Kennan usually concealed the extent of his discontent.
Photographer unknown. From the Shelby White and Leon Levy Archives Center, Institute for Advanced Study, Princeton, NJ, USA.

Kennan in 1975, playing the guitar as television journalist Eric Sevareid looks on
Princeton University Library

Kennan in 1976
onstance Goodman photographer. From the Shelby Vhite and Leon Levy Archives Center, Institute for Advanced Study, Princeton, NJ, USA.

Kennan, shown here in 1981, sported a moustache in his later years.
Herman Landshoff photographer. From the Shelby White and Leon Levy Archives Center, Institute for Advanced Study, Princeton, NJ, USA.

Kennan siblings reunion in 1982. From left, Kent, Constance, George, Frances, Jeanette. *Joan E. Kennan Collection*

Kennan loved to sail.
Joan E. Kennan Collection

Kennan in his nineties
Joan E. Kennan Collection

Kennan gazing out the window of his Institute office in 1997
Photographer unknown. From the Shelby White and Leon Levy Archives Center, Institute for Advanced Study, Princeton, NJ, USA.

Kennan in his nineties, writing in a second-floor bedroom after it became too difficult to climb to his fourth-floor tower.
Collection of Grace Kennan Warnecke

YEAR	
1943	Liberated from Nauheim confinement Sent to Portugal & Azores crisis.
1943-44	London & Rome
1944-46	Moscow with Harriman War College
1947-48	Marshal & Planning Staff
1948	Counselor - Dep't of State
1950	Without pay year - Inst, Resignation, Princeton
1951 -	Korea & ½ year service Purchase of Princeton house Move to Princeton,
1952	Kennedy's offers app'tments. Off to Belgrade.

A year or so before he died in 2005, Kennan attempted a timeline of his career, but his significant errors reveal a failing memory.

Princeton University Library

In his last months, the once prolific writer could no longer write.

Princeton University Library

that no one has interest in the person behind it. I would not mind teaching history except that I find students are not really interested in it. I myself, to tell the truth, am only mildly so, and then mostly when I see it in detail, and become interested in the characters, individually, or when there is some mystery to be unraveled (like that of the Sisson papers).[18] As in my youth, I can take an interest in history only when there is some question to be answered. . . .

Ideally, one should have nothing else seriously on one's mind. Property worries should not be there, nor the frightful succession of prearranged social engagements that throttle American life, nor trips to N.Y., nor the National Institute of Arts & Letters, nor the repairs and greasing of automobiles. One should stroll, sometimes alone, sometimes in company, through shady allées. There should be just enough of the female sex to ease the mind, not enough to destroy it. Can one have these things, in this century? Or can one merely struggle, unsuccessfully, to have them? . . .

What remains, then, is a form of inner, subjective retirement. Do I have the strength to pursue it? This goes beyond just the grand, long-term hopes and ambitions. It reaches into the smaller pockets of life. It means carrying about with you a load of inner sadness, of inner remembrance, of awareness of life's tragic dimensions and limitations. It means keeping in mind at all times that which is physically absent as well as that which is present: the people, dependent on you, whom you do not at the moment see, the responsibilities that do not at the moment impinge themselves on your life & consciousness, your past failures, the appalling acts of weakness of which you have been guilty, the injustices you have done to people, the tragedies that may not yet have happened, but do happen and are bound to; in short, the whole tragic bedrock of existence. The awareness of all this must be your compassion. It must sit, a heavy, relentless burden, on your shoulders as you go through life, slowing your pace, slowing your tongue, whitening the hair (which would whiten otherwise, in any case, but perhaps less impressively).

Do I have the strength and consistency to do this?—I, whose habit it is to walk, bright-eyed and hopeful, into the ensnarement of every passing moment?

One other question troubles me. Would a life of resignation, as just

18. The Sisson papers were forged documents purporting to prove that the Bolshevik revolutionaries had been paid agents of the German imperial government. Kennan wrote a scholarly article that pointed out the forgery.

outlined, not lead to a physical & nervous degeneration? I have often said that a man over 60 needs to be scourged through life, physically & otherwise, if he is not to become flabby and disreputable.

Physically, to a point, I think this is true. But otherwise? The experience of the last year or two suggests to me that an abnormal *Belastung* [burden] of work & effort in the office creates, or better perhaps heightens, an abnormal need for relief & distraction. Would not a more serene mode of life make more easy to bear the self-denial which life forces, willy-nilly, on a man in my position?

My journey, I see, is approaching its end. We are slowly losing altitude, and a shore line which I cannot identify (because it seems to run the wrong way) stretches beneath us. Enough for this long day.

[Hoping to embellish the Johnson administration's reputation with the nation's cultural elite, officials proposed a White House Festival of the Arts. The event was marred, however, by the highly publicized refusal of the poet Robert Lowell and others to participate because they objected to the administration's escalation of the Vietnam War and its military intervention in the Dominican Republic. Kennan, as the newly elected president of the National Institute of Arts and Letters, felt obliged to attend. Indeed, he traveled back to the United States at his own expense. Kennan trimmed from his remarks a passage endorsing the rights of the protesting artists.]

June 14

Washington—no one to meet me. The kidney stone drags. Wearily, I haul my luggage through the seemingly porter-less airport. Taxi to DACOR House.[19] Change clothes. Off to the National Gallery of Art. Write two new paragraphs for the speech: on relation of artists to government policy. Then upstairs to the luncheon.

Seated next to my host . . . Mrs. Johnson on the other side of the podium. Goldman[20] comes to tell me the President will be offended by new passages. I ask "Are we formally his guests?" Goldman says we are. This being the case, I decide to omit them.

Luncheon. I deliver speech—latter very well received, although acoustics are abominable. Mrs. Johnson seemingly very grateful that I didn't mention politics.

19. DACOR is an organization of foreign-affairs professionals.
20. The historian Eric Goldman was a White House aide.

After lunch: flap with the press over missing passages. Then to the White House to attend musical part of program: St. Louis Symphony Orchestra and Roberta Peters singing. All excellent & strangely moving.

Then back to DACOR House. Change clothes. Off, terribly weary, for Dulles Airport, where I admire the terminal building, with its fantastic, tent-like roof, wait 2 hours, & emplane for London.

[Kennan had for years wanted to revisit the Soviet Union. Assured by the Soviet Foreign Ministry that his 1952 expulsion was "no longer valid," he made the trip with his son.][21]

Budapest, June 21

We found our places in a very clean & presentable Soviet sleeping car. What a joy it was to hear, once more, a language you could talk.

The train left at 7:00 p.m., & rattled away through the evening at fairly high speed over a rough road bed, so rough that my kidney stone finally protested at such treatment; & the conductors of our car, coming into our compartment, looked at me and asked me ("I saw it in your eyes," she later explained, "whether I was sick.")

We were woken up about midnight by the first of several border authorities. Between one & two a.m., I suppose it must have been, we stopped at the Soviet frontier station, to change money & to show them my Intourist papers. When I came out, the train was moving away to the place where they removed the standard-gauge tracks & inserted the broad-gauge ones, under the car. Then, we moved off into the night again. Christopher & I both slept through the entire Carpathians. When we awoke, we were running across the fertile Galician plain, south of Lvov, where we arrived (having lost 2 hours to the change of time during the night) about 11:00 a.m. Then all day across the flat lands of the Western Ukraine, behind a powerful diesel locomotive, and on railways obviously vastly improved since my earlier days in Russia. We arrived at Kiev quite on time.

Kiev, June 24

Off early to the airport, with our Intourist guide & a rather slap-happy driver. Soviet jet—100 passenger—to Moscow—comfortable enough—no trouble. The Ambassador's ride, Mr. MacCormack (Princeton, 1956)

21. Gaddis, *George F. Kennan*, 588.

met us at the airport & we were driven over huge wide streets, with endless 8–10 floor apartment houses, to Spaso.[22] The latter now looking absolutely splendid, immensely improved.

We had just time to change before joining the Kohlers[23] in a farewell luncheon they were giving for the departing Israeli Amb. & his wife. We then went for a ride around town, in a car driven by one of the Embassy chauffeurs, interrupting the drive to walk around the Kremlin. . . .

Lunch, informally, at the residence, with Foreign Minister Gromyko[24] & an aide. Pleasant, although positions were stoutly maintained on both sides. I gained a new respect for our visitor, in whom I was obliged to recognize an able & seasoned statesman, not unkind or unreasonable, nor devoid of a sense of humor. (He was accompanied by M. N. Smirnovski, head of the USA section in the Foreign Office. . . .)

Over-excited as I was by the many impressions & associations of today, I read until much too late in the night.

Novgorod, June 26

A very pleasant sight: the wide, flat shore across & up the river towards the lake, studded with the domes of old churches, the long rays of the northern evening sunshine bathing it all, the fresh keen breeze of the Baltic region sweeping across the river, people fishing along the shore, swimming or walking about, in the usual Russian disorder, a sailboat or two, lazily working their way upstream, an outboard race (where did they get the motors?).

Randesund, Norway, August 8

In the evening, reading Edel's[25] account of Henry James' relations with Turgenyev, I became filled with remorse and longing for my abandoned love—Russian history and literature, and I sat down impulsively and wrote a letter to Isaiah Berlin.

August 19

This last night, towards morning, I dreamed that Christopher & I were being carried inexorably towards a sort of a nameless opening, or portal,

22. Since Kennan helped William Bullitt set up the U.S. embassy in 1933–34, Spaso House had been the residence of the American ambassador.

23. Foy Kohler was the U.S. ambassador.

24. Andrey Gromyko had served as Soviet ambassador to the United States during the second half of World War II.

25. Kennan was much taken with Leon Edel's multivolume, psychologically oriented biography of the novelist Henry James.

which I clearly recognized as "the end." I was aware that for me, there was no escape, that all further effort or struggle was useless. Suddenly, it occurred to me, to my great joy and relief, that this did not necessarily apply to Christopher: that he had a right to live, a right to demand life, and that he could well exert himself to make good an insistence on living further. I told him so, and was explaining to him, when the dream faded (or fades now—from my memory) how he might go about it.

Later on, in another dream, I walked with a man, a doctor, whom I knew to be incurably ill. I said to him, casually: "You and I are not long for this world." I waited to see whether, in my own case, at least, he would challenge the assertion. He did not.

I awoke not particularly depressed—above all, not frightened. We shall see now whether the conscious or the subconscious judgment is the more accurate.

Princeton, September 2

Met with Mr. Y. Tsurumi, of International House, Tokyo, now fresh from several weeks of Mr. Kissinger's[26] seminar at Harvard and, prior to that, a visit to Vietnam, where he was much shaken by witnessing the public execution of a Vietcong prisoner. I found both impressive and alarming his account of the extent to which we are sacrificing our position in Japan to the Vietnam undertaking.

November 9

At 6:00 p.m. Annelise tried to tune in on a New York TV news program. She could get no New York station but did find another one; and in this way we learned of the great blackout of the NE part of the country. To McCarter Theatre, in the evening, to see *Hiroshima Mon Amour*, a production from much of which I averted my eyes and the remainder of which I viewed with much distaste. I did not need to be reminded of the horrors of the bombing. I dislike being a witness to other people's intimacies. And the sur-realist touches struck me as contrived & meaningless.

November 23

Into New York, in the afternoon, to see U Thant,[27] with a view to possibly writing a letter, or a piece of some sort, on Vietnam.

26. Henry A. Kissinger was a professor at Harvard before becoming President Richard M. Nixon's national security advisor in 1969.
27. U Thant was secretary-general of the United Nations.

December 2

Wrote a piece on Vietnam. Phoned Kay Graham in late afternoon, & she agreed to take it for the Sunday *Washington Post*.

December 24

[Dream] I was alone—a bachelor again—in some great European city. As in many other dreams, I went out to the outskirts to walk, and then had trouble finding my way back to the city. I was in a sort of a park, where all the other people were colored, and where there were ferocious-looking statues of powerful, hairy African or Asian gods, including one pornographic one. Then, I had rented an apartment, which turned out to be only one large & white bed, elevated in some way over a public square: quite outdoors & exposed. I realized I had overslept, & everyone else around me was already up, & was rather overexposed.

Then, I was eating the white meat of chicken, but when I got to the legs, they turned out to be human in form, like those of a little wax figure; & I gnawed at them without enthusiasm only because A. or someone said I shouldn't waste so much good white meat.

1966

Although unmentioned in the sparse diary entries for 1966, Kennan's testimony before the Senate Foreign Relations Committee in February proved pivotal in widening and in making respectable opposition to the Vietnam War. He was, after all, the author of the containment doctrine in whose name the war was being pursued. Millions of television viewers saw Kennan argue that regardless of the strategic arguments, "the spectacle of Americans" attacking "a poor and helpless people, and particularly a people of different race and color," wreaked "psychological damage" to America's global image. He stressed "that there is more respect to be won . . . by a resolute and courageous liquidation of unsound positions than by the most stubborn pursuit of extravagant or unpromising objectives." He summed up his testimony by quoting John Quincy Adams's famous speech of July 4, 1821: "While America stood as the well-wisher to the freedom and independence of all," she should be "the champion and vindicator only of her own."[28]

Princeton, April 6

[Dream] There was a building like the War College, in Washington: a ponderous, institutional sort of a building. The office diagonally across the corner from mine was that of a man who, I knew from some source, was marked to be murdered in his office. I came out of my office and passed his door as I went out to the steps of the building. I found myself wondering, as I passed the door, whether he had already been murdered—perhaps there was only a dead man in the office.

Out on the great steps of the building, I found myself in the company of a number of other people. I wanted to tell them of all this—suggest

28. *Hearings before the Committee on Foreign Relations United States Senate, 89th Congress, 2nd session, on S. 2793*, February 10, 1966, pp. 334–36.

that they go to the room & look—that they try to prevent it, if it had not already occurred. Then it suddenly occurred to me that I could not do this: they would ask how I knew about it, & why I had said nothing sooner. And I realized then that there was no answer: that I was the prisoner of my own guilty knowledge, the implications of which I had not previously pondered—nay, worse than that: I, by my silence, was an accomplice to the crime.

[Kennan traveled by rail from Chicago to Sacramento to visit Grace and to give a few lectures in the surrounding area. Annelise flew to Sacramento.]

En route to Sacramento, April 11

We were all day in the mountains, & very rocky, barren mountains they were, for the most part, disfigured here and there by the most hideous, trashy sort of human occupancy. Worse sloppiness & ugliness I never saw, and I kept thinking to myself: How these people who live here must hate this country, otherwise they could never treat it so badly.

For the American West, the coming of the white man, my people, was an unmitigated, fearful, irreparable disaster.

En route from San Francisco to Monterey, April 13

Magnificent country it must obviously have been, before the English-speaking white man got after it. What he has done to it I can view only with horror & contempt. I found myself really wishing that some catastrophe might occur that would depopulate this region & permit it to heal its scars & to return to its natural state.

April 16

Again, for the 4th straight day, in most dismal depression. Don't know why California affects me this way. Annelise & I argued bitterly about it at dinner, I trying to explain that this is a foreign & subtly hostile country to me; that if this is right, I am wrong; that if this has value, I am worthless, etc. But I know that part of this is emotional & subjective, & happens to me whenever I am supposed to take a vacation.

Princeton, May 1

I talked to a group of students . . . on problems of conscience connected with Vietnam & the draft.

[Dream] Prague was, as I recall it, the scene of last night's dreams. I was there with some sort of an American delegation—not official, but rather like the delegation to some academic conference. I cannot, I know, remember the main things, but I recall some sort of a meeting, on the last day—social rather than official, a farewell meeting, and there was a Negro woman secretary who had been very fine; & I, in taking leave of her, out of the fullness of my heart (no thought of sexual attraction) leaned over & kissed her, only to become instantly aware that this action was being acutely observed, and with a decided lack of comprehension, by the eagle eye of my good wife.

Cambridge, Massachusetts, May 6

Lunched with Kissinger, who is now fully recovered from the militaristic preoccupations of earlier years—feels that we are, by our German policy, alienating everyone else in Europe and recreating the France-Russian alliance.

1967

On two lecture trips sponsored by the U.S.-based African-American Institute, Kennan reflected on the apartheid system of South Africa, the unilateral declaration of independence from Britain by the white-run government of Rhodesia, the colonial rule of Portugal in Mozambique, and the resentment against such white domination by many Africans. During his trip, the Six-Day War broke out between Israel and its Arab enemies.

Near Johannesburg, South Africa, May 12

Regarding apartheid, the greatest difficulty lay not in the idea of encouraging the various racial communities to retain their identity & to develop separately but in the unfeeling, tactless, rigid, & over-centralized manner in which the idea is carried into execution. . . .

It is clear that the rapid expansion of S. African industry, against a background of a shortage of white labor, is sucking black labor upwards into the labor force at a rapid rate, wherever the blacks can be used at all. This is to some extent in conflict with the aims of apartheid, and worries many people here. On the other hand it serves to increase the dependence of the two communities upon each other and gives to the blacks a stake in the stability and prosperity of the existing industrial establishment which they will ignore at their peril. . . .

Our Consulate General gives each year, for the 4th of July, an interracial reception. (The wisdom & propriety of this last practice I should be inclined to question.)

May 14

[Workers in the gold mines come] right out of the village or the bush. They are much more primitive, but stronger & evidently happier than the town-dwelling Africans around Johannesburg, with whom they have little to do. They come without families & live in the great mining compounds like soldiers in an army camp. Every Sunday morning at each of the mines groups of them perform their tribal dances for the benefit of the others. . . .

We were struck with the fine physical appearance of these African miners, much better than that of the Bantu who live in and around Johannesburg. They were young & strong. While they paid little attention to us whites, there was not observable in their faces any of the sullen deadpan that I, at least, seem to discern in those of their semi-urbanized black confreres.

May 20

In talking with a group of colored intellectuals, all people of high intelligence & dignity . . . it was heart-rending to me to realize how cruelly the artificial ceiling imposed since the last war by the South African Government presses upon these people, particularly the younger ones. The government thinks they will continue to take it, that these efforts will gradually elevate the remainder of their people, and that eventually things will get better. But some of the most able younger ones are already emigrating in despair, & one wonders. It is not just the glaring discrepancy in play, as between them & the whites, but the cumulative effect of a thousand other petty restrictions & discriminations, many of them quite unnecessary and redundant even to the main purpose of apartheid.

Lusaka, Zambia, June 4

I had sympathy, indeed, with the political unhappiness of some of these people, particularly those who came from South Africa and Rhodesia, but I had little sympathy with either their aims or their methods. I had come in South Africa to the conclusion that whereas the Nationalists there had placed themselves in a position where no reasonable person from the Western world could give them any help, it was also ill-advised for foreigners to attempt to bring direct pressure to bear upon them. Foreigners did not have the answers to their problems. They might think they know what was wrong; they could scarcely deceive themselves into believing that they knew what was right. If there was anything certain *not* to bring about an improvement in the situation, it was an attempt to overthrow any of these regimes by force. Yet this was precisely what these exiled political leaders were bent on achieving, and it was in this that they wanted us to help them. Could I now meet with them without appearing to accept their premises? The answer, it seemed to me, was obvious.

June 6

There was now a war on.[29] The radio in the little hotel room had told us that the Sudan had joined in with the Egyptians and six or eight of the Arab countries, including four in Africa, had broken relations with us. There was a terrible possibility that Russia and the U.S. might become involved. Then we would be stuck here for God knows how long. . . .

I realized for the first time in Zambia how violent, how prejudiced, how vindictive, and how unreasonable was the whole emotional "anti-colonial" campaign being waged, with Russian & Chinese encouragement, by the countries of this "Afro-Asian" bloc. The more I saw of it, the more irresponsible I thought it was, and the less respect I had for its authors. I could find no charitable indulgence for these people who in one breath denounced Anglo-American imperialism and the alleged intervention of the great Western powers in the affairs of smaller nations, and then demanded in most violent terms British intervention against a neighboring state, who called for the elimination of the British from the Rhodesian scene and then denounced them for not intervening in it by military means, who demanded sanctions against Rhodesia and then denounced sanctions as a wicked British plot to injure Zambia. I saw the goodwill of our people towards these small nations being abused. They took our aid, it seemed to me, as a sign of weakness and assumed that it was given for ulterior motives, out of fear that they lean to the Russians or the Chinese. They had, I felt, only contempt for us, mixed with dislike. They had no understanding for us and no desire to understand us. They had, in fact, no interest in us rather than an exploitative one. There was no use talking with them. The good will was all on one side. The only thing to do was to leave them alone, withdraw, go our own way, show that we could perfectly well live without them. . . .

I was thoroughly exhausted after nine straight weeks of travel, lecturing, riding around in cars, meeting people, and hotel food: exhausted more nervously than physically, but a bit of both. I was over-reacting,

29. The Six-Day War between Israel and its Arab enemies.

not sleeping, not digesting, suffering—literally—from a touch of jaundice and viewing everything with a jaundiced eye. This was not fair to my hosts, to the countries I was trying to understand, to the African-American Institute or to myself.

Princeton, August 15

Much talk about the Negro riots.[30] It was interesting to see how these had begun to affect everyone's views. It occurred to me, at the end of the evening, and I said to the others, that while today my sympathies were all with the unfortunate firemen and police who were obliged to endure every sort of harassment while they tried to put out fires and restore order, and while I now strongly favored a strong hand in the face of this sort of rioting, I knew that the white backlash, only now developing, would be of such ugliness that a year or two hence I would have to be defending the Negroes.

Blantyre, Malawi, September 16

At a Presbyterian church I found disturbing only the pearly white faces of Christ, the saints and the angels in the stained glass windows, imported, of course, from Britain. They were not even historical, for the people in question, insofar as they ever existed in the flesh, were surely extremely swarthy, but here, in particular, they should have been dark, for the projection of religious belief is an anthropomorphic exercise. . . .

It said very little to me, this semi-tropical scene: the dry, dusty disorder of the hot countries: trash and excrement all over, in the grass and bushes; black faces, the eyes of which studiedly looked past you as though you did not exist. Outwardly, racial relations here are relatively unstrained and equable. One finds very little of the suppressed anger or ostentatious cockiness that pervades the Zambian scene. But there is also none of the happier unselfconsciousness that seemed to us, at least, to mark Lourenco Marques.[31] Or were we wrong?

Dar es Salaam, Tanzania, September 20

Went this morning, alone, to call on the Tanzanian President, Mr. Julius Nyerere. He received me in his office, and had the conversation recorded

30. Riots had broken out in Newark, Detroit, and other U.S. cities.

31. Laurenço Marques was the capital of Portuguese Mozambique before it was renamed Maputo after independence.

by a European lady-stenographer, she and I sitting on the outer side of his large desk. He himself, a small, youthful man with bright eyes, wore a light-colored African robe.

I told him that I . . . admired both the inherent persuasiveness of his internal program and the lucidity with which he had expounded it. The term "socialism" held no terrors for me, and I could see great merit in what he was trying to achieve in the development of his people. For this very reason I was particularly unhappy to find all this associated with a view of my own country which I believed was distorted and unfair. It was of course not his alone. It was one that seemed to be current, generally, in the Organization of African States. It was one which it was difficult for any of us Americans to discuss; we had no reason to feel defensive about ourselves. I would not attempt to discuss it with him this morning. We Americans had many faces. Not all of them were always attractive ones, but the face we had turned to Africa in these recent years seemed to me to have been entirely one of generosity and helpfulness, and it was hard, in the light of this fact, to find our motives still viewed with cynicism and suspicion and ourselves still regarded as imperialists or neo-colonialists. It was my own view that the only dignified response on our part to this state of affairs was withdrawal and long silence. Perhaps when we had taken no initiatives towards East Africa and left people here strictly alone, for a long time, they might be persuaded that we had no sinister designs on them, and then the effort at collaboration could be resumed without inviting the sort of misinterpretation that had encumbered our efforts in the past.

The President's reaction to all this was one of high amusement of the emphatic reiteration of the view that the United States could not withdraw from Africa even if it wished to do so. We were, he said, engaged and involved here: we had no choice now but to stay the course. I did not press the point other than to say that I had become an isolationist of sorts in my old age, and nothing I had seen in Africa had changed my inclination to believe that we could do more good by withdrawal and detachment than by the sort of effort we had been making in recent years.

Accra, Ghana, September 26

I have seen other slums in Africa and elsewhere and am no longer easily surprised by anything in that line, but I cannot recall seeing anything that for sheer filth and stench surpassed these parts of Accra. Recalling the relative decency of the great African township we had visited on the outskirts of Johannesburg, and also what seemed to me the greater wholesomeness even of the native quarter in Lourenco Marques, not to mention the impressive cleanliness of Salisbury, it seemed to me that the black Africans would do well to clean up such conditions in their own countries before they allowed their indignation against the mistreatment of Africans in the south to go beyond a point.

September 28
African Impressions

It is not my purpose here to appear as an apologist for the practices of the South African government in racial questions, but . . . there is on principle nothing necessarily pernicious about the belief that it might be better, in a multiracial society, if each of the various racial communities were to retain its identity as such and if the respective communities were to live and develop side by side, each preserving the integrity of its own social life, each developing and advancing on the principle of separate but equal, rather than being subjected to a process of forced homogenization. People do, after all, prefer as a rule the company of people similar to themselves in origin, in tradition, and in the discipline of human experience. And we Americans, in particular, whose practices seem to lead to the segregation of communities, whatever our high professions of contrary principle (witness what is happening to the public school system of Washington, D.C.) are in a poor position to be critical of people who not only practice "separate development" but confess it as well. One seeks in vain, in any case, for any reason to suppose that a reversal of South African policy designed to force racial integration on a reluctant white population by legislative enactment would have consequences any more attractive than those which just such a policy seems to have produced in many a number of great American cities.

To recognize these considerations, however, is not to say that apartheid, as now practiced in South Africa, is a justifiable or feasible manner of regulating interracial relations in a great modern industrial community. Theory and practice are two different things. It is one thing to talk about apartheid as a concept; it is another thing to put it into practice. It is precisely in this latter respect that the visitor to South Africa is likely not only to find his moral sensibilities shocked but also to be compelled to question whether present practices, even if ethically justifiable, could serve as a basis for the successful development of a national society in the modern age. There are the gratuitous irritations and absurdities of "petty apartheid"—the whole gamut of minor crudities and cruelties that flow from the compulsive fussing over superficials, the obsession with the supposed dangers of physical proximity, the silly signs forbidding certain children to swing on certain swings, the anxious attention to such things as separate buses and toilet facilities, the sort of thing that evoked the famous cartoon of the black man sweeping the church aisle and the white overseer saying: "Go ahead and sweep, but God help you if I catch you praying."

1968

On February 29—a moment sandwiched between the stunning enemy advances of the Tet Offensive begun on January 30 and the New Hampshire primary on March 12—Kennan addressed a rally on behalf of Senator Eugene McCarthy. The Minnesotan had just announced his bid to wrest from Johnson the Democratic nomination for president. Kennan scorned the Johnson administration's policy in Vietnam for forgetting that a country such as ours owed "'a decent respect to the opinions of mankind.'" Kennan offered a ringing endorsement of McCarthy, who deserved "our admiration, our sympathy, and our support."[32]

Although opposed to the conflict in Vietnam, Kennan also faulted the tactics and style of student antiwar protesters. He published his criticism of the protesters and their responses in Democracy and the Student Left *(1968). The family continued its tradition of spending much of the summer in Scandinavia, particularly on sailing trips to and from their summer home near Kristiansand, Norway.*

Princeton, January 30

Suffered much anguish over the problem as to whether I should continue the debate with the students, begun by the recent *New York Times* piece.

Annelise came home from Vermont in late afternoon, & then we listened, on TV, to the appalling news from Vietnam—as though the luncheon conversation had been inspired by premonition.[33]

32. Kennan, "Introducing Eugene McCarthy," *New York Review of Books*, April 11, 1968, http://www.nybooks.com/articles/archives/1968/apr/11/introducing-eugene-mccarthy/.
33. The surprise North Vietnamese and Vietcong Tet Offensive in the cities of South Vietnam initially met stunning success.

February 6

My recent piece in the *New York Times Magazine* (the Swarthmore speech) had brought in an unprecedented volume of correspondence, & the *Times* wanted to make a small paperback book out of the more interesting letters, plus whatever I would write by way of reply or comment. I replied encouragingly. . . .

Horrible & disturbing news from Vietnam & further expansion of the fighting in Saigon: the beginning of the end.

On a sail from Oslo to Kristiansand, June 28

Towards evening, youth, youth international of 1968, youth in the abstract, complete with blue jeans for the boys and levis for the girls, all looking as ragged, dirty, and repulsive as they could contrive to look, gathered on the little square next to the two yachts, and sat down in groups on the cobbles, where they remained, doing nothing in particular, until after midnight. . . .

It occurred to me, as I tried to overcome my distaste for these people that after all they existed: they had to be somewhere, you couldn't just hide them or turn them off like a TV set, and since this was so, there could have been worse places for them to be, and worse things they could have been doing. But one longed to see them full of life and gaiety, interested in Nature and capable of enjoying it, conscious of their own potential beauty as youth and concerned to cultivate it, instead of in this grey, shabby, subdued state. Forty years ago, people of their age would have sailed, picnicked, and built bonfires on the outer skerries, sung songs together. All these possibilities lay open to these, today. Whence, then, this desperate and defeated state of behavior? A reaction to the older generation, they would say. But it was not their parents, surely, who compelled them to dress in rags and to sit all Friday evening on the dusty cobbles of the little wharfside square. The parents who provided them with motorbikes and outboards and the money for hashish were surely not going to deny them the means for healthier and more rewarding forms of recreation. Home, with its TV set and its socially isolated, lonely, satiated parents, might be unexciting. But there were other ways of passing time, even outside the home. There were libraries. And there was the great outdoors, and not just the quayside at Sandøsund.

Kristiansand, July 3

One sees, here in Norway, though in forms slightly less advanced than in the U.S., all the typical phenomena of those places that have participated in the technological revolution of our time. . . .

Whither, one wonders, does all this lead? It leads most surely to a certain material precariousness of civilization, for everything now depends on the supply of motor fuel and electricity. Without the machines driven by these forms of power, men would be largely helpless, incapable of looking after themselves. The skills requisite to a more independent and secure form of life: the skills of agriculture and fishing and the various handicrafts on which men would have to fall back if the machines were ever to fail them, are falling now rapidly into disuse and even oblivion, and the draft animals who played so central a role in the technology of earlier centuries are also now missing. An enlightened society, one could think, would be concerned to keep these skills and these animals in existence, if only on a small scale, in the way that the XVIII century handicrafts are cultivated at Williamsburg, to provide at least a nucleus for possible forced return to a more traditional and primitive technology. Particularly is this the case in a country like Norway, where native resources would be scarcely adequate to the autarchical basis. But no—here, as elsewhere,—one acts as though one had infinite faith in the elaborate division of labor on which this advanced technology depends, and in the soundness of the political status quo of the advanced Western world by which the burden of this division of labor is so largely borne.

Helsinki, August 13

The few characteristics I possess that give any sort of significance to my personality make themselves less in evidence & mean less in Norway than anywhere else. Why is this?

Partly, I think, because the Norwegians, for all their admirable characteristics, are not intellectuals (in some ways, no doubt, this is to their credit) and have small regard for subtleties & refinements of thought. But perhaps, too (and this is less to their credit) they have little feeling for showmanship and I, in certain respects, am a showman.

However this may be, nowhere do I feel less known, less appreciated, and with less to contribute than in Norway.

En route from Kristiansand to Oslo, August 19

I continue to worry away at the problem of my profession, like a dog at a bone. Have been assailed in recent days by a doubt as to whether I would be capable, in any case, of extracting myself from occupation with contemporary affairs, even with the greatest firmness of will & discipline of conduct. Not only could it be done only at the cost of rudeness and discourtesy to many eminent and deserving people, and not only would it cause general bewilderment & meet with misunderstanding in many quarters, but it would involve sacrifices in personal & social life that would have to be borne by Annelise as well as by myself and would constitute a disappointment, and even in some respects a hardship, for my children as well. Nor would I be able to lead a normal scholarly existence in any event. My "image," as that of a person intensely involved with the passing scene, hangs around my neck like a millstone & makes it difficult, if not impossible, for me to be accepted as a historian. I cannot visit any academic campus without being asked & expected to talk about current events, & without bringing bewilderment and disappointment to students if I fail to do so. I cannot visit foreign capitals without being "found out," interviewed, asked to give press conferences, invited to meet with public figures. Even the hospitality offered to me is extended against the background of an assumption of my primary interest in international affairs.

But, if this reasoning be accepted, two bitter problems present themselves: (1) how to reconcile this reality with my position at the Institute for Advanced Study, and (2) how a useful life could be shaped in the light of the acceptance of the role, in which Fate seems to have cast me, of a leader of opinion with relation to public problems. . . .

The more I pursue this inquiry the more I am driven back to the conclusion that scholarship is the only possibility.

I am acutely aware, in the first place, that I need, more than anything else, some solid, prolonged work—a task. I would scarcely find this in the field of contemporary affairs. One would be constantly pressed into the role of a sort of a Greek chorus, accompanying with one's comment a march of events which one cannot directly influence. The subjects one treated would be out of date before one had finished treating them. One would be endlessly buffeted by competing demands for one's time & attention. There would be small sense of purpose, small satisfaction.

Thinking about these matters, I realize that I am in serious danger and trouble, and I say to myself: Look what dilemmas your scattered talents have landed you in, my friend! . . .

More airport reflections.

The extreme unhappiness with which I confront the prospect of returning home arises not just from the hopeless profusion of my obligations and involvements there, but also from awareness of my own personal failings & the lack of success I have had in overcoming them. My congenital immaturity of bearing and conduct, my garrulousness, the difficulty I find rejecting hard liquor when it is offered to me as a part of hospitality, the uncontrollable wandering eye—all these things are unworthy of the rest of me, & they limit what I could make out of myself and what I could contribute in these final years of active life.

Can a man of my age change the structure of habit? Many have tried. Dr. Samuel Johnson tried. Tolstoy tried. Few have succeeded. Certainly, if it is possible at all, then only by the cruelest and most strenuous exercise of the will. Nothing in my previous experience suggests that I am capable of it. It would, of course, be the price of any sense of satisfaction & fulfillment in these final years—a heavy price, but could any be too heavy? What, after all, is the alternative? A long series of trivial gratifications, punctuated by moments of dull, frightening despair.

Do I do better alone, or with other people? To some extent, surely, both situations are necessary, & one should alternate between the two. Neither can be carried to extremes. But it seems to me that in direct personal, oral contact with other people, particularly when it involves any sort of social obligation on my part, I give more than I receive. This in itself is not bad, except that it exhausts and disgusts me, makes me disgusted and bored with myself.

I *must* teach myself the art of living with others through questions, through drawing others out. Could I not make it a rule to let my own ideas be known only by committing them to the privacy of my own journals or other writings, talking with others where I have to, but regarding it as my sole function, in such communication, to draw them out. Operation curiosity . . .

Sadness, reserve, polite inquiry that are coupled, I fear, with a certain mortification and denial of the flesh; that, I suppose, is the recipe?

Is there the faintest possibility that I would be capable of anything of this sort? There would certainly be many failures. Forgetfulness, habit, and, above all, politeness would tend to take over. Perhaps the key to all this is sadness. Only out of sadness can come renunciation.

Stockholm, August 21

We talked uninterruptedly about the events in Czechoslovakia[34] . . . as being of major historical significance and as constituting an error of great gravity on the part of the Russians. . . . I gave out a public statement to the effect that it was a colossal mistake, that the Russian leaders would some day come to regret it, that we would all, in government and out, have to take most serious account of its implications.

En route—plane Copenhagen–Oslo–Bergen–God knows where else, and eventually, New York, August

I have often returned home in a state of depression, but never anything like this.

I am depressed about my work. I see no answer to the problems besetting me: nothing to do but struggle along, spending ⅘ of my time fending off, or meeting, demands peripheral to my real function, unable for this reason to give either adequate time or adequate concentration to my work, and deprived, therefore, of any adequate sense of achievement in it. It has been this way for 15 years, this way it will remain.

I am depressed about the international scene. The Russians, with what they have done in Czechoslovakia, have pretty well disposed of any conceivable improvement in the general international situation. Obviously, we are entering on a period full of dangers, devoid not only of favorable prospects but also of favorable possibilities for action on our own part.

I am depressed about the national scene. The Democrats, now in convention at Chicago, have, with the effective assistance of the North Vietnamese, pretty well fought off the attacks on Johnson's Vietnam policy—have assured that the whole bloody business will continue indefinitely, thus making their position indistinguishable from that of the Republicans. This means, of course, further loss of life, more expense and more taxes, further bitterness & demoralization among the youth, further neglect of domestic problems.

34. On August 20, troops from the Soviet Union and its Eastern European allies marched into Czechoslovakia to crush the "Prague Spring" reform movement.

I am, finally, depressed about myself, bored & disgusted, convinced I should avoid, as far as possible, contact & involvement with other people, aware on the other hand that neither the needs of my wife nor the existing pattern of my obligations will permit me to do so. I must continue futilely, therefore, in my useless, exhausting condition, making a fool of myself, confining productive work to such odd moments—early Sunday morning, moments of enforced travel, etc.—as can be torn from the prevailing general pattern of trivia.

One thing does seem clear to me. I ought, in the interests of my disposition, to avoid as far as possible all confrontation with American life. This means the absolute minimum of travel (and even that, as far as possible, with closed eyes) but also avoidance of the media: radio, TV, newspapers. Anything, in other words, to avoid the sight & awareness of my country. I must learn to live in it as though I did not live in it.

How does one do this?

a) One declines invitations that involve travel.

b) One subscribes to a foreign newspaper—not to the *New York Times*. . . .

c) The farm, of course, has to be visited. Here, evidently, there is no alternative to the automobile. Trains are dirty, slow, & depressing. Allegheny Airlines are exactly what I would prefer not to see. The best thing is travel by turnpike—at night, a wholly useless exercise, to be sure—hours of death subtracted from the hours of life, but better than seeing anything.

What remains of life, in these circumstances?

Outstandingly: trivia . . . with occasional bouts of creative writing (memoirs) and scholarship (Alexander III). Also the farm, with the agreeable, healing childishness of gardening & property upkeep. Scholarship & the farm are the two final refuges, both, significantly, devoid of every sort of involvement with other people—the first devoid even of any involvement with one's own time, the second only partially connected with it.

There will of course be social life. We will be invited. We shall have to invite others. . . .

Whenever I am this depressed, I feel a desire to strip away from life & consciousness everything that is idle, redundant, useless, even food. The mood never lasts. With rest & sustenance, frivolity returns, and vanity, & self-indulgence. The only trouble is that creative work comes hard when one is depressed.

Thoughts for layman's sermon.

1. I don't know whether a pulpit, when occupied (or usurped) by a layman, is a proper place for a mere discussion. It is certainly, in this situation, not a proper place for exhortation, or for religious instruction. This being the case, perhaps you will permit me to expose to you simply a few reflections, controversial ones, admittedly, but honestly-conceived ones, concerning the connection between our Christian faith and the sort of world in which we find ourselves today.

2. Most of us, all of us my age, grew up in the shadow of a general belief in the possibility & even probability of such a thing as human progress. This outlook was taught in the schools, and it came also to pervade the Protestant churches.

3. The Bible is devoid of any suggestions in this direction, especially the New Testament. One will search it in vain for any suggestion that the human predicament could be materially improved by anything men might do, particularly by any manipulation of the social or political arrangement for human life. . . .

4. I hope I do not blaspheme (against?) the holy scripture when I say that I do not think we should give it absolute value. Most of it was written, after all, by men, not by gods. . . . The fact, therefore, that the gospel did not allow for the possibility of progress here below does not alone invalidate a later belief in progress as a possible component of Christian belief.

5. But man's reason, as a God-given quality of his nature, may well invalidate a belief in progress.

There is, in the first place, the tragic element in man's personal predicament: a condition that puts absolutely imperative limitations on the extent to which he can fulfill himself here on earth. But beyond this, turning from the problems of the individual to those of society, we have the grim evidence of the enormous jeopardy into which civilization is itself being carried by man's acquisition of a power over nature dreadfully incommensurate with his power over himself and his capacity for moral responsibility. . . .

The danger of collective catastrophe—from over-population, from exhaustion and pollution of natural resources, from further employment of the nuclear weapon, or from combinations of these things—is so great as to be in part a certainty and in the other part a near-certainty. Actually, the prospects for the future of the human race were more encouraging two hundred years ago, when the overriding danger related only to the longevity of the individual life, than it is today, when it is the continuity of civilization itself, and perhaps even the suitability of this planet as a climate for human existence, that is at stake.

6. In the face of this veritably apocalyptic danger the dream of human progress, in the sense of a betterment of the human condition generally, seems very far away indeed; and from the standpoint of religious thought it must, I think, be discarded altogether. One is struck, in fact, with the similarity of our situation to that of the early Christians. They, as a matter of pure faith, believed in the early end of the world. . . .

7. What, then, is the meaning of all this for Christian outlooks and attitudes? Are we to fall back literally on the teachings of the early church fathers, disregarding the affairs and concerns of this world—falling back entirely on prayer and preparation for another life? This is a matter of individual conscience.

1969

In 1969 and in the next few years, Kennan wrote relatively little in the diary. He continued to ponder what he might do to influence society along the lines of his biting critique of current affairs.

For much of the winter and spring of 1969, the Kennans were in England. George delivered the Chichele Lectures at Oxford and also spoke at Cambridge.

Cambridge University, February 24

I was shown to a very chilly (as yet wholly unheated) suite of bedroom, living room & bath, in a building of Elizabethan vintage—the living room very attractive, actually, in a roomy, antique way, & furnished with two electric heaters, which warmed it, or gave it an effect of warmth, as long as they were going, but upon their being turned off, it reverted at once to the temperature of its massive stone walls, which I dare say has not changed more than 3° since the days of Elizabeth & Essex, when it was built.

February 26

After dinner we sat long in what is called in Cambridge the "combination room," talking about radical students, & I returned to my cold & rather barren quarters deeply depressed over the sudden repudiation by so many of the young not only of my generation of scholars but of the very traditions and conventions and ceremonies by which, for centuries, scholarship has been supported and without which it will lose all form and all dignity.

London, March 8

In the National Portrait Gallery, which I much enjoyed, & where I was very much impressed with the faces of these past generations of Britishers. Amazing that the obvious erosion of the genes, brought about over this past century by the effect of modern hygiene in keeping alive the weak, should be so central a fact of our time, and yet never talked about, as though contemporary Western humanity were afraid of insulting itself.

[The Kennans went on a skiing vacation at Crans, which they did often.]

Crans, Switzerland, March 29

In trying to think out the problems of my future, I realize that there is no one I can talk to about this *in its entirety* except myself.

I am, first of all, not going to produce any major scholarly work. . . .

Secondly, I am not going to affect significantly the trend of public affairs in my own country: the deterioration of physical environment, the trend to racial civil war—in effect, the disintegration and failure of American civilization. It is a question, in fact, whether I should continue to talk about it. . . .

The same applies substantially to what I might call the interior development of European civilization. I am not going to stop the progressive urbanization, motorization, and moral disintegration of Europe.

Not being able to do any of these things—recognizing my inability to do them, I must learn not to resent the phenomena in question, not to react to them, not to be bitter about them, rather to accept them as given and to make the best of them. This, in turn, however, means not exposing myself unnecessarily to the outward evidences of them.

What, then, can I do? . . .

I have, furthermore, the "image" with which life has saddled me: that of a sort of a pundit in public & above all international affairs. I cannot escape this. It may be, as another generation comes along, a declining burden, but for some years it will continue, to some extent, to exist. It is the role in which fate has cast me. . . .

I should not try to teach. Making an effort to approach students of this generation from the standpoint of their standards and values, I should be a hypocrite. Approaching them from my own, I should be a pessimist, and a pessimist should not teach younger people.

All this will not be easy. It means living without purpose, without hope, solely for appearances. And it will be lonely. . . .

Have I the strength of character to do this? God help me if I have not, for there is no other answer to my problem but moral disintegration and shame.

One consolation remains: the improvement of the various properties & the preparation of them as refuges for the children in the hard days to come: the cultivation, that is, of facilities for existence there as independent as possible of the going market economy. This can be health-giving and satisfying & enjoyable.

Doddington, England, May 10

We slept, last night, in the great four-poster bed in the room off the main corridor nearest the wing where our hosts, the Jarvis's, were sleeping. We were thus the only people sleeping in the main body of the great house. I, during the night, had a strange dream. I dreamed I was lying not in the room where I actually was, but in the four-poster bed just the other side of the wall, in the next bedroom. There was a young woman in the room who was pacing about obviously greatly excited and talking wildly. At one point she started to open the door and go out into the corridor, with a view, obviously, to go down towards the wing where the Jarvis's were sleeping. This alarmed me. I feared she would disturb them. I rushed to stop her in the doorway, and pulled her back inside. As I did so, I saw further down the corridor, a small dark creature of some sort, scarcely human (though it might have been a dwarf with a black cape) squatting on the floor outside the room where I was sleeping. I recognized it as an object of unmentionable evil and menace. When I had pulled the young woman back in, she paced up and down the room, in a state of even greater excitement, giving vent to her feelings loudly, with torrent of words. I hushed her down, saying, "You mustn't carry on like that; you will wake the Jarvis's." But then I reproached myself for doing so. "You've frustrated her in two ways," I said. "First you wouldn't let her go out. Now you won't let her voice her feelings. You have left her no outlet. You shouldn't have done it."

(When I told my hosts about this, at breakfast, I saw them pale and exchange quick glances. There was, they explained, a tale, handed down over the generations, that in an earlier century, a young woman, locked up in this room as a consequence of some family conflict, had responded by throwing herself out the window.)

Oxford, May 12

Evening ended with an altercation with two rather ragged Americans who had been impressed with Mr. Alperovitz's insinuations[35]—were reluctant to believe, even on my assurance, that a wicked, pro-fascist U.S. Government had not rebuffed the well meaning advances of a trusting, innocent, & high-minded Stalin.

Princeton, October 20

To the Council on Foreign Relations [in New York City], for a luncheon . . . for the Soviet scientist Kapitsa.[36] I was seated next to him. He knew all about me, treated me with much respect, and even assured me, to my incredulous astonishment, that my book had been translated into Russian & was widely read in the Soviet Union.

What he had to say was partly shrewd & intelligent, partly naïve, & partly the Party line. Pressed by me, for example, to recognize the deterioration in the atmosphere for East-West contacts that had taken place in the last 2–3 years, he laid it all to fears on the Soviet side of a resurgence of German Nazism (which he regarded as a fact), of a military & political collaboration between Germany and China.

35. In *Atomic Diplomacy* (1965), the "revisionist" scholar Gar Alperovitz argued that the primary reason why the United States had dropped the atomic bombs on Japan in 1945 was to intimidate the Soviet Union. Kennan was appalled at the growing appeal of such revisionist historiography in the late 1960s to the 1970s.

36. Pyotr Kapitsa was a Nobel Prize winner in physics.

1970

Although Kennan remained an eminent personage who received multiple invitations to speak at prestigious institutions and participate in international seminars, and although he retained ties with such officials as National Security Advisor Henry A. Kissinger, he remained, to his chagrin, a marginal figure in terms of influence on policy.

January 1

I hereby vow that, barring serious illness or catastrophe, I will make an earnest effort, by way of innovation, to keep this journal up to date throughout the year.

I am beginning it, however, some days after the first of the year; so the record of the first days will be from memory.

Of this particular day, I recall only much weariness from being up to 4:00 a.m., digging out of the snow Svetlana's car,[37] which she had been unable to move from our drive in the wee hours of the morning.

Washington, March 10

Dinner at Polly's:[38] Bohlens & Davies. The Nitzes[39] also came in before dinner. Talked with Paul about the SALT talks & found him as serious as ever about the mathematics of destruction. Otherwise: talk partly on the youth & very depressing, so much so that I had a feeling the ground was shaking under us.

37. Svetlana Alliluyeva, the daughter of Joseph Stalin, was befriended by Kennan soon after she defected to the United States in 1967. She lived for a while at the Kennans' farm and later in her own house in Princeton. Though she turned to Kennan for advice regarding her literary, legal, and financial affairs, she would eventually become estranged from him, as she did with most other people in her life.
38. Polly Wisner, the widow of former CIA official Frank Wisner and the future wife of columnist Clayton Fritchey, was a Washington hostess and supporter of the arts.
39. Paul M. and Phyllis P. Nitze. Paul Nitze had succeeded Kennan as director of the Policy Planning Staff of the State Department. He was at the time of the dinner a U.S. delegate to the Strategic Arms Limitation Treaty (SALT) talks.

But also interesting interrogation of John Davies after dinner—about Mao, whom he describes as combination of earthy, pragmatic peasant and romanticist.

Sørenhus,[40] near Kristiansand, Norway, July 4

In earlier years, I would have flown the stars & stripes from the flagpole at Sørenhus. This year there could be no question of it, for the pole was broken. But even had the pole been intact I would not, I thought, have flown it. Whose country is it, after all? The youth detests what it was to us; we detest what the youth are making of it. . . .

The Norwegians are physically hard, stubborn, sentimental, and simple in their tastes . . . of course, but there is an added measure of complexity in their nature that defies my powers of analysis. There is a certain difficulty they experience in communication with each other.

It is a form of shyness which they overcome or better, perhaps, conceal only with a great outward jollity, but the jolliness is illusory—it is only a protection against themselves. Inwardly, they are melancholy, reserved, and for the most part sensitive.

July 9

I am laid up with stiffness, dampness, & internal cramps.

At this point, after a fortnights' preoccupation with other things, thoughts turn to the various problems and phenomena with which I have been absorbed during this last disastrous year. I realize that the mention of practically any public problem evokes from me only a reaction of cynicism and bitterness. This is obviously unhealthy. What to do about it? . . . I can see only one way out. To write, to state it all, as clearly and compellingly as one can.

In the broad spectrum of political institutions running all the way from the usurping tyrant to the egalitarian democracy, there is only one segment that yields reasonably good government. It is one that combines legitimacy, which means continuity, with the existence of an influential upper class whose composition is made up largely by inheritance but partly by recruitment of able people from other inherited stations, its influence assured by some sort of limited franchise or weighted voting, particularly in national affairs.

40. Sørenhus, a house built in 1935 by Annelise Sørensen Kennan's father, is located on Dvergnestangen peninsula about eight miles from Kristiansand.

[The Kennans interrupted their usual summer vacation in Norway so that George could participate in the International Seminar for Diplomats in Salzburg. He perceived the more liberal attendees as naive and excessively guilty about the Third World.]

Salzburg, Austria, August 8

It was a pleasant luncheon: outdoors, under the trees. The men sat together after lunch and talked about the problems of Western Europe. Before us was the swimming pool; and my recollections of snatches of the conversation (I found myself close, in my views on Europe, to Couve[41]—or at least so it seemed to me) are mixed with impressions of young women in bikinis being courted by other men.

We drove out to a Schloss-restaurant for lunch as guests of Paul & Phyllis Nitze & their daughter & son-in-law, Mr. & Mrs. Scott Thompson—Mr. Thompson being a faculty member at the Fletcher School. . . . All this was very pleasant. (Mr. Gerard Smith, head of our delegation at the SALT talks, being also in the restaurant, it occurred to us that 3 former directors of the Policy Planning Staff were in the room.)

November 23

Made fruitless trip to Washington to lunch with Henry Kissinger who, however, was detained with the President on the unhappy matter of our raid on the empty prison camp in North Vietnam, so that I finally had to lunch with one of his aides, & had only a few moments to talk with him before starting back to Princeton.

41. Maurice Couve de Murville was foreign minister of France from 1958 to 1968.

Chapter Eight

Scholar and Public Intellectual, 1971–80

1971

The diary for 1971 reflects the variety and pace of Kennan's everyday life. The sixty-seven-year-old finished up a small scholarly book,[1] wrote much of what would become his second volume of memoirs,[2] and drafted talks delivered in Europe and America. He also repaired fences at the farm, coped with the problems of his adult children, and conversed with the chancellor and foreign minister of West Germany. He helped select new faculty and members at the Institute for Advanced Study while aiding in the adjustment there of his friend Isaiah Berlin. Kennan was "moved and depressed" at the relative obscurity of another longtime associate, John Lukacs, whom he praised as "America's foremost political-cultural philosopher."[3] When the Kennans traveled to Portugal, Britain, France, Switzerland, West Germany, Norway, and the Netherlands, George did not leave his prejudices behind. He looked with "disgust" at Amsterdam's "enormous population of foreign freaks: rebellious youth . . . foreign workers from the Mediterranean world, and Africans who all looked as though they were here to live off women." He also found offensive the city's "massive pandering to pornographic tastes."[4]

---

1. *The Marquis de Custine and His Russia in 1839* (1971).
2. *Memoirs, 1950–1963* (1972).
3. Kennan diary, January 16, 1971, box 239, Kennan papers. Lukacs wrote a variety of books, including *Historical Consciousness; or The Remembered Past* (1968) and *George Kennan: A Study of Character* (2007).
4. Kennan diary, May 2, 1971, ibid.

Washington, January 11

At 3 p.m. there was a large inner-governmental meeting, at the State Department, to bring together all the available information on *Khrushchev Remembers*.[5]

To Tommy & Jane Thompson's[6] for an intimate supper—a trois.

Princeton, January 22

Started this morning, rather futilely, on Part II of the memoirs, writing a few pages about the appointment as ambassador to Moscow in 1952. (I suddenly have no enthusiasm for this book. Who cares about all this, now? Not even my children).

March 18

[Dream] I donned, for reasons obscure, some sort of huge fish skin, like a dress. Felt there was something living, enclosed by accident between it & me. Looking down, saw something protruding from the bottom that looked rather like an umbilical cord, but semi-transparent. I pulled it all out, & it turned out to be a sort of transparent live snake.

March 19

I glanced at the day's mail, observed, to my horror, that there was one letter from the President, another from the Secretary of Defense, & another from Pampel Walther, in Bonn, intimating that the German Chancellor[7] would like to see me.

September 24

To a dinner (with wives) at Prospect of members of the class of 1925, commemorating our entrance into the University just 50 years ago. That we should have been there was not so remarkable. What *was* remarkable was that we were addressed, with rigor, lucidity, and far greater linguis-

5. Edward Crankshaw (ed.), *Khrushchev Remembers* (1970) was produced from reminiscences of deposed Soviet leader Nikita S. Khrushchev. The material was smuggled out of the Soviet Union and translated by Strobe Talbott, who years later would become the chief Russian expert in the administration of President Bill Clinton. The book was a tell-all sensation that offered Western readers the first detailed look at the personal foibles and political machinations of Kremlin leaders from the 1930s to the 1950s. Kennan was part of the ad hoc team assembled by the State Department to appraise the implications for current foreign policy.

6. Llewellyn E. "Tommy" Thompson Jr. was a former U.S. ambassador to the Soviet Union.

7. Willy Brandt, a friend of Kennan's, had become the German chancellor.

tic coherence than most of us could have mustered, by the professor who then taught the freshman course most of us were compelled to take—Joe Green, now somewhere around 90 years of age.

October 20

I met in late afternoon with a faculty seminar at Columbia, conducted by Zbigniew Brzezinski.[8] The subject was "Stalin as a revolutionary." I held forth and was then gently taken to pieces by a very high-powered group of authorities, which included Mr. Bialer.[9]

The Farm, October 28

Janet[10] phoned me [at] the farm, to say that the Firestone Library [at Princeton University] had been asked by Chip Bohlen to send him a copy of a letter he had written to me in January 1945, which young Mr. ________[11] had discovered among my papers. I was horrified at this news, since I had a vague recollection that Chip had asked me once to destroy my own letter to which his was a reply, and I was sure he would not relish this one being seen by a stranger.

8. A Polish American, Zbigniew Brzezinski became a prominent political scientist at Columbia and then national security advisor under President Jimmy Carter.
9. A former prisoner in Auschwitz and a political scientist at Columbia, Seweryn Bialer is an expert on Soviet and Polish communism.
10. Janet Smith was Kennan's secretary.
11. Kennan did not further identify the researcher.

1972

Kennan never completely abandoned hopes of somehow, sometime, in some way influencing U.S. policy and institutions. After Nixon was elected president in November 1968, Kennan had offered his services, only to be ignored. While deploring Nixon's war in Vietnam, the former diplomat was careful not to burn his bridges to the White House. In particular, he maintained with National Security Advisor Kissinger, who would become secretary of state in 1973, a relationship of mutual respect.

Kennan turned his still considerable energies to other ends, publishing a second volume of memoirs and launching a history of pre–World War I alliance diplomacy. An avid sailor since boyhood, he also took lessons in celestial navigation in preparation for an ambitious trip in European waters.

Princeton, February 6

I once had a dream of what the Foreign Service should be:

An elite corps of the finest the country could produce in way of education, breeding, and character.

Let me explain in greater detail what I mean by these qualities:

(a) **Education**

Broad cultural background, particularly in history, languages, & aesthetics.

History: Western civilization, & particularly in its classical, medieval, and modern-European aspects that tend to provide a common base for all Western cultures.

Languages: at least one of classical ones and one of the three great Western European tongues, in any event French.

Aesthetics: firm knowledge of history of art & architecture. Why? Because powers of observation & of analysis through observation are thereby enhanced. And would stress powers of observation not just in art but in nature.

(b) **Breeding**

By this I do not mean what you may think I do, that one should come from family in social register.

I mean that one should have learned the basic rules of tact, poise, & politeness; should know instinctively when to speak and when to listen and, above all, *how* to speak & how to *listen;* should have some sensitivity to feelings of others & respect for them; should have, in short, a good bearing & good manners. All this can be learned just as well in a poor home as in a rich one. It has nothing to do with the social register. It is something more than just external, & whoever thinks it is not important in diplomacy just doesn't know what he is talking about.

(c) **Character**

Will—this is a hard thing to describe.

Partly a matter of how a man fights his battles with himself, something always invisible to others.

But also of honesty & loyalty in relations with others. They have to be able to depend on him.

Given these three qualities, I would permit most of the technical know-how about foreign affairs & to come in the form of on-the-job training.

I would encourage area specialization or functional specialization, but only on condition that the person in question first fulfilled these more general characteristics.

And then, having adopted & implemented these principles, I would have this be a rigidly professional & highly disciplined service. It would be totally and ferociously non-political. The principles of hierarchical authority would be strictly observed. Discipline would be gentle, considerate, and respectful to the dignity of the individual insofar as the language of communication was concerned, but rigorous in substance. There would be complete freedom of thought and expression in official communication, provided always that good form was observed. But there would be no labor union psychology or activity, no assumption of an antagonism of purpose or interest as between superior & subordinate, no "rights" of the officer except to fair treatment in relation to other officers.

This, then, was my vision of the Foreign Service. I can assure you that had it been consistently invoked over a period of 10 to 15 years (the minimum necessary to make any useful change in a career service) we would have incomparably the best Foreign Service, the most highly respected & most effective for any useful purpose of any in the world.

But whom would it serve? Who would want it? What would be such a service operating against the background of the seamy, disorderly, political establishment which this country produces in Washington, with its provincialism, its low educational level, its narrow introversion? This is no source of an imaginative, effective foreign policy. For the decisions *it* makes and the policies *it* evolves, there is no need of an effective diplomatic instrument. Such a Washington would not recognize a good Foreign Service if it saw one, & would not want it if it recognized it.

March 13

Left, on afternoon bus, for New York, for the weekly night school lesson in celestial navigation.

March 24

Annelise and I studied, into the depths of the night, the charts of English Channel & North Sea that had arrived during the day.

April 15

I finished yesterday, with Janet's help, the reading of the galley-proof of the 2nd volume of memoirs. Now, I feel that I have recorded most of what might be recorded about my life. . . . In the actual moment of appearance and reception of the book, I haven't the faintest interest, so long as it *does* appear, and copies find their way into some of the libraries. I shall be abroad anyway at that time. But of what interest to me is the reaction of the American public, the public of a country surfeited with books, devoid of good reviews and reviewers, a country to which I do not belong, anyway?

To what, then, do I look forward? To the boat. To a bit of historical research next year, if luck is with me. That is about it.

April 16

A. What use is there talking about foreign policy if our main external concern is going to continue to be Vietnam?

B. Well, what would you want us to do in foreign policy if Vietnam did not exist?

A. Withdraw, for the most part, from active participation elsewhere in international life.

B. Vietnam does not prevent that; it rather favors it, in that it rivets to a single area all our passion for involvement, even constitutes an argument against involvement in other places.

A. (Weakly) there are *some* positive things I would like to see us try to do in international affairs.

B. (Scornfully) What, for example?

A. Put a stop to the arms race in nuclear weapons, and thereby if possible, to their proliferation.

B. Vietnam doesn't stop you doing that.

A. Get on with the establishment of international environmental controls.

B. Nor that.

A. Take in hand the problem of the mini-state.

B. That we are not going to do anyway. The image of a world populated by a lot of innocent, virtuous little peoples who love and admire us is much too dear to us. It matters not that 95% of them still hate us or hold us in contempt. We cultivate them not because this produces any positive response. We cultivate them because we look good to ourselves in the mirror, doing it. We will continue to do it, Vietnam or no Vietnam.

A. Then you conclude, do you, that Vietnam doesn't really matter, that it is just a way we like to spend a lot of money and kill a lot of people? And the rest of our lives would go on quite similarly, even if we didn't have it?

B. Substantially.

May 10

I received today, at home, a phone call from a Mr. Harrigan in the White House, who said that the President had charged him with asking for a quick reaction from me about his last pronouncement (May 8) concerning policy towards Vietnam.

I said that I was afraid I could give the President small comfort here. There were important points on which I simply could not go along with him. One was the bombings. I had never seen evidence that strategic bombing was very effective when it came to interdicting the flow of supplies to the battlefield, and to the extent it *was* effective, I thought it was inordinately costly in terms both of extraneous destruction and of our international reputation. Secondly, I thought it likely that the 17 million people of South Vietnam were probably most concerned that the war should stop, and would be willing to pay the price of having a North Vietnamese Communist regime pinned on them, if that would only lead to the cessation of hostilities.

Mr. Harrigan asked me: How about the blockade? I said: Well, it had now been imposed, and that was that; but I thought we ought to do everything possible to limit its dangers when it came to the handling of Soviet shipping, that we ought to keep as closely as possible in touch with the Soviet government and be careful to take no harsher action than we were actually compelled to with relation to any Soviet vessel and then to go out of our way to explain to the Soviet authorities exactly what we were doing and why we were doing it. Nothing in Southeast Asia was as important, I said, as our relations with the Soviet Union, and we should be careful not to jeopardize the latter for the former.

I thought that as far as the future was concerned, we ought to go ahead and get the troops out of there as fast as possible. . . .

I pointed out that I had made no public statements and had associated myself with none of the public attacks on the President over Vietnam. I had restrained myself in this way partly because I had sympathy with him in the problems he faced but partly also because my views about the North Vietnamese were quite different from those of many of his critics and I did not want to invite any confusion as to my own position.

[Accompanied by Annelise, Kennan went to Europe to do research for his history of the origins of the Franco-Russian alliance in the late nineteenth century. It was this alignment, he believed, that undermined the stability sought by German Foreign Minister Otto von Bismarck. The resulting tensions eventually erupted into World War I, destroying the cultural world that Kennan idealized.]

Paris, November 3

Archives all day. In the evening, A. & I went to the movies, to see *The Godfather*, which I (how my children would have been amused) found very good—especially the performance of Marlon Brandon as the father of the family.

Geneva, November 19

We had to pay a call (which I earnestly wished I had not got myself into) on a recent Soviet escapee. . . . I listened with growing despair to his anguished and earnest, but confused talk: his belief that he knew all about the West (he has been out of Russia for some 7 months), his confidence that he understood the faults of both systems and knew just how the Western one could be corrected to put humanity on the right course, his indignation against the West for not blowing defiantly and indignantly at the Soviet Union or (one must suppose) going to war against it. And I thought to myself: "What have you done, you Russian Communists, to create an intellectual atmosphere in which the minds of persecuted opponents are as confused as your own?". . .

I could with the greatest of ease drop everything of my own—research, writing, family, & profession—and devote myself, not only for the remainder of my time here in Europe but for weeks after my return to the U.S., to the task of apprizing the West of the epoch-making event of his arrival and arranging for publication of his book and the arrangement for him of an economically secure existence among us; and he would find not only this an entirely normal expenditure of my energies but would probably end up professing dissatisfaction with the quality of the performance.

1973

Kennan spent much of his time and energy in 1973 and in subsequent years establishing the Kennan Institute to promote the study of Russian history and culture. The Institute was named after the cousin of Kennan's grandfather, another George Kennan (1845–1924), who had won renown from books and lectures about his travels through Russia in the late nineteenth century. The Kennan Institute would eventually become a division of the Woodrow Wilson International Center for Scholars in Washington, DC. Kennan also worked to help contain a rancorous dispute within the Institute for Advanced Study at Princeton.

Princeton, January 14

Went over, at noon, to see Carl Kaysen[12] about tomorrow's meeting. Expressed my wish that whole thing could be postponed for several months & Geertz[13] asked to come up with alternative candidates. Saw, however, that there was nothing to be done, and left with the realization that we were headed for an inescapable conflict.[14]

January 22

The taxi driver greeted me with the news that LBJ (God rest his soul, but only after a little initial chastisement for his egotism, his bullying, and his obscenities) was dead.

March 28

Arose early and set off by rail to Washington, to lunch, at his request, with Henry Kissinger. . . . Together with H. K., walked over, in the

12. Carl Kaysen was director of the Institute for Advanced Study.
13. The anthropologist Clifford Geertz was the first faculty member of the newly established School of Social Science at the Institute.
14. The Institute was embroiled in controversy over the qualifications of a prospective professor in the School of Social Science.

lovely spring sunshine and among the exuberant Washington blossoms, to the Metropolitan Club, where we lunched alone.

[Kennan spent much of the spring and summer in European capitals, including Moscow, doing research for his book on the Franco-Russian alliance. The Kennan family also vacationed at the Sørensen family compound near Kristiansand.]

September 10

Am now on a plane returning from 5 months in Europe. What has happened in the past year and a half? Precisely nothing, except that

1) I am a year & a half older, & that is pretty damned old.

2) I have involved myself, futilely but beyond the point of no return, in an effort to set up in Washington, a national center for Russian studies. . . .

3) I have made such effort as I could to study the history of the Franco-Russian Alliance of 1894, but it was a fragmentary & feeble effort, interrupted constantly by a thousand ulterior preoccupations, and it is clear that at this rate I shall not complete, before retirement, even a first volume.

4) Meanwhile, I have come so far from official thinking in my own views on public problems that I can no longer talk to specific subjects. I have to state the whole thing or nothing. But to admit this merely whets the appetite of the publisher, and invites demands for a book I have neither the privacy nor the time to write.

5) I am still chained to the properties, and they alone are going to take up so much time that I could not think of doing my serious work in addition.

In addition to this, there is the Institute & its problems, which represent a duty; the correspondence & visitors, which I cannot avoid; the remnants of a reputation as a public figure, which I have not been able to bring myself to abandon, & which also mean demands on time; & finally, the family, which is just *there*. . . .

I have perhaps 3–4 years in which I could still write something of some freshness & originality. Should I not simply set aside so & so much time for writing, and let the rest fit in as best it can?—let the cruelty of the bite on the remaining time force its own decisions? . . . The boat would have to go, the farm, too, presumably. It would be a hell of a life, no pleasure but possibly some achievement.

But could I do it to family & children?

Washington, October 18

Went downtown, in the afternoon, first to see Kay Graham, who looked very tired and distracted but to whom I related, as best I could, my endeavors on behalf of a Russian institute. Stopped, on the way back, to see Dick Holbrooke,[15] who loaded me with literature and pressed, as a good editor should, for an article by December.

In late afternoon, went to see Chip, whom I found in bed at his home.[16] Very grey but in some way ennobled by his long and horrible ordeal. Enjoyed the talk with him, and appreciated particularly his assurance that if he could overcome his illness he would gladly help me with the project of a Washington Russian center.

To dinner at Polly Wisner's,[17] where we found to our amazement John Davies and also, not to our amazement but to our pleasure also, Stew Alsop.[18] Henry Kissinger, it was thought, *might* appear—this, in any case, was what his office had given Polly to understand, but he did not do so, being (as we were later to learn) about to take off for Moscow to see what could be done to put an end to the fighting in the Middle East.[19]

Princeton, October 20

We went for dinner to the William Bundy's.[20] While there, the daughter of the house, following the news programs, came in and announced the resignations of Messrs. Richardson and Ruckelshaus as well. . . . It finally penetrated my dense intelligence that we were in the midst of a national crisis.[21]

The day was also notable for the announcement by the Saudis that they are terminating oil shipments to the U.S.[22] Never, I must say, has any news pleased me more. It was obviously the best thing that could have happened to us.

15. Richard Holbrooke, editor of *Foreign Policy*, would serve as a foreign policy operative in several administrations..
16. Chip Bohlen would die two months later.
17. Washington hostess Polly Wisner later married the journalist and public official Clayton Fritchey.
18. Stewart Alsop, the brother of Joseph Alsop, was a newspaper and magazine columnist.
19. The Yom Kippur War was fought between Israel and an Arab coalition.
20. William P. Bundy, editor of *Foreign Affairs* and former assistant secretary of state for East Asian and Pacific affairs, was married to Mary A. Bundy, an artist and a daughter of Dean Acheson.
21. In what became known as the "Saturday Night Massacre," Attorney General Elliott Richardson and Deputy Attorney General William Ruckelshaus resigned in protest over President Richard Nixon's attempts to squelch the investigation of the Watergate scandal.
22. Saudi Arabia was protesting U.S. support for Israel in the October 6–25 Yom Kippur War.

[George and Annelise visited their son, Christopher, who was a student at Yale.]

New Haven, October 27

Thence to the Yale-Cornell football game—very inferior football—a shadow, as it seemed to me, of what used to be played at these institutions. Obviously, these students, with their women, their sophistication, and their past years of drugs and sexual precociousness, do not produce out of their midst quite the same sort of athletes that were produced some years ago. Between the halves, the bands produced the same sort of insults to the president that seem now to pass for humor among the young.

[The Kennans vacationed in Switzerland.]

Icogne, Switzerland, December 26

I have been more depressed before, but never has there been such reason for depression. My public usefulness is finished; my professional accomplishment, as an historian, is negated by the suffocating trivia of life in Princeton. Annelise does not take kindly to the idea of life in the country. I am therefore to stay in Princeton, reading other people's books & manuscripts, receiving visitors & answering mail—a monument to the past and a decoration, of declining attractiveness, for other people's dinner parties.

1974

Kennan spent much of 1974 doing research for a book on the origins of the nineteenth-century Franco-Russian alliance. As usual, the family summered near Kristiansand on the southern coast of Norway. They sailed their boat, the Northwind. *That fall Kennan became a fellow at the Woodrow Wilson Center in Washington. He remained an informal adviser to Kissinger, who had now become secretary of state.*

Brussels, January 14

We were met by the cultural attaché, a pleasant young man of Hungarian-Jewish origin, who took us to the guest house of the American Ambassador to NATO, Mr. Donald Rumsfeld.[23] We unpacked, were served a light lunch, and rested. . . . Dinner, *en famille*, at the Rumsfelds, whom we also liked very much, both Middle-Westerners.

January 15

Listened to an elderly Belgian who told us lovely tales about a lady he had known in her old age who had been the mistress of kings & emperors (Franz-Joseph—very ordinary in bed; Nicholas II—frightfully nervous) as well as of J. P. Morgan.

February 6

Princeton still in the throes of the gasoline shortage and the truckers' strike. It is revealing to observe what an addiction the use of the automobile has become for our fellow citizens, and how furious and ill-mannered they become when anything operates to deny them the privilege of driving their cars.

23. Donald Rumsfeld would become secretary of defense under President Gerald Ford and, decades later, would hold the same position under President George W. Bush.

February 16
Verses by G. F. Kennan on the occasion of his seventieth birthday

When the step becomes slow, and the wit becomes slower,
  And memory fails, and the hearing declines;
When skies become clouded, and clouds become lower,
  And you find yourself talking poetical lines;
When the path that you tread becomes steeper and darker;
  And the question seems no longer whether but when—
Then, my friend, you should look for the biblical marker,
  The sign by the road that reads: Three Score and Ten;
At this point you'll observe, if you care to look closely,
  You're no longer alone on the highway of life;
For there trudges behind you, and glowers morosely,
  A bearded old man with a curious knife. . . .
And you turn to the thoughts of your erstwhile successes—
  How brilliant, how charming, how worthy of fame;
'Til a small voice protests, and the conscience confesses
  What an ass you once were, and how empty the claim;
Then the ghosts of the past find you out in your sadness,
  And gather about and poke fingers of shame—
The ghosts of stupidities spawned by your madness—
  The ghosts of injustices done in your name;
And you grieve with remorse for the sins you've committed:
  The fingers that roamed and the tongue that betrayed;
But you grieve even more for the ones you omitted:
  The nectar untasted, the record unplayed;
But the cut most unkind, and the cruelest teacher,
  Is the feeling you have when, as sometimes occurs,
The wandering eye of some heavenly creature
  Encounters your own, and your own catches hers;
And you conjure up dreams too delightful to mention,
  And you primp and you pose, 'til it's suddenly seen
That the actual object of all her attention—
  This burning, voluptuous female attention—
  Is a fellow behind you who's all of nineteen. . . .
Yet, if given the chance to retread, as you've known it,
  The ladder of life—to begin at the spot

Where the story picked up, and before you had blown it,
Would you take it, dear friends?
I suspect you would not;
So let us take heart; we are none of us friendless;
And fill up your glasses, and raise them again
To the chance that an interval, seemingly endless,
Will ensue
Before you
Become Three Score and Ten.

Washington, April 10

Christopher met me and drove me to Senator Kennedy's[24] house, where the Senator & Mrs. Kennedy were just finishing dinner. . . . I then gave the Senator such advice as I could concerning his forthcoming visit to Eastern Europe and Russia.

Sørenhus, June 4

Suddenly occurred to me today, in a moment of remorse over the way I waste my remaining strength, that now, having so little to lose, I should learn to think of myself from the point of view of and as an instrument of, Him who made me. He did not make me, surely, and particularly he did not give me the talents I have, just to be employed in the service of my own small ego, whose existence and significance will be so soon terminated. He gave them to me to be valued and cultivated and used for purposes wider than my own existence.

Strange, that this ancient and basic religious thought should overtake me so late in life.

Bergen, Norway, June 25

The tendency of the motor age is to overwhelm, subdue, and eventually destroy, in its life-giving qualities, the sea. The harbor of Bergen, with its dearth of ships and its concentration on the oil rig, demonstrates this with a melancholy persuasiveness. The empty docks are the consequence of the replacement of coastal shipping by the road-hauling of freight, for no one wants to use a boat for anything that can possibly be moved by motor vehicle. And the great oil rig will soon join hundreds of its fellows, squatting indecently over the surface of the North Sea, pollut-

24. Senator Edward M. "Ted" Kennedy of Massachusetts.

ing its waters, menacing the navigation on it, and sucking out the riches of its subsoil—all this, with the blessing of peoples and governments, for the internal combustion engine is now king over man. And the assurance of its supply of food is more important, in the eyes of both peoples and governments, than the assurance of the food supply for people. That man should hunger is easier to contemplate than that he should have to restrict himself in the use of his automobile, which he loves above all things in life and for the use of which there is nothing he would not sacrifice.

Ørnes, Norway, June 28

Among the people on the dock, there is a maternal-looking woman with two little children who hold hands with one arm and clutch, in each case, a doll with the other. One of the children is an Oriental, Korean, Annelise thinks. There she stands, the little creature, far from her native soil and culture, a testimony, no doubt, to the sentimentality of some Norwegian missionary. (Nowhere, I think, except in our own Middle West, do the missionaries play such a role as they do in the west of Norway.) How great the prodigality of the Orient, I think to myself, which could produce and cast off no end of these exquisite, intelligent little creatures without even feeling the loss, the prodigality of this great teeming Orient which, in its pitiless vitality, will no doubt some day engulf and enslave whatever may by that time be left of us inane, pampered Westerners, and will teach us (as Custine said of the Western Europeans in the face of the Russians) "how we can and should be ruled."

Svolvaer, Norway

Arriving with the ship, and leaving it at Svolvaer, are two or three examples of the ubiquitous American youth-tourists, complete with straggly long hair, huge knapsacks, rumpled trousers, and sodden tennis shoes. It is impossible, for one of my generation at any rate, to distinguish their sex, and apparently this has little significance. One sees them everywhere. Like the mendicant friars of the Middle Ages, they roam the earth, sleeping in smelly, crowded youth hostels, sitting on the filthy floors of air terminals and bus stations, sharing with their *confreres* of other nationalities the hashish, the guitar-pounding, and all the other hallmarks of their strange international culture. What, I ask myself, could these specimens be seeking, here in Svolvaer? What brought them here? . . . They say we are both Americans, but you are stranger to me than the Hottentots. Benevolently, and with no reaction more negative than a slight shudder, I consign you to your various delights, thankful only that no one compels me to share them with you.

Bardufoss, Norway, July 5

Of the erstwhile rough and picturesque life of northern Norway, so little is left that it is not worth mentioning, and that little is dying. . . . A journey in these parts only intensifies the bitterness of the problem of Norway itself—the country of contradictions, combining so much of the inferior with so much of the superior, vulnerable in exceptionally high degree to the worst influences of foreign urban and industrial culture, governed by political parties that do all in their power to pamper the common man with physical comfort and security, nothing whatsoever to protect and fortify his moral qualities—a country, in short, that is its own worst enemy and cannot be expected, as things now stand, to hold out against the disintegrating tendencies of the modern age.

Sørenhus, August 8

I lay awake, in order to listen, at 2:00 a.m. to Mr. Nixon's speech of retirement, which I found rather odd, since it showed appreciation neither of the real reasons for his personal disaster nor of the significance of it for his future career.[25]

Washington, October 14

Returned to Washington in late afternoon. We took the old road, straight down. In the evening we attended an Italian movie—cynical, despairing, pornographic & full of hatred or contempt for humanity.

The combination of the impressions of the drive through western Maryland and those of the movie & the weird youth in attendance, plus the sights around M Street, where the movie was, left me profoundly depressed. True, the movie was about Italians, could not have been about anybody else. True, also, it was done, obviously, by a talented director. But there was nothing in it to give one the slightest encouragement for the future of Western civilization, & the public assembled to view it was frightening in its decadence.

25. Nixon was forced to resign because of his complicity in the cover-up of the break-in by Republican Party operatives at the Democratic Party headquarters in the Watergate complex.

October 30

Lunched this noon with Professor John Gaddis[26] of Ohio State, who had a lot of questions to ask me about the affairs of the period of my service in Government.

November 3

Hot—85–86 degrees.

Annelise and I drove down and walked for an hour, in late morning, along the river-bank at Haynes Point—I muttering inwardly to myself, in a mixture of anger and despair, over the experience of living in what seemed to me a sort of foreign city, a sort of super Dar-es-Salaam, endowed with a great library, art galleries, and a Kennedy Center, where, once again, a minority of white people was rather sullenly tolerated, while it paid most of the bills.

November 5

In the evening I went to Grace's for supper, after which she took me to a performance at Lincoln Center by the Joffrey City Center Ballet—all fantastically good, I thought. Perhaps Americans, this incoherent people, most of whom are incapable of speaking a clear and grammatical sentence, are destined to find their métier in the ballet.

November 9

Dinner, in the evening, at Joe Alsops.[27] Also there: Joan Braden,[28] who had been having a bad day and spilt her wine, and whom I loved for her reaction to all this; also—Lillian Hellman,[29] whom I liked more, now that we are both older, than I ever did before. She was staying with Joe. The latter was sad and subdued, plans to sell his beautiful house, which seems a great shame.

December 10

Phone call, in early afternoon, from a Miss Chase, at TIME, wanting to know whether I would be disposed to contribute a letter on *détente*. Put

26. The historian John Lewis Gaddis, then of Ohio University, would in 1981 become Kennan's authorized biographer.

27. Joseph Alsop, the newspaper columnist, was married to the former Mary Patten.

28. Joan Braden was a Washington hostess and State Department official.

29. Lillian Hellman, an American playwright, had visited the Moscow embassy during World War II when Kennan was there.

her off. Then phoned to Larry Eagleburger, in the office of Secretary of State, explaining the situation and asking whether the Secretary[30] would like to see the remarks I was going to make tomorrow & to give me advice on their possible publication. The Secretary, it seemed, had left that morning for Brussels, but I was asked to bring the paper over to the Department; they would wire it to him & get his comments. I therefore dropped it off at the Department on my way home. . . .

On return to the hotel, bitter argument with Annelise about the farm, I wanting to put the house on ice, she preferring to sell the whole place. Steadily, as age advances, I feel the choices narrowing around me, and the troubles growing.

December 12

Received call from Larry Eagleburger, who said the Secretary found the speech superb, and left it to me what I wanted to do with it. He appreciated the support.

30. Secretary of State Kissinger.

1975

Kennan, who had now reached his seventies, mused increasingly about what he imagined was a not far-off death. Breaking from his decade-long pattern of confining the diary largely to a calendar daybook, he began also using a notebook that could accommodate longer entries. He believed his detailed explanations of this and that would clarify his own thinking—and that of his posthumous readers. He spent much of the year in Vienna, Helsinki, and other European capitals doing archival research.

Despite his prescience on other matters, Kennan failed to see the long-range significance of the Helsinki Accords signed on July 31, 1975, by the United States and the European nations. In return for formal Western acceptance of post–World War II boundaries, the Soviets acknowledged "the universal significance of human rights." Kennan dismissed the agreement as "a lot of nonsense."[31] *By the 1980s, however, the human rights proviso had developed into a wedge for toppling communist rule in Eastern Europe.*

As in other years, Kennan sailed Norwegian waters aboard his beloved Northwind. *On the water Captain Kennan allowed himself respite from work. Strumming his guitar, he sang such ditties as*

> *Oh mistress Mary, we do believe,*
> *That without sin thou didst conceive;*
> *Oh mistress Mary, still believing,*
> *Teach us to sin without conceiving.*[32]

---

31. John Lewis Gaddis, *George F. Kennan: An American Life* (New York: Penguin Press, 2011), 624.
32. Ibid., 587.

Princeton, January 1

This empty journal was purchased on the last day of 1974 in the belief that if I have anything of real significance to say, not about the details of my comings and goings, but rather about the aspect which the world about me assumes in my eyes, then it is high time, with my 72nd year advancing upon me, that I began to say it.

It will not be easy to find time to write in this journal: I have so much other writing that I have to do, for one reason or another. There is a great lack of time and there is such a thing as writer's cramp. Yet just at this time, when other undertakings seem fleeting and unreal, when not much more is to be achieved or gained from life, when our world dissolves around us, when the end of our civilization seems for the first time scarcely avoidable and probably imminent, and when the new year promises little else for me personally than great waves of trouble and sadness, in these circumstances, surely, an occasional hour of intimate reflection will be no less useful, or have no smaller chances of usefulness, than anything else I might be doing. And there is so little time left in which the real "me," as distinct from the mind alone or the various things I seem to mean to other people, can be expressed.

These words are being written, on New Year's Day, in the bitterly cold tower. I have lit the stove, but it has not yet warmed things up.

Washington, January 8

Attended this afternoon at the Washington Cathedral the memorial service for Walter Lippmann and sat there under the great arches thinking what were, no doubt, highly egoistic and improper, but very human thoughts. For while I had great respect for Lippmann, despite his far smaller regard for me, and would gladly and sincerely have joined in the tributes to him that were read by several of my friends from the pulpit, and while I quite genuinely do not begrudge of him even the smallest part of this posthumous fame, the many things said on this occasion made it impossible for me not to think of myself and of my failure, as great as his success, to make any mark upon the governing establishment of this country. Trying to confront myself with reasonable humility and objectivity, and even in the anguished consciousness of many faults, I am confident that I have had an education broader if less deep than his, a mind no less powerful, a stylistic ability fully as great, and a power of insight into public affairs less practical, less adjusted to the contemporary scene, less immediately useful, but bolder, more penetrating, and more prophetic than his. I have been, in any case, one of the few people who could face him on equal terms on his chosen ground. Yet what I have had to say, while it has fallen on millions of receptive ears in foreign countries and among much of the youth of our own and with individual older figures such as Learned Hand,[33] has fallen in Washington only on deaf ones, and its effect on the public life of this country is undetectable.

Seldom, in these last two or three years, have I even bothered to make the effort to speak publicly on current problems, and when I have, it has been primarily only to make the record, although there was always the sneaking hope that someone might be influenced. Now, I think, I should abandon the effort completely and try to produce one outstanding work of history. Will it make any difference, after all, several decades hence, whether what I wrote about, in this declining, post-Napoleonic world, was my own dreary time or the period of the 1880's?

Washington, January 28

To the State Department for a quiet & pleasant (except for my dreadful head) lunch *à deux* with Henry Kissinger, with whom I talked partly about the sad situation in our foreign policy but partly, also, about Bismarck.

Miami, February 16

First day of the conference.[34] Interesting to see my old colleagues:

Loy Henderson:[35] Handsome, dignified and serene in his old age, quite impressive, in fact. . . .

Durby:[36] Warm, generous, a good friend & comrade, as always, but only semi-coherent, & locked into views that are more 40-year old emotional states than rational opinions;

Henry Shapiro:[37] Thoughtful, serious, the most impressive in depth of his understanding of Soviet-American relations.

Freddy Barghoorn:[38] Much matured, thoughtful, making somewhat hard sledding of it, as usual, but honest, serious, and persistent.

33. Learned Hand was a highly respected judge and judicial theorist.

34. A conference of veterans of the U.S. embassy in Moscow.

35. Loy W. Henderson, a career State Department official, had been senior to Kennan in the Moscow embassy in the 1930s.

36. Elbridge "Durby" Durbrow was a friend of Kennan's from their days in the Moscow embassy in the 1930s. Durbrow was one of the State Department officials who spurred Kennan to write the "long telegram."

37. Henry Shapiro was a longtime United Press International correspondent in Moscow.

38. Frederick Barghoorn had been an official in the press section of the embassy in Moscow in the 1940s.

Vienna, April 24

Vienna looks awfully good to me, these days: the healthiest, most normal, least morbid, most natural, & enjoyable of the great cities of this age. I read very little of the newspapers. They are full, when I do read them, of the collapse of our position in Indo-China, and these impressions join those with which I recently came away from our country, which amounted to an overwhelming sense of the failures of our political system and indeed of our civilization generally.[39] I feel detached from this—I have done what little I could, & it is clear that however I might exert myself, I could do very little more. Write? I *have* written. Write more about domestic affairs, where the real trouble lies? How can you write about domestic affairs when one of the very greatest of the problems is the deterioration of life in the great cities and when one of the major components of the problem this presents is the Negro problem, which is taboo?

Bonn, May 12

On the television was the old movie *South Pacific*, dubbed in German, the regular old American movie. I watched a few moments of it. It seemed like a relic from a civilization separated by centuries from this present age: these fresh, boyish images of American sailors, the harmless inanities of the plot, the heroine's belief in the happy future. All the naivety and innocence and gaiety of the spirit: silly and superficial—yes; inadequate to the test of reality?—yes; and yet . . . and yet. Seeing that, and thinking of today, I found myself suddenly obliged, to my own amazement and amusement, to repress tears. I was, after all, once an American; and if I cannot say, with Oppenheimer: "Dammit, I happen to love this country," I can say that I loved, and love in memory, something of what the country once was. And I supposed that even my present despair is, in a sense, a purely American despair, such as no one other than an American could feel, but then, only an American of *my* generation—the young will never know it.

Kristiansand, June 12

The Norwegians, outwardly so simple, are not really that way at all, and their outlooks reveal some deformations that are positively weird. I

39. The North Vietnamese army, which had remained in South Vietnam after the war ended in 1973, was advancing. The South Vietnamese government would fall on April 30, leading to the reunification of Vietnam.

was particularly struck this time with the anxious, fussy egalitarianism that seems to pervade political thought and to prevail in governmental practice. How is one to explain it? Norwegian society comes closer than any other I know, closer even than the regular "Communist" societies, to the Marxist ideal of the classless society. A few people, very few, have some money and invest it, normally in shipping, but their style of life scarcely varies from that of all the others. I look in vain in the Kristiansand area for a single example of conspicuous affluence. Whence, then, this compulsive preoccupation with questions of relative privilege and prosperity?—this frantic determination to put down and punish an almost non-existent upper class?

Obviously, there is more here than meets the eye. There is also more than one answer, for this is the point where the pseudo-Marxism of the young intelligentsia meets with the religious fundamentalism and provincialism of the rural and small-town elements, particularly along the West Coast. I think I sense, on the part of these latter, a certain cultural jealousy and feeling of inferiority before the relatively cosmopolitan Oslo, an inability to endure the thought that the country should contain others who are better bred, better educated, more discriminating, more independent in taste and habit, more sure of themselves, less vulnerable to the pressure of mass standards in outlook and behavior. . . .

With the young intelligentsia, things are more complicated still. There seems to be a real and burning resentment of Norwegian society as it is, an insistence on seeing it as the ally and instrument of sinister, semi-visible outside forces: imperialism, colonialism, capitalist monopolies, multinational corporations, C.I.A., what you will. Along with this goes an extravagant idealization of the under-developed world, based on the curious syndrome: poverty = virtue, affluence = wickedness. In this last, too, the young Marxists find common ground with the religious fundamentalists, for the missionaries are strong among the latter, and the image of the African tribesman as the noble victim of Western imperialism and accordingly as a fit object of Christian charity is part of their stock in trade. That the present prosperity of Scandinavian civilization might have had something to do with moderate humans and responsible self-government, with industrious habits, with individual self-respect and independence and initiative, and with high levels of integrity in the approach to work, seems never to have entered their heads: they can see this prosperity only as a proof of guilt.

This sort of intellectual primitivism, along with the sweeping urbanization and industrialization of the country, the total surrender to the automobile, the turning-of-the-back on the sea, the failure to learn from the mistakes of the major highly-developed countries and the willingness to ape them in their worst errors—all this is causing me gradually to lose interest in Norway. . . . It simply saddens me, because I have loved the country in a way, and have felt that here, with the magnificent natural setting and the small, hardy population, there was a chance, if there was anywhere, to avoid the worst mistakes of over-development, to retain a healthy relationship between man and Nature, and to preserve the qualities of hardiness, freshness, modesty, and simplicity in people themselves.

[Kennan played no role in the Helsinki talks that concluded in July.]

Helsinki, July

The Foreign Minister entertained me, as guest of honor, at a luncheon at the governmental palace, and on the day after that, our ambassador did the same at his embassy. On each occasion I felt myself transported back, over the years, into the once-familiar world of diplomacy, and I didn't like it. I knew it all. I had had it. I respected the people who were doing it. I could see what was interesting in it. But it was like returning to an old and complex love-affair, now long in the past: no more, thank you, for me. . . .

Aside from the above, my four days in Helsinki were spent in the new library to which the Finns have now transferred their extraordinary collection of XIX century Russian publications. . . . Once immersed in the fine print of these volumes, I am transported into an entirely different world, the world in which I have lived as a historian for some four years—a world as real to me now, in some ways more so, than the modern world that now lies around me. It was only 90 years ago that it existed. A few people now among us were even alive then, albeit as children. To the people of that time the events recorded in these columns, not to mention their own personal experiences, seemed no less momentous than do, to us, the events we witness today. Yet all of this has now faded into the shadows. Empires have disappeared. Names which to the people of that time seemed to reach mountain-high in grandeur and to be assured of a commanding place in history are now known only to a handful of historians like myself. And as my own vicarious XIX-century life runs its course through the perusal of these columns of fine print, it is not that life but the life of our own time that begins to lose actuality.

1976

Kennan's agonizing over how to balance his responsibilities as a scholar, public intellectual, and peace advocate grew sharper in 1976 and in the years that followed. The election of Jimmy Carter in November sparked a backlash that, in turn, spurred Kennan to greater public involvement. Fearing that President Carter would continue the Nixon-Ford-Kissinger policy of detente with the Soviet Union, Paul Nitze—both a friend and rival of Kennan's and his successor on the state State Department's Policy Planning Staff—joined with like-minded hawks to form the Committee on the Present Danger. While Nitze's committee lobbied for increased military spending, especially on nuclear weapons, Kennan grew increasingly alarmed at the prospect of nuclear war.

Princeton, January 17
There is much worry & unhappiness.

Svetlana[40] has again shown signs of emotional stress—impulsiveness, and suspiciousness, and God knows what will come of it.

The newspapers upset me; and I am constantly moved to burst into print on one subject or another, an impulse which I try to suppress in the interests of my work.

I continue to be dissatisfied with myself, not wishing to expose myself to other people, so disliking this "social Kennan," yet knowing that I cannot reform or correct him.

My historical work is my only or almost only solace, the only fully serious & honest thing I do, the thing that no one else is really interested in, the thing that all the remainder of my involvements are in a conspiracy to prevent my doing. But I know that I am fortunate to have it. Many people do not.

40. Svetlana Alliluyeva, Stalin's daughter, whom Kennan had helped adjust to life in the United States.

Washington National Airport, March 13

Things have not improved. Since I last wrote in this journal, 5 weeks ago, I have, in addition to my rather pathetic incidental efforts to write and study history, and other things that escape my memory, done the following:

(1) agreed to write, & written for *Foreign Affairs*, a 13,000 word piece on the history of Soviet-American relations;

(2) attended a meeting in N.Y. of the National Book Award committee;

(3) paid a visit to Washington for conferences with Averell Harriman & others, re my Institute;[41]

(4) spoke for 2–3 hours to a group of 30–40 students at the University;

(5) edited for publication the piece I wrote for Marion Dönhoff (which was privately sent, also, to Henry Kissinger and to Helmut Schmidt);[42]

(6) declined, after some agony, a high-powered appeal to address the Yale-Harvard-Princeton clubs of Washington;

(7) declined, with much less agony, a number of other speaking invitations;

(8) received an award from the Princeton alumni association for service to the nation, and acknowledged it with an unrehearsed statement, delivered to some 1,200 of them—a statement so graceless and stupid that I have been suffering ever since from the recollection of it;

(9) agreed to accept an Honorary Degree on May 8 from Catholic University, in Washington;

(10) agreed, again not without agony, to deliver the National Jefferson Lecture, at the invitation of the National Endowment for the Humanities, in 1977;

(11) agreed, after much uncertainty & hesitation, to write a letter endorsing Senator Frank Church as a candidate for the Presidency and promptly regretted it deeply (however, could hardly bear to refuse);

(12) agreed to go to Cleveland & Chicago, in interests of my Institute, & while in Chicago to address the Chicago Council on Foreign Relations; and, finally,

(13) built & installed, at cost of some hours of physical effort, a new box for the garbage cans—representing, in truth, the only really concrete achievement of these busy weeks.

What does all this mean? It means that, trying to reconcile the writ-

41. Kennan was referring to the Kennan Institute for the study of Russian affairs.

42. Helmut Schmidt was chancellor of West Germany.

ing of history with the playing of the role of a public figure, I am doing neither very well, am being, in fact, quite unsuccessful in the effort to be an historian.

What conclusions are to be drawn from that? . . .

I must finally resolve this dilemma in favor of scholarship, whatever the cost. In a year or two I'll probably be dead or incapacitated anyway, & the public scene will have to get along without me, which it won't have much trouble doing. But perhaps I could contrive in the course of these years to finish my book, & in this way to create something which would, in a minor way, live after me.

Kennedy Airport, New York, May

The West, so far as he could see, was bent on its own destruction, caring little that this probably meant the destruction of civilization per se. The senseless multiplication and proliferation of nuclear weaponry, the obvious addiction of the American political establishment to the cultivation of a Cold War image of the Soviet Union, the equally incurable conviction of the Western Europeans that the Russians were dying to attack them—a conviction bound, if long enough cultivated and acted upon, to make the fancied danger into a real one, the hopeless loss by the Americans of all independence of policy with relation to the Levant, afraid as they were to stand up to the Arabs because of their unwillingness to get along without Arab oil, and their similar unwillingness to stand up to the Israelis for fear of offending the Zionist lobby at home, the equally hopeless inability of the American political establishment to free itself from the pressures of the military-industrial complex, the unwillingness of the entire Western community to do anything serious in the way of putting an end to the pollution of the world oceans—these, and comparable phenomena, were obviously the marks of a doomed civilization, the demise of which, he was obliged to expect, would probably engulf his own children, if not himself.

[The Kennans mixed vacation travel with his participation in a scholarly conference.]

Copenhagen, June 7

His legs bothered him more than ever before. He felt himself moving with the characteristic stiffness of age, and began, for the first time, to wonder whether it would be given to him even to finish the work he had in hand, not to mention taking up anything new. And he thought of the lines from John Donne:

> On a huge hill,
> Cragged and steep, Truth stands, and he that will
> Reach her, about must, and about must go;
> And what the hill's suddenness resists, win so;
> Yet strive so, that before age, death's twilight,
> Thy Soule rest, for none can work in that night.[43]

Princeton, August 29

Knowing that tomorrow I would have to talk with the Secretary of State, I went out early, bought the Sunday *New York Times* and read it dutifully, in a largely vain effort to inform myself of what was going on in the world.

August 30

To Washington for lunch with Henry Kissinger. Found him, not unnaturally, somewhat dispirited, believing that he had failed in his effort to instill into American diplomacy some depth of concept and some subtlety of technique. We found ourselves very extensively in agreement in the matters we discussed—outstandingly, the military mind and its influence on policy, and the affairs of Southern Africa. He is a wise, learned, and agreeable man to talk to, with enormous experience. His memoirs, when he leaves office, will be, by way of rare exception, worth the enormous price the publishers will offer for them.

[The Kennans toured through Eastern Europe.]

Dubrovnik, Yugoslavia, October 8

The debate over foreign policy between Mr. Ford[44] & Mr. Carter. My heart sank, heavily, as I apprehended, from this sparing Serbo-Croatian source, the dreadful fumbling provincialism and electoral frivolity of both men: the fact that Mr. Ford did not know the difference between Yugoslavia, Poland, and Rumania—the fact that Mr. Carter was prepared

43. This poem would inspire the title for Kennan's book *Around the Cragged Hill: A Personal and Political Philosophy*, published in 1993 by W. W. Norton.

44. President Gerald R. Ford assumed office in August 1974 after President Nixon resigned because of the Watergate scandal.

to give an unlimited blank check to the Israelis to dispose of American resources at their will, and that both men were quite prepared to sacrifice our relations with the Soviet Union in order to play up to ethnic minorities among the voters who have at heart all manner of things other than the interests of this country and of world peace; and on top of all this, the fact that neither candidate was willing to take on in any serious way the military-industrial complex.

Rumania, October 20

This vogue of group tourism, in which I myself was for the moment a participant, and which was rapidly crowding out every possibility of civilized individual travel, seemed to me to represent, like the German turnpikes and so many other things, a posthumous triumph of the late Adolf Hitler, who was the great pioneer of this sort of herding about of idle, bored people under the banner of "*Kraft durch Freude* [Strength through Joy]."

Yalta, October 22

Our first point of call was the great palace at Livadia, where we were to see the "Museum of the Crimea Conference."[45] The fine gardens had been well tended and preserved (if only Russian communists, one reflects, cared as much about people as they do about plants), and it was a pleasure to walk through a part of them, despite the cold and the dampness. But the visit to the "museum" consisted only of a shuffling group-walk through the vestibule, with its ghastly painting of all these well-remembered characters associated with the Conference (including a Chip Bohlen, who, I thought, looked more like me; I wondered whether they had confused us), then through the celebrated ballroom, with the large table still standing in the middle of it, then through the now empty wing where the failing FDR had slept. The guide's patter and the surrounding placards still reflected the official Soviet view on that futile and fumbling gathering—the hearty reassuring vision of European and world affairs being soundly reconstructed by the three great statesmen, under the wise and benevolent leadership of Stalin and Molotov.

But I, the while, knowing already all that I wanted to know about the Yalta Conference, kept returning to the image of the coming out ball in

45. At the Yalta summit, Franklin D. Roosevelt, Winston S. Churchill, and Joseph Stalin met from February 4 to February 11, 1945.

May 1913 of the eldest daughter of the last Tsar, the Grand Duchess Olga, held in this same room. I could see it in retrospect. The great French windows thrown open to the view of the sea, the smell of the roses, the brilliance of the candles and the uniforms, the many jewels, and the flowers in the doomed girl's hair, put up for the first time in honor of the occasion. (Fifteen years later she would be shot, with the rest of the family, in the cellar in Ekaterinburg, in the Urals). . . .

On the way back to the ship, the bus descended the narrow street where Chekhov's house still stands. We were able to glimpse, in the gathering dusk and the dripping foliage only a roof and, briefly, a wet stucco façade. I was grateful now for the memory of the visit I had paid to the place 39 years ago, when Chekhov's devoted sister had taken me through the house herself and talked with me about her brother's life.

Mt. Athos, Greece, October 30

We were taken up to see the Greek monastery, Vatopedi. A weird, eerie sight it was, too—this great, nearly deserted place where 800 monks had once lived, and now there were 30, of whom we saw two. I thought of what the life must be: the claustrophobia, the emotional abnormality, the getting-on-each-other's-nerves, the gossip, the snooping, the intrigues; and I thought of the monstrous stillness of the nights in the deserted buildings and courtyards, the terse awareness of the slightest strange sound, and at times, the furtive nocturnal doings of God knows what.

1977

Kennan remained sharply critical of modern industrial society and mourned the passing of what he imagined as an ethnically homogeneous United States. He returned to this critique whether traveling to the Air Force Academy in Colorado, where he gave a talk, or returning from Paris.

Colorado Springs, February 12

The trashy, impermanent habitation of the American West—trailer camps, condominiums, commercial enterprises—all strewn about, with wide expanses of useless, barren prairie between them, and everywhere, of course, the roads, these 4-lane arteries of dark asphalt, stretching endlessly across the emptiness, traffic lights where they cross, in the middle of nowhere—and everywhere the scurrying beetles of cars, whirring drearily along, turning distance into time. Strange people, these Americans: they seek out these places, not really to live but to await death, justifying themselves by the fact that the sun shines and that life is easy—a sort of trancelike unreal state of existence, drugged by the sedatives of advertising, TV, and the wheel of the automobile—all enjoyments vicarious. . . .

I studied the faces of the cadets, where I could see them. Westerners, for the most part (I suppose), from non-wealthy families, they reminded me of the St. Johns cadets of 60 years ago.[46] The Commandant claimed that many of them did outstanding academic work, and occasionally one did indeed see a promising face, but not very often. They were the sons and products of the great American melting pot, in which so little is left of the original pioneer population, although it still shows the fading imprint, linguistic and cultural, of that population on the surface of its life. A lost people, we WASPs, living out our lives, like displaced

46. As a boy Kennan was a St. Johns cadet.

people, in a cultural diaspora, unrelieved even by any consciousness of the existence, albeit far away, of a lost homeland. Our homeland, raped and destroyed by modernity, no longer has any meaning geographically; it has meaning only in time, and has sunk, with scarcely a trace, into history. . . .

People, I am moved to reflect, react more favorably to me as a person than they do to my thoughts. But even then, this view of my person is not one that inclines them even to think of me as a person to whom public responsibility might be given. And perhaps they are instinctively right in rejecting such an association.

[Kennan spent "three miserable (for physical reasons) weeks in Paris"[47] doing research.]

En route, March 21

1. I love my country or at least a great deal of it, but I consider its political system and the intellectual-philosophic level of its political establishment to be, in combination, inadequate to the demands of the present age, and have little hope for it.

2. The country is not all decadent, but the sound stock of it, composed mostly of older people, is so eaten into by decadence that it is doubtful whether it can be saved.

3. Modern urban-industrial man is given to the raping of anything and everything natural on which he can fasten his talons. He rapes the sea; he rapes the soil; he rapes the natural resources of the earth. He rapes the atmosphere. He rapes the future of his own civilization. Instead of living off nature's surplus, which he ought to do, he lives off its substance. He would not need to do this were he less numerous, and were he content to live a more simple life. But he is prepared neither to reduce his numbers nor to lead a simpler and more healthful life. So he goes on destroying his own environment, like a vast horde of locusts. And he must be expected, persisting blindly as he does in this depraved process, to put an end to his own existence within the next century. The years 2000 to 2050 should witness, in fact, the end of the great Western civilization. The Chinese, more prudent and less spoiled, no less given to over-population but prepared to be more ruthless in the control of its effects, may inherit the ruins.

47. Kennan diary, March 30, 1977.

4. I am invited to go out to Aspen, Colorado,[48] and talk with many worthy people. I can see no good in the idea. There is nothing to be gained, for me or for others, by the spreading of my own despair. Beyond which, when people get me talking, really talking, I fascinate them but at the same time I kill the conversation, make them uncomfortable, and—above all—hate myself afterwards. I intensely dislike the garrulous-social Kennan: an over-intense, over-responsive figure, who is less than himself, who forgets his age. It is high time, at the age of 73, that he grew up. Until he does, in any case, he should keep to himself and express his thoughts, if expressed they must be, in writing, not orally.

Sussex, England, June 4

It occurred to me today that the industrial revolution contained the genes (the "signals," in modern scientific terminology) of all that we know today: the modern welfare state, the high degree of industrialization & urbanization, decadence, demoralization, decline of educational standards, vulgarization of the process of public communication, undermining of the genetic qualities of the population. All this was there in embryonic form, and not to be avoided, only if rulers had been perceptive enough to adopt certain principles which even today are too far-reaching to be acceptable, among them: that nothing should be done by machine that could conceivably be done, at no more than reasonable cost in effort by human hand with animal help, and perhaps also, that keeping a person alive by medical means was as much of a responsibility as putting him to death.

Randesund, Norway, June 25

What a pity, I think to myself, that these people found oil off their coasts. Not only is it helping them to ruin the North Sea, but this is making it possible for them to postpone for themselves the desirable day of reckoning, when it will have to be recognized that mankind cannot live by the reckless squandering of energy. In the meantime, great damage will have been done.

Not all the beauty, of course, has gone. Night before last, the night of St. John's Day, the shortest night of the year, no complete night at all in fact, we went out to the summer home of friends, in the islands,

48. He was invited to speak at the Aspen Institute, a group that fostered discussion of public issues.

for the traditional celebration. There was . . . the lighting of the great traditional fire, long prepared, wigwam-like, near the water's edge, fires were burning elsewhere on the shores of the little sound, and there was a great coming and going of motor boats. Then back home by motorboat through the narrow passages of Skippergaten, into the wider leads behind it, where the unceasing glow of the northern sky shone across the water and dim quarter-moon competing feebly with it from the other side. . . .

My recent experience in Germany, where I found myself, on less than a day's notice, being helicoptered to the residence of the German prime minister at his invitation, to discuss international problems with him, convinces me that it is idle to think that I can ever escape the expectation of others that I should be consumed with interest for the passing international scene and able to talk usefully and intelligently about it on demand. The occasions when I shall have to do this may be increasingly rare, but they will occur, and they cannot be avoided. Therefore, however little I like it, however little hope I have for doing or saying anything useful, I must continue to give a good portion of my time to following these subjects, with a view never to be talking about them if I can avoid it, but always to be prepared to talk if I cannot avoid it. This, of course, almost precludes any useful sort of work along other lines, for it leaves no possibility for the necessary concentration. But it is my fate.

Sørenhus, July 26

Still in ill-health & dreadfully depressed. It would probably be a wise policy to avoid trying to think anything out, to make any decisions or resolutions when one is in such a state. I must, in any case, recognize that any views I may now come to are apt to be seriously discolored and to have no more than symptomatic value. But I hate to give up, to let go, when all is chaos & uncertainty inside myself. It is hard to face others in this condition.

So here goes:

1. The first thing I must do, it seems to me, is to face up to the fact that my successes & achievements in earlier life are of no importance. Almost no one knows about them. My son-in-law asked yesterday, whether I had had a ghost-writer to write my last book. I said, "no"—and why did he ask this? "Oh," he said, "it's so well written—in such a fine style." This caused me to reflect that the question was not surprising. How was he to know? My daughter, his wife, had no idea what I had done.

Not only can one not rest on laurels; they lose their meaning. Time passes; memories fade; fame, even modest fame, is fleeting. If one lives long enough, one's achievements are subject to the same oblivion as one's failures & mistakes.

All right: it is objectively true as a matter of ascertainable historical fact that I, once upon a time, had such & such Pulitzer prizes & other awards and honors, that my voice on the radio was once listened to by millions of people, that I had unparalleled lecture successes, that I had an impact, as no other, on policy towards Russia. These things are true, but meaningless. As realities of our time they have no existence. I am an old codger, of whom, occasionally, some one might say: "I was told that he wrote some books at one time about history & politics."

Very well, accept it. These things never happened. Being non-existent, they cannot be leaned on. You (myself) are what you are today, not what you were. All that was a dream.

2. There is no further use in writing anything of a political nature (perhaps of any nature) for the American market, not because the public is unreceptive if something is brought to its attention, but because the low-level of the reviewing stands like a barrier between the public and the author. It is also clear that I, being now largely unknown, have no voice with the government. There is therefore no use in talking or writing publicly.

3. Nevertheless, I must continue and even intensify the effort to keep myself informed in the field of foreign policy. This is because I cannot shake the image that has been formed of me among my friends at home and among people in public life in Europe. They expect me to be interested in this subject and informed about it. . . .

4. I should, in other words, resist being provoked into statements on public questions, but prepared to acquit myself creditably when the resistance is not successful. This, of course, will not be easy: to force one's self to take an interest in a subject in which one is not really interested, in which in fact one sees no element of hope, and where one can make no useful contribution, and this, solely as a matter of self-respect.

August 10

More and more it is borne in upon me how little I have in common with, how little I belong to, this polyglot accumulation of people in the meridial part of North America. My own family's passage there was longer than most, nearly two hundred years when I was born but still it was brief, fleeting, and remote from the general development of the country. Only the Nature, as I look back on it, was mine, as much as it was anybody's. The hot nights of summer in the Middle West of my boyhood, the crickets singing in the grass, the mystery of the great distances thrusting forth in every direction: these were something only an American child of that part of the country could know. They were in his blood. But the human environment of that time and place? Yes, traces of it remain here and there, but they are powerless, like myself—overwhelmed by the totally strange and even hostile life that has grown up around them.

Well, I think to myself: I am quits with this largely foreign country known as the U.S.A. I have written my book.[49] I have offered it what I had. The country didn't need the book or want it or understand it. O.K. It was the best I could do, the product of a lifetime's experience. What is failure? What is success? Who knows?

[Kennan went to Germany to visit friends and to participate in a meeting of Pour le Mérite, a German society that honored extraordinary achievement in the arts and sciences.]

Schloss Crottorf, October 17

This afternoon we were taken to see a former convent, Weinhausen, not far from Celle. It turned out to be a rare experience. It was late afternoon when we arrived. The shadows were already beginning to fall. We were met outside by the most senior of the so-called *Stiftdamen*, a handful of elderly Protestant women who now have custody of the place. She was a strange figure: 87 years of age, tall, bent, wearing a fur coat and a grey wig. While she spoke, the right arm moved up and down in a certain chopping gesture. She proceeded to escort us through the convent: the marvelous church, of which every inch of the walls and ceilings were painted, the galleries, the nuns, dormitory, the cold, dark corridors with heavy board floors. And never have I been more usefully and enjoyably guided, because the old lady loved every nook and cranny, every painting, every sculpture of the place, and wanted nothing more than that we should love and enjoy it with her. In this enthusiasm the ages fell away, as did the religious differences. She identified completely with the little nuns of those earlier centuries. "We," she said, "did this and did that." Her intense joy in the painted and sculpted figures was genuine to the point of a total unselfconsciousness and spontaneity, and the implicit

49. *The Cloud of Danger: Current Realities of American Foreign Policy* (1977).

faith was so unreserved that I turned, at one point, to a companion, and said: "Die kommt in Himmel." (She will go to heaven.) . . .

I came away trying to picture to myself what life must have been like for the nuns (whose average life-expectancy appears to have been only 24 years) in these cold and, for half the year, dark premises, suffering by flickering candle-light the agonizing mysteries of illness and death, compelled to try to replace all normal emotional, feminine demands by the imagined companionship of the absent Bridegroom, whose living form would never be seen, and whose living touch never felt.

Paris, October 29

I worked for a day or two at the Bibliothèque nationale, but had great difficulty with my eyes, and had finally to give it up. . . . A few days earlier I was suddenly overtaken by a strange sense of weakness, bewilderment, and momentary loss of the power of concentration, had to go home & lie down. It passed off by the end of the day, but was disturbing, because I could think of no explanation for it other than a slight stroke.

Princeton, December 14

These last two days have been agitated by the fact that on Monday, Mac Bundy[50] phoned me to say that the Ford Foundation was interested in the suggestion I had made in my Washington speech for a series of briefing sessions on the nature and situation of the Soviet leadership, and would be disposed to help with the realization of such a project.

I phoned Fred Starr,[51] and we agreed that we might advance a proposal for a joint program of the Council on Foreign Relations and the Kennan Institute along this line. . . . I took occasion to speak to the Director, here, about it, and to sound him out on the question of the Institute's acting as host to a very small and quiet preliminary conference, some time next week. His reaction was enthusiastic; he wanted, in fact, the Institute for Advanced Study to be host to the series.

December 15

Worked all day at home, partly on papers, partly on building sawhorses for Christopher.

50. McGeorge Bundy, a former national security advisor in the Kennedy and Johnson administrations, was president of the Ford Foundation.

51. S. Frederick Starr is a historian of Russia who helped organize the Kennan Institute for Russian studies.

1978

Kennan was becoming increasingly involved in the national debate over whether Washington should give first priority to a nuclear arms buildup or to negotiations with Moscow to reduce such weapons. In May, the New York Times Magazine *pitted Kennan against Nitze in a cover story about President Carter's options in dealing with Soviet leader Leonid Brezhnev. In sharp contrast to Nitze, Kennan urged talks to reduce dangerous armaments. He challenged the assumption that Washington was necessarily in the right and Moscow in the wrong. He jabbed at hardliners who seemed to "have a need for the externalization of evil. They have the need to think that there is, somewhere, an enemy boundlessly evil, because this makes them feel boundlessly good."[52] Despite his opposition to Nitze, Kennan tried to keep lines of communication open.*

Princeton, January 3

Talked by phone with Fred Starr. . . . We agreed that I should try to get into touch with Paul Nitze to see how he would react to the suggestion that he should attend some sessions of the sort I had in mind. Tried to phone him but he was in Aspen.

January 16

I live, for the moment, primarily for the completion of the book I have in hand, not that it is much of a book, but it is the fruit of six or seven years of work, at least in my spare time, and I would not like to see it wasted for lack of completion.[53] (When it is completed, I would like to turn, as I claimed last year to do, to aesthetic-literary pursuits. But will I be able to? The demands of friends, family, & people interested in the affairs of the

52. Nicholas Thompson, *The Hawk and the Dove: Paul Nitze, George Kennan, and the History of the Cold War* (New York: Henry Holt, 2009), 270–71.

53. *The Decline of Bismarck's European Order: Franco-Russian Relations, 1875–1890* (1979).

day, will consume any amount of spare time I may have—they would in fact consume the time of ten persons like myself. To claw out a bit of the time for anything worthwhile will continue to be a struggle.)

February 5

It was very cold, damply cold. The air was still, and there was a thin, wintry haze (a skimmed-milk haze, I thought to myself) through which the sun shone, bleakly, without warmth. In the woods, the snow crest was hard and not slippery. Occasionally, there were the tracks of small paws, but no sign of life. The weatherman had predicted snow, and the forest, silent and patient, was waiting for it.[54]

I hid my logs, all but one, behind some trees where I hoped people on the lane would not see them, picked up my tools & saw-back & one symbolic log, and made my way back to the road, not along the lane but across the field, stumbling every two or three steps because the thin icy crust would break and the foot would go through to the uneven, tightly-frozen turf, beneath.

[Kennan traveled to California to raise money for the Kennan Institute for Russian studies and to visit Grace.]

April 24

I sit, in the plane, next to an oriental woman, with a sweet, well-behaved child. I am waited on, or at least offered things, by one colored girl and two or three white ones. I remember that I am to visit, day after tomorrow, the Los Angeles area, where the majority of the births are to people of Latin origin, and where people of British origin, from whose forefathers the constitutional structure and political ideals of the early America once emerged, are not only a dwindling but a disintegrating minority. They are of course lost, as a cultural element and as a source of tradition and identity, but they are no more lost, in this sense, than anyone else. The Latin, Levantine, African, and Oriental elements that now make up so large a part of this population: they, too, are destined, for the most part, to lose their character, their traditions, their unique coloration, and to melt into a vast polyglot mass, devoid of all three things: a sea of helpless, colorless humanity, as barren of originality as it is of nationality, as uninteresting as it is unoriginal—one huge pool

54. The blizzard of 1978 was about to begin.

of indistinguishable mediocracy and drabness. Exceptions may be only the Jews and the Chinese, who tend to avoid intermarriage, and, for a time, the Negroes as well. Could this mean that these three minorities are destined to subjugate and dominate all as an uneasy but unavoidable triumvirate the rest of society—the Chinese by their combination of intelligence, ruthlessness, and ant-like industriousness; the Jews by their sheer determination to survive as a culture; the Negroes by their ineradicable bitterness and hatred of the whites?

. . . On the movie screen, as I write this, a "short" is in progress, a documentary entitled: "The Arabs are Coming." A misleading title, this. Very few of them will come. They will give orders to us—Chinese, Jews and Negroes included—from afar, in all matters that seriously affect their interests, and we will shut our big mouths and meekly obey, because we are the victims of an addiction (the automobile), and they are the people who control the means by which that addiction can be satisfied. They will not come to us. They will merely own us, and prescribe the limits within which our lives are permitted to operate.

San Francisco, April 25

Still ailing, I lay in bed all afternoon, reading Olga Carlisle[55] on the ordeal she and her husband suffered through their efforts to help Aleksandr Solzhenitsyn publish *The First Circle* and the *The Gulag Archipelago* in this country.

Grace gave a dinner for us in the evening. Mrs. Carlisle was among the guests. I sat next to her, and I told her that I had read her book and that I doubted there was anyone in the world who could have read it with more understanding. But what impossible people these Russians are to judge by Solzhenitsyn's: courage, talent, love of humanity in the mass, fortitude, and heroism, all combined with a wholly inexcusable impracticability, ideological self-righteousness, no sense of fairness or tolerance, and a total heartlessness towards those who do not agree with them and even towards those who try to help them but fail, for any reason, to meet their wholly impractical expectations.

[The Kennans were in Europe for much of the summer.]

55. Olga Andreyev Carlisle, who had been born into a Russian literary family, worked with her husband, Henry Carlisle, to translate Solzhenitsyn's works.

En Route from Copenhagen, July 31

Regarding de Tocqueville's memoirs, what did I gain from it, beyond the intense gratification of exposure to the workings of this extraordinarily schooled, perceptive and disciplined mind? Hard to say. The confirmation, of course, of many of my own views: a vivid demonstration of the abundant ironies that mark all parliamentary politics, the realization that it is not only in America that democracy conducts foreign policy for domestic-political reasons. The recognition, too, that while democracy may be, in a country which lives in relative isolation, the least invidious of possible regimes, it is also, even at its best, a highly incompetent one, incapable of seeing more than a very short distance into the future, incapable of perceiving the longer trends of development and allowing for them, bound to lead in the end both to foreign-political helplessness and to financial demoralization, the principal manifestation of which is normally inflation and all its attendant evils.

Taking off from these impressions of Tocqueville, I must say that, with all due effort to avoid exaggerated pessimism and over-dramatization, I can see no salvation for the U.S. either in its external relations nor in the development of its life internally. On the external scene the prospects are simply appalling: an hysterical mishandling of relations with the Soviet Union, a growing dependence on the Arabs & the other OPEC countries for the sources of our energy consumption, situations in at least three regions in other continents where developments are wholly outside our own control or effective influence but where they could easily lead at any time to our own military involvement, a fateful tie to the Israelis from which we have, in contradistinction to the Israelis, everything to lose and nothing to gain, and participation in a mad orgy of exportation of arms to smaller nations, from which no good can conceivably come. But internally, things are not much better: uncontrollable inflation, failure in the cities, declining educational standards, rising cynicism with relation to the federal government; these are not the signs of an effective political system.

What implications do these insights have for my own conduct in relation to other people when I get home this time? It is clear that these things cannot be said publicly. They would arouse only anger, not understanding. Yet people look to me for stimulus, for ideas, for guidance. What to do?

Ideally, the emphasis should be placed in whatever I say on the positive rather than the negative: on what to do, not on what not to do, not on how bad a government we have, but on how to improve it.

In attempting to meet this requirement one confronts at once several dangers and complexities. First, there is the necessity of distinguishing between policies and institutions. There is no use talking about better policies when the system is such that better ones would not be conceivable or comprehensible to those who make policy.

So one turns to the institutions. But here, one is reminded first of all of Tocqueville's admonition that institutions have only a limited importance: that of greater significance are the *manières* or the *moeurs* of a people. True. And about the habits and customs of the American public there is, in the short term, little to be done.

But institutions have *some* importance, and perhaps greater today than in Tocqueville's time, because he was not confronted with one of America's greatest problems: that of bigness, demographic and bureaucratic bigness.

[As someone who prized organic connections in many aspects of life, Kennan had long favored the particular over the general, the regional over the national, and the traditional over the modern.]

In this respect, I *have* something to say, something with which, actually, Tocqueville would presumably sympathize (for he disliked unnecessary centralization), and that is the need for a regionalization—for a break-up, if you will, of the U.S. into regional governments. This, I have tried before to say, with negligible success. For I despair of useful reform of the system at the federal level.

But suppose this regionalization was achieved? How would I have the system of the individual regional unit differ from the sort of federal or state government we have today? And particularly in the face of those very *moeurs*, those customs and habits of thought, to which Tocqueville referred? For surely there is no use recommending institutions to which people are wholly unaccustomed, and for which they would have no understanding. Particularly would this be useless if these changes were of a constitutional nature and required some sort of formal popular acceptance. And I am still just enough of an American to have to reject any suggestion that institutions should be imposed upon people without their consent, even if those institutions should be, theoretically, superior to anything they might conceivably have chosen.

Aspen Institute, Colorado, August 27

I read large parts of Reinhold Niebuhr's *The Children of Light and the Children of Darkness* and was greatly impressed with it: not with all its conclusions, but with its recognition of the flawed nature of all human aspirations and behavior.[56] To my mind, Niebuhr was undoubtedly the greatest moral philosopher of our age, and perhaps of several generations into the past.

I attended a fine lecture by Adam Yarmolinsky[57] on the SALT talks and the other phases of negotiation with the Soviet Union over problems of armament and disarmament: lucid, balanced and enlightened. . . . But I cannot believe that it will be enough, that one calm and sensible man can prevail against the clouds of emotionalism and irrational belligerence that are now being spewed out by the various hardliners. . . .

Curious, that a nation should have permitted its national ideals to have been so extensively shaped, as has been done through the popular literature and the movie industry of this country, by the idealized image of this rough-and-ready, essentially anarchic population—the cowboy image of the silent, nature-hardened, rough-hewn man, romantically independent, courteous to women like a knight of the middle ages, but contemptuous of organized social authority and a law unto himself in his crude but gallant concepts of right and wrong, ready at any time to take up arms in defense of those concepts, awkwardly courteous to strangers at first encounter, but actually arrogant in his contempt for the soft-skin, Eastern "dude." It is, as I say, around the image of this curious and now largely mythical personality, unintellectual, untouched by serious thought, deriving his ethos from a highly untypical and now almost non-existent form of life, that a good deal of the American image-of-self has been, and is being, formed. Small wonder that it does not suffice for the creation of an effective society out of the polyglot population of a highly urbanized and partially over-populated country of the modern age!

. . . As these days in Aspen draw to an end, I continue to chew over the question of my future. Never, it seems to me, have I known greater uncertainty. To whom can I be most useful? To my own country, certainly not. That has been burned into me. Whatever I might have to say,

56. *The Children of Light and the Children of Darkness: A Vindication of Democracy and a Critique of Its Traditional Defense* (1960).

57. Adam Yarmolinsky was an expert on nuclear weapons and a critic of the Vietnam War who served in the Kennedy, Johnson, and Carter administrations.

the media—ignorant, cynical, ill-motivated, and corrupt—would stand between me and it. And its problems are today beyond curing anyway, by anyone. . . .

Russian studies? To give comfort and support and understanding to a few scholars in the fields of Russian history and literature is all very well. It is perhaps the only *surely* useful thing I could do. But is it enough? And does it not mean wasting other possibilities? The Russia that has fascinated me is gone. The Communists have killed it. The old culture is dead. A new one will have to be created. But that will take time. Meanwhile, there is nothing exciting in the life of the Soviet Union, only demoralization of the masses and the decline of an increasingly stupid regime, with nothing hopeful to replace it. The present dreary bureaucracy may very well hold on for decades, for want of anything to replace it. But it will continue to be a dull time in Russian history, duller than the 1880's and 90's, which, after all, drove people like Chekhov to distraction.

I might, of course, have some influence over Russian policy. This would in any case be easier than having any such influence over the policy of my own country. But *they* are not the problem, today; *we* are. They are not going to attack anyone, and if only our good allies to the east and west of the U.S.S.R. could get over their jitters, hold quietly firm against minor encroachments, and not interfere in Russian internal affairs, they would have nothing to fear. It is the West, not Russia, that finds it hard to live with the present ambivalent relationship.

Still, one can never know. The unexpected happens. An expertise about Russia is still, perhaps, the best Archimedean platform I could find for some sort of ulterior usefulness. And this, perhaps, can be maintained, after a fashion, without excessive strain on one of my age.

[During his trip to the Soviet Union, Kennan, feted by Soviet officials and historians, was for the first time in his life taken to the offices of the Central Committee of the Communist Party. In talking with Russians as well as with U.S. and British embassy officials he shared his mounting worries about the nuclear arms race. He also did some research for his ongoing study of the origins of the Russian-French alliance of 1894. Walking the streets of Moscow and Leningrad, he mused about his long, tangled relationship with Russia.]

Moscow, October 10

Moscow has gained in cold, rectangular grandeur, but has lost in the warm coziness of earlier days. Discussion with Georgy Arbatov.[58] We understand each other's position. The only asymmetry—that he has an official position. I don't.

October 17

To the Embassy, then, for lunch with the Ambassador & Mrs. Toon,[59] now both returned from abroad. Tong, the old faithful servant, was there as usual to greet us, and there we stood in the entrance hall, the three of us the last survivors of an earlier generation of inhabitants of Spaso House, wringing each other's hands & recalling times which few others could remember and fewer still would be able to picture in imagination.

Leningrad, October 20

There was night club entertainment, consisting of shatteringly loud music, a la discothèque, a number of very scantily-clad young ladies who danced, two or three similarly clad young men who performed various athletic feats under the guise of dancing, and some singers, whose voices were drowned out by the incredible din of the magnified instrumental accompaniment. . . .

This spectacle, for some reason, saddened me. I could not decide whether I was more disgusted with the Soviet sponsors of this enterprise for choosing this sort of thing to borrow from us, or with us for providing the example. I was never an enthusiast for the Russian Revolution of November 1917, but since a tremendous amount had been subsequently sacrificed in its name, the least they could do I thought would have been to hold to some of the stern, and in their way impressive, Leninist social and personal ideals. And so I found myself, opponent of the system as I am, sharing the well-known reaction of the Leningrad workers at the time of the Kronstadt mutiny.[60] *Za Chto borolis, tovarishchi*? (For what, comrades, did we struggle?).

58. Georgy Arkadyevich Arbatov was a Soviet political scientist, adviser to officials, and founding director of the USA and Canada Institute.
59. Malcolm and Elizabeth Toon.
60. The Kronstadt mutiny of 1921 was a left-wing rebellion against the economic hardships of Bolshevik rule.

1979

Tumult in Iran and in Afghanistan produced problems that would roil international relations for decades. After the forced departure in January 1979 of the pro-American shah, Iranian students and militants in November stormed the U.S. embassy in Tehran and seized dozens of Americans. The resulting hostage crisis would drag on until January 1981. This trampling on traditional diplomatic immunity infuriated Kennan, who urged a declaration of war on Iran. In December, the Soviets marched troops into Afghanistan in an effort to prop up a Marxist government under attack from Islamic militants. The intervention would become a decade-long quagmire, a Soviet "Vietnam." Détente, and any chance of Senate approval of the SALT II nuclear arms limitation treaty, were now dead. Angry at the Soviets, President Carter initiated retaliatory measures and an arms buildup that his successor, Ronald Reagan, would further accelerate.

Worried about the rising risk of nuclear war, Kennan also edged toward bitterness. He believed that his long-standing recommendations regarding domestic energy conservation and policy in the Middle East might have alleviated these and other crises.

Princeton, January 9

Norwegian ambassador-designate to Moscow Dagfinn Stenseth explained that what particularly worried the Norwegians, when it came to their Soviet neighbors, was the possibility that if things in Europe again became tense and there were a danger of military complications anywhere, the Russians might be moved to make territorial demands on them in northern Norway, as they had on Finland in 1939. I told him that I recognized the seriousness of this anxiety, but that in my opinion the Russians would not be apt to behave that way unless they felt in some way threatened, or felt the integrity and security of their rule to be threatened, within their own orbit. The time when they would be dangerous (and this was something our own hard-liners did not understand) would be not when they were doing well, but when they were doing very badly.

I spent most of Wednesday, as I recall it, at the Mudd Library, going through my own papers. . . . I was stunned to realize the quantity of it: something like 10,000 outgoing letters just for the period 1954 to 1968, about half the span of my non-official productive life, and this is aside from several volumes of diaries and several hundred lectures, articles, book reviews, etc. What to do about this I do not know. If you publish a small part of it, you spoil the prospect for anything resembling an eventual "collected works." And even for a small segment of it, I myself could not do the editing, and who else is to do it?

January 14

The assistant pastor at the Nassau Presbyterian Church is a rather beautiful young lady who performs her tasks quietly and competently. For the liturgical aspects of the service, this is all right, but I am not so sure about the sermons. How, I ask myself, does the powerful emotional turmoil of femininity accommodate itself comfortably, in the breast of a good-looking young woman, with the resigned acknowledgment of human imperfection, the recognition of renunciation, that lie at the heart of the Christian faith? I can accept an elderly man, now only too conscious of his own imperfections and as devoid of illusions as he is of unreal hopes, as a spiritual guide and mentor. But a young woman? Women, no less than men, are sinners, but they are, as I see them, seldom repentant. And if they give up hope, it is with bitterness and anger.

January 20

After lunch: a dental appointment (I wish they wouldn't let female dental assistants wear such seductive clothes). . . .

I had a visit from Valentin Berezhkov, former diplomat like myself (we had similar experiences in Berlin in the first years of World War II) and one of Stalin's interpreters at Yalta, now in effect, a representative in Washington of Arbatov's institute in Moscow. He stayed for lunch, and afterwards we had a long talk, which may, one never knows, have some sort of usefulness.

I had a phone call, too, on Friday, from Scotty Reston,[61] who told me that the letter I wrote him some weeks ago had been shown to both the President and the Secretary of State,[62] and that both had agreed with the substance of it. He asked me whether I would be prepared to publish it in the *New York Times Magazine*; and I told him I would give him an answer on Monday.

January 28

I phoned Scotty Reston and told him that I would prefer not to publish my letter at this time. I have since been glad that I made that decision. Measured against the depth of the problem—the power, that is, of the combination of hardline factions intent upon the humiliation or destruction of the Soviet regime, even at the cost of war—measured against the depth of this problem, my little letter, appearing in some organ which not everyone reads, appearing today and forgotten tomorrow, would not be enough to make any serious dent upon the problem, but just enough to land me in more controversy. If one is going to try to mount any serious opposition to these forces, it will take much more than a feeble bleat on my part. . . .

A meeting with Ted Weeks,[63] who wants to publish a volume of these diaries. . . . My instincts are against it. These accounts of sailing cruises (which is for the most part what they are, the ones he has) are too impersonal, too gloomy, too similar one to the other, too devoid of intellectual challenge, to make a book alone. They would have to be at least supplemented by some of my letters of the period. But how, here, would one choose? . . . Is one not simply going to pick off bits of the cream of the entire collection, like a goat nibbling the flowers off the bushes, spoiling it for an eventual publication of the "complete works"?

February 4

The week has been for me a difficult one to stomach: Iran in full revolution[64] and the Pentagon still clinging to the belief that they are going to continue to sell arms there, coupled with a frantic effort to remove or hide the more highly classified ones they have (unwisely) already sold;

61. James "Scotty" Reston was an influential journalist and columnist for the *New York Times*.
62. President Jimmy Carter and Secretary of State Cyrus Vance.
63. Edward A. "Ted" Weeks was an editor at Atlantic–Little, Brown.
64. The shah of Iran, a longtime U.S. ally, was overthrown and replaced by Ayatollah Khomeini, an anti-American fundamentalist.

and then, the country going overboard in its unconquerable fascination with the Chinese, and its indomitable belief that they can someday, somehow, be made to love us. So far as the concern over the classified arms is concerned, which we have delivered to the Persians, I reflect with some bitterness on what I wrote two years ago in my unnoticed book,[65] that you might know into whose hands you delivered arms but you could never know in whose hands they would end up. This was so obvious—could there be any excuse for people not recognizing it?

. . . Somehow or other I must bring myself to come to terms with the painful fact that in what I have written and said in these past three decades I have usually been several years ahead of my time, but by the time the opinion of the journalistic-political establishment begins (sometimes too late) to struggle up to the same opinions, everyone has forgotten I ever voiced them. I find it hard to have been both right in substance, and a failure in effect.

February 23

Dramatic and somewhat menacing events in international affairs: the attack on our Embassy in Tehran, the murder of our ambassador in Afghanistan, the Chinese attack on Vietnam, the beginning of a new price rise and shortage of oil. In the face of all this, our government has behaved in accordance with the worst traditions of American statesmanship: concerned almost exclusively with Congressional opinion rather than with the external affects of its actions—and with hard-line opinion, at that, so that there has been a great deal of verbal flexing of the muscles and militant bravado, all of it directed exclusively to the internal audience, and to hell with its effects abroad. In one day we issued thunderous warnings to the Russians not to attack Saudi Arabia (which they had never even dreamed of doing) and to the Chinese not to attack Taiwan (which was equally far from *their* thoughts). Since then we have also sternly warned the Russians not to intervene in Iran (which we ourselves have been doing for a full two decades). In all these cases we have allowed it to be inferred that if our wishes were not obeyed, we would use force, although in not one of these situations would our military force be the answer to the problem even if we had more than the 20-odd divisions that we now have.

65. *The Cloud of Danger* (1977).

Washington, April 18

I attended a meeting of the Board of the Committee on East-West Accord. . . . A short documentary, emphasizing the terrible nature of the consequences of a nuclear explosion, was non-partisan, reasonable, and quite effective. . . .

The effort of this Committee is a worthy one and, for the most part, without ulterior motive—but a bit pathetic, considering the heavy financial support, and the huge political head of steam, of the factions against which it is contending. I am not comfortable about my membership on it, and especially on its Board, because I don't like to have my own views confused with those of any group of people, however well-intentioned. But I am afraid that for me to leave them would be to bring discouragement to them, and they being the only organized group in the country which is trying to bring balance and good sense into the Soviet-American relationship, I would not wish to do this.

Princeton, May 4

Annelise and I lunched, at the Institute, with Svetlana. She seemed in other respects normal, but reserved and uncommunicative about herself. God knows what goes on in that highly complicated emotional make-up. I wonder whether she realizes how many of her problems are of her own making.

Copenhagen Airport, May 30

In recognizing my failure as a contributor to the public discussion of public affairs, I find myself asking what of value, if anything, I was able to offer if people had cared to listen, I come up in part, with the following:

1) In the case of the Soviet Union, I was one of the first to recognize the essentiality of the ideology to the regime, as the only possible excuse for its own cruelties and excesses, & was the only one to point out, with relation to FDR's mistakes, that you cannot expect to have normal relations with people who have a great deal of blood on their hands.

2) I was one of the first, and the few, to recognize that the weapons of mass destruction invalidated all previous thinking and doctrine concerning the value and uses of armed force in the relations among great industrial nations.

Also, that our adaption of, & persistent adherence to, the principle of "first use" of nuclear weapons not only precluded any significant progress towards the limitation and eventual diminishing of such weapons but assured their proliferation among other powers;[66]

Also, that by the use of such weapons one could further no rational purpose, because the proper aim of warfare was not to inflict blind & useless destruction on others, but to affect the behavior of other regimes in a useful direction, which was not achieved just by destroying their peoples.

3. I was alone in pointing out (to an utterly uncomprehending and uninterested public) that in the cases of peoples living under oppressive political regimes, it was useless for us to attempt by economic means either to help the peoples or to harm the regimes, for the regime in question would find means to take credit for, and to profit from, any aid extended to the people, whereas it would also know how to deflect onto the people any injury aimed at itself, & this in such a way that we would be generally blamed for the result.

I also pointed out that it was very difficult to bring benefit, by foreign aid, to any foreign people as a whole, for any change in the terms of its life such as aid from outside could be expected to produce, would be bound to have adverse effects on the interests of some even if it had welcome effects for many others—that it would constitute, in other words, an external intervention into the affairs of another people, sure to be greeted with at least some degree of misunderstanding and resentment.

4. On questions of general political philosophy: I have pointed out that every ruler and (in a pluralistic society) every governing group, has two qualities, sometimes conflicting, when it appears as the determinant of foreign policy. In the one aspect, it appears as the representative of the entire nation, as the custodian, interpreter, and promoter of the interests of the entire people. In the other aspect, it appears as a competitor in the internal struggle for power, representing the [interests] of one domestic faction against those of opposing factions. It thus has two patterns of motivation, which are sometimes in contradiction when it comes to the formulation of foreign policy. Duty to the national interests suggests one course of action. Self-preservation, as the dominant competitor for power domestically, suggests another, & sometimes quite opposite one.

The more democratic a government is, the less is it able to concentrate on the pursuit of the national interest in foreign policy—the greater the

66. Kennan believed Washington should pledge not to be the first nation to resort to nuclear weapons in a crisis.

priority it must give to its internal-competitive concerns. The more absolute the ruler, the more extensively and exclusively is he able to address himself to the national interest as he confronts the problems of foreign policy. But then, he can address himself to the national interest only as he himself perceives it, so that the definition of it becomes a matter of his own perception and philosophy.

Kristiansand, June 7

In addition to being a political isolationist, I am a believer in autarchy. Not only do I believe that the healthy national society would rigidly eschew the importation of foreign labor and force itself to perform out of its own resources all the functions of its social and economic life, including the menial ones, but I consider that it should restrict to a minimum its economic and financial involvements with other peoples, particularly ones the abrupt alteration or termination of which by action of a foreign government could bring severe embarrassment to itself or could even constitute an effective means of political pressure upon it. Particularly would this apply to the U.S., as the object of so much resentment, of so much reckless denunciation, of so much vicious slander in other parts of the world, and particularly would it apply to relations with Third World countries and Communist countries, where governments are either directly hostile or irresponsible.

June 18

Did I not try to warn Jack Kennedy and Mac Bundy, many years ago, that the best way to approach the problems of reduction of nuclear armaments was not to negotiate treaties which would require legislative ratification but to agree with the Russians, privately, on a series of reciprocal steps, each of which was the pledge of the good faith of the other partner? And have I not for years pleaded the nonsensity of taking seriously the comparisons of fantastic quantities of overkill on which the SALT negotiations have been based? Was I not, too, the first and only one in this country to perceive the dilemmas to which our acceptance of the principle of first use was bound to lead, and to point out that neither could wars be won, nor could our security be promoted, by weapons of this nature—only to be laughed at by Mr. Acheson as one who had no understanding for the uses of power?

And if it be argued that none of what I said could have been done because the Congress would never have accepted or tolerated, or even understood it, then who, I would ask, was it who went around pleading that the occasion of the Bicentennial be used not for costume parades and re-enactments of the Battle of Lexington but for a serious review of the experience we have had over nearly two centuries with our present constitution, with a view to seeing whether it might not now be possible to amend it in certain respects where it was proving to be inadequate to the needs of a great country in the modern age? And again—with total non-effect . . .

The energy problem continues to dominate the news, and someone . . . is saying that we must now urgently consider measures of conservation and of the development of alternative sources of energy. Five years ago, I urged all this in the strongest of terms in my *Cloud of Danger*, without the slightest response. Meanwhile, five years have been lost. Our dependence on the Arabs and other wholly unreliable sources of supply has been permitted to grow rather than being reduced. Our situation today is much more serious than it was then. Not only that, but not five years ago but twenty-five I pointed, in public statements, to the great danger of permitting our economy to become dependent on imports of fuel and raw materials from politically undependable suppliers, and all this—without the slightest response on the part of press or government.

The list could go on for pages.

What of it? Bitterness is a sterile state of mind—one to be avoided. You were confronted over the course of years not just with the temptation but with the duty to ponder the national interest and the general interest of mankind. You came away from the experience with the impression of having done this reasonably well—even better, perhaps, or at least more deeply and far-sightedly, than any American of your generation, except Reinhold Niebuhr, only to find that with the exception of certain of the earliest and least profound of the public statements, such as the X-article and the Chicago lectures,[67] almost nothing you said was appreciated, very little of it noticed at all, and almost none of it understood.

67. Kennan, *American Diplomacy* (1951).

1980

In the 1980s, Kennan's critique of U.S. policies, particularly regarding nuclear weapons, would gain a wider public hearing. Once more he commanded a voice in the national conversation. His stature as a respected man of conscience did not, however, yield the influence in governmental policy that the one-time policy planner in the State Department so earnestly sought. Although he dreaded the prospect of a nuclear catastrophe, a part of him also welcomed the possibility of cleansing the planet of human despoilment.

Having published The Decline of Bismarck's European Order *in 1979, Kennan spent much of the year in various European capitals doing research for the book he would publish in 1984,* The Fateful Alliance: France, Russia, and the Coming of the First World War.

Princeton, February 8

This revival of a diary—or this attempt at one (since I have never had great success in the effort to keep one regularly) owes its inspiration to the realization that in recent days my involvements and problems have been growing over my head, and to the belief that it might be helpful to me in trying to keep them sorted out and to cope with them if I put myself to the discipline of recording them, together with such reactions as they allow.

I might first note, by way of background, that the first volume of my work on the Franco-Russian Alliance (*The Decline of Bismarck's European Order*) appeared in early December. While the publisher (Princeton University Press) seems not to have done very well in getting it onto the bookstore counters, it was well and favorably reviewed initially (the exception being, not unsurprisingly, a piece by A.J.P. Taylor, which I have not yet seen). . . .

Deeply concerned over the appalling militarization of thinking in

Washington and what seemed to one to be the dangerous over reaction there to the Soviet intervention in Afghanistan, I wrote a piece for the op-ed page of the *New York Times*. In addition, I consented to do a TV interview with Mr. Dan Rather for the "60 Minutes" show. . . .

The *New York Times* gave the essay a very conspicuous place and heading and the effect has been sensational. To my own surprise the article seems to have struck into one of those crucial combinations of timing and of public receptivity which multiply the effect manyfold. . . . I was particularly jolted by those who said to me in effect (but sometimes literally): "You must continue to talk. You cannot fall silent. You have become the conscience of the nation in the questions of foreign policy." These appeals, together with the fact that two of the presidential candidates have contacted me with requests for advice as to the positions they should take with relation to the problems in question, have caused me to recognize that I have, in the capacity of critic and commentator in matters of foreign policy, a unique voice, not quite comparable to any other—the nearest thing to the one once possessed by Walter Lippmann, and that it is a shame not to make effective use of so rare an advantage, and one so difficult to acquire. . . .

I have toyed with the thought: should I yield to these pressures? Should I give up history, at least for a year or so, read the papers, "keep up," attend the never-ending stream of meetings with visiting statesmen in New York and Washington, be in the swim, and, on the basis of all this—spend my life speaking and writing on international affairs?

. . . I see no alternative but to struggle along as I have been doing—saying "no" to several hundred invitations and appeals per annum . . . to keep up, after a fashion, on what is going on, and then trying in the face of all this, to continue as a scholar . . . not giving it up, because it provides my basic *raison d'être*, and is, in fact, a part of the image that lends strength to my voice.

Washington, February 28

I went, in late afternoon, to a meeting of the American Committee on East-West Accord: a small group of people crowded together in the Committee's tiny offices near the station. Having been, up to this time, a struggling and largely futile little body, totally outclassed in funds and publicity by three or four hard-line organizations reeking with Texas oil money and dishing out the alarmist talk the politicians love to hear. The staff of the East-West Record Committee now find themselves, they tell me, receiving spontaneous offers of support from foundations and others worried about the recent trend of events. Some of this pleasing change they attribute to me, & the narrow walls of the little office rang with my praises—for the *New York Times* piece & the "60 Minutes" interview. I was told that I had single-handedly "turned things around," that prior to my intervention there had been no focus for the uneasiness so many people were feeling. The Western Europeans, it was said, had been made uncertain not just by what they felt was a binge of hysterical emotionalism on the part of the Administration but also by the fact that there seemed to be no critical response to any of this on the part of the public. I had now provided that response, & the Europeans were relieved.

I was further warmed by the fact that three of those present had just recently been in Moscow, and their reports of what they had heard in that city bore out (even more than I actually deserved) what I had said in my article about the probable background of the move into Afghanistan.

All this was heady stuff, & my head was whirling with it when I left the offices of the Committee. It had been snowing all day. It was now turning cold, & the slush was freezing. So as I slithered back to the station, I reflected on my strange situation, and particularly on how inadvertent have been the few significant contributions I have made to people's thinking about international affairs—how strange and ironic had been the relationship, in these instances, of effect to cause—how difficult it was, for me at least, to calculate this relationship in advance, to achieve what I had hoped or intended to achieve. I fire my arrows into the air. Sometimes, they strike nothing; sometimes, they strike the wrong things; sometimes one or another of them strikes a bell and rings it, loud and clear. And then, if no other purpose is served, people are at least stimulated and helped to think.

[Kennan went to do research in the archives of the Hoover Institution at Stanford University.]

Palo Alto, March 7

Asked to give a layman's sermon, the thought that first springs to my mind is a plea for a limited isolationism—advocacy of the principle that a great nation must learn not to live entirely from its own resources in normal times, but to be able to live within them in abnormal ones, and this, precisely in order that it may not be forced to resort to the use of force for motives going beyond those of immediate defense, as mentioned above.

The objection to this is that it is a line of thought going far beyond anything with which even the more sophisticated portion of the American public is familiar, and a thesis of such complexity that it can scarcely be adequately exposed in 30 minutes.

[Kennan traveled to Europe to do research and visit friends.]

Icogne, Switzerland, Good Friday, April 4

Most human events yield to the erosion of time, and if they survive in memory at all, it is only in the form of dim, distorted myths. The greatest, most amazing, exception to this generalization was what occurred nearly two thousand years ago, on something resembling this same day of the lunar calendar, on the hill of Golgotha. Almost certainly, one must suppose, a man, a Jew, some sort of a dissident religious prophet, was crucified in company with two common thieves. . . .

What was new and of stupendous power in the teachings of this man were two things: first, the principle of charity of love, selflessness, identification with the plight and struggle of the other; but secondly, the possibility of redemption in the face of self-knowledge and penitence—the possibility of reconciliation with one's own ingrained and never wholly eradicable imperfections, with one's animalistic nature and impulses, with man's "original sin." In the combination of these two things: charity and redemption, evoking as they did for the first time the image of a Deity capable of compassion, there lay the origins of the majestic symbolic power of the life and death of the Savior, the power that inspired an entire vast civilization, created a great art, erected a hundred thousand magnificent churches, hung as emblem in token of solace and hope around a host of necks, shaped and disciplined the minds and the values of many generations—placed, in short, its creative stamp on one of the greatest of all flowerings of the human spirit. For the first time man, perched so uncomfortably and on his precarious mountain ledge, somewhere between his animalistic emotional-physical nature on the one hand and his unattainable dreams of beauty and of nobility of spirit on the other, found a source of strength in his struggle against the beast within that threatened to drag him into the abyss, and of solace for his inability to reach the spiritual summit of which he was capable of dreaming.

April 5

I am sick in the consciousness of what awaits my poor children and grandchildren, but otherwise, viewing it from the broader standpoint, I long for the day of the catastrophe in order that the nature of these lovely continents, Europe and North America, now savaged and despoiled by over population and commercialism, may have a chance to breathe, to recover, to cause these atrocities of man's handiwork to decay into the ruins they deserve to become, and to restore to the trees, the natural shrubs, the streams and wetlands, and the self-accommodating, non-destructive animals, the dominion over God's great and beautiful creation which they deserve to have.

Sarlat, France, May 22

I sat myself in the back seat, mildly troubled by an aching kidney-stone, and yielded myself to melancholy reflections, to wit:

1) It was obvious that the trend, both in Western Europe and in the U.S. (but more in the U.S.) was towards war with the U.S.S.R., that all my own efforts to halt it had been futile, and that I had come to the end of my usefulness to my own time. . . .

2) Could I myself have been wrong in my conviction that this was unnecessary, that there were better and safer ways to approach the problem of Soviet power in the post–World War II era? In certain respects, yes, of course. No one is right all the time. But basically: No.

I had been right in saying that once political stability had been established in Europe in the late 1940's and early 1950's, one should attempt to negotiate a departure of both Soviet and American forces from the center of Europe.

I had been right in my opposition to the basing of our defenses, and those of Western Europe, on the worse-than-useless nuclear weapon, and our encouraging of the Russians to do likewise.

I had been right in my belief that the best solution in northeastern Asia would have been a neutralized and demilitarized Japan and Korea.

I had been right in my distrust of a wholly motorized society, in my insistence even 25 years ago, that we should not permit ourselves to become dependent on . . . Middle Eastern oil. . . .

I had been right, finally, in my warnings against the reckless importation into our society or any other highly-developed society, and particularly into our great cities, of masses of people of wholly different cultural habits, traditions, and outlooks, incompatible with our own.

In all of these causes, I have failed, and the result of these failures was the present march of Western civilization, along several paths, into the very jaws of catastrophe.

3) What to do? Acknowledge the total failure as irremediable? Retire silently? Fade out of the picture? Without defense? Without effort at self-justification?

No, one would still like to set the record straight—if only as a matter of self-respect.

Bonn, June 3

I have not much longer to go—a couple of years, probably, at the most (presumably until the 9th of May 1982,[68] to be exact), and so serious is the present international situation, so threatening and terrible to my children and grandchildren (and to millions of other people's children and grandchildren) that anything I could do to diminish this danger would be more important than the best I could hope to do as an historian. Unless the greatest of the dangers can be averted, there will remain few books on history to be read, and there will be few to read them.

September 18

Princeton, with its never-ending pressures, its many other writing tasks (correspondence, especially), and the frequency of travel in every conceivable direction, is a poor place for diaries.

68. Kennan actually would have died on May 9, 1983, if, as he surmised, he had been allocated the precise life span (seventy-nine years, two months, and twenty-three days) as that of the cousin of his grandfather (George Kennan, 1845–1924). In an apparent arithmetical error, he wrote May 9, 1982, in the diary. The two George Kennans shared not only the same birthday and interest in Russia but also many other parallels in their lives.

(3/2/83, continued)

Although this was something of an imposition, I did not have the heart to send her back with her burden, so I took it and undertook to look at it.

Went to the S oviet Embassy for lunch, alone, with Dobrynin. Had no particular purpose, e xcept that I, having once suffered under the fact that xxxxmbxx no one dared come to see me when I was ambassador in the Soviet Union, felt for him in the present dismal state of Soviet-A merican r elations, and thought our country could do a bit better in this respect than the S oviet Union had done by me. So I marched bravely into the old embassy bxxdx building on 16th Street, under the amazed eyes and furiously - clicking cameras of God knows how many agents of the F.B.I. and others of the intelligence fraternity, was kindly and jovially received by my ambassadorial host, lunched and talked pleasantly with him for an hour or so, well aware that the recording devices of both governments were probably noting,xxxxx for the benefit of an official posterity, every word of our rather ixxxx innocuous conversation. I told him about the extraordinary xppxxxxhofxxx approach of Mr. Whitworth, and suggested that perhaps Dobrynin and I could find something else to talk about than politics. Perhaps we could have a mellow, reflective conver ation about our respectives youths or something of that sort. Mr. Dobrynin was skeptical. He found it difficult to imagine Andropov talking to me along these lines. "Our people", he said, tended not to be very communicative about their private lives, viewing this as something not significant from the standpoint of their official positions, and no fit subject for curiosity on the part of foreigners. I knew this, too, and could only recognize the justice of what he said. He did add, however, that he would report this suggestion. Perhaps some day he might get back to me -- but not soon. (I shared, actually, his skepticism.)

Leaving the Soviet Embassy imeidately after lunch, I went to the Dep't of State with our old diplomatic passports, which had expired the previoss day, and got the forms and instructions for the applications for new ones.

Then, in evening, to the Four Seasons Hotel, for a dinner of the ambassadors emeriti with the Secretary of State, Mr. Schultz. Xxbxinx xthexsenioxxofxthexambassadorxx The latter arrived in company with Larr Eagleburger and a young gentleman from California by the name of , who,hadxjustxxecentlyxxx meeting very nicely the usual Reagan requirement that he should have had no previous experience with foreign affairs and should know nothing about them, had just r ecently been named deputy Under-secretary of State -- a position most Foreign Service officers would have regarded as the crowning achievement of 35-40 years of service. I, being the senior of the various ex-ambassadors, was the first to greet and welcome the Secretary of State; and although he is very much an imperturbable person, I thought it jolted him a bit when I gave him the name. The evening passed off pleasantly enough; but I came away doubting that it had been worth his while. He was, as I had expected him to be, patient, quiet, and a good listener, reserving at all times (as I thought quite proper) his opinion on the matters discussed. I found myself liking and respecting him, as most people do; but I foresee something of an ultimate crisis between him and the fanatics in the White House around the President, particularly if he tries to do anything sensible about relations with the S oviet Union.

Chapter Nine

Cold War Critic, 1981–90

1981

Kennan interrupted a European sojourn dedicated to research and to conversations with friends and officials in order to receive the Albert Einstein Peace Prize in Washington on May 19. The award pleased him for several reasons. Though he and Einstein had never spoken, their tenures at the Institute for Advanced Study at Princeton had overlapped. Kennan appreciated the $50,000 check that went with the prize. But most important was the opportunity to argue his case before a wide audience.

Kennan realized that the SALT (Strategic Arms Limitation Treaty) process had come to a dead end. Negotiations had gotten bogged down in arcane, complex details. SALT II remained unratified by a skeptical Senate. The belligerent rhetoric of President Ronald Reagan was further escalating Cold War tensions. Kennan seized the occasion of the Einstein Prize ceremony, which was attended by members of the Reagan administration as well as by the Soviet ambassador, to propose a dramatically new and simple approach to arms control: an immediate across-the-board cut by 50 percent of all nuclear weapons held by the two superpowers. The proposal propelled Kennan further into the limelight, a development that both delighted and dismayed him. Although now seventy-seven years old, he would have to work harder to balance the competing demands of public life and scholarship.

[As indicated in the entries that follow, Moscow, as it had for decades, sparked in Kennan a mix of turbulent emotions.]

Moscow, April 13

I cannot describe the impressions of this day, so many of them deepened by the wisps of memory, the impulses of sympathy and pity, clashing with those of revulsion, the everlasting battle of contradictions.

April 16

The military policies and even more the rhetoric of these two great countries are on a collision course, and I feel quite helpless in the face of this situation. About the Soviet Union, I can do nothing. These people have indulged themselves for 60 years in the habit of polemical exaggeration and distortion. It is as Russian as boiled cabbage and buckwheat kasha. But what about my own government and its state of blind militaristic hysteria? It has not only convinced itself of the reality of its own bad dreams, but it has succeeded in half-convincing most of our allies, and that to such an extent that anyone who challenges that view of the world appears to them as dangerously subversive.

To read what some, most in fact, of our good people are saying makes me feel that I must be going crazy, or they must. Our respective views of reality are simply incompatible.

[Kennan was aghast at Washington's protest of Moscow's threat to intervene against the Solidarity uprising in Poland.]

April 17

What is the inference here?—that this is something new and abnormal? Are we to gather from this that the Soviet Union did not have the capability of intervening in Poland over all these last 15 years?—the Soviet Union, with some 19 divisions in Eastern Germany, with 5 divisions in Czechoslovakia, with dozens more in the western districts of the Soviet Union (or so we are told), and with two divisions already stationed in Poland? Are we supposed to tremble and to wax heroically indignant all of the sudden over a situation that we have peaceably put up with for more than a third of a century?

I feel that I must have been asleep for several decades and have woken up to find it an almost unrecognizable world.

Night before last there was a dinner at the Embassy where the Chargé d'Affaires, Jack Matlock,[1] said in a toast to me the kindest and nicest things I have ever heard from the lips of anyone in this government, enough to make up for all the slights and rebuffs I have had from the U.S. government from John Foster Dulles on down. And today, at a lunch in the Prague restaurant Georgy Arkadyevich Arbatov said equivalently

1. Jack Matlock Jr. was a State Department expert on the Soviet Union who would become ambassador to the Soviet Union from 1987 to 1991.

warm and moving things from the Soviet side, a side from which, too, all has not been posies and compliments in earlier years.

I would not be human if these things did not give me satisfaction. But they are certainly all, if not more, than I deserve. And they are, like the recent [Einstein] Peace Prize, a commitment. May God give me the insight to retain, in the light of my weaknesses, my humility, the strength to do something useful in the remaining time.

April 19

Today, it occurs to me, is the 77th anniversary of the death of my mother, the woman without whose sacrifice and agony I would not have existed.

I never knew her. I try to picture her to myself: beautiful (as I know from the photographs) but provincial. I can more easily imagine her voice, the slow middle-western drawl I can recall from her sister, Aunty Ven. Her passing was a tragedy for the family: for my poor father, who needed her; for my sister, Constance, then 6 years old, who was dependent on her, and who in a way never wholly recovered from the shock of her death; for me, whose relations to women were unfortunately affected by the bewildering succession of female figures who flitted in and out of the house, each taking care of me, in her way, through the years of my infancy and childhood.

Once a few years ago, I dreamed that I saw my mother. I knew it was she. She stood motionless and silent before me. She could not speak. The barrier between the dead and living made it impossible; and I understood that it must be so. . . .

Visiting Tchaikovsky's house I was much moved by the whole encounter, not so much with Tchaikovsky, although I admire a great deal of his music, but rather with these evidences of the period and I came away deploring the fact that I had not been born a hundred years earlier than I was. What a century, that 19th, loaded with meaning, thought, beauty, and tragedy! . . .

The regime of observation over non-resident foreigners has been considerably modified, so that there is no longer much of that indefinable strain, as detectable in the atmosphere as though it had been some sinister odor, that once enveloped the foreigner in this place: the sense that not only was one being constantly followed, one's self by hostile and suspicious eyes, but that those Soviet citizens with whom one had to do, even for unavoidable and authorized reasons, were similarly held under a species of menacing, dangerous observation.

April 21

From these experiences of the day I came away with the sense of having my nose rubbed once more (always a useful experience for one tends to forget) in the incorrigibly dual, ambivalent quality of all Russian political reality: the clash of opposites—the two-headed eagle, the heads looking in opposite directions: the Patriarch, dispensing Christian charity and forgiveness, the Tsar dispensing sheer power in its most terrible forms; the Grand Chancery of Giers'[2] day dispensing current and peaceable policy in the most elegant French, the Asiatic Department conducting its intrigues along the southern borders in the most truculent Russian; the People's Commissariat for Foreign Affairs of the 1930's, behaving like the former Grand Chancery, while the Comintern exerts itself to overthrow the very governments with which the Commissariat is trying to conduct pleasant and frictionless relations, and now—Arbatov and all these others being touchingly kind and nice and this—to me, of all persons, who has no power, has no influence on our government, cannot help them in the least; and on the other hand, the unseen warriors of the Ministry of Defense and the secret police, all of them as convinced of the inevitability of war as were the Tsarist minister of war & chief of the General Staff a hundred years ago—as convinced as are our hard-liners and military planners at home—blinded, all of them, by the unspoken implications of the weapons race in which we are all engaged, fighting in their imaginations and plans . . . rendering inevitable, by the very act of so conceiving it, the very war they profess to wish to prevent—and doubly sinister by virtue of the dense cloak of secrecy and anonymity in which they insist on wrapping themselves. What is one to make of this two-headed phenomenon, which at times can assume the warmth, the capacity for sympathy, of an Arbatov, and at other times the monstrosity of a Stalin?

. . . Obviously, one places some of one's money on both, for however impressed one may be with one side of this personality, one has no right to forget the other. But when and if one has to choose, I would favor giving the edge to the more hopeful side, which is the human and humane one, for it is plainly our best chance—it is in fact our only chance that is less than disastrous. It may have some political disadvantages, the present situation in Afghanistan, for example, but these may be expected to find

2. Nikolay Karlovich Giers was the Russian foreign minister who helped engineer the alliance with France that Kennan was writing about.

their own level with the course of time. Over the long run it is, after all, the "civilizational" capacities of governments that are decisive (as the Russians are now learning, to their sorrow, in Poland). Many a distortion of the moment will find its correction in the slow, mysterious persistence of the underlying cultural habits and capabilities of peoples. But for the horrors of modern war, particularly but not exclusively nuclear war, there is no correction. No one can bring back the lives, the hopes, the cultural values, which a great war destroys.

Copenhagen Airport, April 27

Before leaving Leningrad I walked over to have one last look at the river, for this was, I supposed, my last hour in Russia—ever. So for a few brief moments I drank in the spectacle of what Pushkin called this "majestic" stream, confined among banks which are, to my mind, the finest river banks to be seen anywhere else in the world except Venice, and greater even than these latter in scale and sweep.

The rail trip to Helsinki was comfortable enough. Much snow still lying in the woods, & snow flurries alternating with sunshine all along the route. John Gaddis, the best of the American (and Americanist) diplomatic historians of this generation, now spending a year in Helsinki, kindly met us at the train & escorted us to the hotel. . . . The following day was sunny, but cold. Gaddis and his wife took us to lunch at the very Victorian restaurant in the Park, by the harbor. I felt ashamed to let them do it, for they are young, and Helsinki is an expensive town, but remonstrations were useless.

Returning to Europe after the Einstein prize ceremony, May 27

This last year has changed my life in two ways. The reception of things I have written or said publicly, culminating in the peace prize, has created a situation in which I no longer can or should try to hold aloof from the debates about current questions of international affairs. This being the case, it has plainly become quite impossible for me to do any studying or writing of history. . . . Unless another great war can be prevented, there may be no more history to write about, and, even if there were, no one who could write it, or read it.

The newspapers tell us of President Reagan's speech at West Point. It is a simple world picture that he paints, and a very old-fashioned one. It is so old-fashioned that I ought to love it as he sees it and be thrilled by it. I cannot. I love certain old-fashioned values and concepts—but not *his*.

He stresses the need for a revival of "patriotism." I can imagine that were we ever to meet and talk face-to-face (something which is most unlikely to occur), he might, remembering my evil reputation, look me sternly in the eye and ask: "Kennan, are you patriotic?" What could I say in reply?

I would have to ask in turn: "Do you mean: Do I love my country?" And if so, what do you mean by "country"—the land or the people? If you mean the land, then yes, of course. I love it—loved it as a child, the way it then was—continue to love it today to the extent the people have not yet made a wasteland, a garbage dump, or a sewer out of it. If you and your supporters, who seem to have a positive hatred of all that is natural and beautiful in it, complete the destruction of it (or encourage the developers to complete it, which is the same thing), there will be little of it to love.

And the people? What do you mean: "love" people? I suspect that what you mean, when you speak of "patriotism" is: do I join you in idealizing them, in encouraging in myself and in others the view that there is something wonderful about them, something other people do not have, something that gives them a superior virtue and strength and entitles them to consider themselves leaders in the world, stronger and with greater authority than anyone else? If this is the way the question is put, if this, I am being asked, is the way I view them, the answer is: decidedly no.

Helsinki, July 16

I have been sitting alone with my kind hosts over dinner. I return to my room wholly inebriated, or at least wound up. With what? I had one scotch-and-soda before dinner, a couple of glasses of red wine during dinner, nothing more, before or after. I have had that hundreds of times and never felt inebriated from it. What then? From my own talk, I must conclude. Sometimes, when I sit this way, with a very small circle of listeners, I get going. In some way I overpower them and silence them, or make it difficult for them to speak. And the less they speak, the more I do.

What is it that silences them & leads me on? Fascination? Over-intensity? Astonishment? Whatever it is, I end up like a clock which is about to break because one winds it too tightly.

1982

Despite the extraordinary honors and respect heaped on him, Kennan agonized about his failure to stem the apparent rush toward nuclear war. He saw himself as "a prophet," one who might remain unheeded in his own time. Horror at the prospect of a nuclear holocaust spurred him to question nearly all armed conflict, even the Second World War.

Acting on such conviction, Kennan teamed up with former national security advisor McGeorge Bundy, former secretary of defense Robert McNamara, and arms control negotiator Gerard Smith. In a widely read article in Foreign Affairs, *this "Gang of Four" urged the United States to pledge, as the Soviet Union had done, not to be the first to use nuclear weapons. That assurance could reduce the chances of nuclear war starting through preemption or miscalculation. The Reagan administration, like its successors, refused to make such a no-first-use pledge.*

Princeton, January 10

The year 1981 was what one might call a diary-less year. The reason is obvious. Very active people do not, as a rule, keep diaries—not unless they are so well supplied with clerical help that they can dictate them hastily to secretaries, and so full of the importance of what they are doing that they think their daily doings must absolutely be recorded for history. And for me, 1981 was an "active year." . . .

When I received the Einstein Peace Prize, in Washington, the observations I made by way of acknowledgment of the honor . . . ended up being distributed privately in thousands of copies. When, then, at the end of the summer's vacation in Norway, I was asked to address a special meeting of the Norwegian PEN Club (a gathering much more political than literary), the remarks made on that occasion also went the rounds and ended up, in one form or another, both in *Die Zeit* in Germany and in the *New Yorker* on this side of the water . . . and in the *New York Review of Books*. All of those statements addressed themselves to the problem of nuclear weapons. They produced such an eager response on the part of thousands of people that I was misled into thinking that my word might really carry some weight, and I wrote columns for the *New York Times* op-ed page. . . . I even let myself be wheedled into appearing (a week ago today) on *Meet the Press*.

Today, at the end of this rather pathetic effort to affect governmental policy, I have to recognize its total failure. . . . The *New York Times* obviously understood nothing I said. . . . And for the Reagan administration all this was, at best, a species of slightly annoying mosquito bite, the bite of an insect to be absent-mindedly brushed off and at once forgotten.

So I find myself now in the full consciousness of my failure. I do not regret the effort. My children, if they survive the next five years, which I consider to be doubtful, may at least be able to see that I did my best to head off disaster.

Or was it my best? Would I not have been more effective by far had I, instead of expressing myself as I have, become the politician, said a thousand things I did not mean, cultivated a thousand people for whom I had no respect, mouthed all the fashionable slogans, got myself at least briefly into a position of authority, and then—playing, as the others do, on popular emotions and slogans—wheedled less perceptive people into doing useful things, the real nature of which they would not have understood at all?

The answer to this question is, of course, theoretically in the affirmative. Whoever wishes to lead the masses in a useful direction must learn to deceive, not to appeal to people rationally.

But this answer is actually beside the point. All that was not in my nature. My role, vain as this assertion may sound, was that of a prophet. It was for this that I was born. And my tragedy is to enact this part at a time when it becomes increasingly doubtful that there will, as little as ten or twenty years hence, be anyone left to recognize the validity of the prophecies or whether, indeed, any record of those prophecies will have survived the conflagration to which nuclear war can lead, or any eyes would be there to read it, if it did.

. . . I find myself standing as a witness at the final, apocalyptic self-destruction of this marvelous Western civilization, with all its immense monuments of architecture, music, art, and literature—a civilization which had the vitality to burst out into breathtaking feats of creativity in earlier centuries but lacked the power to live by them, to build on them, and, in the end, even to preserve their surviving monuments.

In the face of this terrible vision, nothing will help except the Christian faith, the Christian faith in its most primitive form, without hope or delusion for the perceived world of our life on earth, its eyes riveted on another life which we are incapable of imagining, and for the reality of which we have only the passionate, inspired, and compelling witness of Christ himself.

There we are! My own role, as a faint and unsuccessful protestor, is obviously at an end. Age would soon have put an end to it anyway, even if discouragement did not. But meanwhile, there is a bit of life still to be lived, a bit to be seen of the tragic beauty and poetry of this world, a bit, in short, to be witnessed, perceived, and recorded.

Whether anyone as old as I am can even observe all this, with his fading eyes, and react creatively and usefully to it with his dwindling perceptiveness, remains to be seen. This journal, being resumed at the moment of final discouragement, will be the answer to that question.

January 11

Bitter cold this morning. Zero, or a bit below (depending on which thermometer you look at). . . .

The morning paper full of stories about the desperate efforts of the Reagan administration to induce others to join them in putting sanctions on the U.S.S.R. over Poland. It is clear to me that the administration has decided that the time has come for an all-out effort to break up the Soviet hegemony in Eastern and Central Europe, and to do it in a manner as humiliating as possible to the Soviet leadership. An unnecessary effort, for the hegemony was disintegrating by itself without our doing, and an immensely risky one, probably leading to war, for Moscow cannot permit so arrogant and dramatic a challenge to its prestige, not to mention to Soviet security. The Soviet leaders will see, at the end of this process, a totally hostile German-American alliance, directed exclusively against them.

January 17

To a visiting Soviet dignitary I imagined saying: "You can say to your people that there is no use in your trying to patch things up with the Reagan administration. They are determined to make things as bad as possible, short of outright war. There is nothing you could do to appease this administration. The only effective way you could handle these people would be to take the consequences of their attitude: to take a deep breath and resolve to live without trade with the U.S., even without the grain, to be prepared for the elimination of all forms of cultural interchange, to insist on a mutual recall of ambassadors, and on a drastic reduction of their staffs, and to settle down to a long period of relations at the lowest and coldest conceivable level short of hostilities, retaining only a readiness to continue with all seriousness the talks on the reduction of nuclear weaponry—to learn, in other words, to live totally independently of the United States, expecting from it only the worst it can do in hostility and vituperation!"

I did not, of course, say one word of any of this, but I would have liked to.

February 16

This, of course, is my 78th birthday. . . . Left to myself, I would give up the Princeton residence, acquire an abandoned farm in the northernmost regions of Vermont or New Hampshire, and settle down to a life of doing the small chores: cutting the firewood, feeding the chickens, baking bread, and carrying water to the horse. Nothing, to me, could sound more inviting.

[The Kennans journeyed to central Europe, where they visited friends and George worked in the archives.]

Prague, March 12

A long ride through central Prague in the Embassy limousine, a Prague not seen for 43 years. It made upon me, even the beautiful baroque facades, an impression of drab and grey sadness. How much of this was a real change, how much the tricks of memory, who could say? To what extent, that is, were these facades really sprucer, brighter, more cheerful, more hopeful and affirmative in that remote year, the last months of Czechoslovakia's real independence when I served here (1938–1939)? Or to what extent did they merely appear so to a far more youthful eye, or did memory now attribute to them a color brighter than any they ever really had?

No fully adequate answer to these questions.

I think without pleasure or pride of the young man I then was: physically healthy as never before (I remember the very sensation of health by which I was overcome in that tragic autumn of 1938), but with great failings, failings so great that I dislike now to remember them. The best I had to offer was not my person, which was weak and inadequate to the private responsibilities it had assumed, but my mind and my capacities for critical observation and judgment, especially for the absorption of impressions and knowledge. I was dreadfully uneducated, but in high degree educable.

These qualities, nevertheless, did not redeem my personal failings, and I find myself wondering what has become of those, other than my wife, who were in one way or another (not always innocently) the victims of them.

Vienna, March 20

The Soviet war memorial . . . surmounted with the heroic figure (and not a bad one) of the Soviet soldier of World War II. It is, I fear, no place of reverence, today—a fatality, in this respect, to the behavior of the Soviet troops in 1945 (the rapes, the plundering, the executions, and other excesses) and to the political brutalities perpetrated upon so much of the rest of Central and Eastern Europe. The Viennese make fun of it, referring to the figure on the top for some reason as the *Erbsen König* (the Pea King). I, alone perhaps in this city of nearly two million, view it with sadness, sympathy, and respect, seeing in it the millions of Russian youngsters who laid down their lives in that war. . . . May those who sent all these men to their death, on whatever side, some day be compelled to account for their action to the God who had caused these victims once to come into this world as sweet, innocent children.

Belgrade, March 28

The image that emerges of the nature of the Reagan regime is more and more appalling. It is not just that it is ignorant, unintelligent, complacent, and arrogant; worse still is the fact that it is frivolous and reckless, and is unquestionably carrying us with great rapidity towards a wholly unnecessary and disastrous war. I return home shaken and deeply concerned.

Washington, April 7

I am devoting this present week to the effort—primarily through an article in *Foreign Affairs* (drafted by Mac Bundy but signed by four of us) to force our government to abandon the option of "first use" of nuclear weapons which it has insisted on retaining for the past 30 years, and to which I have always been opposed. The article was officially released to the press at 6 p.m. this evening. The four of us gave interviews, first, to the European press and then to the American one (about a hundred of them, with the photographers) this morning, and now we are giving individual ones. . . .

Should the effort succeed, I would regard it as the most important thing I had ever had a part in accomplishing.

July 21

As for the Soviet "dissidents," so-called: The thesis is that only Western pressure could cause the Soviet leadership to be more indulgent in its treatment of these people. The record would seem to me to indicate for the most part precisely the opposite. The dissidents are largely Jewish. Their aim is not to overthrow the Soviet government, but to leave the Soviet Union. Because of this desire to leave it, and above all because of their insistent tendency to appeal to the Western press for support, they are stamped in the eyes of the regime as enemies of the Soviet Union and as "agents of the imperialists," meaning the United States and Israel. Any pressure exerted from the Western side on their behalf only confirms this impression.

There are, of course, others—non-Jews—whose opposition to the policies of the regime are of a more political nature, who are trying to bring about useful change by working within the system, who are made to suffer for their efforts, and who deserve Western sympathy and where possible support. It is entirely proper that this sympathy should be made manifest by the Western press and public opinion. It is another thing for the Western government to get into the act and to make an international issue of the treatment of these people at the hands of the Soviet authorities. That is, however one looks at it, interference in the internal affairs of another country. This is seldom useful, and it is inconsistent with our own professions.

July 30

Arthur Schlesinger asked me to participate in a commemorative meeting at the Century Club for FDR. . . . But what do I know about Franklin Roosevelt? An intellectually superficial but courageous and charming man, a gentleman with pronounced liberal leanings, guilty actually, of great mistakes, the greatest of which in my opinion, was the provocation of the unnecessary war with Japan, tying up as it did the forces and energies which, if not thus tied up, might well have and probably would have enabled us to meet the Russians somewhere well east of the line on which we did actually meet them in 1945. But FDR was a man of his time, the captive of its prejudices. If you are going to blame him, you have to go back farther still and blame the American missionary movement, with its powerful pro-Chinese and anti-Japanese bias.

Hanover, West Germany, September 25

I will never get anywhere with most of the Germans until I find some way to argue my point effectively. . . . The scenario conceived by so many of these people (including, I believe, Marion Dönhoff) is simply not the way great powers behave. By this "scenario" I mean the vision of the Russians some day appearing at the door and saying to the West German government: "You do this or that—or else." I know of only one instance in which anything of this sort has actually been done: the night, in March 1939, when Hitler and his henchmen browbeat the elderly, ill, and drugged Czechoslovak President, Emil Hacha. As opposed to this, there have been thousands of instances of serious conflict between stronger powers and weaker ones where this was *not* done. And there is good reason for that, because no serious statesman in his right mind would consent to deal with another government in the face of such a threat because to do so would be to sacrifice all independence of policy. The question would at once arise: If I submit to such pressure today with respect to the particular demand at issue, what will be asked of me tomorrow?

The Farm, October 17

Reunion of five siblings who had not (so far as any of them could remember) been assembled together in any one place for at least sixty years. . . .

It was a momentous occasion. The uncertain lines of fate and experience, which had taken their departure so many years ago from the oddly-positioned, partially dark, and not always happy home on Cambridge Avenue in Milwaukee, had divided us widely and over many years from one another. Yet even at the end of this division we were not strangers. The community of childhood proved stronger in the end than all the intervening ups and downs of life. Memories were kindly and without rancor. Mutual sympathy, for all that life had done to us, the good and the bad, was felt but unspoken. In none of us was there any self-pity, nor was there much of the melancholy of old age. And the reunion was made richer and more reassuring by the presence of the others: spouses, children, grandchildren. Without their youth and strength the occasion would have lost some of its happiness.

Princeton, November 3

Fussed, in the morning, with the reply to a rather persistent young assistant professor from the West Coast who is spending some months here in Princeton, apparently mostly for the purpose of burrowing in my papers at the Mudd Library, and who has unearthed the fragment of a document, apparently written by me in 1938 but never completed or offered for publication, and has built an essay around it.[3] This paper, evidently written in a mood of deep depression over the state of the country and quite immature will no doubt, if published, lend welcome fuel to the fires of my various critics and opponents, but I do not see that I can really object to its publication. I have sent a copy of the young man's essay (his name is David Mayers) and of my proposed reply to John Lewis Gaddis for his comments. The episode raises the question whether I should not ask the Mudd Library to place further restrictions on access to my papers.

Other problems of the morning: Robert Silvers, of the *New York Review of Books*, wanting me to review Cy Sulzberger's book on Yalta.[4] I shouldn't, of course, but oh dear, who else should do it?

[The Kennans traveled to the Caribbean, where they were guests of their friends Bill and Laura Riley.]

Pine Cai, British Virgin Islands, December 24

I thought thoughts. First, about this country and our civilization. Doomed, obviously. Doomed, in the first instance, by the nuclear weapon—this viper which we have seized to our breast in incredible belief that it is our protection because it could bite other people. But then, if the viper should fail to destroy us, we are doomed again by over-population and environmental destruction or degradation. It is not, to be sure, our over-population at this point. Our country is of course some 200% over-populated, but we have at least stabilized our own birth rate, and could perhaps face the future with confidence if we were the only ones concerned. It is the others—the Mediterraneans, the Moslems, the Latinos, the various non-WASPs of the 3rd and the not-quite-3rd worlds—who are destroying civilization with their proliferation, our civilization as well as theirs. . . .

If there could have been any chance of preserving on at least a portion

3. "The Prerequisites: Notes on the Problems of the United States in 1938," in box 240, Kennan papers.

4. *Such a Peace: The Roots and Ashes of Yalta* (1982).

of this planet a reasonably sound and hopeful civilization, as one capable of coming to terms with modern technology in a manner considerate and protective of the natural environment as well as of the human being himself . . . this would have been under the guidance of a body politic made up of people heirs to the traditions and habits, the capacities for self-restraint, and self-discipline and tolerance that have developed historically, in close association with the Christian faith, in and around the shores of the North Sea. One of the great American delusions has been, and is, that these values are readily communicable to others who did not inherit them—that all you had to do was to bring these others to our shores, plunge them into the midst of our civilization, and they would instantly be penetrated by this political ethos and responsive to it in their behavior.

1983

Both the apparent slide toward nuclear war and the resulting public protest gained momentum in 1983. In March, President Reagan publicly castigated the Soviet Union as an "evil empire." Also that month, Reagan announced the Strategic Defense Initiative (SDI), a program to develop and deploy a high-tech shield to protect the United States from Soviet missiles. With such a shield in place, Washington could, observers feared, launch a first strike against Moscow. Though mocked as "Star Wars," SDI threatened a serious escalation of the arms race. In September, Soviet fighter jets shot down a Korean Air Lines plane that had wandered into Russian airspace, killing all 269 passengers aboard. The resulting furor worsened already tense relations. In November, The Day After, *a television movie watched by over a hundred million Americans in its initial broadcast, depicted the effects of a nuclear war on a Midwestern town. Though Kennan did not know it, President Reagan, alarmed at the burgeoning public anxiety, began considering steps to ease tensions with Moscow. The president was encouraged in this effort by Secretary of State George P. Shultz, who had replaced the more hawkish Alexander Haig.*

Princeton, January 4

Helen Caldicott[5] and another lady doctor (both very attractive people) came to lunch and stayed until 4 p.m. It was very interesting to talk with them. They have a program for the peace movement that they are anxious to put forward nationally and for which they would like my support. Dr. C. also described in detail her recent talk (or non-talk, for it was simply hopeless to get through to him) with President Reagan. Terrifying!

5. Helen Caldicott is an Australian physician and antinuclear activist.

Washington, March 2

Went to the Soviet Embassy for lunch alone with Dobrynin.[6] Had no particular purpose, except that I, having once suffered under the fact that no one dared come to see me when I was ambassador in the Soviet Union, felt for him in the present dismal state of Soviet-American relations, and thought our country could do a bit better in this respect than the Soviet Union had done by me. So I marched bravely into the old embassy building on 16th Street, under the amazed eyes and furiously clicking cameras of God knows how many agents of the FBI and others of the intelligence fraternity, was kindly and jovially received by my ambassadorial host, lunched and talked pleasantly with him for an hour or so, well aware that the recording devices of both governments were probably noting, for the benefit of an official posterity, every word of our rather innocuous conversation.

In the evening, to the Four Seasons Hotel for a dinner of the ambassadors emeriti with the Secretary of State, Mr. George Shultz. The latter arrived in company with Larry Eagleburger[7] and a young gentleman from California by the name of [no name specified] who, meeting very nicely the usual Reagan requirement that he should have had no previous experience with foreign affairs and should know nothing about them, had just recently been named deputy Under Secretary of State, a position most Foreign Service officers would have regarded as the crowning achievement of 35–40 years of service. I, being the senior of the various ex-ambassadors, was the first to greet and welcome the Secretary of State, and although he is very much an imperturbable person, I thought it jolted him a bit when I gave him the name. The evening passed off pleasantly enough, but I came away doubting that it had been worth his while. He was, as I had expected him to be, patient, quiet, and a good listener, reserving at all times (as I thought quite proper) his opinion on the matters discussed. I found myself liking and respecting him, as most people do, but I foresee something of an ultimate crisis between him and the fanatics in the White House around the President, particularly if he tries to do anything sensible about relations with the Soviet Union.

6. Anatoly Dobrynin was the longtime Soviet ambassador to the United States.

7. Lawrence Eagleburger was a career diplomat who would later become secretary of state under President George H. W. Bush.

[George and Annelise traveled to Europe for his historical research and to visit their daughter Wendy, who lived with her husband in Switzerland.]

En route from Paris to Zurich, June 10

I am now of an age when I should, on all actuarial probability, have left this life, or at least have forfeited any physical or mental powers that would have permitted me to contribute to it. . . . I must learn, then, to look at my surroundings as I was once forced to do in Moscow: look at them as a disembodied spirit, that is, seeing but unseen, observing that to which the spirit has no relationship, and in which it is not a participant. It is as though one were seeing things that were in one sense the future (because they were occurring subsequent to one's active life) but in another sense the past (because one had left behind the world in which they were occurring).

It was with these thoughts in mind that I boarded the Paris Metro this morning. . . . I heard the train approaching as I was going down the steps and had an impulse to quicken my steps, but then I thought: Why do so? A disembodied spirit has no reason to be in a hurry. Time no longer has, or no longer should have, any serious meaning to him.

Then, perceiving an attractive female figure, I questioned myself again: You, I said to myself, profess to be seeing these women as though you were thousands of miles off in space; what possible difference could it have for you whether or not they are attractive? But then I thought to myself: even if a spirit is disembodied, it may still have yearnings. There is nothing to prevent it from sighing and lamenting, as Justice Holmes[8] once did: "Ah, to be seventy again!"

Zurich Airport, June 13

Flying (but particularly the airports) puts me into the nearest thing to a wholly psychotic depression I am capable of experiencing. "These damned American tourists," so goes my inner protest, "with their lousy clothes—their exposed undershirts, their T-shirts, their California-style 'casual' shirts, their jeans and tennis shoes: Why do they have to be here in the Zurich airport? Why can't they stay at home? There ought to be a law about it." "But," says a still, protesting voice, "you are yourself an American." "The hell I am," says I. "And besides, I have a serious

8. Oliver Wendell Holmes.

reason for being over here in Europe. People who have some legitimate reason for travel—diplomats, business men (provided they can prove their bona fides) and scholars, possibly even a few journalists (if they can demonstrate any educational qualifications), yes. But tourists?—under no circumstances. And the same for the Japanese, with their everlasting cameras. If you could only stop these two nations, the Japanese and the Americans, from touring, and the Germans, too, how much nicer the world would be." . . .

Everything that I have believed in, everything I have urged others to believe in, over the course of the past 30 years has been repudiated by my own government and by every one of the other major NATO governments. . . .

My entire effort of 35 years to exert a useful influence on U.S. foreign policy and international affairs by speaking or writing publicly on Soviet-American relations was misconceived and hopeless, should better never have been undertaken in the first place. Of course, 99% of it was provoked by other people who invited me, indeed pressed me, to speak or to write on various occasions, and it was my nature to state what I thought at the moment was the truth. In a sense, you could say that these people who pressed me to speak were to blame. People listened when I spoke. I made good copy. *They* didn't care whether what I said was useful or not. But I, equally obviously, allowed myself to be provoked, and was fool enough to think that some useful purpose might be served by what I was saying, was fool enough, actually, to believe that policy in a democratic country could be influenced by rational discourse. What is evident from my experience is that this last is quite untrue—that people in the mass are quite incapable of reacting to anything like rational discourse—that if they are to be coaxed into approving and supporting anything worthwhile, it is only by some sort of deceit.

Sørenhus, July 25

Where, at this point, is my great, understanding, forgiving God?

Well, I reflect, He is present, understanding, and forgiving as always. His power is great, and we should be lost without it. But that power is not unlimited. He cannot change the natural order in which it is given to us to live. . . . He, God, cannot—at least, not in our age—work miracles just for the sake of any single individual. He cannot help us by distorting the natural external environment of our lives. He can help us only by working within us, strengthening us to bear up under our own imperfections and the blows inflicted on us from outside, we being confident (because there is no alternative) that in His spirit, in which we are permitted to share, there is in the last analysis the justification and the redemption for all things.

August 5

Normally, the kidney stone merely gnaws and hurts. Today, however, it affected me generally, so much so that after an hour's bout of light work outside, I had no choice but to come in (despite marvelous sunny weather) and lie about for the rest of the day on the sofa, reading (I picked it out from the bookcase) the fifth volume of Leon Edel's magnificent biography of Henry James[9]—a book which is more than the biography of a man, rather—a great picture of the literary-social life of upper-class England and New England in the years of James' maturity.

I find myself, perhaps because it is near to the end of my life, trying as I read it to fit myself into that scene (because I suppose I am a literary person myself, slightly manqué). And in doing so, I also find myself looking at myself, or trying to do so, through other eyes. This helps to gain perspective, and I think now and then that I have a fair idea of the figure: inoffensive but insignificant as a person, erratically and inadequately educated but with a reasonably sensitive, receptive, and clear mind, of which my country could have made better use. One does not, it seems to me, have to be a great personality to see things clearly. It takes, in fact (as Freud observed) a modest man to discern what is real, and to distinguish it from that which is unreal, in this imperfect world. That, with reservations, is the best I could say for myself.

The Farm, September 3

I shall soon be 80 years old. I am not in good health. My days are narrowly numbered.

I can no longer hope to achieve much by what I *do*. I know that what I have to offer is quite insufficient to have any significant impact on the policies of my country, to prevent the deterioration of its internal life or to steer its foreign policy into paths that would have any chance of avoiding a disastrous war.

In my personal life I see nothing but grievous problems and dangers on every hand, in the progressive and physical and emotional degenera-

9. *Henry James: The Master, 1901–1916* (1972).

tion of old age for myself and Annelise, in the failures and tragedies of our children. I know how little I can do to avert these misfortunes.

At the same time, I am impressed and humbled by what, as I am constantly being reminded, my name, and the image they have of me, have come to mean for many thousands of other people. I don't like the term "role model," but I realize that it is just this that I have become for many younger people—students, foreign service officers, writers, what you will.

In these circumstances it occurs to me that if, in these final years, there is little I can achieve by *doing*, there is still something to be achieved by acting creditably the part in which fortune has cast me. This is, it seems to me, the least and the most that I can do: to try to look, at least, like what people believe me to be, to encourage them in the illusion that there really *is* such a person; and, by doing this, to try to add just a little bit to their hope and strength and confidence in life.

September 7

The newspaper columns and the wave lengths have been full of the disaster to Soviet-American relations—the shooting down by the Soviet force of the civilian South Korean plane. It was a great blow to the entire peace movement in this country, and one from which its members will not soon recover. It was a serious blow, too, to my own effectiveness as one appealing for a hopeful and sensible policy towards the Soviet Union. But I am used to that sort of frustration, and have been troubled only on behalf of the thousands of people who have put some confidence in me, who have in effect accepted my intellectual leadership, and who now feel themselves disowned and discredited by the very government, relations with which they were trying to improve. It will be some time before the East-West Accord Committee and the dozens of other organizations working in this field can recover from the blow and again begin to make themselves effective. . . . Our motto, for the moment, should be: we have not allowed ourselves to be discouraged by the blows our own government has dealt us; let us now not be any more discouraged by the one we have just received from the Soviet side.

1984

Although the Cold War was still going full blast, Kennan observed that President Reagan was shifting tone and perhaps even listening to him. In a January speech Reagan stressed that despite differences between their governments, the parents of America and Russia wanted "to raise their children in a world without fear and without war." He imagined a Soviet couple, Ivan and Anya, meeting their American counterparts, Jim and Sally, and finding much in common. "People don't make wars," Reagan affirmed.[10]

Chances for better relations took a step backward, however, after February 9, when Yuri Andropov, who had seemed somewhat receptive to change, died and was replaced with an old-fashioned Communist Party boss, Konstantin Chernenko.

Princeton, January 15

Yesterday afternoon, to my amazement, I received a phone call from Jack Matlock, now serving I believe in the office of the National Security Advisor—in effect, at the White House. He was leaving, he said, in an hour accompanying the Secretary of State on the latter's journey to the Stockholm conference on arms problems.

He wanted, Jack said, to give me an advance briefing on what the President was going to say in the speech on Soviet-American relations he is to give on Monday. This he then proceeded to do. He then told me very interesting things: that the President felt some regret over certain of the things he had said in the early period of his presidency about the Soviet Union, and that the reason why he had been unwilling to deal with the Soviet government at that time was that he had felt that we

10. John Lewis Gaddis, *George F. Kennan: An American Life* (New York: Penguin Press, 2011), 662–63.

were too weak militarily for our word to have any weight. Now, he felt we were stronger, and that he was in a better position to deal with them. So he was (this still according to Matlock) quite sincere in the conciliatory things he would be saying on Monday.

While pleased with this all (for I have high respect for Matlock), I was startled and puzzled by it. The time it was made (on the verge of his departure on an official journey to Europe) showed that the move was not casually undertaken, and the nature of his position leads one to suppose that he must have authorization, and this from a high quarter—either the National Security Adviser or the President to do it. That it was his own initiative I do not doubt, but that the permission was forthcoming is extraordinary.

[The Kennans traveled by rail from New Jersey to Iowa, where Kennan lectured at Grinnell College. Kennan noted that the Amtrak train "compared very poorly with the Russian ones." He liked the town of Grinnell: "ethnicity white, devoid of a demoralized proletariat, essential crimeless (not even a porno shop) . . . But the students arrive here drenched with all the negative influences of American society."[11] The college community was eager to hear Kennan's take on current affairs, which had been occupying his mind.]

Grinnell College, Iowa, January 29

I have a sense that respect for me has recently risen in White House circles, some of them at least, and in the State Department. They will not consult me directly (and I think I should be glad they don't) but I suspect that they listen, if apprehensively, to what I say. (In the President's second speech on Soviet-American relations there were three points taken directly from my recent *New Yorker* article.)[12] And then there was Matlock's call.

I was shaken today by these reflections. Perhaps, I thought, in view of Mr. Reagan's strong position and in view of the mess Russians have made of their relations with most of the Western Europeans, and of their weakness generally, perhaps one should support Reagan and try to work through him for a better relationship. But then I thought of all his other follies and of his unlimited commitment to a military showdown, and I

11. Kennan diary, January 28, 1984.

12. "Breaking the Spell," *New Yorker*, 49 (October 3, 1983), 44–53. Although Matlock had read works by Kennan, it was likely that Reagan had not done so. Gaddis, *George F. Kennan*, 664.

also reflected on my own age and on the limitations that imposes, and I thought: no, the faintly more positive tone of his recent speech is surely no more than a minor tactical concession. He is a stubborn man who, precisely because his political position is a strong one, is unlikely to wander very far from the primitive preconceptions he has already formed. Better, I thought, for you, Kennan, to keep out of this. There is little you can do with Mr. Reagan. And it is impossible to help the Russians when they are so little capable of helping themselves. You are effectively stymied: accept the implications of your old age, and let the tragedy take its course.

[The Kennans traveled to Europe for a number of reasons: George's research, publicity for the French edition of one of his books, meetings with various officials and scholars, sight-seeing, and visiting daughter Wendy, her husband Claude Pfaeffli, and the couple's new son, George's namesake, who was born on February 16, the same date as both Kennan and his grandfather's cousin.]

En route from Geneva to Florence, March 12

I enter without enthusiasm this country of Italy. Of all the great countries of Europe it is, despite its great natural beauty and its marvelous antiquities, for me the least agreeable. There is none other, at any rate, where the life of the contemporary inhabitants strikes me as less interesting and less attractive. . . . When I see what a mess the modern Italians make of their own country, I am less surprised by what the Italian contractors do in New Jersey.

Prague, March 25

How strange and unnatural it seemed to me to see this ancient profoundly European city, once the center of the Holy Roman Empire and indeed the very epicenter of Central Europe, under the influence of the Russians—its street signs and other outward marks of political allegiance confirming to the stale, lifeless, and dreadfully outdated symbols of Soviet power. There could not, it seemed to me, be any permanency in anything so unnatural. And, while I did not say this to them, the great question, I thought, would be whether the recovery of the position of Bohemia-Moravia as a truly central European power, and the ordering of its relationship to all its neighbors, would occur gradually and peacefully or whether the disruption of the abnormal Russian tie would come about only as a byproduct of another great military conflict, which would probably deprive it of all positive meaning.[13]

[Kennan, accompanied by his son, Christopher, flew to the West Coast to raise money for the Kennan Institute for Russian affairs. As on other such flights, he took the occasion to elaborate on his critique of America's society and its place in the world.

In Los Angeles he also met with Dr. Frieda Por, who in 1935 had treated him in the Viennese sanatorium, and who now appeared as "a tiny little aging person but warm bright and happy."][14]

En route to Los Angeles, May 7

What, if I had my way, would be done in place of what is being done. . . .

1. The entire present armed establishment will be, for the most part, replaced by one directed strictly to the defense of our own soil, plus what is required to meet minimum defense assistance needs of our NATO and Japanese allies. The ground force component of this new establishment will be one based on universal national service along Swiss lines. The Navy will be designed for defense of our coasts and for such transport duties as are necessitated by obligations to allies; it, too, while commanded primarily by a professional officers corps, will make maximum use of national service personnel. The most strenuous effort will be made to achieve universal outlawing and removal of nuclear weapons and strategic missiles from national arsenals. Meanwhile, the country will embrace a no-first-use policy and will retain only a minimum nuclear deterrent. . . .

2. First priority will be given to a reduction of population, to a maximum of 200 million, preferably to something more like 175 million. Immigration for permanent residence will be effectively terminated. Illegal immigrants already in this country will be accepted for permanent residence, but no new ones admitted. Border controls will be greatly strengthened. Men having spawned more than 2 children will be compulsively sterilized. Planned parenthood and voluntary sterilization will be in every way encouraged.

3. The principle that the best way to produce is the way that uses the least human labor, the maximum mechanization, the maximum

13. After the Cold War, Czechoslovakia would divide into the Czech Republic (largely Bohemia) and Slovakia (largely Moravia).
14. Kennan diary, May 9, 1984.

computerization, etc., will be rigorously rejected and its application combated. Everything possible will be done to re-primitivize and localize the economic process: encouragement of the handicrafts, restriction of elaborate processing, break-up of the national distribution chains, maximum development of local resources, & local distribution. All development of agricultural land for non-agricultural purposes will be stopped at once. As much as possible of that land that has already been thus developed will be reclaimed and used for settlement of the redundant metropolitan ghetto populations. These will be encouraged and taught to follow a semi-rural, semi-industrial form of life. . . .

Automobiles, except for the most essential purposes, will be in every way discouraged. Public transportation, by the same token, will be encouraged. Air transport will be throttled down & eventually restricted to hardship & urgent cases. So will much of the trucking. The railroad will fill the resulting gap.

Communication, too, will be revolutionized. Most of television will be sacrificed: perhaps one or two public channels operating only in the evening hours, all advertising being either eliminated or restricted to special announced periods and kept quite separate from the legitimate broadcast material. Newspapers will be limited in size and permitted to accept only a limited amount of advertising, something like 10% of the total space, and this segregated into a special advertising section, not mixed with other material.

In agriculture, the small family farm, usually combined with some non-agricultural activity, will be encouraged. The use of artificial fertilizers will be drastically restricted, and with it, of course, the size of the exportable grain surplus. (The beneficiary will be the soil).

Well, enough of this nonsense. The question at once arises: could any of this, even if desirable, be done other than by the most ferocious dictatorship? The answer is obviously: no. It could never be done by popular consent. The "people" haven't the faintest idea what is good for them.

Have I? An imperfect idea—yes; but better than theirs. Left to themselves, they not only would (and will) simply stampede into a final, utterly disastrous, and totally unnecessary nuclear war. And if, by some quirk of fate, that escaped them, they would (and will) complete the devastation of their own natural environment, as they are now enthusiastically doing.

Will I say any of this when I speak tomorrow night? Will I attempt to write it for publication? Obviously not. The one impermissible act is to tell the young that there is nothing to hope for, that all is lost. I might, after all, be wrong—I am bound to be, in any event, partly wrong (for no one is wholly right), but I might even be more wrong than that.

[The Kennans were in Moscow as guests of the U.S. ambassador to the Soviet Union, Arthur A. Hartman and his wife, Donna Hartman. George attended a conference of scholars in the Soviet capital.]

Moscow, June 8

An exciting day full of memories and new impressions, an unreal mixture of the familiar and the unfamiliar. I returned, shaken up with all this emotional and intellectual tossing to and fro. And there, in the Bolshoi, drugged with the music yet high-tuned from the various stimulations of the day, I suddenly saw, more vividly than I had ever seen it before, what a garrulous old fool I really am, and how wholly incorrigible. I am sensitive and intelligent, I know. I see things many others do not see. But I lose balance in the presence of other people. To correct me, you would have to deprive me of all social life, and hence of many possibilities of observation. I would not dry up entirely for I could live, largely, by literature alone, as I have lived in late-19th century Russia. But that, too, is scarcely a practical solution.

Randesund, Norway, July 18

I turn my back, figuratively, on the land and keep my eyes fixed on the horizon of the sea—the abused, raped sea, deprived of its dignity and its mystery by the ubiquitous oil rigs, the monstrous thundering automobile ferries, the airplanes overhead, the pipelines underneath. No wonder that it rises up sometimes in winter and strikes out in its fury against everything that men have been trying to do to it. My heart is with it in these frantic, angry outbursts.

Princeton, August 26

Regarding the U.S. presidential election I have two choices. The first would be to come out publicly before the election, to emphasize the dreadful record of the Reagan administration with respect to Soviet-American relations, and to insist that, all other issues aside, this alone warrants repudiation of Mr. Reagan and the election of a competitor. . . . The other course would be to lie low, and either say nothing at all or at least say nothing critical of the Reagan administration before the election, in the hopes of preserving a faint possibility of being useful to another Republican administration, if one is elected, and if it should by any chance wish to listen to me or to use me in an effort to repair the damage that has been done.

[The Kennans, particularly to meet Annelise's wishes, vacationed in Italy.]

Ischia, Italy, September 23

I thought of the qualities of this place: the incongruous mixture of tolerance, naivety, over-crowding, sociability, family solidarity, localism, acceptance of modernism in its most hideous forms and yet with some sort of an inner self-defense against it—life led, in short, in the small dimension, full of pettiness, no doubt, and not without its small cruelties and injustices, but borne along by the broad, wise, disillusioned charity of the Catholic Church, by the comforting familiarities of family life, and by the unvarying, reassuring support of the Christian sacraments. And I thought to myself: so long as it lasts, imperfect as it is, all this, perhaps, is the best one can hope for—a messy life, full of dirt, overcrowding, confusion, and disorder; but with its failings, like its possibilities, limited by the intimacy of its localistic orientation, and, above all, at least in the personal sense human. Better, in any case, than the great, highly-developed, impersonal societies, with their lordly ambitions, their nuclear weapons, and their vast, technologically-advanced, abuse of the natural environment.

Capri, September 29

Since I, like most diarists, proceed on the theory that someone beside myself will, or may, someday read this diary, and since no one was able, before we came here, to describe this island to me with any reasonable degree of clarity or plausibility, I shall speed its departure from my life with one or two words about it.

[After a medical procedure that removed his kidney stone, Kennan was transported home while reclining in a station wagon piled with pillows and blankets.]

Princeton, November 6

With my eyes too low to follow the road ahead, I was conducted out of New York City in the early afternoon sunshine of a warm November day, seeing everything in a way that I had never seen or appreciated it before: the foliage of Central Park (which never looked more beautiful to me), the smart facades of the uptown buildings, the shabby second floor windows of 11th Avenue tenements, the swift-flowing tiles of the tunnel walls, and finally, the New Jersey of the Hackensack meadows—all quite beautiful so long as one could not see the ground level.

[The Kennans visited friends in Maine.]

Somesville, Maine, December 31

I myself am caught in a strange predicament. I see clearly that this American civilization of ours is headed for terrible troubles, troubles that will complete the destruction of the United States as I have known it. . . .

If left only to myself and free of obligations to others, I would seriously consider moving to Canada and ending my days there, for I am unable to give any serious help to this country and would prefer not to share its conscience. But every time I move around the country as I am now doing, I am made to realize what a great body of supporters I have within it. I cannot estimate the size of this body in numerical terms, but surely it runs into the hundreds of thousands if not millions, of which a large proportion are young people, desperately in need, not of guidance (for they are too independently minded, thank God, to be uncritically led by anyone) but of a figure in whose honesty and good will and moral earnestness and readiness to try to face the facts they can have confidence. I seem, deservedly or not, to appear to them to be that sort of a figure.

If I were to give up the effort here at home and emigrate, I would be saying to all these people (and saying it more eloquently than in words): There is no hope for you, you may as well cut and run, like myself. But I have no right to say this to them. For one thing, they are, by and large in no position to cut and run, and I would therefore only be encouraging them to despair. But, more important still, I have no right to say this to them. I may be wrong. Perhaps, unbeknownst to me, there is no reason for them to despair. Perhaps there is hope which I, seeing things "only through a glass, darkly," cannot see. And what a dreadful crime I would have committed if I had not only urged them, but caused them, to despair needlessly.

No, there is nothing for it. I must stay here and try to carry on, whatever my own judgment tells me, *as though there were hope*. I have, in a way, invited this obligation. Had I wished to avoid it, I should never have been a teacher, should never have written or spoken publicly.

1985

*On March 11, Mikhail Gorbachev, fifty-four, became head of the Communist Party of the Soviet Union. Gorbachev soon announced plans to revitalize his nation with a program of restructuring the economy (*perestroika*) and allowing openness toward opinion (*glasnost*). He was also intent on easing the Cold War. Neither Kennan nor other American experts on Russia foresaw how far-reaching Gorbachev's reforms would extend.*

Washington, April 4

I am questioned [by the director of the State Department's Bureau of Politico-Military Affairs, John T. Chain Jr.] about Mr. Gorbachev and related matters. I answer readily enough. (That is my failing.) My host and his companions are polite and urbane in the best State Department tradition. I am aware that this is the first time in many years that I have been thus consulted in this place, and even if the questioning relates only to information, not to policy, I am mildly pleased to be given this attention. But there is something disturbingly familiar about it—about the place, about the smooth remoteness of my interrogators, about their wariness of me, and mine of them. It puts me in mind of Mr. John Foster Dulles and of his suggestion, on the heels of his firing of me, that I should drop in from time to time and tell him what I thought about conditions; what I had to say, he explained, interested him.

Princeton, April 21

Three more weeks have passed—weeks of such intensive activity that there was no time for a diary. What have I done? Vanity, vanity, vanity! . . .

I attended a small lunch for the Secretary of State. Mr. Shultz, who was relaxed, spoke readily and sensibly about the limited subjects to which the conversation turned, and was distinctly cordial towards me. He even surprised me by inquiring my view as to how the new leadership of the Soviet Union should be approached, to which I replied by pointing out that Soviet leaders are normally in many respects insecure people and require reassurance in the form of respect for their prestige, and that when you negotiate with them it is well to have a clear understanding as to the subject of the negotiations and to stick strictly to that, not confusing them by trying to drag in irrelevant questions.

Charlottesville, April 26

We drove down in the morning (through the hunt club country of Virginia, all relatively unspoiled by commercialism, at least visually, and very beautiful in its spring garb) to lunch with Averell Harriman at his lovely house on the hill. Pamela was away, in Washington, where she had been entertaining some 150 people at a Democratic fund-raising dinner.[15] (I admired her loyalty to this so nearly lost cause; this stoutness reflected, I thought, the Englishwoman in her.)

Averell we found very stooped and fragile, clear enough in mind but not in memory. He was now very much the venerable gentleman of the old school, endowed with that aristocracy of the spirit and demeanor that seems to come with great old age, particularly when supported by wealth and distinction.

Sørenhus, August 14

Christopher has sent me an article from the quarterly entitled *Policy Review*, put out by the Heritage Foundation. . . . It began with the monstrously erroneous statement that I had argued "that containment should be a global strategy, not one restricted to a few areas," a statement that was, as everyone knows who has occupied himself seriously with my works, precisely the opposite of the truth. He would only have had to glance at p. 359 of the first volume of my *Memoirs* to learn this. It was, in fact, precisely this feature of the "Truman doctrine" statement that I objected to.

I agree with Christopher that it would probably be best not to attempt to reply specifically. . . . But, with the forty-year anniversary of the drafting of the X-article coming up, I suppose that at some point I should deal with the criticisms, generally, that have been forthcoming from the right-wing, including this one.

15. Pamela Digby Churchill Harriman was Averell's wife and the former daughter-in-law of Winston S. Churchill.

August 19

As agreed with the German publisher, I received, some days ago, the German translation of the first chapters of *The Fateful Alliance*,[16] sent in order that I might look them over before one went too far with the work.

Oh dear, oh dear! What has happened to the ability of Germans in this age to write their own language? Awkward, pedestrian, painfully literal, word-for-word, and even then many of the words not right—the translation is totally lacking in understanding of the context, and in feeling for the tone and style of the original. I feel sorry for the translator, whom I picture as a young man, fancying that he knows English, and no doubt in need of money (why else would one take on so thankless a task?). But I don't see how I can let the book be butchered after this fashion, and am saying this as tactfully as I can in a letter to the publisher.

Princeton, November 13

Once again, many days have passed since I was able to write in this journal. Why? Because no sooner am I in this place, ostensibly dedicated to scholarship, than I become engulfed in a host of demands, activities, and problems, a few of which are to be sure, related to scholarship in some wider sense, but not to my own researches, and which simply leave me no time for anything resembling a contemplative life. . . .

Never have I felt more strongly the urge to live in the country—in the reassuring company not just of vegetable nature but also of animals: dogs, cats, pigs, cows, horses, what you will. Here in Princeton, what remains of Nature dies its slow suburban death.

November 16

Much of these last two days has gone, however, with the reading of and responding to the massive typescript of a doctoral dissertation written (for presentation at Columbia University) by a man—a Swede, I believe—by the name of Anders Stephanson. He is obviously an erudite man, far beyond the average educational level of our American doctoral candidates, widely read in philosophy and politics generally. I seem to detect a good deal of influence from the Marxist quarter, particularly on the philosophical side, although I do not suspect him of being now a Marxist. He seems to have read with scrupulous (though skeptical)

16. Kennan, *The Fateful Alliance: France, Russia, and the Coming of the First World War* (1984).

care and thoroughness everything he could that I had written, including much from earlier years, and he has picked it all to pieces, mostly from the standpoint of consistency and philosophical profundity, but in my opinion quite fairly. . . . Recognizing it as the most unsparing and impressive critique of my published views I was fascinated by it, couldn't lay it down.

November 27

Another phone call: this time from a congressman, Mr. Seiberling,[17] who wanted to tell me that he had sent to the White House, before the recent summit meeting, a copy of my Einstein Peace Award speech. He knew, he said, that the President never read anything, but he thought perhaps people in his entourage did. In any case, Messrs. Reagan and Gorbachev had agreed on principle, had they not, that a 50% cut in nuclear missiles was desirable? And where had that idea originated except in that Einstein speech?

December 27

I am taking advantage of the unusual quiet to try to assess my own situation and potential usefulness. . . . This past autumn has been no different from many others. There has been the same tension between the effort to study history, conducted in total loneliness in the face of a massive public indifference—all this on the one side; on the other side, the multitudinous pressures and distinctions emanating from people who are anxious, for one reason or another (sometimes commercial, sometimes idealistic), that I should contribute to the discussion of contemporary affairs. . . .

I am becoming a species of myth, particularly for the younger generation. And the less I show myself, as well as the less I talk, the stranger the myth becomes. This is ironic and amazing and puzzling. But it is also a responsibility.

I am in utter despair about this country: despair for its short-term future, despair for its long-term one. I suspect that we are only two or three years from an appalling financial breakdown that will probably wipe us all out. And behind that lie the more serious problems: the nuclear danger, the environmental disaster, the control of the media of

17. John F. Seiberling Jr. was a Democratic congressman from Ohio.

communication by the advertisers, the resulting bemused state of the population, the decadence, the uncontrolled immigration, etc. In the face of all this, however much of a myth I may be to the students, I am helpless. I have influence, you might say, almost everywhere but where it counts.

1986

The year 1986 would be pivotal with regard to historic developments about which Kennan cared. Former ambassador to the Soviet Union W. Averell Harriman, who had both inspired and frustrated Kennan when the latter was his number two in 1944–46, died at age ninety-four on July 26. The passing into history of the generation "present at the creation" of the Cold War, as Dean Acheson had put it, was underscored by the publication of The Wise Men,[18] *a best-selling group biography of Harriman, Kennan, and Acheson as well as of Charles E. Bohlen, Robert Lovett, and John J. McCloy. Even as the origins of the Cold War were receding, the end of that conflict was, in retrospect, becoming discernible in the summit conferences between Reagan and Gorbachev at Geneva in November 1985 and at Reykjavik in October 1986.*

Princeton, January 4

At the moment, of course, the great danger spot is the eastern Mediterranean and the Levant, where the growth of Arab terrorism has produced a crisis now near the breaking point. It is obviously a crisis beyond our ability to solve. Our two great past follies: involving ourselves with the Israelis and tolerating the nationalization of the oil-fields in that part of the world, giving the status of sovereignty to the various sheikdoms and then permitting ourselves and our allies to become dependent on their oil—these two follies are now returning to bite us, and we shall soon have to pay a heavy price, an incalculable one, for our frivolity. . . .

There is a possibility that we may get some snow over night. I always pray for it, too much of it cannot come for my taste. Nothing else, it seems, can stop these people, at least for a few hours, from driving end-

18. Evan Thomas and Walter Isaacson, *The Wise Men: Six Friends and the World They Made* (1986).

lessly about in the cars. It should, when it comes, be a warning to them of the foolishness of permitting themselves to become dependent on this expensive, wasteful, unsociable, and environmentally pernicious mode of transportation.

[The Kennans went to New York to visit friends and to enable George to promote the Kennan Institute and do some research at the Bakhmeteff Archive of Russian and East European Culture at Columbia University.]

New York City, January 31

Regarding the shuttle disaster[19] I feel the same sadness everyone else does for the fate of the victims, but their sacrifice seems to me even more appalling because I have no enthusiasm at all for the activity in which they were to have participated. Only the day before the disaster I had found myself saying to someone that I would gladly trade the entire American space program, in all its forms military and civilian, for a good national telegraph system and railway transportation network such as we used to have. If the space program has served (at such vast expense) any constructive purpose, this has been to teach us that of all the heavenly bodies accessible to our observation and knowledge, our own is the only one suitable for any form of human, animal, or vegetational life, with the lesson that we should value this inestimable blessing and try to fashion our life here below in such a way that we encourage its natural beauty and richness and do not continue to constitute what Bill Bullitt[20] once termed "a skin disease" on its surface.

Princeton, February 5

Annelise and I, yesterday evening, watched the President deliver his State of the Union message. One normally thinks of the demagogue as a cynical, calculating, scheming character, fully aware of the depth of his own duplicity but prepared to step roughshod over all moral principles to assure his own power. What is most terrible about Mr. Reagan is that he is to all appearances an amiable, well-meaning man who probably believes a good part of what he is saying. He is of course enacting a role, but is asking the public to enact it with him, and is triumphing in the cause. The public enjoys enacting this role with him, and is undisturbed

19. On January 28, the space shuttle *Challenger* blew up shortly after takeoff.
20. In 1933–34, William C. Bullitt and Kennan set up the U.S. embassy in Moscow.

by the evidence that it is one that invites nothing other than catastrophe upon the country and the world.

February 11

If salvation is to come for Western civilization, it will come not from this country, committed as it is to the commercial and political cultivation of unreality, and not from a Western Europe bemused by Mr. Reagan's fantasies, and thus plodding blindly along behind us. This, I suppose, is the real reason why I am going to Hungary: to see whether certain of these Eastern European countries, largely immune to the forces of decadence and contrived illusion that are coming to dominate the West, may not by chance stumble on hopeful approaches of which neither of the superpowers is capable.

[Accompanied by Annelise, George traveled to Budapest to visit a Soviet bloc nation that was fast evolving, meet with scholars and officials, and, not least, take advantage of spa medicinal baths for "the treatment of my arthritic knees."][21]

Budapest, March 13

I have not seen in this hotel a single sign, placard, or other marking of any sort to suggest that this is a "Communist" country. This is only one extreme bit of evidence of something that has been obvious now for some years: namely, that as an object of belief, enthusiasm, or even interest, the Marxist-Leninist ideology is embarrassingly dead throughout all of Central and Northern Europe. The heavy hand of Russian military power, while also nowhere in evidence, is still effective throughout this region. And there are no doubt a great many people, particularly in the younger generation, who have accepted the idea of "Socialism," in a wider and vaguer sense, as a commendable ideal. "Capitalism," at least, whatever is meant by it, has come to have negative connotations: selfishness, exploitation, contempt for general humanity, etc. But Communism, as a militant ideology in the Leninist sense, has proved to be empty of meaning, short lived, and spiritually and intellectually powerless, which is the inevitable fate, I suspect, of all would-be secular religions, flowing, as they do, only from the arrogance and presumption of individual human minds, viewing man only as an economic animal, pretending that all his

21. Kennan diary, March 9, 1986.

dilemmas can be resolved by tinkering with his collective condition, and failing to recognize that the deepest of his problems lie within his own individual nature, there to be coped with only by love and faith.

March 28

I must never again visit, so long as the present political situation endures, another country of the Soviet bloc. It puts us all, myself and the local American representatives, into an ambiguous position, but myself in particular. I am looked to by people in the host country for things I cannot deliver—for words of hope in which I do not myself believe. Yet to tell what I know to be the truth: that they have nothing to hope from the United States, is to cross up the local American diplomats, who are only doing their duty and being personally kind to me in the bargain, and to put myself in the position of seeming to be working against my own government in a foreign country, a position in which I never hope to find myself.

[Kennan went to Helsinki to receive an honorary degree.]

Helsinki, May 22

On leafing through the diary for 1983 I was not made entirely happy by what I read. Many of the entries were entirely personal, primarily about myself, only secondarily about my surroundings, and while they were sometimes interesting to me for purposes of self-understanding, they were too plaintive and too repetitious to be of much interest to others, as I would have liked this journal someday to be. For this repetitiveness there was, of course, a reason if not an excuse—the reason being the over-flooding of life everywhere with a type of modernity, drawn largely from the U.S., that I encounter wherever I go and react to negatively and with depression, wherever I encounter it. Aside from the boring subject of myself, there was too much about *peoples*, too little about individual people. And I was made aware in reading these entries that the most valuable things I have written in these recent years have been, after all, my published comments on the contemporary scene, particularly the reactions to my own people and government. Since I have found it best to restrict to a minimum the publication of that sort of material, and since not a day goes by that I do not have thoughts and reactions of that nature that I would like to put on paper, the many blank pages that lie within this new cover would seem to be the best place for them.

Sørenhus, June 11

I agree with Tocqueville, at the start, that more important than the institutions of a people are *"les manières"*[22] (a term which I shall not try, here, to render into English). And I consider that these are something not to be suddenly or violently changed, particularly by legislation. Here only the gradual influences will do, if and when they are needed at all, the principal ones being explication, persuasion, and example. In general, I distrust all efforts to produce abrupt changes in the life of a society. The only changes that can be lasting and useful are the gradual, organic ones, in tune with the slow rhythm of social life. The planets and the pace of our own development as human beings should have taught us that. This is why I dislike and distrust all violent revolutionary upheavals in the lives of peoples and all movements that aim to promote them, whether on the right or on the left.

Secondly, I am a firm believer (as I believe most of the founding fathers of our country were) in *representative* government, as opposed to government by plebiscite, by acclamation, or by direct action of the public. The public is not supposed to know, indeed cannot know, how best to decide the many questions that come before a government. That, as Burke so eloquently argued, is the task of representatives, and particularly those who are able to give to the problems of government their undivided attention, and they should use their own judgment in making the decisions.

But then, those elected to be representatives should have at least minimal qualifications for this responsibility. The public should be able to elect from a panel of candidates, a panel selected in such a way as to assure that its members, if not the best (to assume *that* is impossible) are at least unlikely to be the worst. And who should make this selection? The people at large are incapable of making it; such decisions cannot be made by an inchoate mass. And the bosses of political parties (the ones who make it today) are the last ones to whom this responsibility should be delegated.

Who, then? That, in my opinion, is the central question for American democracy. Our failure to date to find any answer to it is the greatest weakness of our political system. It is not in the election of representatives that the system fails; it is in the process of nomination.

This is an extremely complicated problem. . . .

22. Ingrained behavior, customs, culture.

I view a rule of law, including a reasonable code of civil rights and a proper system of justice, as basic to any tolerable government, and definitely better if you have to choose, than a tyranny of the many.

June 18

The news columns, these days, are full of the problems of South Africa and, even more, of the reaction to these problems in Europe and North America. . . . So little do I see the justification for these demands, so strange are they to my own way of thinking, that I have to ask myself whether I have not missed something.[23] Do all these good people, full of their indignant demands for punitive action against the South African authorities, know something I don't know? They speak of the abolition of apartheid (which is indeed an obsolescent and impractical concept) but they are extremely vague about the alternatives. One is allowed to conclude that what they want is the immediate and extreme centralization of the country under majority rule with a universal franchise, the immediate extension to the black majority, in other words, of full political as well as civil rights.

Do they, I wonder, have any idea of what this would mean? Do they have any reason to suppose that the mass of this black population would have any extensive understanding for such a system of government or any disposition to take upon themselves the qualities of restraint and tolerance such a system implies? Do they really believe that the understanding for such principles of government, and the civic self-discipline that goes with that understanding, are something that any people, regardless of this previous history, tradition, experience, or habit, could don instantly and easily, like a cloak, any day it chose to, and then make it work effectively? If so, do they really believe that the centuries of slow growth of such understanding in the West, and the agonies, the conflicts, and the gradual discipline of experience that went into that growth, were as nothing? . . .

What bothers me most about these demands for pressures and sanctions is the general philosophical shallowness they reveal. Where, here, are the Christian teachings that recognize limits to human wisdom and allow for the existence of genuinely tragic situations, the possible resolutions of which are not readily visible to the human eye? And what has

23. Kennan was referring to pressure to loosen or end the apartheid policies of the white-dominated South African government.

become of the great philosophical insights of such men as Burke and Tocqueville, and particularly the recognition that without an ingrained sense of personal responsibility tyranny can flow just as readily from the will of a majority as from that of a minority or a single man?

Plainly, it seems to me, we are confronted with a generation of people who have never acquired any significant sense of history, and who, lacking that sense, also lack understanding for the reality of tragedy as an ever-present factor of the human predicament.

July 1

The two superpowers are incapable of composing their differences and putting an end to the arms race, or even mitigating its extent. For this, I put by far the greater part of the blame on the United States. I see every reason to suppose that Gorbachev, if given any reasonable amount of political consideration and collaboration from the American side, would have been quite prepared to go in for fairly far reaching accommodations with respect to both nuclear and conventional weapons. This would not have required any readiness on the American side to express agreement to his ideological principles or any acceptances, beyond what has already *de facto* been accorded, to the Soviet hegemony in Eastern Europe.

Given this helplessness of the two superpowers to do anything significant to lower East-West tensions, the question arises as to what the European countries, both east and west of the dividing line, could themselves do to alleviate the most dangerous aspects of the continued division.

Obviously, none of the major European NATO countries is disposed, today, to take any initiative in that direction. Two of them are in the hands of conservative governments that have given Mr. Reagan almost complete support in matters of relations with the Soviet Union. A third, France, has a government headed by a man[24] just as anti-Soviet as Mr. Reagan or Mrs. Thatcher, a government that insists, anyway, on going its own way, is fully and happily committed to the nuclear weapon (a new embodiment of the Maginot Line psychology), and sees nothing greatly wrong with what Mr. Reagan is doing. Most of the other NATO powers are less enthusiastic about American leadership in the East-West relationship, as it has revealed itself in recent months and years, but have been unwilling to mount any vigorous opposition to it. . . .

24. François Mitterrand was the French president.

I see three principal reasons for this complacency. They are:

(a) The feeling that NATO is an end in itself rather than a means to an end, and that therefore the preservation of the outward unity of NATO should take precedence over every other consideration.

(b) The egregious over-rating of Soviet military strength, an over-rating deliberately fostered and encouraged by the Pentagon, with the partial support of the European NATO partners themselves.

(c) The entrenched belief in wide and influential NATO circles that the Soviet leaders ever since World War II have wanted to invade Western Europe, or so intimidate it that they could take it over politically and establish their political hegemony over it, and that it has been only the existence of the American nuclear "deterrent" that has prevented them from taking military action to accomplish this end.

The result of all this is a stalemate that to many people appears quite acceptable. I cannot take this view. The stalemate, in the first place, is not in itself a stable one. The Star Wars project alone, with its many uncertainties, precludes any stability. And the further growth of nuclear arsenals, aside from adding to the already preposterous menace that these arsenals present, cannot be expected to proceed evenly on both sides. Beyond that, there is the growing danger of the unleashing of a nuclear conflict by inadvertence: by human error, by confusion, by misread signals, by computer failure, by nuclear terrorist attack, or, above all, by complications arising from the tragic, deeply-embittered conflicts in various parts of the world where, as a consequence of desperation or inflamed passion, nuclear explosives might be brought into play. In the situations we have before us in southern Africa, in northern Ireland, in the Middle East, in India-Pakistan, and in Korea (potentially one of the greatest danger spots of the world), nuclear-armed powers, or powers possessing the technology for the production of nuclear weapons, are involved. It is only a matter of time, it seems to me, before one or the other of the parties to these conflicts makes use of nuclear explosives, and that when it comes, will be a moment of great danger.

The Chernobyl near-disaster[25] is in one respect a great blessing. It has produced a profound impression on public opinion. It has implications of the most serious nature for both the nuclear power industry and the military development of nuclear weapons. There is a wild absurdity in

25. On April 26, a Soviet nuclear power plant at Chernobyl malfunctioned, releasing a huge amount of dangerous radiation.

the present efforts to achieve international agreement on the means for avoiding the relatively moderate dangers of power plant accidents, on the one hand, and, at the same time, the reckless expansion of the arsenals of nuclear explosives, on the other.

July 23

There has appeared, still at sea but now entering the Kristiansand roadstead, the most extraordinary apparition I can recall ever seeing afloat: an enormous raft, upon which rests a flat horizontal superstructure some 30–40 feet in height, from which in turn, there rise three tremendous steel-skeleton towers, each (according to my estimate) 300–500 feet in height—certainly the highest floating objects I have ever seen, and presumably among the highest ever to have existed—all this towed by a single sea-going tug, the sound of whose pounding diesels can be heard across the 3–4 miles of intervening water. I stare at the apparition through my binoculars. It plainly has something to do with the oil rigs. I see it as a species of modern cathedral: an expression of reverence and submission to the great god of this 20th century, the internal combustion engine and the fuel that feeds it. It is on the altar of this god that there are being sacrificed not only the quality of life of the generation now alive, but through the environmental effects, the very future of civilization.

How sad the real God must be: to see these hundreds of millions of tiny bipeds whom he endowed with intelligence, imagination, and conscience, and for whom he provided this uniquely rich and beautiful planet as a habitat, destroying the planet and the future of their civilization for the childish pleasure of chugging around in their little motorized buggies. And we, the historians and philosophers, are supposed to place our faith in the wisdom of these multitudes, democratically (or so goes the thesis) expressed.

Washington, September 17

The memorial service for Averell Harriman was a tremendous affair in the National Cathedral—a real high-church religious service, this time—very high-church, in fact, with the choir boys singing (not very well). The Almighty, I thought, must have been surprised to be prayed to so ceremoniously and by so many people for the repose of Averell's soul: for Averell as I saw him was the least pious of men. He, I suspect, never doubted from the beginning that he had God's grace, or that he deserved it, and saw no reason why he should pray on Sunday mornings for something that was his by obvious right. I never knew him, in any case, to go to church.

There was a dinner, at Polly Wisner's, where Nancy Kassebaum, Senator from Kansas, now Joany's[26] new boss, was present—all very pleasant. Clayton[27] was full of praise for a book that is about to appear called *The Wise Men*, these latter being Jack McCloy, Bob Lovett, Dean Acheson, Chip Bohlen, and myself. He considered that I came off very well at the hands of its two authors (young Evan Thomas and Walter Isaacson). I myself thought it a dreadful book in a number of respects: shallow, gossipy, supercilious, and most unflattering to myself, who appears as a plaintive neurasthenic and a bad writer in the bargain, the author of masses of "florid" and pretentious prose which bored all those to whom it was submitted. (The account addressed only my governmental service, with a word or two added about the Reith lectures & the testimony about Vietnam on the Hill in 1966. Beyond that, I don't think the authors knew that I had ever written anything in my retirement). I came away from the perusing of the volume, realizing that such is the distance between this generation and my own that if I had ever done or written anything worthwhile, people of this generation (Gaddis, thank God, is an exception) would never be able to recognize it as such.

[The Kennans visited their daughter Wendy and her family in Switzerland.]

Geneva, September 25

I have been enduring, over the past fortnight, some sort of nervous-psychic crisis. It reflects the coming together of a number of causes, of which the simple onset of old age is surely one. But the most marked feature of it is an almost nauseous sense of revulsion not to my former life as an external experience, but to the person of the man that led that life. The book mentioned in the last of these entries had a part in arousing this revulsion, because, unjust, often inaccurate, and superficial as it is, there is just enough truth in this welter of offensive triviality to remind me of the way I was and the way I appeared to others. And while I had been able, in recent years (aided no doubt by all the honors and flattery I had received) to put much of this out of my mind as the psychically healthy person tends to do, I now for some reason find it necessary to

26. George and Annelise's daughter.
27. Clayton Fritchey was a former government official and newspaper columnist.

confront it. The experience of doing so has shaken me so severely that I think things will never be quite the same again.

Princeton, October 15

When I spoke with Mac Bundy on Monday morning, just after the breakdown at Reykjavik,[28] I was much impressed with the suggestion that we should see whether we, as a group, could not find some way to help the President escape successfully from the corner into which he has painted himself.

On hearing his address of last evening . . . as to why we could not give up SDI [Star Wars], I am greatly discouraged over the prospects of any such approach. I saw sitting before the microphone last night only a deeply prejudiced, ill-informed, and stubborn man, not above the most shameless demagoguery, likely to enjoy the acquiescence, if not the convinced support, of a timid political establishment half-knowing that he is talking a lot of nonsense but unwilling to take him on, and a public easily bemused by media showmanship and chauvinistic rhetoric. He is not a man who will be himself in the least impressed by anything that we or any like us will say. It is only pressure from the Congress or from the NATO allies that could possibly move him, and neither seems to be forthcoming in any adequate degree. . . .

I said to Annelise that if it fell to me to talk with Mr. Gorbachev about these matters, and he asked me what he could do to overcome the extravagant suspicion and hostility with which his country is viewed in the United States, I would have to say: "There is absolutely nothing you could do. You could give in to us on every point at issue in our negotiations; you would still encounter nothing but a stony hostility in official American circles; and your concessions would be exploited by the President as evidence that he had frightened you into compliance, and that the only language you understood was the language of force. And what you would be up against would be something wider and deeper than just Mr. Reagan. Powerful elements in the American population feel the need for a totally inhuman enemy. They need that enemy as a foil for what they like to persuade themselves is their own exceptional virtue. The politicians know that, and they, for the most part superficial, narrow-minded, & short-sighted people, will tend to cater to these chauvinistic reactions

28. At their Reykjavik summit meeting, Reagan and Gorbachev talked about possibly banning all nuclear weapons. The discussion was stymied by Reagan's refusal to also ban development of the Star Wars antimissile defense system.

even if this is done at the cost of our relations with other peoples. You, the Russians, largely owing to Reagan's efforts, have been cast in the role of that enemy, & there is nothing you can do about it. You must look elsewhere in the world for the possibilities of normal and satisfactory relationships. Count this country out. Seek peace, trade, and courtesy elsewhere, not here."

November 23

Never has my reputation been greater (for obscure reasons) than just now. Never was the chasm between my real thoughts and state of mind, on the one hand, and the brave front I am obliged to show to the world outside, on the other, been greater. I am faced with the choice between silence and hypocrisy. In these circumstances, I would prefer silence, but the busybody worlds of American journalism and academia keep the pressure on for statements of one sort or another, and some of these pressures are hard to resist.

December 13

The question is whether Mikhail Gorbachev represents something really new, interesting, and hopeful on the Soviet scene, or whether his regime is merely a disguised version of more-of-the-same. Harrison[29] and I hold to the first of these views. The second is vigorously put forward by the cluster of Poles or Polish Jews (Pipes, Ulam, Brzezinski, & Bialer)[30] who, during the Carter & Reagan administrations, have dominated the discussions about Russia in the halls of government and on the pages and screens of the media.

Princeton, December 23

It is borne in upon me by several recent events (Reykjavik, the Iranian arms scandal,[31] and the proposed ABC mini-series on the Soviet "occupation" of the U.S.) that try as I may, try as many others may, you will

29. Harrison Salisbury was a friend of Kennan's and a veteran *New York Times* correspondent in Moscow.

30. Richard Pipes and Adam Ulam were Polish American professors of Russian history at Harvard. Zbigniew Brzezinski, a Polish American international relations expert, had served as national security advisor under President Jimmy Carter. Seweryn Bialer, who had left Poland, is a former Columbia University political scientist.

31. In order to raise money for the "contra" rebels against the leftist government of Nicaragua, White House aides to President Ronald Reagan authorized the sale of weapons to the Islamic Republic of Iran. Because these linked operations violated U.S. laws, they were kept secret—until the scandal broke in November 1986.

never succeed in establishing in American opinion a balanced & sensible view of Russia. We have "adopted" that country as our recognized and official enemy. Having done that, we apply to the Russians our idea of what an enemy should be, quite the same image for the Nazis as for the Communists, the same for the Gorbachev Russia of the 1980's as for the Stalin regime of the 1930's—the same because the image bears little resemblance to reality and arises primarily only from our idea of what an enemy should look like in order to constitute the proper foil for our exceptional virtue.

1987

Even as the Cold War was winding down, Kennan remained pessimistic about the future, particularly concerning America's foreign and domestic policies. His perception of the dilemmas Gorbachev faced made him deeply sympathetic with the embattled Soviet leader. While racking up an astounding record of personal accomplishments and honors, Kennan still regretted his inability to sway the people who mattered most to him—decision makers.

Princeton, January 12

I have been reading over the diary entries from 1964–84, and have derived little pride or satisfaction from the effort. Where they were not personally plaintive, they tended to be repetitive. However, they do (or at least I hope they do) bring out one side of my experience (the aesthetic) of which the memoirs showed very little. So they may have some value.

What strikes me most strongly, in looking over this material, is (1) how little I accomplished, and (2) how little I grew, intellectually and in understanding. Some 40,000 (literally) letters answered over this 20-year period. Two respectable books of diplomatic history produced, but this on a secondary subject. An institute established for advanced Russian studies, but one that has always been, and continues to be, insecurely based, and still has no assurance of permanency. A number of public statements made in one way or another on nuclear arms control and Soviet-American relations, but this wholly unsuccessfully, in a losing cause. And I, now, thinking much the same things and writing the same things I was thinking and writing 25 years ago. . . .

Honors are showered upon me. This is a country of fashions—and I, or rather what people conceive me to be, am part of a momentary fashion. I have the curious experience of being probably the most extensively honored private person in the country and, at the same time, the person least heeded when he speaks. Figure that one out if you can!

Sørenhus, May 22
I take note of the troubles my government is experiencing, and am moved in each case, to respond with that most useless of all statements: "I told you so."

Great anguish is being experienced, for example, over the question of how to arrange for the removal of the medium-range nuclear weapons from Europe. Their uselessness and dangerousness have now become generally recognized. But who was it, let me ask, who precisely 30 years ago, in the 1957 Reith Lectures, pleaded desperately and without avail against the impending decision to base the Continental NATO forces on nuclear weapons?

An American warship has now been nearly destroyed, and 37 lives lost, through attack by an Iraqi aircraft in the Persian Gulf. But what was the warship doing there in the first place? Trying to protect the supply of oil to the West? But who, in early years, called publicly more than once for a determined and drastic reduction of our dependence on Persian Gulf oil? Had that appeal been heeded, there would have been no need for the stationing of American warships there for the purpose of assuring the supply. Or was the ship there ostensibly to protect the Gulf from supposed predatory arms of the Russians with relation to that body of water—and if so, who was it, if not myself, who tried for years to point out that the Russians had no such designs on the Gulf, and had no reason, in their own interests, to entertain any? These were the bases for my view that the stationing of American warships there served no good purpose, was only a provocative exercise of silly and dangerous Reaganite bravado.

Very well. We would all have been far better off if people in government had listened to me. But so what? And why was it that they *didn't* listen? It was not that I wrote badly. They all recognized that I wrote well, even when they were unprepared to give any credence to what I had to say. It was partly, of course, because we—I and they—approached these matters against the background of differing motivations. They were concerned to follow and reflect what they viewed as fashionable and influential opinion in our country, whereas I was concerned to lead that opinion and mold it. But beyond that, they did not understand and could not share the intellectual background against which I was speaking. And nothing, I fear, could have brought them to understand it. To be sure, they, and the media of communication with which they interacted, went through the motions of rational debate about such matters. But it was a debate so deeply colored by accepted preconceptions, so self-conscious, so extensively dominated by the taboo and dictates of a conventional wisdom, that it was simply incapable of responding to what I had to offer. If on occasions, as in the case of "containment," we found ourselves momentarily on the same wave length, this was accidental, fortuitous; and the appearance of agreement was, if anything, more dangerous than the far more numerous instances where what I said did not reach them at all.

What conclusions to draw from this? Was I wrong even to make the effort? . . .

Were I able to relive these recent decades, I would probably do much the same thing all over again. And this is not just because the effort, if it produced no intellectual echo, seems to have earned me a great deal of personal respect (probably also based on misunderstanding). It is rather that much of what I have said has a chance of being re-discovered after my death (if there is anyone to re-discover it), thus to acquire a certain measure of classic quality, and to evoke understanding by that perverse quality of human nature that makes men more inclined to respond to the works of someone long dead than to those of any contemporary.

[Kennan resided at Spaso House, the ambassador's official residence, while attending a conference of Soviet and U.S. historians.]

Moscow, June 20

I observed that the old building was standing there, as it had stood over more of these past six decades, mute and long-suffering, one ambassadorial regime after another performing its brief pretentious act within these silent and unprotesting walls, then packing up—to remove its various paraphernalia—to remove, in fact, most of the traces of its incumbency, including even its memories, and to leave behind it, aside from the occasional forgotten object the successor did not know what to do with, only the curious aroma (perceptible exclusively to the imaginative and sensitive) of the trivial, and occasionally not so trivial, dramas and excitements of which these walls had been the witnesses. Such is the ineffable, tragic, pathetic transience of the profession of diplomacy!

And the remainder of the stay in Moscow?

The sessions of the conference, held in a great highly modern building called the house of tourists, or something of that sort. The room so huge that I could sometimes not even see who was speaking at the other end of the table. Our Soviet counterparts, after producing pathetically poor papers (screened, no doubt, by countless committees), showed themselves warm, friendly, eager for personal contact, and much wiser than the papers they had been permitted to produce. . . .

Everywhere, of course, the ghosts of memory arose to surround me and accompany me. But I was always aware that what I was now observing was divided from those memories by a vast catastrophe, that most of the life I had once known had been destroyed in that catastrophe, and that what I was seeing were the children of the survivors, separated from their parents and grandparents by an abyss no smaller, in many instances even larger, than that which had once separated me, a foreigner, from those same people. The forces of change, in this instance international change, were stronger than the forces of geography and national origin.

There was a day in Riga—highly traumatic. It was 54 years since I had last been there. I had, repeatedly, the sense of one who has been permitted to return from the dead and to see, at the distance of a half-century, what remained of the scenes in which he had once lived. The city itself was crowded, its population more than doubled since I had known it. The amenities were largely gone; the parks and public places, on the other hand, improved. . . .

To me, as a bewildered, foolish, but sensitive young man, this view, this landscape, once had their own mysterious meaning, not to be put into words. How much of this lay in what I was seeing and how much in myself, God alone knows, some, perhaps, in each. . . .

The entire visit was made pleasant by the almost total absence of the reticence and tension which in earlier days, even as little as two or three years ago, had marked all such encounters—a change which we all owed, I am sure, to the courage and good sense of Mikhail Gorbachev. . . .

But, I, I fear, was the only survivor of the odd cast of characters who were then attached to the Legation: partly holdovers from the staff of the pre-Revolutionary American Embassy in Petersburg, partly, like myself, people of the post–World War I professional era, accepting the somewhat provincial amenities of life in Riga but with our thoughts and our efforts of understanding riveted to the great profoundly destabilized country that began two hundred miles to the east of us, with its hostile, defiant government and its greatly suffering population—a spectacle, to us, of horror, drama, and inexhaustible fascination.

Sørenhus, August 5

Gorbachev is easy to criticize. He would be hard, at this point, to replace. But no less interesting than his own fate is the effect of his policies on the non-Russian peoples of the Soviet Union and on the countries of the satellite area. Here we encounter a highly complex picture, with no lack of contradictions and dilemmas. A number of the non-Russian peoples of the Soviet Union, particularly the Baltic countries and the Georgians and Armenians, are better suited than the Russians to make good use of the Gorbachev ideas and efforts than are the Russians themselves, indeed, in some instances they have quietly anticipated them. To the extent that they are able in this way to effect a strengthening of their own economies relative to the Russian one, this should lead to an increase in their importance within the Soviet empire, to a further objective distancing of them from the Russian center, and thus to a heightening of the centrifugal tendencies that had so much to do with the fall of the Tsarist empire in 1917.

More significant still are apt to be the effects of Gorbachev's policies on the relationships of Moscow to the satellite countries. The satellite regimes themselves are still bound to Moscow, of course, by the largely rhetorical but nonetheless politically important ideological bond, and with the exception of Rumania, by the far more solid and important military relationship. But in other respects they had already begun to emancipate themselves, in various & widely differing ways, from strict Soviet tutelage even before Gorbachev's reforms began. Certain of them had even anticipated these reforms even more extensively than had the non-Russian nationalities in the Soviet Union. Their further reactions to "glasnost" and to "perestroika" in the Soviet Union will vary greatly from country to country. Those regimes that feel most secure in their relationship to their own people will welcome the reforms and make the most of them as justification for liberalization on their own part. Others, notably the Czechs and the Romanians, will—in fact, already do—find themselves severely embarrassed. These strains can serve only to widen the already striking differences among the various Warsaw Pact countries and by the same token to produce a further weakening of the general pattern of supposed conformity with the Soviet model of socialism. . . .

Gorbachev is a remarkable man, so remarkable as to be almost inexplicable in terms of his own known professional background. What he set out to do, as he saw it, was no doubt to liberate Soviet society and the Soviet economy from the ill effects of the enduring traces of Stalinist terrorism, on the one hand, and the corrupting system of privilege, on the other, by which the aging Brezhnev and his cronies contrived to hold things together for so many years. But these evils have bitten deeply into the fabric of Soviet society and have mingled and partially fused there with certain of the great distortions brought into the life of the Russian Empire by the Communist revolution of 1917. . . .

It is this, in essence, that Gorbachev is running up against, whether he realizes it or not, as he sets out to correct what he sees as the enduring evils of Stalinism and Brezhnevism in Russian life. He probably thinks this is all he has to correct. But he may find, before he is finished, that in some respects he has to correct the mistakes and the blind spots of the Bolshevik seizures of power in 1917, and even to take upon his own shoulders some of the unfinished business of the old Tsarist regime. Russia has no lack of past follies that cry out for correction and will require correction if Gorbachev is to make out of Russian society what he would like to make of it.

Princeton, Thanksgiving, November 26

The approach of Mr. Gorbachev[32] depresses me profoundly. I cannot understand why he consented to come. Here he will only be stifled by the crowding in of several thousand reporters and photographers and insulted by the Reaganite political establishment. And he will return empty-handed, having seen precious little of this country, but cordially hating all he has seen.

Washington, November 30

I was startled to gain the impression from this talk and from the morning Washington papers that people in Washington are much more optimistic about the forthcoming summit meeting than I have been. Could it really be, I ask myself, that something more might come out of it than the intermediate-range missile treaty which Mr. Reagan was once moved to propose supposing that the Russians would never agree to it, and which, even if signed, forces a ratification battle that will destroy much of the good feeling it might conceivably have produced?[33] If so, it means that

32. Gorbachev was coming to Washington for a summit conference with Reagan.

33. At their December 7–10 summit meeting, Reagan and Gorbachev signed a treaty that would eliminate the intermediate-range nuclear missiles in the U.S. and Soviet arsenals. Contrary to Kennan's prediction, the treaty sailed through the Senate by a 93–5 vote in May 1988.

Gorbachev is weaker than I supposed him to be. Or could it be that he is even smarter? There is nothing that so upsets the NATO conservatives, Mr. Reagan among them, than a sudden and unexpected consent to their more outrageous demands.

Princeton, December 17

Some weeks ago I took to New York and delivered to Harriet Wasserman[34] the five binders containing items from my diaries and letters describing scenes and landscapes. The idea that a collection of these might be published originated with John Lukacs,[35] who strongly urged me in that direction. . . .

[William Shawn, the reader for the publisher,] was concerned and upset because he had found in it nothing from my war years in Germany.[36] He suspected, I gather (it was all very vague) that I must have been concealing something from that time. She did not want to say more over the telephone, and insisted that she would come out here on the 18th—i.e., tomorrow—to talk to me about it.

I don't know what it is really about, but sense that it all bears some relation to my views, or lack of views, or suspected views, on the fate of the German Jews. I will find out tomorrow, in any case, what it is all about. But today, to prepare myself for whatever the trouble is, I spent most of the day in the Mudd Library, reading over my diary notes and letters from that period, numbers of which I cannot recall seeing since the days when they were written, more than forty years ago.

It was a strange experience: being suddenly moved back in this way into the atmosphere, the stresses, the moods, expectations, dreams, and emotional trials of that period. . . .

The image of myself as I was 45 years ago and as was reflected in these papers left me unhappy and unsatisfied, partly, I suppose, because I could not wholly distance myself from it (too much of it left in me today) but partly, too, because in these notes and letters I also see that image partly from the outside, and derive a certain distaste from what I see. It would be easier, I expect, for others bearing in mind my nature, background, and experience to be lenient about the shortcomings of that distant figure than it is for me.

34. Harriet Wasserman was Kennan's literary agent.
35. John Lukacs is a historian and was a close friend of Kennan's.
36. William Shawn was a former editor of *The New Yorker.*

December 20

Well, day before yesterday Harriet Wasserman came out to Princeton, it was her insistence, and told me about this episode. It was, more or less, as I suspected. Shawn had seemed very upset about the absence of any diary items from the period of my service in Germany. The Farrar Company, for which Shawn now works, had declined the manuscript, and the latter had been returned to her. She suspected it had had something to do with references to "Jews" in the early diary entries (all, incidentally, from my service in Germany and the Baltic states in the years before the Nazis were even in the picture). She was herself furious about this but also, I thought (and understandably), concerned over the question of how it might reflect on her and on her business. She was going to talk to them further about it, and Shawn had said he was going to phone me about it at some point. (The head of the Farrar firm, I should have noted, had said something to her about Kennan's "German problem," whatever that may have meant.)

I am much concerned about this whole episode, but for Harriet's sake rather than for my own.

1988

As the Soviet Union under Gorbachev began to withdraw, in some cases unilaterally, from various Cold War contests, Kennan was prescient in perceiving that the United States, by contrast, would not pull back from its forward military positions around the globe. Nor would Washington sharply cut its contracts or ambitions for ever-more sophisticated and powerful weapons. In sum, the groundwork was already in place for America's decade-long transition from a preoccupation with the Cold War to a focus on the global "war on terror."

Princeton, January 10

Gorbachev, with his statements, actions, and proposals, has done us all one great favor, which was to demonstrate that for a great many people in the West, including the heads of three of the most important Western governments, and for a considerable number of politically influential people in our own country, the reason for supporting the present absurdly high and terrifying levels of nuclear weaponry is not really the need for balancing off the comparable levels of such weaponry held on the Soviet side; that this declared rationale was only an excuse; that the Soviet holdings and further cultivation of these weapons and the Soviet positions in the various arms talks and negotiations have actually had very little to do with these attitudes; and that the persons in question have a deep emotional commitment to nuclear weaponry, quite aside from anything the Russians might do in either the cultivation or in the abandonment of it. . . .

What we now have to turn our attention to is no longer the perception of the relative strength of the Russians and ourselves in this form of weaponry but rather

(a) the sources of the peculiar morbidity of the human spirit that inspires the Manichaean view of international relations and this anxious clutching at weapons of this nature, despite their suicidal and apocalyptic qualities, as though there could be disasters worse than those which any sort of use of these weapons would draw upon us; and

(b) how we are to develop and inculcate into American opinion a much more mature and sophisticated understanding of the problem of the balance in "conventional" weaponry, one that takes into account the intentions as well as the capabilities of the supposed adversary, and one based on the recognition that there can be no salvation for any of us in another major war fought with such weapons—that here again we are ultimately dependent on the intentions, rather than the capabilities, of the adversary, the influencing of which is primarily a political and psychological, not a military, problem.

[The Kennans vacationed on Barbados.]

Barbados, March 10

Where would I, with this torn nature, & with this incongruous mixture of strength and weaknesses, where would I have been without a firm, quiet, sensible but sensitive and loyal wife at my side? . . .

How persistently the English, in their own self-confident Victorian and Edwardian manner, shaped the lives of what must have been as little as two or three generations back a population of African slaves: converted them to a species of Anglican Christianity, established for them and then bequeathed to them a firm system of humane justice as well as a proper structure of education, taught them cricket to absorb as much as possible of the old Adam in the men, and turned them loose, to govern themselves under the benevolent eye of a rather helpless governor-general, the Queen's representative, who nevertheless incorporates the grandeur of the inimitable civilizational ideal, namely the British crown, in the name of which all this took place. Not perfect, of course. Not unaffected by the modern age, who is? But if to be judged, then only by the criterion: "Compared with what?"

En route to the Farm, May 9

What I find it hard to adjust to is the acceptance of my own failure: of the failure, that is, to exert any useful influence on the dominant trends of official American thought and policy and, secondly, the dreadful and dangerous extent of my alienation from the prevailing intellectual currents of my own time.

First the failure. I have been unable to prevent the militarization, and particularly the nuclearization, of American and NATO policy. There has, in these respects, been a consolidation during the Reagan years of precisely these trends in the American political consensus that I oppose. And I see neither in the prospects for the succession to the Reagan presidency nor in the outlooks of the American press & media (and the same is largely applicable to the European ones as well) any sign of the leadership required to overcome these tendencies. Similarly, I had not been able to lay the groundwork in public or official opinion for any sanification and long-term improvement of Soviet-American relations. The possibilities for that improvement are plainly present on the Soviet side. On the American side they are lacking. I have also failed (& here, I suppose it could be said that I have not tried as much as I could have) to gain any understanding or acceptance for my own concept either of the desirable thrust of American domestic policy or of the principles that should, in my opinion, govern our relations with the remainder of the world.

Well, failure is failure. All men fail to some extent. One should learn to accept it. . . . But I am, for better or for worse, not dead yet. I still live, and live in a human environment that looks to me for communication, for intellectual interaction. Here is where the alienation comes in. . . .

I have no hope that a nuclear disaster can be avoided. As for Soviet-American relations: were I to talk frankly with Mr. Gorbachev, I should have to advise him to address no hopes to his relationship with this country, rather, to wish it off in his foreign policy concepts—to try neither to injure it nor to appeal to it for any positive contribution to world affairs, but also not to fear it (its bark will be worse than its bite), simply to leave it alone and to look elsewhere, primarily to the Far East, for any constructive contributions to international life.

Similarly, of course, I can look for no useful American leadership in world affairs generally. I can have no confidence in a country that (a) is as vulnerable as this one to pressures for a militarized view of its external relationships, and (b) places its foreign policies so extensively at the service of the emotions and prejudices of ethnic minorities. What good can a man such as myself, who can look at these problems only from the standpoint of national interest & world peace, hope to do in the face of such distortion of the official American vision. . . .

Not a morning passes that I don't bridle at something in the morning paper or the radio news, & am seized with the desire to write something about it. But where? . . . One answer, theoretically, is a book. And the effort will be made. But it is not the whole answer.

[Since the 1930s, Kennan had deplored what he saw as American society's excessive individualism, commercialization, and exploitation of the environment. He also bemoaned the politicization of foreign policy. Lacking much confidence in democracy, he developed the notion of a council of highly respected individuals who might offer wise advice to the executive and legislative branches of government. Kennan would eventually include these and other recommendations in his 1993 book *Around the Cragged Hill: A Personal and Political Philosophy*.]

Kristiansand, July 25–26

I produced a chapter delineating five specific problems of American society, all serious ones, which if neglected could lead to serious deterioration of American life. I argued (this was not hard to do) that with none of these problems was the American political establishment, as it now stands, capable of coping. . . .

The only expedient I could recommend was the establishment, by act of Congress, of some sort of advisory council of state, to be composed of men chosen by presidential appointment from among a national panel of distinguished citizens, known not only for their integrity, experience, and good sense but for their total lack of political involvement or ambition. If, I thought, there were to be conferred on such a body, situated not within the regular political establishment but at the side of it and accepted as advisory to both executive and legislative branches of the government, sufficient prestige to lend authority to its findings, then, I thought, there was a possibility that it might stiffen the regular establishment to the point where it could address more successfully the problems I had mentioned and others like them. It was obvious, however, that all this would take time, years if not decades. Meanwhile, we would remain at best a nation sorely and dangerously tried by domestic problems, a nation that had shown itself capable of coping with the task of developing (however wastefully) the resources of a great, fertile continental region of the northern temperate zone, but had still to prove that it could cope with the far sharper and more subtle challenges of a world of high technology, nuclear power, and environmental deterioration. . . .

But (and here came the dilemma) it was no use telling people that their situation was hopeless—that there was nothing they, with their small strength, could do about it—that they might as well resign themselves for the worst. Not only was there no use in my telling them that, there was also no excuse for it. I had long since recognized, in earlier moments of despair, that it was incomprehensible and indefensible to tell young people that there was no hope. For one thing, I might be wrong. There might be hopeful possibilities I did not see. If *that* was the best I could do, then better shut up. . . .

The problem was complicated at just this time by the developing political situation. The reports of the Democratic convention, together with Mr. Dukakis' own statements, his choice of a vice-presidential running-mate,[37] and his obvious reference to the various aggressive ethnic minorities, struck me as being susceptible of no other interpretation than as evidences that Mr. Reagan, notwithstanding all his inadequacies, his mistakes, and his reverses, had really won in the end—won in the sense that his right-wing view of America's place in the world had prevailed. The Democratic Party, unprincipled and ready to place itself at the disposal of any faction that would promise to bring it money or votes, had surrendered in advance to the well-heeled, loud-mouthed, and brutal forces of the southwestern right-wing—arrogant, chauvinistic, and militaristic. These were now the dominant political forces of the country. Mr. Bush,[38] running around the country trying desperately to conceal the fact that he had ever had anything to do with education or culture (those abhorred features of an effete East coast society) had already long been the captive of these forces. Now, Mr. Dukakis was joining him. Did it matter which of them was elected? And what conceivable connection did I have with their world of feeling and (if you can call it that) thought? If this was *their* country, as it apparently was, could I plausibly claim it as mine?

Aboard a plane, August[39]

Were I to be asked by a responsible Soviet official: "What could we in Moscow do that we have not done, within the limits of political realism, to change this situation?", I should have to reply along the following lines:

"There is nothing you could do that would really change it. The American political establishment conceives of itself as an actor on a

37. Michael Dukakis was governor of Massachusetts and Democratic candidate for president. Senator Lloyd Bentsen of Texas was the vice presidential candidate.

38. George H. W. Bush was the Republican candidate for president.

39. Kennan later noted that the entry "was written probably on a plane & probably in August 1988."

stage facing an audience, which is American opinion, and enacting some sort of a passion play. It has cast itself in the role of a knight in shining armor, championing the cause of the innocent virtuous maiden which is the American people. For this role to achieve plausibility there is required a foil, an Evil Spirit, a wicked sorcerer, if you will, from whose threatening advances the maiden must be protected, otherwise no use for the knight.

The sorcerer, dear Russian friend, is of course, you. This is the role in which you have been cast. You cannot help it. For a number of reasons, you qualify for it as no one else could. It is in part related to what you once were; it has very little relationship to what you now are. But without it, the play could not go on. . . . This is a stage drama, not a reality. It is the appearance of victory they are after, not victory itself.

Princeton, September 17

Notification that I am to receive the Toynbee Prize.[40] The honor will require a speech. . . . Now, how could this have been avoided? Only by declining the honor. In the future, then, I must decline them, although this is late in the game. But I think I can now do it. I have had all the significant ones except the Nobel Prize, & I am most unlikely to receive that.

And, oh yes, I forgot to mention, among the things done, a rather short piece I wrote for the *New York Review of Books* on Gromyko's[41] memoirs. Here, again, I was the prisoner of my own past, for I was the obvious person to write it, being virtually the only one who could.

40. Named after the historian Arnold J. Toynbee, the Toynbee Prize honors those who have acted from a historical perspective to further the social sciences.

41. Andrey Gromyko, wartime Soviet ambassador to the United States and longtime Soviet foreign minister, wrote *Memoirs* (1989).

1989

For decades Kennan had believed that the Cold War would eventually end. Yet as that happy day approached, the former diplomat groused that Washington's persistent unwillingness to negotiate had unnecessarily prolonged the conflict. Moreover, he worried about the instability that could ensue from the demise of the communist system and the freeing of the Soviets' empire in Eastern Europe. Critical as ever of U.S. society and the West, Kennan despised any tendency toward Cold War triumphalism.

With the inauguration of the administration of President George H. W. Bush, Kennan understood that U.S. policy might change. So he made it a point to share his viewpoints with select media and with the Senate Foreign Relations Committee.

Princeton, February 5

It must be a half a year since I have written in this journal. . . .

The month of January has been most unnaturally warm. There has been much speculation as to whether this is not attributable to the warming trend the scientists believe themselves to have discovered, affecting the entire planet.

February 12

At a dinner inaugurating the institute for the study of diplomatic history that John Gaddis is setting up at Ohio University . . . there was the usual sense of encouragement from the Midwestern scene: the unassuming kindliness, the pervasive cheerfulness, the modesty and simplicity. And Gaddis, with his intelligence, his strength, his decency, and his relative youth, is the hope of the country for the understanding of the past and the future of the country's position in the world. And his wife: a fine intelligent woman, herself a scholar, but also a good quiet mother. Altogether, it was a heartening experience, one that left a good taste in your mouth. . . .

The summit meetings[42] were rather silly media events without political substance. The INF agreement was a minor step in the direction of arms reduction, accepted with reluctance by our major European allies and by many in the President's own political entourage, a small petard on which Mr. Reagan had hoisted himself by some of his earlier propagandistic statements, and from which he found no other way to extract himself.[43]

Otherwise, things have remained much the same. Throughout the later years of his presidency, Mr. Reagan tried to appeal to both of two mutually irreconcilable consistencies: his hard line supporters, on the one hand, for whom the cultivation of the image of the "evil empire," dedicated to our destruction, appears to be an emotional necessity, and, on the other hand, the great body of moderate, well-meaning, but somewhat bewildered people in this country who would like to see relations with the Soviet Union improved and a military showdown avoided. Drawing on his remarkable ability to wiggle through the sticky places and to impress others with his one-line absurdities, however mutually contradictory, he has largely succeeded in this effort, waging war with Russia verbally out of one pocket and peace out of the other. But there has never been much room for doubt about the direction in which his own inclinations were leading. He has succeeded, with his extraordinary genius for over-simplification and for establishing the slogan at the expense of the thought, in gaining wide acceptance, not only in the public but even in the ranks of his Democratic opposition, for a whole series of propositions that are quite incompatible with any serious improvement of Soviet-American relations and particularly with any significant further progress in arms control. . . .

[In what follows Kennan refers to the controversy in December 1987 over publishing extracts from his diary.]

Harriet, if I remember correctly, had thought it possible that the book would be published by the very Jewish firm of Straus & Farrar, for which,

42. At their December 1987 summit meeting in Washington, Reagan and Gorbachev signed the Intermediate-Range Nuclear Forces (INF) treaty that eliminated intermediate-range missiles from Europe. The two leaders had previously met in Geneva in 1985 and in Reykjavik in 1986.

43. At a time when the Soviets had already deployed intermediate-range missiles in Eastern Europe and the United States had not yet installed such missiles, Reagan had proposed a "zero-zero" solution. Moscow would have to dismantle existing weapons while Washington could stand pat. To wide surprise, Gorbachev accepted the deal.

at that time, Mr. Shawn was functioning . . . as a consultant. But Straus & Farrar then declined to publish the book, giving as a reason (in a letter to Harriet) "this German thing" on Kennan's part.

I have never been anti-Semitic, but I must admit that this episode brought me as close as I have ever been to becoming one. Those of us who served in the Berlin embassy during the war were under no illusions about the Nazis. We had not chosen this assignment, which for some of us was a strenuous and exhausting one. Why should it be thought that I should have burst out in prose, expressing my horror of the Nazis? I was not a reporting officer, but an administrative one. To whom should I have addressed such outpourings? To the government? How? Through my superiors in the Embassy? They would have thought I was mad. They knew what the Nazis were as well as I did. So did our government. Who would have been enlightened? And what good would it have done? A weird idea these critics of 1988 had of life and work in the Foreign Service in Berlin, 1940!

February 16

Today was my 85th birthday. Yesterday, I went to New York simply for a pleasant luncheon with Arthur Schlesinger. No strain & no particular fatigue. . . . But I was utterly drained out, good for nothing. I looked at the drafts of two articles written in the past few days. Neither, I realized, was adequate to its purpose. Both would have to be wholly rewritten, and this under pressure of time. And then, for the first time in my entire life, the thought occurred to me: What if I simply can't, anymore? What if the battery has finally run out? What if this is "it"? And if so, how does one, being still physically alive, convey this situation to others? I am not here, I would have to say, for any of the things you expect me to be here for, I must now go my own way: no opening mail, no answering phone calls, no involvement in the life around me, no social occasions. Could one? Or must one?

Washington, April 3

In view of the change of administrations and the possibility of influencing the new one, I have tried to put my word in where I could. It is, after all, a crucial time—with new and more intelligent people in and around the White House, and in the aftermath of Mr. Gorbachev's sensational unilateral cuts in conventional arms. I thought: if I don't say something now, and the new people go the wrong way, I will never know whether something I could have said and didn't would have made a difference. So I gave two interviews on the McNeill-Lehrer program, wrote an article for the *New York Times* weekly magazine, and another one on Germany for publication elsewhere, and accepted an invitation to appear tomorrow, April 4, before the Senate Foreign Relations Committee as the lead-off witness in a series of hearings on the future of Soviet-American relations. And all this has been complicated by the forthcoming appearance of my book[44] of excerpts of travel sketches from my diaries, and [in] particular by the appearance of selections of them in *The Atlantic* some days ago, an event that I regretted but could not prevent.

The hearings take place tomorrow morning. I have prepared for them as well as I could. But I dare not be optimistic. I have not been feeling well, particularly in the mornings. I don't think I do so well, anyway, under this sort of questioning.

> [When Kennan finished his two and a half hours of testimony before the Senate Foreign Relations Committee, everyone in the room, including the stenographer, gave him a standing ovation. The journalist Peter Jennings commented that if "anyone is entitled to call off the Cold War, it is George Kennan, the man who invented the Western strategy for winning it."][45]

Princeton, April 9

The Senate hearings were dramatized by the appearance in the *Washington Post* the same morning of a two-page spread with bold headline and photograph . . . the *Atlantic* excerpts, and the forthcoming book so that . . . Washington's attention, if not that of the *New York Times*, was drawn to my person (comparatively speaking) in no small way. And the hearing, 2½ hours in length, ended, surprisingly and somewhat embarrassingly, with something that was I am told unprecedented in the experience of that eminent committee: a standing ovation in which even the remaining senators took part.

I must be careful not to overrate the significance of that unusual occurrence. The senators who participated were mostly Democrats (though even the Republicans who attended, including Jesse Helms, were extraordinarily polite and respectful). The *New York Times*, true to

44. *Sketches from a Life* (1989).
45. Gaddis, *George F. Kennan*, 672.

its custom, wholly ignored the event. Except for one cable channel, the television people, for some reason known best by themselves, were not there. But the *Washington Post* reported the event quite handsomely, the following morning. *Newsweek*, I am told, is about to give it prominent attention in its next issue. The *New York Times*, somewhat shamefacedly, ran the bulk of my initial statement (by arrangement with the Committee, not with me) on the op-ed page of today's Sunday edition, following a spate of stories about the various efforts to prod President Bush into clarifying his views about how, if at all, we are to react to the changes in Russia. So I feel that I did succeed in giving at least a palpable jolt to the complacency of the new administration. . . .

This, however, has led me into what may prove to be deeper water. . . . I received a phone call from General John Galvin, Supreme Commander of NATO inviting me to come to Mons in Belgium and to address there the annual SHAPEX conference of the NATO Pact. This is a closed meeting (not open to press or visitors) which brings together all the senior members of the NATO community.

The Farm, April 16

I brought along a thick bundle of reading material bearing on the Gorbachev regime and what it could, or should, mean for American policy, and after just this first day's immersion in it (and the reading has only begun) I find myself startled by the recognition that not only is the standard NATO outlook dated and no longer relevant to the emerging situation in Russia and Europe but so, in a way, is my catalogue of grievances against that NATO outlook. We are all being overtaken by a new and dangerous situation, the end of which we cannot foresee, and when we argue about what we have known in the Cold War period, we are arguing, historically, about the past.

Kennedy Airport, May 5

A strange experience: this sudden wave of attention coming over me in my old age. In its present form, this is the combined product of the surprising effects of the Senate testimony and the appearance in the bookstores and in the reviewer's columns of the new book, *Sketches*. It is for me hard to assess. In part, it is explicable simply by my age. I am living amid a generation of people who knew very little about me and have suddenly discovered that I exist. The slenderness of this knowledge explains the primitive naivety of their enthusiasm. Also, there is not much competition.

The political significance is harder to assess. The success of the appearance before the senatorial committee was a personal one, but had little effect on governmental policy. The senator did not ask me about arms control questions, the only area where I could have come to grips with those aspects of policy where I could perhaps have contributed something.

Well, here I now am, en route to Brussels, to speak at the SHAPEX exercise. This is more serious. The event could not have been more crucially planned. A fortnight later there is to take place a NATO summit meeting. The central question to be confronted at that meeting is that of whether the range of the Lance missiles deployed by us, the Americans, on German soil should be greatly increased, raised practically to that of the medium-range missiles we were supposed to have removed on the basis of the agreement that Mr. Reagan concluded with the Russians before leaving office, or whether we should not better negotiate with the Soviet Union an agreement which would result in the removal of this type of weapon (of which the Russians have deployed in Germany far more than we have) altogether. Obviously, anyone who had the slightest interest in lowering the tension of the military confrontation in the center of Europe would opt for the second of these alternatives. But neither Mrs. Thatcher or Mr. Bush want to go in that direction, and behind the entire dispute there lies the deeper question as to whether these latter two, and the people around them, really want anything of the olive branch Mr. Gorbachev has been holding out to them, or whether they have taken the Cold War so tightly to their bosoms that they cannot even contemplate life without it.

En route from Brussels, May 11

I come away from this meeting with the NATO establishment more discouraged than I have been for years. I see no ray of hope in their attitudes, nor in those of the major governments that support them, only an indefinite continuation and development of the military and nuclear competition of the Cold War as we have known it for four decades, with my own government, together with that of Britain, in the lead. Depressing, above all, is the deep and unreasoning devotion to the nuclear weapon. The indifference to its proliferation, the irresponsibility involved in its cultivation decade after decade, when we have no satisfactory means of disposing of the nuclear wastes, and when our continuation of this cultivation is bound to prolong indefinitely the proliferation of it that is now in progress.

Bonn, May 30

Within an hour I am to call on President Weizsäcker.[46] These thoughts by way of preparation for this meeting.

I am extremely glad that things went well at the crucial NATO summit meeting yesterday, and it is good that a confrontation was avoided over the nuclear weapons. I share in the general sense of relief that things went as well as they did. But the problems that led to the recent tension are by no means solved, and unless there are changes in the attitudes of both British & Americans, I think NATO will have further difficult times to go through.

Kristiansand, June 29

President Bush was disposed to bestow upon me on the evening 6th of July a high honor.[47] I am to receive it together with three other elderly worthies (I, incredible as this seems, am the youngest of the lot). The ceremony (a very brief one) is indeed to take place in the Rose Garden next Thursday morning, and is to be followed with a small luncheon given by the President and Mrs. Bush. We, the honorants, are (thank God) not expected to respond.

I am somewhat bewildered by this development. It is true that the President did speak kindly of me in a public statement some weeks ago, including my name among those of certain of the "Wise Men" of forty years ago. It is also true that my name has probably come to his attention in several other ways in recent weeks. It remains a rather strange circumstance that he should be undertaking this gesture towards one whose views on a number of important subjects are known to be so little in accord with those that he represents.

Princeton, July 4

Tomorrow, we go to Washington for the brief Rose Garden ceremony.

As this brief and relatively insignificant ceremony approaches, I have two reactions.

First: I realize that what is involved here is a gesture of respect for my person, not for my views or my efforts over the years to influence public policy. So obvious is this that I am led to the suspicion that this is a species of consolation prize given in recognition not of my success but

46. Richard von Weizsäcker was president of the Federal Republic of Germany.
47. Kennan was awarded the Medal of Freedom.

of my failure, that without the failure, in effect, it would never have been accorded.

Secondly, I am afflicted with a disturbing sense of emptiness. Talking a day or two ago with Christopher, I was obliged to recognize that there was no way I could, of my own initiative, capitalize on this latter-day notoriety any further than I have done. Nor am I expected to.

But if not this, then what?

Back, presumably, to diplomatic history. But not at once.

[After the White House ceremony, the Kennans headed back to Kristiansand for their summer vacation.]

Copenhagen Airport, July 8

The White House ceremony and the following luncheon were graciously conducted by the President & Mrs. Bush. The former confirmed my sense of the motivations for the invitation to myself. When I remarked to him that I particularly valued this gesture because I was aware that my visions had never accorded entirely with those of any administration since Harry Truman, he replied that the honor was not one accorded for ideological reasons.

I sat on the 2nd place to the right of him at lunch, the intervening chair being occupied by the former senator, Margaret Chase Smith. The President seemed, I thought, a bit hurried and tense, more so than I would have thought he would be just after his 4-day holiday in Maine, and also, less surprisingly, somewhat removed and distracted. Despite his excellent health, the cares of office, I suspected, were weighing upon him.

[On November 9, the Berlin Wall came down. Kennan felt overwhelmed, not by joy but rather by the pressures of responding to requests for comments. While unwilling to give up his public standing, he longed to focus on his scholarship. He was thinking about writing a third volume of his history of the pre–World War I Franco-Russian alliance.]

Princeton, November 14

For the last two or three weeks, after nearly two years of interruption of my historical work, I finally got my desk cleared of the usual trivia—cleared to the point where, on a number of days, I could go over to the Institute library and return to history.

I loved the experience, every minute of it, was happy in it, in fact. But it was a fight. The old web of ulterior involvements of every sort continued to lie heavily upon me. The hours in the library had to be literally clawed out of this web, day after day. To do this clawing was a tour de force. The pressures were intensified by the dramatic events occurring in eastern Europe, in Germany above all.[48] Precariously, almost desperately, I continued the struggle. Liz,[49] at the telephone, was obliged to fight the good fight even more fiercely than myself. The phone rang all day with requests for interviews, TV appearances, articles, statements, you name it.

November 15

Very well. Agreed. They win; I lose. I am defeated—defeated, not by lack of strength or talent, but by the power of the entourage—by the power of an entourage that has little interest in serious things, that values the entertaining "quickie" more highly than the sustained effort, values the emotional reaction more highly than thought, and image more highly than reality. It is an entourage that wants performers more than it wants scholars. But there it is; and so pervasive is its power, even at the end of the telephone line in the Institute for Advanced Study, that no one in my position can withstand it except at a cost that would involve real violence to his own social life and to that of his family.

Where, then, do we go from here?

I went, last evening, for a long lone walk through the empty nocturnal Princeton streets, trying to think out the answer to that question. I could, I thought for a time, see myself wandering through life, from here on out, purposelessly and distractedly, taking things as they might come, observing little things and deriving amusement from them, reserving my comments, as a rule, mostly for this journal, anticipating nothing, expecting nothing.

But this, upon reflection, proved not as easy as it sounded. In response to the many appeals to do this or that, choices would have to be made. But by what criteria? If things are insignificant, how does one choose among them?

48. He published an op-ed in the *Washington Post* warning that it was premature to think of German reunification.

49. Elizabeth Stenard was Kennan's secretary and aide.

November 18

I received a call from Washington to the effect that the President wished to see me, together with three other ex-ambassadors to the Soviet Union, on Friday (yesterday) at 2 p.m.

So down I went, on the familiar trek to Washington, showed up (by the grace of God, because the Amtrak train was nearly a half hour late) in the White House at the proper time, met with my former colleagues Tom Watson, Arthur Hartman, and Mac Toon,[50] and was ushered with them into the Oval Office, where we were greeted by the President and joined by four or five other people, three of whom I recognized as the Secretary of State, the Vice President,[51] and the Security Advisor (whose name, always on the tip of my tongue, I can never remember—but, oh yes, now it comes to me: Mr. Brent Scowcroft, I believe). There followed a series of contributions, including my own, than which (but for different reasons in my case) I can think of nothing more useless and trivial.

A curious man, Mr. Bush. You talk with him—he is courteous, relaxed, reasonable in what little he says, and charming. You leave him, and what he says to the public bears not the faintest mark of what you had said, and what he had appeared to listen to quite respectfully. I, in any case, came away quite favorably impressed with him, though not at all impressed with the usefulness of the exercise we had just been through. But in the morning paper I read the record of words from his lips that could scarcely have escaped those lips had he had the faintest knowledge of what I wrote in last Sunday's *Washington Post*, or had what I said to him yesterday made the faintest impression on his mind.

Thanksgiving Day, November 23

I have been obliged to recognize, over this past week, a change in myself—an unpleasant change, which I suspect of being irreversible. How can I describe it? Not only physical weakness, jitteriness, unsteadiness, etc., but also emotional reactions—lack of buoyancy, moments of impatience and irritation, other moments of dark apprehension of I know not what, and a sense of being not fully in control of my own reactions and behavior.

Ah ha, I say to myself, the onset of senility. But that sets up contradictory questions and reflections. If you recognize in yourself the signs of

50. Thomas Watson was ambassador to the Soviet Union from 1979 to 1981, whereas Arthur Hartman served from 1981 to 1987 and Malcolm Toon from 1976 to 1979.

51. James A. Baker was secretary of state. Dan Quayle was vice president.

senility, can you be really senile? Or can you be senile, knowing that you are in a state of senility, yet being unable to control the manifestations of it? I fear, alas, that you can.

What sort of conduct, then, does this dictate?

Small undertakings, I would suggest, not large ones . . . and, above all, a minimum of self-exposure to larger gatherings of people.

November 29

I continue to feel the ulterior involvements of my life, trying as I may to avoid them, growing upon me, and being less and less coped with. They have been increased by the dramatic happenings of the time: the sudden self-emancipation of Eastern Germany and Czechoslovakia from Communist rule, and (of minor interest to me but the occasion for great excitement among the gentlemen of the press and media) the meeting, 2 or 3 days hence, of Messrs. Bush and Gorbachev on their respective naval ships near Malta. The telephone, by consequence, has been ringing constantly, here and in the office, bearing requests for interviews and appearances. All these have been declined, except an invitation to appear once more, alone, in January before the Senate Foreign Relations Committee. Perhaps I should not have accepted it. . . . But I am one of the very few people they seem to trust. And there are, I think, a few things I can usefully tell them. So there we are.

December 3

A weekend grandly wasted for the most part, much of it spent watching Messrs. Becker, Edberg, and McEnroe[52] play tennis—while the Communist domination of Eastern and parts of Central Europe was going up in flames, and Messrs. Gorbachev and Bush were meeting in the midst of a Mediterranean near-hurricane, at Malta. My reason for this frivolity was the last effects of the ill-health that has held me in its dreary grip over this past fortnight.

I must, I know, now begin the effort to inform myself seriously about what has been going on these days in Russia and Europe, in preparation for speaking at the Council on Foreign Relations later this month. This revolution in the Communist world fails, for some reason, to excite me very greatly. I can fairly say that I saw it coming. I was trying to

52. Boris Becker, Stefan Edberg, John McEnroe.

tell the government, as early as in the late 1940's and early 1950's, that Russian Communism as an ideology had entirely lost its hold on the Soviet people. And it is years ago, before Gorbachev came on to the world scene, that I began trying to persuade people that the structure of Soviet authority in Eastern Europe was seriously undermined and would, if challenged, prove unable to stand up against any pressure. (I often compared it to a thin sheet of ice on a pond which looked quite solid but would, if stepped upon, prove unable to bear any weight.) But of course I could not see when the disintegration would come, or how suddenly.

It is to my mind a pity that it did come so suddenly. It overtakes everywhere a generation which, through no fault of its own, is wholly unprepared for self-government—does not even have any viable political parties to take over from the Communists. Not only that, but none of these excited peoples seem to have learned, as they could have learned from the sensible Finns, that the only safe way to establish their true independence is to show a decent respect for Soviet security interests. If they do not come to that realization, and if they couple their demands for independence with a challenge to Soviet security, they will simply destroy Gorbachev, the man who has given them the large measure of independence (or, in the case of the Baltic States, of autonomy) they have so recently achieved.

December 16

Four days hence, I must address a meeting of the Council on Foreign Relations, supposedly a regular, serious occasion, but actually a special Christmas meeting, to which members may take, I understand, their older children. The news of the occasion has got around. There is going to be a great crush. And people expect great things of me. I am assured that all that is expected is ten or fifteen minutes of extemporaneous remarks, to be followed by questions. Painless, one might suppose, but far from it in actuality. Europe is in the throes of the greatest upheaval since World War II and a many-sided rapidly-moving one, at that. What can one say about it in 10–15 minutes?

As these days go by, I am increasingly preoccupied with the thought of an unavoidably abrupt and final act of liberation from this futile and exhausting bondage that causes me to spend week after week either saying "no" politely to importunities of every possible sort, or yielding occasionally to the odd unrefusable one and having then to deal with the new crop of requests it produces.

I think this, and say it, in full awareness of the many times I have said it before. But it is now a question [of] whether the ultimate act of liberation comes by my own initiative or by death. Since the time available is limited in my case, why not by my own initiative?

1990

For several decades already, Kennan had suspected that he was about to succumb to death or at least to senescence. Nevertheless, the eighty-six-year-old remained sharp and active, and he would live for another fifteen years.

Kennan remained uneasy about the rapid changes sweeping through the tottering Soviet empire and South Africa. Nor was he happy about the decline of the old international system of unquestioned national sovereignty and the rise of a new international regime of, at least in theory, universal human rights.

THE GREAT EGRET (*Casmerodius albus*)[53]

Please stand aside a moment
For the haughty Great Egret.
He's the well-acknowledged leader
Of the long-legged beauty set.
And if you should fail to show him
The respect he thinks you owe him,
He might choose to disregard it,
but
He won't forget.

Princeton, January 21

The first three weeks of this New Year have been taken up with the liquidation of the remaining obligations of what I hope now to be able to regard as my old life.

The encounter with the Council on Foreign Relations, just before

53. Bill and Laura Riley, friends of the Kennans', often hosted them at North Haven, Maine, or at Captiva Island, Florida. Kennan penned this and similar verses in appreciation of the Audubon prints in the guest cottage.

Christmas (a huge affair which, because of the number of members and offspring who showed up, had to be removed to the theater of Hunter College) was, to judge by all the reactions, a great success. Then, on the 5th of January, there was a huge affair given by the State of New Jersey, at which again I was among the honorants. Three days ago, after much preparation by reading and writing things I would otherwise never had read or written, I made my appearance before the Senate Committee (which, on this occasion, consisted of a simple senator, Mr. Biden, which reduced somewhat the dramatic quality of the event), and acquitted myself to my own satisfaction, whatever the others in attendance or the press and public may have felt. And with all of this, I consider my contribution to the public life of my time to have been substantially ended.

The period of this contribution was a clearly delimitated period, some 44 years in extent. That it is now ended, and that a wholly new one is beginning, is obvious. What I could contribute to the new one would be, at best, brief and not greatly significant.

January 25

All over the world, strange and dark things happening: Russia disintegrating, drifting into the collapse of the traditional Russian Empire, experiencing the failure of perestroika and the ruin of Gorbachev, moving into a new Time of Troubles. This country on the verge of financial disaster, with incalculable consequences.

February 4

Evening before last we saw on television the Prime Minister of South Africa announcing, to a troubled and silent parliament, the removal of the ban on the African National Congress and promising the early, but definite, release of Mr. Mandela.[54]

Concerning the second of those undertakings, I have no special feelings. I know nothing about Mr. Mandela, other than he has been imprisoned for a very long time and has resolutely refused to abandon the use of violence to obtain for his movement the power he would like it to have. I know of no pearls of wisdom that have fallen from his lips, or of any other evidences of great nobility or high statesmanlike qualities on his part. That he is better off, from everyone's standpoint, outside of prison than in it I have no doubt. That he will be brought to Washington,

54. Nelson Mandela had been imprisoned by the all-white government for his agitation for racial equality in South Africa and an end to the segregationist rule of apartheid.

permitted to address the Congress, and given an ovation by people who know nothing about him but want to curry political favor with black voters, is obvious and of little importance, just another manifestation of American domestic political posturing. . . .

I have no confidence in the prospects for anything like a mingling of the races in South Africa, nor can I permit myself to hope that the whites will be permitted to retain very much of the quality of their own lives, or indeed of the vitality of the economy, in a country dominated, on the principle of one-man, one-vote, by a large African majority. I would expect to see within five or ten years' time only desperate attempts at emigration on the parts of the whites, and strident appeals for American help from an African regime unable to feed its own people from the resources of a ruined economy.

Captiva Island, Florida, February 11

I suddenly realize how tired I was of all the things that absorbed my interest in Princeton: the remaining involvements, the obscure struggle with the inevitable bewilderments of advanced age, the spectacle of the tragically-disintegrating Russia.

Princeton, March 7

George Shultz, honorable and amiable man that he is, spoke at a dinner here day before yesterday. In the *tour d'horizon* he gave us, he placed much stress on what he viewed as the success of our government in persuading or compelling other governments to respect "human rights."

This statement sets an entire chorus of dissenting, or at least questioning, bells clanging away in my mind. . . . Do we claim, as a feature of our sovereign status, the right to govern ourselves as we like, deferring to the traditions, tastes, concepts, and customs of our people? And would we resent an effort by any other government to prescribe for us changes in this governmental system? If so, do we nevertheless claim, on the basis of some supposed superiority of our own system, the right to intervene in just this way in the lives of other peoples and governments?

And is it our view, in this connection, that our particular institutions have universal value? That they represent the best possible response to the need of all peoples, regardless of their traditions, tastes, etc., regardless of their history, regardless of their stage of development?

And do we consider that individuals have "rights" of citizenship, independent of any duties or responsibilities this citizenship might also involve? Does a man require only to be born, to assume human form, that is, in order to become the beneficiary of these "human rights"? Is nothing to be required of him? Is it that he may be as selfish, as nasty, socially as negative, uncooperative, and burdensome to others as he likes, but as long as he contrives to stay within the law, he can claim all the benefits of these rights?

I am sure the answer of most Americans to this last question would be an emphatic "yes," and perhaps unavoidably so. But the disparity between a total irresponsibility and an unearned privilege continues to bother me.

March 12

I am probably the most widely honored person, outside the entertainment industry and the political establishment, in this country. How could this have happened? And how to put it in its proper place?

I am at a loss to answer those questions. I have had occasional insights—yes, and most of them ahead of their time, so much so as to render them, at the time of their conception, substantially useless. Also, I have been extremely lucky: favored by fortune even in most of those experiences that seemed at the time to be disasters. But I am well aware of my own weaknesses. . . . I am being honored, in large part, not for what I really am but for what people think I am. But that in itself is significant. Not only is it significant, but it is an obligation. Finding myself thus costumed, like an actor acting the part of someone other than himself, I must try to live up to the costume and to the part. My role is to sustain other people's illusions.

March 17

We have been enjoying nearly a week of real summer weather, without precedent (for the high temperature) in this part of the country. One wonders, of course, whether this is not one of the first evidences of a real and menacing warming of the planet. In any case, the forsythia, not unnaturally, is in bloom.

[Although the dissolution of the Soviet Union into its constituent republics by December 1991 would develop without serious violence, the breakup could have spawned chaos and bloodshed. That worried Kennan, who had never lost his passionate feelings for Russia.]

April 5

Today is a day of black despair. Part of this, no doubt is physical. . . .

There was also politics: the realization that the foolish Lithuanians, determined to kill the goose that lays the golden egg, have evidently succeeded in pushing poor Gorbachev back into the arms of, and into a dependency upon, the army, the police, and the Russian hard-liners, and thus putting the final end to his real independent leadership in Russia. Accordingly, there will grow up an increasing breach between him and the U.S., produced by the movement of this country into the position of *the* great patron of any and every entity that expresses a wish to leave the Soviet Union—the adoption by this country, in other words, of a policy of promoting and accepting a share of responsibility for, the break-up of the traditional Russian Empire, with all the chaos, bloodshed, and horror that is going to mean.

May 5

Our government was preparing, under pressure from our hard-line NATO partners, primarily the French and British, to exploit the present confused and precarious situation in Russia with a view to excluding the Russians from all participation in the security problems of the continent and leaving them confronted, as the final result of their great military effort in World War II, with a Europe dominated militarily by a Germany, representing in itself the greatest military power on the continent, and in a state of alliance with the United States, Britain, and France, to the bargain. . . . I thought it always a mistake to take advantage of the momentarily weakened position of another great power to obtain advantages one could not have obtained under normal circumstances. To do this, I said, was something that always revenged itself at a later date.

June 1

Last evening: the state dinner for Gorbachev at the White House. It was, I thought, very nicely and tastefully done. Annelise looked, I thought, very beautiful in her multi-colored chiffon dress. I kept meeting people I knew or faintly recognized. Henry Kissinger greeted me with real warmth, which moved me. Gorbachev, as on the first occasion when I met him, gave me the embrassio,[55] and told me that he had seen the

55. Gorbachev literally embraced Kennan.

statement I recently made (the Milwaukee statement, presumably), and so jolted me by this greeting that I, distracted, failed to notice Mesdames Bush and Gorbachev standing a little back from the President & had to be yanked back by Annelise to greet them. . . .

Altogether, a creditable evening on the American side, showing that we, the Bush White House, at least, know, when challenged, how to do this sort of thing. But I was never unaware of the sharpness of the differences that are going to have to be talked out tomorrow morning, particularly in connection with Germany, the problems of European security.

En route to Norway, June 17

Some way or other the time has to be spent, not wasted.

Well, then: I had thought to write, this summer. Why not start now? . . .

The most important thing to be said is that man (even the best of him) is an imperfect creature, a cracked vessel. This does not mean that he is not capable of fantastic efforts of creativity or virtue. It means only that those who are capable of such things (a small minority at that) find their efforts frustrated or corrupted by certain powerful impulses in themselves that are in conflict with all creativity and all virtue.

These impulses fall into two categories, both deriving their power from Nature's insistence that those born into her family should be concerned for the preservation, or in more practical terms the multiplication, of their species. One of these impulses is the instinct of self-love. The other is the sexual urge. Let us take first the sexual urge, as the simpler and most primitive of the two. What may be said about it? Sometimes, like self-love, assuming many forms, even disguising itself, it remains an urge of enormous power. And it is, above all, in conflict with civilization: with order, with reason, even with human dignity. So silly is it, by all rational standards, so destructive and so self-defeating, that it fits poorly with even the most rudimentary requirements of an orderly, responsible life and sometimes even with those of its partner—self-love. Its manifestations oscillate between the extremes of the tragic and the ludicrous.

It is often confused with love. The two do indeed sometimes meet, though seldom for very long, and when they do and as long as they do, and only then, the sexual urge is relieved of its sordidness and in some way ennobled. Ennobled, because here, love (if it is real love) becomes the master; and the sexual urge, in taking second place, gains dignity from the service, and from that which it serves. But those moments do not mark all lives, and are not long-lasting even when they do. But meantime, this urge remains the chaotic, anarchic force that we know it to be: beastly, demeaning, mocking the dignity of its helpless victims, always grist to the mill of the cynical and the scoffers, but leaving everywhere, a trail of shame and frustration in its path.

Self-love, the other compelling, elementary force which mars the perfectability of the human species, is quite different: more pervasive (for there are, for good or for bad, a few that seem to escape the sexual urge), more subtle in the devices it employs to hold its victims in its grip, far cleverer in disguising itself, less flagrant in its attack on the good order of society, even insinuating itself into the most widely accepted and even respected inventions of civilized behavior.

The Farm, September 16

It is clear that I am, whether slowly or rapidly, but in any case with increasing acceleration, dying. . . .

Whether there is "life" after death is a question that does not trouble me. It is clear to me that the soul, while of course dependent upon the body for its presence and activity in this world, is not identical with the body; and there is no particular reason why it should cease to exist just because the body has been abandoned by the functions of life and is no longer a human being but only a rotting substance.

> [Accompanied by Annelise, George flew to Europe so that he could visit friends at Crottorf Castle, attend the Pour le Mérite for Arts and Sciences meeting in Würzburg, catch a glimpse of reunited Berlin, and then travel to Moscow, where he was a guest of the Soviet Academy of Sciences. They stopped off in London on the way home.]

En route to Europe, September 25

There are weighty reasons why one should be very careful about any complete disappearance of a central Soviet authority, not the least of them being the danger of fragmentation of the responsibility for custody of the nuclear weaponry now in Soviet hands.

Crottorf, West Germany, September 29

Four days from now Germany is to be re-united. The change has come much too suddenly for its effects to be in any way foreseeable or predictable. Beyond this, lies the immense and menacing uncertainty of the situation in what is now called the Middle East (it is really the *Near* East). So great, so baffling, are these uncertainties that here in these last days they have scarcely been discussed at all. Life, aside from the sudden rise in the price of gasoline, takes its usual course. And one lives from day to day. The papers have been full of German politics, particularly the unification of the western Social Democratic Party with its sister party from the east. But these are all short-term developments, viewed only as such. The future of Germany and of all Western Europe is recognized as being greatly sensitive to the world outside. And the world outside is unstable and inscrutable in the highest degree.

En route to London, October 8

The day of German unification, Annelise and I took a *Stadtbahn* train to the Friedrichstrasse, in what was, until today the eastern sector of Berlin, whence we joined the tens of thousands of people shuffling along in two great streams, in opposite directions, on Unter den Linden. We joined the west-going stream, and continued with it for one or two miles (we had no choice, in fact, for we could, over all this distance, find no other means of transportation than our own legs, of which my right one complained rather emphatically over the unusual demands being placed upon it). . . . The crowds, made up mostly, I suspected, of East Germans, were quiet and undemonstrative (many of them a bit hung-over, perhaps from the more strenuous celebrations of the night before). It was impossible to know what they were thinking. I had the impression that their principal reaction to this historic day, beyond a good deal of curiosity, was a certain paralyzing bewilderment in the face of the suddenness and unexpectedness of the entire recent stream of events. I saw no signs of any triumphant chauvinistic or even nationalistic emotion.

Altogether, upon leaving Germany, as we did the following morning, my principal reaction to the situation there was the recognition that this situation was, in the longer-term sense and from the standpoint of American policy, essentially out of control. The unification of the country, in the way and at the time it came about, was not the result of anyone's foresight or of an agreed policy on the part of the powers that were allied in the Second World War. It was the result of spontaneous action on the parts of several tens of thousands of young East Germans, motivated by the hope of getting better jobs, making more money, and bathing in the fleshpots of the West. Everyone cheered, of course, and expressed satisfaction, but was this, over the long term, what we really wanted?—the establishment of a united and armed Germany as incomparably the greatest economic and potentially the greatest military power in Europe?—and this before there was any really significant framework of European unification into which Germany could be firmly integrated?

. . . What is most disconcerting is the fact, demonstrated by these recent events, that there is no longer any sort of central control over the march of events in Europe. If chance, in the form of spontaneous outbreaks of impulse on the part of poorly informed and unreflective people, proved to be the dominant engine of change during this recent crisis, sweeping aside every sort of sober reflection and judgement on the part of the responsible governments, who is to say that things will be any different in the years ahead? Even if the German government contrives to take things in hand (and its leaders are almost the only ones who possibly could), our own ability as Americans to affect the course of events has been reduced to almost negligible dimensions.

Be that as it may, we proceeded on October the 4th to Moscow, where we were met at the airport by representatives of the Central Committee (of the Party) and of Arbatov's Institute. . . .

The following morning I was driven to the Kremlin for the scheduled meeting with Alexander Yakovlev, a vice-president of the governmental structure (as opposed to that of the Party), member of the Politburo of the party, and a man known not only as the only intellectual in Gorbachev's entourage but as one very close, intellectually at least, to Gorbachev himself. . . . Most of the discussion was conducted in Russian on both sides. Occasionally, when I had something I particularly wanted to be careful about, I went over briefly to English. I had warned Yakovlev in advance that I would not be in a position to discuss with him the present situation in his country, which is developing with frightening precipitation, and which I had made no effort to follow in detail, and would be prepared only to talk with him about the history of Soviet power and of its place in Russian history. He had said that he would welcome this, and indeed it was to this subject that he directed the first part of the 2–3 hours conversation. . . .

The Soviet Union is indeed today in a dreadful and most alarming state. The most critical and threatening aspect of this situation is of course the immediate condition of the economy, particularly (but not exclusively) the breakdown of the official production and distribution system for food and other consumer goods. The American media correspondents in Moscow have been giving what may have been a somewhat over-sensationalized picture of this situation by concentrating their reports on the official food stores and neglecting the open markets, where food seems to be comparatively quite abundant. But even taking this into account the situation is serious and even scary.

For the state of affairs I have just described demands immediate and drastic attention. Instead of giving it that attention, Gorbachev (and here, I fault him, too) and the other governmental leaders have been giving most of their time to the other more long-term problems of the switch from the Party's previous monopoly of power to an elected-governmental system and to the similar transition from a command economy to a free-enterprise one. Both of these are of course tremendous problems, but less urgent than the immediate collapse of the economy. And the concentration upon them by the leadership reminds me of what General Marshall said about the situation in Europe just before the Marshall Plan initiative: "The doctors deliberate while the patient fades." . . .

The whole picture is overshadowed by something else that is of greatest importance, and to which the leadership, in my opinion, is also giving insufficient attention, which is the progressive disintegration of the Soviet Union itself. . . . So far-reaching has been this process of spontaneous decentralization that Gorbachev, I fear, is going to wake up one of these mornings to discover that while he has largely in place a new and ostensibly democratic apparatus for the governing of the Soviet Union, there is no such thing as a Soviet Union left to govern.

That the three Baltic countries would demand their independence and act in many respects as though they already had it, was only to be expected, and the same could be said about some of the others, particularly in the Black and Caspian seas region. But much trouble lies ahead in connection with the Ukraine, parts of whose population are stridently demanding independence, whereas the country is in a number of respects very poorly fitted for it. And even more important, but also more alarming, is the vigorous movement toward independence in the Russian heartland of the country . . . under Boris Yeltsin's leadership. For if in this great territory, more than half of that of the U.S.S.R., and comprising roughly half of its population, the center of real political vitality moves from the all-union Soviet level to that of the republican government, as it now threatens to do, the question will arise as to whether there will be enough left in the way of subordinate territory to justify the maintenance of any central authority at all. I have pointed out in an article about to appear in the November edition of *Foreign Affairs* that anything of that sort would hold great dangers for everyone involved, including ourselves.

This whole problem is now greatly aggravated and complicated by the evidence that in many respects the other great problems I have mentioned—the political transition, the movement to free enterprise, and even the mastering of the present difficult economic situation—could probably be approached more effectively at the separate-republican level than at that of the now relatively helpless central government. For this reason, the problem of the decentralization of the previous empire also demands new and urgent attention—attention which, so far as I can see, it is not receiving. The best solution would be a loose confederation that would involve extensive economic and financial cooperation, somewhat along the lines of the present European Economic Community, and possibly the continuation of a common currency, but also a new ordering of military relationships that might allow for local militia, but also for something in the nature of a central military organization, possibly along the lines of NATO, and particularly one that could continue to bear sole responsibilities for the nuclear weapons now in Soviet hands.

One could well blame Gorbachev for much of this. He clearly did not foresee (nor did any of us) how quickly and dangerously things would fall apart in Russia once the strong disciplinary hand of the Party was relaxed. What he did in destroying the old system was a great historic service to Russia and the world. And nobody else could have done it. But he is not a good politician in the democratic sense. He has no adequate inter-action with the people at large. Yeltsin, not an intellectual but quite intelligent, is far ahead of him in these respects. He, Gorbachev, is a man of ideas, and a very courageous one, but he is not a good administrator and is anything but an effective demagogue. If the decentralization of the country continues at the present pace, Gorbachev's role in Russian history may turn out to be completed, for he has hitched his star to the development of the central all-Union government, and this may soon fail and disappear under him, like a horse under its rider, leaving him without much of any function at all. But here, too, I may be mistaken. This is no time for prophets or predictions. Gorbachev is a resourceful man, with a great and deserved international reputation. Russia, whether united or not, needs him. Perhaps he will rouse himself betimes and contrive to take charge both of the economic situation and the re-ordering of the relations among the republics. I hope so. But I cannot be sanguine.

Princeton, December 16

Mr. Bush continues to entangle us all in a dreadful involvement in the Persian Gulf to which no favorable outcome is visible or even imaginable. In addition, he has, by forcing through the UN resolution mentioning January 15, created his own deadline.[56] At the moment, it is hard to see anything ahead but a military-political disaster.

56. The Bush administration had helped push through the United Nations a resolution demanding that Saddam Hussein's Iraqi forces evacuate Kuwait, which they had occupied since August.

Chapter Ten

At a Century's Ending, 1991–2004

1991

Kennan continued to take pride in his accomplishments even as he despaired at the limit of his influence. He criticized the war against Iraq as unnecessary and as diverting resources and attention away from desperately needed rehabilitation of America's domestic infrastructure and finances. Nevertheless, he was impressed with the spectacle of U.S. military might. Contrary to what one might expect, he said little about the final collapse of the Soviet Union.

Princeton, January 15

Today, January 15, is of course the day on which the UN ultimatum to Iraq expires and Mr. Bush receives carte blanche to inaugurate hostilities whenever and however it suits him. There is every reason to assume that at some time during the next hours or days he will do just that, thus locking us into a quite unnecessary adventure which is bound to preempt our attention and our resources for many months, if not years to come, and for which no ultimate favorable outcome is visible or even imaginable.

This, coming only a little more than a year after the effective ending of the Cold War, cancels out the respite which that development might have provided for us, including the opportunity to undertake the restoration of our shattered finances and endangered economy.

One might wonder whether so great and weird an error could be anything other than the reflection of some sort of a subconscious death wish on the part of American society in general. But this would be an over-simplification. The American public at large had no impulses of that nature. Nor, in this case (and this is a significant change) did the Congress. (The sole bright spot in this entire dismal business has been the high quality—troubled, thoughtful, and dignified—of the Congressional debate over the resolution giving the President authority to go ahead and inaugurate hostilities.) No, the impulse to which this strange behavior was a response was one concentrated overwhelmingly in the mind set of the President himself. And this, as I see it, was the product of two factors: one, our unfortunate involvement with the part of the world in question (now called the Middle East, though this is a geographic misnomer), as this has been shaped in the years since World War II; the other, the belief, so deeply inculcated through the false attitudes of the Cold War and so strongly supported subsequently by the Reagan administration, in the ability of America's armed strength to solve all serious international problems and to assure the political glory of any president bold enough to employ it.

I, during this entire recent crisis, have not said a single word publicly about the Gulf crisis. . . . But I have had to ask myself whether I could not have foreseen this crisis and done something to help hold it off.

I look back over my own record, and I see that in the case of every fundamental component of this present situation I did in earlier years express myself as forcefully as I could. As far back as 1954 . . . I stressed the folly of turning these Persian Gulf oil resources over to the local sheiks and then establishing their sheikdoms in the quality of sovereign states, beholden to nobody. . . .

None of this had the faintest effect. . . .

An attempt, as Chief of the Planning Staff, to warn the U.S. government in 1948 of the fact that in co-sponsoring the establishment of the state of Israel in the face of the continued opposition of the Arab leaders we were creating a problem to which we could have no peaceful answer, had no result other than to earn me a reminder from the Undersecretary of State that ours was a country in which domestic political considerations, even when involving the interests of only a minority of our citizens, took priority over considerations of national interest. . . . My efforts, finally, to persuade people, over the Cold War years, that war with the employment of great modern forces could, in this modern age, serve no positive purpose. . . .

All these efforts turn out once again, as Mr. Bush's decision now proves, to have made no perceptible impact at all on our official thinking, or even on public opinion.

How, then, to reconcile this with the startling fact that I find myself, at the age of nearly 87, if not the most extravagantly honored private individual in this country, then one of at the most two or three of whom that could be said? Is there not here a grotesque anomaly between the esteem bestowed on the person and the scant regard for his views? And if so, is this not evidence of some delinquency on his own part? Is there not, in other words, some way I should have conducted myself that would have assured to my thoughts a public attention commensurate with the respect paid to my person?

February 6

The situation in Russia, too, is unmitigatedly dreadful. There, the future is wholly unpredictable. The best that could be said is that it will probably take years before things sort themselves out, and what may happen in the meantime is fearful to contemplate.

. . . When I am asked, "What do I think of the situation in Russia?," my reaction is: "How lovely it would be to live somewhere deep in the country."

February 3

This past fortnight has been from the personal standpoint a very difficult one: much physical weariness and deterioration, a more rapid succession of heart palpitations. . . . I am now really and rapidly growing old. . . .

I did write this last week, and published in today's *Washington Post*, an article on recent events in the Baltic countries and on the other aspects of the problem of what is to become of the traditional Russian, recently Soviet, empire. I wrote it, really, to be read by Mr. Gorbachev (as I rather expect it will be). I wanted to urge him, in his own interests and in those of Russia herself, to give the Baltic states their independence and to meet the other restless republics half-way in their desire for a much greater autonomy and a looser set of ties to Moscow. I wrote it as a matter of duty, without any very high expectation that it will have any effect. But even this was an exertion.

En route to Captiva Island, February 12

The dreadful, fateful involvement in the Persian Gulf is approaching its climax, which can be anything but a favorable one. Mr. Bush continues to place his bets, and his own political prospects, on a thrilling military victory, disregarding the appalling effect the war is having on opinion throughout the Arab and Muslim world, a development that would appear to prejudice increasingly the chance for anything resembling a satisfactory peace.

Princeton, February 27

The President announced this evening the suspension of hostilities in Iraq about 2 hours from now, on condition that the Iraqis respond in kind. One way or another, this marks, I am sure, the termination of a brilliantly successful military campaign, and one, incidentally, which puts us into a new age in respect to the art of warfare.

We shall now have to face the multitudinous problems of designing a new sort of a peace to take the place of the precarious one that existed prior to this war in the Middle-Eastern region. This will be very hard, and it is not a problem to which I could contribute in any very useful way, even if I were asked to do so. Those who have created this problem will have to come up with the ideas as to how they are to cope with it. I only hope that they will not pay too much attention to Arab and other Moslem opinion, and will not go too far out of their way to appease it. The one strong feeling I have gained from watching the Gulf War on television over these long weeks is that so far as the Arabs are concerned, I would rather have their respect than their affections—and their respect, in particular, for our military power and prowess, for they seem to understand little else. Their friendship would rest at best on fickle and hysterical foundations. Let them hate us, if they will, so long as they regard us, as this war should have taught them to do, as a serious force, a military force if not a political one, in world affairs.

September 4

A strange psychic state: moments of apprehension of I know not what, a lack of emotional elasticity, great discontent with myself, regrets for the callousness I showed towards others when I was young, general dissatisfaction with myself, and lack of enthusiasm for life. These, I suspect, are clear signs of age, and even of approaching death. This last I do not mind. It is, generally speaking, high time that I died. But I would like first to finish the book and I feel every day that in my effort to finish the book, I am racing against death . . . and must be sure that I can complete this last task, for, as John Donne said, "none can work in that night."

[In Washington Kennan addressed a dinner at the Library of Congress held in honor of the one hundredth anniversary of Averell Harriman's birth. He also spoke at St. Alban's School, where he received the first peace prize given by the Episcopal Diocese of Washington.]

Washington, November 15

For nearly two and a half months this personal diary has been neglected in favor of the completion of the as yet unnamed book.[1] The latter was taken to New York and delivered to Harriet Wasserman ten days ago. She delivered it (on the same day, I believe, to Donald Lamm, the chief of the Norton publishing house). He read it, as did some of his associates, and pronounced it, according to Harriet, "the most important book he has ever written"—a pronouncement which, well-intentioned as I am sure it was, would have had more weight in my eyes if I considered that any of the 19-odd books I have written was of any importance—in the sense, that is, of what I would suppose "importance" to mean to him, whom others have declared (and which I readily believe) to be the best in the trade.

[The Kennans traveled to Boston where doctors examined George's heart palpitations, which had recently worsened.]

Boston, November 21

I fear, in particular, the reviewers. Where could you find people, particularly in this country, who could understand such a book?

Actually, I know, that is not what is most important. More important will be the people, if there are any, who will pick the book up and read it fifty to a hundred years hence. If they find nothing intelligible in it, then it will indeed have been written in vain. In this sense it should be regarded, as have so many other books, as something written for those who came after me, and perhaps, given the prospective state of Western civilization in this coming period, long after.

[The Kennans went to Bermuda for a vacation.

In contrast to the many readers of the Mr. X article of 1947 who lauded Kennan for his prescience about the eventual fall of the Soviet Union, the author of that essay evinced no such pride. He believed that Washington had foolishly expanded the geographical scope of containment and had passed up many opportunities for negotiations that might have eased or ended the Cold War.]

1. *Around the Cragged Hill: A Personal and Political Philosophy* (1993).

Bermuda, December 26

Yesterday evening before dinner, we went over to the Lodge to watch, on their TV set, Gorbachev giving his resignation speech, in which he conceded that the Soviet Union had come to an end. The lowering and removal of the Soviet flag over the Kremlin was also showed. A historic moment, if there ever was one!

Today, here, things are much like the other days—drifting cloud masses and sunny-intervals. Wind has gone further around to the north. One begins to become lazy.

Lay awake this morning, pondering question of what should be the basis of American foreign policy. Fell to thinking of a dilemma: far, wide, and interdependent vs. small, intimate, only local dependence. My own preference, of course, for the latter. But realistic?

Considering the total undependability of our world environment, my first reaction is: surely, we should seek, together with a complete cessation of immigration, as extensive a national autarchy as we could possibly achieve. . . . Why, I asked myself, if we are going to talk about autarchy, limit it to the national dimension? I have in my book suggested the break up of the country into a dozen smaller entities. Why not autarchy in them?

1992

While finding himself increasingly bothered by the frailties of his aging body, Kennan remained razor sharp in his commentary on events past and present. Walking the streets of Washington prompted a frank appraisal of his now deceased associates. Kennan looked askance at Washington's growing tendency in the post–Cold War world to use troops in dealing with humanitarian disasters overseas. He perceived that what the generals called "mission creep" could entangle the United States in thorny problems. Moreover, such military involvement helped postpone what he saw as the need to reallocate financial resources toward domestic needs.

Princeton, January 14

After two months of journeys to Washington and Boston, several cardiograms, some anxiety, and Lord knows how many thousands of dollars, I am precisely back where I was before. The only difference is that I know that what I have are not just the usual palpitations but something usually known as atrial fibrillation, which can be (although they think it is not in my case) much more dangerous. . . .

Began today, though feeling wretched, the rewriting of the chapter in my book on foreign policy—a hard job!

March 11

I was moved to receive, here at my home, a courtesy visit from the new Russian ambassador, Vladimir Lukin, who was here in Princeton ostensibly to address a dinner at the Woodrow Wilson School, but his leading assistant at the Embassy, Vladimir Pechatnov, had told Liz that he would accept the invitation from the school only if I could receive him while he was here. He had only been in this country for 3 or 4 days, and had not yet presented his official credentials at the White House. It gave me an unusual satisfaction to reflect that he had, so to speak, presented his credentials to me before presenting them to Mr. Bush.

March 17

Curious changes are occurring in me, these days. I went this morning to Firestone Library to pick up, among other things, a copy of a volume of English translations of Chekhov's stories, one of which Annelise and a friend wanted to see. On finding the book in the stacks, I found myself glancing at the translation, in it, of "The Steppe," fell to reading it, standing upright between the narrow stacks, was so moved by it that I finally had to tear myself away, then went home and, the house being empty, sat down in the library and burst out sobbing (something that had not happened to me for years) over the sheer beauty of the tale. But in this outburst of senile emotion, I suddenly saw myself and my present life as, I suspect, they really were rather than as I was accustomed to seeing them—saw myself as the old emaciated scarecrow that I am, going through the motions of trying to hold together a personal and professional life as though I were 68 instead of 88, leading this life instead of vegetating somewhere far out in the country, cultivating my garden patch and tending my chickens, as a man of my age ought to be doing.

April 9

Strange, I observe, are the effects of old age upon a man, not the physical ones, of course, but the psychic and emotional. . . . I am tired of the things with which I was only recently more intimately involved: the Cold War and its history, the Kennan Institute and its problems, the record of my own life, etc.

May 16

The ordeal of having the pace maker inserted was somewhat enlivened by questions being put to me by an assistant surgeon who had read one of my books and who now bombarded the helpless me with questions about Russia. I replied as best I could in muffled tones from underneath the blankets that had been placed over my face.

Washington, October 5

I pursued my elderly limping walk through the inner streets, encountering at every turn the houses in which there had once lived friends and acquaintances: Joe Alsop, the Bohlens, the Achesons. . . .

While I knew all these people, and some of them quite well, I was never properly a member of what was called the Georgetown set. I was for much of the time too poor, and too little urban. I spent my weekends elsewhere normally after the war, out at the farm. Thus I missed all the weekend entertaining. But it was more than that. While some of these friends knew me quite well, professionally if not personally, they all, I thought, looked at me slightly askance. Joe Alsop, being himself a fine writer, recognized what he thought was a similar quality in myself, and respected it. Beyond that he knew little about me, and what he thought he knew was mostly wrong. Chip Bohlen, himself not a good writer and quite uninterested in the quality of writing as distinct from its content, regarded me, in an anguished way, as a brother, if only for our mutual interest in Russia, and followed me with an anxious eye, lest I depart from the correct interpretation of trends and events in that far country. Dean Acheson, like Alsop, recognized me as a good writer, but viewed that quality with a touch of suspicion, sensing that it fitted ill with the world of politics and the law that was his natural habitat. He viewed me, I suspect, with a sort of amused personal affection, but I never commanded on his part the same sort of respect he accorded to the law. There was, in his view, nothing better or higher than the latter profession; the American Foreign Service did not even come within sight of it. For these, and for all the others, I hovered uncertainly on the horizon, a strange occasional social phenomenon, over-intense, seldom relaxed, to be fitted into no known category, to be approached with a certain respect but also with a certain wariness. You never knew, they thought, when I would fall out of the proper tone, or in some other way violate the rules. And they were not wrong. I never knew it, myself. . . .

At a play based on selections from my *Sketches from a Life* the only unpleasant moment of the evening came when my host, who was Jewish, turned to me and whispered something unpleasantly critical about the passages referring to the Germans. I was puzzled by this, and replied that perhaps she should read the full text, but she made no reply and turned away. I still remained puzzled by this, and at a loss to know to what she was referring. It could scarcely have been the mention of the shock I experienced when first seeing Jews in Berlin wearing the yellow stars, unless it be my observation that a great many Germans, too, were shocked and troubled by the same spectacle. (But this was true.) As for the other passages: Could she have been offended by my feeling for small German children who, amid the ruins of Berlin, still believed in fairies?

If so, then we are really in trouble, for whoever despairs of the children, despairs of civilization itself. Or could it have been my sense of outrage over the realization that we, the Western allies, had destroyed seventy-five thousand civilians, people of all kinds and ages, in the fire-bombing of Hamburg? Did she think I did not know that the Germans, too, had bombed cities and that the Nazis had burned even greater numbers of innocent civilians? But had I not referred to, and rejected, the screaming non sequitur "they did it to us?"

My host's reactions left me with a lingering sense of concern. . . . I had an exposure greater than that of many others to the terrible sides of Nazi rule, and needed instruction from few. With this exposure, too, I tried, as with the comparable exposure to the cruelties and abominations of Stalinist rule in Russia, to come to terms in my own way, bearing in mind the weaknesses, the blind spots, the helplessness of great masses of people in the hands of totalitarian rulers, and hope I have done this with reasonable fairness and sense of humanity. But if I thought these were things I could never hope to discuss freely with my many Jewish friends—that this was a sort of getting-off place beyond which communication and understanding was no longer possible—it would be a source of deep discouragement to me. For my entire literary life, as I now see it, has been one long effort to gain understanding for the outlooks of others and to reach their understanding for my own.

Princeton, October 22

The New York dinner honoring Arthur Schlesinger on his 75th birthday must have included more than a hundred guests and was elaborate and replete with celebrities and noise. I, given the first male place to the right of the host, was seated between Jackie (Kennedy) Onassis and Evangeline Bruce, with both of whom I enjoyed talking (albeit for different reasons).[2] But when 10:30 came, and we had still not come to the dessert, and it was clear that a large part of the program still lay ahead, I, aware that I would have to travel to Washington and to face another dinner there the following night, fled, thus abandoning most ungallantly, my two distinguished ladies but seeing no alternative.

November 14

These last weeks have been busy ones. I wrote and published in the *New York Times* op-ed page one piece protesting the Bush administration's

2. Evangeline Bruce was the elegant wife of the diplomat David Bruce.

wild and despairing claim to have "won the Cold War." It brought in a number of responses, all favorable, except for one letter by Richard Pipes, published on the same paper's editorial page, taking issue with my piece, on the grounds that I myself had said, in the X-article, that we had it in our power to influence the course of events in Russia. (Pipes failed to note that the five pages immediately preceding the sentence he quoted had been filled with material about the underlying weaknesses of the Soviet regime and the uncertainties that hovered over its future, and that the quoted sentence was only an introduction to a paragraph asserting my view that the way we could influence Russia was by the power of example, not—by implication—military threats and intimidation.)

A week later, I published, in the Outlook section of the *Washington Post* a column that . . . I took steps to see was made known to the State Department (through Frank Wisner)[3] and to the Clinton entourage (through Tony Lake).[4] . . .

I voted for Clinton. I did so without enthusiasm, for I disapproved of some of his statements about domestic affairs, and found others of them not greatly persuasive. But Mr. Bush had never impressed me very much in the first place, and I felt that he and his entourage, in addition to being poorly in touch with parts of the population, particularly the more intelligent youth, were worn out and devoid of any adequate positive program. I have no means of knowing what the Clintonites will do about foreign affairs.

The Farm, November 26

As we left for this Thanksgiving visit to the farm, I picked up from a bookcase in Princeton a book of Reinhold Niebuhr, which I had never used, brought it along, and have read it here.[5] Have read it, in fact, with intense interest, not only for its own value (which is at the impressive elevation that marks all Niebuhr's works) but for the light it shed on my own recent book, now about to appear.[6]

We share, I am thrilled to see, a number of insights into the condition of man. How many of these, in my own case, were ones inspired or induced by other reading of Niebuhr's works, I cannot say. Certainly, I

3. Frank G. Wisner is a businessman and diplomat. He is the son of Frank Wisner, an official at the Offices of Strategic Services and the CIA.

4. Anthony Lake was President Bill Clinton's national security advisor and is, by happenstance, a son of the former Eleanor Hard, to whom Kennan had been engaged before he married Annelise.

5. *Man's Nature and His Communities* (1965).

6. *Around the Cragged Hill: A Personal and Political Philosophy* (1993).

was significantly influenced by him. But this present reading gives me the impression that in some ways I may have gone beyond him, if only because the developments of the years since his death have confronted us with dimensions of reality that were less conspicuous in his time. . . .

There was our common recognition of the dangers of collective impulse and reaction over those of the individual. I had fancied that my own recognition of this factor was original. I was thrilled to see that Niebuhr had also recognized it, although not nearly so sharply as had I, or had he attributed to it the same significance.

Princeton, December 9

The television screen is showing live pictures of the Marines going ashore, in the grey dawn of another African day, in Somalia. . . . I regard this move as a dreadful error of American policy; and I think that in justice to myself I should set down at this point, if only for the diary, my reasons for this view.

The purpose of this exercise is, we are told, to take charge of the channels of transportation and to assure the movement of food to certain aggregations of starving people. . . . The supply lines by which it would have to be delivered are subject to harassment on the part of armed bands and individuals along the way, as a result of which much of the food is plundered and lost before it can reach its destination. . . . Why, then, is our action undesirable? First, because it treats only a limited and short-term aspect of what is really a much wider and deeper problem. . . . The situation we are trying to correct has its roots in the fact that the people of Somalia are wholly unable to govern themselves and that the entire territory is simply without a government. The starvation that we are seeing on television is partly the result of drought (or so we are told), partly of overpopulation, and partly of the chaotic conditions flowing from the absence of any governmental authority. . . .

This dreadful situation cannot possibly be put to rights other than by the establishment of a governing power for the entire territory, and a very ruthless, determined one at that. It could not be a democratic one, because the very prerequisites for a democratic political system do not exist among the people in question. Our action holds no promise of correcting this situation. . . .

Secondly, this is an immensely expensive effort. What we are pouring into it must run, in the monetary sense, into hundreds of millions if not billions of dollars. This comes at a time when our country is very deeply indebted. . . . There are many needs at home, particularly in the condition of our cities and of the physical infrastructure of our society, which are not being met, ostensibly for lack of money. . . .

The dispatch of American armed forces to a seat of operations in a place far from our own shores, and this for what is actually a major police action in another country and in a situation where no defensive American interest is involved—this, obviously, is something that the founding fathers of this country never envisaged or would ever have approved. If this is in the American tradition, then it is a very recent tradition.

December 14

Have had spells in recent days of a type of depression I have never before experienced: not, this time, the over dramatization of my own ills that used once to overtake me from time to time, but rather an extreme awareness and distaste for American civilization as I now see it around me. Since the external environment has not greatly changed, I suspect that the recurrence of these moments are attributable, not surprisingly, to some sort of physical changes within myself.

How I long to be living somewhere in the country, real country, if such a thing were to be found. But this would, I suspect, depress Annelise as much as the absence of it depresses me.

1993

Kennan's lifelong ambition to influence domestic and foreign policy flared up anew with the commercial success of his book on political and personal philosophy, Around the Cragged Hill.

Princeton, January 3

The first review of the new book appeared today in the *New York Times* book review. It was not a serious review. If the author (George Will) had read the entire book, the review does not suggest it. It was a kindly piece, but not serious, reflecting, as it seemed to me, the view: "Kennan is not a bad old chap. Let us be indulgent of him. Every old man is entitled, after all, to a few intellectual oddities, and some of his are even here or there amusing."

I was pleased, of course, that the review was not nasty. But I came away from the reading of it with the idea that I would rather be severely criticized by someone who took the book seriously than be treated with such benevolent condescension by some one who did not.

January 22

The presidential inauguration seemed a happy national fiesta, rather moving, in fact. I was particularly affected by the spectacle of Mr. and Mrs. Clinton accompanying Mr. Bush, on foot, to his helicopter and wishing him Godspeed on his return to private life. And again, the receiving by Mr. & Mrs. Clinton in the White House after the parade, of some 600 people, chosen by lot from applicants from all across the country, and the kindness and respect shown to these people and particularly to the little children, by the President and his wife. True: all of this was bound to be followed the next day (and was so followed) by the brutalities of "politics as usual." But there was in all of this happy ceremony, normal-occurring in so vast a country, a certain magnificence, and there were moments when I found it hard to repress the tears. . . . It yielded for me a moment of pride and affection for my country such as I am not often permitted to enjoy.

[The Kennans traveled from Washington, where George had met with Frank G. Wisner and Strobe Talbott,[7] to Princeton to New York. While on babysitting duty with Annelise in New York, George tried his hand at genealogical research at the New York Public Library. He was thinking about doing a family history of his ancestors.]

New York City, February 2

Frank Wisner, whose most recent post had been, as I understand it, Under Secretary of State for Security Affairs, had now, in the last post-inauguration days, moved over to a similar position in the Pentagon. Strobe T., on the other hand, had just received a high position in the State Department, where he was to have overall charge of all affairs having to do with Russia. It was to be the first official position he had ever occupied.

Both men were extremely kind to me, yet I came away from the encounter a bit chastened and saddened. . . . Frank heard me out on Russia with apparent respect, but I felt as did Henry Adams[8] (according to one of his diary notes or letters) when he wrote that he and John Hay[9] were now regarded as "sages," by which he evidently meant that they were to be treated with respect but that their observations were not to be taken seriously when it came to public policy. This being the case, it was time, Adams wrote, for the two of them to make their exit as gracefully as possible.

Princeton, April 7

The extraordinary and wholly unexpected commercial success of my recent book. For full three weeks (if I remember correctly) it surprised us all, publisher, agent, author, and many others, by appearing on the *New York Times'* national best seller list. And it will again appear there (after a week's absence) on the coming Sunday. It is selling massively across the country, and noticed almost everywhere, except by the U.S. government and the media. A strange fate, mine: to move so many compatriots, but never those in power.

Well, more and more I am being made to realize that this is not my

7. After a career in journalism, Strobe Talbott became deputy secretary of state with special responsibility for relations with Russia.

8. Henry Adams, the grandson of John Quincy Adams, was a historian and an acerbic commentator on public affairs. His *Education of Henry Adams: An Autobiography* (1918) remains a literary monument.

9. John Hay was secretary of state under Presidents William McKinley and Theodore Roosevelt.

epoch. I enjoy a greater prestige than I had ever expected to enjoy. I am, like Henry Adams (who, someone pointed out, was born on the same day of year as myself), also being viewed as some sort of a sage. And I find myself being, or at least so I am led to suppose, the most elaborately-honored non-political and non-governmental personage in this country, yet totally without influence where it counts. I drift along on some sort of an elevated magic carpet, far above the fray, but so appalled by the little I see of it that I am beginning to lose my interest in it, give scarcely more than a glance at the morning paper, and do my best to retire into a really private life.

April 29

In spite of the commercial success of the book, neither the Clinton administration nor the media have shown the faintest interest in its contents—not even in the suggestion for a Council of State, and the administration has never gotten into touch with me about anything. But this, too, is something to which I am accustomed, after 40 straight years of such treatment. Had that kind of frustration been the cause of my present troubles, this would have revealed itself years ago.

What troubles me is a state of weakness so extreme that at least one of each 3 or 4 days I am not even able to do any normal mental work. That is new, and there must be some reason for it other than the sort of depression the doctor suspects.

My interest in life, in an epoch which is not my own and which I can do nothing to affect or improve, is fading. . . . I would prefer to have a small place in the country, live there alone, keep a dog, feed some chickens, and stumble about among the remains of what was once a garden.

September 12

I am rather disgusted with myself for all the time wasted over these three weeks, particularly watching the U.S. Open. But that comes only once a year; and it is almost my sole frivolity. (Everyone, it seems to me, is entitled to at least one major frivolity per annum.)

November 2

To celebrate my 90th birthday, the Council on Foreign Relations was expecting to invite three ex-presidents and 5 or 6 ex-secretaries of state of the United States. Whether any of these will accept and come is of course a question, but at least two or three of them presumably will. In any case, the mere fact that it was thought fit to invite them, and this to a dinner in my honor, jolts me severely. I know my weaknesses. I am accustomed to receiving honors in the academic world, but this moves me out of my accustomed orbit, and causes me to realize that I now have a different sort of an image—an image to which I not only have to try to live up outwardly but inwardly as well. This sobers me, and causes me to think that I must try, in this final bit of my life, to put behind me a number of my principal weaknesses, to accept the importance of the image that has been formed of me, and not to play the part but to live it.

I emphasize this last. Have talked with Annelise about it. She, sensible woman, says, "Oh, just be yourself. Being yourself has brought you where you are today. Let it carry you through the dinner." Sound advice only in the sense that I am not the man to pretend to be anything other than myself. But it is the self that is insufficient and ought, at long last, in these few short weeks, to be changed. It ought to be more collected, more composed, more deeply thoughtful, not just spewing out the insights of the moment but putting together all that I have, confronting the tragic elements in what I see around me but without yielding to despair. I must, without losing my modesty, respect all that within myself that has caused others to respect me. But if I find that what invites their respect is in part an image that fails to correspond entirely to the reality, I must, at any rate, respect the image and try to live up to it, not by dissembling the reality but by trying to bring it closer to the image.

1994

On reaching ninety, Kennan resolved to retire from public life. Yet he kept going. He also could not stop regretting his failure to instigate change in the policies and governing structure of the United States.

Princeton, January 6

Realizing that for one reason or another, I had not been able to keep this diary regularly over this past autumn, I decided to use some of the days of the Institute's Christmas holiday to write a summary account of the doings of these last 3–4 months. . . .

There was a trip to Washington at the invitation of Strobe Talbott, to talk with people in various departments of the government who were concerned with Russian matters at the working level, and to attend a dinner he was giving at his home for the Secretary of State, Mr. Warren Christopher. One could well ask what I, having not been officially concerned with Russian matters for forty years, and informed of the passage of events in that country primarily only through the daily press, could have to offer to these various people, who literally lived in this subject. But they were mostly experts, each with his limited professional competence. Strobe assured me after the session that what I was able to do for them, and what they appreciated, was to put everything together and look at the entire subject in a way they themselves were unable to do. This, I suspect, precisely because of my greater distance from the subject, was largely true. As for the Secretary of State, with whom I had previously never had anything more than a nodding acquaintance, I found him, in this more intimate atmosphere, a much warmer and more engaging a personality than when he puts on his characteristic attorney's mask and appears before the press and the public. Altogether, I welcomed this chance to establish acquaintance with those who now have responsibility for Russian affairs in Washington. I was, after all, for some twenty-six years a member of the American Foreign Service. I have some feeling for the situations of those I was meeting. And I would rather have a relationship of personal acquaintance and mutual confidence with them than to be obliged to feel myself regarded as a hostile and suspect outsider. . . .

At the Institute for Advanced Study I spoke about the enormous damage—social, spiritual, and even genetic—which seven decades of Communist power had done to the Russian people, what this had cost them, how far it had set them back, and what now remained: a confused, genetically and economically impoverished population, shaken, humiliated, and traumatized, without much confidence in itself, and without the leadership to give it that confidence. Whoever could not recognize this background and bear it in mind, had little chance of understanding what is now taking place in that tragically injured and spiritually diminished country. . . .

Mr. Clinton, in speaking publicly some months ago at the Seattle meeting of various heads of state, attributed some of the success he conceived us to have had in the immediate aftermath of the Second World War to "visionaries like Truman, Marshall, and Kennan"—a kind remark, even though "visionaries" was not exactly what we three gentlemen were. . . .

What concerns me most deeply are two phenomena, obviously closely connected, which have something to say to us about the mental and emotional state of large portions of our population. The first is the unrestrained decadence that has overcome so much of our social and cultural life: the delivery of most of the process of journalistic, electronic, and cultural communication into the hands of the entertainment industry and then the dreadful uses that industry makes of its near monopoly, not merely the low intellectual level but the shameless pornography, the pathological preoccupation with sex and violence, the weird efforts to claim for homosexuality the status of a proud, noble, and promising way of life, and in general the sweeping permissiveness and lack of moral leadership on which these distortions thrive.

Beyond this, there is something that is to my mind even more menacing, and that is the evidence of real emotional instability in considerable portions of our population, particularly in the universities and among young faculty and portions of the student body. I have in mind the bizarre effects of such contagious hysteria as "political correctness," but also something that is an unavoidable component of such hysterias, namely the total loss of a sense of humor. This, in fact, carries very far, even beyond the instances I have just mentioned. In whole or in part it pervades the magazine world, the political cartoons, the behavior of students en masse at sporting events, and a great deal of the movie and television outlook. Since I have always regarded a capacity for appreciation and enjoyment of the ironic and the absurd as an essential component of mental and emotional health, particularly in people with our cultural inheritance, I can only regard the extensive disappearance of it as a sign of something very significant and very disturbing in the mental and intellectual life of the people affected.

All of this gives to me the impression that ours is indeed in significant degree a sick society. And I cannot imagine where, in a country which has consigned a great portion of cultural leadership to the electronic media, the cure for this malady is to be found.

February 7

Difficult days. I have been trying, rather desperately, to clean up the papers staring me in the face from both my desks, the one in the office and the one here at home, in view of my determination that my 90th birthday, now less than ten days off, shall be the cut-off date for the effort, the never-ending effort, to cope decently and courteously with the stream of demands from the outside that I should do things others have wanted me to do. I wanted to prepare for this by having before me, when the day arrived, a clean slate: no further engagements, no unanswered correspondence, no obligations to others. I worked over the past weekend at this, even skipping church to find time to do it. Thought I was, at least as far as the office was concerned, on the verge of success. But no: by noon today the desk was covered with new demands, some of them relatively urgent.

New York City, February 15

The Council on Foreign Relations birthday dinner was for about a hundred people, fully eighty percent of them my friends or people with whom I was well acquainted. In view of what the event meant for me, I shall try to include in this account a list of the guests. The affair was presided over by Leslie Gelb,[10] but present, too, were Peter Tarnoff, Under Secretary of State for Political Affairs, and Pete Peterson, Chairman of the Council on Foreign Relations.

I was seated next to Madeleine Albright, the present ambassador to the UN, who, I gathered, represented the White House. She read aloud

10. A former journalist and official in the State and Defense Departments, Leslie Gelb is the former president of the Council on Foreign Relations.

and presented to me a letter from the President the drafting of which he himself had drafted. There was then read, and presented (I blush to say that I can't remember by whom) a similarly kind letter from the Secretary of State, Mr. Christopher, together with the bestowal of the Department of State's Distinguished Service Award (which is, I believe, the highest recognition that Department can give to any individual). There followed the announcement, by Peter Peterson of the establishment of an endowed Distinguished Fellowship for Russian Studies at the Council, to bear my name. Something in the order of a million dollars had already been raised. . . . Most moving toast of all: from Marshall Shulman,[11] calling attention to my work as a scholar. In short, they poured it on, and left me not only overwhelmed but unable to think of any even approximately adequate response.

Princeton, February 25

An effort to get up off the bed found me, to my dismay, simply incapable of doing this. Legs would not hold, and such was the state of vertigo that I could no longer stand or walk. Annelise, seeing that things were getting no better, called Dr. Wei, who appeared somewhere around seven p.m., and, after examining me, pronounced my condition to be the evidence of a stroke.

March 24

I have had two mornings in the office. I have answered x-number of letters (another x-number still remain, and will be replenished every day). I have fielded a request from Senator Bill Bradley for a foreword for a part of his forthcoming book. I have received Henry Kissinger's 590-pp. book and also a phone call from his office suggesting an early lunch at the Century (and what do you suppose he has on his mind?). . . . I have struggled with a newly-installed, state-of-the-art telephone system on my office desk, all the complexities of which I have not mastered and have no intentions of mastering. . . . I am making arrangements to attend the semi-annual meeting of the American Philosophical Society, later in April.

Life, in other words, has been resumed precisely as it was before my recent 90th birthday, before my stroke, exactly as it was, in fact, thirty years ago. No allowance is made for my age or my condition. I have felt

11. Marshall D. Shulman was a scholar of the Soviet Union, adviser to U.S. officials, and founding director of the W. Averell Harriman Institute for Advanced Study of the Soviet Union at Columbia University.

poorly for most of the last five days, sometimes even close to the edge. But I went to the cardiologist this afternoon, and was pronounced fit as a fiddle. A few pills each day; otherwise, don't spare yourself, lead life as you always have. Obviously, if I am nearing death, I am the only one who suspects it.

Sørenhus, June 29

About a week ago, I got word that the President's speech-writer, Mr. Robert Boorstin (nephew, as I understand it, of the recent Librarian of Congress of that name) was trying to reach me. Reason? The President was shortly going to Riga for a meeting with the three Baltic presidents, & there had been talk of my being asked to accompany him, or, if that proved impossible, perhaps send a greeting through his party, to the staff of the embassy at Riga. I therefore roused myself, although still not in the best of health, drafted a message of greeting as requested. The first secretary of the embassy in Oslo, made a brief visit down here to discuss the matter & receive the handwritten draft of the greeting, and thus we were off.

I have since drafted another two or three-page paper containing some of my thoughts on the situation in the Baltic countries and on some of the views about Russian-Baltic relations to which the President may well be exposed when he comes to Riga, and sent it the same way. The probabilities were that they never will reach him, but I am too old to be greatly concerned about this. I am still too much the diplomat, too much the servant of our government, to fail to respond when thus challenged.

July 2

I came here this summer armed with a great volume of Shakespeare's collected works and resolved to read them all through, time permitting. Well, I have now read, for the first time relatively seriously and completely, the first of the plays in this book's arrangement: *The Tempest*. . . . The question whether Shakespeare was really at heart a Christian, whether he was not more deeply influenced by the tragic mysteries of the Greek concept of a humanity at the mercy of the power of a variety of semi-human Gods. I shall keep this question open as I go on with the reading.

July 7

I received a very pleasant phone call from Mr. Boorstin, who told me that the very private thoughts I had written out and dispatched through the Oslo embassy had been shown to the President, that he had had them checked from the factual side by the governments experts & had encountered only corroboration on that quarter, and that as President, he wanted Boorstin to transmit his thanks for my pains.

[In the following entry Kennan reflected on a recent State Department dinner in his honor.]

Princeton, October 14

I could not, of course, be unmindful throughout the evening that this was the building from which, on one summer day, years ago, I departed after being casually dismissed by Mr. Dulles, thus ending a career of 26 years in the Foreign Service, and that there was no one in the building whom I knew well enough to say good-bye to except the charming 5th floor receptionist.

[The Kennans traveled to Barbados for a vacation.]

Barbados, December 28

In the personal sense, melancholy is heightened by the fate of my last book. A national best-seller for a couple of weeks, it seemed to sell best the farther you were from Washington or New York (one exception: the excellent review by Arthur Schlesinger in the *New York Review of Books*), and it appears to have been read extensively everywhere but in the two circles to which it was addressed: the press and the government. Here I was preaching to a mixture of the deaf and the inattentive.

1995

Kennan's strong feelings for Russia continued to shape his thoughts. He worried about the Chechen rebellion and about the ethnic prejudice of many experts on Russia. He thrilled at the chance to accompany President Bill Clinton to Moscow to celebrate the fiftieth anniversary of V-E Day. He ended up, however, declining the invitation, apparently fearing that his frailty would render him a spectacle.

His thinking remained wide-ranging and robust. In response to the public debate that erupted on the fiftieth anniversary of the atomic bombing of Hiroshima and Nagasaki, Kennan mused that the most basic question in August 1945 had been "our obligation to ourselves—to our sense of what it was suitable and decent for such a country as ours to be doing." We should "have swallowed our militant pride and consented to sound out the Japanese on the possibilities . . . of compromise."[12] *He penned incisive critiques of St. Augustine, Felix Frankfurter,*[13] *Walter Lippmann, and Dean Acheson. He also tried to explain his own failure, as he saw it, to devote adequate effort to the diary.*

Princeton, January 13

I follow with increasing dismay and heaviness of heart the ill-considered action now in progress against the Chechens. They are a people for whom I have no admiration, and for whose nationalistic aspirations I have no sympathy, but there were far better ways that the situation could have been handled. One hears in many quarters alarmist prognostications that this will be the end of democracy in Russia, that Yeltsin will use this episode to impose a complete dictatorship. I doubt that this sort

12. Kennan to Freeman Dyson, January 20, 1995, Freeman Dyson papers (in private possession).
13. Felix Frankfurter was an influential Supreme Court justice and an occasional adviser to presidents, especially Franklin D. Roosevelt.

of thing will, or could, happen. Things have gone too far in Russia, and the imposition of that sort of discipline on the Russian people, after all that has happened in the past six years, would encounter too many forms of obstruction and resistance.

February 4

I gave a telephone interview to National Public Radio, responding to some three questions I had asked them to give me in writing in the advance of the event. I did this because the questions they wanted to put were about history, the beginning of the Cold War, and not about me personally. The questions were themselves illustrations of the paucity of historical knowledge on the part even of the intelligent editors at NPR. It was evident that my questioner understood very little of the situation that existed in Soviet-American relations at that time, and had even been influenced by the subsequent right-wing charges that President Roosevelt had at the Yalta Conference deliberately delivered Poland and Eastern Europe into the hands of the Stalin regime, for them to do what they wanted with. And this, although there was an abundance of published evidence (Chip Bohlen's book[14] alone would have sufficed) to show the unsubstantiality of that charge. The complacency with which we had witnessed (not caused) the Soviet advance into Eastern Europe and the consolidation of their fearfully oppressive rule over that area, actually flowed from (a) the genuine naivety of FDR and certain of those around him; (b) the extent to which our government had succeeded in persuading many Americans that the Stalin regime was composed of well-meaning people, whose wartime aims were not really too different from our own; (c) and most importantly, the incorrigible persistence of our military leaders in refusing to give any attention to political considerations while the war was on. This last factor, incidentally, was strongly supported by the White House, not least because of FDR's unshakeable impression that if he only had sufficient time to talk with Stalin and to expose the latter to the charm of his own personality, he could cause this leopard to change his spots.

March 9

The only other guests at a dinner in New York City were the well-known George Soros and his wife Susan, he, of course, if not the world's richest man, then certainly one of the three or four richest. I had of course heard

14. *Witness to History, 1929–1969* (1973).

of him, but knew very little about him, and wondered what manner of man he would be. To my surprise and pleasure I found a charming and unpretentious Central European, impressively well informed of all that was going on in Central and Eastern Europe, and very shrewd in his judgment of the situations, the problems, and the leading personalities involved. I had, after dinner, a long and pleasant talk with him. And I was moved to wonder whether his relaxed and normal manner did not have something to do with his realization that I, in contrast with so many others that he meets, wanted nothing from him financially and appreciated him (I hope, anyway, that he sensed this) not for what he owned but for what he was.

April 4

Woke up today feeling very poorly . . . and then in mid-morning a phone call from Strobe Talbott, now virtual Under Secretary of State, to tell me that the President wanted me not just to be with him at the commemoration of the ending of World War II in the Arlington Cemetery, but also to accompany him, that same evening, on the presidential plane to Moscow, to be with him in attendance of the Russian ceremony for the same event. . . .

I would of course have liked to go. I was, after all, the senior American official present in Moscow on that memorable day. And it would give me much satisfaction to be there as an honored and friendly guest of the government in the Kremlin in place of the dangerous enemy that I was always supposed to be, not only on that historic occasion when I stood off the base of one of the pilasters and addressed the cheering Soviet crowd.

April 8

I have struggled over the question: to join or not to join President Clinton on his forthcoming journey to Moscow. Everybody urges me to go (except Annelise, who wisely gives no advice, but only makes it known that if I went, she would expect to accompany me). Christopher, who is here this weekend with his little son, Oliver, feels especially strongly about this—says it would be stimulating, would perk you up, & you would go through it famously. Grace would say the same thing. If I try to tell them that I don't feel up to it, they say, "Oh, we've heard all that." If I go to the doctors (went to one on Wednesday) they can only say that except for the failing heart and the arthritic knees they can find nothing wrong with me. Yet every morning, when I get up, I find myself in such a condition that I say to myself: "Never, never. Under no circumstances, should I ever attempt anything like that."

June 8

I have been torn, this week between the demands of my scholarly undertaking and those of watching the French Open (tennis tournament), bits of which are shown, unfortunately, only in the mornings, the only time when I can do any good writing. Watching good tennis is my only frivolous hobby. But should anyone be without one such? Only by something of this sort can we keep our sanity in this crazy and unpromising time.

June 12

Poor old Russia. Having had no sufficient emigration of real Russians, it has no real Russian diaspora. The people abroad who write about it for publication are surely 90% people who came from Russia (or whose parents did) and established themselves in the West, but who are everything else but true Russians. They are people of Jewish, Polish, German-Baltic, or other kinds of *near* Russian but not *of* Russian, origin. Generally speaking, if they don't hate Russia, they strongly dislike it, and want the remainder of Western opinion to share their feelings. I am one of the very few American WASPs who have any great interest in that country and would like to see it fairly treated. But to someone such as myself, the Russians, themselves, are no help. They are not really much interested in what is not Russia.

Sørenhus, July 5

I brought along the *Confessions of St. Augustine*, and I am, at this moment, deeply into them. . . . I find in these confessions a great deal, a stupendous amount, in fact, of attention given to the relationship of man to God, but very little to the relationship of man to man. And this fails to satisfy me, for I find myself asking whether the greatest service individual man is capable of making to God will not be found in whatever useful service he can render, during his short time on this globe, to his fellow man.

Also, I find myself somewhat disturbed by the extremely personal nature of St. Augustine's relationship to God, and by the demands this relationship implicitly places on the concern and attention of the Deity for the situation of a single man. . . . God's mercy and understanding are comprehensive, not exclusive, and there must have been a great many others who needed them, and upon whom, precisely because of their significance and helplessness, they had also to be expended. You, St. Augustine, were undeniably a great man of your time. But it was not for you, as you advanced your claims for God's attention, to assume this, to assume for yourself, that is, as high a place in the measure of God's values.

I may be nearing the margins of sacrilege, but I cannot help my mind's turning, in this connection, to the humble graffiti affixed, I was told, to a religious placard somewhere in England, consisting only of the words "Jesus saves," to which some irreverent person (or was it really a reverent one?) had added the words: "Jesus is tired. Save yourself."

[The Kennans went to Maine for a vacation as guests of their friends Bill and Laura Riley.]

North Haven, Maine, August 28

Among the books that our thoughtful hostess, Laura Riley, left before us in this cottage was a book of taped interviews. . . . I opened it at random, and fell upon the interviews with Felix Frankfurter, Walter Lippmann, and Dean Acheson, all older men and celebrities of the time when I was in my Planning Staff period. I knew Acheson the best, of course, but occasionally met the other two as well, and talked with them: several times with Lippmann, once (quite futilely for both our parts) with Frankfurter. Younger than all of them, and for long a subordinate of Acheson, I was impressed by their reputations and their authority in their respective fields. Now something of a minor celebrity myself, and one who still regards himself, as he then did, as the intellectual equal of any of them, it amuses me to think back on the deference with which I treated them all, a deference largely justifiable in view of my greater youth, and concealing no doubt a generous measure of conceit on my part. And I now review in my mind the ways in which I viewed them, and they viewed me, in those long-gone days.

For Frankfurter, I had the least regard: a sharp and aggressive legal mind, certainly, a wily and formidable denizen of a political center dominated by lawyers, but neither a philosopher nor an impressive personality.

In Lippmann, a man who had carried journalism into something much greater than what that term generally describes, a fine writer with a brilliant mind and an impressive store of what I might call liberal erudition, mildly affable on the outside but cold and in a curious way defensive on the inside. He analyzed public questions with great maturity of judgment and literary style, but, yielding to the normal compulsions of a columnist, wrote too often and too much, his formidable critical quality sometimes carrying him around in circles until he found himself chasing his own tail. Lippmann greatly resented me for my arrogance in writing the X-article, and, above all, writing it for *Foreign Affairs*, a journal for the contributing to which he had disqualified himself for personal reasons. He felt challenged and provoked by the fact that an unknown pip-squeak such as myself should have written, on a subject of which he saw himself as the dean of commentators, an article that became the object of such massive public attention. I never lost my respect for him. He remained for me, of course, over the ensuing years a committed intellectual opponent, yet one whose sharp and logical criticism probably did me more good than harm.

Acheson was something entirely different. I viewed him as a man of honor in the highest degree, and felt for him, as our association in the State Department ran its course, much respect and even a certain remote affection (remote, because of the differences in age and position that divided us). He was seen by many, and not always unjustly, as a cold and haughty person, capable of cutting people down, when he thought they deserved it, with a single stroke of his razor-sharp tongue. But he was actually a very warm person within the relatively small circle on whom his capacity for friendship or affection was bestowed. He was in fact a man of intense dislikes but also of fierce loyalties, and I respect him for all of it.

By education, training, and profession, Dean Acheson was in every inch a man of the law. His world was that of American lawyers and courts and of the American political system in the doings of which lawyers and courts were as a rule so deeply involved. Ours was, after all, a political system run by legal decision rather than by the wide range of administrative discretion that played so large a part in most European governmental operations. That being the case, Acheson had little understanding for his administrative responsibility as head of the Department of State. He dealt with individuals rather than with bureaucracies, to which category the State Department outstandingly belonged. He knew nothing about the American Foreign Service, at that time conceived by many of us, its members, as an hierarchical, disciplined institution like the army or the navy. He must have known that he had, in theory at least, the highest direct administrative authority over the members of that service, but he had difficulty in viewing them otherwise than as citizens, subject individually to the laws, the courts, and the workings of the political system, like everyone else. . . . When, then, as occasionally happened, these officers, fell afoul of the workings of prominent parts of the political system, as in the case of certain of the "old China hands,"[15] he could see no obligation on the part of the State Department or the Secretary of State, personally, to defend them. There were laws and courts, were there not?

Princeton, December 12

Fell to thinking, this last day or so, about the question: Why do I have such difficulty in finding the time to give attention to this journal? And it occurred to me that the most obvious answer is: because I have for years given precedence to my correspondence with other people and with other writing tasks—all of it, on the wholly unrealistic premise that when I get my desk cleaned up, then I shall return to the diary. But of course, come to think of it, the desk has never been entirely cleaned up and never will be. And this means that this journal, as a species of correspondence with myself, will never achieve its full purpose unless and until I consent to regard the correspondence with myself as more important than the correspondence with others, which perhaps, especially in present circumstances, and for such purposes as may be reasonable and promising for a man of my age, it really could be.

But it is possible that I have not thought through the question of just what sort of a diary this should be, if it is to have any utility. A diary can serve more than one purpose. It can be only what I think of as a calendar diary: a bare record of what one did on a given day, to serve as an aid to memory, and no more, useful perhaps at some date long in the future for a biographer or a family historian anxious to establish the time when a given event occurred.

Or it can be a notebook of sorts, such as many writers of fiction seem to have kept, to remind them of curious things they have heard or seen or might otherwise unrecord.

Or it can be a journal of ideas, of thoughts evoked by experiences of the day. I have tried to hold this diary as close as possible to the latter cat-

15. "Old China hands" refers to State Department officials who had based their careers on their familiarity with China. Kennan was referring to such China experts as John Paton Davies Jr. and Edmund Clubb, whom Acheson had failed to defend when they were unfairly attacked by Senator Joseph McCarthy and others seeking scapegoats for the 1949 defeat of Chinese leader Chiang Kai-shek.

egory. But this approach is not normally fueled by any sense of urgency. Beyond which, I know, from experience, that many thoughts come to me only when I sit down to write something for some very specific ulterior purpose, for something I had not thought to record for myself alone.

Had I ever asked myself, and compelled myself to decide, just what sort of a journal this was meant to be, what could be expected of it, why, in short, keep it, I might have given it more faithful attention.

1996

Though convinced that his life could not last much longer, Kennan worked to refine his thinking on matters concerning the future, such as the developing world roles of China and of Russia. He also reiterated long-held notions, such as the benefits of what he called an "isolationist" foreign policy.

Princeton, March 20

There are sometimes moments in the transition zone between sleep and the waking state, and particularly when one is wakening in the morning, where insights occur that are indeed subject to a degree of logical coherence, but are also the products of some deeper, more emotional, in part subconscious forms of awareness, and deserve a more serious recognition than they normally get. . . .

Yesterday morning, lying in just that sort of transitional state, I was aware of the fact that there is a gap between, on the one side, my ability at this age to go about at least a considerable number of normal activities, and, on the other side, the complete loss of that ability, which is The End—Death. . . . The gap has this outward semblance of stability, but I know that it is a very fragile sort of stability, and could at any time be abruptly and totally destroyed. . . . It is in a sense like a profound abyss, on the edges of which I lead a life of pretense, of pretense that I am really as normal and robust as I appear to be.

April 13

Highly unsatisfactory television interview with David Gergen:[16] pleasant enough personally, but he was totally unprepared, had only the flimsiest of acquaintances with the book (if it could be called that at all),

16. A former White House adviser, Gergen has become a television journalist and frequent commentator on public affairs.

and made no mention of it at all, to my memory, in the interview.[17] He launched us instead into the dreadfully hackneyed subject of "containment" and used the whole 15 available minutes pressing me to discuss it, which I did wearily and very badly. He plainly had no knowledge of what I had been doing over the past 30 or 40 years, and was, I suspect, surprised to find me alive and publishing a book at this great age.

April 28

I looked again, this morning, at parts of my book, particularly the chapter on non-military foreign policy, which I had almost forgotten I ever wrote. And I came away from the experience boiling over with indignation. Why? Because I, looking at it from this distance, found large parts of it where deep problems of political philosophy were well addressed and worthy of note, yet I could not find the faintest response on the part of the media or the government to the points I had raised. I had not expected these views to be met everywhere with agreement. On the contrary, I realized that some of them would be little short of provocative. But I thought them worthy of public attention and of critical response. And the fact that there was none of this is what most upsets me. I would much rather that my views had been disputed than that they be ignored.

I consider these views, more frankly stated, to have been major contributions to the development of political philosophy in our age, and to have this go wholly unrecognized is a bitter disappointment.

But I am not sorry that I stated them. I could do no other—or, at least, had I done any other, I would never have ceased to reproach myself for the omission.

May 16

Annelise complains, even to others, that I complain too much about my health. I know why she does it: she does not want to admit, to herself or to anyone, that it is weakening. She is no doubt right, at least in one respect. I ought never to complain. But what I am complaining about is not the discomfort of old age itself—that I would, and probably should, bear and grin. It is that people are asking me and expecting me to perform as though I was not 92 years of age but 62. . . . *Could* one not have, at the age of 92, a few moments of repose?

17. Kennan is referring to *Around the Cragged Hill*.

June 13

By virtue of a consent delicately extracted from me over many months by John Gaddis, I received in my office a television crew sent over (or so I gather) by the BBC for the purpose of interviewing me about the history of the Cold War. The reason for this interview had to do with an undertaking of the BBC to produce, in partnership with the Turner broadcasting empire (or whatever it is called) of this country, an "educational" film of at least 20 hourly segments on the history of the Cold War. In vain I had argued with Gaddis that I didn't like this medium, that I did not trust its claimed educational capacity, that the watching of such films was the lazy student's way of studying history, that I was a writer, not an actor; that I disliked my own appearances of TV films as much as I disliked the medium itself, that every answer I might give to the questions such appearances evoked would be an egregious oversimplification—bad acting, bad history.

His answers were, but you can't stop: it is a part of the modern age. The film will be produced whether you contribute or not, but if you don't contribute, it will be even worse than you envisage it as being. It will be worsened, in particular, because you yourself have a unique relationship to the Cold War and a unique view of it.

Sørenhus, July 21

I have listened to the news of the two explosions, the one on the plane off Long Island and the one in Atlanta,[18] and I naturally wonder what the more lasting effects on American policy are going to be. On domestic affairs—probably unfortunate, but on American attitudes on foreign affairs—perhaps not all bad. If these events can wean Americans from their common belief that we have only to give our civilization maximum exposure across the world, and people will come to love us, perhaps the bombing, aside of course from their tragic and unforgivable human consequences, will have useful effects.

Princeton, September 21

I have completed the small (96 pp.) history of the Kennan family.[19] . . .

Much of my plight is explicable by the fact that as I have moved into

18. The investigation into the crash of TWA Flight 800 concluded that the cause was not terrorism but rather an explosion of fuel vapors resulting from a short circuit. The deadly bomb at the Atlanta Olympics was the work of a domestic terrorist.
19. It would be published by W. W. Norton as *An American Family* (2000).

the condition described as "old age," the various aspects of my personality have not developed in unison. Each of them—the physical, the mental, the emotional-sexual, the imaginative, the control over the nervous structure, etc.—has advanced, or regressed, at its own pace, so that now, at this age of 92½, they no longer relate to one another as they should. There is a lack of the normal coordination. They jar each other, disregard each other, strive from moment to moment for ascendancy. And the result is a mess, in both the way I conduct myself and see myself, and in the way I am seen by others.

November 25

Waking up yesterday morning, I fell to asking myself whether I could properly be called, in the vocabulary of this epoch, an "isolationist." . . .

The answer is: yes. Being guided strictly by consideration of national interests as opposed to a plethora of other ones, I am indeed an isolationist, though with certain important reservations. I would urge fidelity to the requirements of our two (and only) formally contracted alliances, those with NATO and Japan. . . . I see great portions of the international community, embracing almost all of Latin America, Africa, and southern Asia, where governments are led mainly by exploitative attitudes towards us—attitudes as devoid of any gratitude or appreciation for what we may give them as of any particular concern for the maintenance of our world position. To these, as I see it, we owe nothing but the dictates of our national interest.

The two great countries of China and Russia present, admittedly, special problems. In the case of China: I see that country as the seat of a great culture which deserves our highest respect. Its people, from all I have been able to observe or have learned of them, are of very high intelligence—higher, I should think, than could be said of our own—but extremely ruthless when crossed, and essentially xenophobic. For this latter quality, I do not blame them. It is their privilege to be that way, and I think that those of their people who have migrated to this country have played a positive role here and will play an even stronger, and not invariably positive one, in future years. But I cannot see that we have anything to gain from a closer government-to-government relationship with that country. I would like to see us treat them on the diplomatic level with the most impeccable courtesy (which they would understand) but to have, beyond that, as little as possible to do with them, and, in the areas where we have to deal with them, to treat them with no smaller a firmness than they are accustomed to putting forward in their relations with us. This would apply in no less measure in problems of trade than anywhere else. We should guard against allowing our business world to develop any extensive dependence on China in commercial matters, even if this should force them to moderate their hopes for occupying a prominent place in what they insist on viewing as the "great Chinese market." And finally, I would urge that our government should desist, finally and completely, from any and every effort to press the Chinese government, now or in future, in matters of human rights. That is their concern, not ours.

In the case of Russia, things are more complicated. In its traditional religious and intellectual culture, Russia belongs very largely (not entirely) to the Western world. In its relations with the West it will continue to have things to contribute as well as things to learn. Its civilization has been seriously weakened by the vicissitudes of this passing century, including outstandingly the exactions and abuses of seven decades of Communist control, and it is now going through a hard time, the outcome of which we cannot foresee.

There will, I think, always be useful and enjoyable contacts between Russia and this country at the higher levels of arts and letters. That says little, however, about the quality of governmental rule in both countries. At its worst, in Russia, it could cause much trouble for Western Europe and for us. At its best, Russia could become a useful factor in the preservation and strengthening of Western European society. And this is for us of great importance, for Western Europe remains, in my view, the only part of the planet to which we can look, with some confidence, for the support of our civilization.

1997

Kennan regarded the extension of NATO to the borders of Russia as a shortsighted policy that would antagonize Russia. Although he succeeded in helping to stir up opposition to this policy, the Clinton administration went ahead anyway.

Princeton, January 4

Should I make any New Year's predictions? So far as I can recall, I have never done this. And what I could offer would be less in the way of predictions than of expectations. So far as the public arena is concerned, they would not be pleasant ones.

That the Russians will not react wisely and moderately to the decision of NATO to extend its boundaries to the Russian frontiers is clear. They are already reacting differently. I would expect a strong militarization of their political life, to the tune of a great deal of hysterical exaggeration of the danger and of falling back into the time-honored vision of Russia as the innocent object of the aggressive lusts of a wicked and heretical world environment. Beyond that, and more realistically conceived, there will be efforts by the Russian leadership (a) to persuade the members of the "Commonwealth of Independent States" (meaning a portion of those that broke off or were pushed off from the Soviet Union in 1991) to transform the relationship with Russia into one of an out-and-out military alliance, and (b) to develop much closer relations with the neighbors to the east, notably, Iran and China, with a view to forming a strongly anti-Western military bloc as a counter weight to a NATO pressing for world domination.

Thus will develop a wholly and even tragically unnecessary division between East & West and in effect a renewal of the Cold War.

Beyond that, since I am speaking of expectations, I would think it unlikely that the "peace process" in what is now called the Middle East will come to a favorable conclusion. Israel, by insisting on its present position, will become increasingly isolated among its Moslem neighbors, not all of whom in other circumstances would necessarily have positioned themselves as its enemies. And if all this should deteriorate into the area of military conflict, then our country will be asked to take over the bulk of the military burdens—something the politicians might prefer, for the usual domestic political reasons, to do, but which might split public opinion in a most undesirable and painful manner.

But enough of my gloomy expectations. Let us, and me and mine along with all the others, hope for the best but prepare for the worst, and take what comes.

January 28

The deep commitment of our government to press the expansion of NATO right up to the Russian borders is the greatest mistake of the entire post–Cold War period. I feel that I should state that view publicly. But then it would be wrong to do this without notifying the few friends and potential friends I have in government, and giving them, at least hypothetically (they won't do it), a chance to correct their course.

In an effort to be fair, I stretched my mind, through the early morning hours, trying to find any reason for this colossal blunder. I could find none. But in the insistence on doing this senseless thing I saw the final failure of the effort to which I have given so large a portion of my life: the effort to find a reasonable area of understanding and sympathy between the great Russian people and our own.

But how old I am! How weak! How helpless!

February 3

I have drafted and sent to Strobe Talbott my letter warning him that I had it in mind to come out publicly against NATO expansion (as now planned). And I have drafted and sent my letter to the *New York Times* (where, to my surprise, it was received with cheers). It should appear before the end of this week. I cannot predict what the reaction will be. Someone or other may want me to come down to Washington to discuss it. But I doubt it. Just as they, without consulting me, have nailed their flag to their mast, so must I nail my flag to mine. Let them see how they can extract themselves from the mess they themselves have created.

February 8

The results of the *New York Times* op-ed piece, in this age of instant communication, were surprising. Before the day was out, a German publisher

(*Die Woche*) was checking in on the fax channels, wanting to publish an excerpt from it. Then came a word from Grace's office, where she had checked in electronically (presumably from St. Petersburg) to say that she had heard of it there. And later the same day, the French Prime Minister, who had been to Moscow for a brief visit with Yeltsin, came out with a suggestion that there be a summit meeting of the leading NATO powers in the near future. The relationship of this last event to the appearance of my own article was, I am sure, purely fortuitous. But in any case, the article could not have appeared at a better moment. And I came away with the feeling that if I did not change American policy by this intervention, I at least set the policy makers . . . back on their heels.

April 15

John Gaddis is about to assume his professorship at Yale, where, I predict, he will be very busy, much appreciated, and happy. But I, for my part, am concerned. It must be now more than 20 years ago, that he and I signed a brief and simple agreement designating him as my authorized biographer. He has, I know, done some work on it, interviewing most of my family (except Christopher) and close friends and assembling, I suspect, mountains of material. But in the meantime, I have no signs that the biography has even been undertaken.

I don't find this surprising. He would no doubt have preferred to write it when I am dead, as I should, in the natural order of things, long since have been. But I am also aware that during this long interval, his own position and reputation have progressed from that of a relatively modest scholar at a minor Ohio place of learning to one of great academic prominence and distinction, with all that this means in this country in the way of pressures not only from other academic circles but from the media, particularly television, whose hunger for screen material is unappeasable. So I begin to wonder whether he will ever get down to the task of writing the biography. Not, I fear, unless I should do him the favor of dying immediately at this present point, allowing him time to put the work together in the coming spring & summer, before he starts in at Yale—not, God knows, an impossibility (particularly if I go on feeling as I have today), but also not exactly in the realm of probability.

Sørenhus, July 11

I have been rendered most unhappy by the press reports of the NATO meeting in Madrid where the formal decision was taken to admit Poland, the Czech Republic, and Hungary to membership in NATO, which meeting was taking place precisely while we were conducting our unhappy air flight. I had of course expressed publicly my decided disapproval of this measure. . . .

How, one asks, are the Russians to take this? What NATO missions are there for which the new NATO members have to be so suitably armed? How is this to be reconciled with the assurances to the Russians that they need not worry, that the extension of NATO's borders to the east has no military implications?

July 31

The past 24 hours have been the most unhappy of any similar period I can recall.

First, there has been the growing recognition that has been growing on me for the past week or so, that my own condition—physical, mental, and emotional—is now deteriorating rapidly, and has progressed to a point where, in addition to being physically crippled, I can no longer trust either my memory or my mental coherence. . . .

To add to the sadness and pain of all this (and perhaps partly as an illustration of some of it) the last night was an intensely unhappy one. I had phoned Marion Dönhoff on another matter during the day, and there was a casual mention by myself of the Polish hatred of Russia, which prompted an immediate and emphatic response from her to the effect that this, as I knew, was something on which she could not agree with me at all.

I woke up at 1 a.m., recalled this reply, recognized it as evidence that she saw nothing wrong with the recent and future extensions of NATO's borders to the Russian ones. This, in turn, caused me further to recognize that I have failed completely to put forward effectively my own views on this subject, that the Polish view of it has triumphed in Western opinion, and that if I could not persuade Marion (and my own wife) of its unjustifiable and terrible implications, the entire thrust of my activity as an official and a publicist must be regarded as misguided and useless. With that recognition my entire view of myself, my work, and my life collapses.

I lay, then, from 1 to 5 in the night, pondering the recognition. And when I asked myself what I should say to Marion if I was to say anything at all, I could think only of the bald statement: "Marion, I am simply heartbroken over what is now occurring. I see nothing in it other than a new Cold War, probably ending in a hot one, and the end of the effort to achieve a workable democracy in Russia. I see also a total, tragic, and wholly unnecessary end to an acceptable relationship of that country to the remainder of Europe."

Princeton, September 7

The week that has just passed has been one in which the news was dominated by the tragic death of the English Princess Diana. So extraordinary were the reactions of this event that it becomes, it seems to me, a challenge to any thoughtful person to find the reasons why it is so extraordinary. . . .

I can see it only as the reflection, and a very disturbing reflection, of the effects of the television and the computer age on the public in general but particularly on the youth now just coming into what should have been the age of personal maturity and responsibility. That the response we now have before us contains a very considerable component of mass hysteria cannot be doubted. This form of hysteria is always a dangerous phenomenon. It is particularly dangerous when it is informed and encouraged by the television media. . . . The great majority, after all, of those who have shared in this reaction to the Princess's death had never seen her except on film. Their whole relationship to her, in other words, was vicarious. But this is of course precisely what the business of TV is—to convey to great masses of people vicarious emotional stimuli devoid of any responsibility on the part of the viewers to react in any way to the challenges with which these stimuli confront them. The result of this is the promotion of personal immaturity on a vast scale, feeding a "voyeur's" idle curiosity but holding no answers to the real dilemmas and challenges of personal life.

November 4

On reading the article in the *New York Review of Books* by Theodore Draper on the Hiss-Chambers[20] matter of some 40–50 years ago. I was interested in this matter at the time, not just because Hiss was the darling of the Eastern establishment of that day, and first and foremost of

20. In 1948, as Cold War tensions were increasing, Whittaker Chambers, a former member of the Communist Party of the United States, publicly accused Alger Hiss, a respected State Department official, of having passed secret documents to a Soviet agent in the late 1930s. Though Hiss was found guilty of perjury in 1950, controversy about his guilt or innocence persisted.

Dean Acheson, but particularly because it was he who was taken along on that last sad Rooseveltian journey to Yalta and it was he, knowing nothing about Russia, who was allowed to stand at the President's side and to advise him on how to confront Stalin, whereas Chip Bohlen was used primarily as an interpreter, and I, ill with the effects of a difficult Moscow winter, was left in temporary charge of the Embassy there, and nothing was further from the thoughts of the President and his entourage than to consult me about anything at all.

Later, in the 1950's, when Whittaker Chambers' charges against Hiss attracted great attention and were used (not least by Richard Nixon) as a means of attacking the Democratic "liberals," I was fascinated by the conflict and even assembled a small collection of the books which then began to appear about the case. It did, after all, involve the Soviet Union as the supposed instigation and master of Hiss's Communist connections.

In summary, I never trusted either of the two men. Both were too perfect in their respective roles. Hiss, as the bright, promising, and admiringly successful New Dealer, with his Georgetown residence and his easy proximity to the great of the Rooseveltian world. Chambers, as the repentant, and therefore pure and courageous one-time denizen of the Communist horror, from which, by noble agony, he had now liberated himself, and for whom a devotion to the truth had left no other alternative than to expose and denounce his former comrade in the Communist conspiracy. These poses, for anyone who knew something about the Russian-Communist intelligence apparatus, were too vulgarly pretentious to be wholly plausible.

Princeton, December 2

I had a dream that rocked me as nothing of this sort has rocked me within my memory. . . . I was, clearly, carried back to a time more than fifty years ago. The dream was built around a real emotional dilemma of that time. It was not, in the dreamlike version, realistic. The elements of the dilemma were brought out in a vision of great beauty and horror: a weird semi-nocturnal scene of a great, tireless, cold, and deserted plateau, with only one tiny human figure—far away—lost, abandoned, and desperate. The plight was, in some way, my doing. I also could have helped, if anyone could. But circumstances prevented my doing so. Here was the dilemma . . . and I was unable (perhaps not strong enough) to solve it.

And this helplessness was a fatal flaw in the integrity of my emotional life. And a long-lasting one, as long-lasting as has been myself. . . . I was still torn apart by the unresolvable dilemma. And I was appalled by it. The whole unpitying bite of it was still upon me, more dreadful than ever.

1998

Kennan rendered judgment on his own sexual improprieties and on those of President Bill Clinton, who was trying to survive the Monica Lewinsky scandal. As he had in his 1993 book, Around the Cragged Hill, *Kennan pondered the human relationship with God.*

Princeton, March 8

The scandal of Mr. Clinton's relationship to his Jewish girl intern[21] is grinding, more and more sordid and wearisome every day, towards what I believe will be its inconclusive termination. I have seen no reason to revise the opinion I held & expressed to Annelise at the outset of this episode, some 3 weeks ago: namely that I thought Mr. Clinton should step down, taking the position that a man cannot be expected to cope at one & the same time both with the fending off of this sort of legal harassment and with an adequate performance of his normal presidential duties. But he has made serious mistakes in responding to this challenge, and no one can now help him.

On the foreign policy front . . . I found myself wondering why we cannot regard another country, in this case Iran, as just that, as one more country which we would regard as neither friend or foe, with whom we are prepared to deal on a day-to-day basis, neither idealizing it nor running it down, keeping to ourselves (here, of course, I am speaking about our government) our views about its domestic political institutions and practices, and interesting ourselves only in those aspects of its official behavior which touched our interests—maintaining, in other words, a relationship with it of mutual respect and courtesy, but distant.

May 3

Fell to reflecting on Christ's profoundly deep-seated conviction that he was the Son of God, as well as the "son of man." But of what God? What

21. An investigation would conclude that President Clinton had lied about his affair with Monica Lewinsky.

was God "like?" Where was he seated? Had Jesus ever really been there? Of all this, we are told nothing. And since he was born of woman, must have passed infancy and childhood in this world, and since there are no evidences of long absences in his life as a youth, how and when could he have known God? have been recognized by the latter as his son, and assured himself of the filial relationship?

They are, of course, silly, inept questions, ignoring and sidestepping the element of divine mystery, without which there could have been no real Christianity. And they could easily be misinterpreted. But they and similar questions suggest to me that the God of whom Jesus spoke was, whether or not he himself was aware of this, a concept of his own creative imagination. This sounds, of course, as though I were saying that his God did not really exist, that he was only a figment of his imagination. But things were more complicated than this. The vision Jesus had of God was one not only of imagination but of intuition and of super-conscious conviction, and it was a vision of such power and magnificence that he could see only some deeper meaning in his very awareness of it—that it must have had some ultimate reality, and that he was in some way selected as the conveyor of it to the life of his time.

May 11

Can it really be, I ask myself, that a man of my age cannot be spared the humiliation of being dragged, like a semi-inert body, through the stresses and strains of social life in this town and in its various outreaches, required to ask himself daily: "Should I, must I, do this or that?"—and this at a time when all I really want is rest and solitude? And must I accept the added burden of never-ending concealment of the condition I am in? A life, that is, without joy or self-respect? . . .

How easy it is, when you have no other choice, to fall back on the usual, familiar externally-oriented personality—the show personality, nurturing the impression that one is the same brave figure, striding confidently through the minor trials, challenges, and obstacles of life in the manner to which family, friends, and acquaintances have all become accustomed!

May 28

Partly, perhaps, it is sheer laziness, but there are other reasons, too, why I have of late written so little in this journal. One is of course the effects of sheer old age, and particularly the physical and nervous difficulty I experience in the very effort to write by hand. But another, and also no doubt the reflection of old age, is not that I have too little to say, but rather that I have too much. The mind seethes with thoughts, but many of them are at least in part repetitive of thoughts I have long since expressed in print, usually quite uselessly. On the other hand, there is of course a time for everything.

One of the reasons why those thoughts, expressed so long ago, fell upon deaf ears or dim, little attentive eyes, was that they were put forward at the wrong time, a sin that is indeed rarely forgiven. But it is now too late for me to put them publicly forward. The effort would be beyond my strength. And I would not know where and how, in this advertisement-ridden culture, to place them. I cling to the faint hope that someone may some day, perchance by sheer inadvertence, pick up one of my books (by my preference *Around the Cragged Hill*) and note what I was talking about.

Aboard a cruise ship, June 29

Two extraordinary dreams I recently had. Both appear to me to have taken off from the extraordinary dream I had at some date in the last weeks of 1997 which revealed to me so vividly and sadly the split personality that I now know myself to be—a division dating, I am sure, from the day in April 1904 when my infantile relationship to my mother was suddenly torn apart by her sudden and tragic death.

Now, in the first of these two recent dreams, I found myself confronting scenes that were too silly and ludicrous to bear retelling (dreams have little or no sense of humor), but which suddenly confronted me with all my sexual emotional delinquencies of the past, not, thankfully, the recent past but earlier reaches of my life. The dream brought home to me the extent to which they inflicted, or could have inflicted, suffering or injuries on relatively innocent persons of the other sex. Despite the absurdity of the examples that the dream offered, I was, by the time it was approaching its close, wracked with a sense of repentance. And I remember asking, just before it ended: "What, then, should I do, being the worthless person you have just shown me to be? Should I destroy myself?" And here, quite properly, I answered my own question promptly and correctly, by saying: "No. That would serve no good purpose whatsoever. You must go on living with yourself and making the best of it." But it was meant, I am obliged to conclude, as a reminder (coming to me from where?) of the corruption and helplessness that I shared with so much of the remainder of humanity, and of the continued need for placing myself, and whatever talents I may possess, into a perspective in which these weaknesses and inadequacies would never be ignored or underrated.

The second dream occurred only two or three nights before our departure. . . . There was nothing facing me but an absolutely blank wall, not totally black but dark and wholly without decoration. And before it there stood, in three dimensions, like a sculpted object, but real, the crucifixion—the cross and nailed to it the living body of the tortured Christ. Nothing else, no sound, no word of comment or explanation. I was simply confronted with this scene; it was left to me how to react to it.

I felt, in the case of the other dream just mentioned, that the dream was not the product of just my own subconscious emotional life—that some external force was at work here—that someone, and someone capable of shaping my dreams, was trying to tell me something that I was otherwise not apt to know. And now, I had the same feeling about this other dream: that it was not something of my own emotional subconscious manufacture, that behind this stark wordless confrontation, and through it, someone was trying to say something to me. But what?

Princeton, September 24

Poor Mr. Clinton! He has not been a bad president, in the times when he could keep his hands off women, and, I should say, "as they go." But he is the outgrowth of a seriously decadent and spoiled society. He is tactically nimble and impressively industrious at his job. But he is shallow in his philosophical background and in his human relationships. And he has, unfortunately, little or no understanding of the true grandeur and dignity of the presidential office. For that, you would have to have been born into more than he appears to have been born into.

October 20

An agonizing and absurd evening, wrangling with Annelise about my life here. I, complaining that the effort to live at the same pace as at this age of 94, as I did at the age of 64, is telling on me. I can live reasonably well with one or two engagements or involvements staring me in the face, but not with 5 or 6 of them on my mind at one time. I must, I feel, come to a point where I make a fool of myself.

On the other side of the marital table—no understanding for any of this. "You," is the usual refrain, "do all right."

I say to myself: "If you go on this way, you will break down, and the end will be hastened." "Well," responds the alter ego, "you want the end to be hastened, don't you? You long for it every day." True enough, and if it were to be sharp and swift and not too atrociously painful, I would not complain. But I begin more and more to suspect that that is not the way people like myself die. The old heart, half asleep–half dead, if you will—plugs along under the incessant needling of the pace-maker, dragging after it the tired, protesting old body, and allowing it no rest from its labors. More and more, the physical frame becomes a silly, offensive, half-conscious old scare crow, a miserable slave of habit, a burden to all those around it.

I think often of the final lines of the first paragraph of Pushkin's great poem, "Eugene Onegin," in which the gallant, young aristocratic playboy, charged with caring for his dying uncle, sighs and thinks to himself, "When in hell is the Devil finally going to take you?" How many people will be thinking that, I ask myself, before this silly, unthinking old heart relaxes its unpitying grip and permits what Churchill called "just old death" to do what it was meant to do?

1999

As Kennan at the age of ninety-five felt himself "coming apart," he hoped the diary might help with holding himself together. Despite his diminishing powers, he tried to adhere to a high standard.

Captiva Island, February 27
I am writing in this diary simply in the hope that to write in it in this way and in this time will help me to put myself together at a moment when I feel myself badly unstrung and disoriented, as a result, I suspect, of fatigue overtaking me after yesterday's day of travels.

Princeton, May 20
Phoned Terrie,[22] first thing this morning, & asked her to fax following message to Grace:

We have, evidently unwisely, junked your old fax machine and replaced it by a new and much fancier model. Having wasted an entire day trying in vain to understand the 45 pages of instruction for its usage and to send you a message on it, I have decided it is not for me and that there is an abiding mutual hatred between us two. I therefore neither expect nor desire to touch it again. However, I suspect that if you were to fax me on the usual number, the beast, taken unaware, would probably transmit it, and suggest you try.

Love,
Daddy

Washington, May 24
Dinner, I being escorted to the fine 6th floor reception room of the State Department, in a wheel chair. Seated next to the Secretary of State, Mme. Albright, with whom I had a good serious conversation—on my other side, an equally intelligent woman—Mme. Christine Sarbanes, wife of

22. Terrie Bramley was Kennan's secretary and aide.

the ex-Senator. I had to speak for several minutes, without notes and without (I must say) any particular preparation, but I think I coped creditably & things went well. The attendance at the dinner: approximately 200, of whom I knew only a few.

Sørenhus, July 2

A Federal Express package containing 5 copies of the *New York Review of Books* for August 12, containing as its leading article, I was startled to see, the interview I gave, most unhappily, to Dick Ullman.[23] I was even more startled upon reading further in the same issue when I came upon, and read with pleasure three other articles, all of which I found far better than my interview.

I was disappointed, too, by the fact that nowhere did the *Review* point out, in connection with the interview, that I was 95 years old. We oldsters should, of course, not coquette with our age. And certainly it cannot be misused as an excuse for weaknesses we have had over most of our lives. But there are certain handicaps connected purely with advanced age. And of these our readers might at least be reminded.

July 13

I have, incidentally, recently come to feel that the English, with all their faults, are really, have been at least, the greatest of peoples of post–15th century Europe—this, at least, in their literary and scholarly upper-class. Their civilization was of course erected on great and unfeeling class distinctions. But the members of the upper-class were in many instances no less cruel to each other than to those beneath them. And somehow or other, they produced, out of the unfeeling but firmly disciplined society, some of the greatest of world thought and literature.

I don't "like" the English any more than they like us. But I recognize their qualities—am, myself an heir to some of them—and am grateful for this inheritance.

August 3

Spent a good part of the day just lying around and pondering the question: What do you do when there's nothing you have to do?

I am far from a solution to the question. The mind grasps at all sorts of responses (I will not call them answers). There are certain injunctions

23. Richard Ullman was a professor of international affairs at Princeton and a friend of Kennan's.

on behavior, but there are ones that would prevail even if you had something you ought to be doing. . . . Example: Make yourself scarce. Don't spend a minute more in the company of others than politeness requires you to do. Then, quietly absent yourself. Never forget that you are a goddamn bore, and for this reason, when you cannot avoid being in the company of others, don't speak more than you have to, more than politeness requires.

Princeton, October 23

Because I have had, in these last weeks and days, a feeling that I was in a curious way coming apart, I feel a need to put together again at least that part of me that is still, if only out of decency, respect for my environment, and self-respect, worth holding together. And perhaps (or so I think at the moment) the orderly discipline of keeping this journal will be a help in that respect.

October 25

A question that presents itself when it comes to the possibility of "putting myself together" is: To what extent the disintegration is a matter of nerves and the will, and to what extent it is simply physical? Certainly, the second of these questions demands a serious answer. This was borne in on me this morning, when I was driven first to the Institute, and then downtown for a couple of errands on Nassau Street. I returned from this expedition resolving never to undertake this sort of thing again. The shopping visit involved, by my estimation, no more that some 450 feet of walking, which only a month ago would have presented no problem at all. This time I was, by my own sensation, on the verge of collapsing before I made it back to the parked car. And I was aware that in the shop, where I bought a book, I was a feeble caricature of my former self.

The question in my mind is: Does so rapid a physical and nervous decline mean the rapid descent to the end? I would like to ask the doctor about this, but will not do so. It would be unfair to him. I have no desire to prolong this condition. I am fairly sure it would be better for wife and children if it were not prolonged beyond the immediate future.

November 27

I have just re-read the gospel of John. And here I am drawn to wonder over the great emphasis placed, not only by St. John but by other Christian thinkers down to Calvin and the modern Protestant church, on the qualifications of faith alone as an assurance of salvation. Faith, belief—yes. But why should people have been asked to believe? Heathens that they presumably were, they were now being asked to believe not only in the supreme power of God, but in the divinity of a man claiming to be God's son. How, and on what basis, was this supposed innovation in their belief to take place? . . .

Ah, one may say—you forget the miracles. (At this point, I was obliged, by sheer physical weakness, to break off the writing, move across the room, & lie down until lunch time. Had I been physically better off, I would have gone on to explain why I saw the miracles as a partial reason, of course, but only for a limited number of people, and even for them not fully persuasive. For an even more limited number of people who knew Jesus and talked with him personally, there was, I suspect, a more serious reason for faith, and that was the great apparent power and persuasiveness of his personality. But this, for hundreds, and eventually thousands of others, could have been no more than a matter of hearsay. More about all this, if I live that long and in adequate condition, at another time.)

Christmas Day, 1999

The unquestionable decline of my own powers: partly intellectual powers, but beyond that, going into the personal, the inability to confront the small distractions of life, the decline of memory, the limits of concentration. I see myself surrounded in this house by great piles of demands upon me, demands that I don't see in myself the power to cope with. Many of these arise from expectations encouraged by things I have done in the past, coming from people who have no idea of the inner frailties of old age. I am, in this sense, the victim of my own past.

The lesson of all this is, I am sure, that I have lived too long, have outlived myself. I have no defense against the refrain flung at me by so many: "You look all right." I try, in the face of all this, to do my best. But it is not good enough. And the awareness of its inadequacy is what weighs most heavily upon me.

2000

Although Kennan was, as he put it, "sour on everything," he remained mentally engaged in almost everything. He followed national and international politics. He worked on the revisions of his family history. And he reflected on his relationship with his biographer, John Lewis Gaddis.

Princeton, January 22

This journal . . . has plainly suffered a longer neglect than usual, and that for the usual reasons: poor health and a formidable overburden of mail on my desk. I would like to revive it, and will make an effort to do so, but handwriting becomes increasingly hard, and sheer physical exhaustion insists on its rights. The details of declining powers make depressing reading, so let it go at that.

February 13

I am also aware (lest any reader of this journal think I am not) that I am steadily forgetting how to spell. And this—after writing twenty books.

March 3

Eight days have elapsed, as I now make it, from my return from the hospital. None of them have been easy ones. . . . Harriet and the publisher, panting, evidently, with determination to get on with the book,[24] have pressed me day after day to get on with this or that. My own self-respect as an author has compelled me to rewrite, almost in entirety, an entire chapter.

March 25

Oh dear—oh dear! I finished the rewriting, as it turned out, of two chapters of the book. . . .

But I have stood the effort, with all its side effects and demands on

24. *An American Family.*

attention, poorly. And today, after spending half the day in bed, I came to realize that I am in a state not just of nervous exhaustion but of deep depression. And in this (and I suppose it is always that way) it is not just my own condition but what I see of the state of the country that is involved. I see everything in black. The President tearing around in India and Pakistan doing things and saying things that are neither necessary nor useful; the poor but valiant old Pope paying his visit to what he (not the present inhabitants) regards as holy places; the stock market jumping up and down at its absurd and dangerous heights; the press and much of the public absorbed with its annual mock ceremony for the "Oscars," a ceremony as empty, silly, and decadent as the films and glamour of the moving picture industry they are trying to glamorize.

I am sour on everything. And the acme of my alienation from my time came when the strike of a portion of the American Airways (or something like that) cabin personnel was settled at the last minute. I found myself disappointed by this outcome because the company, failing a solution of the conflict with the employees, had vowed to shut down all its operations everywhere. And this, I thought, would be just dandy. The public ought to be taught, I thought, to understand what an unreliable, uncomfortable, dreadfully polluting, and basically unnatural and expensive means of travel the airplane really provides.

I was, I suppose, just about the only person in the country who regretted the avoidance of this strike.

And is that not depression?

The Farm, April 22

I would like to set forth such views as I, at this advanced age entertain—views, that is, on global, regional, and national problems—views highly adverse to the prevailing assumptions of the relatively liberal culture of which I see myself as a part.

I could not hope to do this for publication. What I might have to say would far exceed the dimensions of any op-ed page in the daily press, probably exceed the dimension of any magazine article as well (nor would it be widely noted there). In book form? Some of these views were set forth in my book *Around the Cragged Hill* some years ago, and I doubt that anything I wrote in all my literary career ever fell flatter and received less public attention than did these particular views. . . .

Even then, I would still like to get my views down on paper (never mind for whom), if only as part of my political-literary legacy. But this, if only handwriting were to be used as the medium, would require weeks of uninterrupted concentration. And with the typewriter? That could be done only at home. And such life as can be led there is highly unconducive to such an effort. There are endless interruptions: phone calls, invitations, visits, daily correspondence, press readings, etc. The ancient typewriter is in the most intensely habited room in the house, together with the television and the telephone. I could, and perhaps will, try, but with few favorable prospects.

Princeton, April 29

A visit from John Lukacs. He, too, I thought, had changed a bit, had been ill for a time. But I can talk with him as with no other visitor. Each of us sees in the past work of the other elements of profundity which, in both instances, have never achieved anything resembling recognition by the critics or by readers in general. . . .

Bunny Dilworth sent over to me yesterday afternoon, a great heavy bundle of materials connected with myself, which her late husband, Dick,[25] had squirreled away, during the years of our acquaintanceship. Among them, whether she was aware of it or not, was the typed record of an interview between Dick and my appointed biographer, John Gaddis, all dealing with myself and my foibles (of which Dick, I thought, showed a more lively and painful awareness than did his interlocutor). The subject of the talk was purely my person. There was no reference to anything I had ever written or otherwise achieved. And I realized that to Dick, and perhaps in a sense to both of them, the person was more important than the achievement. Which is a pity, as I see it. For while the person did indeed have foibles, and while it was no doubt good for me to be thus confronted with the recognition of them, and humbled by it, the person was beyond comparison less important than the work as a writer and thinker. The person alone would never have justified the sort of effort that Gaddis is preparing to put into the account of my life.

May 2

These last two days have been extremely painful ones for me. For the text of Gaddis's interview with Dick Dilworth had shown me that the former, at least at that time, had no idea of what was really at stake in

25. J. Richardson Dilworth, a lawyer for the Rockefeller family, and his wife, Bunny, were friends and neighbors of the Kennans'.

my differences with the Western (French and British) governments and our own—differences that marked the years of the decade from 1948 to 1958. These were the crucial years in my efforts to be of use to my own government, and indeed to all of Western Europe, in our encounter with the Russia of the aging Stalin. That I was a total failure in those efforts is clear, and should have been even clearer to me at the time. I learned, in any case, to accept the failure and, after 1958 (the Reith lectures being the final and conclusive episode), to abandon the effort and to go my own way as a scholar. But the lone battle I was waging in those years—a battle against the almost total militarization of Western policy towards Russia—was one which, had my efforts been successful, would have, or could have, obviated the vast expenses, dangers, and distortions of outlook of the ensuing Cold War, and would have left us in far better shape than we are to face the problems we now confront. That this battle should not be apparent even to the most serious of my postmortem biographers means that the most significant of the efforts of the first half of my career—namely to bring about a reasonable settlement of European problems of the immediate postwar period—will never find their historian or their understanding.

And this is hard.

June 6

We received a luncheon visit from John Gaddis. . . .

The visit has asked me to reflect on the shortly-to-be-written biography. I have never regretted the decision to charge him (among many of others who would like to have tried their hand at it) with this biographic task. He is incomparably better informed than anyone else about the diplomacy of those postwar years when I was performing governmental service. He is a thoroughly honorable person. He will relate what he knows and finds significant of that time. Whether he will take a similar interest, and attempt to depict with no less insight, the post-governmental phases of my life and experience—the personal ones recorded in the *Sketches*, or the political philosophical reflections set forth in *Around the Cragged Hill*—I am not so sure. But I consider myself more fortunate than most of those who have biographies written about them.

Sørenhus, July 23

Is there, I find myself asking, any use in continuing this sort of a journal?

Well, there have been, as I then perceived it, both personal and non-personal reasons for doing so. On the personal side, there was the belief that this sort of a record, when reviewed periodically by the writer, gave the latter a certain distance of view on himself—his weaknesses, complaints, useful and useless hopes and reactions of the day, warned him about things to be better avoided, kept him from pursuing erroneous roads, leading nowhere.

Princeton, August 27

From Harriet and the publisher, I learn that the editors of *The New Yorker* were (don't ask me how) impressed with the uncorrected proof of my little book, which they must have seen some time ago, and they want to send one of their number out to Princeton in one of the approaching days, to do what they call a "profile" on me. This puts me under a strange sort of dilemma. I am, unquestionably, depressed. But should I receive this editor in that condition? Obviously not. But so pleased am I with the interest that magazine has shown in that little book that I feel it would be ungracious on my part to decline to receive the gentleman. This means, however, that I must, in the interval before he comes, pull myself together and restore, so far as I can, my sense of humor.

August 28

I watched the Democratic convention. While not in agreement with Al Gore in all respects, I did feel that in his final acceptance speech the real person finally began to overcome the political actor. (Others seem to have gathered a similar impression, for his rise in the polls was quite striking.) I am still not very happy about his choice of a vice-president, but continue to recognize its demonstrable political advantage.

September 25

I suffered (it was very small suffering) what I believe to have been a small heart attack. (The heart, by the feel of things, was in any case certainly involved in it.) But it involved for someone of my age, the familiar problem: either you do too much, and are then sharply and unpleasantly reminded of your frailty, or you do too little, in which case you tend to vegetate, which is actually worse for everyone involved. On the edge of this fragile balance, my life proceeds.

2001

Kennan resolved to relax his standards for the diary. He would no longer bother to record significant or otherwise important events and thoughts, he told himself. Nonetheless, he could not refrain from noting some key international developments. Nor could he resist making the diary into a potentially useful medical record.

The summer of 2001 would prove the last that Kennan spent in Norway.

Princeton, February 4

I am giving up any and all effort to make this into a serious literary journal, and will use this and ensuing pages simply for jottings of daily events in these final weeks of my life—events of no interest to others than myself, and to myself only as matters of record that may help me to keep action and memory in some sort of useful relationship to each other.

April 30

Realizing that it will presumably not be long before it becomes unsuitable and un-useful that I should bear the main responsibility for making decisions or plans for Annelise and myself about the various "displacements" of her body and mine, and that these questions would be ones to be decided between the doctor and the children (principally Christopher), I thought that I should as a possible aid to them keep some sort of a brief record of major matters of health they might like to know about when they assume that responsibility.

June 5

Woke up, knowing that the day was to be a bad one, and was struck by a total recognition—total, unquestionable, and susceptible of no doubt or vacillation—that I was a dying man. How long it would be before the end, I could not know ("Man knoweth not his time"), but it could not be very far off. And meanwhile, this awareness should govern all my decisions and behavior.

Pursuant of this conviction, and, whether it was cause or effect, feeling shaky and confused in the extreme, I made a morning trip to the old Institute office and completed the examination of the papers that had been left there, disposing of the circumstances of their removal from the room, and coming home with the feeling: "That, at least, is now done." Whether well done or badly, I could not say. Nor need to ask.

[On September 11, 2001, nineteen terrorists hijacked four U.S. airliners and crashed two of them into the World Trade Center buildings in New York and one into the Pentagon. As passengers in the fourth aircraft tried to gain control of the plane, it plowed into a field in Pennsylvania. A few weeks later, President George W. Bush launched a war in Afghanistan, where the terrorists, belonging to al Qaeda, had trained. Kennan did not refer to the 9/11 attacks in the diary.]

The Farm, November 20

I will not worry further about the multiple, unnecessary, and grave dangers into which Mr. Bush is now so light-heartedly leading us. I am like someone on a ship crossing a great ocean. I know that the course taken by those on the bridge is dreadfully incorrect, but having been neither consulted nor allowed to feel that my opinion, even if volunteered, would be welcome or respected, why should I worry beyond a point? I can only be inwardly prepared for what is coming, and mumble helplessly, as did the discarded and dying Bismarck, "*Wehe meinen Enkeln.*" (God help my grandchildren.)

November 21

Regarding the war in Afghanistan I find myself more of an isolationist than ever, reflecting that we, as soon as we can detach ourselves from that imbroglio, should concentrate our efforts on developing at home alternatives to the importation of Middle Eastern, and especially Saudi Arabian, oil—this, in place of further efforts to play a role in that particular region.

2002

Kennan suggested through a friend that if people in the State Department wanted his views on current problems, they should send a representative to talk with him. Although the State Department did arrange such a meeting, he did not mention the encounter in his diary. Even with his strength ebbing, the old warhorse never ceased wanting to influence public affairs.

Princeton, March 22

I have also had in mind the curious idea trying, in this coming period, to set forth, in the dimensions of a small book, to be entitled something like an *Old Man's Dream*, partly facetious, some of the bizarre thoughts on public problems of a man of my age. Today, I sat down and asked myself to give this more serious thought. The result of that effort persuaded me that, attractive as was this idea, it was wholly impractical and silly. I no longer have the strength for any such involvement, and it could even make life harder for me if it were tried and failed.

June 22

I woke up early this morning and thought that I would, if strength permits, resume the keeping of a diary. . . .

In what now will be written (if the effort succeeds at all), there will be none of the pretenses or affectations of earlier diaries: no deep thoughts, no logical conclusions, no strivings for literary color. I am, for good or for bad, beyond all that. My mind is a hodgepodge of random, uncoordinated, impulses and reflections. Let them flow as they may, like water slowly seeping through a swamp.

July 6

I find myself in a state of rapidly advancing deterioration of both body and soul. Whether it is in my power, in the power of will and understanding, to halt this or to slow it down, remains to be seen. If not, what lies ahead is of course unpredictable, but I hope will be short.

But does not the very awareness of this process evidence that it can, at least by strength of will, be at least slowed down and made less disreputable? Let us see. . . .

Is effort, even if unsuccessful, its own reward—even clumsy effort? And even at this age? I quail at the questions.

July 13

What a time, and what an age, at which to try to keep a diary! . . .

I watch, but this too only half-heartedly, the political arguments on TV, hoping against hope that the President will soon begin to be called to account for his grievous and abundant follies. God help us if he is not.

[Citing what would turn out to be false evidence that Saddam Hussein's Iraq possessed weapons of mass destruction, the administration of President George W. Bush was pushing for war with that nation.]

Washington, September 15

I have been urged, by at least one friend, to write another X-article, urging patience and avoidance of violence even with regard to Saddam Hussein & his Iraq. And here, with relation to . . . the question of military violence overtly initiated by ourselves or its opposite, I have a few views, centering on the question of nuclear weapons, that I would like to voice.

But I am simply not in any position, at this stage in my life, to involve myself in public controversy. So the matter stops at that point.

Princeton, December 16

I now live, beginning with my own children, in a circle of resistance to anything more than a certain level of sympathy for the ailments of the very old. I sense this as well in the case of my two excellent physicians (Drs. Wei and McCain) who have at one point or another given me their attentions in recent months. Both have examined me. Neither has found anything seriously wrong with heart, lungs, urinary, or digestive systems. What, then, am I complaining about? But I notice that while, in these recent weeks and days, I have been careful not to bother either of them, neither of these physicians has made any inquiries as to how I was getting on.

My situation, then, is what could most accurately be described as one of a lonely personal discomfort, which I must learn to accept.

2003

The diary for 2003 evidences a sudden decline in the near centenarian's mental faculties. By December, he was desperately trying to hold himself together by marking the passage of hour-long increments of time. Nevertheless, earlier in the year he noted with revulsion President Bush's war of choice in Iraq. Kennan had also taken the opportunity when in Washington to explain to a group of reporters why he opposed the war.

Princeton, March 18

The launching of the war in Iraq—the first firing in cold blood—is now, the President has told us, only some 36 hours off.

July 31

I am, at this moment, totally confused about time—the calendar, that is, not to mention a no lesser confusion about myself.

What bothers me about the calendar is simply that it is hard for me to believe that the attack on Iraq and its immediate consequences could all really have occurred in the four and some months of April through July of this present year.

As for myself: after completing a truly disturbing awakening after a night of weird and threatening dreams, I fell to pondering the implications of that misery for my relations with those around me, and was preparing to set to paper some of the thoughts that pressed upon in that connection when I picked up this long-neglected diary. . . .

Any complaints of these discomforts, voiced to others, fall on highly deaf & totally unsympathetic ears. All of them—doctors, children, friends—have come to regard me as one incorrigible and incurable hypochondriac. And such is the extent of their unanimity in this conclusion that I have no choice but I accept it, at least for all objective purposes. They are not fools. There must be reason for their attitudes. I must keep my physical complaints studiously to myself, and that I shall be at pains to do.

But this resolve imposes certain restraints on them as well as on myself. They must not send any others to see me. They should not (unless they want to make a liar of me), address to me the question (or encourage others to address to pose it), "How are you today?" I might be provoked into admitting that I did not feel entirely well.

December 17

I have lived through the most terrible night in memory, its agonies sharpened by extreme dizziness and weakness, which frustrated several efforts to get into a standing position to cope with the trials of the night.

Well, after successfully shaving in late afternoon, I have again lived through the trials of the half-hour, and am still confronting them. Let me begin by noting certain of the insoluble aspects of the problem.

(a) My limit of successful effort is the single 60-minute hour, or, if the strain is not too great, a single uninterrupted succession of such hours but no more.

(b) This, the single hour, can be endured and lived through without physical or nervous discomfort. And its limits are marked by the every half-hour passage of the hour in question.

(This effort to come to terms with my problems was supposed to have been inaugurated with the passage of the 9:30 half-hour mark. But the clock across the room shows it to be, at this moment, not 9:30 but 11:30—a difference of 2 hours. And still no 9:30 notation. What has happened to mock my good intentions?)

December 18

Where do we go from there? And what becomes of my good intentions? Only, perhaps, to make another start, & see: What then? It is, in any case, now shortly before noon. Anna[26] will soon be arriving, with that unwanted but relentlessly prepared and served challenge to this communication with myself. To give it up? Nothing left, then, than the end—So: struggle along.

December 19

Another of the hourly passages is now upon me. I am determined to continue to build my life around these regular hourly marking points.

26. Anna was a caregiver.

2004

Kennan clung desperately to his failing memory. He dictated the February 6 entry, which appears to have been polished a bit by the typist. He then tried to write down the years of each stage of his career and life—but getting the chronology right proved too much for his fading mind. He abandoned the timeline midway through.

Princeton, February 6

To aid in matters of memory, I append a list of the apparent challenges to reality that have marked some of my recent days—all of these for noting under the title of "Reality and Unreality in my Recent Memory." It is incomplete but will serve its purpose.

Some days ago I read in the paper of observations made publicly by the president to various journalists. I had seen a part of these in the morning *New York Times*. . . . I had thought, however, that he went on to speak at greater length about these matters. . . . On receiving the actual text of the paper, I found in it nothing of that sort and was obliged to conclude that all the further testimony to the press represented nothing more than my own imagination.

YEAR	
1943	Liberated from Nauheim confinement[27]
	Sent to Portugal—Azores crisis
1943–44	London—home
1944–46	Moscow with Harriman
	War College
1947–48	Marshall & Planning Staff
1948	Counselor—Department of State
1950	Without pay year—Institute

27. Kennan was liberated from Bad Nauheim in 1942, not 1943.

	Resignation. Princeton
1951	Korea & ½ year service
	Purchase of Princeton house
	Move to Princeton
1952	Kennedy offers appointments
	Off to Belgrade[28]

Kennan put enormous effort into pulling himself together for the one hundredth birthday celebration held in his honor at the Institute for Advanced Study on February 18, 2004. At the gathering he stressed his continuing gratitude, a half century later, at being appointed a faculty member despite his lack of professional credentials.

Kennan in his last year could not write in the diary. John Lukacs saw him near the end: "His head, resting on a pillow, now had a skeletal beauty; he could speak only a little, forcing out a few words with increasing difficulty."[29] *He died peacefully at home on March 17, 2005, one year, one month, and one day after his one hundredth birthday. Although Annelise survived him by three years, she had succumbed to dementia even while George was still alive. So ended the journal begun by the eleven-year-old:*

> In this simple, little book,
> A record of the day, I cast;
> So, I afterwards may look
> Back upon my happy past.

28. Kennedy offered Kennan the ambassadorship to Yugoslavia in 1961, not 1952.

29. John Lukacs, *George Kennan: A Study of Character* (New Haven: Yale University Press, 2007), 188.

Notes

Where Kennan Lived and Wrote

1. George F. Kennan, interview with John Lewis Gaddis, August 24, 1982, box 15, George F. Kennan papers (hereafter "Kennan papers"), Seeley G. Mudd Manuscript Library, Princeton University, Princeton, NJ.

2. Jeanette Kennan Hotchkiss, interview with Joan Elisabeth Kennan, November 2, 1972 (in private possession).

3. Kennan to Jeanette Kennan Hotchkiss, November 16, 1930, box 23, Kennan papers.

4. Kennan to Jeanette Kennan Hotchkiss, November 1, 1931, box 24, ibid.

5. Kennan, "Fair Day Adieu," [1939–40], box 240, ibid.

6. Kennan to Jeanette Kennan Hotchkiss, February 10, 1935 [included in the diary], box 231, ibid.

7. Kennan to Jeanette Kennan Hotchkiss, April 5, 1935, box 24, ibid.

8. Charles B. Burdick, *An American Island in Hitler's Reich: The Bad Nauheim Internment* (Menlo Park, CA: Markgraf, 1987), 43.

9. Joan Elisabeth Kennan to author, July 10, 2013.

10. Kennan to Martin E. Segal, Faculty Series, box 19, Shelby White and Leon Levy Archives Center, Institute for Advanced Study, Princeton, NJ.

11. Grace Kennan Warnecke to author, July 20, 2012, and July 3, 2013.

12. Wendy Kennan to author, July 1, 2013.

13. Christopher Kennan to author, July 14, 2013.

Introduction

1. Richard H. Ullman, interview with John Lewis Gaddis, September 30, 1987, p. 14, box 1, John L. Gaddis papers (hereafter "Gaddis papers"), Seeley G. Mudd Manuscript Library, Princeton University, Princeton, NJ. For an online link, see http://findingaids.princeton.edu/collections/MC256.

2. For a discussion of Kennan as "organic conservative," see Anders Stephanson, *Kennan and the Art of Foreign Policy* (Cambridge, MA: Harvard University Press, 1989).

3. Robert R. Bowie, interview with Gaddis, December 10, 1987, p. 1, box 1, Gaddis papers.

4. Constance Goodman, interview with Gaddis, December 10, 1987, p. 1, ibid.

5. Kennan to Jeanette Kennan Hotchkiss, October 8, 1944, box 24, George F. Kennan papers (hereafter "Kennan papers"), Seeley G. Mudd Manuscript Library, Princeton University.

6. Paul Nitze, interview with Gaddis, December 13, 1989, p. 1, box 1, Gaddis papers.

7. Kennan diary, May 15, 1958, box 233, Kennan papers.

8. Kennan, interview with Gaddis, August 24, 1982, box 16, ibid.

9. Ships and passenger trains, however, he liked. He saw rail travel as efficient and as supportive of community, in the rail car and in the housing clustered around the station.

10. Loy W. Henderson, interview with Gaddis, September 25, 1982, p. 7, box 1, Gaddis papers.

11. Jeanette Kennan Hotchkiss, interview with Gaddis, December 21, 1982, p. 12, ibid.

12. Kennan, interview with Gaddis, December 13, 1987, p. 38, box 15, Kennan papers; John Lewis Gaddis, *George F. Kennan: An American Life* (New York: Penguin Press, 2011), 294–95, 316–19.

13. Department of State, *Foreign Relations of the United States: 1946* (Washington, DC: Government Printing Office, 1969), 6:708.

14. Kennan interview with Gaddis, September 8, 1983, p. 9, box 16, Kennan papers.

15. William P. Bundy and Mary A[cheson] Bundy, interview with Gaddis, December 6, 1987, p. 13, box 1, Gaddis papers.

16. Grace Kennan Warnecke, "Daughter of the Cold War" (unpublished manuscript), 250.

17. *Around the Cragged Hill: A Personal and Political Philosophy* (New York: W. W. Norton, 1993).

18. Albert Eisele, "George Kennan Speaks Out about Iraq," George Mason University's History News Network, August 8, 2005, http://hnn.us/articles/997.html.

19. Robert C. and Evgenia Tucker, interview with Gaddis, September 4, 1984, p. 14, box 1, Gaddis papers.

20. Henderson, interview with Gaddis, September 25, 1982, pp. 2–3, ibid.

21. Kennan to Jeanette Kennan, May 18, 1923, box 23, Kennan papers.

22. Kennan to Jeanette Kennan Hotchkiss, June 28, 1935, box 24, ibid.

23. Sir Isaiah Berlin and Lady Berlin, interview with Gaddis, November 29, 1992, p. 21, box 1, Gaddis papers.

24. Kennan to Jeanette Kennan Hotchkiss, September 3, 1928, box 23, Kennan papers.

25. Ibid., May 13, 1935, box 24.

26. Martha Mautner, interview with Gaddis, September 24, 1983, p. 1, box 1, Gaddis papers.

27. Dorothy Fosdick, interview with Gaddis, October 29, 1987, p. 2, ibid.

28. Berlin and Berlin, interview with Gaddis, November 29, 1992, p. 18, ibid.

29. Bundy and Bundy, interview with Gaddis, December 6, 1987, p. 13, ibid.

30. Wilson D. Miscamble, *George F. Kennan and the Making of American Foreign Policy, 1947–1950* (Princeton: Princeton University Press, 1992), 353. See also Gaddis, *George F. Kennan*, 265–336.

31. Tucker and Tucker, interview with Gaddis, September 4, 1984, p. 5, box 1, Gaddis papers.

32. J. Richardson Dilworth, interview with Gaddis, December 6, 1987, pp. 1–2, ibid.

33. Constance Goodman, interview with Gaddis, December 10, 1987, pp. 5–6, ibid.

34. Ibid., p. 16.

35. Dorothy Fosdick, interview with Gaddis, October 29, 1987, pp. 1–2, ibid.

36. Given his personal and professional interest in the private lives of top officials, Hoover probably noted Kennan's wrought-up emotions while talking with Fosdick. During the McCarthyite hysteria, Kennan testified on behalf of Robert Oppenheimer at the latter's security hearing. Kennan was also a public supporter of the State Department's China expert John Paton Davies Jr., who was hounded out of government by false aspersions on his loyalty. Although Kennan was investigated by the FBI, he was never accused of any misconduct. Indeed, "the Bureau has had cordial relations with him," Hoover affirmed. As a State Department employee, Kennan had furnished information to the bureau. He had even reported on the activities of two "minor employees." Gaddis, *George F. Kennan*, 496–97.

37. Dorothy Fosdick, interview with Gaddis, October 29, 1987, pp. 1-2, box 1, Gaddis papers.

38. Miscamble, *Kennan and the Making of American Foreign Policy*, 35.

39. Berlin and Berlin, interview with Gaddis, November 29, 1992, p. 30, box 1, Gaddis papers.

40. Ullman, interview with Gaddis, September 30, 1987, p. 5, ibid.

41. Kenneth W. Thompson, interview with Gaddis, December 6, 1982, p. 1, ibid.

42. Nicholas Thompson, *The Hawk and the Dove: Paul Nitze, George Kennan, and the History of the Cold War* (New York: Henry Holt, 2009), 205.

43. Gaddis, *George F. Kennan*, 592–93; Costigliola, "Is This George Kennan?" *New York Review of Books*, December 8, 2011, p. 6.

44. Gaddis, *George F. Kennan*, 671–72; Thompson, *Hawk and the Dove*, 311.

45. Christopher Kennan, interview with author, September 22, 2012.

46. John H. Elliott, interview with Gaddis, December 7, 1992, p. 8, box 1, Gaddis papers.

47. Bundy and Bundy, interview with Gaddis, December 6, 1987, p. 2, ibid.

48. Arthur S. Link, interview with Gaddis, September 5, 1984, p. 9, ibid.

49. Kennan, interview with Gaddis, December 13, 1987, p. 26, box 16, Kennan papers.

50. Kennan to Jeanette Kennan, Thanksgiving Day, 1921, box 23, ibid.

51. Frances Kennan Worobec, interview with Gaddis, June 28, 1984, p. 11, box 1, Gaddis papers.

52. Hotchkiss, interview with Gaddis, December 21, 1982, p. 4, ibid.

53. "But I don't think she was" cruel, countered Kennan's sister. It was just that Louise "wasn't at all an earthy person." She did not understand young boys. "Any little thing that [George] did that was awkward—you could see her wince." Hotchkiss, interview with Gaddis, December 21, 1982, p. 6, ibid.

54. Kennan, interview with Joan Kennan (ca. 1972), p. 3, Joan Elisabeth Kennan papers (in private possession).

55. George F. Kennan, *Memoirs, 1925–1950* (Boston: Little, Brown, 1967), 4.

56. Kennan, interview with Gaddis, August 24, 1982, p. 11, box 15, Kennan papers.

57. Kennan, interview with Joan Kennan (ca. 1972), pp. 1, 4, Joan Elisabeth Kennan papers.

58. Gaddis, quoted in "Kennan '25 Honored as Hundredth Birthday Nears," *Daily Princetonian*, November 12, 2003.

59. Kennan to Jeanette Kennan Hotchkiss, January 3, 1931, box 23, Kennan papers.

60. Ibid., April 28, 1931.

61. Ibid., July 9, 1931.

62. Gaddis, *George F. Kennan*, 60–61.

63. Annelise Sørensen Kennan, interview with Gaddis, August 26, 1982, p. 3, box 15, Kennan papers.

64. Ibid., pp. 3–5. In a letter to his sister Jeanette ("Netty") a few months later, Kennan spelled out the scope of his worries:

"We have no 'foreign policy.' The foreign policy of each administration is the sum total of the reflections of its internal party politics in the foreign field. . . .

"The America I know and love and owe allegiance to is Father's America—the America of George Kennan the elder, and John Hay and Henry Adams and [Theodore] Roosevelt and Cleveland and the *Atlantic Monthly* and the *Century*. That is the world we were brought up in on Cambridge Avenue, after all, and it stood for certain ideals of decency and courage and generosity which were as fine as anything the world has ever known, and for a certain maturity and intelligence besides. Where is it all, now, and how much part does it play in the life of the country? . . . I am not expatriated, Netty. I am very home sick—for the autumn in Wisconsin, for football games, for Sunday morning waffles, for loyal, generous people, and for a thousand memories of the U.S. I always am, over here, when autumn comes on. But I can treat myself to no illusions as to whom I am representing in these European countries. They are the readers of the tabloids and the great American advertisements. They are the people who believe that you will be charming if you don't have halitosis, who are 'puzzled by conflicting tooth-paste claims,' and who let their thought be seriously affected by the question of whether their ice-box ejects its cubes immediately. . . . What can you do for such a people? What good does it do to 'represent' them? If they could have their toys taken away from them, be spanked, educated, and made to grow up, it might be worthwhile to act as a guardian for their foreign interests in the meantime.

But when one can do none of these things . . . ?" Kennan to Jeanette Kennan Hotchkiss, October 18, 1931, box 24, ibid.

65. Bundy and Bundy, interview with Gaddis, December 6, 1987, p. 34, box 1, Gaddis papers. See also Dilworth, interview with Gaddis, December 6, 1987, p. 4, ibid.

66. Bundy and Bundy, interview with Gaddis, December 6, 1987, p. 35, ibid.

67. Kennan to Jeanette Kennan Hotchkiss, December 31, 1934, box 24, Kennan papers.

68. Kennan, interview with Gaddis, August 25, 1982, p. 6, box 15, ibid.

69. John and Patricia Davies, interview with Gaddis, December 7, 1982, pp. 9–10, box 1, Gaddis papers.

70. Gaddis, in his interview with Ullman, September 30, 1987, ibid.

71. Grace Kennan Warnecke, interview with author, April 30, 2012.

72. Bundy and Bundy, interview with Gaddis, December 6, 1987, p. 1, box 1, Gaddis papers.

73. Ibid., p. 11.

74. Ullman, interview with Gaddis, September 30, 1987, pp. 13–14, ibid.

75. Kennan, interview with Gaddis, August 25, 1982, p. 3, box 15, Kennan papers.

76. Ibid.

77. John Lukacs (ed.), *Through the History of the Cold War: The Correspondence of George F. Kennan and John Lukacs* (Philadelphia: University of Pennsylvania Press, 2010), 137.

78. Bill Riley, interview with author, May 18, 2013.

Index